Urban Religion
in
Roman Corinth

D0731585

HARVARD THEOLOGICAL STUDIES
53

Series Editors

François Bovon
Francis Schüssler Fiorenza
Peter B. Machinist

Managing Editor for This Volume
Gene McGarry

CAMBRIDGE, MASSACHUSETTS

Urban Religion
in
Roman Corinth

Interdisciplinary Approaches

Edited by
Daniel N. Schowalter
and
Steven J. Friesen

DISTRIBUTED BY
HARVARD UNIVERSITY PRESS
FOR
HARVARD THEOLOGICAL STUDIES
HARVARD DIVINITY SCHOOL

Urban Religion in Roman Corinth: Interdisciplinary Approaches

Managing editor: Gene McGarry
Copy editor: Gene McGarry
Typesetters: Gene McGarry, Glenn Snyder, Carly Daniel-Hughes
Proofreaders: Glenn Snyder, Margaret Studier
Indexers: Rachel Billings, Cory Crawford, and Margaret Studier
Production liaison: Margaret Studier
Cover design: Eric Edstam
Cover photograph: Corinth forum, view of the Archaic Temple above the Northwest Shops. Photo by Daniel N. Schowalter. Reproduced by permision of Archaeological Resources for New Testament Studies, Harvard University.

The foreign language and transliteration fonts used in this book are available from Linguist's Software Inc., PO Box 580, Edmonds, WA 98020-0580 USA. Tel: (425) 775–1130. Website: www.linguistsoftware.com.

Library of Congress Cataloging-in-Publication Data
Urban religion in Roman Corinth : interdisciplinary approaches / edited by
Daniel N. Schowalter and Steven J. Friesen.
    p. cm. -- (Harvard theological studies ; no. 53)
    Summary: "Seventeen essays on the history, archaeology, urban development,
and religious practices of ancient Corinth, with special attention to the
early history of Christianity. Topics include burial customs, water supply,
city planning, and sociology. Results of an interdisciplinary conference
held at Harvard University, January 2002--Provided by publisher.
  Includes bibliographical references and indexes.
  ISBN 0-674-01660-2 (alk. paper)
  1. Corinth (Greece)--Religion. 2. Corinth (Greece)--Antiquities. 3.
Corinth (Greece)--Church history. 4. Christianity and other
religions--Greek. 5. Church history--Primitive and early church, ca.
30-600. I. Schowalter, Daniel N., 1957- II. Friesen, Steven J. III. Series.
  BL793.C6U73 2005
  200'.938'7--dc22
                    2004029899

| Contents

Acknowledgments   ix

Abbreviations   xi

Introduction   3
Daniel N. Schowalter

CHAPTER ONE
Urban Corinth: An Introduction   11
G. D. R. Sanders

CHAPTER TWO
Urban and Rural Planning in Roman Corinth   25
David Gilman Romano

CHAPTER THREE
Favorinus's "Corinthian Oration":
A Piqued Panorama of the Hadrianic Forum   61
L. Michael White

CHAPTER FOUR
Fountains and the Formation of
Cultural Identity at Roman Corinth   111
Betsey A. Robinson

CHAPTER FIVE
Religion in Corinth: 146 B.C.E. to 100 C.E.   141
Nancy Bookidis

CHAPTER SIX
Rites for Melikertes-Palaimon
in the Early Roman Corinthia   165
Elizabeth R. Gebhard

CHAPTER SEVEN
The Stones Don't Speak and the Texts Tell Lies: 205
Sacred Sex at Corinth
John R. Lanci

CHAPTER EIGHT
Roman Corinth: The Final Years of
Pagan Cult Facilities along East Theater Street   221
Charles K. Williams II

CHAPTER NINE
Unquiet Graves:
Burial Practices of the Roman Corinthians   249
Mary E. Hoskins Walbank

CHAPTER TEN
Placing the Dead:
Funerary Practice and Social Stratification in the
Early Roman Period at Corinth and Ephesos   281
Christine M. Thomas

CHAPTER ELEVEN
Paul's Letters to Corinth:
The Interpretive Intertwining of
Literary and Historical Reconstruction   307
Margaret M. Mitchell

CHAPTER TWELVE
The Silence of the Apostle   339
Helmut Koester

CHAPTER THIRTEEN
Prospects for a Demography of the Pauline Mission:
Corinth among the Churches   351
Steven J. Friesen

CHAPTER FOURTEEN
Paul's Assembly in Corinth:
An Alternative Society   371
Richard A. Horsley

CHAPTER FIFTEEN
Civic Identity in Roman Corinth
and Its Impact on Early Christians   397
James Walters

CHAPTER SIXTEEN
Archaeological Evidence for Early Christianity
and the End of Hellenic Religion in Corinth   419
G. D. R. Sanders

CHAPTER SEVENTEEN
Ecclesiastical Ambiguities:
Corinth in the Fourth and Fifth Centuries   443
Vasiliki Limberis

Bibliography   459
Maps   499
Illustration Credits   507
Index   511

Acknowledgments

The organizers express profound gratitude to all who participated in the "Urban Religion in Roman Corinth" conference, and especially to everyone who supported both the conference and the publication of this volume. Dr. Kathleen Warner Slane and Dr. Nancy Bookidis were extremely helpful during the planning process. The primary sponsors of the conference were the Department of Classics and the Institute for the Study of Antiquity and Christian Origins at the University of Texas at Austin, along with the Foundation for Biblical Studies and the Shive Foundation, both of Austin, Texas. Given the concerns about security and the difficulties in raising funds in the months after 9/11, it needs to be said that without the encouragement of L. Michael White and the support of these organizations, the conference would not have taken place.

Major funding and very comfortable meeting space was provided by Harvard Divinity School. The Sackler Museum and the Department of Ancient and Byzantine Art and Numismatics at the Harvard University Art Museums graciously hosted the opening lecture and reception and helped with publicity. Additional funding for the conference was provided by the Society of Biblical Literature, Stonehill College, and Carthage College.

A final word of thanks to the Boston Museum of Fine Arts, and to John Herrmann, curator of ancient art. Not only did Dr. Herrmann host an enjoyable and informative tour of the Museum's collection, he also arranged a special exhibit featuring items relevant to the Corinthia.

Publication of this volume was made possible by a sabbatical leave from Carthage College and by the hospitality and resources of the Blegen Library of the American School of Classical Studies in Athens, and of Hill House in Corinth. We would like to thank Charles K. Williams II and the

New Testament and Archaeology Research Fund for their contributions to the production costs of the volume. We are grateful to François Bovon, Margaret Studier, and all of the staff of the *Harvard Theological Review* and Harvard Theological Studies for their encouragement and assistance in the publication of this volume. We further acknowledge the exceptional editing done by Gene McGarry. Gene's professional skill, scholarly acumen, and patient support played a major role in bringing this book to press.

This volume is dedicated to Helmut Koester and Charles K. Williams II with respect and deep regard for their erudite scholarship, interdisciplinary cooperation, and unfailing support.

Abbreviations

For abbreviations not included here, see *The SBL Handbook of Style* and *The Oxford Classical Dictionary*, 3d ed.

AA	*Archäologischer Anzeiger*
AB	Anchor Bible
ActaAth	Acta Instituti Atheniensis Regni Sueciae
Agora	The Athenian Agora
AJA	*American Journal of Archaeology*
AM	Asia Major
ANF	*The Ante-Nicene Fathers.* Edited by Alexander Roberts and James Donaldson. 10 vols. 1885–1896. Repr., Grand Rapids, Mich.: Eerdmans, 1969–1973.
ANRW	*Aufstieg und Niedergang der römischen Welt: Geschichte und Kultur Roms im Spiegel der neueren Forschung.* Edited by Hildegard Temporini. Berlin: de Gruyter, 1972–.
AntK	Beiheft zur Halbjahresschrift Antike Kunst
ArchDelt	*Archaiologikon Deltion*
ARNTS	*Archaeological Resources for New Testament Studies*
ASCSA	American School of Classical Studies at Athens
BCH	*Bulletin de correspondance hellénique*
BCHSup	Bulletin de correspondance hellénique. Supplement.
BÉFAR	Bibliothèque des écoles françaises d'Athènes et de Rome
BerMatÖAI	Berichte und Materialien des österreichischen archäologischen Instituts

BETL	Bibliotheca ephemeridum theologicarum lovaniensium
BEvT	Beiträge zur evangelischen Theologie
BHG	*Bibliotheca hagiographica graeca.* François Halkin. Brussels: Société des bollandistes, 1977.
BHT	Beiträge zur historischen Theologie
BICS	*Bulletin of the Institute of Classical Studies*
BICSSup	Bulletin of the Institute of Classical Studies Supplement
BSA	*Annual of the British School at Athens*
BTB	*Biblical Theology Bulletin*
BWANT	Beiträge zur Wissenschaft vom Neuen Testament
CBQ	*Catholic Biblical Quarterly*
CIG	*Corpus inscriptionum graecarum.* Edited by A. Böckh. 4 vols. Berlin, 1828–1877.
CIL	*Corpus inscriptionum latinarum*
Corinth	Corinth: Results of Excavations Conducted by the American School of Classical Studies at Athens
CP	*Classical Philology*
Delos	Exploration archéologique de Délos faite par l'École française d'Athènes
DOP	*Dumbarton Oaks Papers*
EKKNT	Evangelisch-katholischer Kommentar zum Neuen Testament
EPRO	Etudes préliminaires aux religions orientales dans l'empire romain
FiE	Forschungen in Ephesos
FRLANT	Forschungen zur Religion und Literatur des Alten und Neuen Testaments
GRBS	*Greek, Roman, and Byzantine Studies*
HNT	Handbuch zum Neuen Testament
HNTC	Harper's New Testament Commentaries
HUT	Hermeneutische Untersuchungen zur Theologie
ICC	International Critical Commentary
ICSB	*Institute of Classical Studies Bulletin*
ICSBSup	Institute of Classical Studies Bulletin Supplement
ILS	*Inscriptiones Latinae selectae*

Isthmia	Isthmia: Excavations by the University of Chicago under the Auspices of the American School of Classical Studies at Athens
IvE	*Inschriften von Ephesos*
JAARSup	*Journal of the American Academy of Religion Supplement*
JdI	*Jahrbuch des deutschen archäologischen Instituts*
JBL	*Journal of Biblical Literature*
JHS	*Journal of Hellenic Studies*
JR	*Journal of Religion*
JRA	*Journal of Roman Archaeology*
JRASup	Journal of Roman Archaeology Supplement
JRS	*Journal of Roman Studies*
JSNT	*Journal for the Study of the New Testament*
JTS	*Journal of Theological Studies*
KEK	Kritisch-exegetischer Kommentar über das Neue Testament
LCL	Loeb Classical Library
LIMC	*Lexicon Iconographicum Mythologiae Classicae*. Edited by Hans Christoph Ackermann and Jean-Robert Gisler. Zürich: Artemis, 1981–1997.
LSJ[9]	Liddell, H. G., R. Scott, and H. S. Jones, *A Greek-English Lexicon*. 9th ed. with revised supplement. Oxford: Oxford University Press, 1996.
LTUR	*Lexicon Topographicum Urbis Romae*
MAAR	Memoirs of the American Academy in Rome
MEFRA	*Mélanges d'archélogie et d'histoire de l'École française de Rome*
NA[27]	*Novum Testamentum Graece*, Nestle-Aland, 27th ed.
NCP	F. W. Imhoof-Blumer and P. Gardiner, *Ancient Coins Illustrating Lost Masterpieces of Greek Art: A Numismatic Commentary on Pausanias* (ed. A. N. Oikonomides; repr.; Chicago: Argonaut, 1964).
NovT	*Novum Testamentum*
NovTSup	Novum Testamentum Supplements
NTAbh	Neutestamentliche Abhandlungen
NTS	*New Testament Studies*

OCD	*The Oxford Classical Dictionary.* Edited by Simon Hornblower and Antony Spawforth. 3d ed. Oxford: Oxford University Press, 1996.
ÖJh	*Jahreshefte des österreichischen archäologischen Instituts in Wien*
PBSR	*Papers of the British School at Rome*
PCPS	*Proceedings of the Cambridge Philological Society*
PG	Patriologia graeca. Edited by J.-P. Migne. Paris, 1857–1886.
PMAAR	*Papers and Monographs of the American Academy at Rome*
Pompeii	Pompei: Pitture e mosaici
Prak	*Πρακτικὰ τῆς ἐν Ἀθήναις Ἀρχαιολογικῆς Ἑταιρείας*
PW	*Paulys Realencyclopädie der classischen Altertumswissenschaft.* New edition by G. Wissowa. 49 vols. Munich, 1980.
RA	*Revue Archéologique*
RGG	*Religion in Geschichte und Gegenwart.* Edited by Hans Dieter Betz. 4th ed. Tübingen: Mohr Siebeck, 1988–.
SBLDS	Society of Biblical Literature Dissertation Series
SBLSP	*Society of Biblical Literature Seminar Papers*
SBLTT	Society of Biblical Literature Texts and Translations
SHA	Scriptores Historiae Augustae
SIMA	Studies in Mediterranean Archaeology
SÖAW	*Sitzungsberichte der österreichischen Akademie der Wissenschaften*
SR	*Studies in Religion*
ThLz	*Theologische Literaturzeitung*
WUNT	Wissenschaftliche Untersuchungen zum Neuen Testament
YaleClSt	Yale Classical Studies
ZNW	*Zeitschrift für die neutestamentliche Wissenschaft und die Kunde der älteren Kirche*
ZPE	*Zeitschrift für Papyrologie und Epigraphik*

Urban Religion
in
Roman Corinth

Introduction

Daniel N. Schowalter

Urban Religion in Roman Corinth follows in the interdisciplinary path of its predecessor volumes on Ephesos and Pergamon.[1] These volumes provide the documentary record of conferences that brought together leading archaeologists from the respective sites, as well as scholars whose main focus is the literary evidence for early Christianity. The resulting dialogue is like few other academic conversations. Instead of debates between scholars using similar methodology to discuss much the same evidence, this format invites experts in a variety of different fields to consider specific and essential pieces of data, be they literary evidence or material remains. The engaged presence of scholars with different training and experience means that even long-established truths need to be explained, defended, and in some cases modified or discarded. Almost three years later, participants from both sides of the dialogue continue to talk about the questions and new perspectives first raised at the conference. In many cases, the published versions of their papers reflect this ongoing dialogue.

The "Urban Religion in Roman Corinth" conference was organized by the steering committee of the Archaeology of Greco-Roman Religion Section of the Society of Biblical Literature. It was held at Harvard University in January 2002, and proved to be a lively gathering of scholars discussing from a variety of disciplines and perspectives one of the most significant cities of

---

[1] *Ephesos, Metropolis of Asia: An Interdisciplinary Approach to Its Archaeology, Religion, and Culture* (ed. Helmut Koester; HTS 41; Valley Forge, Pa.: Trinity Press International, 1995; repr., Cambridge, Mass.: Harvard Divinity School, 2004); and *Pergamon, Citadel of the Gods: Archaeological Record, Literary Description, and Religious Development* (ed. Helmut Koester; HTS 46; Harrisburg, Pa.: Trinity Press International, 1998).

the Roman world. The papers addressed a number of important approaches to evaluating the material culture and textual evidence for religious practice in Corinth, and opened up theoretical discussions on how those who work predominantly with texts can be informed by those who deal with archaeological remains, and vice versa. The interdisciplinary nature of the volume is reflected in the bibliography, which shows the wealth of resources that the contributors have consulted.

The collected papers from the conference distill knowledge compiled by scholars who have devoted decades to excavating and analyzing the material remains of the Corinthia. In some cases, their contributions feature previously unpublished findings or interpretations. In other cases, they include easily accessible summaries of important information on the current state of knowledge regarding Corinth and its surroundings, or new perspectives on long-debated topics and theories. In every case, the essays represent some of the latest thoughts on how the archaeological evidence from Corinth informs the study of ancient religion.

Scholars working predominantly from the religious studies perspective also examine a variety of vital questions. Some focus on the Pauline letters, or on other texts from the New Testament. Other essays consider the interplay between religion and various aspects of culture and society in ancient Corinth. Finally, several consider specific aspects of archaeological evidence and ask how an enhanced knowledge of material realities—including burial practices, water supply, and city planning—strengthens our understanding of religious identity and practice in the ancient city.

In order to understand what was happening among the early Jesus followers in Corinth, one cannot simply read the surviving letters of Paul or other textual information and "let the message sink in." As with other ancient peoples, movements, and civilizations, it is essential to consider the material remains of the culture in order to comprehend the context within which the events were taking place. The challenge comes when differences of language, variations in the interpretation of symbols, and the distances of place and time make it difficult to gain access to the details of an ancient community. This challenge confronts scholars who attempt to understand any aspect of an ancient society. The ability to see into the past, however, can be greatly enhanced if, as in this volume, scholars from different disciplines are able to put aside long-standing obstacles and work together.

The volume begins with an introductory essay by Guy Sanders, director of the Corinth Excavations. He surveys the physical situation, geographical formation, and natural resources of ancient Corinth, and he also describes the history of excavations at Corinth and the current status and focus of excavations. Sanders concludes with a review of the main areas of excavation and how the analysis, interpretation, and conservation of the monuments have developed over time.

Three essays focus on the physical arrangement of ancient Corinth either on a macro scale or with an eye to a more defined area. David Romano reports on a systematic survey of the Corinthia conducted by the Corinth Computer Project under the auspices of the Mediterranean Section of the University of Pennsylvania Museum of Archaeology and Anthropology. On the basis of this survey, Romano discusses his analysis of the system of city planning used by the Romans when they established Corinth as a colony in 44 B.C.E. He also presents evidence for a new city plan at the time of the refoundation of the region as *Colonia Iulia Flavia Augusta Corinthiensis*, during the reign of Vespasian (69–79 C.E.), and he suggests that some of the new colonists were captives from the Jewish revolt in Palestine who had been brought to the region by Nero to work on his project of building a canal across the isthmus.

L. Michael White considers a distinct portion of the city as he discusses the layout of the forum in Corinth in approximately 130 B.C.E., during the reign of Hadrian. His argument combines archaeological data with rhetorical analysis of an address by Favorinus, his "Corinthian Oration." White argues that a nuanced reading of the oration reveals that Favorinus is using the physical surroundings of the Corinthian forum as important elements of his address. White thus provides the reader with rhetorical, social, and topographical insights into Corinthian life in the early second century.

Betsey Robinson narrows the focus even further to two specific locations in Roman Corinth, the Peirene and Glauke fountains. She gives an excellent overview of the physical features and history of the fountains. Robinson is most interested, however, in discussing the way in which these installations relate to the ancient Greek mythical legacy of Corinth and the new Roman identity of the city. Her work takes into consideration extensive modern research on the movement and delivery of water in the ancient Mediterranean world.

Several essays consider various aspects of polytheistic religion in Roman Corinth, starting with an insightful overview of evidence for religious practice in Corinth by Nancy Bookidis. She examines the question of how that evidence reflects change and continuity in religion from the Hellenistic to the Roman phases of the city. Bookidis argues convincingly that religious influences from the Hellenistic city have had more influence on Roman Corinth than has often been assumed. While specifically Roman cults were gathered especially in the forum of the Roman city, cults with Greek roots were reconstituted (perhaps in a Roman aspect) in other areas in and around the city.

Elizabeth Gebhard comes to a similar conclusion as she examines the evidence for a specific cult practice: the worship of Melikertes/Palaimon at the sanctuary of Poseidon in Isthmia. Her analysis of the archaeological evidence suggests that the Roman colonists who re-established rites for Melikertes/Palaimon built a new sanctuary and combined ancient Greek practice, such as a funeral dirge, with new rituals familiar from mystery cults. Gebhard argues that there was both continuity and change in cult practice between the rites observed in the Greek Corinthia and in the Roman colony.

John Lanci raises questions about one of the most frequently cited religious practices of ancient Corinth: temple prostitution in the Aphrodite cult on Acrocorinth. Not only does Lanci challenge common assumptions about the existence of the practice at Corinth, he also considers the evidence for cultic prostitution in the context of the broader Mediterranean and Near Eastern world. This line of inquiry also allows for general reflection on the nature of so-called fertility goddesses and their cults. Lanci pursues several angles that call for a reconsideration of how modern scholars view both these goddesses and the women who worshiped them.

A re-evaluation of Aphrodite also plays a major part in the essay by Charles K. Williams II, director emeritus of the Corinth Excavations. Williams discusses previously unpublished material from excavations east of the theater in Corinth. The architecture, decorations, and small votive objects found in this location illustrate what Williams describes as "religion of the common people in an everyday place." He argues that the presence of votive material related to Aphrodite/Venus does not necessarily indicate prostitution, but could rather reflect the concerns of married women in the community. Williams also details how finds from that site inform us about the decline of polytheistic worship and the growth of Christian influence at the end of the third century C.E.

In addition to religious ritual and everyday life, two essays consider evidence for burial practice and how it illustrates the beliefs of the Corinthians. Mary Walbank provides an initial report on a series of graves excavated in a Roman cemetery north of the city. These are not elaborately decorated funerary monuments, but rather what Walbank refers to as "ordinary graves of very ordinary people." Because these burials are of different types and date from the early colony to the sixth century C.E., they represent an important spectrum of evidence. Walbank and Kathleen Slane are preparing a volume on these tombs for publication in the Corinth series. That volume will be the first detailed examination of the burial practices of the Roman Corinthians, and Walbank's essay gives the reader a preview of the evidence and their analysis of it.

Christine Thomas also looks at burial practice, but draws on her experience with funerary remains in Asia Minor to undertake a comparative study of burial practices in Corinth and Ephesos during the Late Republican and Early Roman Imperial periods. Not only does Thomas survey the ways in which burial practices changed in each region, she also suggests that those changes are indicative of local response to the imposition of Roman authority in the eastern Mediterranean. Specifically, she argues that changes in the prevalence of cremation burials indicate differing social and political hierarchies in Ephesos and Corinth, and divergent ways of interacting with Roman authority.

Several essays discuss specific questions about the New Testament letters of Paul in light of archaeological research. Margaret Mitchell suggests a new arrangement of the documents that make up the composite letter known as 2 Corinthians. At the same time, Mitchell offers an enhanced view of the entire spectrum of Paul's interaction with the community, and how the letters—understood in their proper sequence—shaped that interaction for good or for ill. She concludes with seven questions addressed to archaeologists who study Corinth, in which she inquires about parallels between the people who made up Paul's *ekklēsia* and adherents of other religious associations in Corinth.

Helmut Koester also focuses on the Corinthian *ekklēsia* when he compares what we would like to know about Paul and the church in Corinth with what can actually be learned from literary and archaeological evidence. Koester documents the difficulties in trying to draw conclusions about the community based on Paul's letters, the book of Acts, and other texts. He emphasizes Paul's concern to build up the "body of Christ" in Corinth into a just and peaceful community where no one takes precedence over anyone else, and everyone lives in harmony anticipating the return of Jesus. According to Koester, understanding Paul's realized eschatology is essential to gaining a more nuanced view of Paul's letters and the communities to which they were addressed.

Examination of the history of scholarship leads Steven Friesen to criticize recent attempts to analyze the social structure of the Pauline communities. Friesen argues that such analysis has been hampered by two shortcomings: a narrow focus on an inherently limited New Testament database, and a lack of engagement with modern research on society and economy in the Roman Empire. To counteract these tendencies, Friesen demonstrates the value of compiling a complete listing of all known members of Pauline communities, along with any indication of their poverty or wealth. His data leads him to conclude that the vast majority of members of Paul's communities lived at various levels of poverty. This profile conforms to economic reality in the broader Roman society.

Two essays look in detail at the relationship between members of the community addressed by Paul and the broader culture of Roman Corinth. Richard Horsley questions long-standing assumptions about the language used to talk about Paul's churches, and explores how the countercultural claims of the assembly of Jesus followers in Corinth would have challenged the Roman imperial order of the city. In fact, Horsley argues, the movement promoted by Paul should be seen as an "international anti-imperial movement of communities." This movement was empowered and emboldened by the expectation that God was bringing about the end of Roman power and the beginning of a new age.

James Walters looks at the relationship between the Jesus followers and the Roman authorities from the opposite perspective. He suggests that while the cultic and administrative presence of Rome in the colony had a significant impact on the Corinthian believers, there does not seem to be much evidence that the Roman authorities exerted external pressure on the community. In dialogue with recent scholarship on the Corinthian believing community, and on social relationships within the broader empire, Walters posits that the lack of external pressure explains the presence of factions and conflict within the *ekklēsia*. It seems that believers like Erastus (Rom 16:23) were able to participate in the Jesus community without jeopardizing their status in the Corinthian ruling class. Therefore, greater social diversity within the *ekklēsia* contributes to the tensions within the community addressed by Paul in 1 Corinthians.

The last two essays in the volume examine aspects of Corinth as a Christian city. Guy Sanders studies the transition from Roman to Christian Corinth, discussing both the most recent analyses of pottery and other evidence for dating that transition. Sanders's excavations in the Panayia Field, southeast of the forum, and his review of Christian burial material and basilicas from across the ancient city reveal that the worship of Hellenic deities continued up to the end of the fourth century C.E. Public displays of Christian piety are not obvious in the archaeological record until the late fifth century C.E.

Vasiliki Limberis provides a complement to Sanders's archaeological analysis by offering an overview of the status and development of the Christian church in Corinth during the fourth and fifth centuries. Using primarily literary sources, she introduces the cast of characters who are remembered as the leading figures of Christian Corinth. Limberis looks at episcopal records and hagiography in order to illustrate the internal workings of the institutional church in Corinth, as well as its relationship to other churches and ecclesiastical bodies around the empire.

Each of these essays contributes to a growing consensus that studying the religious development of Roman Corinth offers enormous potential for those who seek to understand Roman religion and the early churches. It only takes a brief walk around the site of ancient Corinth to realize the depth and complexity of its material remains. From a single vantage point, it is possible to view structures representing over 1,500 years of civilization. And even a cursory glance at the site guide reveals that most of the visible remains are related in some way to religion. Of course, it is only a more careful consideration of the evidence that yields an appreciation of how religious observance and practice were integral to every aspect of life in ancient Mediterranean culture generally and urban centers like Corinth in particular.

In the late stages of editing the present volume, the twentieth volume in the Corinth series, *Corinth: The Centenary, 1896–1996,* was released.[2] Corinth XX is a treasure trove of recent research on a variety of Corinthian topics. *Urban Religion in Roman Corinth* includes essays by several contributors to that volume and provides a sharpened focus on issues of religion that are raised in Corinth XX.

One comment concerning nomenclature is in order. Some recent commentators have taken issue with excavators of Corinth who use Greek names for divinities and locations. Their contention is that if one is to take seriously Corinth as a Roman colony, it is necessary to use Latin designations wherever possible. While this observation is important and in many ways helpful, it has been our experience that the archaeologists represented in this volume have gone out of their way to emphasize the Roman nature of colonial Corinth, and have encouraged those of us who study religion and the early church to do likewise. The issue is complicated by the fact that so much of the discussion of places and deities is shaped by the descriptions of Pausanias, who wrote in Greek. It hardly seems appropriate to Latinize the language of an ancient source in order to conform to modern perceptions or preferences.

In both teaching and research, the organizers of this conference attempt to investigate the nature and extent of the religious dimensions of ancient

---

[2]Charles K. Williams II and Nancy Bookidis, eds., *Corinth: The Centenary, 1896–1996* (Corinth XX; Princeton, N.J.: ASCSA, 2003).

society. Sometimes our goal is to illustrate the context in which early Christianity developed, and at other times we seek to understand the veneration of a particular ancient divinity on its own terms. In every case, however, we strive to understand ancient religious practice without judging it through a lens of confessional doctrine or historical success. In this regard, it is particularly important to examine evidence from material remains in conjunction with and in addition to surviving literary records. While such remains must also be analyzed and subjected to scholarly perspectives, they have often escaped centuries of interpretation and the layers of meaning accumulated over that time. It is for this reason that we are especially grateful to our colleagues who have uncovered and begun to interpret the material remains from Corinth, and we welcome any opportunity for dialogue and discussion with them. The contents of this volume are the literary remains of just such a dialogue.

CHAPTER ONE

Urban Corinth: An Introduction

G. D. R. Sanders

THE GEOGRAPHY OF CORINTH

Corinth is located 80 km west of Athens on the south side of the Isthmus of Corinth, a narrow neck of land connecting the Peloponnese to mainland Greece (see map 1). The isthmus separates the Corinthian Gulf from the Saronic Gulf, and thus the Ionian Sea from the Aegean. The local geology is dominated by marine and lacustrine sediments laid horizontally in bands of porous sandy and pebbly limestone interbedded with impervious marl clays. Older Jurassic limestone entities, such as Acrocorinth, extrude through the later deposits to heights of over 570 m. Local uplift of the land relative to the sea has created a series of broad terraces terminating in raised beaches marked by vertical cliff faces. The city is situated on two of the terraces—one about 60 m, the other about 90 m above sea level—at the foot of Acrocorinth, about 3 km from the coast of the Gulf of Corinth.[1] At the exposure of the interfaces of the limestone and underlying marl at the edges of the terraces are several natural springs of abundant freshwater.[2] These springs are notably absent from the region of the isthmus to the east, which to the present has always been sparsely populated and cultivated. By contrast, the land in the plain to

[1] Chris L. Hayward, "Geology of Corinth: The Study of a Basic Resource," in *Corinth: The Centenary, 1896–1996* (ed. Charles K. Williams II and Nancy Bookidis; Corinth XX; Princeton, N.J.: ASCSA, 2003) 15–42.

[2] Mark E. Landon, "Beyond Peirene: Toward a Broader View of Corinthian Water Supply," in *Corinth: The Centenary, 1896–1996* (ed. Charles K. Williams II and Nancy Bookidis; Corinth XX; Princeton, N.J.: ASCSA, 2003) 43–62.

the west is fertile and well watered by springs and the seasonal rivers that descend from the Ayios Vasilios valley and Mount Ziria to the south.

Not only did geology determine why Corinth is located where it is, but the geological makeup of the Corinthia also provided the basic materials for the city's construction. The oolitic limestones of the marine sand bars extend from Kenchreai on the Saronic Gulf to Sikyon and have been extensively quarried for stone.[3] Quarries can be seen to the east and west of the Temple of Apollo. The freshly exposed portion of this rock is so soft that it can be cut with woodworking tools; indeed, there is evidence that early builders used carpentry techniques in stone construction on the site.[4] On exposure to air, the stone gradually forms a hard but brittle surface. So good was this stone, with its rich reddish-yellowish color, that it was exported in bulk at great expense to Delphi and Epidauros and doubtless elsewhere for the construction of temples.

Certain of the marl beds are a rich source of mortar and ceramics. The calcarious marl is easily dug and reduced to a fine powder. A little heat applied for a short duration is all that is required to calcine this powder to calcium oxide. The addition of water reduces the oxide to hydroxide, and the result is a white lime cement. These marls were also excavated, powdered, slaked with water, and dried to a malleable clayey consistency. The clay was formed into light-weight vessels, painted, fired in a kiln, and then probably doused in water. Whether these vessels should be called ceramic or cement is still being investigated.[5] In certain periods, they were exported widely in the Eastern Mediterranean and as far as Spain to the west.

Finally, the tectonic fragmentation of the region has ensured the perennial threat of earthquakes. Some of the more severe of these earthquakes have destroyed major structures and have even disrupted the flow of local springs. Scholars have spiced up the written history of Corinth with a liberal garnish of real and imaginary seismic events; these have served to explain disruptions in the archaeological record. Ongoing research by Nicholas Ambraseys, a leading authority in seismic engineering, has shown, however, that we now need to reconsider every seismic event that has been invoked to explain the

[3]Chris L. Hayward, "High-Resolution Provenance Determination of Construction-Stone: A Preliminary Study of Corinthian Oolitic Limestone Quarries at Examilia," *Geoarchaeology* 11 (1996) 215–34.

[4]Robin F. Rhodes, "The Earliest Greek Architecture in Corinth and the 7th-Century Temple on Temple Hill," in *Corinth: The Centenary, 1896–1996* (ed. Charles K. Williams II and Nancy Bookidis; Corinth XX; Princeton, N.J.: ASCSA, 2003) 85–94.

[5]This research is being undertaken by G. D. R. Sanders, Louise Joyner, and Ian Whitbread.

destruction of various phases of the city. His findings, which have been generally accepted by geologists and seismologists alike, are that earthquakes in
Greece rarely exceeded a magnitude of 6.5 and never exceeded 7.0 on the
logarithmic Richter scale. According to Ambraseys and J. A. Jackson, the
nature of faults in Greece is such that the range of damage wrought by an
earthquake of such a magnitude is limited to a few tens of kilometers from the
epicenter. Thus, an earthquake such as the 551/52 C.E. earthquake recorded by
Procopius at Chaironeia in central Greece clearly did not have the catastrophic
effect on Corinth that three generations of scholars have claimed.[6]

Corinth possessed four harbors. Schoenus and Poseidona were presumably
fairly simple docking facilities that served either end of the Diolkos.[7] The
Diolkos was a paved portage road built across the 6-kilometer width of the
isthmus, with an average gradient of about 1.5%. It was probably constructed
by the tyrant Periander in the sixth century B.C.E., and is scored by the wheels
of transport vehicles whose wheelbase averaged 1.5 m across. On either side
of the paved portion were earthen roads. Historical sources mention six
attempts—five successful and one unsuccessful—to portage warships over the
isthmus between 428 and 30 B.C.E. Niketas Oryphas, revealing his familiarity
with ancient literature, effected a sixth successful crossing in 881 C.E.

Most commentators insist that the Diolkos was used principally for military
purposes, but from the vulgar humor of the *Thesmophoriazusae* of Aristophanes,
one gets a very different impression.[8] Mnesilochos, an interloper among women
and himself disguised as a woman, hides his masculinity by pushing his huge
stage prop penis back between his legs. When Kleisthenes attempts to find
it from behind, Mnesilochus pushes it to the front. This action is repeated
several times. Finally, Kleisthenes cries in exasperation, "You have a sort of
isthmus, bro', hauling your prow to and fro more often than the Corinthians
[haul ships across the Diolkos]." We can surmise that the Diolkos was actively
and regularly used for merchant ships, or else there would be no humor in
Kleisthenes' quip. The triremes that crossed the Diolkos were comparable in
size and capacity to the Kyrenia ship (14 m long x 4.2 m wide, laden weight
ca. 39 tons). Mr. Sarris, the shipbuilder of the Kyrenia replica, assures me
that, properly supported by the keelsom, a ship of those dimensions could be

[6]N. N. Ambraseys and A. Jackson, "Seismicity and Associated Strain of Central Greece
between 1890 and 1988," *Geophysics Journal International* 101 (1990) 663–708.

[7]G. Raepsaet, "Le Diolkos de l'isthme à Corinthe: sa trace, son fonctionnement,"
BCH 117 (1993) 233–56.

[8]Aristophanes, *Thesmophoriazusae* (ed. Benjamin Bickley Rogers; LCL; Cambridge,
Mass.: Harvard University Press, 1924) line 648. Since Rogers did not translate the passage,
the rendition that follows is mine.

moved considerable distances—even with its full cargo aboard—without the slightest damage.[9]

Such traffic must have kept a society of wagoners and their teams of oxen fully occupied. The portage proved so valuable that efforts were made to replace it with a canal. The emperor Nero actually began work on the canal by personally dumping the first shovelful of earth into a golden bucket, using a golden shovel. He died before much progress could be made, but not before his image as the god Herakles had been inscribed in one wall of the cutting. Under Vespasian, about 800 yards of canal were excavated to a depth of 90 feet, using 6,000 Jewish slaves captured in the sack of Jerusalem, before the project was finally abandoned.[10] Herodes Atticus, the Athenian teacher of philosophy and wealthy patron of extravagant monuments, briefly contemplated the completion of Nero's and Vespasian's work but demurred on the grounds that it was hubristic to succeed where emperors had failed. By the time the canal was finally completed in 1893, the Levant trade had waned.

Kenchreai on the Saronic Gulf and Lechaion on the Corinthian Gulf were altogether different kinds of harbors. Kenchreai was excavated by the American School of Classical Studies in the 1960s.[11] It consists of a settlement on the south slopes of a promontory with a pair of harbor moles encircling a round basin facing southeast. Architecture, pottery, and coins derive from many centuries of occupation and include shrines of the gods (one perhaps dedicated to Isis) and a small early Christian basilica of the sixth century. Lechaion must be considered the principal harbor. Located on the coast north of the city, the harbor consists of a series of landlocked basins accessible from the sea by a narrow channel. The outer works of the harbor included three long moles, two for a square basin and the third to protect the entrance to the inner harbor. Sporadic excavations in the area indicate that the associated settlement was extensive. The most concentrated campaign of archaeological work, that of the Greek Archaeological Society in the 1960s, revealed an enormous early Christian basilica between the inner harbor and the sea.[12]

[9]M. L. Katzef, "The Kyrenia Ship," in *A History of Seafaring Based on Underwater Archaeology* (ed. George Fletcher Bass; London: Thames and Hudson, 1982) 50–52; and idem and S. W. Katzef, "Building a Replica of an Ancient Greek Merchantman," in *Proceedings of the 1st International Symposium on Ship Construction in Antiquity* (ed. H. E. Tzalas; Athens: n.p., 1989) 163–75.

[10]On this point, see the essay by David Gilman Romano in this volume (pp. 25–59, esp. 27–29).

[11]Robert L. Scranton, Joseph W. Shaw, and Leila Ibrahim, *Topography and Architecture*, vol. 1 of *Kenchreai, Eastern Port of Corinth* (Leiden: Brill, 1978).

[12]D. I. Pallas, "Korinth," *Reallexikon zur Byzantinischen Kunst*, vol. 4 (Stuttgart: Hiersemann, 1990) 745–811.

Together these four harbors attest the sheer volume of Corinth's commercial interests at various times.

Traffic moving north and south across the isthmus was channeled into narrow corridors along the Kakia Skala or over Mount Geraneion. At one end of the corridor, routes fanned out to Athens and to Thebes and beyond. At the other end, the routes led along the coast west towards Patras, east to Epidauros, and through passes on either side of Acrocorinth into the Peloponnese, to the Argolid and Arcadia. The historical communications network of southern Greece has recently been treated purely as a problem in graph theory. This is an application most useful to economic geographers and perhaps familiar to most of us as the particular talent of the title character in the film *Good Will Hunting*. Corinth was unsurprisingly found to be at the mathematical and geographical center of the Roman province of Achaia.[13]

As in modern commerce, whether building a cement factory or opening a downtown bar, location has always been important to commercial success. This much may have occurred to the apostle Paul when he chose Corinth for his ministry. In the middle of the first century C.E., Corinth was a perfect place for the dissemination of goods and ideas—a multilingual, polytheistic, cosmopolitan community visited by travelers, merchants, and seamen from all over the Mediterranean. It is not difficult to imagine why the moral condition of commerce-oriented Corinth, its inhabitants, and visitors still concerned Paul deeply some two hundred years after the infamous cult of Aphrodite on Acrocorinth had closed its doors.[14]

Well-watered, overlooked by an imposing acropolis, flanked by a large fertile plain to the north and northwest, and located between two seas, Corinth commanded the principal nodal point in the land and sea communications of southern Greece. Its strategic and commercial position was supplemented by valuable natural resources for export, including building materials, excellent clays for ceramics and mortars, wood, and agricultural produce. It was not so much Corinth's own riches that were being moved, however. The importance of Corinth was as an entrepôt through which the produce of other regions was shipped.

---

[13]G. D. R. Sanders and I. K. Whitbread, "Central Places and Major Roads in the Peloponnese," *BSA* 85 (1990) 333–61.

[14]On Corinthian Aphrodite, see the essays by John R. Lanci (pp. 205–20) and Charles K. Williams II (pp. 221–47) in this volume.

History of the Corinth Excavations

The American School of Classical Studies at Athens has been excavating at Corinth since 1896. Over the course of the twentieth century, scholarly interests have changed considerably. The earliest excavators were largely concerned with ancient topography and planned to reveal as much of the center of the pre-Roman city as they could. While they revealed large portions of the center of Corinth, their task was made more difficult by Mummius's sack in 146 B.C.E. and by the foundation of a Roman colony in 44 B.C.E., when the city plan was re-engineered and settlers covered or even tore out the core of the Classical city.

The years between 1925 and 1940 saw continued but rather more systematic clearance of the theater and forum areas. Interest shifted from topographic to taxonomic and chronological concerns. At the time, however, it was still generally the practice to excavate with large teams of nonspecialist laborers under limited supervision. They dug from topsoil to forum level, a depth of 3–4 m, in a single season, and although the recovery of data was far superior to the earlier campaigns, it was not what one would now demand. The excavators generated a large number of books and articles on urban history, buildings, inscriptions, sculpture, ceramics, and minor objects. This literature has shaped present popular conceptions of Corinth and set many of the standards on which archaeologists in the Eastern Mediterranean still rely.

From the mid-1960s to the present, the archaeological study of Corinth has undergone a sustained period of ideological and methodological evolution if not revolution. During this exciting intellectual passage, scholars have begun to focus on the human rather than the monumental side of antiquity, and post-Classical archaeology has come into its own. Despite the sheer volume of work undertaken in these forty years, the overall plan of the site has changed remarkably little. Our understanding of the urban and historical landscape, however, has been transformed. Systematic excavation by small teams of trained technicians supervised by a recording archaeologist has permitted close control of the stratigraphic sequences. New procedures for the recording of finds were instituted, context materials and not just remarkable objects were saved, and preliminary reports of work appeared annually in the journal *Hesperia*. It would be fair to say that now equal portions of the research are done by descriptive scientists with hand lenses and microscopes and by researchers engaged in the painstaking archaeological autopsy of earlier records.

Coins have been supplanted by pottery as the currency of chronology. Coins are common and survive well, and they provide refreshingly specific information about their date of issue—but the right coin is rarely found in the right place. Until comparatively recently, ceramics specialists tended to concentrate on fine wares, because the accepted bias was that coarse wares were not worth studying because they were not diagnostic. Coarse wares, however, comprise the large majority of finds from any context. Some periods were neglected simply because they were unfashionable, and Late Roman pottery assemblages are a case in point. The study of Late Roman Corinth was driven by coins and disasters until the publication of a Late Roman fine pottery survey by John Hayes in 1972.[15] Unfortunately, the heroic efforts of Demetrios Pallas in the basilicas and James Wiseman at the gymnasium came too early to benefit from Hayes's volume.[16]

Pottery is ubiquitous in archaeological contexts and can be used to date phases of activity with a fair degree of precision. Kathleen Slane's volume on the Demeter sanctuary and her specialist articles have given us some idea of what Corinthian pottery looked like through the Roman period.[17] It was only with the excavations east of the theater in the 1980s that sufficient quantities of well-excavated deposits, many retained in their entirety, enabled Slane to undertake a thorough diachronic survey of Roman pottery from the foundation of the colony to the beginning of the seventh century.[18] This study is based on statistical analyses of number and weight by type and on stratigraphic relations.[19] The final publication, which is eagerly anticipated, will be the first complete overview of Roman pottery typology for a Greek site. It will show how the proportions of different pottery types changed over time; also, analysis of imports will allow researchers to identify shifts in economic contacts. This tool will enable scholars to reassess old contexts and redraft our history of the city. Its impact should be felt well beyond Corinth and even Greece.

[15]J. W. Hayes, *Late Roman Pottery* (London: British School at Rome, 1972).

[16]Pallas, "Korinth"; and James Wiseman, "Excavations in the Gymnasium Area. 1969–1970," *Hesperia* 41 (1972) 1–42.

[17]Kathleen W. Slane, *The Sanctuary of Demeter and Kore: The Roman Pottery and Lamps* (Corinth XVIII.2; Princeton, N.J.: ASCSA, 1990).

[18]Charles K. Williams II and Orestes H. Zervos, "Corinth, 1988: East of the Theater," *Hesperia* 58 (1989) 1–50; for bibliography, see the essay by Charles K. Williams II in this volume (pp. 221–47).

[19]Kathleen W. Slane, "Corinth's Roman Pottery: Quantification and Meaning," in *Corinth: The Centenary, 1896–1996* (ed. Charles K. Williams II and Nancy Bookidis; Corinth XX; Princeton, N.J.: ASCSA, 2003) 321–36.

The way in which we look at dead Corinthians has also changed. Charles Williams's excavations south of the Museum encountered a packed cemetery dating to the Frankish period.[20] To cope with the excavation and analysis of this complicated mass of evidence, anthropologists Art Rohn and Ethne Barnes were invited to excavate and study the burials.[21] Rohn has not only trained our specialist pickmen to articulate burials and then remove them; he has also begun to examine changes in burial practice through time. Barnes is able to discern in bones repetitive stress patterns that betray regular heavy exercise of different kinds. She can also recognize the effects of genetics, illness, malnutrition, and violence. Although they started with Medieval and continued with post-Medieval burials, Rohn and Barnes now include Roman and earlier material in their research. Corinth now has such a range of fascinating pathologies that a special facility was recently opened to house a comparative collection for study.

Despite the excavation of many hundreds of Roman tombs, only individual tombs have occasionally been published. In the 1960s, Henry Robinson was invited to excavate in advance of the construction of a drainage channel along the edge of the north terrace of Corinth, where he found several significant graves dating from the first through fifth centuries C.E. Mary Walbank and Kathleen Slane are in the final stages of producing a book-length publication of these discoveries.[22]

The topography of the Corinthia has received rather patchy coverage, but a comprehensive picture is gradually emerging. James Wiseman's important extensive survey of the region put many sites on the map.[23] Other investigators added topoi to this basic work; two new doctoral theses and a third nearing completion have examined the borders of Corinth with Epidaurus, Sikyon, and Argos.[24] The recently completed Eastern Corinthia archaeological survey was an intensive survey of a much smaller territory that will add a new dimension to our understanding of the historical geography. Mary Walbank was the

[20]Charles K. Williams II, L. M. Snyder, Ethne Barnes, and Orestes H. Zervos, "Frankish Corinth, 1997," *Hesperia* 67 (1998) 223–81.

[21]Ethne Barnes, "The Dead Do Tell Tales," in *Corinth: The Centenary, 1896–1996* (ed. Charles K. Williams II and Nancy Bookidis; Corinth XX; Princeton, N.J.: ASCSA, 2003) 435–43.

[22]See the essay by Mary E. Hoskins Walbank in this volume (pp. 249–80).

[23]James Wiseman, *The Land of the Ancient Corinthians* (SIMA 50; Göteborg: P. Åström, 1978).

[24]Y. A. Lolos, "The Hadrianic Aqueduct of Corinth," *Hesperia* 66 (1997) 271–314; and Michael D. Dixon, "Disputed Territories: Interstate Arbitration in the Northeast Peloponnese, ca. 250–150 B.C." (Ph.D. diss., Ohio State University, 2000).

first to discuss Roman land division in the Corinthia.[25] David Romano and Panos Doukellis have since independently extrapolated different schemes of mensuration on the basis of crop marks, field boundaries, and roads.[26] In the past couple of years, resistivity survey has added much of topographical interest to the picture presented by the excavated remains.[27]

The American School has also been active in excavation outside of the city but within its territory. Elizabeth Gebhard and her colleagues have continued the excavations and publication program started by Oscar Broneer at the major Corinthian sanctuary dedicated to Poseidon and Palaimon at Isthmia.[28] Timothy Gregory and his colleagues have continued Paul Clement's work in the Late Roman fortress and Roman baths, also at Isthmia.[29] Robert Scranton excavated above and below the water line at Kenchreai.[30] In addition to the American work, the British School excavated and published the sanctuary of Hera at Perachora under Humfry Payne and later Richard Tomlinson.[31] Many of these diverse threads of more recent research have already appeared as books, as articles in *Hesperia*, and elsewhere. The most important new synopsis is the volume originating in the 1996 centenary conference.[32] It contains twenty-seven papers by active students of Corinth's archaeology

[25]Mary E. Hoskins Walbank, "The Foundation and Planning of Early Roman Corinth," *JRA* 10 (1997) 95–130.

[26]David G. Romano, "City Planning, Centuriation, and Land Division in Roman Corinth: *Colonia Laus Iulia Corinthiensis* and *Colonia Iulia Flavia Augusta Corinthiensis*," in *Corinth: The Centenary, 1896–1996* (ed. Charles K. Williams II and Nancy Bookidis; Corinth XX; Princeton, N.J.: ASCSA, 2003) 279–301; Panagiotis N. Doukellis, "Le territoire de la colonie romaine de Corinthe," in *Structures rurales et sociétés antiques: actes du colloque de Corfou, 14–16 mai 1992* (ed. Panagiotis N. Doukellis and Lina G. Mendoni; Paris: Belles Lettres, 1994) 359–90; and Mary E. Hoskins Walbank, "What's in a Name? Corinth Under the Flavians," *ZPE* 139 (2002) 251–64.

[27]The results of this ongoing survey will be published in *Hesperia* by G. D. R. Sanders and M. Boyd.

[28]For bibliography, see the essay by Elizabeth R. Gebhard in this volume (pp. 165–203).

[29]Timothy E. Gregory, *The Hexamilion and the Fortress* (Isthmia V; Princeton, N.J.: Princeton University Press, 1993); and *The Corinthia in the Roman Period: Including the Papers Given at a Symposium Held at The Ohio State University on 7–9 March 1991* (ed. Timothy E. Gregory; JRASup 8; Ann Arbor, Mich.: Journal of Roman Archaeology, 1993).

[30]Scranton, Shaw, and Ibrahim, *Topography and Architecture*.

[31]R. Tomlinson, "Perachora," in *Le Sanctuaire Grec* (ed. Albert Schachter and Jean Bingen; Entretiens sur l'Antiquité classique 37; Geneva: Fondation Hardt, 1992) 321–51. For a more recent appraisal of the temple and cult, see B. Menadier, "The Sixth Century BC Temple and the Sanctuary and Cult of Hera Akraia, Perachora" (Ph.D. diss., University of Cincinnati, 1995).

[32]Charles K. Williams II and Nancy Bookidis, eds., *Corinth: The Centenary, 1896–1996* (Corinth XX; Princeton, N.J.: ASCSA, 2003).

stating their current ideas and features a complete bibliography of Corinth from the Neolithic to Late Medieval periods.

In his early years as director, Williams concentrated on the reinterpretation of some seventy years of scholarship by restudying the earlier excavation records and by undertaking new excavations in and around the forum. Over the course of fifteen years he was able to document how the city developed over time, and a brief overview of his synthesis follows below.[33]

Development of the Urban Area

The area of the site opened to date concentrates largely on the Roman forum and its surrounds. This zone is the transition, marked by a steep slope (10–20% grade over 15 m) between the two terraces on which Corinth was built. Here the natural drainage pattern and spring line has created a fairly broad valley and a relatively easy transition for wheeled and pedestrian traffic between the terraces. The upper valley is occupied by the forum and the lower valley by the Lechaion Road.

There is ample evidence for prehistoric settlement dating from the Neolithic to sub-Mycenean periods. Corinth is reckoned to have synoecized—that is, emerged as a polity—in the eighth century B.C.E., sending out trading colonies to Syracuse and Corfu. Archaeologically at Corinth there is little evidence for the form and extent of the city. The earliest Geometric period is represented by domestic debris in the valley floor, graves, and a well. In the second half of the eighth century, however, burial was kept separate from the residential area. At the same time, the first stone architecture becomes evident and the watercourses of the springs are artificially channelled. Evidence of roads survives. These roads direct traffic from the south and from the southwest towards the north at the mouth of the valley.

In the seventh century B.C.E., the first temple was built on the rise to the north of the forum.[34] The street plan developed with the addition of roads parallel to the Geometric streets; these roads also channeled traffic from the south and west towards the north. The Sacred Spring was elaborated and perhaps at

---

[33]A full bibliography can be found in ibid., which also includes plans illustrating changes in the forum area over time; see maps 4 and 5 in this volume. For more detail, see Williams's publications in *Hesperia*.

[34]For a survey of Corinth's sanctuaries with pertinent bibliography, see Nancy Bookidis, "The Sanctuaries of Corinth," in *Corinth: The Centenary, 1896–1996* (ed. Charles K. Williams II and Nancy Bookidis; Corinth XX; Princeton, N.J.: ASCSA, 2003) 247–60.

this point first had cult associated with it. In the mid-seventh century, a small house with a well was constructed to the south of the spring. In the Lechaion Road valley, the Cyclopean fountain was constructed and houses now faced the road towards Acrocorinth. In the sixth and early fifth centuries, the early temple was destroyed (ca. 580 B.C.E.) to be replaced about forty years later by the Archaic temple that still stands on the site today. The formal approach was from the northeast, but access was supplemented by a monumental ramp leading up from the street that ran past the Sacred Spring to the southeast. To the east of the temple, at the base of the cliff separating it from the valley, a small stoa was built. A cluster of proto-Geometric graves received a temenos, and a small underground shrine was established alongside a new road to Acrocorinth.

The later fifth and early fourth centuries saw a rapid, organized, and formalized development that gives the impression of a thoroughly urban space. The Peirene Fountain received draw basins, Temple A was constructed to the north, and the Sacred Spring was further developed with a triglyph and metope wall and a curious apsidal temple. A racecourse more or less followed the southernmost Archaic road, and the houses that flanked it were replaced by larger complexes. To the west, the house of a merchant dealing in imported fish fillets was constructed and subsequently removed, and finally a bath complex was established. The main changes in the following period were a realignment of the racetrack and the construction of the South Stoa.

A question that has constantly arisen is the location of the agora. By analogy with the Athenian agora, many would point to the racetrack as evidence that the Corinthian agora was the predecessor of the Roman forum. In the Greek period, however, this area had a relatively steep and continuous slope from the Sacred Spring up to the South Stoa, interrupted only by the racetrack. All roads found to date channel traffic in a general northward direction, while the water supply also supplies the area towards the north. Although it might be argued that the lack of inscriptions in the area of the forum is to be expected in a tyranny, and later an oligarchy, as opposed to a democracy, it is notable that what inscriptions have been found are concentrated at the northeast side of Temple Hill. A better hypothesis, therefore, is that the agora was located immediately to the north of the excavated zone. If it was not an agora, then what were the main functions of the excavated area of the later forum in the Classical period? According to Williams, it was largely dedicated to cult (especially non-Olympian cult), housing, and minor industry. The evidence for cult includes fragments of inscriptions, buildings, temenoi, a racetrack, and twenty-six hero reliefs. The cults attested tend to be of deities with local rather than pan-Hellenic significance and include not only Hellotis, celebrated with a torch race on the race track; her sister Kotyto, honored perhaps in the Sacred Spring; Artemis Korithos; and Peirene; but also Poseidon and Aphrodite, and perhaps Dionysos, Hermes, and the nymphs. Cults of heroes include Zeuxippus and various unknown dead ancestors.

In 146 B.C.E., after defeating the Achaian League led by the Corinthians at Lefkopetros on the Isthmus, the Roman general Mummius sacked Corinth. He killed the male population and sold the women and children into slavery. Thereafter Corinth was no longer a political entity but at best an almost-deserted ghost town occupied by a small non-Corinthian population engaged in cultivation of the agricultural land. Finds identified from this interim period amount to forty-two knidian amphorae stamps, some Megarian bowls, and over ninety coins. The prestige and income from the Isthmian games devolved to Corinth's northwest neighbor, Sikyon, and the rich agricultural land was auctioned off as *ager publicus* every two years in Rome. The city was refounded in 44 B.C.E. by Julius Caesar as a colony for 16,000 colonists. Its territory was measured out into portions for the colonists and the city was redeveloped on an orthogonal plan. There is little reason to believe that many of Corinth's religious traditions survived. Nancy Bookidis has dealt briefly with three of the cults that were resurrected: those of Apollo, Asklepius, and Demeter.[35]

In the early Roman period, the forum was a huge open space measuring about 200 m east-west and 100 m north-south, and taking its orientation from the surviving South Stoa, which defined its southern edge. The South Stoa was modified, some of its smaller spaces being converted into larger rooms, but it retained its colonnade. Dominating the skyline to the north, the Archaic Temple of Apollo on Temple Hill was flanked by colonnades to the north and south. The colonists had rotated its orientation by 180 degrees to face an approach from the road out of the forum to the west. Its interior colonnade was removed and re-erected in a line running north from the west end of the South Stoa along the road to Acrocorinth. Also to the north was a long basilica flanking the Lechaion Road on one side and the cliff of Temple Hill on the other. The Lechaion Road, entering the forum from the north, ascended a broad stairway through a three-bayed monumental arch. East of the Lechaion Road, Peirene Fountain had been refurbished and extended. The former simple façade of the draw basins was walled off with a series of arches. A rectangular two-story court enclosing a rectangular pool was added to the north.

---

[35]See Bookidis's essay in this volume (pp. 141–64).

On the east side of the forum stood the Julian Basilica. At forum level this was a cryptoporticus basement. The first story, approached by a staircase of fourteen steps leading up to a porch, was an open rectangular space measuring 38 x 24 m, with Corinthian columns supporting a clerestory and a marble dado. Inside were sculptures of the imperial family, including Augustus in Pentelic marble, dressed in a toga with a fold draped over his head, and portrayed engaged in sacrifice. He was flanked by his adopted sons Caius and Lucius Caesar, each portrayed in heroic nudity with a chlamys over the shoulder, perhaps as the Dioscuroi. Clearly this building had some high civic function.

To the west of the forum stood Temple E, a 6 x 11–column peripteral temple on a low base with long stoas flanking it to the north and south. The identification of the temple has been hotly debated. Some think that it was dedicated to Jove or Zeus based on its size and location, while others regard it as the temple of Octavia. In front of the temple was a range of more typically Roman temples and monuments. Two prostyle temples, F and G, were dedicated to Venus and to Clarion Apollo, respectively. Built in the Roman style, they stood on high marble-clad podia of concrete and rubble that were approached from the east by a stair. To the north was a fountain house dedicated to Poseidon, decorated with a statue of the god and dolphins, and a circular monument decorated in the Corinthian order and dedicated by Gnaius Cornelius Babbius. South of center in the forum was the rostra, considered by many to be the bema in front of which Paul was brought by the elders of the Jewish community (Acts 18: 12). A second topos for those following the travels of Paul in Greece can be found east of the theater, also remodeled to suit Roman taste. An inscription found there reads: ERASTUS PRO AEDILIT[AT]E S(ua) P(ecunia) STRAVIT ("Erastus, in return for his aedileship, laid the pavement at his own expense"). Since the office of aedile can be pretty much equated with that of *oikonomos*, it is thought that this could be the *oikonomos* Erastus whose greetings Paul forwards in his letter to the Romans (16:23).[36]

A hundred years later, the plan of the forum remained much the same, receiving additions such as the odeion, another temple at the west end of the forum, shops to the west of the rostra, and a new basilica south of the South Stoa.

---

[36]For more on Erastus, see the essays by Helmut Koester (pp. 339–49), Steven J. Friesen (pp. 351–70), and James A. Walters (pp. 397–417) in this volume, as well as Steven J. Friesen, "Poverty in Pauline Studies: Beyond the So-Called New Consensus," *JSNT* 26 (2004) 323–61.

Finally, in the Late Roman period Corinth seems to have been radically transformed. Earthquakes in the late fourth century C.E. and a social call by Alaric and his Goths seem to have reduced the city. The great sanctuaries of the Hellenic deities Demeter and Asklepios, already under legislative pressure to close, apparently did not survive. Efforts were made to refurbish the area of the forum, however—most notably by reappointing Peirene Fountain[37] and the west shops, and by converting the central shops into the broadest stairway in the Roman world. In the early fifth century, a city wall was laid out, encompassing the heart of the city. Remote-sensing survey suggests that this wall enclosed only about 25% of the area hitherto envisioned, and as-sertions about the relationships of cemeteries and churches to the city center will clearly have to be revised. The sixth century saw the construction of the first buildings to be dedicated to Christian worship. A huge church, the length of two football fields, was built at Lechaion, and smaller basilicas were erected at Kraneion, Skoutela, and in the plain just north of the city. At what should have been an auspicious time, Christian Corinth fell victim first to bubonic plague and its high mortality levels, and subsequently to a deep economic depression that lasted, as the archaeology of the site witnesses, for five hundred years.[38]

[37]See the essay by Betsey A. Robinson in this volume (pp. 111–40).
[38]See my other essay in this volume (pp. 419–42), as well as my "Problems in Interpreting Rural and Urban Settlement in Southern Greece, AD 365–700," in *Landscapes of Change: The Evolution of the Countryside from Late Antiquity to the Early Middle Ages* (ed. Neil Christie; Aldershot: Ashgate, 2004) ch. 5.

Chapter Two

Urban and Rural Planning in Roman Corinth

David Gilman Romano

Introduction

Since the beginning of work at ancient Corinth in 1896 by the American School of Classical Studies, various elements of the Roman city have been excavated and studied, including buildings, monuments, roadways, villas, and tombs. Aspects of the Roman city plan have been known for many years, but only recently has it been possible to place accurately all of these sometimes disparate aspects of the city together on a single map in order to create an overall sense of what the Roman city looked like and to answer some important questions. How large were the urban and rural areas of the colony? Where was the forum located within the urban area? What was the relationship of the Roman colony to the former Greek city on the same site? How did the Roman city develop and change over time?

The Corinth Computer Project was initiated in order to study the Roman planning of Corinth and its territory.[1] The specific objectives of the project

[1]This essay is based on the work of the Corinth Computer Project (1988–), a research and field project of the Mediterranean Section of the University of Pennsylvania Museum of Archaeology and Anthropology in Philadelphia, carried out in conjunction with the Corinth excavations of the American School of Classical Studies at Athens. For permission to carry out this work at Corinth and for friendly and helpful assistance, I thank Dr. Charles K. Williams II, director of the excavations until 1997, and Dr. Guy Sanders, director from 1997 to the present. I also thank the staff of the Corinth excavations for their sustained assistance

as outlined in 1988 include the following: to study the nature of the city planning process during the Roman period, to gain a more precise idea of the order of accuracy of the Roman *agrimensor* (land surveyor), and to create new, highly accurate, computer-generated period maps of the heart of the ancient city.[2] The research has included a computerized architectural and topographical study of the Roman city and its immediate environs. This work also facilitates understanding of the organization and development of the excavated remains and recording the location of the known antiquities in the general area.

HISTORICAL INTRODUCTION

The Greek city of Corinth, which led the Achaian League against the coming of Rome in the second century B.C.E., was defeated by the consul Lucius Mummius in 146 B.C.E. From Pausanias we learn that the male citizens were killed, while the women, children, and freedpersons were sold into slavery.[3] The archaeological record indicates that there was a partial and selective destruction of Greek structures and the city walls. As a result, Corinth was deprived of its civic and political identity. For all practical purposes, the city ceased to function.[4] Following the defeat of Corinth, the Roman Senate sent

---

and interest in this project. Finally, I am grateful to the over 100 University of Pennsylvania students who have assisted me with this project during the past fifteen years, both in Corinth and in Philadelphia.

[2]A number of publications describe the results and the methodology of the Corinth Computer Project. A listing of many of these may conveniently be found in David G. Romano, "City Planning, Centuriation, and Land Division in Roman Corinth, *Colonia Laus Iulia Corinthiensis* and *Colonia Iulia Flavia Augusta Corinthiensis*," in *Corinth: The Centenary, 1896–1996* (ed. Charles K. Williams II and Nancy Bookidis; Corinth XX; Princeton, N.J.: ASCSA, 2003) xix–xx, 279–301. See also idem, "A Tale of Two Cities: Roman Colonies at Corinth," in *Romanization and the City* (ed. E. Fentress; JRASup 38; Portsmouth, N.H.: Journal of Roman Archaeology, 2000) 83–104, esp. 83 n. 4. Since January 1997, a website (http://corinth.sas.upenn.edu) has been devoted to discussing some of the methodology of the project as well as to disseminating the results of the research of this project. The final publication of the project will appear as a volume in the Corinth series and will include a text volume, CD-ROMs, and an atlas and gazetteer.

[3]Pausanias 7.16.8.

[4]On the damage sustained by the city, see James Wiseman, "Corinth and Rome I: 228 B.C.–A.D. 267," *ANRW* II.7.1 (1979) 491–96.

ten commissioners to assist Lucius Mummius in the settlement of Greece.[5] This work included the sale of property confiscated from those who had been prominent in the fight against Rome.

During the century that passed between the capture and colonization of Corinth (146–44 B.C.E.), the land that had been under its control became largely *ager publicus,* although several ancient authors suggest that Sikyon had taken over care of part of the land of Corinth.[6] The *lex agraria* of 111 B.C.E., passed in Rome by the assembly of tribes, indicates that some parts of the Corinthian territory were measured out for sale and boundary stones erected.[7] The Roman colony of Julius Caesar, located on the site of the former Greek city, was not founded for 102 years, more than three generations after the defeat.[8]

ROMAN *AGRIMENSORES*

When the earliest settlers from Rome arrived in Corinth in 44 B.C.E., they likely brought with them detailed plans for both the urban and rural design of Julius Caesar's colony, *Colonia Laus Iulia Corinthiensis.*[9] It is probable, however, that an advance contingent of Roman *agrimensores* had visited the site on one or more occasions in order to prepare the way for the arrival of the colonists. Roman colonies typically were well planned, and Corinth was no exception in this regard.[10]

[5]Pausanias 7.16.9; Polybius 39.4.1; 39.5.1. For a discussion of the economic conditions following the Achaian War in Greece, see J. A. O. Larsen, "Roman Greece," in *An Economic Survey of Ancient Rome* (ed. Tenney Frank; 4 vols.; Baltimore, Md.: Johns Hopkins University Press, 1938) 4:259–498. See also Erich S. Gruen, *The Hellenistic World and the Coming of Rome* (Berkeley: University of California Press, 1984) 523–27.

[6]Livy 27.1; Cicero, *Leg. Agr.* 1.2.5; 2.19.51.

[7]For the *lex agraria,* see M. H. Crawford, ed., *Roman Statutes* (2 vols.; BICSSup 64; London: University of London, 1996) 1:139–80; and A. W. Lintott, *Judicial Reform and Land Reform in the Roman Republic* (Cambridge: Cambridge University Press, 1992) 171–285.

[8]Greece was not converted into a province until 46 B.C.E. under Julius Caesar, and then again in 27 B.C.E. under Augustus.

[9]There is considerable literary, historical, and numismatic evidence concerning the foundation of the colony of Julius Caesar at Corinth. For literary accounts, see Strabo 8.6.23; Plutarch, *Caesar* 57; Dio Cassius 43.50.3–5; and Appian, *Punica* 136. For numismatic evidence, see Michel Amandry, *Le monnayage des duovirs corinthiens* (BCHSup 15; Paris: de Boccard, 1988) 26–28. See also the recent article by Mary E. Hoskins Walbank, "The Foundation and Planning of Early Roman Corinth," *JRA* 10 (1997) 95–130.

[10]For general discussion of the practical aspects of the colonization process, see E. T. Salmon, *Roman Colonization under the Republic* (London: Thames and Hudson, 1969) 13–28. For a

Several sources describe the activity of the *agrimensores*. The *Corpus Agrimensorum Romanorum* is a collection of ancient land surveyors' manuals originally compiled in the fifth century C.E., but including texts as early as the first century C.E. In these documents we have detailed accounts of the techniques of the surveyors and various elements of their work.[11] A number of illustrations, likely based on earlier Roman drawings, accompany certain of the texts and relate to the topics described. Fragments of ancient stone maps from Orange (ancient Aurasio) also illustrate the agricultural division of land—*limitatio* or centuriation. In addition, physical evidence for Roman land division has been found in many parts of the Roman world.[12]

The *agrimensores* used as their principle surveying instrument the *groma* (fig. 2.1). A very simple device, the *groma* comprised a vertical staff with two horizontal crossbars connected by a bracket. Each of the ends of the crossbars supported a cord, which was held vertical by a plumb bob. Roman surveyors were skilled in using this instrument, together with sighting rods (*decempeda*), to create straight lines and right angles.

In preparation for a colonial foundation, the *agrimensores* would have typically worked under the direction of the commissioners and would have been given several responsibilities: to delimit the boundaries of the territory of the colony, to measure the *limites* of the city, and to survey and subdivide into sections the urban areas as well as the *territorium* of the colony. Only then could the actual allotments of land, both urban and rural, be measured out and assigned to the individual colonists.[13] These procedures were customary

---

recent account of Roman colonies in Achaia, see A. D. Rizakis, "Roman Colonies in the Province of Achaia: Territories, Land and Population," in *The Early Roman Empire in the East* (ed. Susan E. Alcock; Oxford: Oxbow Books, 1997) 15–36.

[11]For a translation of the *Corpus Agrimensorum Romanorum* with commentary, see Brian Campbell, *The Writings of the Roman Land Surveyors* (London: Society for the Promotion of Roman Studies, 2000).

[12]For Orange, see A. Piganiol, *Les documents cadastraux de la colonie romaine d'Orange* (Gallia Sup 16; Paris: Centre national de la recherche scientifique, 1962); and F. Salviat, "Orientation, extension et chronologie des plans cadastraux d'Orange," *Revue Archéologique de Narbonnaise* 10 (1977) 107–18. For discussion and interpretation of centuriation studies from different parts of Europe, see Monique Clavel-Lévêque et al., *Atlas historique des cadastres d'Europe*, vols. 1–2 (Publications of the Action COST G2 "Paysages anciens et structures rurales"; Luxembourg: Offices des publications officielles des Communautés européennes, 1998–).

[13]The land allotment per colonist at Corinth is not known, nor do we know how many colonists settled the colony. Appian (*Pun.* 136) mentions that 3,000 colonists were sent to Carthage in 44 B.C.E., and some have assumed that the same number would have been sent to Corinth. For the size of Roman colonies in Italy, see L. Keppie, *Colonization and Veteran Settlement in Italy, 47–14 B.C.* (London: British School at Rome, 1983) 97–100.

Fig. 2.1 Drawing of a *groma*.

in colonial foundations, and the Roman land surveyors were usually a part of the forward team of any new colony.

Although we do not have any records that document the work of the Flavian surveyors in Corinth, the name of one of the surveyors who was working in the Peloponnesos at about this time is preserved in an inscription found in Messenia:

> I, Titus Flavius Monomitos, a land surveyor and freedman of the Roman Emperor Vespasian, in the consulship of L. Ceionius Commodus and D. Novius Priscus, on the 14th day of December, A.D. 78 in Patras, have checked and certified the aforementioned boundaries.[14]

The boundaries in question were between Laconia and Messenia.

Evidence for the work of Roman surveyors at Corinth may be arranged chronologically in three divisions: (1) an interim period lasting from the sack of Corinth in 146 B.C.E. until the foundation of the Caesarian colony in 44 B.C.E. and including the evidence from the *lex agraria* of 111 B.C.E; (2) the time of the foundation of the Caesarian colony of 44 B.C.E., *Colonia Laus Iulia Corinthiensis*; and (3) the time of the foundation of the Flavian colony of the 70s C.E., *Colonia Iulia Flavia Augusta Corinthiensis*. I will first discuss the evidence for the Caesarian colony, then introduce evidence associated with the earlier interim period and the *lex agraria*, and then turn to the evidence for the Flavian colony.

---

[14]*Inscriptiones Graecae* V 1431.40; translation in Jack L. Davis, *Sandy Pylos: An Archaeological History from Nestor to Navarino* (Austin: University of Texas Press, 1998) xxix.

COLONIA LAUS IULIA CORINTHIENSIS

The Roman land surveyors' plan for Julius Caesar's colony included a measured design for the overall urban limits as well as the location and dimensions for other specialized areas of the city. The "drawing-board plan" of the urban area was composed of 4 centuries, each measuring 32 x 15 *actus* or 240 *iugera* (fig. 2.2). The original divisions of the city were likely to have been 1 x 2 *actus* units,[15] and the principle orientation of the colony was approximately 3° west of north.[16] Each of the 4 centuries of the urban colony was characterized as having the capacity for 29 *cardines* and 29 one-*actus*-wide *insulae* (fig. 2.3), although the implementation of the colonial design may not have been completed in all areas of the city. The *cardo maximus* occupied the westernmost *insulae* of the eastern centuries. The width of the excavated *cardines* varies from 8 to 24 feet; the overall average was likely to have been 12 feet. Each century was also designed to have had the capacity for 6 *decumani*, with an average width of 20 feet. The urban centuries of the colony were organized according to the legal formula *iter populo non debetur*, meaning that the road widths were added outside of the regular *insula* measure.[17] The overall size of the planned urban colony was 240 ha (593 acres), and it fit largely within the area of the Greek fortification walls.[18] Only in the northwest corner of the city did the plan for the colony extend outside the Greek circuit walls.

The *cardo maximus* of the urban colony was the Lechaion Road, which has been excavated to the north of the propylaia at the entrance of the forum. It is described by Pausanias as the roadway that led north out of the forum directly to the Lechaion Harbor.[19] By modern measurement we know that the distance is approximately 3,150 m from the rostra in the forum to the harbor. The *cardo maximus* is the widest excavated roadway in the urban colony; the paved roadway proper is 24 Roman feet wide where it joins the steps at the north entrance to the forum.[20]

---

[15]There are also examples of 1 x 3 and 1 x 4 *actus* unit *insulae*.

[16]The surveyed orientation of the east curb of the *cardo maximus* of the city is 3°3′46″ west of north.

[17]Charles Saumagne, " 'Iter populo debetur' . . . ," *Revue de Philologie*, 3d series, 2 (1928) 320–52. This was the normal type of organization for urban areas.

[18]For comparison of the size of some Roman cities, see the table in Pierre Grimal, *Roman Cities* (trans. and ed. G. M. Woloch; Madison: University of Wisconsin Press, 1983) 334–35. Rome inside the Servian walls measures 450 ha, Lyons 127 ha, Nimes 320 ha, and Turin 51 ha.

[19]Pausanias 2.3.4.

[20]The width of the roadway of the *cardo maximus* tapers from north to south.

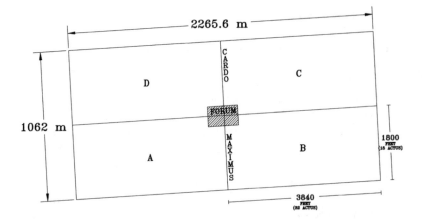

Fig. 2.2 Schematic drawing of the four quadrants of the urban colony at Corinth, each of which measures 32 x 15 *actus* (240 *iugera*; 3840 x 1800 feet) with centrally located *forum* and *cardo maximus*.

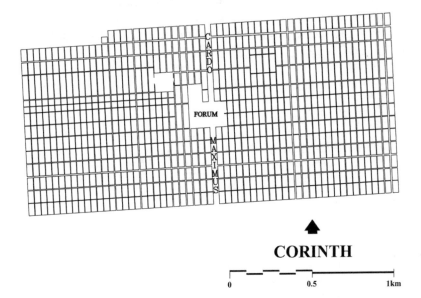

Fig. 2.3 Drawing-board plan of the urban colony of Corinth, 44 B.C.E.

FORUM PLANNING

Within the area of the urban colony of Julius Caesar, the forum area as a whole was designed to occupy 24 *actus*[2] or 12 *iugera* in the topographical center of the urban colony, measuring 6 *actus* east-west and 4 *actus* north-south (fig. 2.4).[21] This large area included important elements of the former Greek city in the Upper Lechaion Road Valley, including the imposing South Stoa, over 164 m long; the Hellenistic racecourse; and the precinct of the Sacred Spring (see pp. 43–46 and figs. 2.5 and 2.12, pp. 35 and 47). Many of the most important civic, political, and religious buildings of the Roman colony would be constructed within this space. The open area of the forum was eventually paved in the first century C.E., and it measured approximately 13,000 m[2], or approximately 40% of the reserved 6 x 4 *actus* area.[22] This was a relatively large space for a forum.[23] During the Augustan period, the Julian Basilica and what appears to have been an administrative building adjoining it to the south, the Southeast Building, were constructed at the east end of the forum, tucked neatly into the available space and close to the rising ground to the east.[24] At the west side of the forum were Temple F, likely dedicated to Venus Genetrix, and the Fountain of Poseidon.[25] A monumental triple-bayed arch was built where the forum met the *cardo maximus*, the Lechaion Road.[26]

---

[21]This measurement of area does not include the planned roadways between *insulae* that were not constructed in the forum.

[22]Vitruvius (5.1.2) recommends a forum size with a proportion of 3 x 2. The area of the entire (6 x 4 *actus*) forum space is equal to approximately 33,000 m[2]. For the paving of the forum in the first century C.E., see Robert L. Scranton, *Monuments in the Lower Agora and North of the Archaic Temple* (Corinth I.3; Princeton, N.J.: ASCSA, 1951) 148–51.

[23]For comparison, the Forum of Trajan in Rome was approximately 11,000 m[2] in size.

[24]For the Julian Basilica, see Paul Scotton, "The Julian Basilica at Corinth: An Architectural Investigation" (Ph.D. diss., University of Pennsylvania, 1997). For the Southeast Building, see S. S. Weinberg, *The Southeast Building, the Twin Basilicas, and the Mosaic House* (Corinth I.5; Princeton, N.J.: ASCSA, 1960).

[25]Scranton, *Monuments,* 6–73. See also Charles K. Williams II, "The Refounding of Roman Corinth: Some Roman Religious Attitudes," in *Roman Architecture in the Greek World* (ed. Sarah Macready and F. H. Thompson; Society of Antiquaries of London, Occasional Papers, n.s. 10; London: Society of Antiquaries of London, 1987) 26–37; idem, "A Re-Evaluation of Temple E and the West End of the Forum of Corinth," in *The Greek Renaissance in the Roman Empire: Papers from the Tenth British Museum Classical Colloquium* (ed. Susan Walker and Averil Cameron; BICSSup 55; London: University of London, 1989) 156–62; and Charles K. Williams II and Orestes H. Zervos, "Excavations at Corinth, 1989: The Temenos of Temple E," *Hesperia* 59 (1990) 351–56.

[26]C. M. Edwards, "The Arch over the Lechaion Road at Corinth and Its Sculpture," *Hesperia* 63 (1994) 263–308.

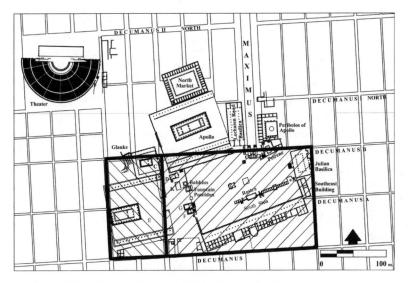

Fig. 2.4 Early Roman forum planning, illustrating original 6 x 4 *actus* area with additional 2 x 4 *actus* area to the west, corresponding with the early phase of Temple E of the late first century B.C.E.

Along the north boundary of the forum toward the northwestern corner, a new stoa was constructed, approximately 101 m long, known today as the Northwest Stoa.[27] From the earliest days, the *rostra* would have been located on the south side of the open space of the forum.[28] A large altar was placed approximately in the center of the open area of the forum. Just outside the 6 x 4 *actus* space of the forum were constructed Temple E, Temple C, and the West Shops, probably in the late Augustan period or slightly later; a western appendage of 2 x 4 *actus* was added to the forum to accommodate these buildings, possibly in the late first century B.C.E. (fig. 2.4).[29]

It is clear to anyone looking at the plan of the Roman forum at Corinth that the Roman surveyors picked an orientation for many of these Augustan and later structures that was not in keeping with the urban *insulae* grid of the

[27]Richard Stillwell, "The Northwest Stoa and Shops," in *Architecture* (ed. Richard Stillwell, Robert L. Scranton, and Sarah Elizabeth Freeman; Corinth I.2; Cambridge, Mass.: ASCSA, 1941) 89–130. The Northwest Stoa was built in the late Augustan period or slightly later. See Charles K. Williams II, "Roman Corinth as a Commercial Center," in *The Corinthia in the Roman Period* (ed. Timothy E. Gregory; JRASup 8; Ann Arbor, Mich.: Journal of Roman Archaeology, 1993) 33.

[28]Scranton, *Monuments*, 99–111.

[29]This area was enlarged in the 70s C.E. to 3 x 4 *actus*.

new Roman colony, approximately 3° west of north. Although the overall space reserved as the forum was rectilinear, and designed with reference to the city plan, most of the new Roman buildings and structures added inside this space were not oriented with respect to the urban grid. Only the Augustan triple-bayed arch at the head of the Lechaion Road conformed to the urban insular orientation (see the summary of orientations in fig. 2.6, p. 37).

Individual buildings in the forum were constructed on several orientations (fig. 2.5). One orientation was that established by the alignment of the existing sixth-century B.C.E. Temple of Apollo on Temple Hill and the fourth-century South Stoa (fig. 2.5, identified at 0°). These two buildings dominated the Greek city—the Temple of Apollo due to its elevated location on Temple Hill, and the South Stoa due to its immense size.[30] In the Early Roman period, the *rostra* and the Southeast Building[31] were clearly constructed with respect to, and at virtually the same orientation as, the South Stoa, just as the Central Shops would be in the first century C.E. Temple F, the Fountain of Poseidon, and the Julian Basilica were built in the Augustan period according to an orientation approximately 8° east of the Greek orientation; this orientation was likewise adopted for the other temples to be built in the west forum, including Temple G, Temple D, Temple K, and Temples C, E, H, and J.[32] The orientation of the Northwest Stoa (fig. 2.5, identified at +4°) along the north edge of the forum lay midway between the earlier Greek orientation that framed the north and south sides of the forum and the Augustan orientation that framed the east and west sides. The Early Roman altar[33] located approximately in the middle of the forum was built at an orientation midway between the orientation of the *rostra* on the south and that of the Northwest Stoa on the north (fig. 2.5, identified at +2°). The Roman surveyors could have oriented all of these structures with respect to the South Stoa and the Temple of Apollo, but they chose not to do so.

---

[30]For the Temple of Apollo, see C. A. Pfaff, "Archaic Corinthian Architecture," in *Corinth: The Centenary, 1896–1996* (ed. Charles K. Williams II and Nancy Bookidis; Corinth XX; Princeton, N.J.: ASCSA, 2003) 112–15. See also H. N. Fowler and R. Stillwell, *Introduction, Topography, Architecture* (Corinth I.2; Cambridge, Mass.: ASCSA, 1932) 115–34. For the South Stoa, see Oscar Broneer, *The South Stoa and Its Roman Successors* (Corinth I.4; Princeton, N.J.: ASCSA, 1954).

[31]The entrance to the Southeast Building was from the west, but the general orientation of the building was in keeping with that of the neighboring South Stoa.

[32]A significant similarity in orientation is shared by a number of major Roman buildings in and around the forum between the Augustan and the Claudian periods (27 B.C.E.–54 C.E.).

[33]Scranton, *Monuments*, 139–41.

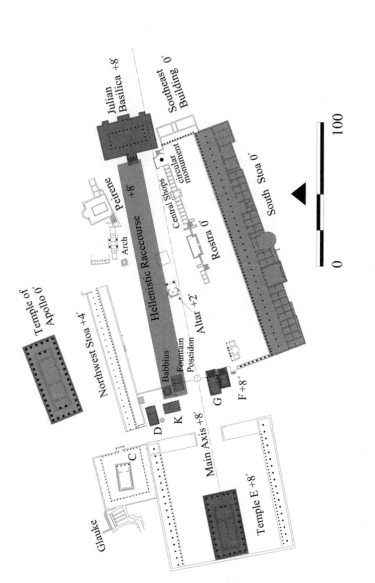

Fig. 2.5 Schematic drawing showing the main axis of the Roman plan of the forum and the difference in orientations of buildings and structures in and near the forum around the middle of the first century C.E.

The Roman east-west axis in the forum was a line that joined the central east-west orientation of Temple E in the west to the east end of the forum— specifically, to the south aisle of the Julian Basilica. This line falls just north of the Circular Monument.[34] The orientation of this axis was approximately 8° different from the earlier Greek orientations of the Temple of Apollo and the South Stoa, but it was the same as the Greek orientation of the Hellenistic racecourse that served as the predecessor to the forum space itself, located ca. 15 m north of the line of the Roman east-west axis (fig. 2.5). The Roman architects chose the average between existing orientations of buildings for new buildings and structures that were built on the north and south sides of this major east-west axis. As the spaces between the buildings were diminished, the major orientation difference between structures was cut from approximately 8° to 4° to 2°.

As long ago as 1960, Saul Weinberg observed that the similar orientation of the Julian Basilica and the temples in the western end of the forum described an axis spanning the forum, and he concluded that the Roman surveyors had probably followed an earlier Greek orientation.[35] Weinberg knew that the Hellenistic racecourse running through the forum area takes this very orientation, as does the North Building on the earlier Greek Lechaion Road to the north of the forum; other structures may have shared this orientation.[36] For whatever reason, the Roman surveyors chose to follow this well-established Greek orientation when aligning the new Roman temples and the Julian Basilica. One nearby Greek structure, although at a lower elevation, that did not share the same orientation was the Peirene fountain house, which received several Roman renovations while retaining its earlier Greek orientation.[37] Of course the Romans leveled off and covered from view the Sacred Spring and its associated monuments.

[34]The date of the construction of the Julian Basilica is likely to have been in the Augustan period. See the abstract of a paper by Paul Scotton, "An Augustan Tribunal: A Seat for Gallio," *AJA* 106 (2002) 278. Since the earlier phase of Temple E may be late first century B.C.E. or a little later, it cannot be said that this axis was necessarily original to the earliest forum plan. See n. 65, below.

[35]Weinberg, *Southeast Building*, 37–38.

[36]From the excavation of the Hellenistic racecourse it was clear to the excavator that "the racecourse goes out of use with the destruction of Corinth in 146 B.C.E." (Charles K. Williams II and Joan E. Fisher, "Corinth, 1970: Forum Area," *Hesperia* 40 [1971] 22–23). It would have been perfectly clear to the architects and engineers who were responsible for the design and construction of the Julian Basilica that the orientation of the building and the Hellenistic racecourse were the same, since the foundations for the staircase of the building overlap the starting line of the Hellenistic *dromos*. See Weinberg, *Southeast Building*, 42 and plate 19.1.

[37]Bert Hodge Hill, *The Springs: Peirene, Sacred Spring, Glauke* (Corinth I.6; Princeton, N.J.: ASCSA, 1964) 64–105. For recent work on Peirene, see Betsey A. Robinson, "Fountains and the Culture of Water at Roman Corinth" (Ph.D. diss., University of Pennsylvania, 2001).

Greek Structures

Temple of Apollo	E-W axis sighting lines (average)	N68°55'07"E
South Stoa	E-W stylobate	N69°48'53"E
Hellenistic Racecourse	N-S starting platform	N13°02'49"W
	E-W south water channel	N77°41'32"E
North Building	N-S foundation	N12°49'25"W

Roman Structures

Julian Basilica	E-W foundation	N76°46'48"E
Temple E	E-W south foundation	N77°52'13"E
Temple F	E-W foundation	N77°05'27"E
Temple C	N-S peribolos wall	N13°41'15"W
Triple-Bayed Arch over the Lechaion Road	E-W foundations (average)	N86°26'23"E
	N-S foundation	N03°47'45"W
Rostra	E-W foundation	N69°35'03"E
Southeast Building	E-W wall	N69°39'38"E
Northwest Stoa (average)	E-W foundation	N73°04'58"E
Altar	E-W foundations (average)	N71°26'40"E
Long Rectangular Building	N-S foundation	N06°04'11"E
Arch at Southwest Forum	N-S foundation (average)	N04°56'21"E
Cardo Maximus (Lechaion Road)	East curb	N03°03'46"W

Fig. 2.6 Summary of orientations of selected Greek and Roman structures.

From what we currently know of the excavated city, it is clear that from the Augustan period through the third century C.E. the Romans clustered their temples on the west side of the forum.[38] In addition to these, the Romans constructed in the first century C.E. three prostyle tetrastyle Ionic temples to the south of the urban colony, on the lower northern slope of Acrocorinth—specifically, on the upper terrace of the Sanctuary of Demeter (see pp. 55–58, below).

Immediately outside the limits of the forum, the location and plan of the Lechaion Road Basilica, built in the Augustan period, is totally in keeping with the orientation of the urban grid. It also occupies a portion of one *iugera* of space in the grid. Immediately across the Lechaion Road, the Augustan *macellum* was also built with respect to the urban plan.[39] To the north of the Lechaion Road Basilica, it is possible that another Augustan *macellum* was built within the urban insular organization.

THE ROMAN FOOT MEASURE

It has been possible to measure the width of a Roman *insula* within the area of the southwest forum, between *cardo* II and *cardo* III west. Between the exterior west face of the Roman Cellar Building and the exterior east face of the building immediately west of *cardo* II west, the surveyed distance measured is 35.486 m, or 120 Roman feet of 0.295+ m (fig. 2.7).[40] This *insula* interval, derived from the overall plan of the city, remained constant within both the urban settlement of 44 B.C.E. and the area modified during the late first century B.C.E.[41]

---

[38]See the discussion of the planning of Corinth in Pierre Gros and Mario Torelli, *Storia dell' Urbanistica, il mondo Romano* (Rome: Laterza, 1994) 391–96.

[39]Williams, "Commercial Center," 31–46.

[40]The Roman foot measured for this *insula* is very close to 0.2957 m.

[41]See pp. 32–34, above.

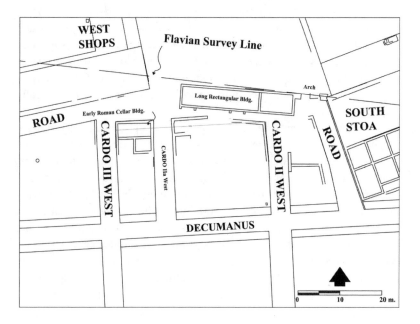

Fig. 2.7 Detail of the area of the southwest forum, between *cardo* II to *cardo* III west and the *decumanus*; the dashed line illustrates the points at which the surveyed measurement was taken. The Long Rectangular Building is almost aligned with the likely location of the Flavian survey line (see p. 54, below).

City Planning outside the Forum

A regular network of roadways was constructed within the limits of the urban colony, according to the insular plan of the Roman urban colonial organization.[42] The past century of excavations has revealed twenty-two distinct Roman roads within the urban limits of Roman Corinth, in addition to four interim-period roads (fig. 2.8). It is clear that many were built as *cardines* and *decumani* of the colony, aligned parallel and at right angles to the *cardo maximus*, the Lechaion Road.[43] In some cases, the construction of the straight Roman roads required builders to modify the landscape. Such is the case, for instance, where *decumanus* III north passes close to the area of the Greek gate near the Cheliotomylos hill. Here Roman engineers cut through a low rise in the ground specifically to allow the road to pass.[44]

An amphitheater and a circus were part of the design of the colony from the Augustan period. Both structures find their closest parallels in contemporary structures elsewhere.[45] Both were found at the edges of the city: the amphitheater at the northeast corner of the planned colony, over a kilometer away from the forum; and the circus at the northern edge, close to the gymnasium and the theater, and close to the Sanctuary of Asklepius at the northern limit of the Greek city. Both the amphitheater and the circus were built with respect to the Roman grid and fit neatly within its system. The amphitheater with its surrounding area occupies 8 *actus*^{2} or 4 *iugera*, and the circus covers 18–20 *actus*^{2} or 9–10 *iugera*. Both would have been utilized for different kinds of Roman festivals. The amphitheater would have been the locale for gladiatorial games (*munera*) and wild beast shows (*venationes*), although it is known that such events were also held in the theater at Corinth.[46] Also, the Corinthian Caesarea festival and the Panhellenic Isthmian games were sometimes held in Corinth, and it is probable that the equestrian aspects of these contests were held in the circus.

[42]For a color drawing showing the evidence for this grid, see Romano, "City Planning," 284, fig. 17-3.

[43]Some Roman roads utilized existing Greek roadways.

[44]This feature is discussed by Rhys Carpenter and Antoine Bon (*The Defenses of Acrocorinth and the Lower Town* [Corinth III.2; Cambridge, Mass.: ASCSA, 1936] 63) as feature D, "an outcropping of rock with abundant traces of a Roman cement paving running through a central depression." The roadway was found to be slightly less than 8 m wide.

[45]For the amphitheater, see Katherine Welch, "Negotiating Roman Spectacle Architecture in the Greek World: Athens and Corinth," in *The Art of Ancient Spectacle* (ed. Bettina Bergmann and Christine Kondoleon; Studies in the History of Art 56; Washington, D.C.: National Gallery of Art, 1999) 133–40. For the circus see David G. Romano, "A Circus in Roman Corinth," *Hesperia* (forthcoming).

[46]Richard Stillwell, *The Theatre* (Corinth II; Princeton, N.J.: ASCSA, 1952) 84–98.

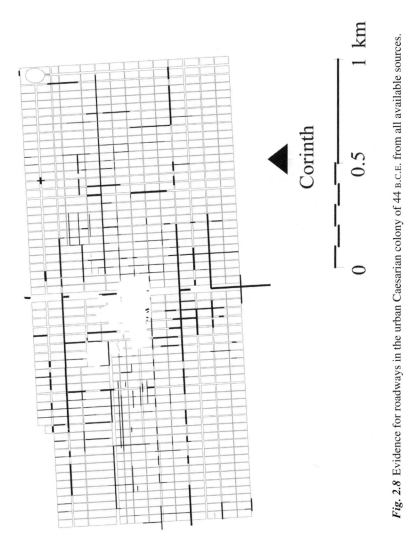

Fig. 2.8 Evidence for roadways in the urban Caesarian colony of 44 B.C.E. from all available sources.

Figure 2.9 summarizes the measurements, sizes, and areas of the urban colonial plan of Julius Caesar:

Basic Areas

The urban colony comprised four quadrants.

Area of one quadrant of the urban colony in *actus²*	480 *actus²*
Area of one quadrant of the urban colony in *iugera*	240 *iugera*
Area of the urban colony (excluding planned roads) per quadrant	203 *iugera*
Area of the urban colony in *actus²*	1920 *actus²*
Area of the urban colony in *iugera*	960 *iugera*
Area of the urban colony (excluding planned roads)	812 *iugera*
Area of the forum (excluding planned roads)	12 *iugera*
Area of the urban colony excluding planned roads and without forum (excluding planned roads)	800 *iugera*
Area of *cardo maximus* in urban colony	12 *iugera*
Area of circus (excluding planned roads)	9–10 *iugera*
Area of amphitheater (excluding planned roads)	4 *iugera*
Area of addition of Temple E precinct	4 *iugera*
Area of second addition of Temple E precinct	3 *iugera*
Area of odeion addition	2 *iugera*

Relationships Between Areas

Area of planned roadways (total) to area of urban colony (including roads)	$148/960 = 15.4\%$
Area of forum to area of urban colony	$12/812 = 1.48\%$
Area of *cardo maximus* to area of urban colony	$12/812 = 1.48\%$
Area of circus to area of urban colony	$11/812 = 1.35\%$
Area of amphitheater to area of urban colony	$4/812 = 0.5\%$
Area of paved forum floor to area of planned 6 x 4 actus forum	$13{,}000\text{m}^2/33{,}000\text{m}^2$ $= 39\%$

Fig. 2.9 Summary of Corinth colonial planning in drawing-board terms. (1 *actus* = 120 feet; 1 *actus²* = 14,400 ft²; 2 *actus²* = 1 *iugerum* = 28,800 ft²).

TERRITORIUM OF THE CAESARIAN COLONY

It was typical for a Roman colony to have under its control agricultural land outside of the urban center. This land was called the *territorium* of the colony, and it was usually divided up in a very regular manner to facilitate both the distribution of land to colonists and the assessment of taxes. The evidence for centuriation outside the urban colony indicates a division of land into large units of 16 x 24 *actus* at the same orientation as the city, or 3° west of north (fig. 2.10, p. 44). These large units were divided into smaller sections. For instance, a large concentration of vestiges of these field lines was found in the area between the Greek Long Walls[47] to the north of the city as far as the Lechaion Harbor, an area of approximately 6 km². Here the major subdivision appears to be one-*actus* units with smaller subdivisions. The overall area of the centuriation in the Corinthia is approximately 340 km², and the area extends from the Longopotomos River near the coastline, and from the area of the Nemea River at higher elevations, to well beyond the modern canal in the east. Vestiges of the same system of centuriation can also be found in the southern Corinthia in the area of Tenea and further to the west in Kleonai.[48]

INTERIM PERIOD, 146–44 B.C.E.

Archaeological evidence for the period between 146 and 44 B.C.E. suggests that the Roman division of land in the area between the Greek Long Walls of Corinth should be associated with the work described in the *lex agraria* of 111 B.C.E. As mentioned above, after the victory of Mummius in 146 B.C.E., Corinthian land became largely *ager publicus*.[49] From the *lex agraria* it is known that some parts of the Corinthian land were measured out for sale or rent and boundary stones were erected. A roadway that was in use between 146 and 44 B.C.E. passed through a break in the Greek circuit wall near

---

[47]By the "Long Walls" I mean the excavated and published East Long Wall (Carpenter and Bon, *Defenses*, 84–127) and a West Long Wall that I have suggested stood at approximately the same distance to the west of the *cardo maximus*, the Lechaion Road, as is known to exist to the east of it. See David G. Romano, "Post 146 B.C.E. Land Use in Corinth, and Planning of the Roman Colony of 44 B.C.," in *The Corinthia in the Roman Period* (ed. Timothy E. Gregory; JRASup 8; Ann Arbor, Mich.: Journal of Roman Archaeology, 1993) 26.

[48]Romano, "Two Cities," 92–95; and idem and N. L. Stapp, "Piecing Together the City and Territory of Roman Corinth," *Archaeological Computing Newsletter (Institute of Archaeology, Oxford)* 52 (1998) 1–7.

[49]For qualifications in Livy and Cicero, see n. 6, above.

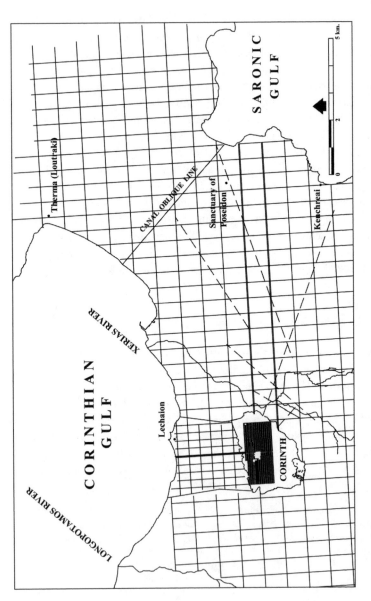

Fig. 2.10 Corinthian colony, 44 B.C.E., north and east of Corinth, including the rural land division composed of 16 x 24 *actus* units (8 x 12 *actus* units between the long walls) and including oblique lines of the canal and suggested roadways.

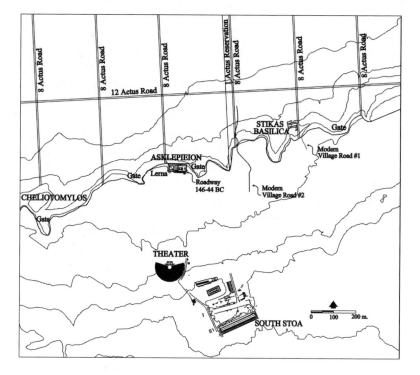

Fig. 2.11 Greek Corinth, 146–44 B.C.E., with northern Greek circuit wall and interim-period Roman land division to the north of the city. Portions of the two modern village roads are indicated. Contour lines are at intervals of 10 m.

the Asklepieion and joined outside the wall with one of the 8-*actus* north-south roadways that have been identified north of the city (fig. 2.11, p. 45). This new road is fairly close to the locations of two of the Greek gates of the city, and it is likely that the Romans built a new road in this location in order to facilitate the division of land to the north of the city. Also, within the former city and in the area that would become the Roman forum, there is archaeological evidence for two additional interim period roadways (fig. 2.12).[50]

Further evidence for the development of the colony north of the city is found 8 *actus* farther east, where there is a one-*actus* reservation of land between the units of 8 x 12 *actus*. This 120-foot reservation of space is on the axis of the *cardo maximus* within the urban colony, and it was probably set aside for the extension of this important roadway through the plain to the harbor.

If these preparations had been made in the area to the north of the city in 146–44 B.C.E., it seems very likely that the new colony was taking shape long before the colonists arrived. The process of centuriation preceding the actual colonization would have laid the groundwork for the settlement of a new population. Andrew Lintott has argued that the *lex agraria* provided for the centuriation of some elements of Corinthian land, which suggests that a colony was planned for the site.[51] The archaeological evidence in turn suggests that this land, or at least a portion of it, was the land between the Long Walls to the north of the city. In the rest of the area for which there is evidence of centuriation, larger divisions of 16 x 24 *actus* were employed.

COLONIA IULIA FLAVIA AUGUSTA CORINTHIENSIS

Physical vestiges within both the city of Corinth and the surrounding rural area attest to a second Roman land division that may be equated historically with *Colonia Iulia Flavia Augusta Corinthiensis*, a refoundation in the time of Vespasian. This titulature is known from epigraphic and numismatic sources, although the evidence for a centuriation that can be associated with this new colony has been presented only recently.[52] This first-century C.E. system of

---

[50]See Romano, "City Planning," 279–83 and fig. 17.2.

[51]Lintott, *Judicial Reform,* 87, 99. Crawford (*Roman Statutes,* 180) finds no textual evidence for centuriation at the time of the *lex agraria.*

[52]See the discussions in Romano, "Two Cities," 96–104; and idem, "City Planning," 291–99. For a summary of the numismatic evidence, see Mary E. Hoskins Walbank, "Aspects of Corinthian Coinage in the Late 1st and Early 2nd Centuries A.D.," in *Corinth: The Centenary, 1896–1996* (ed. Charles K. Williams II and Nancy Bookidis; Corinth XX; Princeton, N.J.: ASCSA, 2003) 337–49.

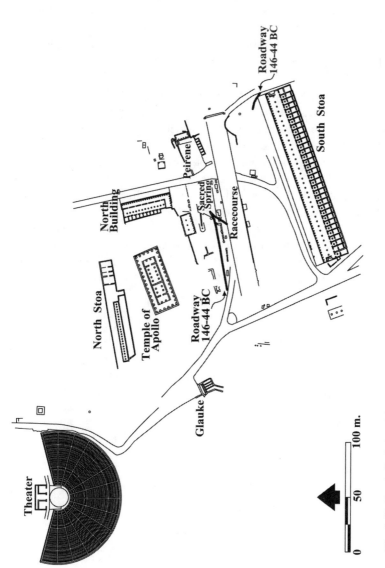

Fig. 2.12 Greek Corinth, 146–44 B.C.E., illustrating the locations of two east-west interim-period roadways.

centuriation extended over a large area to the south of the Corinthian gulf, from the north of Sikyon to the east shore of the Saronic Gulf, and it also included areas in the southern Corinthia and to the north of the modern Corinth canal east of Loutraki. The total area covered is approximately 300 km^2. The Caesarean and Flavian centuriations overlap for approximately 140 km^2, especially in the areas immediately neighboring the urban colony and in the southern Corinthia.

The Flavian system is characterized by a fan-shaped grid that is divided into ten differently oriented units in the plain immediately to the south of the Corinthian Gulf. These units are designated A1–A10 in fig. 2.13. Each of the units corresponds to a specific area of the coastal plain, and all of the units—with the exception of A8—are linked and are related to each other by the simple ratio of the arctangent of 1:4, equal to the angle of 14°2′10″.[53] Each of the ten units is roughly parallel to the coastline and perpendicular to the river of the area—Longopotomos, Nemea, Asopos, or Elisson.[54] The length of the stretch of Flavian centuriation along the south coast of the Corinthian Gulf, from the northwest of Sikyon to the east of the Corinth canal, is approximately 30 km (fig. 2.14). This kind of linking of centuriated units of land is known from other regions of the Roman Empire and is specifically a Roman technique of land division.[55]

A1	Sikyon	N62°26′52″E
A2	Sikyon, coast region	N48°24′42″E
A3	Nemea river area	N34°22′32″E
A4	Longopotamos river area	N20°20′22″E
A5	Corinth, Lechaion to Kenchreai	N6°18′12″E
A6	Corinth to Kenchreai, southern corridor	N20°20′22″E
A7	Xerias river area	N7°43′58″W
A8	West of Isthmus	N34°22′32″E
A9	West of Isthmus	N21°46′8″W
A10	East of Isthmus	N35°48′18″W

Fig. 2.13 Orientations and locations of Flavian centuriation south of the Corinthian Gulf.

[53]The Roman surveyors achieved this orientation by creating a right triangle with short sides of 1 *actus* and 4 *actus*. See Romano, "City Planning," 291–93. Unit A11 is related to the A series grid in a ratio of 2:9 but may have been created as a result of Nero's canal project; see pp. 51–53, below.

[54]This organization of the land with respect to the curving coastline and the rivers of the area would have allowed the most efficient use of the division of the land.

[55]For a discussion of comparative systems of Roman centuriation, see Romano, "City Planning," 299.

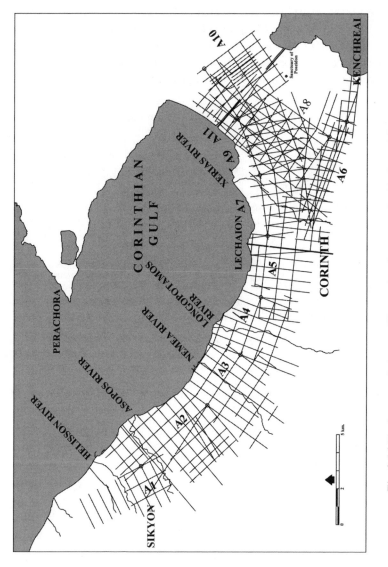

Fig. 2.14 Flavian centuriation, ca. 70 C.E., showing restored grid of 16 x 24 *actus* units.

Clearly the new areas of centuriation—that is, those areas that were not cen-turiated as a part of the Caesarian colony of 44 B.C.E.—are those to the west of the Longopotomos River, reaching all the way to Sikyon and beyond. Vestiges of this work survive in a heavy concentration of modern field and property lines; there is also evidence for a long and straight roadway leading from Sikyon to Corinth. Traces of the same orientation of centuriation are also found to the south of Corinth, in the areas of Tenea and Kleonai. Here, of course, there is no coastline, and the systems of land division seem to be more mixed.[56]

---

[56]A recent article by Mary E. Hoskins Walbank ("What's in a Name? Corinth under the Flavians," *ZPE* 139 [2002] 251–64) has called into question the research methods as well as the results and interpretation of this study of the proposed Flavian centuriation in the Corinthia. While I am eager to receive comments and criticism from serious and interested scholars, there are aspects of Walbank's discussion that need to be corrected and other as-pects that should be clarified. First of all, Walbank refers to, but does not cite, the series of methodological articles that I have written over the past ten years explaining in some detail the techniques that I have followed in this research. I mention this specifically because she is critical of my methodology. See David G. Romano and B. C. Schoenbrun, "A Computerized Architectural and Topographical Survey of Ancient Corinth," *Journal of Field Archaeology* 20 (1993) 177–90; Romano, "Post 146 B.C. Land Use," 9–30; David G. Romano and Osama Tolba, "Remote Sensing, GIS and Electronic Surveying: Reconstructing the City Plan and Landscape of Roman Corinth," in *Computer Applications and Quantitative Methods in Ar-chaeology 1994* (ed. Jeremy Huggett and Nick Ryan; BAR International Series 600; Oxford: Tempus Reparatum, 1995) 163–74; idem, "Remote Sensing and GIS in the Study of Roman Centuriation in the Corinthia, Greece," in *Interfacing the Past, Computer Applications and Quantitative Methods in Archaeology CAA95* (ed. Hans Kamermans and Kelly Fennema; Analecta Praehistorica Leidensia 28; Leiden: Brill, 1996) 457–63; and Romano and Stapp, "Piecing Together the City," 1–7. In addition, the Corinth Computer Project's website includes a detailed methodological discussion (see n. 2, above).

Part of Walbank's confusion about my interpretation of the evidence may be directly related to the fact that she is not familiar with the methodology that has been followed. She makes a series of assumptions about my research and methodology that are simply not true. For instance, whereas she states that I have not taken into consideration the evidence of the Venetian presence in the Corinthia, I have indeed, and this element will be included in the final publication. Walbank also states that I have not taken into consideration the evidence of the "archival material, such as maps, cadastral registers or the accounts of early travel-ers." She should note the section of the Corinth Computer Project website that is devoted to "Ancient Corinth, 1676–1923." This portion of the website was written by Dr. Leslie Kaplan, research assistant of the Corinth Computer Project, 1991–1995.

There are additional inaccuracies in Walbank's summary of my proposal that should be clarified here. As I have outlined above, I identify two systems of Roman centuriation. She presents an inaccurate and incomplete listing of my results ("What's in a Name," 253). Interested readers should refer to Romano, "Tale of Two Cities," 96–104; and idem, "City Planning," 291–99. Walbank's argument is misleading and in error when she states that I am not citing the dating evidence for the two systems of centuriation (note Romano, "City Planning," 293–98). Walbank questions whether the orientation of the three Roman Ionic prostyle temples in the Demeter Sanctuary have anything to do with the Roman centuriation

Traces of the Flavian surveyors' work can also be seen near the Lechaion Harbor. Survey lines in the form of very shallow trenches are clearly visible in a low-level balloon photograph taken by Dr. and Mrs. J. Wilson Meyers in 1986. The land is divided into strips of *insulae,* one *actus* (120 Roman feet) in width, separated by 30-foot-wide strips, presumably for roadways. The general organization of this area can be reconstructed by mapping the survey lines (fig. 2.15, p. 52).[57] This would appear to be the outline for a harbor installation that was never completed.

Another unfinished maritime project aligned with the Roman grid was Nero's attempt to build a canal across the isthmus of Corinth in 66–67 c.e.[58] The planned canal followed an oblique line that crossed an existing 16 x 24 *actus* centuriation grid (fig. 2.10).[59] Because the canal was oriented to the grid, it was possible for the builders to begin work on both ends at the same time. Josephus[60] tells us that Vespasian assembled Jewish captives in the stadium at Tiberias in September 67 c.e. and sent 6,000 of the strongest young men to the isthmus, presumably for the canal project.[61] Although the canal was not

---

in the area, pointing instead to a close orientation of Greek structures. She fails to note that the Hellenistic propylon in the Demeter sanctuary was reoriented by 3.5° when it was rebuilt by the Romans (see ibid., 296 n. 75). See also pp. 55–59, below. Walbank cites the recent results of excavation in the area to the southeast of the forum, where a road predicted on my urban grid plan failed to materialize during the excavation (G. D. R. Sanders, "A Late Roman Bath at Corinth: Excavations in the Panayia Field 1995–96," *Hesperia* 68 [1999] 444). It should be mentioned that another north-south road on my restored urban grid was discovered in a neighboring area of the same excavation, in a location predicted by me, although this road was not reported by the excavator.

To my knowledge, Walbank has not undertaken a scientific study of urban planning in Corinth or of rural centuriation in the Corinthia and therefore is in a relatively poor position to judge the merits of this research. She states that she was the "first to recognize in the early 1980's the existence of centuriation at Corinth," but her recognition was not based on a qualitative or quantitative study. Walbank has also challenged my statements regarding the "likelihood" that a second system of centuriation would be imposed on an earlier system. Here she should note the existence of this phenomenon in other parts of the Roman Empire. There are examples from Arausio, Nola, and Béziers. See Romano, "Two Cities," 102 n. 64; and idem, "City Planning," 299. See also Clavel-Lévêque et al., *Atlas historique des cadastres d'Europe,* vols. 1–2.

[57]There is evidence for 1 x 3 and 1 x 4 *actus* units.

[58]See the discussion in Romano, "City Planning," 297–98.

[59]See p. 43, above.

[60]Josephus, *B.J.* 3.540.

[61]There were also many limestone quarry sites in and around the isthmus, and it is possible that some of the Jewish slaves may have been worked there. For a discussion of some of these quarry locations, see C. L. Hayward, "Geology of Corinth: The Study of a Basic Resource," in *Corinth: The Centenary, 1896–1996* (ed. Charles K. Williams II and Nancy Bookidis; Corinth XX; Princeton, N.J.: ASCSA, 2003) 15–42.

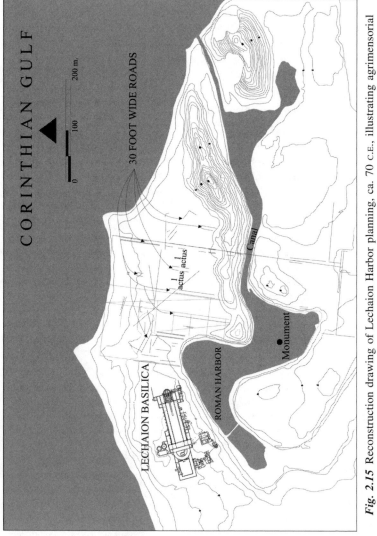

Fig. 2.15 Reconstruction drawing of Lechaion Harbor planning, ca. 70 C.E., illustrating agrimensorial lines. Contour lines are at intervals of 1 m.

finished by Nero, nor by Vespasian, enough of the canal was completed that we can reconstruct its plan as well as other details of its construction.[62]

I have suggested elsewhere that the importation of these Jewish slaves may be related to the refoundation of Corinth as a Flavian colony.[63] The size and extent of the Flavian centuriation suggests that the planners of the city aimed to enable an increased population to farm underutilized portions of the agricultural land. It is very likely that there would have been some re-arrangement of populations and cities, similar to what happened at Patrae, an Augustan colony in the northwest Peloponnesos.[64]

Perhaps some of the new Corinthian colonists were Sikyonians or relocated citizens of other neighboring cities. It is also possible that some of the new labor came from the ranks of the slaves who had worked on the canal project. The slaves may have been given their freedom together with plots of land in the neighborhood of Corinth. Alternatively, they may have become tenant farmers for the new colony. Whether or not the slaves at the isthmus became farmers in the refoundation, certainly the inhabitants of Corinth, including its well-known Jewish community, would have been aware of the Jewish slaves working nearby in the late 60s C.E. Julius Caesar's colony of 44 B.C.E. was originally a combination of veterans and freedpersons, and although we do not know for certain the composition of the Flavian refoundation, portions of the population may likewise have been veterans and freedpersons.

THE FORUM

After the Augustan period, several modifications and additions occurred in the area of the forum. First, the size of the forum was enlarged twice. During the first construction of Temple E, possibly as early as the late first century B.C.E., the western limit of the forum was extended an additional 4 *iugera* (also including space for Temple C); when Temple E was enlarged in the Flavian period, the western limit was further extended by an additional 2 *iugera*, for a total of 6 *iugera*. This enlarged the area of the forum by one

---

[62]See N. M. Verdelis, "Der Diolkos am Isthmus von Korinth," *AM* 71 (1956) 51–59.

[63]Romano, "Two Cities," 101–4.

[64]Patrae, *Colonia Augusta Aroe Patrae*, was established under Augustus in 16 B.C.E. in order to settle the veterans of the tenth and twelfth legions, as well as to provide for other neighboring settlements. See Susan E. Alcock, *Graecia Capta: The Landscapes of Roman Greece* (Cambridge: Cambridge University Press, 1993) 132–45.

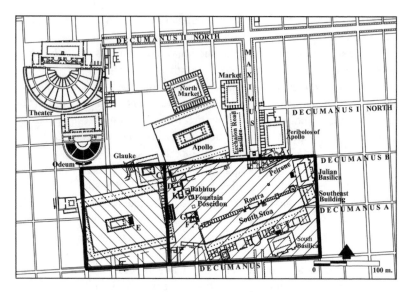

Fig. 2.16 Roman forum planning, illustrating original 6 x 4 *actus* area with additional 3 x 4 *actus* area to the west, corresponding with the later phase of Temple E (70s C.E.). For a larger view of this area, see fig. 2.18, p. 57.

half of its previous size (fig. 2.16).[65] A number of modifications to the city grid were necessary once Temple E was sited.[66]

In the southwest forum, the orientation of the Long Rectangular Building introduced a new orientation in the forum, but one that was in keeping with the major Flavian centuriation of the area, A5 (fig. 2.14). Adjacent to this building was a monumental arch that served as an entrance to the forum (fig. 2.7). The building and the arch were dated by the excavator to the period of Nero and may be related to the Flavian refoundation in the 70s C.E.[67]

From an examination of the modern field and property lines that preserve vestiges of the ancient land division in and around Corinth, it is clear that the original extent of the drawing-board plan of the colony of Julius Caesar

[65]For Temple E, see Scranton, *Monuments,* 126–236; and Williams, "Re-Evaluation of Temple E," 156–62. Mary E. Hoskins Walbank ("Pausanias, Octavia and Temple E at Corinth," *BSA* 84 [1989] 361–94) dates the extension of the forum to the second century during the reign of Hadrian or possibly Antoninus Pius. See Romano, "City Planning," 287–88 nn. 50–51.

[66]*Cardo* III west was closed and a new north-south street, *cardo* IIa west, was inserted in the plan. See ibid., 287–88.

[67]Charles K. Williams II and Joan E. Fisher, "Corinth, 1975: Forum Southwest," *Hesperia* 45 (1976) 126–37, figs. 3–5. See Romano, "Two Cities," 96–98; idem, "City Planning," 296.

had not been realized by the 70s C.E., and that the limits of the urban colony as originally planned had contracted by about 40%. Thus, the population and size of the city never achieved the promise of its first-century B.C.E. foundation.

In the first century C.E., the forum floor was paved with hard limestone, as were many of the city's roadways.[68] Construction of the Central Shops had begun on the east end, and several more rooms of the South Stoa were refurbished. The *cardo maximus* now exited the South Stoa through one of the reused rooms.[69] The odeum, located immediately to the south of the theater, was constructed during the Flavian period, and its location and design were in keeping with the Roman urban grid, occupying 2 *iugera* of space.[70] The theater was refurbished at about the same time or a little later.[71] The restored Roman city plan, ca. 150 C.E. is illustrated in fig. 2.17 (p. 56) and the restored Roman city center in fig. 2.18 (p. 57).

Outside the Urban Limits

To the south of the city on the lower slopes of Acrocorinth, three parallel prostyle tetrastyle Roman Ionic temples were built on the upper terrace of the Sanctuary of Demeter (fig. 2.19, p. 58).[72] The temples identified with Demeter (western), Kore (central), and possibly the Morai (eastern) are datable to the period after the earthquake of the 70s C.E., and all have a primary orientation in keeping with the major Flavian centuriation in the area, A5.[73] I have suggested that these three temples were intentionally oriented with respect to the Flavian centuriation in the same area.[74]

[68]Scranton, *Monuments*, 135–36.

[69]For the Central Shops, see ibid., 112–17; for the South Stoa, see Oscar Broneer, *The South Stoa and Its Roman Successors* (Corinth I.4; Princeton, N.J.: ASCSA, 1954) 128–29.

[70]Oscar Broneer, *The Odeum* (Corinth X; Cambridge, Mass.: ASCSA, 1932).

[71]Richard Stillwell, *The Theatre* (Corinth II; Princeton, N.J.: ASCSA, 1952) 41–83. See also recent work from the theater, published by Charles K. Williams and O. H. Zervos, "Corinth, 1987: South of Temple E and East of the Theater," *Hesperia* 57 (1988) 113, 115. Williams gives the date as "late 1st or very beginning of the 2nd century for the laying of the construction fill" for the addition of new buttresses to replace earlier ones along the east side of the cavea. This reconstruction possibly occurred in the time of Domitian. See Stillwell, *Theatre*, 135–36.

[72]Nancy Bookidis and Ronald S. Stroud, *The Sanctuary of Demeter and Kore: Topography and Architecture* (Corinth XVIII.3; Princeton, N.J.: ASCSA, 1997) 436–37.

[73]A setting line on the top surface of the east wall of the central temple was found to differ by only 3.5' of 1° from the Flavian centuriation of this area (A5), which was determined by independent means.

[74]Romano, "City Planning," 296 n. 75.

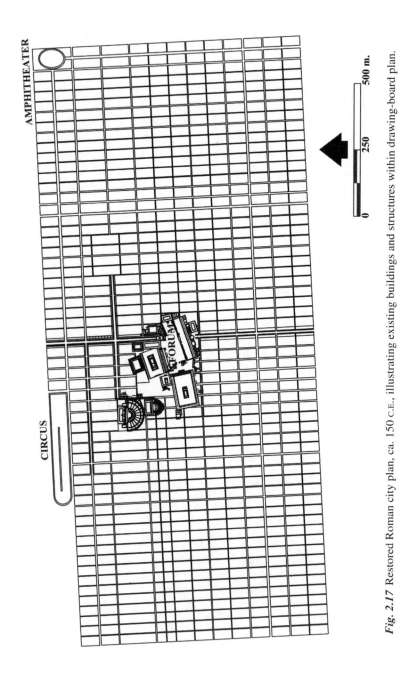

Fig. 2.17 Restored Roman city plan, ca. 150 C.E., illustrating existing buildings and structures within drawing-board plan.

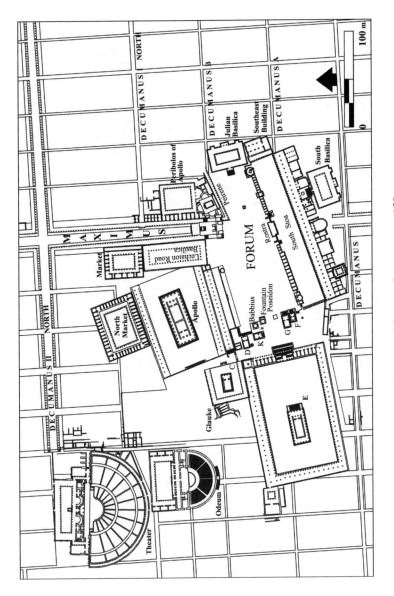

Fig. 2.18 Restored Roman city center, ca. 150 C.E.

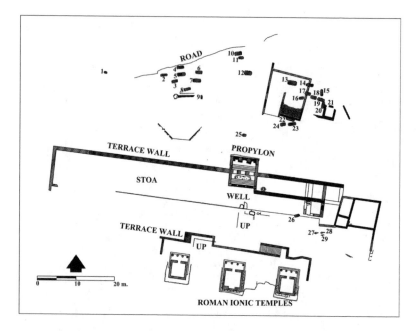

Fig. 2.19 Roman phase of the Sanctuary of Demeter and Kore, restored plan, illustrating locations of Roman Ionic temples.

Several Roman villas that have been excavated can be located in the context of the development of the Roman colony during the first and second centuries C.E. Within the limits of the urban colony, there is one villa to mention, located approximately 740 m southwest of the rostra in the forum. It is situated south of an east-west roadway, *decumanus* II south. The villa had three phases of occupation: an early Roman phase, a first-century C.E. phase with which the mosaics are associated, and a later Roman phase.[75] Northwest of the urban colony, outside of the Greek circuit wall, is a second Roman villa that can be dated to the first and second centuries C.E.[76] It is located near an east-west roadway that passed through the Greek wall at its northwest corner and is found at a distance of 1403 m from the *rostra* in the forum.

[75]H. S. Robinson, "Excavations at Corinth," Chronika B1, *ArchDelt* 18 (1963) 76–80 and plate 92c. See also the notice in *BCH* 87 (1963) 725–26, fig. 10. For a report of the mosaic found in the villa, see Stephen G. Miller, "A Mosaic Floor from a Roman Villa at Anaploga," *Hesperia* 41 (1972) 332–54. Miller's article includes a plan of phase 2 of the villa, after J. Travlos (ibid., fig. 2, p. 335).

[76]T. L. Shear, *The Roman Villa* (Corinth V; Cambridge, Mass.: ASCSA, 1930).

Roman tombs are located in the areas immediately outside the Greek circuit walls, and they are sometimes found in the scarp immediately below the line of the Greek wall. For instance, a large and important Roman tomb was excavated in the 1960s on the outside of the north city circuit, near the Cheliotomylos hill.[77] Other tombs have been found immediately outside the city circuit wall to the north and east. Further north of the city is a large cemetery that was used in the Roman period, in an area that likely extends to the Greek North Cemetery.[78] To the east of the city, a large built Roman tomb is located 1770 m to the east of the southeast gate of the city, near the road to Hexamilia.[79]

Conclusions

There can be little doubt that the Romans planned both the urban and rural elements of the successive Roman colonies at Corinth. The planning itself was based on the tradition and methods of the Roman *agrimensores*, who we know worked in the Corinthia on several different occasions. By using the *groma* to create straight lines and right angles, and by employing some basic trigonometry to deal with whole number ratios of *actus* units, the *agrimensores* laid out both the urban colony and the rural *territorium* according to the principles of Roman city and landscape planning. The Romans chose to align the forum—the political, commercial, and religious focus of the colony—with an earlier Greek orientation, although the overall space of the forum fit neatly into the Roman insular plan of the Caesarian colony. The work of the *agrimensores* is one of the most enduring physical manifestations of Roman influence on the former Greek city and its landscape.

[77]G. Daux, "Chronique des Fouilles," *BCH* 89 (1965) 694–97.
[78]Carl William Blegen, Hazel Palmer, and Rodney S. Young, *The North Cemetery* (Corinth XIII; Princeton, N.J.: ASCSA, 1964).
[79]Fowler and Stillwell, *Introduction*, 77–78.

CHAPTER THREE

Favorinus's "Corinthian Oration": A Piqued Panorama of the Hadrianic Forum

L. Michael White

An ancient traveler come to Corinth, and the record of what he saw. We wish we had records from others besides Pausanias and Paul—the two most frequently mentioned ancient travelers to Corinth—since neither of them has left an unproblematic account. Charles Williams and others have amply demonstrated so in regard to Pausanias's descriptions of various parts of the city.[1] Still, he is a valuable source. Paul is another matter, precisely because he himself says so little about the actual city. By contrast, the account that does mention specific monuments—namely, the portrayal of Paul's visit in Acts 18 (written roughly forty years or more after the fact)—is beset by numerous historical difficulties.[2] Nonetheless, the possibility of evaluating

---

[1]Charles K. Williams II and Joan E. Fisher, "The Route of Pausanias (1)," in "Corinth, 1974: Forum Southwest," *Hesperia* 44 (1975) 25–29; Charles K. Williams II and Orestes H. Zervos, "The Route of Pausanias (2)," in "Corinth, 1983: The Route to Sikyon," *Hesperia* 53 (1984) 101–4; and Georges Roux, *Pausanias en Corinthie (Livre II, 1 à 15)* (Paris: Belles Lettres, 1958). For individual monuments as viewed by Pausanias, see the specialized studies, e.g., Nancy Bookidis and Ronald S. Stroud, *The Sanctuary of Demeter and Kore: Topography and Architecture* (Corinth XVIII.3; Princeton, N.J.: ASCSA, 1997) 1–8. On Pausanias's method of survey and description in general, see Christian Habicht, *Pausanias' Guide to Ancient Greece* (Berkeley: University of California Press, 1985) 20.

[2]For an analysis of the treatment of the analogous case of Philippi (another Roman colony) in Acts, see L. Michael White, "Visualizing the 'Real' World of Acts 16: Toward

ancient literature alongside the archaeological record is the focus of this study of Favorinus's "Corinthian Oration," or *Korinthiakos*. Preserved traditionally as *Oration* 37 among the speeches of Dio Chrysostom,[3] the *Korinthiakos* has, since the early nineteenth century, been attributed to Favorinus instead.[4] Despite renewed interest in Favorinus in recent years, this speech has not

---

Construction of a Social Index," in *The Social World of the First Christians: Studies in Honor of Wayne A. Meeks* (ed. L. Michael White and O. Larry Yarbrough; Minneapolis: Fortress, 1995) 234–64; for a similar analysis of the treatment of Ephesos, see Richard Pervo, *Profit with Delight: The Literary Genre of the Acts of the Apostles* (Minneapolis: Fortress, 1987) 9–11. The main point in both cases is that even while the author of Luke-Acts seems to have direct knowledge of elements of local culture particular to these cities, this fact does not necessarily mean that the events described regarding Paul are historical, as assumed by Ramsay and others. Instead, it appears that much of the Lukan author's "local color" may even date from after the time of Paul (as in the use of the title νεωκόρος at Ephesos), even when it is historically accurate to the particular city. See Steven Friesen, "The Cult of the Roman Emperors in Ephesos: Temple Wardens, City Titles, and the Interpretation of the Book of Revelation," in *Ephesos, Metropolis of Asia* (ed. Helmut Koester; HTS 41; Valley Forge: Trinity Press International, 1995) 232 and L. Michael White, "Urban Development and Social Change in Imperial Ephesos," in ibid., 36–37.

[3]In the remainder of this study, I shall simply refer to it as *Korinthiakos* (abbreviated *Kor.*), using the paragraph numbers now well established in critical editions of Dio since that of Hans von Arnim [Johannes de Arnim], *Dionis Prusaensis quem vocant Chrysostomum quae exstant omnia* (2 vols.; Berlin: Weidmanns, 1893–1896). Von Arnim's edition has been termed "the turning point for modern study of the text of Dio's extant speeches"; so B. F. Harris, "Dio of Prusa: A Survey of Recent Work," *ANRW* II.33.5 (1991) 3854. Since the text of the speech has received significant—and in some cases erroneous (as discussed below)—emendations, it is worth mentioning that *Orations* 32–41 are contained in only three (out of twelve) of the main manuscripts of Dio—Cod. Urbinas 124 (11th cent.), Cod. Parisinus 2958 (14th cent.), and Cod. Meermannianus [Leidensis 67] (16th cent.)—all of which come from a common archetype and reflect similar textual corruptions; see von Arnim, *Dionis Prusaensis*, 1:xxv–xxxiii.

[4]That Favorinus was the actual author was first proposed by Adolph Karl Wilhelm Emperius, *De Oratione Corinthiaca falso Dioni Chrysostomo adscripta* (Braunschweig: G. Westermann, 1832), repr. in *Opuscula philologica et historica* (ed. F. G. Schneidewin; Göttingen: Librariae Dieterichiana, 1847) 18–49. The view was repeated in Emperius's critical edition, *Dionis Chrysostomi Opera graece* (Braunschweig: G. Westermann, 1844). This conclusion was soon challenged in the Utrecht dissertation of Johannes Leonardus Marres, *Dissertatio de Favorini Arelatensis; vita, studiis, scriptis. Accedunt fragmenta* (Trajecti ad Rhenum: Kemink et filium, 1853). As a result, Ludwig Dindorff simply chose to place *Or.* 37 at the end (among the doubted works) of his first Teubner edition of Dio: *Dionis Chrysostomi Orationes* (Leipzig: B. G. Teubner, 1857) 2:293–307. Despite being convinced that *Or.* 37 was not by Dio, von Arnim (*Dionis Prusaensis*, 2:iii), following Dindorff, nonetheless preferred to list it as "anonymous," even though he returned it to its traditional numerical position (2:17–29). This cautious ascription was followed by Guy de Budé in his correction of Dindorf's Tuebner edition (*Dionis Chrysostomi Orationes* [2 vols.; Leipzig: B. G. Tuebner, 1916–1919] 2:22–38), even though he acknowledged Emperius's argument (2:ix). Ernst Maaß

been explored in detail for what it can tell us about the physical remains of Corinth and its life.[5] This study is, therefore, divided into three distinct parts. In the first, I focus on the speech itself. I examine its rhetorical stance and performative features on the grounds—both figuratively and literally—that it might thus be understood to reflect an actual historical situation and location in Corinth. In the second part, I deal with the archaeological evidence from Corinth. Finally, in the third part I ask whether and how the archaeological record might be illuminated by other clues within the oration.[6]

THE ORATOR FAVORINUS AT CORINTH: A FATEFUL VISIT

An ancient traveler come to Corinth . . . Nor was it his first visit. Favorinus tells us he had been there twice before, over a period of ten years, and to great acclaim. Given the circumstances of his third visit, however, this time he must have skulked into town somewhat surreptitiously, but we shall return to that later. We do not know precisely how he arrived, whether by the main road from Athens or by ship. At least one of his comments may favor his arrival via the harbor at Kenchreai,[7] in which case we might assume that he sailed

---

("De Favorini oratione Corinthiaca" in *De biographis Graecis quaestiones selectae* [Philologische Untersuchungen 3; Berlin: Weidmannsche Buchhandlung, 1880] 133–38), however, vigorously defended Emperius's identification, and this position was given its imprimatur by Eduard Norden in an important analysis of Favorinus's distinctive style (*Die Antike Kunstprosa* [1912; 2 vols.; repr., Darmstadt: Wissenschaftliche Buchgesellschaft, 1958] 1:422–27; see also Albin Lesky, *A History of Greek Literature* [2d ed.; New York: Thomas Y. Crowell, 1966] 834). Since that time Favorinus's authorship has not been seriously challenged; see the remark of H. Lamar Crosby, trans., *Dio Chrysostom* (LCL; 5 vols.; Cambridge, Mass.: Harvard University Press, 1932–1951) 4:1. See also Adelmo Barigazzi, *Favorino di Arelate: Opere: Introduzione, Testo Critico e Commento* (Testi greci et latini con commento filologico 4; Florence: Lelice Le Monnier, 1966), esp. 81–85; idem, "Favorino di Arelate," *ANRW* II.34.1 (1993) 573; and n. 12 below.

[5]The recent study by Jason König, "Favorinus' *Corinthian Oration* in its Corinthian Context" (*Proceedings of the Cambridge Philological Society* 47 [2001] 140–71), deals with the "context" in terms of identity formation (Greek vs. Roman), but does not discuss the physical or social situation of the city or the speech itself. The speech was discussed briefly by Saul Weinberg (*The Southeast Building, the Twin Basilicas, and the Mosaic House* [Corinth I.5; Princeton, N.J.: ASCSA, 1960] 11–12) in conjunction with his identification of the Southeast Building as the possible library; however, he assumed that the speech belongs to Dio.

[6]Let me add my thanks to Charles Williams, Nancy Bookidis, and the Corinth excavations both for their hospitality during my periods of field work there and for their body of scholarship, which naturally plays a central role in the second part of my paper.

[7]So *Kor.* 8 [= Dio 37.8; see n. 3, above], in reference to his second visit.

from his adopted home in Ephesos, where he was one of the most illustrious men in town. On this occasion, however, he came to Corinth under a cloud. I imagine him making the trek into the city from Kenchreai, passing by the Craneum and the tomb of Diogenes the Dog, and entering the city by the "back" route. Perhaps he had stayed the night with friends, if he had any left, before coming to the forum, where he would deliver this particular speech.

Favorinus claimed to be a disciple of Dio Chrysostom.[8] He was certainly a regular in Plutarch's circle, one of the set of younger members that included Plutarch's own sons.[9] Among this younger set, around whom the Second Sophistic was spawned, he was an early standout; later he became the teacher and intimate of Herodes Atticus.[10] More to the point, he was one of the two most famous sophists during the reign of Hadrian.[11] Born circa 80 C.E., a member of the equestrian order, and originally from Arelate (Arles) in Roman Gaul, Favorinus had moved to Athens and then to Ephesos, where he became the city's pre-eminent rhetorician.[12] As Philostratus tells us, his

[8]Philostratus, *Vit. Soph.* 1.8 (490a).

[9]See *Quaest. conv.* 8.10 (734D–735C). On this occasion Favorinus is involved in a dinner discussion of Aristotle with the sons of Plutarch, who would be closer in age to Favorinus himself. In 734E there appears to be a reference to Sosius Senecio in this connection, who likewise is made a part of this "younger set" of Plutarch's associates. See Sven-Tage Teodorsson, *Commentary on Plutarch's Table Talks* (3 vols.; Gotheborg: Acta Universitatis Gothoburgensis, 1990) 3:283. Some of these prosopographical connections may become significant to understanding Favorinus's situation both in Athens and in Corinth, since Senecio was related by marriage to the Euryclids of Sparta and Corinth. Favorinus was also the dedicant of Plutarch's *De prim. frig.*; the *Lamprias Catalogue* of the works of Plutarch lists a "Letter to Favorinus concerning friendship" (no. 132); and one of Favorinus's recorded works is titled Πλούταρχος ἤ περὶ τῆς Ἀκαδημαικῆς διαθέσεως. See Christopher. P. Jones, *Plutarch and Rome* (Oxford: Clarendon, 1971) 35, 61.

[10]Philostratus *Vit. Soph.* 1.8 (490b): "[Favorinus] was very intimate (ἐπιτηδειότατος) with Herodes the sophist, who considered him both teacher and father and wrote to him, 'When shall I see you; when shall I lick your lips?' " The last phrase may be a paraphrase from Aristophanes frag. 231 (ed. T. Kock, *Comicorum Atticorum fragmenta* [3 vols.; Utrecht: HES, 1976]), also found in Dio *Or.* 52, where it refers to Euripides tasting the eloquence of Sophocles. Given the context in Philostratus, one suspects a double entendre at the very least. At his death, says Philostratus, Favorinus bequeathed to Herodes his library, his house in Rome, and a favorite slave, Autolecythus, who was a favorite distraction (or "pet," ἄθυρμα) at their symposia. Even so, Philostratus's report (*Vit. Soph.* 1.25 [537a]) of the relationship between Herodes and Polemo bears striking verbal similarities to that between Herodes and Favorinus.

[11]On the Second Sophistic, the study of Glen W. Bowersock, *Greek Sophists in the Roman Empire* (Oxford: Clarendon, 1969), remains indispensable; for Favorinus, see esp. 35–36, 51–53, and 90–93.

[12]The majority of Favorinus's speeches are lost or known only by the title (see Aulus Gellius, *Noc. Att.* 17.21.1; 18.1); however, a few, like the *Korinthiakos*, have been preserved

principal rival was Marcus Antonius Polemo (ca. 88–144 C.E.), an aristocratic Laodicean whose family claimed descent from both Polemo, king of Pontus, and Mark Antony. Antonius Polemo served as chief rhetorician and public advocate for Smyrna.[13] As with Dio, the major cities courted these orators for their fame, for their influence with emperors and governors, and for their wealth. Most of the famous sophists—such as Herodes Atticus (at Athens and Corinth)[14] or Flavius Damianus (at Ephesos)[15]—were also important civic

---

among the manuscripts of Dio's orations (see n. 4, above). Favorinus's speech in praise of Fortune is preserved as Dio's *Or.* 64. While Dio's *Or.* 30 is also generally considered spurious, efforts to assign it to Favorinus have not been so successful. For example, von Arnim relegated *Or.* 30 to the doubtful works as No. 80 (*Dionis Prusaensis*, 2:295–308). A number of other works of Favorinus are known only from extracts and comments preserved in other writers. Two other philosophical works that may be by Favorinus, the *Memorabilia* (Ἀπομνεμονεύματα) and *Miscellaneous History* in twenty-four books (*Omnigena historia* or Παντοδαπὴ ἱστορία), were important sources for later writers, such as Diogenes Laertius (5.5), but these are only fragmentarily known from extracts and citations. All of these have been collected and edited by Barigazzi (*Favorino*), who also discusses the identification and authorship issues; see also Barigazzi's article, "Favorino di Arelate," 556–81; and Eugenio Amato, *Studi su Favorino: Le orazioni pseudo-crisostomiche* (Salerno: Edisud, 1995). A Vatican manuscript (P. Vat. Gr. 11.1) discovered in 1931 also contains an authentic speech of Favorinus reflecting on his exile. The text, now called *De exilio,* was published by Barigazzi, *Favorino,* 375–409; see also Maude W. Gleason, *Making Men: Sophists and Self-Presentation in Ancient Rome* (Princeton, N.J.: Princeton University Press, 1995) 147–57. See also now C. K. Callahan and A. Bertini Malgarni, "Übersehene Favorin-Fragmente aus einer Oxforder Handschrift," *Rheinisches Museum für Philologie* 129 (1986) 170–84, which presents eight new fragments that traveled under the name of Favorinus.

[13]Philostratus, *Vit. Soph.* 1.25 (530–45). On the competition with Favorinus, see Bowersock, *Greek Sophists,* 90–93; for Polemo's surviving works, see William W. Reeder, *The Severed Hand and the Upright Corpse: The Declamations of Marcus Antonius Polemo* (SBLTTS 42; Atlanta, Ga.: Scholars Press, 1996).

[14]Active from Hadrian to Marcus Aurelius, he rebuilt the Peirene fountain and the Odeion; see Philostratus, *Vit. Soph.* 2.1 (546–56, esp. 546b–52a) for his wealth and civic benefactions; for statuary and honorifics at Corinth see John Harvey Kent, *The Inscriptions 1926–1950* (Corinth VIII.3; Princeton, N.J.: ASCSA, 1966) nos. 128–29; *SEG*[3] 854 (= *IG* II².3604); A. B. West, *Latin Inscriptions, 1896–1926* (Corinth VIII, ii; Cambridge, Mass.: Harvard University Press, 1931) no. 58; see also G. P. Stevens, "The Fountain of Peirene in the Time of Herodes Atticus," *AJA* 38 (1934) 55–58; Walter Ameling, *Herodes Atticus* (2 vols.; Hildesheim: Georg Olms, 1983); Paul Graindor, *Un milliardaire antique: Hérode Atticus et sa famille* (Cairo: L'Université Égyptienne, 1930); and Jennifer L. Tobin, "The Monuments of Herodes Atticus" (Ph.D. diss., University of Pennsylvania, 1991).

[15]For Damianus, see Philostratus, *Vit. Soph.* 2.23 (605–6); among his benefactions, Philostratus reports that he built a marble colonnade along the processional route from the temple of Artemis to the Magnesia gate; for the inscriptions, see *IvE* 672a–b; 676a; 735.14; 811; 2100; 3029.26; 3051; 3080; 3081.3; and *PIR²*, F 253. For an honorific statue, see fig. 3.2, p. 76.

officeholders and benefactors. In turn, the orators could expect adulation, respect, and public honors of the sort that only leading provincials and noble Romans could normally achieve.[16]

What was the immediate situation that precipitated the *Korinthiakos*?[17] Favorinus tells us (in §§1, 8; see appendix A) that on his two previous visits to Corinth he had met with unbounded adulation by the Corinthians, so much so that on the second trip the magistrates tried to convince him to take up residence there instead of Ephesos. When he declined, they erected a bronze statue of him and placed it in front of the library. Now, on his third visit, he faces a different response: he has fallen into public disrepute, and his statue has been torn down. It seems that a principal factor in Favorinus's loss of favor with Hadrian and the public was the spread of imputations about his masculinity.[18] Delivered during the latter half of Hadrian's reign, the *Korinthiakos* is Favorinus's response to this shift in his fortunes.[19]

[16]Bowersock, *Greek Sophists,* 59–88.

[17]I have provided a translation of key passages, the framing sections, in appendix A. The traditional translations of the *Korinthiakos* (such as that of Crosby in the LCL) have missed much of its barbed irony and even its basic rhetorical strategy, as reflected in numerous unwarranted emendations. Key examples will be indicated in the following notes, as well as in appendix A.

[18]Even his name was something of an irony. Favorinus was known to be a "hermaphrodite" from birth (διφυὴς δὲ ἐτέχθη καὶ ἀνδρόθηλυς, Philostratus, *Vita Soph.* 489a). Philostratus attributes his unique personal and rhetorical style, including a beardless face and high-pitched voice like that of a eunuch, to his physical nature. On the other hand, Philostratus also indicates that Hadrian's disapproval arose from Favorinus's amorous involvement with a senator's wife at Rome, for which he was charged with adultery (*Vit. Soph.* 489b). Apparently his condition was a disorder known now as Reifenstein's syndrome, whereby a male is born with a penis but no testicles (Gleason, *Making Men,* 3, citing H. Mason, "Favorinus' Disorder: Reifenstein's Syndrome in Antiquity?" *Janus* 66 [1979] 1–13).

[19]The speech probably dates from after 125/6 C.E., perhaps around 128–131/2 when Hadrian made his second visit to Greece. In §35, Favorinus makes a veiled reference to an "accuser" (perhaps Polemo himself) and someone he calls "the Agonothete." The latter may well be Hadrian, who, on his first visit (in 124 C.E.), had participated in the City Dionysia at Athens and served as its Agonothete (IG II².3287 and Dio Cassius 69.16). Based on extant inscriptions, Hadrian does not seem to have held the title of agonothete at Corinth or in conjunction with the Isthmian games (Kent, *Inscriptions,* 30–31). Among other momentous events on Hadrian's second visit to Greece, the Olympieion at Athens was dedicated, and Antonius Polemo delivered the dedicatory address (Philostratus, *Vit. Soph.* 1.25 [533]). A statue of Favorinus at Athens was also removed at about this time; see Philostratus, *Vit. Soph.* 1.8 (489–92).

Favorinus's Rhetorical Strategy

In the *Korinthiakos*, Favorinus adopts the rhetorical ploy of defending his now missing statue (§23) as a way of indirectly defending himself against the calumnies of the Corinthians. In so doing, he also rebukes them.[20] He accuses the Corinthians of being fickle friends who have mistreated his "friend," the poor statue. In this way he effectively defends and praises himself, while rebuking them for a serious breach of social etiquette that borders on moral turpitude.[21] Favorinus couches these ideas rhetorically in terms of the reciprocal bonds of obligation that should attend friendship. He begins (§1):

> When I sojourned (ἐπεδήμησα) in your city the first time, . . . and shared a measure (μετέδωκα) of my speeches with your demos and magistrates, I seemed to be an intimate friend (ἐπιτήδειος) to you[22] to a degree not exceeded even by Arion of Methymne. Yet you did not make a figure (τύπον) of Arion.

Then, after a digression on Arion and other famous "visitors" of old, he comments on his second visit to Corinth (§8):

> But when we sojourned (ἡμᾶς δὲ ἐπιδημήσαντας) [with you] a second time, you experienced such gladness (ἀσμένως ἐπείδετε) that you tried very hard to keep me, but then, seeing that to be impossible, you instead made a physical likeness (τὴν εἰκὼ τοῦ σώματος), and taking this you set it up (or "you dedicated it," ἀνεθήκατε) *in the library* (βιβλία), *in a front seat* (προεδρίαν), where you thought especially

---

[20]So also Gleason, *Making Men*, 9. Gleason argues that beneath the Corinthians' contempt, expressed by the removal of the statue, runs an undercurrent derived from Polemo's denigration of his masculinity. Philostratus (*Vit. Soph.* 490b–91a) describes their bitter personal rivalry and laments that it resulted in numerous public insults in their speeches, especially in Rome. Bruce Winter (*Paul and Philo among the Sophists: Alexandrian and Corinthian Responses to a Julio-Claudian Movement* [2d ed.; Grand Rapids, Mich.: Eerdmans, 2002]) compares the rejection and reaction to that of Paul in 2 Corinthians; see also idem, "The Toppling of Favorinus and Paul by the Corinthians," in *Early Christianity and Classical Culture: Comparative Studies in Honor of Abraham J. Malherbe*, (ed. John T. Fitzgerald, Thomas H. Olbricht, and L. Michael White; NovTSup 110; Leiden: Brill, 2003) 291–306.

[21]The following discussion of Favorinus's rhetorical strategy is based on my treatment of the speech in comparison with Paul's letter to the Galatians: "Rhetoric and Reality in Galatians: Framing the Social Demands of Friendship," in *Early Christianity and Classical Culture: Comparative Studies in Honor of Abraham J. Malherbe* (ed. John T. Fitzgerald, Thomas H. Olbricht, and L. Michael White; NovTSupp 110; Leiden: Brill, 2003) 307–49.

[22]Reading ἔδοξα ἐπιτήδειος εἶναι [ἔτι δὲ] ὑμῖν, after von Arnim (followed by de Budé). I have not followed Crosby (LCL 4:4) here in emending the text with οἰκεῖος before ὑμῖν. Wilamowitz-Moellendorff had deleted ἔτι δέ after εἶναι, but von Arnim retained the words in brackets (so *Dionis Prusaensis*, 2:17.3), while Crosby restored them to the text to reinforce the addition of οἰκεῖος.

it might summon (προκαλέσασθαι) the youth to follow the same pursuits as we do. For you bestowed such honors not as one of the many
who annually disembark at Kenchreai[23] as merchants, or festival-goers,
or ambassadors, or travelers, but rather as a beloved friend (ἀγαπητόν),
who at last appears after much time.

Favorinus starts by rehearsing his own prior experiences with the Corinthians, and their displays of friendship and honor toward him. He is a "beloved
friend" who produces the joy of true friendship in their hearts when they see
him return.[24] His honored status is signaled by the placement of the statue in
a προεδρία ("front seat") in the library, and this comment is the focal point
of the second part of this study. The Corinthians had thereby honored him
with the status of a "first man," i.e., a leading citizen and civic benefactor.
Yet, paraphrasing Homer,[25] he notes ironically that such civic honors may
be fickle and fleeting (§9).

Next (§9) he begins to turn the screws on the Corinthians:

So that I stand *perplexed* (ἐν ἀπόρῳ καθεστάναι) both in regard to my
own case and now, by Zeus, in regard to that of yet another man too,
wondering whether I did not see truly—the things taking place being
not a waking appearance but a dream—or whether the things taking
place were accurate in every detail, both the zeal of the crowd and the
judgment of the council, but the statue (ἀνδριάς) chanced to be a work
of Daedalus and escaped us unnoticed.

Favorinus is saying: I, the orator (i.e., the one who brings words to visual
reality), now doubt my own vision of these events.[26] He adds that it is not
only his case that is perplexing but that of "another man." At this point he
starts to shift the rhetorical ploy of the speech; indeed, the entire rest of the
speech—well over half—will now focus on the experience of this "other
man," namely the statue of Favorinus that has now disappeared from sight, as
if, he says, it were one of the mythical, magical works of Daedalus (§10).

Next he plays with this idea of magically endowed statues in a kind of ring
composition (§§10–21),[27] which allows him to ask why, in fact, even if the

---

[23]This is the allusion to Kenchreai that I noted earlier (n. 7) as evidence that Favorinus
himself had reached Corinth by sea.

[24]For this joy at the return of the long-absent friend, see Hans Dieter Betz, *Galatians*
(Hermeneia; Philadelphia: Fortress, 1979) 226–28; compare Gal 4:13–15.

[25]See appendix A, n. 116, below.

[26]Compare also the element of "seeing" truly and "with his own eyes" with the references to seeing in both Gal 4:15 (a long-debated passage in Paul) and Gal 3:1 (a reference
to Paul's earlier preaching).

[27]Notice how Favorinus uses the framing addresses in relation to the mythical/historical

statue could flee the city, it would choose to do so, seeing that Corinth is such a beautiful place. So if "he" (the statue) fled, there must be something wrong with the city, or more precisely, with its inhabitants. But no, he concludes (in §§20–21), the statue did not flee at all, nor did it ever intend to leave the city; therefore, something else must have gone wrong. Why, "he" must have been banished instead! This allows Favorinus to turn the rest of his speech into a defense of the "accused" (i.e., the statue), as if he were speaking in court, and to cast his audience in the role of the jury.[28]

So Favorinus, like a true friend, now leaps to the defense of the poor statue:

> Then if some sort of decree that statues be called to account were to be passed by you [Corinthians]—or rather, if you will, supposing that such has been decreed and a trial (ἀγῶνος) has begun—permit me, yes *permit me* to make a [defense] speech before you as though in court on behalf of this very man (αὐτοῦ) [i.e., the statue].[29]

> Men of the jury, they say one must expect anything in the course of time; but this man (οὗτος) is, in a brief span, at risk of being put up (τεθῆναι), on the one hand, as the noblest of the Greeks; and on the other, of being put down (ἐκπεσεῖν) as the vilest. Now then, to prove that he was put up (ἐστάθη)[30] well and justly and profitably for your city and all the Greeks, I have much to say. (§§22–23)

He begins with irony by creating a double entendre: "he" (the statue) was, indeed, *put up* worthily but *banished* (or *put down*) unjustly. The two verbs τιθέναι and ἐκπίπτειν create a wordplay, since both can be used not only of legal actions taken by a *dēmos* or *boulē* (meaning "to award or vote in favor

---

digressions. The latter occupy the bulk of the speech, but the former are the key points. The digressions help him to make and illustrate his key arguments, while also showing off his rhetorical artistry.

[28] In §§23–47 the speech pretends to be a real forensic defense, but this too is a rhetorical ploy.

[29] Here I follow the manuscripts and read ὑπὲρ αὐτοῦ, "on behalf of him" (so also von Arnim and de Budé), as opposed to Crosby's emendation (LCL 4:22–23), ὑπὲρ αὑτοῦ, "in my own behalf." Here and throughout the speech, Crosby's unwarranted emendations have Favorinus speaking about himself, but that is not his rhetorical strategy. He is speaking about "the other man," i.e., the statue; see Norden, *Antike Kunstprosa,* 1:423. Gleason (*Making Men,* 13 and n. 51) observes the same problem of erroneous emendation.

[30] The manuscripts all give the first person (ἐστάθην) here; however, both von Arnim and de Budé accepted Emperius's correction to the third person (ἐστάθη), as demanded by the preceding sentence: οὗτος . . . κινδυνεύει τεθῆναι ("this man . . . is at risk of being put up"). Even so, Crosby (LCL 4:27) reverts to the first person ("I was set up fairly and justly"), citing only Emperius's correction. This change forces him to strain the translation

of someone at trial" and "to banish," respectively), but also of the acts of "setting up" and "taking down" a statue as in a temple (hence, "to dedicate or set up" and "to tear down," respectively). This wordplay will continue to the end of the speech (see §§37, 47).

In the process, Favorinus adopts two further rhetorical ploys through the friendship *topos*. In §37, he says it is out of his own sense of friendship for the Corinthians that he is pointing out their errors of judgment in "banishing the statue." Here again is the motif of frankness: a true friend will not refrain from delivering a rebuke when needed. In §36, he even uses the term παρρη-σία ("frank criticism") in this regard. Then in §§46–47, Favorinus concludes the speech by offering consolation to the statue as to a friend, and he calls for the "right" verdict in the "case."[31] So Favorinus, not the Corinthians, is the true friend after all. Of course, the "jury" (i.e., the audience) is supposed to recognize its previous error and to shout its acclamation in favor of the statue. Whether this was the outcome and the Corinthians returned Favorinus to favor is unfortunately not recorded.[32]

Now I want to return for a moment to Favorinus's expression of disbelief and perplexity at the beginning of this section (§§9–10). To some extent it must be understood as a ploy, part of the dramatic quality of Favorinus's rhetorical display as he stands beside the empty statue base. I shall return to this passage in the third part of this study, since it may also give us a hint about the location of the statue base within the city. Apropos the rhetorical effect, the point is this: even if his "perplexity" here is in some sense feigned, nonetheless it is meant to heighten the concrete situation of social tension and to facilitate Favorinus's ironic rebuke. It does so precisely because such perplexity in relationships is the exact opposite of how true friends ought to deal with one another. In other words, Favorinus is saying that his "emotional state" of perplexity is the direct result of their breach of the obligations of

---

of the preceding sentence by reading οὗτος thus: "This one *who stands before you*." This forced reading of the text is in keeping with his tendency to take many of the demonstratives (referring to the statue) as reflexives (referring to Favorinus himself); see the preceding note. Note also von Arnim's emphatic comments on the use of the first person (*hic intolerabilis*—"here it is intolerable") in regard to the parallel and related use of ἐστάθη[ν] in §27, where it similarly follows immediately on a demonstrative (τοῦτον) referring to the statue (*Dionis Prusaensis*, 2:23.25, s.v. App. Crit.); von Arnim seems to view the first person in both instances as erroneous scribal emendation (see n. 3, above).

[31]See the notes to appendix A for discussion of several key word plays.

[32]Crosby, in the introduction to the LCL edition (4:2), proposes that the occasion was the unveiling or dedication of a new statue, but this seems most unlikely. Favorinus's final words are entirely metaphorical. So also Gleason, *Making Men,* 20.

friendship; it is a moral judgment on the audience for their past actions. He charges them with having turned friendship into enmity. Then in a deliciously satirical twist, Favorinus says that if he himself is *perplexed*, imagine how the poor statue must feel!

Although Favorinus's speech has an apologetic function, as Maude Gleason has noted,[33] it should be classified formally as epideictic with a high degree of irony, as he blames the Corinthians for having transgressed the social and moral obligations of friendship by removing his honorific statue. Even the title, Κορινθιακός, is an ironic form of epideictic, since such a title would usually imply a speech in praise of the city—i.e., an encomium, the other type of epideictic oratory, as we see in both Dio and Aelius Aristides.[34] Likewise, the ostensible court speech (§§23–47) is not the real form, function, or setting of Favorinus's oration, but a rhetorical ploy in order to make the rebuke effective.[35] The framing elements (as given in the selections in appendix A) are the real key to understanding the speech and its rhetorical strategy.

Later, when Favorinus turns to console his absent "friend" at the end of his speech, he concludes with these words addressed to the missing statue:

> Accordingly, I wish now to offer consolation (παραμυθήσασθαι) to him, as to one possessing sensation: "O silent image of my oratory, will you not show yourself? . . . I myself will raise you up (ἀναστήσω) before the goddess [Fame], whence nothing will cast you down (καθέλη)—*neither earthquake nor wind, neither snow nor rain, neither envy nor enmity*—but even now do I discover you risen up (ἑστηκότα)." (§§46–47)

This is actually a double use of friendship motifs. In form, it is a consolation, as to a friend. Then near the end (in §47), in saying "I'll raise you . . . and nothing will cast you down [again]," he describes the dangers that have been overcome in the process: earthquake, wind, snow, rain, etc. The central pair (*neither snow nor rain*) is an allusion to Herodotus's famous tribute to

---

[33]So also Gleason, *Making Men,* 9: "In effect, he has to combine the activities of apology and invective without appearing to perform either." Gleason also discusses the rhetorical problems of self-praise, as reflected in Plutarch's *De se ipsum citra invidiam laudando* (*Mor.* 539A–547F).

[34]Compare Aelius Aristides, *Or.* 43, Ῥοδιακός ("The Rhodian Oration"); however, Dio Chrysostom uses the same title for his customary form of corrective symbouleutic speech in *Or.* 31, Ῥοδιακός (which also deals with mistreatment of statues, §§95–97), and *Or.* 33, Ταρσικός A; see Bargiazzi, "Favorino," 573.

[35]Similarly, Favorinus's speech on Fortune ([Dio] *Or.* 64) is epideictic "structured as defense"; so Gleason, *Making Men,* 150 n. 73.

the Persian couriers, now better known as the unofficial motto of the United States Postal Service.[36] Presumably the audience was supposed to catch the allusion, as well as Favorinus's irony: now, his "flighty" statue will become as steadfast as a Persian courier. But to this Favorinus adds two more pairs of "dangers," one at the beginning and one at the end. At the beginning he refers to *earthquake* and *wind*; these allude to an earlier point in the speech where Favorinus muses on what could possibly have made the statue go away.[37] Then comes the Persian courier allusion, a lighter piece of irony. Finally, Favorinus adds two more dangers—*neither envy nor enmity* (οὐ φθόνος οὐκ ἐχθρός)—and these are more to the real point. Rather than natural disasters that can topple a statue, they are pitfalls that destroy friendship.[38] On the basis of the structure[39] and allusions within this line, then, one can imagine how it was delivered rhetorically by pairs—the first pair spoken earnestly but softly, the second rather whimsically, and the last with biting intensity. It would have "sounded" something like this:[40]

---

[36]Favorinus's version reads οὐ σεισμός, οὐκ ἄνεμος, *οὐ νιφετός, οὐκ ὄμβρος*, οὐ φθόνος, οὐκ ἐχθρός, whereas the passage in Herodotus (8.98) reads τοὺς οὔτε νιφετός, οὐκ ὄμβρος, οὐ καῦμα, οὐ νὺξ ἔργει μὴ οὐ κατανύσαι τὸν προκείμενον αὐτῷ δρόμον τὴν ταχίστην. It is no more than an allusion, but it is meant to be recognizable, and thus humorous. Favorinus mentions Herodotus (who is listed as one of the famous visitors to Corinth) by name at several points in the speech; see §§7, 18.

[37]See §20: "But then did someone overturn the dedication [i.e., the statue] of the city? Well if it were a whirlwind (στρόβιλος), or a hurricane (πρηστὴρ), or a thunderbolt falling on it (σκηπτὸς ἐμπεσών) . . . ."

[38]For envy as a cause of enmity, and enmity as the opposite of friendship, see Plutarch, *De capienda ex inimicis utilitate* 1, 9 (*Mor.* 86C, 91B) and *De invidia et odio* (Mor. 536C–38E). The latter may be dependent on Aristotle, *Rhet.* 2.4.30–32. See also Dio, *Or.* 77/78.32–39 and *Or.* 38.22 (enmity as the opposite of friendship and concord between cities, as discussed above). Compare also Gal 4:16; in relation to the use of "enemy" there, Betz (*Galatians,* 229 n. 102) cites the definition of Ammonius, *De adfinium voc. diff.* 208: "the 'enemy' is the one who was formerly a friend." See also Peter Marshall, *Enmity at Corinth: Social Conventions in Paul's Relations with the Corinthians* (WUNT 2.23; Tübingen: Mohr Siebeck, 1987) 35–69.

[39]Notice the precise parallelism created by careful word selection (all masculine nouns ending in -ος, beginning with and without consonants) so that it yields an alternating pattern of οὐ and οὐκ in three pairs.

[40]One cannot do justice in print to the sound of the Greek. I have arranged the lines in rhythmic segments corresponding to what I imagine to be Favorinus's inflections; the vertical bars represent pause beats (where ˈ = .5 beat, | = 1 beat, and ‖ = 2 beats). In brackets I give Norden's scansion of Favorinus's rhythm in these lines (*Antike Kunstprosa,* 1:427).

ἐγώ σε ἀναστήσω | παρὰ τῇ θεῷ,   [⌣́ U U ⌣́ U _]
ὅθεν οὐδείς σε ' μὴ καθέλῃ—   [⌣́ U ⌣́ U U _]
  οὐ σεισμός, | οὐκ ἄνεμος,   [⌣́ U ⌣́ U U U]
    οὐ νιφετός, | *οὐκ ὄμβρος,* [U̇ U U ⌣̣ ⌣́ U]
      οὐ φθόνος, ‖ **οὐκ ἐχθρός**   [⌣́ U U ⌣̣ ⌣́ U]
—ἀλλὰ καὶ νῦν σε ' καταλαμβάνω ' *ἑστηκότα.*   [⌣́ U ⌣́ _ ⌣́ U U]

Favorinus has accused the Corinthians—and especially his detractors—of betrayal, by marking how their former friendship has turned into envy and enmity.[41]

THE FORUM AT CORINTH: ARCHAEOLOGICAL CONSIDERATIONS

. . . and the record of what he saw. I will now argue that Favorinus's rhetorical strategy clearly presupposes a specific location in Corinth, where the orator could gesture and point at specific monuments as he rehearsed numerous aspects of the city's history and tradition. The speech lasted approximately forty-five minutes when performed, and it took much of its rhetorical force, as I have tried to show, from Favorinus's interaction not only with his audience but also with the missing statue. Thus, Favorinus must have been standing beside the empty statue base while he delivered the speech. I turn now to the statue itself and its location; later, I shall examine more carefully what Favorinus might have been looking at as he spoke.

The Disposition of Favorinus's Statue

At a number of points in the speech, notably in §§25 and 46, Favorinus indicates that the statue was in bronze.[42] It should be noted that Corinthian bronze was famous and that bronzeworks for statuary dating from the first century C.E. were discovered in earlier excavations.[43] As to the location and

---

[41]In §35, Favorinus seems to make an allusion to Hadrian and some unnamed "accuser," possibly even Polemo himself. On the other hand, there may be local detractors implied as well.

[42]In §§21, 25, and 30, bronze is mentioned as a symbol of its intended permanence, while §46 suggests that the statue has already been melted down.

[43]See the comments of James Wiseman, "Corinth and Rome I: 228 B.C.–A.D. 267," *ANRW* II.7.1 (1979) 512, citing his own excavation work reported in "Excavations at Corinth, The

disposition of the statue, the key reference comes in §8. Here again is the central portion:

> And taking this [the statue] you set it up in the library, in a front seat (ἀνεθήκατε εἰς τὰ βιβλία, εἰς προεδρίαν), where you thought it might especially summon the youth to follow the same pursuits as we do (οὗ μάλιστ᾽ ἄν ᾤεσθε τοὺς νέους παροκαλέσασθαι τῶν αὐτῶν ἡμῖν ἐπιτηδευμάτων ἔχεσθαι).

There are two ways to interpret these comments.[44] The first is to take the term προεδρία literally and assume that he means an actual "front seat" in the library proper.[45] Since we know of other statues located in libraries, this might fit, but the mention of a "seat" could still refer to either a standing or a seated figure. If Favorinus refers to a seated figure here, then I would imagine something like the seated figure of C. Julius Philopappos (another member of Plutarch's sympotic circle), in the dress of the philosopher, installed in the central niche of his funerary monument on the Museion Hill in Athens (fig. 3.1).[46] On the other hand, a number of references within the speech, and indeed even the rhetorical ploy of the final scene, suggest that it must have been a standing statue in the pose of a rhetor.[47] Based on the stated function for which Corinth erected the statue—"to summon (προκαλέσασθαι) the youth of Corinth" (§8)[48]—I imagine a sculpture like those of the orators of old, such as the Roman copy of a third-century B.C.E. portrait of Demosthenes (now in the Vatican Collection).[49] Examples of later orators in similar pose

---

Gymnasium Area, 1965," *Hesperia* 36 (1967) 38; "Excavations at Corinth, The Gymnasium Area, 1966," *Hesperia* 36 (1967) 413–16; and "Excavations in Corinth, The Gymnasium Area, 1967–1968," *Hesperia* 38 (1969) 67–69. The foundry was located in the area adjacent to the Peirene and the Peribolos of Apollo.

[44]Saul Weinberg takes a third option, following A. Langie (Weinberg, *Southeast Building,* 12 and n. 27): namely, that the term προεδρία refers to the "City Hall," i.e., in the administrative buildings of the forum. Such usage is unattested and seems most unlikely.

[45]Crosby (LCL, 4:11 n. 2) seems to take the phrase metaphorically in this way.

[46]For discussions of the monument and the statuary composition, see Diana E. E. Kleiner, *The Monument of Philopappos in Athens* (Rome: G. Bretschneider, 1983).

[47]As discussed above. So note the closing line of the speech: ἣ κατ᾽ ἄνδρα μοι ὀρθὸς ἔστηκας ("by which [judgment] to me you stand aright, like a man"). This is another word-play, since ὀρθός here can mean either "right" (as used also to signify the affirmative verdict in a court case) and an "erect" posture.

[48]Compare §26, where Favorinus describes his divinely inspired gifts for "arousing [Greeks] to join him in pursuing philosophy" (ἐπῆρε συμφιλοσοφεῖν αὐτῷ).

[49]See John Boardman, *Greek Art* (New York: Praeger, 1964) 225, fig. 205.

Fig. 3.1 Athens: funeral monument of C. Julius Philopappos (d. ca. 113 C.E.). Detail of seated portrait statues.

Fig. 3.2 Ephesos: honorific marble statue of the sophist and benefactor
T. Flavius Damianus, from the East Gymnasium (Antonine Period).

are certainly known, as in the case of the statues of Herodes Atticus from Athens, or Flavius Damianus from Ephesos (fig. 3.2). Yet, it must be noted that these statues are all in marble. Bronze would offer an even more expressive medium for the execution of Favorinus's "imploring" pose: compare the bronze of Lucius Mammius Maximus (fig. 3.3, p. 78, first century B.C.E.) or the contemporaneous bronze of Camillus (fig. 3.4, p. 79, Hadrianic period).

Now, such a statue might have been located in the library itself, presumably up front or in a niche. We might also, however, understand προεδρία more metaphorically as a reference to an honored position, but in the area "*in front of* the library (εἰς τὰ βιβλία)"—just outside the entrance to the library, perhaps in a portico or just beyond—and this is where I would locate the speech. I think that while delivering his speech, Favorinus was standing beside the base where both he and his audience knew his statue had stood. This conjecture brings the rhetorical strategy of the speech to life: Favorinus defended, then consoled and extolled, his absent "friend" in front of the library and before the Corinthian crowd.

The Library

But where was the library of Corinth? I have suggested that it was somewhere in the forum, or in some conspicuous public area in the central city, on analogy to the location of libraries in other Greek cities. To date, however, no building at Corinth has been conclusively identified as the library, and no excavated building conforms to the architectural form seen in other known libraries of the period.[50] Closest in date and location to Favorinus are the library of Celsus at Ephesos,[51] the library of Pantainos in the

---

[50]See the survey by Heinz Kähler, "Biblioteca," *Enciclopedia dell'arte antica, classica e orientale* (Rome: 7 vols.; Enciclopedia Italiana/Instituto dello Stato, 1959) 2:93–99; E. Makowiecka, *The Origin and Evolution of Architectural Form of Roman Library* [sic] (Warsaw: Wydawnictwa Uniwersytetu Warszawskiego, 1978); N. Purcell, "Atrium Libertatis," *PBSR* 61 (1993) 125–55; V. M. Strocka, "Römische Bibliotheken," *Gymnasium* 88 (1981) 298–329.

[51]Dates to ca. 105 C.E. (Trajanic). See Wilhelm Wilberg et al., *Celsusbibliothek* (Forschün-gen in Ephesos 5.1; Vienna: Österreichische Verlagsgesellschaft, 1944); Burkhard Fehr, "Archäologen, Techniker, Industrielle: Betrachtungen zur Wiederaufstellung der Bibliothek des Celsus in Ephesos," *Hephaistos* 3 (1981) 107–25; Friedmund J. Hueber, "Beobachtungen zu Kurvatur und Scheinperspektive an der Celsusbibliothek und anderen Kaiserzeitlichen Bauten," in *Bauplanung und Bautheorie der Antike* (Diskussionen zur archäologischen Bauforschung 4; Berlin: Deutsches Archäologisches Institut, 1983) 175–200; and Lora L. Johnson, "The Hellenistic and Roman Library: Studies Pertaining to Their Architectural Form" (Ph.D. diss., Brown University, 1984).

Fig. 3.3 Herculaneum: bronze statue of Lucius Mammius Maximus (1st c. B.C.E.).

Fig. 3.4 Rome: Hadrianic bronze statue of Camillus (117–136 C.E.).

Athenian agora,[52] and the library of Hadrian at Athens;[53] not as widely known is a similar edifice from the agora of Thessalonika dated to the time of Antoninus Pius.[54] Yet, Favorinus's speech offers further evidence that there

[52]Early Trajanic in date (before 102 C.E.), privately dedicated by T. Flavius Pantainos who, with his son and daughter, "dedicated the outer colonnades, the peristyle, the library with its books, and all the furnishings at their own expense" (τὰς ἔξω στοὰς, τὸ περίστυλον, τὴν βιβλιοθήκην μετὰ τῶν βιβλίων, τὸν ἐν αὐτοῖς πάντα κόσμον, ἐκ τῶν ἰδίων . . . ἀνέθηκε, *SEG* XXI.703, lines 3–4). The "library" proper is a large square room off one side of the peristyle. Since the inscription also refers to Pantainos as the son of a "head of the school" (διάδοχος), it might be appropriate to think of the larger building as the school hall, with one room serving as a "library," albeit with public access. The inscription was first published by Benjamin D. Meritt, "Greek Inscriptions," *Hesperia* 15 (1946) 233, no. 64. See also James H. Oliver, "Flavius Pantaenus, Priest of the Philosophical Muses," *HTR* 72 (1979) 157–60; repr. in *The Civic Tradition in Roman Athens* (Baltimore, Md.: Johns Hopkins University Press, 1983) 62–65; Michael Woloch, *Roman Citizenship and the Athenian Elite, A.D. 96–161: Two Prosopographical Catalogues* (Amsterdam: Hakkert, 1973) 231–33, no. 53; Simone Follet, *Athènes au IIe et au IIIe Siècle: Études chronologiques et prosopographiques* (Paris: Belles Lettres, 1976) 56–57; and Daniel J. Geagan, "Roman Athens: Some Aspects of Life and Culture, I. 86 BC–AD 267," *ANRW* II.7.1 (1979) 385. Another inscription gives the rules and hours for the use of the library, with the provision that books may not be taken out. For both texts, see Richard E. Wycherley, *Literary and Epigraphical Testimonia* (Agora III; Princeton, N.J.: ASCSA, 1957) 150, no. 464. For plan, photographs, and discussion, see Homer A. Thompson and Richard E. Wycherley, *The Agora of Athens: The History, Shape, and Uses of an Ancient City Center* (Agora XIV; Princeton, N.J.: ASCSA, 1972) 114–16; and John M. Camp, *The Athenian Agora: Excavations in the Heart of Classical Athens* (2d ed.; London: Thames & Hudson, 1992) 187–91.

[53]Probably dates to his second visit, ca. 128–131/2 C.E.: *IG* III.18 = II².1094; see Pausanias 1.18.9 and Vitruvius 5.11.2. See also Ida T. Hill, *The Ancient City of Athens: Topography and Monuments* (2d ed.; Chicago: Argonaut, 1969) 245–47; Wolfram Martini, "Zur Benennung der sogennanten Hadriansbibliothek in Athen," in *Lebende Altertumswissenschaft: Festgabe H. Vetters* (Vienna: Adolf Holzhausens, 1985) 189–91; Dietrich Willers, *Hadrians panhellenisches Programm. Archäologische Beitrage zur Neugestaltung Athens durch Hadrian* (Beiheft zur Halbjahresschrift Antike Kunst 16; Basel: Vereinigung der Freunde Antiker Kunst, 1990) 14–21; A. Spetsieri-Choremi, "Library of Hadrian at Athens: Recent Finds," *Ostraka* 4.1 (1995) 137–47; I. Baldini Lippolis, "La monumentalizzazione tardoantica di Athene," *Ostraka* 4.1 (1995) 169–90; and Ioannes Travlos, "Τὸ τετράκογχο οἰκοδόμημα τῆς βιβλιοθήκης τοῦ Ἀδριανοῦ," *ΦΙΛΙΑ ΕΠΗ ΕΙΣ ΓΕΩΡΓΙΟΝ Ε. ΜΥΛΩΝΑΝ* (4 vols.; Athens: Ἡ ἐν Ἀθήναις Ἀρχαιολογικὴ Ἑταιρεία, 1986–1989) 1:343–47.

[54]For the excavation report, see Charalambos Bakirtzis, "Περί του συγκροτήματος της Αγοράς της Θεσσαλονίκης," in *Archaia Makedonia II* (Thessaloniki: Institute for Balkan Studies, 1977) 257–69. The building has a comparable apsidal niche and columns around the walls, and a statue of Athena was found nearby, which seems to belong in the niche; see Georgios Despines, "Το αντίγραφο της Αθηνάς Medici του μουσείου Θεσσαλονίκης," in ibid., 95–102. A fuller discussion of the architectural form, with comparisons to other libraries, is given by Evangelia Kampouri, "Δημόσιο κτίσμα των ρωμαϊκών αυτοκρατορικών κρόνων στο χώρο του συγκροτήματος της αρχαίας Αγοράς Θεσσαλονίκης," in

was indeed a library of some sort at Corinth. Judging by the criteria of size and location, either of the Twin Basilicas might suffice, although they have generally been thought to have had some sort of commercial function. Room A of the South Stoa is similar in shape to the library of Pantainos at Athens; however, it is usually thought to be the chambers of the *Hellanodikai* (so Oscar Broneer)[55] or perhaps the earlier *bouleuterion* (so Mary E. Hoskins Walbank).[56] In part, the question of the location of Corinth's library turns on some important archaeological issues concerning the architectural development of the forum itself.

The Southeast Building

The only building that has been suggested as the library during the course of the Corinth excavations is the so-called Southeast Building, located at the eastern end of the South Stoa (map 5).[57] It was also adjacent to, but slightly above, the Julian Basilica, which stands immediately to its north and on a slightly different axis. Together the Southeast Building and the Julian Basilica framed the eastern end of the Roman forum and blocked off what would have been the earlier roadway past the South Stoa and the Circular Monument.[58] The Southeast Building lies perpendicular to the South Stoa on the same axis and on the ground level of the upper terrace between the Stoa and the central shops, while the Julian Basilica stood on the forum floor, oriented toward the Western Terrace and Temple E.[59]

Broneer was the first to propose that the Southeast Building was the *tabularium* of Corinth based on excavations in 1946–1947.[60] Among the finds of

Η ΘΕΣΣΑΛΟΝΙΚΗ 1 (1985) 85–109. In a recent study, however, Theodosia Stephanidou-Tiveriou ("Une téte colossale de Titus au Forum de Thessalonique," *BCH* 125 [2001] 389–411) identifies this building as a temple instead. My thanks to Dr. Bakirtzis, Ephoros of Byzantine Antiquities in Thessalonika, for providing me with these references and this valuable piece of comparative data.

[55]Oscar Broneer, *The South Stoa and Its Roman Successors* (Corinth I.4; Princeton, N.J.: ASCSA, 1954) 110.

[56]Mary E. Hoskins Walbank, "The Foundation and Planning of Early Roman Corinth," *JRA* 10 (1997) 95–130, esp. 119.

[57]See Wiseman, "Corinth and Rome I," 514, followed by Donald Engels, *Roman Corinth: An Alternative Model for the Classical City* (Chicago: University of Chicago Press, 1990) 68.

[58]This was the earlier entrance to the central city via the Kenchreai road.

[59]On the issue of the different axes in the plan of the forum, see the discussion of Walbank, "Foundation and Planning," 114–16.

[60]Oscar Broneer, "Investigations at Corinth, 1946–1947," *Hesperia* 16 (1947) 237.

that season was a single fragment of the Ionic epistyle frieze in white marble bearing the inscribed letters *NIA* (from *colonia*) at the end of a line.[61] Earlier, A. B. West had pieced together three other architectural fragments bearing similar inscribed letter forms;[62] together these fragments formed the epistyle inscription for the Southeast Building (see appendix B.1). Broneer restored in the missing portion of the text the word *tabularium* ("library" or "records office"). While it seems likely that the word(s) in the inscription just before *et porticum* contained the ancient identification of the Southeast Building, this particular restoration remains highly conjectural. On the other hand, the restoration of the name "Gnaeus Babbius Philinus" is equally important, because he is the same as the dedicator of the Babbius monument at the west end of the forum.[63] The proposed restoration of the name was based on the fact that he is the only magistrate of Corinth known (from other inscriptions) to have held the titles of both *duovir* and *pontifex*.[64] As to date, the letter forms point to sometime between 25 and 50 C.E., while the usual dating for Babbius Philinus (following Kent)[65] would place him in the Augustan to early Tiberian period.

A second inscription (Kent, *Inscriptions,* no. 327; see appendix B.2 and fig. 3.5) seems to confirm the association of the family of Babbius with the Southeast Building, and further supports Broneer's identification (followed

---

[61]Ibid., 237; see also Kent, *Inscriptions*, no. 323 and plate 29.

[62]See West, *Latin Inscriptions,* no. 122.

[63]Ibid., no. 132; and Kent, *Inscriptions,* no. 155. See appendix A.3.

[64]So West, *Latin Inscriptions,* no. 122, but accepted by Kent (*Inscriptions,* 130). While restoring the name "Cn. Babbius Philinus" based on the role of his son, Cn. Babbius Italicus (to be discussed below), is most likely correct, it should be noted, however, that at least one other Corinthian is now known to have held the two titles *pontifex* and *duovir*: T. Manlius Iuvencus, whom Kent dates to the end of Tiberius's reign (Kent, *Inscriptions,* 25 and no. 154). It is worth noting, moreover, that the inscription honoring him for his innovation in scheduling the Caesarean before the Isthmian games was found in Room C (the Agonotheteion) of the South Stoa, and that it dates from a period later than the time of his duovirate, i.e., probably sometime in the reign of Claudius. As a result, he too would be contemporary with the epistyle inscription of the Southeast Building.

[65]Kent, *Inscriptions,* 25. For fragmentary inscriptions bearing the name "Cn. Babbius" from the area of the Julian Basilica, see also West, *Latin Inscriptions,* nos. 98–101; and Kent, *Inscriptions,* no. 364. For a marble stele apparently commemorating the revetment work of the Julian Basilica, see West, *Latin Inscriptions,* no. 130 (compare no. 13). For possible family connections of the Julian Basilica to the Babbii, see also ibid., no. 14, which could conceivably yield the name "Cn. [Babbius] Pius," possibly the father of Philinus, in the context of some sacred function related to the Augustan imperial cult located in the Julian Basilica. See appendix B.5 for further discussion of this inscription, with epigraphic evidence for the name Babbius Pius.

Fig. 3.5 Corinth: inscription of Gnaeus Babbius Italicus from the Southeast Building.

by Saul Weinberg in *Southeast Building*) of the building as the library.[66] As restored by J. H. Kent, the inscription preserves the name of "Gnaeus Babbius Italicus, son of Gnaeus"—that is, Babbius Philinus; it apparently commemorates the marble revetting of the Southeast Building by the younger Babbius. But this would place the date sometime later, at least during the time of Claudius or Nero. Notably, Broneer had restored the final word in line 3 as [*scr*]*ipta* ("library"),[67] whereas Kent[68] later restored the last word as *pr*[*aescr*]*ipta* (presumably referring to the "orders" for the work).

Phases of Construction in the Southeast Building

A renovation and/or redecoration of the Southeast Building by the son of Babbius Philinus is quite consistent with the archaeological record, which indicates two distinct architectural phases and some secondary renovations. The first phase of the Southeast Building (map 4) is usually associated with the early rebuilding of the South Stoa at the time of the founding of the colony as suggested by Weinberg (following Broneer),[69] and followed by Wiseman and Walbank.[70] According to Weinberg, the rectangular hall measured 26.70 m in length (N-S) and 18.20 m in width, with a portico 5.20 m wide along its west side.[71] In more recent plans (fig. 3.6), however, the size and shape of the earlier building has been modified (both longer and narrower) from that proposed by Weinberg and Broneer; however, these new data have not been published. Even so, the first Southeast Building seems rather clearly to predate the construction of the Julian Basilica, since the line of the northeast corner of its foundations was interrupted when the basilica was built.[72]

When the first building was destroyed, much of its foundation material was dismantled and reused; as a result, the limited remains have been interpreted differently in recent years. Weinberg thought the first building was destroyed during the time of Tiberius or slightly later to make room for the

---

[66]Weinberg, *Southeast Building*, 27–28.

[67]Ibid., 28, following Broneer, *Corinth Excavations*, 237.

[68]Kent, *Latin Inscriptions*, no. 327.

[69]Weinberg, *Southeast Building*, 13.

[70]Wiseman, "Corinth and Rome," 514; and Walbank, "Foundation and Planning," 112 and plan; Walbank does not otherwise discuss this dating of the building.

[71]Weinberg, *Southeast Building*, 5, fig. 1, shows Weinberg's plan of the early building, which differs from more recent plans. See fig. 3.6, opposite.

[72]Ibid., 7–9. Much of the known building material from this first phase seems to have been reused from buildings of the earlier Greek/Hellenistic period (ibid., 5–6).

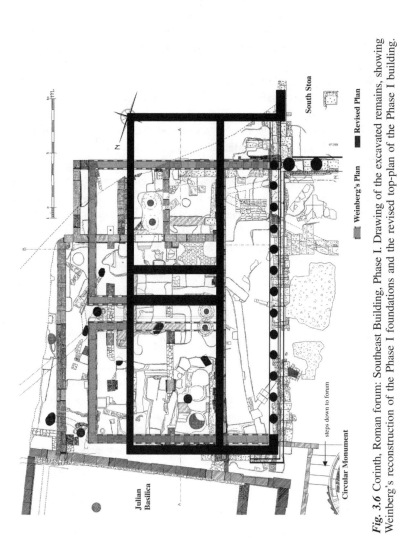

Fig. 3.6 Corinth, Roman forum: Southeast Building, Phase I. Drawing of the excavated remains, showing Weinberg's reconstruction of the Phase I foundations and the revised top-plan of the Phase I building.

Julian Basilica. Afterward, the Southeast Building was rebuilt on the same axis but with a different plan. Weinberg thus associated the construction of the second building with Babbius Philinus at about the same time as the construction of the circular Babbius Monument.[73] The building of Phase II was 1.60 m shorter in overall length (25.10 m) due to the encroachment of the Julian Basilica, but the portico on the west kept its original dimensions (fig. 3.7). The new building was divided into two rooms: the north room measured 17.80 x 14.50 m and was divided by columns into three aisles; the south room measured 6.10 x 13.20 m and was connected to the north room by a central door.[74]

Weinberg associated the marble revetment of the second building with other projects in the forum during the reign of Claudius.[75] Later still, it seems, the Southeast Building saw another major renovation following apparent damage to the north, west, and south walls of the colonnade. On the basis of the mosaic pavement of the north room and ceramic finds, Weinberg dated this rebuilding to the time of Hadrian or later, and he associated the work of Babbius Italicus with this later phase (IIB).[76] Also associated with Phase IIB are a new mosaic floor and the repainting of the walls with frescoes and dipinti.[77] Weinberg's dating would make these renovations later than the time of Favorinus.

Further Archaeological Considerations

Since the 1970s, the dating of these later phases of construction has been generally—though not yet conclusively—reconsidered. It seems preferable to identify the work of Babbius Italicus with the renovation of the Phase II building. While a date under Claudius or Nero is possible for this renovation, Babbius Italicus might have been active well into the Flavian period, which saw a major renovation of the forum area after the earthquake of 77/78 C.E. In fact, this date might also be consistent with the inscription of Babbius Italicus. If so, one might propose that the construction and the original portico

---

[73]Ibid., 13, 28–29. Engels (*Roman Corinth*, 68) assumes a date under Tiberius for both the Babbius Monument and the Southeast Building, but does not discuss whether there was an earlier phase.

[74]Weinberg, *Southeast Building,* 26.

[75]Ibid., 28.

[76]Ibid., 29–31.

[77]Ibid., 29 and 10–11, respectively. New evidence regarding the frescoes will be discussed below.

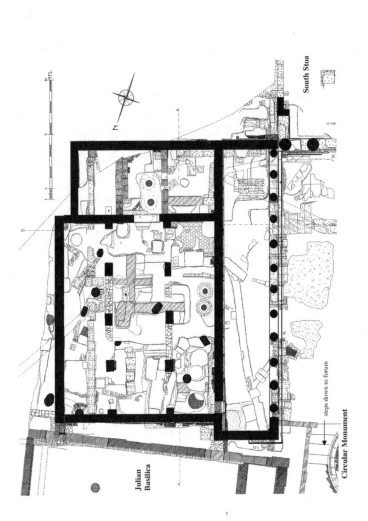

Fig. 3.7 Corinth, Roman forum: the Southeast Building, Phase II. Drawing of the excavated remains showing Phase II plan.

of Phase IIA under Tiberius (14–37 C.E.) or, more likely, under Claudius (41–54 C.E.), was the work of his father, while the younger Babbius paid for repairs and/or rebuilding plus decoration (marble revetments, frescoes, mosaics) of the entire complex in honor of his father during the time of Nero (54–68 C.E., or slightly later?).[78] Given the importance of the elder Babbius in the earlier period and his clear presence in the development of the west end of the forum,[79] one might well speculate that the Southeast Building project (and other work in the eastern end of the forum) comes from later in his career. It is even possible that projects begun by the father, Philinus, were continued or completed by the son, Italicus, in the middle part of the century. The "unusual" form of the Southeast Building might then be a result of the fact that it antedates the other known Roman libraries (already listed above) of the imperial period by some fifty years or more. If the Southeast Building was indeed the library or *tabularium,* it would have been the natural location for Favorinus's piqued panorama of the forum.

That the epistyle frieze of the Southeast Building contained an epigraphic designation for the building (thus, NN *et porticum*), as proposed by Broneer,[80] is supported by the other fragmentary building inscriptions preserved in the area of the forum, especially for some rooms of the South Stoa. Many of these inscriptions are from the epistyle or architraves along the eastern end of the forum (see appendix B, section C). It is quite unfortunate that they were so badly preserved that none of them have so far been permanently "reattached" to any particular building.[81] They indicate nonetheless that the decoration and repair of the southeast area of the forum continued throughout the first and into the early second century, especially during the time of Nero and again just after the earthquake of 77/78 C.E.

---

[78]Kent (*Inscriptions,* 21, 133) argues cautiously for a date under Nero and places the marble revetment of the building to "either the second or the third building period" (ibid., 133). I take his terms "second" and "third" to correspond to my designations of IIA and IIB respectively.

[79]Charles Williams has shown that the development of the west terrace, having begun probably under Tiberius, continued into the period of Claudius. He argues also that Temple E postdates both the Babbius Monument and the Fountain of Poseidon. See Charles K. Williams II, "A Re-Evaluation of Temple E and the West End of the Forum of Corinth," in *The Greek Renaissance in the Roman Empire* (ed. Susan Walker and Averil Cameron; BICSSup 55; London: University of London Institute of Classical Studies, 1989) 156–62. Since he argues, further, that the Fountain of Poseidon was the earlier of the two monuments constructed by Babbius Philinus, one might see in the Babbius Monument a commemorative or honorific for his role in this early phase of the development of the west end of the forum.

[80]See appendix B.1.

[81]The lone exception is possibly no. 12, which may go with the South Basilica.

As noted in the commentary in appendix B (section C), dating many of these fragmentary inscriptions is just as difficult as assigning them to a particular building. Many of the names fit the Flavian period as easily as the Julio-Claudian.[82] These facts prompt me to make some final, tentative observations on the archaeology of the east end of the forum. First, the orders of the exterior colonnade of the South Stoa in the early Roman period are Doric, while those of the inner colonnade are Ionic. These orders clearly preserve and emulate that of the early Greek form of the Stoa, but there is also evidence of later Roman "copies" or replacements for some of the elements in the second Roman phase (dating to the late Augustan or Tiberian period).[83] Renovation and decoration of the rooms of the South Stoa continued into the second century C.E.[84] The marble revetment of the bema and of the Fountain House in the South Stoa (Room E), which show stylistic similarities, are usually dated to the Claudian period, near the middle of the first century, although some of the comparanda cited by Broneer date to the Neronian period.[85] Recent work on the ceramic deposits in the South Stoa may well cause further reconsideration of these dates.

Second, the orders of the portico of the Southeast Building (Phase II) are Ionic (fig. 3.8, p. 90) and were compared by Weinberg to those of the Babbius Monument as well as the bema.[86] Many of the fragmentary building inscriptions from the eastern area of the forum also come from Ionic epistyle friezes (see appendix B, section C). It should be remembered, however, that the exterior colonnade of the adjacent South Stoa was Doric. In other words, Phase II of the Southeast Building would seem to be from a distinct project in the Roman development of the forum. The orders alone, however, do not yield a narrow range of dates for the construction. For example, the Ionic orders of the marble colonnade of the Peribolos of Apollo are very similar in profile to those of the

---

[82]Kent (*Inscriptions*, 128) dates one of these (no. 321 = Appendix B.12, found in the southeastern area of the forum) to the Augustan period on the basis of "the characteristic tail of the letter Q"; however, the two markets referred to in the inscription (probably corresponding to the Peribolos of Apollo and the South Basilica) were not built until later.

[83]Broneer, *South Stoa*, 102.

[84]The athlete mosaic of Room C, the Agonotheteion, dates from the late first or early second century C.E.; so ibid., 108–9.

[85]Ibid., 127–28. Broneer's principal Greek comparanda for the flooring technique in the Fountain House come from Athens—the Odeion of Agrippa in the Agora and the Neronian rebuilding of the Theater of Dionysus. But see also the comments of Kent in *Inscriptions*, no. 322.

[86]Weinberg, *Southeast Building*, 28.

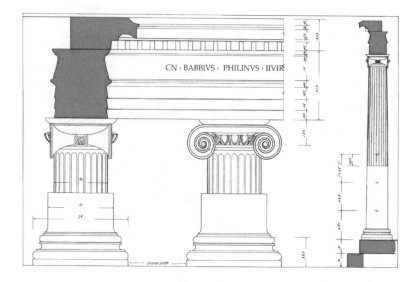

CN › BABBIVS › PHILINVS › IIVIR

Fig. 3.8 Corinth, Roman forum: marble colonnade of the Southeast Building, Phase II. Drawing of restored elevation with inscription of Gnaeus Babbius Philinus.

Southeast Building.[87] The epistyle frieze also contains numerous inscribed segments commemorating the construction and decoration of the Peribolos of Apollo, but it dates to the Flavian rebuilding after the earthquake of 77/78 C.E.[88] As a result, we can be confident that the form and decoration of the Southeast Building (and the eastern half of the forum) was set by the time of Favorinus, in the early second century; however, some caution is due if we try to push them much earlier than the middle of the first century. One wonders, then, if the renovations and decorations of the Southeast Building undertaken by Babbius Italicus were not part of a larger program of refurbishments in the forum, perhaps including the revetment of the bema and the Fountain House.[89] Several inscriptions from the eastern forum indicate provisions for *tutela*, endowments for upkeep, which likewise would indicate a large-scale project.[90] More work needs to be done on the architectural development of the forum, especially in the third quarter of the first century: this includes the entire reign of Nero, who made the first imperial visit to Corinth in 64 C.E., and continues to the eve of the earthquake of 77/78 C.E.

[87]Richard Stillwell, Robert L. Scranton, and Sarah Elizabeth Freeman, *Architecture* (Corinth I.2; Cambridge, Mass.: ASCSA, 1941) 38–49.

[88]For the inscriptions, see ibid., 45 and fig. 29; and West, *Latin Inscriptions*, no. 123.

[89]For the revetment of the bema, see Kent, *Inscriptions*, no. 322.

[90]Ibid., nos. 314, 317 (appendix B.8, 10).

The Physical Setting of Favorinus's Oration

Of course, my suggestion for the setting of Favorinus's oration, while tempting, remains rather speculative. Perhaps we ought to look elsewhere and give up on the Southeast Building and the forum altogether for the setting of Favorinus's speech. But I am not quite ready to do that.[91] Other allusions within the oration seem to confirm a setting in the forum.

First, it should be noted that Favorinus's designation for the "library" as τὰ βιβλία is somewhat unusual; in fact, it is the lone example of this meaning cited in *LSJ*. The more usual term, of course, is βιβλιοθήκη in both Greek and Latin, as found in the inscriptions for the library of Celsus at Ephesos and the library of Pantainos in Athens.[92] In the papyri, βιβλιοθήκη is also used for the local records offices (i.e., equivalent to the Latin *tabularium*) of the administrative districts of Roman Egypt.[93] On the other hand, τὰ βιβλία would be an appropriate Greek equivalent for the Latin *scripta*, were that the proper restoration of the Babbius Italicus inscription, already discussed. Was this the local designation for the Southeast Building in its capacity as both records office and library? Weinberg thought so.[94]

Second, clues that Favorinus delivered his *Korinthiakos* in this area of the forum may be found in the way he cites local landmarks and traditions in service to his rhetorical points. These occur throughout the speech, chiefly in the form of digressions set between the main framing sections.[95] For example, Favorinus opens the speech (§1) by referring to Arion, the legendary inventor of the dithyramb, who was famed at Corinth but did not merit a statue

---

[91]In conversation, Charles Williams suggested to me that the one other building in the area of the forum that might fit the physical situation outlined in the first part of this study would be the rooms at the western end of the Northwest Stoa adjacent to Temple D and the Babbius Monument. This section of the Northwest Stoa seems to be a single project dating to the time of Augustus or slightly later, in conjunction with the Roman layout of the western terrace and the area of Temple E. See Charles K. Williams II and Orestes H. Zervos, "The Temples of the West Terrace: Recent Observations," in "Excavations at Corinth, 1989: The Temenos of Temple E," *Hesperia* 59 (1990) 351–56. Such a location would indeed fit the rhetorical play of the speech as I have outlined it above. Even so, it seems that the evidence assembled here favors the Southeast Building, and this view will be strengthened by the following considerations.

[92]For Ephesos, see *IvE* 3009.4–5; 5101.2; 5113.4, 10, 18–19 (all dating to ca. 105 C.E. or shortly thereafter); for Athens, see the inscriptions cited in n. 52, above.

[93]*P.Tebt.* 389; *BGU* 79.1; *P.Ryl.* 291.1 (all dating from the second or third century C.E.).

[94]Weinberg, *Southeast Building*, 11.

[95]See appendix A for the structure of these framing sections and the intervening digressions, also discussed in n. 27, above.

when he visited. Of course, this opening is meant to show the high regard that Favorinus had earned when the Corinthians erected his statue (§8). In §§2–7, Favorinus follows his opening comment about Arion with a kind of digression on such ancient notables as Arion and Solon who had visited Corinth during the time of Periander but received no statue. In §§2–4, he rehearses the legend of Arion, who, like Palaimon at Isthmia, was rescued from the sea by a dolphin. The digression ends with a reference to the statue dedicated by Arion at Taenarum of himself riding on the back of the dolphin.[96] But how would Favorinus have known that there was never such a statue of Arion at Corinth? Depictions of Palaimon and the dolphin were certainly displayed in Corinth and could have easily been taken for Arion.[97] The answer lies, I suggest, in the monuments of the forum itself. At the west end of the forum, just to the south of the Babbius Monument, stands the Fountain of Poseidon, which, as recent archaeological work has shown, was decorated with dolphins on either side. As it turns out, the fountain, too, was dedicated by Cn. Babbius Philinus and was still standing in the Hadrianic period (fig. 3.9).[98] In other words, Favorinus need only have pointed at the dolphins as if to say, "See, just dolphins; there's no statue of Arion."

A second example of Favorinus's use of monuments in the forum to punctuate his speech comes from his second main digression (§§10–15), where he muses on how a statue might disappear. After remarking on his own perplexity and doubts about his "vision" of what had happened (§9), he quips that the statue must have been one of the magical works of Daedalus, whose statues were so lifelike they could move;[99] his statue just stole

[96]For the legend, see Herodotus 1.23–24. Pausanias (3.25.7) attests to the presence of the bronze statue in Taenarum.

[97]Pausanias (2.3.4) comments on a monument of Palaimon at Corinth in the Lechaion Road baths. I will not enter into a digression on the associations of the Palaimon legend with the temple of Poseidon at Isthmia, as they are now well known from the recent Isthmia excavations. See the essay by Elizabeth R. Gebhard in this volume (pp. 165–203). Surely Favorinus would have known them, too, but they do not fit his needs. It is also worth noting that there are architectural similarities between the monopteral Palaimon monument at Isthmia and the Babbius Monument; however, recent work suggests that the Palaimonion itself dates only to the early second century. See Helmut Koester, "Melekertes at Isthmia: A Roman Mystery Cult," in *Greeks, Romans, and Christians: Essays in Honor of Abraham J. Malherbe* (ed. David L. Balch, Everett Ferguson, and Wayne A. Meeks; Minneapolis: Fortress, 1990) 355–66.

[98]The fountain was later destroyed, but it was still standing when Pausanias toured the city (2.2.8); see Williams and Zervos, "Corinth 1989," 353–55 and fig. 5. For the dedicatory inscriptions by Babbius Philinus, see appendix B.4.

[99]See Euripides, *Hec.* 839; Plato, *Euthyphr.* 11C–D; and Suidas, s.v. Δαιδάλου ποιή-ματα.

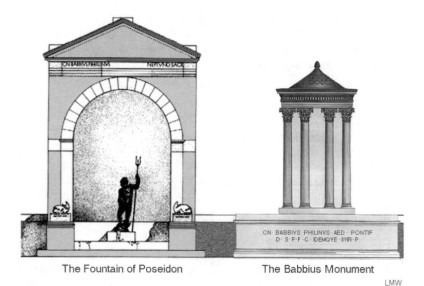

The Fountain of Poseidon   The Babbius Monument

LMW

Fig. 3.9 Corinth, Roman forum: restoration drawing of the façade of the West Terrace with the monuments of Gn. Babbius Philinus (first–second century C.E.).

away while no one was watching (§10–11). Pausanias (2.4.5) says that near Corinth's Temple of Athena Chalinits, which is close to the theater, stands a wooden statue of Herakles "said to be a work of Daedalus." In the light of recent work on the area around the theater, this statement would place the statue somewhere in the area of the Sikyon Road on the terrace above East Theater Street and near the later Odeion (map 5).[100] While a direct view of this area from the forum would have been blocked by Temple C (and by the Fountain of Glauke immediately behind it) to the left of the Sikyon road, and by the escarpment of the Archaic Temple to the right, the comment of Pausanias clearly presupposes that the "Herakles of Daedalus" was a local landmark along this important route into the forum. As a result, we have little difficulty imagining Favorinus's allusion here: a mere gesture in that direction would have sufficed.[101]

[100]See Williams and Zervos, "Corinth, 1983: The Route to Sikyon," 101–4, esp. 103; see also ibid., 89–92.

[101]On the assumption that Favorinus was standing on the upper terrace in front of the Southeast Building, it is worth mentioning that the original orientation of the Hellenistic foundation for the Circular Monument at the east end of the Terrace Shops (and just beside the north end of the portico of the Southeast Building) is on a direct axis with the Fountain

There are numerous other minor allusions in the speech that may refer to monuments in Favorinus's immediate view.[102] One final example, however, drawn from the third major digression of the speech, will be necessary for the purposes of this study. Immediately following his quip about a magical statue of Daedalus (§10, discussed above), Favorinus again shifts the rhetoric by asking:

> But even if [the statue] were of the ancient craft of Daedalus, what is amiss that he should flee your city, over which the two gods, Poseidon and Helios, are said to quarrel, the one being lord of fire and the other lord of water? And when they had quarreled, they turned the decision over to a third, older god, whose *"heads were many, yea many too his arms."*(§11)

The poetic allusion here is to Briareos (also called Aegaion), "the hundred-handed one" (ἑκατόγχειρον), who according to Homer protected Zeus from the cabal of Hera, Poseidon, and Athena.[103] In this case, however, we have a local foundation myth in which Briareos mediated between Poseidon and Helios when they fought for possession of Corinth. Pausanias (2.1.6) reports the same story and says that Briareos "assigned the Isthmus and adjacent areas to Poseidon, and to Helios the heights (τὴν ἄκραν) above the city [i.e., the Acrocorinth]."[104] In addition to the Sanctuary of Poseidon at Isthmia, this

---

of Glauke (see map 5). I have confirmed this fact in my previous fieldwork at Corinth. This means that the sightline from the terrace in front of the Southeast Building and adjacent to the Circular Monument looked naturally across the forum to the West Terrace, where the Babbius Monument and Fountain of Poseidon stood, and immediately above them visually would have been the area of the Fountain of Glauke and the statue of Herakles mentioned by Pausanias.

[102]In §33, for example, in the context of a catalogue of mistreatments suffered by other statues, even those of the gods, he refers to the myth of Artemis and Actaeon (see Apollodorus, *Bibliotheca* 3.4.4); the Corinthian audience might naturally follow his gesture toward Acrocorinth. He also refers to Hephaestus "nearly making a mother out of the Virgin [Athena]." While the story is a legend associated with the founding of Athens by Erechtheus (see Apollodorus, *Bib.* 3.14.6), an immediate context for the comment might easily come from the monumental statue of Athena that stood in the center of the lower forum (see Pausanias 2.3.1).

[103]Compare Homer, *Il.* 1.402–4. The phrasing of Favorinus is closer to that of Hesiod, *Theog.* 147–51 (τῶν ἑκατὸν μὲν χεῖρες . . . κεφαλαὶ δὲ ἑκάστῳ πεντήκοντα), where he is one of the monstrous sons of Ouranos and Ge (compare Apollodorus, *Bib.* 1.1.1). The precise poetic line as used by Favorinus is not identified, and may be his own.

[104]An allegorical interpretation of Briareos that makes him the mediator between fire and water is given by the first century Stoic, L. Annaeus Cornutus, in his *Theologiae Graecae Compendium* 17.2 (ed. Lang, 27), a commentary on the myths of Homer and Hesiod. As his *gentilicium* indicates, Cornutus was a freedman of the family of the Senecas; he served as

peculiar local myth is reflected in a variety of monuments within the area of the forum. The Fountain of Poseidon on the West Terrace, dedicated by Babbius Philinus, has already been mentioned (see Pausanias 2.2.8). Pausanias also says (2.3.2) that two gilded statues of chariots—one bearing Helios and the other Phaethon, son of Helios—adorned the sides of the *propylaeon* at the entrance to the forum from the Lechaion Road. So, Favorinus could have easily gestured toward these monuments as part of his extended paean to the superiority of Corinth—a city with two patron deities.[105]

To sum up, it should be noted that these three appeals to local tradition comprise the first three major digressions in the speech. This fact leads me to conclude that Favorinus was, indeed, standing in a conspicuous place in the forum where he could actually point to these monuments while rebuking his audience for having taken down his statue. Even so, it does not tell us exactly where Favorinus stood in the forum, and thus point us to the library. A little-known artifact of Corinth, however, may shed new light on this last allusion to the mediating Briareos and point to the immediate vicinity of the Southeast Building, supporting the identification of this building as the library.

In a passing comment on the earlier excavations in the Southeast Building, Weinberg reported that the walls of the interior were painted with a dominant red and yellow field, but that many fragments of the frescoes showed signs of having been painted over.[106] He continues:

---

paedagogue to some of the nephews of the younger Seneca, such as Lucan and particularly Persius Flaccus. The *Theologiae Graecae Compendium* may well have been addressed to the latter, who in turn eulogized Cornutus in his *Sixth Satire*. This connection to the family of Seneca is of significance for three additional reasons: (1) the brother of the younger Seneca, L. Junius Gallio, was proconsul of Achaea and thus based in Corinth in 51/52 C.E. (see *SIG*³ 801D; compare Acts 18:12); (2) Cornutus's discussion of Briareos was roughly contemporaneous with the construction of Phase II of the Southeast Building; and (3) Cornutus's allegorization seems to depend directly on some knowledge of the Corinth myth. The last point is suggested by the fact that even though his reference to Briareos is given in the context of the passage from Homer, Cornutus allegorizes his identity by making him the natural balance between "fire and water" (i.e., Helios and Poseidon), each of which might swallow up the cosmos if not checked. In service to his allegorical technique, Cornutus frequently makes use of such local legends and variations on Homer and Hesiod. In turn, the comment of Favorinus regarding the two gods—that they are the lords of fire and water, respectively—may be taken to indicate that he was aware of this kind of philosophical allegorization, and perhaps knew the work of Cornutus directly. It would also be consistent with Favorinus's reputation as a philosopher who enjoyed engaging in technical discussions. (See n. 9, above; and *Kor.* 25, discussed briefly below.) For a different allegorization of the Briareos passage in Homer, see (Ps.-)Heraclitus, *Quaestiones Homericae* 21.2; 25.6–11.

[105]The digression continues through §15, but it turns to other legends after the beginning of §13.

[106]Weinberg, *Southeast Building*, 10.

This later decoration seems to consist largely of geometric patterns, but among the pieces found in 1931 Whittlesey mentions one section which showed a pediment painted in white on the yellow ground and had shadows indicated with purple paint. At the same time was found a fragment with letters *BRIA* painted in black on a light blue ground.[107]

While he does not further discuss this interior wall decoration of the Southeast Building, Weinberg implies that this fresco belonged to the redecoration of Phase II, and perhaps even Phase IIB, when the later mosaic floor was installed.[108] If so, this would link the fresco with the redecoration work of Babbius Italicus. In a personal communication, Nancy Bookidis reports that, indeed, this is now thought to be a late-first-century C.E. fresco from the Southeast Building depicting the contest of Poseidon and Helios over Corinth. The partial dipinto discovered so many years ago must refer to Bria[reos], who is also depicted in the scene.[109] Favorinus's coy allusion to Briareos, whom he does not call by name, would make much more sense rhetorically if he could simply point to this painting of the "many-headed and many-armed god." In light of this evidence, it would seem that the Southeast Building may well be the *Biblia* of Corinth after all, and that Favorinus was standing in its portico or just outside—on the upper terrace near the Circular Monument—when he delivered his *Korinthiakos*.

FINAL REMARKS

In closing, I want to reflect on the apparent importance of the several conspicuous monuments of Babbius Philinus and his family in the rhetorical play of Favorinus's speech. In addition to the performative elements and local monuments already discussed, they might also point us to other social connections in the time of Hadrian. For example, at least one other descendant of this family, a woman named Babbia, is known from the Hadrianic period. She was married into another prominent colonial family, the *Publicii*, and she is mentioned in an inscription honoring her father-in-law, Cn. Publicius Rusticius, *duovir* and *agonothete* under Hadrian.[110] The Babbii were still

[107]Ibid. Weinberg reports the letters in Roman characters as above, but does not state whether they reflect a Greek or Latin dipinto. I have not been able to locate a published version of the 1931 season report to which Weinberg refers.

[108]Ibid., 30.

[109]Nancy Bookidis first mentioned this fresco to me when I presented this essay at the "Urban Religion in Roman Corinth" conference. My thanks to Charles Williams and Nancy Bookidis for allowing me to use this as yet unpublished information. An article on the fresco is under preparation by Umberto Papallardo.

[110]Kent, *Inscriptions*, no. 176 (appendix B.6). A woman named Karpime Babbia, "weaver

visible in Corinthian society at least into the Antonine period.[111] This leads me to wonder whether Favorinus still had other friends, as well as foes, at Corinth. One may consider the likes of prominent Corinthians such as Antonius Sospes or the younger Julius Eurycles Herculanus, who, like Favorinus, were in Plutarch's circle. They, too, were part of the "Greek renaissance."[112] Later, Herodes Atticus unabashedly portrayed himself as a pupil of Favorinus and dedicated a statue of his wife Regilla beside the Temple of Tyche (Temple D) and the Babbius Monument on the West Terrace.[113]

Finally, Favorinus's speech shows one more thing about the public demeanor of the forum. Despite its thoroughly Roman form, by the Second Sophistic it was beginning to celebrate its Greek heritage more and more. Even though he had fallen out of favor with the philhellenic Hadrian, Favorinus was nonetheless a proponent, if not an agent, of the Greek renaissance. Thus, we may close with one final comment from Favorinus himself, referring in the same breath to both his own "hellenization" and that of Corinth. We may now more clearly imagine him scanning the magnificently marbled forum as he says (§25):

> But if someone who is not a Lucanian, but a Roman, not one of the masses, but of the equestrian order, who has emulated not only the language but also the sensibility and the manner and the dress of the Greeks . . . in order to achieve this one thing above all else, namely both to appear and to be Greek, then should this man not deserve to have a bronze statue set up by you [Corinthians]? Yes, he even deserves one in every city—by you, on the one hand, because he, though a Roman, has been thoroughly *hellenized* (ἀφηλληνίσθη), *just as your very own patria has been* . . . , and, on the other hand, by all the Greek cities, because he pursues philosophy and has both aroused many of the Greeks to join him in the pursuit of philosophy and has caused not a few of the barbarians [to do likewise]. Why, it seems he has been equipped by the gods for just such a purpose.

---

of garlands," shows up on three curse tablets found in Room 7 (location of the ritual deposit) of the Sanctuary of Demeter. The stratigraphy of this room indicates that they must belong to either the first Roman phase (before 77 c.e.) or the second Roman phase (after 77 c.e.) of the sanctuary. See Bookidis and Stroud, *Sanctuary of Demeter*, 282. One wonders if she might belong to the same family, or if the first name is some form of ritual epithet associated with the Thesmophorian cult.

[111] A Marcus Babbius, *duovir, agonothete*, and *sodales Augusti* (i.e., priest in the local imperial cult), and his wife (?) Babbia are possibly named in an inscription from the reign of Antoninus Pius; see Kent, *Inscriptions*, 27 and no. 185. For a son with praenomen Marcus, while the father's name is Gnaeus, compare ibid., no. 176 (appendix B.6).

[112] For Antonius Sospes, see ibid., nos. 170, 226; for C. Julius Eurycles Herculanus (L. Vibulius Pius), see ibid., no. 212, and comments on no. 314. See Plutarch, *Quaest. conviv.* 8.4.1–4 (*Mor.* 723A–B); and 9.5.1, 12 (*Mor.* 740A, D).

[113] Philostratus, *Vit. Soph.* 1.8 (409b); Kent, *Inscriptions*, nos. 128–29.

Appendix A

Favorinus's *Korinthiakos*: The Framing Sections[114]

§1   Ὅτε τὸ πρῶτον ἐπεδήμησα τῇ πόλει τῇ ὑμετέρᾳ, ἀφ᾽ οὗ δέκα ἔτη σχεδόν, καὶ τῶν λόγων μετέδοκα τῷ δήμῳ καὶ τοῖς τέλεσι τοῖς ὑμετέροις, ἔδοξα ἐπιτήδειος εἶναι ἔτι δ᾽ [ ][115] ὑμῖν οὕτω σφόδρα ὡς οὐδὲ Ἀρίων ὁ Μηθυμναῖος. Ἀρίονος μέν γε τύπον οὐκ ἐποιήσασθε....

§8   Ἡμᾶς δὲ δὶς ἐπιδημήσαντας οὕτως ἀσμένως ἐπείδετε ὥστε μάλιστα μὲν ἐπειρᾶσθε κατέχειν, ὁρῶντος δὲ ἀδύνατον ὄν, ἀλλά γε τὴν εἰκὼ τοῦ σώματος ἐποιήσασθε καὶ ταύτην φέροντες ἀνεθήκατε εἰς τὰ βιβλία, εἰς προεδρίαν, οὗ μάλιστ᾽ ἂν ᾤεσθε τοὺς νέους προκαλέσασθαι τῶν αὐτῶν ἡμῖν ἐπιτηδευμάτων ἔχεσθαι. οὐ γὰρ ὡς ἕνα τῶν πολλῶν καὶ κατ᾽ ἐνιαυτὸν καταιρόντων εἰς Κεγχρεὰς ἔμπορον ἢ θεωρὸν ἢ πρεσβευτὴν ἢ διερχόμενον, ἀλλ᾽ ὡς μόλις διὰ μακρῶν χρόνων ἀγαπητὸν ἐπιφαινόμενον, οὕτως ἐτιμήσατε.

§9   *τιμὴ δ᾽ ἥτ᾽ ὄνειρος ἀποπταμένη πεπότηται (Od.* 11.222)

ὥστε ἐμὲ ἐν ἀπόρῳ καθεστάναι καὶ πρὸς ἐμαυτὸν καὶ νὴ Δία ἤδη πρὸς ἕτερον, πότερ᾽ ὡς ἀληθῶς οὐκ ἔβλεπον, οὐδὲ ὕπαρ ἀλλὰ ὄναρ ἦν τὰ γιγνόμενα, ἢ τὰ μὲν ἦν ταῦτα ταῖς πάσαις ἀκριβείαις, σπουδῇ τε τοῦ πλήθους καὶ κρίσις τῆς βουλῆς, ὁ δ᾽ ἀνδριὰς τῶν Δαιδάλου ποιημάτων ἔτυχεν ὢν καὶ λαθὼν ἡμᾶς ἀπέδρα....

§11   Ἵνα δὲ καὶ τῆς ἀρχαίας τέχνης ᾖ τῆς Δαιδαλείου, τί παθὼν ἂν ὑμῶν ἀπηλλάγη τῆς πόλεως...;

§16   ἀλλ᾽ οὔτε ἀπέδρα οὔτε ἐπεχείρησεν οὔθ᾽ ὅλως ἐμέλλησε· καταλείπεται τοίνυν αὐτοὺς τοὺς Κορινθίους ἐκβαλεῖν αὐτὸν μήτε κρίσεως προτεθείσης μήθ᾽ ὅλως αἰτίαν ἔχοντας ἐπενεγκεῖν....

---

[114]The speech is preserved as (Ps.-)Dio Chrysostom, *Or.* 37; it dates from the later part of the reign of Hadrian, after Favorinus had fallen into disfavor; see Philostratus, *Vit. Soph.* 1.8 (489–92). Translations mine.

[115]I have not followed Capps here in emending the text with οἰκεῖος before ὑμῖν.

§1 When I sojourned in your city the first time, nearly ten years ago now, and shared a measure of my speeches with your *demos* and magistrates, I seemed to be an intimate friend to you to a degree not exceeded even by Arion of Methymne. Yet you did not make a figure of Arion. . . .

> There follows a digression (through §7) on Arion, Periander, and Adeimantus, ancient heroes who were honored by Corinth.

§8 But when we sojourned [with you] a second time, you experienced such gladness that you tried very hard to keep [me, as a citizen], but then, seeing that to be impossible, you instead made a physical likeness, and taking this you set it up in the library, in a front seat (προεδρίαν), where you thought especially it might summon the youth to follow the same pursuits (practices or professions) as we do. For you bestowed such honors not as one of the many who annually disembark at Kenchreai as merchants, or festival-goers, or ambassadors, or travellers, but rather as a beloved friend who at last appears after much time.

§9 *But **Honor**, like a dream, has taken wing and flown away.*[116]

So that I stand perplexed both in regard to my own case and now, by Zeus, in regard to that of yet another man too, wondering whether I did not see truly—the things taking place being not a waking appearance but a dream—or whether the things taking place were accurate in every detail, both the zeal of the crowd and the judgment of the council—but the statue chanced to be a work of Daedalus, and escaped us unnoticed. . . .

§11 But even granting that he [the statue] were of the ancient craft of Daedalus, what is amiss that he should have fled your city . . . ?

> There follows a digression (through §15) on the divine foundations of cities in myth and history. What lovelier a place than Corinth for a statue to dwell?

§16 Well no, then; neither has he [the statue] run away, nor attempted to, nor even had any intention to do so; therefore, it yields the conclusion that the Corinthians themselves banished him, without even holding a trial or having any kind of charge to bring against him.

---

[116]Favorinus has replaced Homer's ψυχή with τιμή. This anticipates one of many wordplays and puns in the speech, as Favorinus will later return to speak to the status as a "soulless" (ἄψυχον, i.e., dead) friend, whom he refuses to desert (cf. §46 below).

§22 Εἰ δὲ γένοιτο καὶ παρ' ὑμῖν ψήφισμά τι τοιοῦτον, ἀνδριάντων εὐ-
θύνας εἶναι, μᾶλλον δ' εἰ θέλετε καθάπερ ἐψηφισμένον γε τοῦτο καὶ
ἀγῶνος ἐνεστηκότος, δότε μοι, δότε τοὺς λόγους ὑπὲρ αὐτοῦ[117] πρὸς ὑμᾶς
οἷον ἐν δικαστηρίῳ ποιήσασθαι.

Ἄνδρες δικασταί, ἅπαντά φασι δεῖν προσδοκᾶν ἐν τῷ μακρῷ χρόνῳ·
οὗτος δ' ἐν τῷ βραχεῖ κινδυνεύει τεθῆναι μὲν ὡς ἄριστος Ἑλλήνων,
ἐκπεσεῖν δ' ὡς πονηρότατος. §23 ὅτι μὲν οὖν καλῶς καὶ δικαίως καὶ
συμφερόντως τῇ πόλει τῇ ὑμετέρᾳ καὶ πᾶσι τοῖς Ἕλλησιν ἐστάθη,[118]
πολλὰ ἔχων εἰπεῖν . . .

§25 Εἰ δέ τις οὐ Λευκανὸς ὤν, ἀλλὰ Ῥωμαῖος, οὐδὲ τοῦ πλήθους, ἀλλὰ
τῶν ἱπποτρόφων, οὐδὲ τὴν φωνὴν μόνον ἀλλὰ καὶ τὴν γνώμην καὶ τὴν
δίαιταν καὶ τὸ σχῆμα τῶν Ἑλλήνων ἐζηλωκώς . . . ἵν' αὐτῷ περιῇ ἓν ἀντὶ
πάντων Ἕλληνι δοκεῖν τε καὶ εἶναι· εἶτα τοῦτον οὐκ ἐχρῆν παρ' ὑμῖν
ἑστάναι χαλκοῦν; §26 καὶ κατὰ πόλιν γε· παρ' ὑμῖν μέν, ὅτι Ῥωμαῖος ὢν
ἀφηλληνίσθη, ὥσπερ ἡ πατρὶς ἡ ὑμετέρα, . . . παρὰ πᾶσι δέ, ὅτι φιλοσο-
φεῖ καὶ πολλοὺς μὲν ἤδη τῶν Ἑλλήνων ἐπῆρε συμφιλοσοφεῖν αὐτῷ, οὐκ
ὀλίγους δὲ καὶ τῶν βαρβάρων ἐπεσπάσατο. ἐπ' αὐτὸ γὰρ τοῦτο καὶ δοκεῖ
ὑπὸ τῶν θεῶν οἷον ἐξεπίτηδες κατεσκευάσθαι. . . .

§35 Παρρησίαν δὲ ἄγω διπλῆν, ἑνὸς μὲν τοῦ συνειδότος, ἑτέρου δὲ τοῦ
ἀγωνοθέτου. . . .

---

[117]Here I am reading ὑπὲρ αὐτοῦ ("on behalf of him") following the original manuscript,
as opposed to ὑπὲρ αὑτοῦ ("on my own behalf") as emended by Crosby (LCL).

[118]Both von Arnim and de Budé accepted Emperius's correction to the third person
(ἐστάθη), while Crosby (*Dio* LCL 4:27) reverts to the first person ("I was set up fairly and
justly"). See n. 30, above.

There follows a digression (through §19) on the legendary justice of the Corinthians, and (§§20–21) on trials conducted against statues at Syracuse.

§22 Then if some sort of decree that statues be called to account were to be passed by you [Corinthians]—or rather, if you will, supposing that such has been decreed and a trial (ἀγῶνος) has begun—permit me, yes permit me to make a [defense] speech before you as though in court on behalf of this very man [the statue]:

"Men of the jury, they say that one must expect anything in the course of time; but this man is, in a brief span, at risk of being put up (τεθῆναι), on the one hand, as the noblest of the Greeks; and on the other, of being put down (ἐκπεσεῖν)[119] as the vilest. §23 Now then to prove that he was put up well and justly and profitably for your city and all the Greeks, I have much to say . . .

§25 "But if someone who is not a Lucanian, but a Roman, not one of the masses, but of the Equestrian order, who has emulated not only the language but also the sensibility and the manner and the dress of the Greeks . . . in order to achieve this one thing above all else, namely both to appear and to be Greek, then should this man not deserve to have a bronze statue set up by you [Corinthians]? §26 Yes, even in every city—by you [Corinthians] on the one hand, because he, though a Roman, has been thoroughly hellenized (ἀφηλληνίσθη), just as your very own patrimonial city has been . . . , and, on the other hand, by all the cities [of the Greeks], because he pursues philosophy and has both aroused many of the Greeks to join him in the pursuit of philosophy and has caused not a few of the barbarians [to do likewise]. Why, it seems he has been equipped by the gods for just such a purpose.

Favorinus then describes how cities erect statues, both of gods and humans, with sacred intent.

§35 "But I hold frankness of speech to be two-sided: one, that of the person who has a glimpse [of the situation]; the other, that of the agonothete. . . ."

[119]There is a wordplay here on the two verbs τίθημι and ἐκπίπτω. When appearing in tandem as here, these two words can be used of public or legal actions (meaning "to award or vote in favor of at trial" and "to banish," respectively); at the same time they may refer to setting up and taking down a statue as in a temple ("to dedicate or set up" and "to tear down," respectively). This wordplay will continue to the end of the speech: see §§37 and 47.

§37 Καὶ ταῦτα μὲν ὑπὲρ τῆς πόλεως, ἣν οὐ δεῖ παρὰ τοῖς Ἕλλησιν αἰσχύνην ὀφλεῖν, ὅταν[120] τὸν ὑφ' ὑμῶν ἐκπεπτωκότα πάντες ἄσμενοι καταδέχωνται οὐ μόνον, ἀλλὰ καὶ καλῶσι καὶ διπρεσβεύωνται καὶ τιμαῖς, ταῖς τε ἄλλαις γεραίρωσι καὶ δὴ καὶ τῇ τῶν εἰκόνων ἀναθέσει. . . .

§46 ἡμεῖς δ' οὐ παρέχωμεν τὸν ἀνδριάντα χωμεύειν, κἂν αἰσθάνηται· νῦν δ' ὁ μὲν κρείσσων αἰσθήσεως, ἐγὼ δὲ κατὰ τὴν Εὐριπίδου Λαοδάμειαν

οὐκ ἂν προδοίην καίπερ ἄψυχον φίλον.

βούλομαι οὖν αὐτὸν ὡς αἰσθανόμενον παραμυθήσασθαι. ὦ λόγων ἐμῶν σιγηλὸν εἴδωλον, οὐ φαίνῃ· οὐδὲ γὰρ ὁ πρὸ σοῦ Ἀριστένς·[121] . . . ἀλλὰ καὶ τότε καὶ νῦν καὶ πρὸς ἄπαντα τὸν χρόνον ἔζη Ἀριστένς.

§47 μνάσεσθαί τινά φᾶμι καὶ ὕστερον ἀμμέων.

πάνυ γὰρ καλῶς εἶπεν ἡ Σαπφώ· καὶ πολὺ κάλλιον Ἡσίοδος·

φήμη δ' οὔτις πάμπαν ἀπόλλυται, ἥντινα λαοὶ
πολλοὶ φημίξωσι· θεός νύ τίς ἐστι καὶ αὐτή.[122]

ἐγώ σε ἀναστήσω παρὰ τῇ θεῷ, ὅθεν οὐδείς σε μὴ καθέλῃ, οὐ σεισμός, οὐκ ἄνεμος, οὐ νιφετός, οὐκ ὄμβρος,[123] οὐ φθόνος, οὐκ ἐχθρός, ἀλλὰ καὶ νῦν σε καταλαμβάνω ἑστηκότα. λάθα μὲν γὰρ ἤδη τινὰς καὶ ἑτέρους ἔσφηλε καὶ ἐψεύσατο, γνώμη δ' ἀνδρῶν ἀγαθῶν οὐδένα,[124] ᾗ κατ' ἄνδρα μοι ὀρθὸς ἔστηκας.

---

[120]The Greek here is ὅταν, but the sense seems to be causal (as a contraction for ὅτι ἄν), a usage more typical in later Hellenistic Greek; so LSJ, s.v. ὅταν 1.b. Compare Dio Chrysostom, Or. 7.105.
[121]Cf. Herodotus 4.13–15.
[122]Op. 763–64, but with a variant: ἥν τινα πολλοὶ λαοί.
[123]Herodotus 8.98.
[124]Apparently a paraphrase from Sappho, so Crosby (LCL) following Edmonds, Lyra Graeca I, 236 (LCL), who sees it as a continuation of the passage from Sappho quoted just above.

§37　Now these foregoing remarks have been offered on behalf of the city, which ought not to bring disgrace on itself before the Greeks, since not only would all [the Greeks] welcome with delight (ἄσμενοι καταδέχωνται)[125] this one who has been banished by you, but they would also summon him and send out embassies and would grant him honors of this sort and that and, what is more, even by the dedication of statues. . . .

> There follows a digression on the fate of statues in other cities, followed by a digression on stories of punishment with some speculation about the fate of body and soul.

§46　Then, shall we yet not present the statue for melting, even though it might possess sensation? No. Although he is now superior to sensation, yet I, in the words of Euripides' *Laodameia*,

> *would not abandon my friend, though devoid of soul.*

Accordingly, I wish now to offer consolation (παραμυθήσασθαι) to him [the "friend"—i.e., the statue], as to one possessing sensation:

"O silent image of my oratory, will you not show yourself? No, neither did Aristeas before you. . . . But Aristeas lives both then, and now, and for all time.

§47　*Someone, I say, will at last memorialize even me,*

as Sappho so beautifully says. And even more beautifully Hesiod:

> *But Fame is by no means utterly destroyed, which is also what many people report, who [i.e., Fame] is even now herself a god.*

I myself will raise you up before the goddess [Fame], whence nothing will cast you down—neither earthquake, nor wind, nor snow, nor rain, nor envy nor enmity—but even now do I discover you risen up. *Aye, for now Oblivion has tripped and cheated sundry others, but judgment* (γνώμη)[126] *does no harm to good men,* by which [judgment] to me you stand aright, like a man (ἦ κατ' ἄνδρα μοι ὀρθὸς ἔστηκας)."[127]

---

[125]Compare the wording in §8 above.

[126]A wordplay, since γνώμη can mean both the mental faculty of judgment and the vote of the assembly.

[127]Another wordplay, since ὀρθός can mean both the affirmative verdict in court ("to be judged right" and thus meaning "just") and standing erect or "upright."

Appendix B

Selected Inscriptions

Inscriptions from the Southeast Building

1. West, *Latin Inscriptions*, no. 122; supplemented in Kent, *Inscriptions*, no. 323.

Several fragments of Ionic epistyle in white marble that formed the architrave inscription above the colonnade of the Southeast Building. Section B of the text comprises two blocks (one found near the Circular Monument in 1896 and the other found in the portico of the Southeast Building in 1915); the join is confirmed both by the fit of the two blocks and by the match in the inscribed text. Section A was discovered in 1915, reused in the medieval wall of Peirene. Section C was discovered in 1946–1947 during excavation of the Southeast Building. The position of C at the end of the line is confirmed by the blank space at the right end of the block. For photo of these materials, see Kent, *Inscriptions*, plate 29 (showing sections A and B only, and not in the correct order). See also fig. 3.8 (p. 90). Letter height 0.10 m.

[Cn. Babbius Philinus, IIv]IR • PONT[ifex, tabularium]

A

ET • PORTICUM • C:OLONI[ae ? – – – – – ? colo]NIA

B^1 : B^2 C

The above restoration of the name as Cn. Babbius Philinus, the dedicator of the Babbius Monument on the west end of the forum, is given further support by the following inscription, which also comes from the Southeast Building. Its dedicator is given as Cn. Babbius Italicus, the son of the Babbius above. The dates for the elder Babbius are late Augustan to Tiberian; his service as duovir is recorded in West, *Latin Inscriptions*, no. 152 (cf. nos. 2, 3, 98–101, 131, and 132) and Kent, *Inscriptions*, no. 155 (the Babbius Monument). The dates for the younger Babbius are probably Neronian, though they could stretch into the early Flavian period. Later members of the family are known from the time of Hadrian where they are intermarried with the prominent family of the Pubilicii; see Kent, *Inscriptions*, no. 176 (compare no. 153), reproduced as inscription 6, below.

2. Kent, *Inscriptions*, no. 327.

A total of 21 fragments of a thin marble revetment slab with inscription. All fragments were found in the southeastern end of the forum, and seven from the Southeast Building itself. The fragments join to form ten segments (a–j) of the inscription, which seems to come from the wall revetment of the Southeast Building, probably in the portico or from the interior. Because the relationship of the various segments is uncertain, only the first line is relatively secure. Even though some of the other individual readings are likely correct, the overall restoration of the last two lines is conjectural. For photograph of the fragments, see fig. 3.6 (p. 85), which arranges the fragments in order according to the reconstruction below, as taken from the individual photos of Kent, *Inscriptions*, plate 30 (not in order). Letter height: line 1 = 0.081 m; lines 2–3(?) = 0.063–0.068 m, with the exception of the T in line 1 (fragment c) = 0.098 m and that in line 3 (?, fragment j) = 0.072 m, while the A = 0.035 m.

[Cn] BABBIUS • CN • F • AEM [• i]TALIC[us] •
    a   d   b   c   e

OB [–]AE [–] ENV – – – – – – – – a]VGVS[t – –]
f   a   d   c   e

[– –] II • VI[ris – –]O • AN[– –]O • PR[aescr]IPTA
     g   h   i   j

In addition to the name of the dedicator (see the commentary on inscription 1, above), the other important piece of information relative to the Southeast Building appears in segment j, which Broneer restored as [*scr*]*ipta* (i.e., "library" [in Weinberg, *Southeastern Building,* 28]), whereas Kent restores it as above, by combining it with segment i to read *pr*[*aescr*]*ipta.* In either case, this likely places the renovation and revetting of the building in the time of Nero (or Vespasian?).

Other Inscriptions from Cn. Babbius Philinus and His Family

3. West, *Latin Inscriptions*, no. 132.

Blue marble circular epistyle block from the top of the Babbius Monument, found near the area of the western forum in 1907. Letter height: line 1 = 0.08 m; line 2 = 0.07 m.

[C]N(aeus) • BABBIVS • PHILINVS • AED(ilis) • PONTIF(ex)
D(e) • S(ua) • P(ecunia) • F(aciendum) • C(uravit) •
    IDEMQVE • IIVIR • P(robavit)

Gnaeus Babbius Philinus, Aedile, Pontifex,
cared for the construction from his own funds
   and approved it himself, being duovir.

Compare Kent, *Inscriptions*, no. 155, which gives the same inscription on the marble base for the Babbius Monument. For other inscriptions bearing the name of Babbius from architectural fragments, see West, *Latin Inscriptions*, nos. 98–101. Even though none have identifiable provenience, they attest to the fact that Babbius's name was visible on numerous buildings in the area of the forum. See also fig. 3.9 (p. 93).

4. West, *Latin Inscriptions*, nos. 2–3.

Two blocks of blue marble, similar in size, one found near the area of the Babbius Monument in 1907 and the other found north of the Propylaea in 1925. Both bear the same inscription. These are now known to be the bases on the sides of the Fountain of Poseidon on which the dolphin statues rested. Letter heights range from 0.35–0.45 m.

> CN(aeus) BABBIVS PHILINUS
> NEPTVNO • SACR(um)

> Gnaeus Babbius Philinus.
> Sacred to Neptune (Poseidon).

The new understanding of these blocks came after the discovery of the marble epistyle of the fountain bearing the same inscription. For the new reconstruction of the Fountain of Poseidon, where these blocks are visible on the sides, see Charles K. Williams II, "The Temples of the West Terrace: Recent Observations," *Hesperia* 59 (1990) 353–55 and the description of the fountain by Pausanias (2.2.8). See also fig. 3.9 (p. 93).

5. West, *Latin Inscriptions*, no. 14.

A small white marble base found in the Julian Basilica in 1915, which appears to be from the imperial cult. The inscription may date during the lifetime of Augustus or shortly after his death. Letter height: line 1 = 0.056 m; line 2 = 0.042 m; line 3 = 0.034 m.

> AVGVST[O SACR(um)
> CN • CN • CN [– –
> PIVS • PON[– –

> Sacred to Augustus.
> Gnaeus [—] and Gnaeus [—, sons of ?] Gnaeus [Babbius?]
> Pius, Pontifex . . . .

West, *Latin Inscriptions*, no. 13 depicts an inscribed slab of marble revetment which may be restored [*La*]*ribus Augustis Sacrum* ("Sacred to the Lares of Augustus"), an indication that the Augustan imperial cult was housed in the Julian Basilica. The text above (no. 14) seems to represent the local Corinthians who had a hand in dedicating the imperial cult sanctuary. West proposed that the three men named Gnaeus are most likely a father and two sons. He also argues that the name "Pius," visible on line 3 is the cognomen of the father. We include the inscription here because it is just conceivable that "Gn. [—] Pius" could be the name of Babbius Philinus's father, if the gentilicium were restored. The name Babbius Pius is now attested (as restored) on a marble revetment slab from the South Basilica; see Kent, *Inscriptions*, no. 391. The name Gnaeus Babbius [—] is also found on a slab of marble revetment perhaps from the Julian Basilica; see Kent, *Inscriptions*, no. 364. If Babbius Philinus's father were so named in an Augustan inscription, it could possibly date him among the original colonists, and might then explain why Babbius Philinus held such an important position in the development of the city in the later Augustan and Tiberian periods.

6. Kent, *Inscriptions*, no. 176.

Four fragments of a grayish marble statue base, found in the South Stoa in 1936. The fragments fit together to preserve the entire left side of the inscribed face. The inscription dates from the time of Hadrian. Letter height: line 1 = 0.06 m; line 2 = 0.047 m; lines 3–5 = 0.04 m; lines 6–10 = 0.035 m.

```
      CN PVBLIC[io]
      M • F • M • N • PR[on •]
      AEM • RVST[ico •]
      II • VIRALIBVS • [et quinquen •]
  5   ET • AGONOT[het • ornamentis • ]
      HON[orato • et – – – – – – – – uxori •]
      PO[st • obitum ? – – – – – – – – – – ]
         M • PV[blicius • cn • f • et • – – – ]
      BABBIA • V[xor • eius •]
 10                    PARENT[ibus •]
            D • [d •]
```

To Gnaeus Publicius Rusticus,
son of Marcus, grandson of Marcus, great-grandson of Marcus,
of the tribe Aemilia,
duovir, duovir quinquennalis,
who was honored with the perquisites of agonothete;
and to [– – – – his wife].
Marcus Publicius [son of Gnaeus and – – –]
Babbia, his wife,
made this monument to their parents after their death (?),
by decree of the decurions.

Other Building Inscriptions from the Southeastern Forum

7. Kent, *Inscriptions*, no. 332.

Two fragments of Ionic epistyle in white marble with inscription. From the southeastern area of the forum; building unknown. Letter height: 0.10 m. Compare West, *Latin Inscriptions*, no. 122 (inscription 1, above).

> – – –] RIS • L [– – –
> – – –] S • IL [– – –

8. Kent, *Inscriptions*, no. 314.

Fifteen fragments of a revetment slab in white marble found in the southeastern area of the forum. The letter forms seem to be Augustan; however, the donor, Eurycles Herculanus (line 5), might be either of two known benefactors to Corinth, one from the Augustan age and one from the Hadrianic. The building has not been identified, but the possible restoration of *tutelam et statua* are suggestive of a major building project. See also Kent, *Inscriptions*, no. 317 (inscription 10, below). Height of letters: line 1 = ca. 0.042 m; line 2 = 0.05 m; line 3 = 0.043 m; line 4 = 0.038 m; line 5 = 0.033 m; line 6 = 0.042 m.

> – – – –] CR [– – – –] IS [– – – – – – – – – –
> HIC [– – – – – – – – – – – – – – –] R • A [– – –
> COLONIAE • LAVD[i • iuliae • cor]INTH[iensi •
> [tute?]LAM • ET • STAT[uam ? – – –] G N [– – – –
> 5   euryc]LIS • HER[c]VLAN[i – – – – – –] • SIGN[. .
> . . . . .]MQVE • OR[navit (?) – – (?) ii • vir • [pr]OBAVIT
>   prob]ANTE PATRE

9. Kent, *Inscriptions*, no. 316.

Nineteen fragments, thirteen with inscribed letters, of Ionic frieze in white marble found in the southeastern area of the forum. These can be joined into four segments that formed part of a single line inscription with donor names and dedication for another building, but uncertain which one. Letter height: 0.067 m, except segment b = ca. 0.06 m.

> a   – – – – –] ARIVS • PYLADIS • CA [– – – – – –
> b   – – –] • L • HESYCHVS • AVGVSTA [– – – –] SACR
> c   – – – – – – – –] ET • L [– – – – – – – – – – –
> d   – – – – – – – – –] ILI [– – – – – – – – – – – –

10. Kent, *Inscriptions*, no. 317.

Fragment of Ionic frieze in white marble found in the southeastern area of the forum. Letter height is close to parts of no. 327 (inscription 2, above) while the nature of the crown molding suggests a similar pattern of building inscription to that in nos. 314 and 316 (inscriptions 8 and 9, above). Even so, it must be from a different inscription than either of these. Letter height: not given.

$$- - - -] \text{ M} \bullet \text{TUTEL[am} - - - -$$
$$- - - - - - - - - - - - - - - -$$

11. Kent, *Inscriptions*, no. 318.

Thirteen fragments of an Ionic frieze in white marble, all found in the southeastern area of the forum or in the South Stoa. The inscription seems to have been a single line below the crown molding, but the nature of the fragments, grouped into eight segments, does not allow for a suitable restoration except for individual words. Segment c should be the end of the text, while segment d may well be near the beginning (assuming that it should be restored as "son/daughter of Quintus"). The building from which it came cannot be precisely identified. Letter height: 0.09 m, except for T = 0.107 m.

a	$- - - - -$] ET $\bullet$ COLO[$- - - - - - - -$
b	$- - - - -$ orna]MENTAQUE $\bullet$ O [$- - -$
c	$- - - - - - - -$]VNT $\bullet$ S $\bullet$ P $\bullet$ F $\bullet$ C
d	$- - - - - - - -$] Q $\bullet$ F [$- - - - - - - -$
e	$- - - - - - - -$] OOTO [$- - - - - - - -$
f	$- - - - - - - -$] ONIA [$- - - - - - - - -$
g	$- - - - - - - -$] TIOL [$- - - - - - - - -$
h	$- - - - - - - -$] EA [$- - - - - - - - -$

12. Kent, *Inscriptions*, no. 321 (supplementing and correcting West, *Latin Inscriptions*, nos. 124–125).

Thirteen fragments of three slabs of white marble, found in the southeastern area of the forum; one was found in the South Basilica. Dated by West to the late Augustan or Tiberian periods; however, the name of Maecianus might also be associated with the Flavian rebuilding. According to Kent, the cognomen indicates Greek *liberti*. The inscription mentions a meat market and a fish market (restored). West identified the fish market with the Peribolos of Apollo just north of Peirene. It is possible that the meat market should be associated with the South Basilica. Letter height: 0.058 m.

Q • CO[r]N[elius • [.] • f • a[EM • SECVNDVS • et
MAEC[ia • q]• F • VXOR • [eius • [.] • cornelius • secundus •
   m[A]e[CIANVS •F • Q • CORN[elius
SECV[nd]VS • F • [co]RN[elia • secunda • f • eius • uxor • q •
   m]A[e]CI • Q • L • CLEOGEN[is
MACELLV[m – – – – – – –– – – cum – – – – –] ET • P[iscario
   – – – –
5   INEA • LOC –
   – – – –

Quintus Cornelius, son of [– – –], of the tribe Aemilia, together
with his wife Maecia, daughter of [Quintus Maecius], his son
[– – – Cornelius Secundus] Maecianus, his son Quintus Cornelius
Secundus, his [daughter] Cornelia [Secunda, the wife of Quintus]
Maecius Cleogenes, the freedman of Quintus [Maecius], [built?] the
meat-market [– – –] along with [– – –] and a fish-market [– – – – –].

CHAPTER FOUR

Fountains and the Formation of Cultural Identity at Roman Corinth

Betsey A. Robinson

> *Salve, fons, ignote ortu, sacer, alme, perennis,*
> *vitree, glauce, profunde, sonore, inlimis, opace.*
> *salve urbis genius, medico potabilis haustu*
> *. . . fons addite divis.*
>
> Ausonius, Ordo urbium nobilium[1]

That freshwater springs were considered sacred in the Greco-Roman world is well known. In the lands ringing the Mediterranean Sea, fresh water has always been a precious resource, its existence to be honored, its spirits propitiated. Ancient writers and archaeological finds indicate widespread spring-veneration in the dedication of votives, in the use of springs for prenuptial rites, and in the celebration of annual feast days like the Roman

---

[1]Lines 30–33: "Hail, fountain of source unknown, holy, gracious, unfailing, crystal-clear, azure, deep, murmurous, shady, and unsullied. Hail, guardian deity of our city, of whom we may drink health-giving draughts . . . a fountain added to the role divine" (trans. H. G. Evelyn-White; LCL; Cambridge, Mass.: Harvard University Press, 1919). Unless otherwise noted, translations from Greek and Latin are from the LCL. This article draws from my dissertation, "Fountains and the Culture of Water in Roman Corinth" (Ph.D. diss., University of Pennsylvania, 2001). My understanding of Roman Corinth benefited greatly from a year spent in Rome as the Oscar Broneer Fellow in Classical Studies, for which I warmly thank the Luther I. Replogle Foundation and the American Academy in Rome. For input on topics discussed herein, I am particularly grateful to Charles K. Williams II, Elizabeth Gebhard, and Ann Kuttner, as well as my fellow conference participants. All shortcomings remain my own.

Fontanalia and the festival of Anna Perenna.[2] Excavations at Corinth have attested to a pre-Roman cult at the Sacred Spring, as well as the Late Antique practice of casting lamps into the Fountain of the Lamps; yet for the Roman period, neither archaeology nor history provides evidence that springs were a focus of organized religious activity.[3] Thus, for this volume on urban religion in Roman Corinth, I turn to two Corinthian fountains that, while giving little insight into Corinthian "cult," have much to offer on Corinthian culture.

The fountains of Peirene and Glauke provide fascinating case studies in the monumental history of Corinth in the early Roman period (figs. 4.1 and 4.2, pp. 114–15).[4] The two structures were "survivors" from pre-Roman Corinth, resuscitated soon after the refoundation of the city as a Roman colony. Both were high-capacity fountains that must have served as primary watering points in Roman Corinth, a city that would be noted for being "well watered," as it had been since the Archaic period.[5] Despite their utilitarian kinship, Peirene and Glauke seem to have followed very different developmental paths in the Roman period. The ancient fountain house at the Peirene spring would

---

[2]Votives: Pausanias 10.8.9 (cakes for Castalia); Strabo 6.2.9 (wreaths for the Apheios and Eurotas); Cicero, *Ver.* 2.4.107 and Diodoros Siculus 5.4.2 (small gifts to Cyane, near Syracuse). Prenuptual rites: René Ginouvès, *Balaneutiké: recherches sur le bain dans l'antiquité grecque* (Paris: de Boccard, 1962) 265–82; and S. E. C. Walker, "The Architectural Development of Roman Nymphaea in Greece" (Ph.D. diss., University of London, 1979) 107–13. Fontanalia: Varro, *Ling.* 6.22; Anna Perenna: Ovid, *Fast.* 3.523–696. For spring-reverence in general, see Louise Adams Holland, *Janus and the Bridge* (PMAAR 21; Rome: American Academy in Rome, 1961) 8–20; and Naomi Miller, *Heavenly Caves: Reflections on the Garden Grotto* (New York: G. Braziller, 1982) 13–17.

[3]For ritual deposits at the Sacred Spring, see A. Steiner, "Pottery and Cult in Corinth: Oil and Water at the Sacred Spring," *Hesperia* 61 (1992) 358–408; for the Fountain of the Lamps, see James Wiseman, "The Fountain of the Lamps," *Archaeology* 23 (1970) 130–37; and D. R. Jordan, "Inscribed Lamps from a Cult at Corinth in Late Antiquity," *HTR* 87 (1994) 223–29.

[4]For the authoritative publication on Peirene and Glauke, see Bert Hodge Hill, *The Springs: Peirene, Sacred Spring, Glauke* (Corinth I.6; Princeton, N.J.: ASCSA, 1964). For broader studies of fountains in Greece and Corinth, see Walker, "Roman Nymphaea"; Franz Glaser, *Antike Brunnenbauten (KRHNAI) in Griechenland* (Vienna: Verlag der österreichischen Akademie der Wissenschaften, 1983); Mark E. Landon, "Contributions to the Study of the Water Supply of Ancient Corinth" (Ph.D. diss., University of California, Berkeley, 1994); Sandrine Agusta-Boularot, "Fontaines et fontaines monumentales en Grèce de la conquête romaine à l'époque flavienne: permanence ou renouveau architectural?" in *Constructions publiques et programmes édilitaires en Grèce entre le IIe siècle av. J.-C. et le Ier siècle ap. J.-C.*, (ed. Jean-Yves Marc and Jean-Charles Moretti; BCHSup 39; Paris: de Boccard, 2001); and Robinson, "Fountains."

[5]Simonides (Bergk 96; Diehl 90), quoted frequently, as in Hill, *The Springs*, 1; see Pausanias 2.3.5 on Corinth's many fountains.

be one of the first Corinthian structures to be refashioned—and in overtly Roman architectural terms. In contrast, Glauke was renovated, but apparently never "Romanized."

The keys to understanding the individual histories of these two fountains, and their meaning for the city of Corinth, lie in their mythological and historical associations. In the Roman period, Peirene and Glauke were both "historiated" landmarks, places where important events were believed to have taken place. Indeed, as early as the Archaic period, the spring of Peirene was celebrated as the site where heroic Bellerophon tamed the winged horse, Pegasos, a story that would have been well known to the class of Romans that was instrumental in planning the Roman colony. Writing in the mid-second century C.E., Pausanias offers an equally venerable history for Glauke: the fountain was named for Jason's princess bride, the first victim of Medea's rage at Corinth.[6] Pausanias is, however, our only source for this tradition, and I shall suggest that while the fountain of Glauke was probably built in the fourth century B.C.E., its "history" was an invention of the Roman colony-builders.

To see these fountains for what they were in the early years of Roman Corinth, it is worthwhile to view their architecture and ornament, as known through archaeological study, within a context that includes their rich literary, visual, and imaginative heritage. Local coins and works of art are illuminating, but it is likewise important to examine Corinthian themes as represented farther afield. Taken together, the architecture and imagery may help to understand the extent to which the new Corinthians, those "youngest of the Peloponnesians," understood ancient Corinthian traditions, how they connected with them, and how they incorporated them into their own designs.[7] The parallel histories of Peirene and Glauke document the selective appropriation of ancient "Greek" Corinthian traditions as an important process in the re-creation of Corinth as a Roman colony, and in the formation of its collective identity.

The Corinthian landscape was dramatically transformed in the early Roman period, when what had once been a largely sacred and ceremonial zone was laid out as the colony's civic center. By the mid-first century C.E., central Corinth was dominated by very "Roman-looking" buildings—a triple-bayed arch at the head of the Lechaion Road, at least two prostyle podium temples, the rostra, and two basilicas.[8] A new fountain stood at the western side of

[6]Ibid., 2.3.6.

[7]Ibid., 5.1.2 (trans. W. H. S. Jones).

[8]See the essay by Nancy Bookidis in this volume (pp. 141–64); and Mary E. Hoskins Walbank, "The Foundation and Planning of Early Roman Corinth," *JRA* 10 (1997) 95–130.

Fig. 4.1 The Fountain of Peirene

Fig. 4.2 The Fountain of Glauke

the forum, with a bronze statue of the Roman sea god Neptune under a monumental triumphal arch façade.[9] Latin was the language of inscriptions, and the cults in the center were not so much those of old Corinth's Upper Lechaion Road Valley, but new foundations, backed by the increasing presence of the imperial cult.[10] Without underestimating the *romanitas* of early Roman Corinth, it is important to remember the selective restorations of pre-Roman structures in the new city center, like the South Stoa, the Archaic Temple, and the fountains of Peirene and Glauke. Such adaptive reuse of major Greek structures was paralleled in the cultural sphere, particularly in the return of the Isthmian games to Corinth as early as 40 B.C.E.; imperial cult games would soon be joined to the Isthmia.[11]

PEIRENE

The fountain of Peirene, preeminent among Corinth's many springs, was well known to Pindar, Euripides, Plautus, and Cicero.[12] In its pristine state, the spring of Peirene was probably a cave-sheltered source, feeding a perennial stream that ran downhill towards the Corinthian Gulf.[13] By the time of Corinth's destruction in 146 B.C.E., the site of the spring was the product of centuries of development (fig. 4.3).[14] Facing onto an open court was a broad cave sheltering an elaborate system of basins, reservoirs, and tunnels. Masonry walls, probably added in the fourth century B.C.E., supported the

---

[9]Charles K. Williams II, "A Re-Evaluation of Temple E and the West End of the Forum of Corinth," in *The Greek Renaissance in the Roman Empire: Papers from the Tenth British Museum Classical Colloquium* (ed. Susan Walker and Averil Cameron; BICSSup 55; London: University of London, 1989) 156–62; and Charles K. Williams II and Orestes H. Zervos, "Excavations at Corinth, 1989: The Temenos of Temple E," *Hesperia* 59 (1990) 325–69.

[10]See the essay by Bookidis in this volume (pp. 141–64), with bibliography.

[11]Elizabeth Gebhard, "The Isthmian Games and the Sanctuary of Poseidon in the Early Empire," in *The Corinthia in the Roman Period* (ed. Timothy E. Gregory; JRASup 8; Ann Arbor, Mich.: Journal of Roman Archaeology, 1993) 78–82. From ca. 30 B.C.E., probably beginning as Actian victory games, thymelic *Caesarea* were included in alternate celebrations of the biennial *Isthmia*. *Sebastea* were added from the time of Tiberius. See A. B. West, *Latin Inscriptions, 1896–1926* (Corinth VIII.2; Cambridge, Mass.: ASCSA, 1931) esp. 64–66; Nancy Bookidis and Ronald S. Stroud, *The Sanctuary of Demeter and Kore, Topography and Architecture* (Corinth XVIII.3; Princeton, N.J.: ASCSA, 1997) 28–31.

[12]Pindar, *Ol.* 13.60–86; Euripides, *Med.* 68–69; Plautus, *Aulularia* 557–59; and Cicero, *Att.* 12.5; see Hill, *The Springs*, 2–4, 7–11.

[13]See Charles K. Williams II, "Corinth, 1969: Forum Area," *Hesperia* 39 (1970) 35.

[14]The following summary of pre-Roman developments follows Hill, *The Springs*, 18–63.

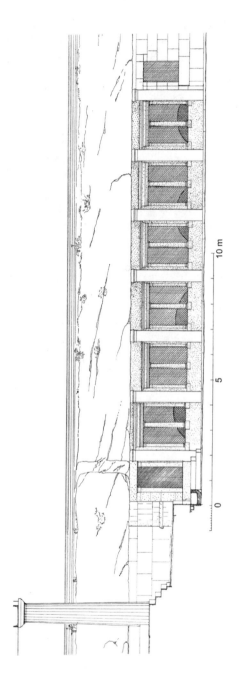

Fig. 4.3 The Fountain of Peirene: restored elevation, Greek period.

cave's thick bedrock roof and divided the space within into six open-ended chambers. To collect spring water, people would pass underground into one of the chambers, then dip water from three long, deep basins of the sixth or fifth century B.C.E. Visible behind the basins were the mouths of four ancient rock-cut reservoirs, extending about twenty meters south into the darkness. Water flowed into the reservoirs through hundreds of meters of tunnels in the aquiferous bedrock.[15]

Indeed, Euripides must have been imagining the situation of his times when, in the *Medea*, he depicted "sacred" or "hallowed" Peirene as a busy city fountain, where old men sat playing games, talking and watching the traffic of water-bearers.[16] That this favorite people-watching venue and public utility was also a sacred place is underscored by the discovery of *kalouria*, little clay votive rings, in Classical deposits near the fountain.[17]

As mentioned above, Peirene's greatest claim to fame was its enduring reputation as the place where the Corinthian hero Bellerophon tamed Pegasos with the help of Athena. The association was early, strong, and widely advertised. The heroic duo appear on local pottery from the seventh century B.C.E., and the "Peirenian colt" was a constant of Corinthian coinage from the sixth.[18] The earliest preserved narrative of the taming is in Pindar's *Thirteenth Olympian Ode* of 464 B.C.E., written for the Corinthian Xenophon. After honoring the victor's city with praise of shrewd Sisyphos and Medea, Pindar recalls Bellerophon,

> who once suffered much indeed in his yearning
>   to yoke Pegasos, the snaky Gorgon's
> son, beside the spring,
> until, that is, the maiden Pallas brought him the bridle
> with the golden bands, when his dream suddenly became reality.[19]

[15]Ibid., 19–25.

[16]Euripides, *Med.* 68–69; see Athenaeus 13.558c–e on Apelles and his cohort watching the girls go by.

[17]The rings were found together with red-figure base fragments in 1910; Williams uncovered more examples in excavations in the Peribolos of Apollo in the 1960s (personal communication). For a sample of these rings, see G. R. Davidson, *The Minor Objects* (Corinth XII; Princeton, N.J.: ASCSA, 1952) 335 and 339, no. 2920.

[18]Euripides, *El.* 475. For artistic representations, see J. L. Benson, "Human Figures in Later Protocorinthian Vase Painting," *Hesperia* 64 (1995) 174, for two examples of the Middle Protocorinthian II period (660–650 B.C.E.); T. J. Dunbabin, "Bellerophon, Herakles and Chimaera," in *Studies Presented to David Moore Robinson* (ed. G. E. Mylonas and D. Raymond; 2 vols.; Saint Louis: Washington University, 1953) 2:1164–65; and M. L. Schmitt, "Bellerophon and the Chimaera in Archaic Greek Art," *AJA* 70 (1966) 341–47.

[19]Pindar, *Ol.* 13.65–67 (trans. W. H. Race).

A wall painting from a Pompeiian triclinium of the early first century C.E. is perhaps the most evocative pictorial counterpart of Pindar's poem to come down to us.[20] Still *in situ* in the Casa di Virnius Modestus (IX 7,16), the painting is poorly preserved, but its details are recorded in the 1891 watercolor shown in figure 4.4. Bellerophon and Athena approach Pegasos,

Fig. 4.4 The Fountain of Peirene. Landscape with Pegasos, Bellerophon, and Athena, from a Pompeiian wall painting of the late first century B.C.E. Watercolor of 1891 condition, Casa di Virnius Modestus (IX 7,16).

[20]*LIMC*, s.v. "Peirene," 7/1:231, no. 2 (C. Lanara); and ibid., s.v. "Pompei," 9:794–95, figs. 21, 22 (V. Sampaolo). See also W. Klein, "Pompejanische Bilderstudien II," *ÖJh* 19–20 (1919) 273–74; Christopher M. Dawson, *Romano-Campanian Mythological Landscape Painting* (YaleClSt 9; New Haven, Conn.: Yale University Press, 1944) 83, no. 7; Karl Schefold,

who drinks from the spring of Peirene, while a reclining figure, the nymph of the spring, looks on. The panel captures Pindar's dreamy mood and suggests his resolution:

> The gods' power easily brings into being even
> what one would swear impossible and beyond hope.
> And indeed powerful Bellerophon,
> eagerly stretching
> the soothing remedy around its jaws, captured
> the winged horse.[21]

With Athena's help, Bellerophon succeeds in his heroic task. He thus becomes an exemplar of the pious and enterprising Corinthian; by analogy, Xenophon and Corinth are honored and elevated.

Over time, Peirene's significance grew, and the Corinthian fountain, real or imagined, became the proverbially inexhaustible source cited by Plautus and Cicero, and also a source of inspiration, as in the verses of Statius and Persius.[22] Moreover, from the Hellenistic period, Peirene evolved into a metonym for Corinth and for the Isthmian games, a connection that would be embraced and reiterated by Latin poets of the Golden and Silver Ages.[23] So too Peirene, who, allegorized as a nymph, may have appeared in poetry as early as Bacchylides' Archaic verse; she flourished in Roman literature and art: she is the vital force of the spring, a numinous presence.[24] The related

---

Die Wände Pompejis: Topografisches Verzeichnis der Bildmotive (Berlin: de Gruyter, 1957) 269; idem, "Origins of Roman Landscape Painting," *Art Bulletin* 42 (1960) 87; Stefan Hiller, *Bellerophon: Ein griechischer Mythos in römischer Kunst* (Munich: W. Fink, 1969) 22–27, fig. 9; Karl Schefold and Franz Jung, *Die Urköniger, Perseus, Bellerophon, Herakles und Theseus in der klassischen und hellenistischn Kunst* (Munich: Hirmer, 1988) 125; and B. Bergmann, "Rhythms of Recognition: Mythological Encounters in Roman Landscape Painting," in *Im Spiegel des Mythos: Bilderwelt und Lebenswelt* (ed. Franceso de Angelis and Susanne Muth; Wiesbaden: L. Reichert, 1999) 98–99.

[21]Pindar, *Ol.* 13.83–86 (trans. W. H. Race).

[22]Plautus, *Aulularia* 557–59; Cicero, *Att.* 12.5; Statius, *Silv.* 2.7.2–4; idem, *Theb.* 4.59–61; and Persius, *Satires*, prologue.

[23]Callimachus, *Victory of Sosibius* [384] 21–32; Ovid, *Met.* 7.391; *Pont.* 1.3.75; and Statius, *Silv.* 1.4.25–30.

[24]Bacchylides 9.62. The first indisputable visual representation of the nymph appears on an Italian silver cup of the early first century C.E.; see Ernest Babelon, *Description historique et chronologique des monnaies de la République romaine vulgairement appelées monnaies consulaires* (2 vols.; Paris, 1885–1886); and *Trésors d'orfèvrerie gallo-romains: Musée du Luxembourg, Paris, 8 fevrier-23 avril 1989* (ed. F. Baratte, K. Painter, and F. Legge; Paris: Éditions de la Réunion des musées nationaux, 1989) 79–80, 84–85, no. 18. For the nymph Peirene on high-Imperial "Bellerophon" sarcophagi and on Corinthian coins of the Antonine and Severan periods, see Robinson, "Fountains," 199–202, with bibliography.

story that human Peirene was Poseidon's lover, transformed into a spring because of her incessant weeping for their dead son, is first attested by Pausanias, although it recalls Hellenistic *aitia*.[25] Finally, this inexhaustible source of fresh water inspired a wealth of further musings: that subterranean veins linked the center city spring to "Upper Peirene" high on Acrocorinth, and that this spring complex was engendered by a blow from the hoof of Pegasos.[26] To conclude, the literary and pictorial references to Peirene document early traditions, continuous accretions, and ever a strong sense that this spring was a very special place.

Within a few decades of Corinth's refoundation, there came the first of many Roman-era modifications to the façade of Peirene. An ornamental screen wall in two stories was erected across the front of the old Greek spring house (figs. 4.1, p. 113, and 4.5, p. 122).[27] At ground level, a continuous parapet with an elaborate cap molding stretched across the fronts of the six antechambers, which were thereby converted into basins. An arcade rose from the parapet, its six arches framing the new basins. Doric half-columns flanked the arches, standing on "pedestals" formed by projections of the parapet. The second order was Ionic; little survives. The building material was local oolitic limestone with a lustrous surface of painted stucco. Although the builders hardly touched the ancient walls within, their additions transformed the fountain, both visually and functionally. With the conversion of the antechambers into basins, people no longer passed into the old subterranean fountain house, but remained outside, leaning through the arches to lift water from within.

The façade was an impressive composition, all the more so considering that it seems to have been among the colony's earliest monumental projects; my reading of the archaeological evidence puts it in the 20s or 10s B.C.E.[28] Within the first decades of the first century C.E., further "improvements" were

---

[25]Pausanias 2.3.3. P. M. C. Forbes Irving (*Metamorphosis in Greek Myth* [Oxford: Clarendon, 1990] 13–20) notes that transformation stories of this type are only applied "on a large scale" from the Hellenistic period forward; however, it remains uncertain whether these were largely new inventions, or the expression of long-lived *topoi*.

[26]Strabo (8.6.21) is the first to use the name Peirene to refer to the spring on Acrocorinth and to assert its connection to the spring in town below. For Pegasos's creation of Peirene, see Statius, *Silv.* 1.4.25–30; 2.7.2–4; and idem, *Theb.* 4.51–69. For Upper Peirene, see Carl William Blegen, Oscar Broneer, Richard Stillwell, and Alfred Raymond Bellinger, *Acrocorinth, Excavations in 1926* (Corinth III.1; Cambridge, Mass.: ASCSA, 1930) 31–60; Glaser, *Antike Brunnenbauten,* 18–19, no. 10; and Landon, "Water Supply," 154–62.

[27]See Hill, *The Springs,* 64–68 for preliminary Roman interventions at Peirene, focusing on the stabilization of standing architecture and maintenance of the water supply system.

[28]Robinson ("Fountains," 44–45) reconsiders the numismatic evidence; compare Hill, *The Springs,* 64.

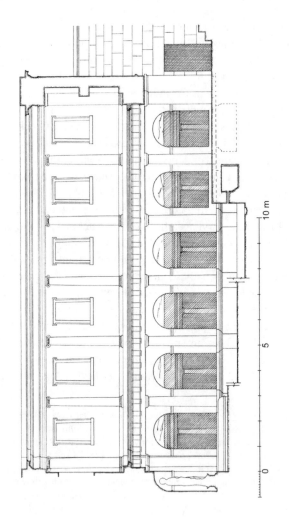

Fig. 4.5 The Fountain of Peirene. Restored elevation, early Roman period.

undertaken as the neighborhood developed.[29] The space in front of Peirene was enclosed by straight walls on the east and west, and on the north by a wall punctuated by an apse. Like the main façade, the new walls were two stories high, with superimposed orders. Thus Peirene would remain until sometime around the turn of the second century c.e., when the court and façade of the spring house were redecorated in marble.[30] Throughout the Roman period, Peirene was periodically renovated, so that its appearance was always kept "up to date."

Early Roman Peirene speaks clearly for itself of the forces that shaped it, reflecting, above all, an infusion of Italian ideology and tastes. As every Roman schoolboy knew, Peirene was a venerable ancient source, a numinous locale charged with meaning. Back in Rome, the emperor Augustus and Marcus Agrippa were responsible for renovations of the most sacred sources in the heart of the city: the *Lacus Servilius*, the *Lacus Iuturna*, the *Lacus Curtius* and the *Lupercal*.[31] Like Peirene, these were all historiated springs—places long associated with historical events. This attention reflects the efforts of Roman leaders to express their piety by promoting the continuity of such sources, while at the same time tapping into their symbolism. Whether prompted by imperial designs or undertaken by the local elite, the renovation of Peirene, like that of the pre-eminent springs in Rome and others scattered throughout the young empire, is an extension of this phenomenon.[32]

In their efforts to realize Peirene's full decorative and symbolic potential, Corinth's "inheritors" likewise betray strong Roman aesthetics. Repeating arches were already the most distinctive motif in Republican Roman architecture; one has only to think of the great vaulted substructures of Republican Latium.[33]

[29]Ibid., 79–88; see also Robinson, "Fountains," 36–41, with further bibliography.

[30]Hill, *The Springs,* 92; Robinson "Fountains," 58–75.

[31]Ibid., 51–54; for reviews of recent scholarship, see *LTUR* 3:166–67 (s.v. *Lacus Curtius,* C. F. Giuliani); 168–70 (s.v. *Lacus Iuturnae,* E. M. Steinby); 172–73 (s.v. *Lacus Servilius,* A. La Regina); and 198–99 (s.v. *Lupercal,* F. Coarelli).

[32]For early Augustan hydraulic interventions at Glanum (Saint Rémy de Provence), see Claude Bourgeois, *Divona* (2 vols.; Paris: de Boccard, 1991–92) 2:226; Jean-Michel Roddaz, *Marcus Agrippa* (BÉFAR 253; Rome: L'École française de Rome, 1984) 396–97. For early Imperial Nîmes, see A. R. Congès, "Culte de l'eau et dieux guérisseurs en Gaule romaine," *JRA* 7 (1994) 402; and Roddaz, *Marcus Agrippa,* 398–99.

[33]See W. L. MacDonald, "Empire Imagery in Augustan Architecture," in *The Age of Augustus: Interdisciplinary Conference Held at Brown University, April 30–May 2, 1982* (ed. Rolf Winkes; Providence, R.I.: Center for Old World Archaeology and Art, Brown University, 1985); and F. Coarelli, *I santuari del Lazio in età repubblicana* (Rome: La Nuova Italia Scientifica, 1987).

Still closer to Peirene's seriated arches and superimposed orders, however, are the buildings that dominate the center of Rome itself, such as the Late Republican Tabularium and the Early Augustan Theater of Marcellus, to name just two examples. In Peirene's new façade, I see a deliberate quotation of the architectural language of the new imperial capital, a clear and early Greek example of what William L. MacDonald has aptly called "empire imagery."[34]

Choices made by Peirene's architects indicate that other very Roman sensibilities were also at work behind the façade. Just as the gaze of every modern visitor is drawn up to the arches and into the dark recesses behind, so too did the ancient visitor behold Peirene's grottoes, which even in the second century C.E. would still look "like caves" to Pausanias.[35] Rather than covering the lip of bedrock that extended behind the arches, the Early Roman architects seem to have left it exposed for visitors to see—living rock encrusted with water-worn pebbles and fossil shells. Moreover, just beyond the basins and their walls of fine Greek masonry loomed dark, rock-cut recesses in plain view. The sense that the space behind the façade belonged to another realm would have been accentuated by the moist air exhaled from these grottoes, cool in summer, warm in winter. Comparative evidence, particularly from Italy, suggests to me that the architects' preservation of views into the interior of the spring was purposeful, a tribute to the resident spirit and the memory of the taming of Pegasos.

Numinous grottoes were places of reverence, passage, and of magical events. When Peirene was transformed in the late first century B.C.E., the grotto was already a well-worn motif in literature, art, and architecture in Rome and Italy. Up and down the Italian coast, on lakefronts and in rustic vales, caves were improved with man-made walls, artificial stalagmites, sculpture, and even seats for nymphs.[36] Such places were also fondly reproduced in the decorative arts.[37] A well-known example appears in a wall painting from the villa of P. Fannius Synistor at Boscoreale, from the mid-first century B.C.E.[38]

[34]MacDonald, "Empire Imagery."

[35]Pausanias 2.3.3.

[36]Norman Neuerburg, *L'architettura delle fontane e dei ninfei nell'Italia antica* (Naples: G. Macchiaroli, 1965).

[37]See A. Kuttner, "Looking Outside Inside: Ancient Roman Garden Rooms," in *Studies in the History of Gardens and Designed Landscapes* 19 (1999) 3–35.

[38]M. L. Anderson, "The Villa of P. Fannius Synistor at Boscoreale," *Metropolitan Museum of Art Bulletin: Pompeian Frescoes in the Metropolitan Museum of Art* (1987/88) 16–21; and Phyliis Williams Lehmann, *Roman Wall Paintings from Boscoreale in the Metropolitan Museum of Art* (Monographs on Archaeology and Fine Arts 5; Cambridge, Mass.: Archaeological Institute of America, 1953) 114–17.

On the rear wall of an elaborately painted *cubiculum*, two craggy-edged caverns interrupt the cultivated landscape and its vine-covered trellises. Within the shadowy reserve of the right-hand cave, better preserved than its pendant, the touch of humanity is also apparent: a marble basin catches and redistributes spring water, while a little statue of a deity stands in the shadows, at once alluding to both the sanctity of the cave and the reverence paid to it by humans.[39]

Nature, divinity, and humanity are again the subject of a painted panel of the mid-first century C.E. from a Pompeiian triclinium in a modest edifice in Pompeii (fig. 4.6, p. 126).[40] The viewer is transported back to Corinth to witness the taming of Pegasos, depicted here not as the easy triumph of Pindar's verses, but as a fierce struggle. At center, Bellerophon, actively aided by Athena, strives to overcome the panicked beast. The rough lip of a cave fills the left-hand side of the painting: the lair of Peirene. The story of Pegasos's taming, and its Corinthian locale, were very much the subject of "table talk" among the classes of people who transformed Rome, Italy, and Corinth.

Indeed, similar imagery was alive in Roman Corinth from the start, as illustrated by bronze coins of 43 or 42 B.C.E., which show the taming of Pegasos as a struggle before Peirene (fig. 4.7, p. 127).[41] On the coins, a Roman arch replaces the rustic cave of the Pompeiian painting. Thus, the Corinthians "reactivated" Pegasos, the old symbol of autonomous Corinth, and thereafter he was almost always accompanied by Bellerophon. Meanwhile, Peirene's inheritors created a very modern Roman monument that clearly evoked the poetic past and the sanctity of the source—where people had only to gaze into the dark to see what might have been the vestiges of the pristine grotto, the place where Pegasos and Bellerophon first met. Just as the honor of Pindar's victor and his city-state had been enhanced by association with the pious hero and his great coup, the Roman colony at once grounded itself in, and was elevated by, that same narrative, and the reputation of hallowed Peirene.

---

[39]Ibid., 114–16; and Kuttner, "Looking Outside," 18–19.

[40]From the Termopolio e Casa di L. Vetuzio Placido, and now in Naples (Museo Archeologico Nazionale, inv. no. 20878). See Hiller, *Bellerophon*, 34–36, plate 12; N. Yalouris, *Pegasus: Ein Mythos in der Kunst* (Mainz: Philipp von Zabern, 1987) 82–83, no. 61; *Pompeii*, 1:802–3, 825, figs. 37–38 (V. Sampaolo); Pietro Giovanni Guzzo, ed., *Pompeii: Picta fragmenta: Decorazioni parietali dalla città sepolte* (Torino: Umberto Allemandi, 1997) 119–20, no. 69 (M. Mastroroberto); and A. d'Ambrosio, "Termopolio e Casa di Le Betuzio Placido," in *Pompei: Abitare sotto il Vesuvio* (Ferrara: Ferrara arte, 1996) 109 and plate 41.

[41]As dated by Michel Amandry (*Le monnayage des duovirs corinthiens* [BCHSup 15; Paris: de Boccard, 1988] 32–33), this is the second coin type to be minted by the new colony.

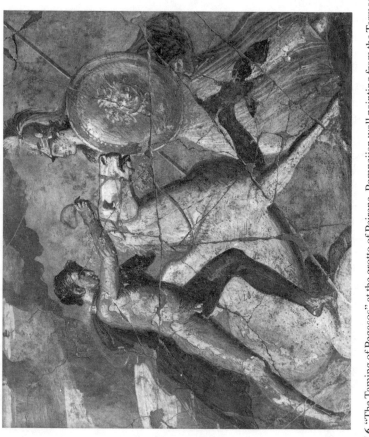

Fig. 4.6 "The Taming of Pegasos" at the grotto of Peirene. Pompeiian wall painting from the Termopolio e Casa di L. Vetuzio Placido (I 8,8), now in Naples (Museo Archeologico Nazionale, inv. no. 20878).

Fig. 4.7 "The Taming of Pegasos." Reverse of a Corinthian coin issued between 43 and 42 B.C.E. by Corinthian *duoviri* P. Tadius Chilo and C. Iulius Nicephorus. Obverse: Seated Poseidon.

GLAUKE

About eighty meters west of the Archaic Temple, a monolithic cube of oolitic limestone juts out of the landscape: the Fountain of Glauke (fig. 4.2). We owe this identification to Pausanias, our only ancient source on the monument. Here, he reports, the Corinthian princess Glauke, Jason's bride, threw herself into the water, trying to save herself from Medea's "wedding gift" of poisoned garments.[42] I shall return to the story, but the material remains require some comment.[43]

The fountain house was accessed from the Sikyon Road, which ran more or less east-west in front of the fountain. Users would have climbed up a set of stairs across the front of the building to reach a covered porch cut into the rock (now collapsed) with a parapet along its southern edge (figs. 4.8 and 4.9, p. 130). Behind the parapet, four large reservoirs were cut into the rock, with a tripartite basin across the front. With Glauke, we are faced with two difficult questions: what is the date of the fountain, and when was it first given a history? As to the first question, stratigraphic data offer little insight. While the early excavators assumed the fountain to be the work of the Archaic Corinthian tyrants, the most recent excavator in this area, Charles Williams, has suggested that the fountain was actually a Roman creation.[44]

Indeed, as Williams has shown, formal and practical criteria indicate that the creation of Glauke came considerably later than originally posited; nonetheless, the evidence still favors a pre-Roman date. First, as noted by the excavators and authoritatively described by R. Siddall, a typically "Greek" mortar underlies patches of Roman terracotta-rich waterproofing inside the fountain's reservoirs.[45] Other factors further support a pre-Roman date.

---

[42]Pausanias 2.3.6.

[43]For detailed descriptions of the fountain house, see G. W. Elderkin, "The Fountain of Glauce at Corinth," *AJA* 14 (1910) 19–50; Hill, *The Springs*, 200–28 [Elderkin]; Richard Stillwell, Robert L. Scranton, and Sarah Elizabeth Freeman, *Architecture* (Corinth I.2; Cambridge, Mass.: ASCSA, 1941) 143–46, 156–65 (including a discussion of the ancient testimonia); Glaser, *Antike Brunnenbauten* 72–73, no. 52; and Robinson, "Fountains," 206–34.

[44]R. B. Richardson, "The Fountain of Glauce at Corinth," *AJA* 4 (1900) 470–71; compare Charles K. Williams II and Orestes H. Zervos, "Corinth, 1983: The Route to Sikyon," *Hesperia* 53 (1984) 97–101 and 104; and Williams, "Refounding of Roman Corinth," 34–35.

[45]In the Roman period, the waterproof lining of choice was *opus signinum*, a terracotta-rich mortar. For a detailed study of hydraulic mortars at Corinth, see R. Siddall, "Lime Cements, Mortars and Concretes; The Site of Ancient Corinth, Northern Peloponnese, Greece; I: Preliminary Results from Morphologic and Petrographic Analyses (Weiner Laboratory Internal Report; Athens, 1997)," unpublished manuscript; for Glauke, see ibid., p. 47.

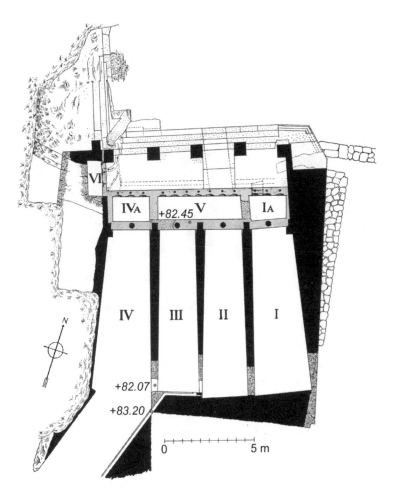

Fig. 4.8 The Fountain of Glauke. Plan at stylobate level of inner porch.

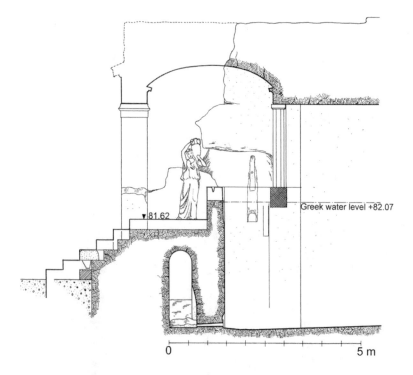

Fig. 4.9 The Fountain of Glauke. North-south section through porch.

The major axes of the fountain are more closely aligned with the remaining buildings of pre-Roman Corinth than with Roman-era foundations.[46] The flat-chisel work on finished blocks is also typical of pre-Roman practice at Corinth. On the other hand, Glauke departs from the early rupestral fountains of the Corinthia in one important way: it stands well above the water table, and it was pipe-fed from some distance, probably from the spring of Hadji Mustafa, uphill.[47] The distant water supply and subtle deviations from stylistic norms indicate that Glauke was not among the earliest Corinthian fountains. The design finds close parallels in other hydraulic installations at Corinth and

[46]This should be evident in fig. 2.5, p. 35. I thank David Gilman Romano for his work and input on the orientations of buildings and other features at Corinth.

[47]See P. A. MacKay, "The Fountain at Hadji Mustafa," *Hesperia* 36 (1967) 193–95; and Landon, "Water Supply," 174–77.

Perachora of the fifth and fourth centuries B.C.E., and a date in the latter half of the fourth century B.C.E. is most appropriate.[48] Such a date would put the construction of this high-volume, state-of-the-art fountain in a time of significant architectural development at Corinth—from the construction of the theater and South Stoa to the refurbishment of the Asklepieion and Peirene.[49]

There is not enough evidence to reconstruct more than a rough outline of the fountain's evolution, yet I think it is possible to suggest a Roman-period starting point. Extensive quarrying transformed the topography of the area west of the temenos of the Archaic Temple and south of the theater in the early Roman period. This work ended in the mid-first century C.E.; there followed the construction of Temple C and its temenos beside Glauke, and the routing of an east-west road past the northern temenos wall and the façade of the fountain.[50] This wave of development offers the most logical opportunity for the refurbishment of the fountain.

Before or during the Roman quarrying operations, Glauke was pared down to the freestanding cube we see today. Like G. W. Elderkin, I would blame injuries to Glauke's westernmost reservoir on the Roman quarrymen and assign the construction of a retaining wall within, as well as the first recognizably "Roman" waterproofing, to the period immediately after the cessation of quarrying.[51] Likewise, damage to Glauke's steps was probably mended at this time, and the space before the fountain paved with diamond-shaped tiles, hiding many of the scars of the Roman operations and providing access from the adjacent roadway. The fountain would not have stood in isolation as it does today. The temenos of Temple C abutted the eastern face of Glauke, and its northern perimeter wall ran east from the fountain's porch. Unfortunately, the architectural history of the area just west of Glauke is not well understood.

The Roman-period condition of the fountain house is a matter of educated guesswork. I am inclined to believe that it was still intact. As Williams has pointed out, the porch and façade bear no signs of Roman remodeling, but surely

---

[48]Compare R. A. Tomlinson, "Perachora: The Remains Outside the Two Sanctuaries: The Storage Chambers and the Fountain House," *BSA* 64 (1969) 196–218; and Oscar Broneer, *The South Stoa and Its Roman Successors* (Corinth I.4; Princeton, N.J.: ASCSA, 1954) 12–17.

[49]Ibid., 98; Hill, *The Springs*, 39; Richard Stillwell, *The Theatre* (Corinth II; Princeton, N.J.: ASCSA, 1952) 131–33; Charles K. Williams II, "Archaic and Classical Corinth," in *Corinto e l'Occidente: Atti del trentaquattresimo convegno di studi sulla Magna Grecia* (Taranto: Istituto per la storia e l'archeologia della Magna Grecia, 1995) 44–45; Charles K. Williams II and Joan E. Fisher, "Corinth, 1971: Forum Area," *Hesperia* 41 (1972) 153, 169–71; and idem, "Corinth, 1972: The Forum Area," *Hesperia* 42 (1973) 23–27.

[50]Williams and Zervos, "Corinth 1983," 98.

[51]Hill, *The Springs*, 224.

the stone surfaces would have been maintained—probably with painted stucco, as it is clear that the facade was never revetted with marble.[52] As Corinth was transformed from a city of stuccoed *poros* to one of marble-clad monuments, the impression of the fountain as a Greek holdover would have been magnified.

By the time of Pausanias's visit in the mid-second century C.E., then, Glauke would have looked its age of five hundred years, if not older. By then, too, the Medea legend was already a complex of contradictory traditions, their common denominator being that Jason and Medea came to Corinth, where their stay ended tragically in the deaths of their children, an event located by the oldest preserved account in the sanctuary of Hera Akraia.[53] Pausanias uses Glauke mainly as a springboard for retelling the stories of Medea at Corinth, quickly segueing to the monument of Medea's children, which he saw somewhere by the Odeion.[54] Local tradition seems to have blamed the children's deaths on vengeful Corinthians, and according to Pausanias, the locals paid for their ancestors' crime with rites to appease the children's uneasy spirits until the Mummian destruction.[55]

---

[52]Williams and Zervos, "Corinth, 1983," 98–99.

[53]According to the Bacchiad historian Eumelos (Pausanias 2.3.6–7), Medea hid her children in the sanctuary to make them immortal, but they died. Scranton (Stillwell et al., *Architecture*, 151–65) supposes that the sanctuary of Hera Akraia and the tomb of Medea's children stood on the crest of the hill over (or on top of) Glauke; Georges Roux (*Pausanias en Corinthie (Livre II, 1 à 15): texte, traduction, commentaire archéologique et topographique* [Paris: Belles Lettres, 1958] 120–22) suggests that the sanctuary of Hera Akraia was originally located in the area of the Odeion, but was moved when the Romans quarried out the area. Charles K. Williams II ("Pre-Roman Cults in the Area of the Forum of Ancient Corinth" [Ph.D. diss., University of Pennsylvania, 1978] 47) has stated that "it is enough to say that the original temenos of Hera Akraia and 'tomb' of the children of Medea probably should be put north or northwest of the Fountain of Glauke, in the vicinity of the Roman Odeion." For the plausible suggestion that the mythic Sanctuary of Hera Akraia was at Corinthian Perachora, see B. Menadier, "The Sixth Century BC Temple and the Sanctuary and Cult of Hera Akraia, Perachora" (Ph.D. diss., University of Cincinnati, 1995); Sarah Iles Johnston, "Corinthian Medea and the Cult of Hera Akraia," in *Medea: Essays on Medea in Myth, Literature, Philosophy, and Art* (ed. James J. Clauss and Sarah Iles Johnston; Princeton, N.J.: Princeton University Press, 1997) 44–70; and Domenico Musti and Mario Torelli, eds., *Pausania. Guida della Grecia* II (Milan: Fondazione Lorenzo Valla–Mondadori, 1986) 226–27.

[54]Pausanias 2.3.6–7; see Williams and Zervos, "Corinth 1983," 102–4.

[55]As recorded in schol. Euripedes *Med.* 264, Parminiskos (second century B.C.E.) blames the deaths of fourteen of Medea's children on Corinthian women who rejected Medea's rule, while Kreophylos writes that Medea killed Kreon, then fled, and his kin avenged him by killing the children whom Medea had left behind at the altar of Hera Akraia. The tradition recounted by Apollodorus (*Bibl.* 1.9.28) is similar, although "the Corinthians" in general are accused. See Stillwell et al., *Architecture*, 159; Denys L. Page, ed., *Euripides: Medea* (Oxford: Oxford University Press, 1967) 4; compare Aelian, *Var. Hist.* 5.21; *Schol.* Euripides *Med.* 9–10 (Parmeniskos).

Euripides' *Medea* of 431 B.C.E. made Medea's reputation as a child-murderer, and it is the earliest preserved source to include the princess. By his account, after years in Corinth, Jason tired of Medea and chose to wed the daughter of Kreon, king of Corinth. Facing exile, Medea sent two of her boys to visit the bride, bearing heirlooms from their grandfather, Helios. Donning the tainted robe and diadem, the princess collapsed, then perished in flames; her father succumbed with her. Medea then killed her boys to save them from more hostile hands and took off in a chariot drawn by winged snakes. Euripides never mentions the princess's name, leaving it for his scholiasts and later writers to fill in: Glauke or Kreousa.[56]

Countless discussions have focused on untangling the different threads of tradition. The *idea* of the princess seems to have preceded Euripides.[57] The place of her death in all visual and literary sources except for Pausanias is the palace, not a fountain. If any structure associated with water had a place in the early Corinthian traditions of Medea's revenge, it is certain that the "original" was not the Late Classical or Early Hellenistic fountain house we see today. Conversely, did this new Fountain of Glauke take the place of an earlier, "authentic" fountain and reputed place of death, either on the same site and subsequently destroyed by quarrying, or elsewhere in Corinth?[58] The pre-Roman date of the structure in question renders this scenario unlikely as well. As S. E. Alcock and others have noted, Greek peoples were actively restoring and "historiating" old monuments well before the Roman period, yet it is difficult to imagine that this new urban monument, a state-of-the-art fountain when it was constructed, could or would have been passed off as an "original" before the Roman period.[59] The ancient cultural memory and institutions of the city remained unbroken. Life was still embedded in the old religious and historical topographies.

I suggest a new working hypothesis: on inheriting this monument, Corinth's rebuilders selected it to become another place where fragments of Corinthian history could be localized in the new urban landscape, and

[56]For Glauke, see schol. Euripides *Med.* 19; Apollodorus, *Bibl.* 1.9.28; Pausanias 2.3.6; and *Anth. Pal.* 5.228 (Gaetulicus, probably early first century C.E.). To Propertius, Ovid, Seneca, and Athenaeus, she is Kreousa or Creusa.

[57]See Page, *Medea*, xxv-xxvi.

[58]The possibility is noted by Williams, "Refounding of Roman Corinth," 35.

[59]Susan Alcock, "The Heroic Past in a Hellenistic Present," in *Hellenistic Constructs* (ed. Paul Cartledge, Peter Garnsey, and Erich Gruen; Berkeley: University of California Press, 1997) 20–34.; idem, "The Pseudo-history of Messenia Unplugged," *TAPA* 129 (1999) 333–41; and see J. G. Pedley, "Reflections of Architecture in Sixth-Century Attic Vase-Painting," in *Papers on the Amasis Painter and His World* (Malibu, Calif.: J. Paul Getty Museum, 1987) 63–80, for a sense of the excitement accompanying the construction of fountain houses in sixth-century C.E. Athens.

thereby incorporated within the collective imagination of the new city. E. J. Hobsbawm suggests that the invention of new traditions "occur[s] more frequently when a transformation of society weakens or destroys the social patterns for which 'old' traditions had been designed."[60] Indeed, coming more than a century after the destruction of old Corinth, the Roman reconstruction provides the most opportune "moment" for the attachment of the name "Glauke" and the associated narrative to the fountain. Like their Hellenistic forebears, the Early Imperial Romans of the classes that oversaw the rebuilding of Corinth understood the usefulness of harnessing local mythology, and they recognized that the legendary past became that much more powerful when connected with visible landmarks.

Although I differ from Williams on the original date of the monument, my interpretation has much in common with his. Williams argues that Glauke's treatment in the Roman period reflects "the literary spirit of the educated Roman colonist, who wanted to be able to show a monument of ancient Corinth, as he saw it . . . [namely,] the myth of Medea as it was passed down, even into the time of Pausanias, perhaps justifying the local version of the tragedy over that set down by Euripides."[61] That the *Medea* saga was well known to a broad cross section of Roman society becomes clear in an examination of the Latin sources and, moreover, in an exploration of their visual counterparts in Roman art.

I turn now from the ancient Greek traditions per se to their reception and reinterpretation in Roman circles. By the Imperial period, Jason and Medea, much like Bellerophon and Pegasos, were very much part of common Greco-Roman culture. While the peculiarly Corinthian versions of Medea's story were clearly known by imperial writers, *their* perspective seems to have derived mainly from a narrative *koine* that may have begun with Euripides' tragedy but continued to flower in literature and art under Roman republican and imperial patronage.[62]

---

[60]E. J. Hobsbawm, "Introduction: Inventing Traditions," in *The Invention of Tradition* (ed. E. J. Hobsbawm and T. Ranger; Cambridge: Cambridge University Press, 1983) 4.

[61]Williams, "Refounding of Roman Corinth," 35; compare F. K. Yegül, "'Roman' Architecture in the Greek World" (review of *Roman Architecture in the Greek World* [ed. S. Macready and F. H. Thompson; London 1987]), *JRA* 4 (1991) 349.

[62]Scranton (Stillwell et al., *Architecture,* 164) explains Aelian's remark (*Var. Hist.* 5.21) that the Corinthians offered sacrifices to the children "up until now," as an anachronistic reference from an earlier source. The same could be true for an epigram by Gaetulicus, *Anth. Pal.* 7.354: "This is the tomb of Medea's children, whom her burning jealousy made the victims of Glauce's wedding. To them the Corinthian land ever sends peace offerings, propitiating their mother's implacable soul" (trans. W. R. Paton). This epigram probably dates from the first century C.E.; see Denys L. Page, *Further Greek Epigrams* (Cambridge: Cambridge University Press, 1981) 49.

Italian interest in the story is apparent from the earliest Latin rewritings of Greek tragedy, and in the numerous versions of the early empire. Ennius first dealt with Medea at Corinth; Pavinius and Accius soon introduced other episodes, and these works would become classics by the imperial period.[63] In the early years of the empire, Ovid and Pompeius Macer wrote tragedies, now lost, and Maecenas is rumored to have done so. Tragedies by Lucan, Curiatus Maternus, Bassus, and the younger Seneca followed, but of these only Seneca's *Medea* (ca. 62 C.E.) is preserved.[64] To what extent the lost and fragmentary works dealt with Medea at Corinth remains a question, but still other works by Ovid, Horace, Martial, and Valerius Flaccus give a strong sense of Medea's hold on Roman imagination.[65] Medea is a beauty, terror, cuckold, avenger, traveler, exile, mother, killer, sorcerer. Meanwhile, even in the Roman sphere, Kreousa/Glauke is never more than a minor player.

In the arts, Caesar's display of Timomachos's painting of Medea in the Temple of Venus Genetrix in Rome offered a potent moral and artistic exemplar. Of this *Medea*, and its pendant *Ajax*, Pliny recalls that "it was the Dictator Caesar who gave outstanding public importance to pictures by dedicating [the two paintings] at the *aedes* of Venus Genetrix."[66] Pliny's remark underscores the significance of the subject matter at the time of Corinth's refoundation, as well as its familiarity for the Roman populace. Medea would become a remarkably popular subject of Roman art, particularly wall paintings.[67]

Likewise, whereas the Corinthian princess was a minor player in the art of Greece, she also comes into her own in that of Rome. Preserved in

[63]See André Arcellaschi, *Médée dans le théâtre latin d'Ennius à Sénèque* (Collection de l'École française de Rome 132; Rome: L'École française de Rome, 1990), with extensive bibliography. For Ennius's readership, Roman philhellenism, and the education of the Republican elite in Greek language and culture, see Erich S. Gruen, *The Hellenistic World and the Coming of Rome* (2 vols.; Berkeley: University of California Press, 1984) 1:255–60; for the continued popularity of the early plays, see H. D. Jocelyn, ed. and comm., *The Tragedies of Ennius: The Fragments* (Cambridge: Cambridge University Press, 1967) 47–57.

[64]E. Künzl, "Der augusteische Silberkalathus im Rheinische Landesmuseum Bonn," *Bonner Jahrbücher* (1969) 377; and J.-M. Croisille, *Poésie et art figuré de Néron aux Flaviens* (Collection Latomus 179; Brussels: Latomus, 1982) 42–43.

[65]Ovid, *Trist.* 2.525–28; Horace, *Epod.* 3.9–14; Martial 10.35.5; see Croisille, *Poésie et art figuré*, 43.

[66]Pliny, *Nat.* 35.26 (trans. H. Rackham); compare Cicero *In. Verr.* II 4.60.135. For Timomachos, see Robert Schilling, ed. and trans., *Pline l'Ancien: Histoire Naturelle* (Paris: Belles Lettres, 1977) 195–96; Croisille, *Poésie et art figuré*, 44–46; and *LIMC* 6/1, s.v. "Medeia," 388, no. 7 (M. Schmidt).

[67]For a selection of Pompeiian paintings, see *LIMC* 6/1, s.v. "Medeia," 388–89, nos. 8–13 (M. Schmidt); and Croisille, *Poésie et art figuré*, 48.

isolation among artworks of the first century C.E., scenes of Medea's children presenting gifts to Glauke and of Medea's contemplation of infanticide come together in a brief burst of *stadtrömische* sarcophagus production in the later second century C.E.[68] In the sarcophagus reliefs, these scenes are reinserted into a visual narrative that includes the death of Glauke, as well as Medea's escape in a chariot drawn by winged snakes. The formulaic visual narratives on the sarcophagi indicate a common prototype, and an example of the "gift presentation" scene on an Early Imperial silver cup demonstrates that a model existed and was well known by the first century C.E.[69]

Figure 4.10 illustrates a typical "Medea" sarcophagus of ca. 150–160 C.E.[70] The narrative begins on the left, as Medea's children bring the poisoned robe and crown to the seated princess; at center, Kreon helplessly watches as Glauke perishes in a frenzy; and to the right, Medea prepares to kill her children, then makes her exit with their dead bodies thrown over her shoulder. The scale of horror rises as we move from left to right, from prologue to murder, to the consumption of the princess, and finally to the mother's murder of her own children. Within this progression, Glauke's death is often the centerpiece, and it is never far from center.

The sarcophagi restore to Kreousa/Glauke a central place within the ancient narrative cycle; perhaps they also shed some light on what lay behind the treatment of the Fountain of Glauke in the Roman period. The ultimate inspiration for these works may have been Euripides' *Medea* and lost Greek masterpieces, but recent authors have been right to emphasize the fertility of Roman imagination as a source of fresh details.[71] For the transmission and perpetuation of the imagery, lost sketchbooks are a likely vehicle, as are new spectacles. By the second century C.E., Lucian records the "Death of

[68]Published examples date from ca. 150 C.E. to ca. 210 , according to V. Gaggadis-Robin, *Jason et Médée sur les sarcophages d'époque impériale* (Rome: L'École française de Rome, 1994) 138–45 and 197, table 5. See also Croisille, *Poésie et art figuré*, 53–56; and *LIMC* 6/1, 120–27, s.v. "Kreousa II," with bibliography (G. Berger-Doer).

[69]The drinking-cup was found at Xanten, Germany; *LIMC* 6/1, s.v. "Kreousa II," 123, no. 13, with illustration (G. Berger-Doer); Künzl, "Der augusteische Silberkalathus"; H. Froning, "Ikonographische Tradition mythologischer Sarcophagreliefs," *Jahreshefte des Österreichischen Archäologischen Institutes in Wien* 95 (1980) 330–31; and Erika Simon, *Augustus: Kunst und Leben in Rom um die Zeitenwende* (Munich: Hirmer, 1986) 228–31.

[70]The pictured sarcophagus was found in a tomb on Via di Porta Maggiore, and is now in the Museo Nazionale Romano (inv. no. 75248); see A. Giuliano, ed., *Museo Nazionale Romano: Le Sculture I, 8, Parte I* (Rome: De Luca, 1985) 279–83, no. 6.8 (L. Musso); and Guntram Koch and Hellmut Sichtermann, *Römische Sarkophage* (Munich: C. H. Beck, 1982) 159–60.

[71]Croisille, *Poésie et art figuré*, 56, 64–65; Gaggadis-Robin, *Jason et Médée*, 145; C. Isler-Kerényi, "Immagini di Medea," in *Medea nella letteratura e nell'arte* (ed. Bruno Gentili and Franca Perusino; Venice: Marsilio, 2000) 132.

Fig. 4.10 "Medea" sarcophagus. Museo Nazionale Romano, inv. no. 75248.

Glauke" among subjects of dance or pantomime.[72] The image of the dying princess was well known and widely dispersed; the Corinthians would only have had to find a place for it.

As a landmark of the Corinthian finale to the Argonaut saga, Glauke did not exist in isolation. Although not itself a religious building, the fountain was an earnest memorial to Glauke, thematically associated with a cult site of Medea's children near the Odeion.[73] The memory that the Argo had been retired and dedicated to Poseidon on the Isthmus survived, if not the great ship itself.[74] The educated elite knew such traditions, and less "cultured" colonists would learn them through retellings at the relevant sites.

Old Glauke was meanwhile thoroughly integrated into the new urban landscape. To Romans, a fountain like Glauke, marking an entrance to the city center, would have seemed as "normal" as the historiated springs that ringed Rome's forum, or Peirene across Corinth's. Thus, for people approaching the city from the west, Glauke, together with the Archaic Temple—which retained at least its original exterior colonnade (and with it, the look of great age) despite extensive changes within—would have presented a sort of antique urban façade.[75] Just as Glauke "passed" as an Archaic landmark for genera-tions of Corinthian excavators, it would have had an air of antiquity for the inhabitants of the Roman city. As Corinth's monumental center filled with marble and marble revetment, the effect would have been that much stronger. The naming of the place, the preservation of an appropriately "old-fashioned" monument, and the retelling of the associated tales and their consequences made the connection to the past seem tangible, and in effect *real*.

---

[72]Lucian, *Salt.* 42; Robert Turcan, "Les sarcophages romains et le problème du symbolisme funéraire," *ANRW* II.16.2, 1722–23; *LIMC* 6/1, s.v. "Kreousa II," 121.

[73]Pausanias 2.3.6–7.

[74]The *Argo* is said to have been on display at the Isthmus until 146 B.C.E., perhaps longer. See Dio Chrysostom, *Orat.* 37.15; P. L. Couchoud and J. Svoronos, "Le monument dit 'des taureaux' à Délos et le culte du navire sacré," *BCH* 45 (1921) 276–77; and N. Purcell, "The Ports of Rome: Evolution of a *Façade Maritime*," in *'Roman Ostia' Revisited: Archaeologi-cal and Historical Papers in Memory of Russell Meiggs* (ed. Anna Gallina Zevi and Amanda Claridge; Rome: British School at Rome, 1996) 269.

[75]For early Roman renovations to the temple, see H. S. Robinson, "Excavations at Corinth: Temple Hill, 1968–1972," *Hesperia* 45 (1976) 236–38; Williams, "Refounding of Roman Corinth," 31–32; and Walbank, "Foundation and Planning," 122. Although the internal columns were removed and the interior dramatically rearranged, the stocky archaic columns of the exterior order would have continued to give the temple the appearance of great antiquity.

MONUMENTS, MEMORY, AND IMAGINATION

As in the case of Peirene in Euripides' day, the utilitarian purposes of Peirene and Glauke in the Roman period in no way diminish their cultural import. The archaeological record, however, offers no evidence to suggest that they functioned as sites of organized worship. Excavations have uncovered no signs of religious objects or inscriptions from Roman contexts at Peirene and Glauke—nothing like the oil and water vessels associated with the Sacred Spring, the inscribed lamps of Late Antiquity in the Fountain of the Lamps, and not even the Classical *kalouria* that were once left around Peirene. Perhaps ephemeral goods were given to the springs, like the cakes thrown into Delphic Castalia, the wreaths given to the Alpheios and Eurotas rivers, or milk and honey poured into the source of the Camenae near Rome.[76] Lacking the data to answer such questions, I prefer to characterize these fountains as "numinous," a term that connotes the presence of a numen or spirit without conjuring the organized practices implied by the term "cult."

Transients, tourists, and pilgrims might have stopped to see Peirene, to drink its fine water, and to wash off the dust of the road. Others "burning up" after a long hike into town might have stopped to take, or perhaps just to gaze into, the waters where Glauke was said to have met her fiery end. Events and festivities helped to keep these images alive, tying the fountains into the life of Corinth and linking past and present: think of Glauke's dance of death (perhaps performed in the theater just downhill from her fountain), and Apuleius's burlesque of Pegasos and Bellerophon within the Isis procession at Kenchreai: "an ass with wings, glued on his back, walking beside a decrepit old man, so that you would call the one Bellerophon and the other Pegasus, but laugh at both."[77] This pair was funny precisely because their models were so familiar.

As important public amenities and landmarks at least *recalling* a heroic age, the fountains of Peirene and Glauke offer insights into the extent to which Corinthian cultural memory was severed by the Mummian destruction and the following century of near-abandonment, as well as some of the sensibilities that shaped the new cityscape after Corinth's refoundation. It seems that the Roman builders capitalized on the aspects of Corinthian culture that they knew well—that is, the traditions that by then belonged to Greco-Roman patrimony. Peirene was a ready-made hit, and as this fountain was maintained and constantly updated, the individuals associated with it

---

[76]See nn. 2, 3, and 17, above.
[77]Apuleius, *Met.* 11.8 (trans. J. A. Hanson).

figured prominently in the adornment of the city and on its coins. By localizing an episode from the saga of Medea at an urban landmark, the Roman colonists again articulated a connection to Corinth's legendary past, one that would become stronger with each retelling of the story. Thus, the Corinthian princess Glauke, together with Medea and her children, was remembered alongside Peirene, Pegasos, and Bellerophon, recalling the Greek city's past in the service of the Roman successor city.

CHAPTER FIVE

Religion in Corinth: 146 B.C.E. to 100 C.E.

Nancy Bookidis

The first colonists to settle Corinth arrived in 44 B.C.E. or shortly thereafter and found a city that was partially inhabited; Hellenistic buildings survived, although they probably lacked roofs and timbers. The famed Mummian destruction of the city in 146 B.C.E., celebrated—or mourned—by many an ancient author, was less thorough than has been thought. Looted of her portable riches, Corinth nevertheless still stood. That the visible remains of the old city influenced the new one is shown quite plainly in the choice of site and layout of the new forum, which took its orientation from the South Stoa rather than from true north. In this essay I will attempt to show that the influence of the Hellenistic city on Roman Corinth was not limited merely to the forum, for the new Roman colony was not established on the site of a city that had been utterly destroyed, buried, and forgotten. For one hundred years, members of the Corinth excavations have vacillated on the issue of cultural, and in particular of cultic, continuity between the Hellenistic city and the Roman colony. As this essay will demonstrate, the issue is far from dead. My interest is primarily in the cults of the Roman city of the first century B.C.E. and the first century C.E., but a brief review of the Hellenistic religious presence may help to give the setting for the Early Roman city.[1] I have left the study of religion in Isthmia to others.

[1] I wish to express my indebtedness to Charles K. Williams II, who offered me much valuable advice on this essay and who is responsible for most of the work that has been

CULTS OF HELLENISTIC CORINTH

I begin by reviewing what cults may have been practiced at the center of the city in the Hellenistic period. One must remember that the available sources are extremely fragmentary and uneven. I will thus make some leaps of faith with which the reader may or may not agree. Written evidence is limited to that contained in brief literary sources and the all-too-few inscriptions, which include part of an archaic ritual calendar.[2] I will also concentrate on the archaeological evidence recovered from several excavated sanctuaries, in particular the evidence for the cults of the Roman city. Much of our understanding of the Greek city center is colored by the fact that the agora has not yet been found. Thus, it is difficult to know what we should expect in the way of civic cults at the center of the city, and to what extent we may take democratic Athens as a model for oligarchic Corinth. One fact stands out, however. Within the limited corpus of Hellenistic public inscriptions, the greatest number derive from the excavations of the northeast slope of the Archaic sanctuary on Temple Hill.[3] This concentration suggests that the agora lay to the north of the hill and probably not at a great distance from it. If this was indeed the case, then Apollo would have been the god who overlooked the agora and oversaw civic order. The names of several deities have been associated with the Archaic temple—Apollo, Zeus, Zeus and Hera together, or

---

done in Corinth in recent years on the subject of cult, as will be obvious. I would also like to thank Kathleen Slane, who has been responsible for opening my eyes to the subtleties of the Roman period. A basic source for this paper has also been the very useful unpublished dissertation by Robert Lisle, "The Cults of Corinth" (Ph.D. diss., Johns Hopkins University, 1955). A review of the history of Hellenistic and early Roman Corinth, as well as a discussion of the interim period, appears in James Wiseman, "Corinth and Rome I: 228 B.C.–A.D. 267," *ANRW* II.17.1 (1979) 438–548. My intention in this paper is to present a quick overview of what is known of the cults of first-century Corinth. It is not meant to present an in-depth study of the practice of Roman religion. It is, moreover, hampered by the fact that our major source for so many of the monuments is Pausanias, who cites these by their Greek names. Simply to translate these into their proposed Roman equivalents is to offend "Romanists," who accuse "Hellenists" of equating Hellenistic and Roman cults. To leave them in their Greek form is to further offend the "Romanists," who then criticize the "Hellenists" of not thinking in Roman terms at all. It is important that both sides be aware of the limitations of the sources. I have chosen, in my estimation, the least satisfactory solution of all, giving both, unless I specifically cite Pausanias.

[2]For the calendar, see John Harvey Kent, *The Inscriptions, 1926–1950* (Corinth VIII.3; Princeton, N.J.: ASCSA, 1966) 1–2; and Sterling Dow, "Corinthiaka," *AJA* 46 (1942) 69–72; see H. S. Robinson, "Excavations at Corinth: Temple Hill, 1968–1972," *Hesperia* 45 (1976) 249–50, fig. 11, for an additional fragment of the calendar.

[3]These are to be published by Professor Donald Laing.

Athena.[4] A most recent rediscovery, however, may provide further evidence. It is a small terracotta object, possibly a pinax, that was excavated in 1902 in late fill just east of the sanctuary. The pinax appears to bear part of a painted epichoric dedication to Apollo dating to the sixth or early fifth century B.C.E. Never published, it is preserved in a drawing made by Samuel Bassett in his excavation notebook. Undoubtedly washed down from the top of the hill, the tablet is, in my estimation, of prime importance for the association of the Archaic temple with the worship of Apollo.[5]

Assuming that the agora was positioned a relatively short distance north of the Temple of Apollo and east of the theater, at least two other major sanctuaries were located nearby. The further away of the two is the Asklepieion, with its two-tiered temenos, which abutted the north city wall north of the presumed location of the agora.[6] The second is a Doric temple, larger than the Temple of Apollo, and of the late sixth century, fragments of which were built into the fifth-century C.E. city wall.[7] Given the size of the architectural elements and their location, it is tempting to assign these fragments to the temple of Zeus Olympios, mentioned by Pausanias as having burned in 398 B.C.E., although there is no conclusive evidence for this.[8] The temple was situated either south of the Asklepieion and therefore near the agora, in the area of the so-called gymnasium, or further to the west.

---

[4]For a discussion of these various identifications, see Wiseman, "Corinth and Rome I," 475, 530; and Nancy Bookidis, "The Sanctuaries of Corinth," in *Corinth: The Centenary, 1896–1996* (ed. Charles K. Williams II and Nancy Bookidis; Corinth XX; Princeton, N.J.: ASCSA, 2003) 247–60. Some scholars have argued that Apollo is not a sufficiently prominent figure in Corinthian mythology to warrant such an imposing temple. But see Plutarch (*Aratus* 40) for an account of a gathering between Aratos and the citizens of Corinth in the Sanctuary of Apollo. It is also from the Sanctuary of Apollo at ancient Tenea that the first settlers set out for Syracuse.

[5]Nancy Bookidis and Ronald S. Stroud, "Apollo and the Archaic Temple at Corinth," *Hesperia*, forthcoming.

[6]Carl Roebuck, *The Asklepieion and Lerna* (Corinth XIV; Princeton, N.J.: ASCSA, 1951).

[7]W. B. Dinsmoor, "The Largest Temple in the Peloponnesos," in *Commemorative Studies in Honor of Theodore Leslie Shear* (Hesperia Supplement 8; n.p.: ASCSA, 1949) 104–15. The temple is also discussed by C. A. Pfaff, "Archaic Corinthian Architecture," in *Corinth: The Centenary, 1896–1996* (ed. Charles K. Williams II and Nancy Bookidis; Corinth XX; Princeton, N.J.: ASCSA, 2003) 95–140; Pfaff notes Roman plaster on some fragments.

[8]Lisle ("Cults of Corinth," 121–22 and nn. 187–88) cites A. B. Cook (*Zeus: A Study in Ancient Religion* [3 vols. in 5; Cambridge: Cambridge University Press, 1914–1940] 2:915 n. 2), who favors this interpretation. Pausanias (3.9.2) states that the temple was burned in 398 B.C.E. Theophrastos (*De causis plantarum* 5.14.2) mentions a district of the city called "Olympion." As Wiseman ("Corinth and Rome I," 530) observes, some scholars would associate this temple with that on Temple Hill. Others would assign it to a burned temple seen by Pausanias (2.5.5) outside the city on the road to Sikyon.

Whereas major sanctuaries stood to the north and south of the agora, south of the temple of Apollo the picture is rather different. Here lies the so-called Upper Valley of the Lechaion Road, which, over its long history, was shaped from a rather uneven breach in the marl, conglomerate, and limestone ridge into a much gentler slope. In the Hellenistic period, a sizable part of that valley was given over to cult but, without exception, to cult of a very local character. At the base of the hill lay the Sanctuary of the Sacred Spring. Now much reduced in size from its Classical form, it nonetheless continued to function, along with its spring cult; its water was now supplied by an underground channel, and its open temenos and apsidal building were possibly used for initiation rites. Charles Williams has suggested that the sanctuary was dedicated to the worship of Kotyto, a Corinthian heroine who, with her sister Hellotis, was killed during the Dorian invasion of Corinth.[9] Whether she was, like her sister, joined with another deity such as Athena or Artemis is unknown.

A racecourse for torch races and a semicircular platform for boxing and wrestling lay to the south and east of the spring and were probably connected with the worship of Hellotis, or Athena Hellotis as she is called by Pindar (*Ol.* 13.82).[10] Extending across the length of the valley, the racecourse provided a focal point for the cults set around it. South of the Spring and racecourse lay the small Heröon of the Crossroads. This was built over a Protogeometric graveyard as an open-air enclosure that was typical of local cults.[11] Another enclosure lay at the west end of the South Stoa. This was furnished with the quintessential Corinthian stele, which may have once been painted with an image of the attendant deity.[12] Several examples of

---

[9]For the sanctuary in this phase, see Bert Hodge Hill, *The Springs: Peirene, Sacred Spring, Glauke* (Corinth I.6; Princeton, N.J.: ASCSA, 1964) 192–99; Charles K. Williams II, "Excavations at Corinth, 1968," *Hesperia* 38 (1969) 36–63, esp. phase 8; and idem, "Pre-Roman Cults in the Area of the Forum of Ancient Corinth" (Ph.D. diss., University of Pennsylvania, 1978) 125–27.

[10]Excavated in 1937, then again in 1980, the racecourse is discussed in C. H. Morgan, "Excavations at Corinth, 1936–37," *AJA* 41 (1937) 549–51; Charles K. Williams II and P. Russell, "Corinth: Excavations of 1980," *Hesperia* 50 (1981) 27–29; and David G. Romano, *Athletics and Mathematics in Archaic Corinth: The Origins of the Greek Stadion* (MAPS 206; Philadelphia: American Philosophical Society, 1993). For an extensive discussion of the torch-races and attendant cults, see S. Herbert, "The Torch-Race at Corinth," in *Corinthiaca: Studies in Honor of Darrell A. Amyx* (ed. Mario A. Del Chiaro; Columbia: University of Missouri Press, 1986) 29–35.

[11]Charles K. Williams II and Joan E. Fisher, "Corinth, 1972: The Forum Area," *Hesperia* 42 (1973) 2–12; Charles K. Williams II, J. MacIntosh, and Joan E. Fisher, "Excavation at Corinth, 1973," *Hesperia* 43 (1974) 1–6; and Williams, "Pre-Roman Cults," 79–87.

[12]Ibid., 56–66; and Charles K. Williams II, "Corinth, 1977: Forum Southwest," *Hesperia* 47 (1978) 2–12.

such shrines were also found in the Potters' Quarter,[13] but these were no longer functioning in the second century B.C.E. The importance of hero or heroine cults in the Upper Valley is further shown by several deposits of Hellenistic terracotta figurines, some of which depict horse-and-riders and reclining banqueters;[14] several inscriptions on pots;[15] and twenty-five marble hero reliefs of Hellenistic date.[16] Three more hero reliefs have been found in the area now being dug southeast of the forum.[17] One more shrine, more monumental than the Heröon of the Crossroads but probably also heroic, underlay the Roman Peribolos of Apollo. Originally comprising a small prostyle temple and a covered semicircular altar, it was limited to a baldachino over the temple foundations and a covered altar in the second century B.C.E.[18] Other cult places were buried when the South Stoa was built, primarily the Underground Shrine,[19] which was probably associated with the same graveyard as the Heröon of the Crossroads, and Building I.[20] One of

[13]Charles K. Willliams II, "The City of Corinth and Its Domestic Religion," *Hesperia* 50 (1981) 408–21; A. N. Stillwell, *The Potters' Quarter* (Corinth XV.1; Princeton, N.J.: ASCSA, 1948) 22–28, 31–32, 41–42, 49–53, 72–76; and S. P. Morris and J. K. Papadopoulos, "Phoenicians and the Corinthian Pottery Industry," in *Archäologische Studien in Kontaktzonen der antiken Welt* (ed. Renate Rolle and Karin Schmidt; Göttingen: Vandenhoeck & Ruprecht, 1998) 251–63.

[14]Oscar Broneer, "Hero Cults in the Corinthian Agora," *Hesperia* 11 (1942) 128–61; G. R. Davidson, "A Hellenistic Deposit at Corinth," *Hesperia* 11 (1942) 105–27; and Williams, "Pre-Roman Cults," 36–38.

[15]Ibid., 49–53. A potsherd from the theater bears a graffito reading ΗΡΩΟΣΙΑΡΟΣ (C-28-131).

[16]These are discussed by Williams, ibid., 30–36. See also two reliefs dedicated to Pan and the Nymphs in C. M. Edwards, "Greek Votive Reliefs to Pan and the Nymphs" (Ph.D. diss., New York University, 1985) 771–76, S-2690 and S-1441. In addition, the ivory forearm of a life-size or greater chryselephantine statue was found in a basin at the west end of the racecourse, in fill dated to 146 B.C.E. With what statue or monument this piece was once associated is unfortunately no longer known. See Richard Stillwell, "Excavations at Corinth, 1934–1935," *AJA* 40 (1936) 43–45, figs. 22–25, MF-4366; Kenneth Lapatin, "Pheidias Ἐλεφαντουργός," *AJA* 101 (1997) 665–66, fig. 3; and idem, *Chryselephantine Statuary in the Ancient Mediterranean World* (New York: Oxford University Press, 2001) 129 and 149, no. 44. Lapatin identifies the gender of the piece as female, based on the lack of prominent musculature or veins.

[17]S-2617, S-1997-3, -4.

[18]Compare Richard Stillwell, Robert L. Scranton, and Sarah Elizabeth Freeman, *Architecture* (Corinth I.2; Cambridge, Mass.: ASCSA, 1941) 3, 9: fourth century B.C.E.; and Charles K. Williams II, "Pre-Roman Cults," 13: fifth century B.C.E.

[19]Morgan, "Excavations, 1936–37," 543–45; and Williams, "Pre-Roman Cults," 67–78.

[20]Williams and Fisher, "Corinth, 1972," 151–65. Morgan's so-called Tavern of Aphrodite was subsequently reidentified by Williams as a private house, Building III. See C. H. Morgan, "Investigations at Corinth, 1953—A Tavern of Aphrodite," *Hesperia* 22 (1953) 131–40; Charles K. Williams II and Joan E. Fisher, "Corinth, 1971: Forum Area," *Hesperia* 41 (1972) 173–74; and Williams and Fisher, "Corinth, 1972," 19–27.

these may have been the recipient of a fourth-century B.C.E. bronze statuette dedicated to Artemis Korithos.[21] It is unclear whether any of these cults were transferred to the South Stoa, rebuilt in the open at the new Hellenistic level, or simply abandoned.

Two other shrines, those of Medea's children and Athena Chalinitis, are mentioned by Pausanias (2.3.6–4.5) after the Fountain of Glauke and near the odeum and theater. That the worship of Medea's children existed in Greek times is clear not only from Pausanias, but also from Diodorus Siculus and other sources, commenting on Euripides' *Medea*.[22] The evidence for a Greek cult of Athena Chalinitis is somewhat more tenuous. Pindar (*Ol.* 13.82) mentions Athena Hippia, who gave Bellerophon the bridle by which he was able to capture Pegasos. If this cult can be assumed to be the same as that of Athena Chalinitis ("the bridler"), which is mentioned only by Pausanias, then that cult lay slightly west of the Greek theater.[23]

A number of cults were gathered on the north slope of Acrocorinth, in much the same way that sanctuaries were gathered on the slopes of the Athenian acropolis. Our chief source here is Pausanias,[24] whose account is augmented by excavations. Ascending Acrocorinth, Pausanias mentions possibly four sanctuaries of Isis and Sarapis; an altar to Helios; and temene to Ananke and Bia, Mother of the Gods; the Fates; Demeter and Kore; and Hera Bounaia, as well as a temple to Eilithyia near the Teneatic gate. Excavation of a well at the base of Acrocorinth, to the west of the fountain of Hadji Mustapha, yielded a small marble tripod base that bears an inscription to Isis and Sarapis. Of Hellenistic date, the inscribed base attests to the existence of at least one of these

---

[21]Williams and Fisher, "Corinth, 1971," 153–54, no. 16 (MF-71-51), and plate 23.

[22]Diodoros Siculus 4.55.1–2; Euripides, *Medea* 1379; Parmeniskos, apud schol. Euripides *Medea* 264 [ed. Schwarz]; and Lisle, "Cults of Corinth," 113–14. Scholarship has been divided as to whether the Sanctuary of Hera Akraia was in Corinth or only in Perachora. See B. Menadier, "The Sixth Century B.C. Temple and the Sanctuary and Cult of Hera Akraia, Perachora" (Ph.D. diss., University of Cincinatti, 1995); and Sarah Iles Johnston, "Corinthian Medea and the Cult of Hera Akraia," in *Medea: Essays on Medea in Myth, Literature, Philosophy, and Art* (ed. James J. Clauss and Sarah Iles Johnston; Princeton, N.J.: Princeton University Press, 1997) 44–70.

[23]On Athena, see Williams, "Pre-Roman Cults," 42–43. In 1925–1926 it was thought that this sanctuary had been found. See T. L. Shear, "Excavations at Corinth," *AJA* 29 (1925) 388–91; and idem, "Excavations in the Theater District of Corinth in 1926," *AJA* 30 (1926) 1–6. But recent excavations by Williams east of the theater have exposed remains of Roman buildings. See his essay in this volume (pp. 221–47).

[24]Pausanias 2.4.6–5.4. For a discussion of the topography of Acrocorinth, see Nancy Bookidis and Ronald S. Stroud, *The Sanctuary of Demeter and Kore: Topography and Architecture* (Corinth XVIII.3; Princeton, N.J.: ASCSA, 1997) 4–8.

sanctuaries before the destruction of Corinth and allows us to place it in the flat area at the base of the mountain where the later Canopus probably lay.[25]

Excavations have demonstrated that the sanctuary of Demeter and Kore existed from the eighth century B.C.E. on.[26] Ananke and Bia are found together only here at Corinth and in Pisidia, where they appear with Apollo at the entrance to a Greek oracle.[27] They and the Fates are all sufficiently tied to early Greek mythology to make their Greek origins likely. Ananke appears in some traditions as the mother of the Fates,[28] which may shed some light on her placement near that sanctuary. Moreover, Ananke, Bia, the Fates, and Demeter and Kore all have chthonic connections. Thus, their topographical grouping here makes sense. Indeed, it may be these underworld associations that relegated them to the outskirts of the city. Pausanias states that it was not customary to enter the hieron of Ananke and Bia, nor could one see the cult statues of the Fates or of Demeter and Kore; again, a common regulation, at least, seems to unite those cults. The Mother of the Gods is attested in Classical Athens and in fourth-century B.C.E. Olympia and could well have existed in Hellenistic Corinth. The cult of Helios is less clear. As for Hera Bounaia, her epithet is a Corinthian one, for Pausanias (2.3.10) tells us that the temple was established by Bounos, the son of Hermes and Alkidameia and one of the early rulers of the city.

At the top of Acrocorinth was the sanctuary of Aphrodite, Corinth's city goddess. We know very little about her sanctuary and little about her cult apart from the well-known references to temple prostitutes. Excavations in 1926 at the summit exposed some cuttings and blocks that might belong to a small prostyle Doric temple.[29]

Two other small shrines lay on the outskirts of the north city wall. One was situated near a spring by the Sikyonian Gate at the northwest edge of

---

[25]I-2650. See H. S. Robinson, "Excavations at Corinth," Chronika B1, *ArchDelt* 21 (1966) 139, plate 129c–d. The piece was found in a well, in a stratum dated to the first century C.E. See also Françoise Dunand, *Le culte d'Isis dans le bassin oriental de la Méditerranée* (3 vols.; EPRO 26; Leiden: Brill, 1973) 2:18, with earlier references.

[26]Bookidis and Stroud, *Sanctuary of Demeter*, 15–17, 424–25.

[27]*CIG* 4390.O.

[28]PW, s.v. "Ananke" (Wernicke). Also *LIMC* 1:757–58, s.v. "Ananke" (Simon); and ibid., 2:115–16, s.v. "Bia et Kratos" (Simon).

[29]Carl William Blegen, Oscar Broneer, Richard Stillwell, and Alfred Raymond Bellinger, *Acrocorinth: Excavations in 1926* (Corinth III.1; Cambridge, Mass.: ASCSA, 1930) 1–28. For a discussion of the cult of Aphrodite, see Charles K. Williams II, "Corinth and the Cult of Aphrodite," in *Corinthiaca: Studies in Honor of Darrell A. Amyx* (ed. Mario A. Del Chiaro; Columbia: University of Missouri Press, 1986) 12–24; and the essay by John R. Lanci in this volume (205–20).

the city, present-day Kokkinovrysi. Comprising a stele or shaft for a small statue, and a favissa that chiefly contained figurines of circle dancers, the shrine may have been dedicated to Pan and the Nymphs.[30] Two tall shafts of the fourth or early third century B.C.E., with cuttings for small statues, may belong to a second shrine in the northeast corner of the city.[31]

The picture that emerges from these sources is one of traditional Olympian cults mixed with others that were peculiarly Corinthian.[32] Without specific epithets, Apollo, Asklepios, and Poseidon, or even Zeus Olympios, could have existed in any city. But Athena Chalinitis or Hippia, the bridler, and Hera Bounaia are associated with local heroes. Demeter at Corinth bore the unique cult title of Epoikidia.[33] Hellotis and Kotyto were two Corinthian sisters killed during the return of the Herakleidai, and Medea's connection with the city is all too well known. In addition, various cults of heroes, now nameless, dotted the Classical and Hellenistic city. Indeed, based on the evidence for this period that we have today, local Corinthian cults far exceeded those of the traditional Olympians.

In 146 B.C.E., Corinth, as head of the Achaian league, was destroyed by the Romans under the general Mummius. In the past, because of the literary testimonia, the prevailing view was that the city had been wholly abandoned for 102 years—except for visits from neighbors like the Sikyonians, who simply looted what the Romans had left and dismantled buildings for stone. Since Virginia Grace's work on stamped amphora handles and Williams's excavations in the east and west ends of the forum, we can now speak with some certainty of occupation during this interim period. As seems clear from the excavations, however, this occupation did not resume immediately after

[30]The deposit is as yet unpublished. See Williams, "Corinth and Its Domestic Religion," 409–10. For a reused inscription from the excavation, see N. Robertson, "A Corinthian Inscription Recording Honors at Elis for Corinthian Judges," *Hesperia* 45 (1976) 253–66. It is not clear whether this shrine lasted until 146 B.C.E., although in Williams's opinion, its location by a spring makes this likely. See H. S. Robinson, "Excavations at Corinth," Chronika B1, *ArchDelt* 18 (1963) 77–78; and idem, "American Excavations at Corinth," Chronika B1, *ArchDelt* 19 (1964) 100–2. Robinson interpreted the deposit as a favissa used only once and associated it with a nearby, and undiscovered, shrine. For the plan, see Bookidis, "The Sanctuaries of Corinth," 237, fig. 14.8.

[31]A-70-91, -92. Both are tall slender shafts with a depression in the top for the plinth of a dedication.

[32]Other deities and shrines are attested in literary or epigraphical sources only. These include Dionysos, in whose honor the first dithyrambs were developed in Corinth (Pindar, *Ol.* 13.18–19) and who is attested in the Sanctuary of Demeter and Kore (Bookidis and Stroud, *Sanctuary of Demeter*, 247, 259); Ares (Pindar, *Ol.* 13.23); and a shrine of the Nymphs in which was kept a likeness of the coroplast Butades of Sikyon.

[33]Hesychios, s.v. ἐποικιδίη; and PW 6/1 (1907) 228, s.v. "Epoikidia" (Jessen).

Mummius's attack, for the portable remains (in the form of imported Knidian and Rhodian amphoras, Ionian moulded bowls, and coins) indicate that the reoccupation began after only forty or fifty years of abandonment following the Roman sack.[34] Most recently, the evidence has been summarized by Elizabeth Gebhard and M. W. Dickie.[35] What we know about the sanctuaries can be stated briefly as follows.

The Sacred Spring was abandoned. During this period a well-trafficked road ran diagonally across the middle of the sanctuary. The extent of its use is shown by the wheel ruts that wore down the top of the triglyph retaining wall and adjacent monument base. Furthermore, a wall was built over the south side of the abandoned sanctuary. The wall dates to no earlier than ca. 86 B.C.E., for a Roman republican coin of C. Censorinus was found therein. The wall was dismantled when the forum was built.[36] Similar wheel ruts cut through a part of the Asklepieion, beginning at the northwest corner of the Lerna Square, then passing through the lower gateway and up the ramp south of the temple. A Knidian stamped amphora handle, recovered from the Roman ramp fill, dates to the interim period, but is by itself of little use in positing continuing worship.[37] Finally, in the Sanctuary of Demeter and Kore, a single Roman silver denarius of 106 B.C.E., two West Slope vases, a possible West Slope plate with offset rim, and two Ionian bowls suggest the possibility of interim use.[38] But

[34]Williams, "Corinth 1977," 21–23; Williams and Russell, "Corinth, 1980," 27–29; and Wiseman, "Corinth and Rome I," 494–96.

[35]Elizabeth R. Gebhard and M. W. Dickie, "The View from the Isthmus, ca. 200 to 44 B.C.," in *Corinth: The Centenary, 1896–1996* (ed. Charles K. Williams II and Nancy Bookidis; Corinth XX; Princeton, N.J.: ASCSA, 2003) 261–78.

[36]On the wheelruts, see Williams, "Corinth, 1968," 52, 60–61. A second coin of Censorinus was found in fill that covered the racecourse south of the Sacred Spring. Pottery from that fill, however, dates as late as the first quarter of the first century C.E. (Lot 5805). It is therefore unclear from this deposit whether the racecourse was covered in the interim period or early in the life of the Roman colony. Two distinct layers separate the latest track from the overlying paving (Charles K. Williams II, personal communication). For both coins, see Williams and Fisher, "Corinth, 1970," 22, 35, 45, nos. 181–82, coins 68-1112 and 69-63 respectively.

[37]Roebuck, *Asklepieion,* 82–84. The Knidian stamp is that of Hipparchus Dionysiou Epiphaneus (C-31-383), for which see also V. R. Grace, "Stamped Amphora Handles found in 1931–1932," *Hesperia* 3 (1934) 251, no. 132. For the most recent dating of this official, see idem, "The Middle Stoa Dated by Amphora Stamps," *Hesperia* 54 (1985) 35, period VIA.

[38]Elizabeth G. Pemberton, *The Sanctuary of Demeter and Kore: The Greek Pottery* (Corinth XVIII.1; Princeton, N.J.: ASCSA, 1989) 4, 108, no. 191 (C-65-486); 164, nos. 472–73 (C-65-319, -609); and 163, nos. 462–63 (C-65-303, -647). The coin is published in Nancy Bookidis and J. E. Fisher, "Sanctuary of Demeter and Kore on Acrocorinth. Preliminary Report V: 1971–1973," *Hesperia* 43 (1974) 303, no. 67 (73-530). The issue

Susan Rotroff's recent study of West Slope ware from the Athenian Agora has now raised the date of three of those pieces to before the Mummian attack,[39] leaving the two Ionian bowls, which could belong to this period, and the coin. In the opinion of Ronald Stroud and myself, this does not constitute sufficient evidence to posit resumed cultic activity before the Roman colonization of Corinth, especially since the site lay along one of the routes up Acrocorinth. At the same time, the three pieces do attest to some brief presence.

This abandonment of cult places indicates to me that the so-called squatters cannot have been returning Corinthians. Indeed, they probably were people without previous connections to the Greek city who lacked either the interest or the financial ability to support her cults.[40] These people may have been brought in to serve the interests of Roman exploiters of the land. At the same time, I emphasize again that little evidence for Mummius's destruction has been found anywhere within the city walls of Corinth, despite the graphic accounts of looting and burning preserved in the ancient sources. A stratum of destruction debris, perhaps owing to Mummius, has been found in the area of the racecourse, as well as in the columnar hall at the west end of the Upper Valley,[41] but for the most part what excavations have recovered is "Mummian clean-up": Hellenistic ceramic, architectural, and other debris, mixed in with Early Roman wares, primarily in the South Stoa wells and around the Lechaion Road Basilica, is thought to represent removal of the destruction debris during the early phases of the Roman colony.[42] Virtually

---

is that of Q. Lutatius Cerco, possibly minted in Sicily. See also Bookidis and Stroud, *The Sanctuary of Demeter and Kore*, 434.

[39]Susan I. Rotroff, *Hellenistic Pottery: Athenian and Imported Wheelmade Table Ware and Related Material* (Agora XXIX; Princeton, N.J.: ASCSA, 1997) 64 (dating of cross-hatching as early as 240 B.C.E.), 122 (West Slope amphoras).

[40]On the issue of whether some Corinthians might have come back to the city during the interim period, Wiseman ("Corinth and Rome I," 493–94, 496) notes that Cicero (*Tusc. disp.* 3.22.53) refers to "Corinthians" who were presumably living there ca. 79–77 B.C. and suggests that some survivors and their descendants returned. M. Piérart ("Panthéon et hellénisation dans la colonie romaine de Corinth: la 'redécouverte' du culte de Palaimon à l'Isthme," *Kernos* 11 [1998] 85) argues that Cicero met "Corinthians" elsewhere, in Argos, for example. "Corinthians" also could simply have meant people living at Corinth. In addition, several inscriptions testify to the presence of Corinthians elsewhere.

[41]Williams and Russell, "Corinth, 1980," esp. 27; and Charles K. Williams II, "Corinth, 1976: Forum Southwest," *Hesperia* 46 (1977) 53–58.

[42]See, for example, G. Roger Edwards, *Corinthian Hellenistic Pottery* (Corinth VII.3; Princeton, N.J.: ASCSA, 1975) 189–90. For quarry filling beyond the northwest corner of Temple E, see J. K. Anderson, "Corinth: Temple E Northwest, Preliminary Report, 1965," *Hesperia* 36 (1967) 2.

all other assumed instances of vandalism and destruction must be regarded as hypothetical, except for the possible dismantling of stretches of the city wall.[43] As a result, much of Greek Corinth may still have been standing in some form or other. Certainly, no evidence of destruction was found in the Sanctuary of Demeter and Kore.

CULTS OF ROMAN CORINTH

In or around 44 B.C.E., the new colony of *Laus Iulia Corinthiensis* was established. We have limited information about this event, apart from the fact that a certain number of freedmen and veterans were sent out from Rome.[44] Therefore, in attempting to reconstruct the evidence for civic religion in the early colony, we are faced with several problems. First, as with Hellenistic Corinth, both literary and epigraphical resources for the Roman period are few, and the inscriptions are quite fragmentary. As a result, we are forced to turn to Pausanias, who came to Corinth 212 years after its foundation, to try to determine what might have existed in the first century C.E. Second, most of the forum was excavated early in the twentieth century. Thus, precise stratigraphic, ceramic, and numismatic evidence that could have helped to date monuments has been lost. Without this documentation, buildings must be dated individually on the basis of architectural details; or relatively, as Williams has shown with Temples F and G; or according to a scholar's concept of the way in which the colony must have developed. While reconstructions of an Augustan-period forum have been frequently and indeed reasonably proposed, Kathleen Slane has observed that there is a dearth of pre-Claudian pottery in the forum. As a result, I have generally avoided tackling the issue of chronology. At the same time, in dealing with those cults that have possible Greek connections, I have tried to concentrate on those clearly attested in the first century C.E. Finally, I have hesitated to use the word "civic" in some cases because of the lack of a local calendar for the Roman colony.

I begin with the fact that the new Roman city of Corinth was founded by a number of freedmen and some veterans who were sent out from Rome. The official language of the city was Latin. At the same time, a certain number of

---

[43]Rhys Carpenter and Antoine Bon, *The Defenses of Acrocorinth and the Lower Town* (Corinth III.2; Cambridge, Mass.: ASCSA, 1936) 126.

[44]Wiseman, "Corinth and Rome I," 497–500; and A. J. S. Spawforth, "Roman Corinth: the Formation of a Colonial Elite," in *Roman Onomastics in the Greek East: Social and Political Aspects* (ed. A. D. Rizakis; Μελετήματα 21; Athens: Research Center for Greek and Roman Antiquity; Paris: de Boccard, 1996) 167–82.

graffiti on the undersides of first-century C.E. pottery show that there was a substructure of Greek that, by the time of Hadrian, became, with encouragement, a dominant element. The structure and organization of the early city was Roman. Some idea of what this must have been is provided by the *lex coloniae genitivae*, the statute that provided for the foundation of the Caesarian colony of Urso in Spain. With regard to the colony's cults, it tells us that within ten days of the foundation, the *duoviri* and *decuriones* must agree on the festivals and sacrifices to be celebrated. It also specifies how contracts are to be allotted for organizing sacrifices and spectacles and what money is to be paid by whom.[45] Presumably, the land allotted to civic sanctuaries would also have been defined at or by this time. Until the voting mechanism was in place, the first officials and priests would have been brought from Rome, and a sacred calendar established. As was the case in Rome, I assume that other cults could gradually be added to the calendar.

Organized planning is clearly evident at Corinth. The Upper Lechaion Valley was picked as the site for the administrative center, perhaps to take advantage of the standing South Stoa. It was leveled and landscaped into a two-tier forum in the Augustan period, as sherds from the cement surface under the pavement suggested to the early excavators.[46] All of the earlier monuments between the South Stoa and the Northwest Stoa were covered over, as was the Hellenistic racecourse. On the Lechaion Road, the hero shrine north of Peirene was also covered, and for a short period a bronze foundry existed just to the northeast.[47] The Romans then laid out their cults around the periphery of the lower forum. As Williams has shown by reading the route of Pausanias counterclockwise, the Roman temples were located as follows:[48] at

---

[45]M. H. Crawford, ed., *Roman Statutes* (2 vols.; London: Institute of Classical Studies, 1996) 1:393–454, no. 25. Those articles dealing with religion are LXIIII, establishment of cults; LXV, money collected from penalties to be used for sacrifices; LXVI–LXVIII, prerogatives of pontiffs and augurs; LXIX, allotment of contracts for sacrifices and religious functions; LXX–LXXI, organization of spectacles for Jupiter, Juno, Minerva, and the gods and goddesses; and LXXII, money brought into a sanctuary to be spent there.

[46]Robert L. Scranton, *Monuments in the Lower Agora and North of the Archaic Temple* (Corinth I.3; Princeton, N.J.: ASCSA, 1951) 148–49. The marble paving was later. Although not closely datable, the pottery under the paving bedding dates to at least the first or second quarter of the first century C.E. (lot 5805).

[47]Stillwell et al., *Architecture,* 27–31.

[48]Charles K. Williams II and Joan E. Fisher, "Corinth, 1974: Forum Southwest," *Hesperia* 44 (1975) 25–29. A useful chart of the various identifications of these buildings can be found in Wiseman, "Corinth and Rome I," 540–41, table 4. For the monuments of the forum, see Scranton, *Monuments.*

the west end from north to south are Temple D, dedicated to Tyche / Fortuna;[49] an aedicula to all the gods and a fountain of Poseidon / Neptune,[50] both built by Cn. Babbius Philinus; Temple G, dedicated to Clarion Apollo, progenitor of Augustus; and Temple F, dedicated to Venus, mother of the colony and of the Roman nation. All of the small temples are proper Roman podium-style buildings that were fronted by steps on which stood an altar.[51] All three cults, moreover, had close ties to the *gens Iulia* and to Rome. At the west end of the south side of the forum lies the three-room temple to Hermes / Mercury the market god, a head of whom was found nearby. Unlike the podium temples, this is flush with the forum. In her unpublished dissertation, Mary Walbank sees in this building a further connection with Augustus, who, after Actium, identified himself with Mercury as a god of peace.[52] In the center of the forum is a large platform for an early altar that was paved over in the time of Claudius.[53] On the north side of the forum is a monopteros that may have been dedicated to either Artemis / Diana or Dionysos / Bacchus. Suggestive of the latter may be the over life-size marble head of Dionysos found nearby, as well as a base for a Roman tripod dedication set up a short distance to the southeast over the Classical triglyph wall of the Sacred Spring.[54] It is also useful to remember Marc Antony's identification with that deity.[55] The monopteros was constructed directly over the south side of the apsidal building located near the Sacred Spring; a segment of the foundation of the apsidal building was removed in the process, thus raising a question

---

[49]For a discussion of the cult and associated sculpture, see C. M. Edwards, "Tyche at Corinth," *Hesperia* 59 (1990) 529–42.

[50]Charles K. Williams II, "A Re-Evaluation of Temple E and the West End of the Forum of Corinth," in *The Greek Renaissance in the Roman Empire: Papers from the Tenth British Museum Classical Colloquium* (ed. Susan Walker and Averil Cameron; BICSSup 55; London: University of London, 1989) 158–59, plates 60–62.

[51]Charles K. Williams II, "The Refounding of Roman Corinth: Some Roman Religious Attitudes," in *Roman Architecture in the Greek World* (ed. Sarah Macready and F. H. Thompson; Society of Antiquaries of London: Occasional Papers, n.s. 10; London: Society of Antiquaries of London, 1987) 26.

[52]Mary E. Hoskins Walbank, "The Nature and Development of Roman Corinth to the End of the Antonine Period" (Ph.D. diss., Open University, London, 1986) 170–71.

[53]Scranton, *Monuments*, 139–41.

[54]For the head, see Franklin P. Johnson, *Sculpture, 1896–1923* (Corinth IX; Cambridge, Mass.: ASCSA, 1931) 31–32, no. 25 (S-194). The tripod base is published in L. T. Shoe, "The Roman Ionic Base in Corinth," in *Essays in Memory of Karl Lehmann* (ed. Lucy F. Sandler; New York: Institute of Fine Arts, New York University, 1964) 302–3, ill. 3, figs. 2–3; and Charles K. Williams II, "Corinth, 1969: Forum Area," *Hesperia* 39 (1970) 28–30, fig. 8.

[55]Plutarch, *Antonius*, 14.3, 16.3, 60.2–3, 75.3.

of intentional continuity between the apsidal building and the monopteros. Without certain identification of the cult, the issue cannot be settled. My own feeling, however, is that the continuity was unintentional since all other cult places beneath the forum were filled in.[56] The site of the monopteros was relegated slightly to the north of the Northwest Stoa and northwest of the North Basilica in an area where space was limited. In addition, the natural ground level here was high.

Each of these temples is small and opens directly onto the forum without any enclosing temenos. Three other temples differ from these. The first is the Archaic temple on the hill north of the forum, which I argued above was associated with Apollo in Hellenistic Corinth. That it continued to be associated with Apollo in the Roman period is attested by Pausanias, who mentions it as he leaves the forum by the Sikyonian Road (2.3.6). No later than the time of Claudius, the apparently intact interior columns were removed and transferred to the southwest corner of the forum. Whether the cella thereafter retained its division into two chambers is unclear. The foundations of a base, now visible in the smaller western chamber, have been dated both to the original building as well as to its Roman reconstruction. The roof was also redone.[57] At this time the orientation of the building may have shifted to the west, but this must remain speculative, for the arrangement of the Roman interior is no longer apparent. Colonnades framed the north and south sides of the large temenos, and an entrance, possibly axial, was placed on the west side.

West of the temple and across the street stood Temple C, a tetrastyle prostyle Doric temple in the Greek style, lacking a podium but within a sizeable colonnaded peribolos. Passed over by Pausanias without mention, the temple remains unidentified. Scranton thought that the Fountain of Glauke could be accessed from its peribolos, and he therefore associated the two structures with the cult of Medea's children.[58] But Williams has observed that the wall separating the two was unbroken. Moreover, from Pausanias it is clear that the monument to Medea's children lay further to the northwest along the Sikyon Road.

---

[56]Williams (Charles K. Williams II and Orestes H. Zervos, "Excavations at Corinth, 1989: The Temenos of Temple E," *Hesperia* 59 [1990] 351–56) had earlier suggested that there may have been a direct relation between the structures, but subsequently rejected this opinion ("Pre-Roman Cults," 27). The importance of this building is shown by the fact that in the second century C.E., when the Northwest Shops were built, the monopteros was dismantled and replaced by a similar structure a short distance to the southeast; see Hill, *The Springs*, 151–52.

[57]Robinson, "Excavations: Temple Hill," 237–38. For Roman tiles stamped PONT, see W. Dörpfeld, "Der Tempel in Korinth," *AM* 11 (1886) 297–308, esp. 304, plate VIII.

[58]The temple is discussed in Scranton, *Monuments*, 131–65.

Abutting the south side of Temple C is the temenos of Temple E, which dominates the west side of the forum.[59] Williams has restored at least two, and possibly three, successive temples. The first was a peripteral Doric temple with a three-stepped crepidoma in the Greek style, dating no earlier than the reign of Augustus and no later than that of Claudius. Its reconstruction is based on impressions of Doric columns and capitals, larger than any other structure in Corinth, that were preserved in the concrete podium of the later temple.[60] This Doric temple was replaced sometime after the earthquake in the 70s C.E. by a Roman-style podium temple with Corinthian peristyle and pedimental sculpture that depicts, among other figures, Roma, Apollo, and Tyche/Fortuna.[61] Set in a large temenos, the precinct was enclosed by a colonnade on all four sides.[62] The area enclosed by the peristyle was as wide as the lower forum and nearly two-thirds its length. Clearly, this was a very important temple, but its identification is not certain. Standing in the middle of the forum, Pausanias (2.2.3) states that above or beyond it (ὑπέρ) is the temple of Octavia. Logically, this should be Temple E. Yet Octavia, sister of Augustus and wife of Antony, would not have been honored in such a way. Two opinions are current: Freeman, Walbank,[63] Ward-Perkins,[64] and Torelli[65] assume that Pausanias is mistaken and reidentify the temple as a Capitolium,

[59]The original publication is Stillwell et al., *Architecture,* 166–236.

[60]Williams, "A Re-Evaluation of Temple E," 156–62. Williams bases his identification of this structure as a low, Greek-style temple on the absence of a cement core abutting the interior face of the south foundation course of this building (personal communication).

[61]Williams posits two possible phases here: the marble building standing today he would place in the second century C.E., perhaps in the time of Antoninus Pius. This, however, may replace an earlier Corinthian stage built of limestone, from which some of the capitals are preserved. For the sculptures, see Stillwell et al., *Architecture,* 210–30, and, in particular, 216, no. 5 (S-1540), and 221, no. 17 (S-1504); and Johnson, *Sculpture,* 21–22, no. 11 (S-827, here labeled "Enyo?").

[62]In actuality, the earlier peribolos consisted of colonnades on three sides because the Doric temple was built up against the back wall. In the later rebuilding, the west peribolos was pulled back, leaving the temple freestanding. For the discovery of the southern side, see Williams and Zervos, "Excavations at Corinth, 1989," 326–31.

[63]Mary E. Hoskins Walbank, "Pausanias, Octavia and Temple E at Corinth," *BSA* 84 (1989) 361–94.

[64]J. B. Ward-Perkins, *Roman Imperial Architecture* (New Haven, Conn.: Yale University Press, 1981) 256–57: "probably to be identified as the Capitolium."

[65]Domenico Musti and Mario Torelli, eds., *Pausania. Guida della Grecia II* (Milan: Fondazione Lorenzo Valla/Mondadori, 1986) 222. Torelli places the Temple of Octavia east of the Julian Basilica.

which, it is argued, should have been of prime importance to the early colony.[66] Dinsmoor,[67] Roux,[68] Wiseman,[69] and Williams[70] assume that Pausanias is essentially right, but they associate the temple with the imperial cult.

As Mary Walbank has demonstrated, evidence for the imperial cult in first-century C.E. Corinth is considerable.[71] The well-known group of Julio-Claudian portraits, assembled in the Julian Basilica at the east end of the forum, together with two fragments of decorated small altars, gives some indication of cult in that building, possibly in the form of sacrifices to the Genius Augusti.[72] At least sixty-two inscriptions make reference to the imperial cult, beginning with an altar to the Divus Iulius. A statue in the middle of the forum was erected by the Augustales to the Divus Augustus. Dedications to the Lares Augusti, the Genius Augusti, Saturnus Augustus, and subsidiary cults such as Providentia Augusti, Salus Publica, and Victoria Britannica were also all related to the imperial cult. There are also epigraphical references to the *flamen divi Iulii* and the *flamen Augusti*, as well as to the various agonothetes responsible for both the Isthmian and Caesarean games. An interesting dedicatory inscription on an Ionic epistyle frieze block, found roughly on the east side of the modern village square, mentions an *aedes* and statue of Apollo Augustus, as well as ten shops or *tabernae*. Smaller in size than an epistyle from Temple G,[73] the block could have been part of a small shrine that stood within a market complex, rather like the macellum at Pompeii.[74]

[66]Against this view, J. Rufus Fears ("The Cult of Jupiter and Roman Imperial Ideology," *ANRW* II.17.1 [1981] 59–60) argues that the Capitoline cult was relatively unimportant under Augustus.

[67]Dinsmoor, "Largest Temple," 115 n. 22.

[68]Georges Roux, *Pausanias en Corinthie (Livre II, 1 à 15): texte, traduction, commentaire archéologique et topographique* (Paris: Belles Lettres, 1958) 112–16, 126–27.

[69]Wiseman, "Corinth and Rome I," 522.

[70]Williams, "Re-Evaluation of Temple E," 156–62.

[71]The evidence is presented in Mary E. Hoskins Walbank, "Evidence for the Imperial Cult in Julio-Claudian Corinth," in *Subject and Ruler: The Cult of the Ruling Power in Classical Antiquity* (ed. Alastair Small; JRASup 17; Ann Arbor, Mich.: Journal of Roman Archaeology, 1996) 201–14.

[72]The possible altar blocks appear in Johnson, *Sculpture,* 145–46, nos. 314–15. The sculptures are published in John Pollini, *The Portraiture of Gaius and Lucius Caesar* (New York: Fordham University Press, 1987).

[73]A. B. West, *Latin Inscriptions, 1896–1926* (Corinth VIII.2; Cambridge, Mass.: ASCSA, 1931) 94–95, no. 120 (I-37) = *CIL* 3:534. The height of the block is 0.50 m as compared with 0.69 m for the height of a similar block from Temple G.

[74]August Mau, *Pompeii: Its Life and Art* (rev. ed., 1899, trans. Francis W. Kellsey; repr., New Rochelle, N.Y.: Caratzas Bros., 1982) 94–103; and Lawrence Richardson Jr., *Pompeii: An Architectural History* (Baltimore, Md.: Johns Hopkins University Press, 1988) 198–202, fig. 32.

Because of this association of Augustus with Apollo, Walbank would place the imperial cult in the Temple of Apollo. I forego a discussion of this important issue, which cannot be resolved without substantive evidence. My only suggestion would be to look at the sculpture from the pediment of Temple E to see whether Apollo, Roma, and Tyche / Fortuna might not make more sense on a temple dedicated to Augustus rather than on one dedicated to the Capitoline Triad.[75] According to this interpretation, Apollo would then remain alone in his Archaic temple.

To these major civic cults can be added a shrine in the center of the East Central Shops,[76] and a long building in the southwest corner of the forum, probably to be associated with an inscribed Ionic epistyle restored to read *Sacerdos Genii Coloniae*.[77] One further building across the street to the west from this is of considerable interest: the so-called Cellar Building, dating to the earliest days of the colony. A bronze couch fulcrum and fine table wares found within it indicate that meals were taken there.[78] But standing as it does to one side of the forum yet outside of all the temene, it probably served a Roman organization or society of some sort.

How were these civic cult places used? Again, without literary or epigraphical sources, only general comments are possible. Insofar as the material remains can be interpreted, the cults in the forum are nearly all closely tied to the Roman state. Therefore, we can assume that ceremonies and sacrifices pertaining to the emperor and to state cults were performed at the same time and in the same way as in Rome. But given the different sizes of the temples and their different spatial allotments, these celebrations must have taken different forms. Since the small temples at the west end were located in close proximity and without temene, I presume that sacrifices, led by state-appointed priests and augurs, were carried out periodically at the small altars that must have stood on the steps before each of these buildings, and

---

[75]The other issue, of course, is the building's architectural form. If Williams is correct in his restoration of the earliest phase of Temple E, then a low-set, Doric peripteral temple would hardly suit the Capitoline Triad. Even the later peripteral plan, although now with Corinthian columns, is not customary for Capitolia. See I. M. Barton, "Capitoline Temples in Italy and the Provinces (Especially Africa)," *ANRW* II.12.1 (1982) 259–342.

[76]Scranton, *Monuments,* 114–15.

[77]For the building, the so-called Long Neronian or Rectangular Building, see Charles K. Williams II and Joan E. Fisher, "Corinth, 1975: Forum Southwest," *Hesperia* 45 (1976) 127–35. The inscription was published by T. R. Martin, "Inscriptions at Corinth," *Hesperia* 46 (1977) 180–83.

[78]Williams, "Corinth, 1976," 58–62. The pottery is published in K. S. Wright, "A Tiberian Pottery Deposit from Corinth," *Hesperia* 49 (1980) 135–77. The couch fulcrum appears in C. C. Mattusch, "Corinthian Metalworking: An Inlaid Fulcrum Panel," *Hesperia* 60 (1991) 525–28.

that public attendance was not necessary. The larger temene suggest that larger public gatherings were held within them, together with more elaborate sacrifices and processions. The role of communal dining in these sanctuaries is unattested. That consumption of the sacrifice did take place in imperial Rome has been convincingly argued by J. Sheid, and it should be expected here, too.[79] Nevertheless, facilities for such dining do not seem to be preserved within the temene that have been fully excavated, unless a room with an atrium at the northwest corner of the temenos of Temple E served such a purpose for a small group.[80] At the same time, elaborate spectacles and games were also sponsored in the theater, in the amphitheater at the east end of the city, and possibly in the forum, and at these assemblies food may have been distributed to the populus.[81] In 1985, Williams excavated two buildings by

[79]See J. Scheid, "Sacrifice et banquet à Rome: Quelques problèmes," *MEFRA* 97 (1985) 193–206. In addition, Robert Schilling ("Le sanctuaire de Venus près de Casinum," in *Perennitas: Studi in onore di Angelo Brelich* [Rome: Edizioni dell'Ateneo, 1980] 445–51) cites evidence for kitchens in a number of Italian sanctuaries.

[80]The room was partially excavated in 1933 by Sterling Dow, and further explored in 1965 by J. K. Anderson. It has never been published. For a plan and brief notice, see Anderson, "Corinth: Temple E," 1–3; and Robinson, "Excavations [1966]," 135, plan 1. Based on the quarry fill over which it was built, it should date no earlier than the 30s C.E. In 1933, several inscriptions were found in the room, including a dedication to the deified Augusta or Livia from the time of Claudius (Kent, *Inscriptions,* 33, no. 55 [I-1282]), as well as an under life-size head of Dionysos (S-1669) and a colossal finger.

[81]On the subject of large-scale public feasting, see J. H. D'Arms, "P. Lucilius Gamala's Feasts for the Ostians and Their Roman Models," *JRA* 13 (2000) 192–200. According to D'Arms and others, the practice did not begin until Julius Caesar, who used it to further his political aims. The subject of sacrificial meat in the Roman period is one that is near and dear to Pauline scholars because of Paul's comments on the subject (1 Corinthians 8 and 10). See H. J. Cadbury, "The Macellum at Corinth," *JBL* 53 (1934) 134–41; M. Isenberg, "The Sale of Sacrificial Meat," *CP* 70 (1975) 271–73; and Wendell L. Willis, *Idol Meat in Corinth: The Pauline Argument in 1 Corinthians 8 and 10* (SBLDS 68; Chico, Ca.: Scholars, 1985). Regrettably, no architectural setting for ritual dining was found in the Roman-period sanctuary of Demeter and Kore. The abundance of domestic and table pottery found, together with transport/storage amphoras and a few terracotta grills, suggest that there may have been dining at the site, but if so, it is not clear where it took place. The existence of butcher shops in the Roman period seems to be in contrast to the lack of them in Greek times. A quick review of the Greek words for butcher or butcher shop in Liddell and Scott (κρεοθέτης, κρεοποιός, κρεοπωλέω, κρεοπώλης, or κρεοπώλις) produces no examples of pre-Roman date. This subject, however, needs to be examined more thoroughly. See also n. 77, above; and on Greek sacrificial practice, M. H. Jameson, "Sacrifice and Animal Husbandry in Classical Greece," in *Pastoral Economies in Classical Antiquity* (ed. C. R. Whittaker; PCPSSup 14; Cambridge: Cambridge Philological Society, 1988); and Guy Berthiaume, *Les rôles du mágeiros: étude sur la boucherie, la cuisine, et le sacrifice dans la Grèce ancienne* (Mnemosyne 70; Leiden: Brill, 1982). Two market sites have been identified in Corinth,

the theater where food was clearly prepared in ovens and served up or sold. In one of these he found over 176 kg of butchered animal bones, chiefly goat, with some cattle and less pig, that could well be the remnants of such a public celebration.[82]

If we turn now to the cults outside the forum, the remains are less homogeneous. At least four cults are attested in the first century C.E., three of which had certainly existed in the Greek city.[83] One of the earliest in the Roman city is that of Asklepios/Asculapius, which was re-established in its Hellenistic temenos.[84] The Hellenistic temple was repaired by Marcus Antonius Milesius, whose name was inscribed on the epistyle and later erased. At some stage, access to the lower temenos was severely restricted by the construction of cross-walls in the ramp. Although the first priest may have come from Rome, Gaius Vibius Euelpistos, honored in the second century as physician and priest, was probably a native of the colony.[85]

Four inscriptions, including one of Augustan date, were set up in the forum in honor of the *theocolus* of Jupiter Capitolinus, while a fragment of a fifth

---

both along the Lechaion Road. One may have underlain the Peribolos of Apollo (Stillwell et al., *Architecture*, 32–38, although the market is not so identified there). With it has been associated a set of inscriptions referring to the macellum (West, *Latin Inscriptions*, 100–2, no. 124). The second market site lay in the so-called hemicycle, further down the road to the west (Stillwell et al., *Architecture*, 142–47). Here was found a second set of inscriptions referring to the Macellum Piscarium (West, *Latin Inscriptions*, 103–4, no. 125).

[82]Charles K. Williams II and Orestes H. Zervos, "Corinth, 1985: East of the Theater," *Hesperia* 55 (1986) 132, 136–37, 146; and D. S. Reese, "A Bone Assemblage at Corinth of the Second Century after Christ," *Hesperia* 56 (1987) 255–74.

[83]Lisle ("Cults of Corinth," 168) lists seventeen cults that survived the interim break. Of those cited by Lisle, three—Poseidon, Palaimon, and Artemis—are attested at Isthmia and therefore not included here, and three—Ares, Helios and Nike—have no clear Greek prototypes. Although Dionysos is attested together with Demeter and Kore in the Acrocorinth sanctuary, to date no evidence has been found for him in the center of the city. The Sanctuary of Hera Akraia at Perachora did not continue into the Roman period. Hercules may appear in the late-second-century temple built to Commodus; the date of the temenos to Bellerophon, mentioned by Pausanias (2.2.4), is uncertain.

[84]It should be noted that, in addition to Pausanias's citation, the deity's name appears only on two second-century C.E. inscriptions written in Greek. The Greek name of the deity is used in both inscriptions.

[85]Roebuck, *Asklepieion*, 39, 77–82, 90–91. According to Roebuck, although the colonnades surrounding the lower area were not rebuilt by the Romans, the court was still in use. Pottery overlying the floor was Late Roman in date. Presumably, once the ramp building was built, restricted access was through the abaton building, or along the city wall. See ibid., 155. The inscription is published in ibid., 156–57 (I-1035). Dedications of Roman date are confined to one more fragment of a dedicatory inscription (ibid., 156 [I-1040]), and several large-scale statues and small-scale statuettes (ibid., 145, nos. 4–12).

had been built into a medieval grave on top of Temple E.[86] Pausanias (2.4.5) mentions one temple to Zeus Capitolius or Koryphaios after the theater and before the Asklepieion. Two finds from the excavations of the Asklepieion suggest that it lay close by, perhaps where the gymnasium has been identified.[87] One is a head of Zeus/Jupiter from a herm, and the other is a neo-Attic relief with an enthroned Zeus, belonging to a statue base.[88] Less clear is whether Jupiter Capitolinus and Greek Zeus Olympios were served by one and the same cult in the same place. It is curious, however, that the Greek term (θεοκόλος) is used for Jupiter's priest in the Roman period.[89]

A third sanctuary is that of Demeter and Kore. Here evidence for the date of the foundation of the cult is less definite, for pottery and lamps are at odds with coins: the pottery and lamps suggest a date no earlier than ca. 50 c.e., while the coins indicate the time of Augustus.[90] Once again, worship was established in the Hellenistic temenos, respecting the same terraces, and initially using still-standing buildings. Modifications were made to the layout, however, and I will discuss them below.

The fourth sanctuary is that of Aphrodite/Venus on Acrocorinth which, like the Asklepieion, must have been revived immediately, for a *naidion* is mentioned by Strabo (8.6.21), who visited in 29 B.C.E.[91] In the time of Pausanias, the cult statue group consisted of Aphrodite armed (Oplismene), Helios, and Eros with a bow. A marble head of Eros found near Upper Peirene might

[86]Kent, *Inscriptions*, nos. 152 (I-1267), 69–70; 194 (I-1435), 86–87; 196 (I-1443), 87–88; and 198 (I-1411), 88. The fragmentary inscription is no. 195 (I-1171), 87.

[87]Against those who would suggest that Pausanias was looking back toward Temple E when he mentioned this temple, Williams has argued persuasively that Temple E would not have been visible at this point. Pausanias's mention of the temple in a sequence of monuments on the terrace below the forum makes its placement there the more logical one.

[88]The relief appears in Roebuck, *Asklepieion*, 145, no. 139 (S-1440); and Olga Palagia, "Meaning and Narrative Techniques in Statue-Bases of the Pheidian Circle," in *Work and Image in Ancient Greece* (ed. N. Keith Rutter and Brian A. Sparkes; Edinburgh: Edinburgh University Press, 2000) 73, fig. 12. It was built into a Byzantine wall at the east side of the temenos. For the herm, which was actually found south of the Asklepieion, see J. DeWaele, "The Sanctuary of Asklepios and Hygieia at Corinth," *AJA* 37 (1933) 439; and Edward Capps, Jr., "Pergamene Influence at Corinth," *Hesperia* 7 (1938) 544–45. For references to the temple of Zeus Olympios, see n. 8, above.

[89]The title is best known at Olympia, but it is also used in other parts of the Greek Mainland, chiefly in the Greek period. See PW, s.v. "theokolos" (L. Ziehen); and Walbank, "Pausanias, Octavia and Temple E at Corinth," 383.

[90]For the evidence see Bookidis and Stroud, *Sanctuary of Demeter*, 272–75, 435. In point of fact, there is some evidence for pottery before the second half of the first century C.E.

[91]Interestingly, Strabo (8.6.21, 8.6.23) twice refers to Corinth being restored again.

be from that group.[92] Coins, a marble statuette from southeast of the forum, a wall painting from east of the theater, and two second-century C.E. lamps all reproduce an identical image of Aphrodite: standing semi-nude, and using a shield as a mirror.[93] If this image is that of the cult statue, then her association with prostitution on Acrocorinth seems a thing of the past.[94]

As for the rest, we are left with the testimony of Pausanias: the Mnema of Medea's children; Athena Chalinitis; Sarapis and Isis; Helios; Ananke and Bia, the Mother of the Gods; the Fates; and Eilithyia. If I am correct in assuming that most of these had Greek sources, it may be that they were re-established early on, but it is also possible that they were new cults that were only added gradually as Greek elements in the city became more pronounced.

The five cults of Apollo, Asklepios/Asculapius, Zeus/Jupiter, Aphrodite/ Venus, and Demeter/Ceres and Kore/Proserpina, which are attested early, can all arguably be derived from Rome. They were cults that had been recognized by the Romans and incorporated into their own worship at a time already in the past. In addition, Asculapius and Ceres and Proserpina would have been of considerable importance for the well-being of the colony. Having been a canonical sanctuary with temple, altar, and columnar peribolos in the Hellenistic period, the Asklepieion must have looked familiar to the new colonists, and they therefore easily reused the existing buildings.

The plan of the sanctuary of Demeter and Kore, however, had to be altered. There was no canonical temple in the Greek sanctuary;[95] sacrifices were made in a deep pit set some distance from the temple,[96] and the dining halls were also unsuited to Roman practice.[97] Here, therefore, major changes were brought about, especially after the earthquake in the 70s C.E.[98] Canonical small prostyle temples were built, which might even have resembled podium temples when seen from below;[99] the small theater for initiates was covered

---

[92]S-1320, unpublished.

[93]For a discussion of the type, see Williams, "Corinth and the Cult of Aphrodite."

[94]See the essay by Charles K. Williams in this volume (pp. 221–47).

[95]The Hellenistic candidate for a temple is Building S-T:16–17 (Bookidis and Stroud, *Sanctuary of Demeter,* 267–71).

[96]See the discussion of Pit B in ibid., 243–45, although it is possible that this had been filled in by the middle of the third century B.C.E.

[97]For these see ibid., esp. 393–420.

[98]Donald Engels (*Roman Corinth: An Alternative Model for the Classical City* [Chicago: University of Chicago Press, 1990] 94–95) incorrectly states that the sanctuary suffered heavy damage from neglect and theft of building materials. There is little evidence for or against this idea.

[99]Bookidis and Stroud, *Sanctuary of Demeter,* 337–71.

by a monumental staircase.[100] The customary votive offerings of miniature pottery and figurines were replaced by occasional larger-scale honorific statues and, for a limited period, the thymiaterion.[101] The dining rooms that had covered the hillside were abandoned. Only one Hellenistic dining room was refurbished as a cult place for the deposition of curse tablets in the last quarter of the first century C.E.[102] Lying below the main Middle Terrace, this building may have been a part of the sanctuary or it may have been a separate one. Once introduced, the custom of depositing curse tablets continued to be practiced there for over one hundred years.

A question that has been raised by Barbette Spaeth and considered by myself is whether the cult was the same in both the Greek and the Roman periods. Three Roman temples certainly suggest the cults of Ceres, Liber, and Libera. But in my opinion, four points argue against this. One is the lack of evidence for this triad in Greece and the Eastern Mediterranean. A second is the discovery in the central temple of a curse tablet of the late first or second century C.E., addressed to Lady Demeter.[103] A third is the occurrence of the name "Neotera" in a mosaic inscription of the second or early third century, which is paralleled at Eleusis as an epithet of Persephone.[104] A fourth is the existence of the cult of Demeter and Kore together with Dionysos, Eueteria, Artemis, and Kore in the Sacred Glen at Isthmia.[105] In addition, the name of Persephone in its Latin form of Proserpina occurs on a new bilingual

[100]For the staircase, see ibid., 371–78.

[101]Ibid., 435; and Kathleen W. Slane, *The Sanctuary of Demeter and Kore: The Roman Pottery and Lamps* (Corinth XVIII.2; Princeton, N.J.: ASCSA, 1990) 64–71. On the paucity of Roman figurines, see Gloria S. Merker, *The Sanctuary of Demeter and Kore: Terracotta Figurines of the Classical, Hellenistic and Roman Periods* (Corinth XVIII.4; Princeton, N.J.: ASCSA, 2000) 311–19. Of the more than 24,000 fragments of figurines found in the sanctuary, only 29 could be identified as Roman. Engels (*Roman Corinth*, 101) wrongly states that "the small shrine was especially popular among the poor, as is shown by the quantities of inexpensive votive offerings found in Roman deposits." The offerings to which he refers are of Archaic to Hellenistic date, and the sanctuary is not small.

[102]The Building of the Tablets, in Bookidis and Stroud, *Sanctuary of Demeter,* 277–91.

[103]The curse tablets will be published by Ronald S. Stroud. This tablet was found in a late context over the temple but was, quite likely, disturbed from its original place of deposition in or around the temple. In the destruction and post-destruction levels of the temple was a considerable amount of earlier material, some of which directly joined with pottery from the foundation fills or on the floor of the temple.

[104]Bookidis and Stroud, *Sanctuary of Demeter,* 362–66.

[105]See Oscar Broneer, *Isthmia: Topography and Architecture* (Isthmia 2; Princeton, N.J.: ASCSA, 1973) 113–16. The names of the deities are as given in the inscription.

inscription from the forum of Corinth.[106] There is no reason to posit a different set of deities in the Roman sanctuary. Ronald Stroud and I have discussed elsewhere how the Acrocorinth cult underwent modifications in the course of its Roman history.[107] The changes, however, came from the East rather than from the West, and manifested themselves iconographically in symbols familiar from the worship of Isis and Sarapis: vestigia, palm trees on an antefix from the roof of Kore's temple, and marble horns or elephant tusks. But this syncretism, if so it may be called, may have been a phenomenon of the later periods.

CONCLUSION

I recognize three different simultaneous levels in the operation of religion in Early Roman Corinth. The first is that of the official Roman cults of the mother city, which were chiefly gathered in the forum. These drew their inspiration, in large measure, from the house of Augustus and possibly Marc Antony. The second level is that of cults, like those of Apollo, Aphrodite, Asklepios, and Demeter and Kore, that had Greek roots in the city but were by the first century C.E. a part of Roman civic religion. Reinstated in their original places, they were organized according to the needs and customs of the new practitioners.[108] The third level is that of the fringe Greek cults. Pausanias tells us quite clearly about the monument to Medea's children: "But after Corinth was laid waste by the Romans and the old Corinthians were wiped out, the new settlers broke the custom of offering those sacrifices to the sons of Medea, nor do their children cut their hair for them or wear black clothes."[109]

---

[106]Michael D. Dixon, "A New Latin and Greek Inscription from Corinth," *Hesperia* 69 (2000) 335–42. Henri Le Bonniac (*Le culte de Cérès à Rome, des origines à la fin de la République* [Paris: C. Klincksieck, 1958] 295) states that Ceres and Libera were not a couple, but that Latin authors customarily used the name of Proserpina when referring to the daughter of Ceres/Demeter.

[107]For a review of the history of the sanctuary, see Bookidis and Stroud, *Sanctuary of Demeter,* 423–44.

[108]Piérart ("Panthéon et hellénisation") argues that in the addition of Greek cults a certain role must have been played by wealthy erudites who familiarized themselves with the earlier history of Corinth. While this may have played a role in the late first or second centuries, it cannot have done so in the early phases of the colony.

[109]Pausanias 2.3.7 (trans. W. H. S. Jones; LCL; Cambridge, Mass.: Harvard University Press, 1918). Pausanias's statement is usually taken to mean that nothing more was being done

In other words, a monument still stood to give testimony to Corinth's mythical past, but the now meaningless practices were abandoned. Pausanias tells us elsewhere (2.2.7) of the *xoana* of Dionysos that were made from the tree in which Pentheus hid from the women on Kithairon. And he recounts the myth of the contest between Helios and Poseidon for the control of Corinth, in which Briareos awarded Acrocorinth to Helios and the Isthmus to Poseidon. This myth was depicted in a painting on the wall of the Roman Southeast Building, at the southeast corner of the forum, fragments of which were recovered in 1930. It is clear, then, that at some stage before the middle of the second century the Romans were concerned to give their colony Greek roots. They did this by means of reputedly "old" monuments and by means of cults tied to Corinth's mythical past. Prime among these would have been Aphrodite on Acrocorinth; in the past she had been city goddess and one source of Corinth's great repute. But her image apparently had changed. In the case of cults like Athena Chalinitis or Medea's children, I have assumed that there was a Greek prototype. This assumption may or may not be correct. But I would also return to the observation that Hellenistic Corinth was not completely destroyed in 146 B.C.E. Monuments and inscriptions may still have given some indication of what had existed. Written descriptions and histories of the city certainly also still existed. Otherwise, how could Pausanias have known as much as he did? When the new colony retained the name of Corinth in its title, it laid claim to a long and rich history that could be manipulated in many and different ways. Thus, we find that in the fourth century C.E., Libanius can say, in his defense of Aristophanes to the emperor Julian: "First, sire, he is a Greek . . . however, his city's name inspires even more respect, for he is from Corinth."[110]

---

there in his day. Two other citations, however, suggest that some sort of rites continued to be practiced, unless the citations were simply literary topoi. See Piérart, "Panthéon et hellénisation," 87 and n. 18. Possibly in Pausanias's time, "old rites" were replaced by new.

[110]*The Julian Orations* 14.27 (trans. A. F. Norman; LCL; Cambridge, Mass.: Harvard University Press, 1969). For a discussion of Corinth as a member of the Panhellenion in the second century C.E. and its implied Hellenization, see James H. Oliver, "Panachaeans and Panhellenes," *Hesperia* 47 (1978) 191.

CHAPTER SIX

Rites for Melikertes-Palaimon in the Early Roman Corinthia

Elizabeth R. Gebhard

In memory of Oscar Broneer, on the fiftieth anniversary of his excavations at the Isthmus, and of John Hawthorne, who first addressed the problems raised for the cult of Melikertes-Palaimon by those excavations.

INTRODUCTION[1]

It is generally believed that the shrine of Melikertes-Palaimon, uncovered on the Isthmus, represents a new, Roman version of his cult, created by the settlers some time after the foundation of the colony at Corinth. Marcel Piérart has recently argued that the rites described by second-century C.E. authors were the product of learned inquiry.[2] Helmut Koester, following John

[1]My thanks are due to many colleagues: Hans Dieter Betz, Nancy Bookidis, James Hanges, John Hayes, Fritz Hemans, George Huxley, David Jordan, Corinne Pache, David Reese, Betsey Robinson, Sara Strack, Mary Sturgeon, Charles Williams, and Orestes Zervos; and to Daniel Schowalter and Steven Friesen for bringing the Corinthians together. A full study of the cult and archaeology of the sanctuary is in preparation for the *Isthmia* series. Versions of this paper were read at a seminar on hero cults at the University of Chicago (February 2002) and at a colloquium at the German Archaeological Institute in Athens, "Sanctuaries and Cult Practice in Roman Greece" (September 2002). I am grateful to all who have discussed these problems with me and offered valuable suggestions; errors remain my own.

[2]M. Piérart, "Panthéon et hellénisation dans la colonie romaine de Corinth: la 'redécouverte' du culte de Palaimon à l'Isthme," *Kernos* 11 (1998) 85–89.

Hawthorne, saw no direct connection to an earlier cult; he took the view that the rites were a manifestation of the general enthusiasm for mystery cult in the empire.[3]

The literary sources for the myth are well known.[4] Recent studies of the texts and archaeological remains of the shrine suggest that a more nuanced interpretation of the cult is in order.[5] Two aspects of Melikertes-Palaimon may be distinguished: a child who died in the sea, was buried on the Isthmus, and received heroic honors including the Isthmian Games; and an immortal sea-god and savior who was associated with Poseidon. He joins other figures, such as Heracles and Asclepius, Achilles and Trophonius, who began as mortals and received apotheosis at their death but were also worshipped as heroes. With respect to the Isthmian Games, it is his heroic aspect that most concerns us, but there are elements in his Roman shrine that suggest also his worship as an immortal deity of the sea. I shall argue that not only did the essential elements of his rites exist before 146 B.C.E., but that they were continued by

[3]J. Hawthorne ("The Myth of Palaemon," *TAPA* 89 [1958] 92–98) reviews the primary ancient sources; Helmut Koester, "Melikertes at Isthmia: A Roman Mystery Cult," in *Greeks, Romans, and Christians: Essays in Honor of Abraham J. Malherbe* (ed. David L. Balch, Everett Ferguson, and Wayne A. Meeks; Minneapolis: Fortress, 1990) 355–66.

[4]Basic studies: Lewis R. Farnell, *Greek Hero Cults and Ideas of Immortality* (Oxford: Clarendon, 1921) 35–47; Albin Lesky, "Melikertes," PW 29 (1931) cols. 514–21; Edouard Will, *Korinthiaka: recherches sur l'histoire et la civilisation de Corinthe des origines aux guerres médiques* (Paris: de Boccard, 1955) 168–80, 210–12, 217–19; and Walter Burkert, *Homo Necans: The Anthropology of Ancient Greek Sacrificial Ritual and Myth* (trans. Peter Bing; Berkeley: University of California Press, 1983) 196–204.

[5]Recent publications: Archaeology: Elizabeth R. Gebhard, "The Isthmian Games and the Sanctuary of Poseidon in the Early Empire," in *The Corinthia in the Roman Period* (ed. Timothy E. Gregory; JRASup 8; Ann Arbor, Mich.: Journal of Roman Archaeology, 1993) 89–93; Elizabeth R. Gebhard, F. P. Hemans, and J. W. Hayes, "University of Chicago Excavations at Isthmia, 1989: III," *Hesperia* 67 (1998) 428–54; Gunnel Ekroth, "Altars in Greek Hero-Cults: A Review of the Archaeological Evidence," in *Ancient Greek Cult Practice from the Archaeological Evidence* (ed. R. Hägg; Stockholm: Svenska Institutet i Athen, 1998); and Elizabeth R. Gebhard and D. Reese, "Sacrifices to Poseidon and Melikertes-Palaimon at Isthmia," in *Greek Sacrificial Ritual, Olympian and Chthonian: Proceedings of the Sixth International Seminar on Ancient Greek Cult, Göteborg University, April 1997* (ed. R. Hägg; ActaAth 8, 17; Stockholm: 2004) 125–54. Cult: Elizabeth R. Gebhard and M. W. Dickie, "Melikertes-Palaimon: Hero of the Isthmian Games," in *Ancient Greek Hero Cult: Proceedings of the Fifth International Seminar on Ancient Greek Cult, Göteborg University, 21–23 April 1995* (ed. R. Hägg; ActaAth 8, 16; Stockholm, 1998) 159–65; R. A. Seelinger, "The Dionysiac Context of the Cult of Melikertes/Palaimon at the Isthmian Sanctuary of Poseidon," *Maia* 50 (1998) 271–80; Piérart, "Panthéon et hellénisation"; and C. Bonnet, "Le Culte de Leucothéa et de Mélicertes en Grèce, au Proche-Orient et en Italie," *Studi e Materiali* 10 (1986) 33–71.

the colonists of Roman Corinth when they assumed administration of the Isthmian Games. By claiming the city's right to host the Panhellenic festival and by reinstituting worship of the Isthmian deities, the settlers reaffirmed one of the city's most ancient traditions.[6]

Melikertes-Palaimon, the sea-god, seems to have been known at Corinth from the archaic period; he was also worshipped at Tenedos. At Rome, Ovid links him with the harbor god, Portunus; the poet connects his mother, Ino, with the Italian goddess Mater Matuta. Both mother and son are at all periods associated with the infant Dionysos.[7] References to his mysteries (*teletai*) appear in the first century C.E. and grow more explicit in the second.[8] Although his myth and rites stretched from Italy to the coast of Asia Minor, his principal shrine and the only one yet discovered belongs to the Sanctuary of Poseidon on the Corinthian isthmus. Its identification with the god rests on Pausanias and on representations of the boy, his dolphin, and his temple on second-century Corinthian coins. The traveler also saw his altar by a pine tree on the shore of the Saronic Gulf, not far from the sanctuary (2.1.3; figs. 6.1a and 6.1b, p. 168).

---

[6]Jason König, "Favorinus' *Corinthian Oration* in its Corinthian Context," *Proceedings of the Cambridge Philological Society* 47 (2001) 148–53. The city's early response to its Isthmian heritage is an indication that the process of hellenization began at once, even as the colony established itself as a Roman city. The Argive complaint about Corinthian pleasure in less traditional forms of entertainment and sport shows another side (Ps.-Julian, *Letters* 198); see A. J. S. Spawforth, "Corinth, Argos, and the Imperial Cult. Pseudo-Julian, *Letters* 198," *Hesperia* 63 (1994) 211–32.

[7]See Nonnos, who is drawing from the earlier traditions; Timothy Gantz, *Early Greek Myth: A Guide to Literary and Artistic Sources* (2 vols.; Baltimore, Md.: Johns Hopkins University Press, 1993) 176–80; and Robert Shorrock, *The Challenge of Epic. Allusive Engagement in the Dionysiaca of Nonnus* (Mnemosyne Supplement 210; Leiden: Brill, 2001) ch. 2. Images of Ino and Athamas receiving the infant Dionysos occur from ca. 460 B.C.E.: *LIMC* 5/2, s.v. "Ino," nos. 10–12. T. H. Carpenter identifies Ino, Melikertes, and Athamas as the figures accompanying Dionysos and Ariadne on the Derveni krater (third quarter of the fourth century B.C.E.), arguing that they and the imagery of the vase as a whole belong to an iconographic tradition reaching back to the fifth and perhaps the sixth century B.C.E. but without explicit reference to mysteries of Dionysos; see his "Images and Beliefs: Thoughts on the Derveni Krater," in *Periplous: Papers on Classical Art and Archaeology presented to Sir John Boardman* (ed. G. R. Tsetskhladze, A. J. N. W. Prag, and A. M. Snodgrass; London: Thames and Hudson, 2000) 54–58. Compare Seelinger, "Dionysiac Context."

[8]Plutarch, *Thes.* 25.4; see discussion below. See also Koester, "Melikertes," 364–66.

Fig. 6.1a Altar of Melikertes and pine tree, Poseidon at right (coin of Marcus Aurelius, *NCP*, plate B vi). Scale 1:1.

Fig. 6.1b Athlete holding torch and palm, pine tree, and dolphin with Melikertes at right (*NCP*, plate B v). Scale 1:1.

MYTH

The life of young Melikertes was abruptly ended when his mother leaped with him into the sea. In one version, Hera is the cause of it all. She becomes angry because Athenas, father of Melikertes and husband of Ino, showed kindness to Dionysos; she strikes Athamas with madness,[9] so that he kills his older son, Learchus, and pursues Ino and Melikertes to the Molonian cliffs in the Megarid, where she throws herself with the child into the sea.[10] In other accounts, Ino likewise becomes mad and kills Melikertes by throwing him into a boiling cauldron before her leap into the sea.[11]

[9]The complex figure of Athamas had earlier roots in Thessaly as well as being known as ruler of Boeotian Orchomenos; see Gantz, *Early Greek Myth*, 176–80.

[10]The fullest narratives, representing different versions, appear in Apollodorus 1.9.1–2; 3.4.3; Pindar, *Isthm.* hyp. a–d (ed. Drachmann, 3:192–195); Pausanias 1.44.7–8; 2.1.3; Ovid, *Met.* 4.416–542; *Fast.* 6.473–550; and Hyginus, *Fab.* 4 (also 1, 2, 3). The sea-leap and death of Ino and her sons comprised but one of three separate stories wound around the house of Athamas. Ino was known as early as the *Ehoiai* (Hesiod, frag. 70.6–7, ed. West) and the *Odyssey* (5.333–35), receiving further treatment in the fifth century B.C.E. at the hands of Pherecydes, Aeschylus, Sophocles, and Euripides (Gantz, *Early Greek Myth,* 179). In some accounts, Ino suffers her fate for contriving the death of Phrixis and Helle, Athamas's children by another wife. It is the Theban story of Semele and Dionysos, however, that the Corinthians connected with the Isthmian hero cult of Melikertes.

[11]Euripides likens her to Medea for killing both her sons (*Medea* 1282–89). The cauldron (λέβης) is mentioned in Apollodorus and *Isthm.* hyp. d.; Pindar in a fragmentary *threnos* appears to refer to the same story (fr. 128d, ed. Snell/Maehler, discussed in n. 47, below). In a variant, Ino places the dead Learchus in the pot before going mad herself and making the sea-leap with Melikertes (schol. ad Pindar, *Ol.* 1.37–40).

The plunge has two consequences. Mother and son are immediately made immortal: she becomes the goddess Leukothea, received by the Nereids; Melikertes becomes the marine deity Palaimon, associated with Poseidon.[12] At the same time, a dolphin carries the dead boy's body to the Isthmus, where Sisyphus, ruler of Corinth, buries him and celebrates the first Isthmian Games at his funeral.[13] According to some sources, Ino shared the heroic honors and also was buried on the Isthmus. The Megarians too claimed her tomb and offered her annual sacrifices; at Chaironeia she had a *sēkos*.[14] On the other hand, for Pindar and later poets such as Callimachus and Euphorion who were interested in the origins of the major athletic festivals, it was the dead

[12]Variations: sailors assign them new names (Apollodorus); Leukothea is made a goddess by the Nereids (Pindar, *Isthm.* hyp. d) or Neptune/Poseidon (Ovid, *Met.* 539–42); Palaimon is a *daimon* (Pindar, *Isthm. Hyp.* a). One account holds that they both died (Pindar *Isthm.* hyp. c; schol. ad Lycophron *Alex.* 107). For Ovid (*Fast.* 538–52), divinization takes place only after Ino and Melikertes arrive in Rome. Aelius Aristeides says they were never mortals but always divine (*Or.* 46.34). Neither Ovid or Aristeides connect Melikertes-Palaimon with the Isthmian Games.

[13]Development of the Isthmian founding legends: K. Schneider, "Isthmia," PW 9 (1916) 2248–49; Will, *Korinthiaka*, 168–80; Bonnet, "Culte de Leucothéa," 57–63; Albert Schachter, *Cults of Boiotia* (4 vols.; BICSSup 38.1–4; London: University of London, Institute of Classical Studies, 1986) vol. 2, appendix; Gebhard and Dickie, "Melikertes-Palaimon"; Elizabeth R. Gebhard, "The Beginnings of Panhellenic Games at the Isthmus," in *Olympia 1875–2000: 125 Jahre Deutsche Ausgrabungen* (ed. Helmut Kyrieleis; Mainz am Rhein: Philipp von Zabern, 2002) 225–28, table 2. In a fragment of the *Korinthiaka* attributed to the Corinthian poet "Eumelos," it is Poseidon and Helios who establish the first Isthmian games with the Argonauts and other heroes as contestants; see M. L. West, "'Eumelos': A Corinthian Epic Cycle?" *JHS* 122 (2002) 122–23, 130–31.

[14]Tomb on Isthmus: Statius, *Theb.* 12.131; shared cult: schol. ad Lycophron *Alex.* 107; tomb at Megara: Pausanias 1.42.7. The yearly offering (*thysia*), central location, and elaboration of her shrine at Megara, as well as their claim to have been the first to call her Leukothea, show the importance of her worship. Whether the monument and rites reported by Pausanias are a continuation of an ancient cult or were more recently established is impossible to say, although her discovery by the daughters of "Kleson, son of Lelex" echoes the finding of Melikertes, discussed below. The heröon surrounded by a *thrigkos lithon* recalls the shrines of Opheltes at Nemea (Pausanias 2.15.3) and Pelops at Olympia (ibid., 5.13.1), where the stone fences belong to the Hellenistic period. Nemea: Stephen G. Miller, ed., *Nemea. A Guide to the Site and Museum* (Berkeley: University of California Press, 1990) 104–7; idem, "The Shrine of Opheltes and the Earliest Stadium of Nemea," in *Olympia 1875–2000: 125 Jahre Deutsche Ausgrabungen* (ed. Helmut Kyrieleis; Mainz am Rhein: Philipp von Zabern, 2002) 239–50. Olympia: Alfred Mallwitz, *Olympia und seine Bauten* (Munich: Prestel-Verlag, 1972) 133–34; Helmut Kyrieleis, "Zu den Anfängen des Heiligtums von Olympia," in *Olympia 1875–2000: 125 Jahre Deutsche Ausgrabungen* (ed. idem; Mainz am Rhein: Philipp von Zabern, 2002) 213–20. Shrine at Chaironeia: Plutarch, *Quaest. rom.* 16 (267d); Schachter, *Cults of Boiotia*, 2:62–63. The myth and rites resemble those for Mater Matuta at Rome: Ovid, *Fast.* 551–62.

child and his funeral games on the Isthmus that drew their attention. They constitute our primary source for the rites celebrated to him as a hero.[15]

As divinities, the mother and son were popular figures—Ino much more so than Melikertes-Palaimon—and endowed with a wide range of powers.[16] Both resemble other deities who changed form and gained divinity in the sea.[17] Worship of the boy as a sea-god in the company of Poseidon is attested by plaques representing a youth riding dolphins and other aquatic creatures; these plaques were found at a shrine to Poseidon and Amphitrite at Penteskouphi, west of Corinth.[18] His power as a marine deity in the fifth

[15]Pindar: frag. 6.5(1) (ed. Snell); see Gebhard and Dickie, "Melikertes-Palaimon." Callimachus: *Aitia* book 3, frags. 54–59, 384 (ed. Pfeiffer); see also P. M. Frazer, *Ptolemaic Alexandria* (2 vols.; Oxford: Clarendon, 1972) 725. A variant places the sea-leap and recovery of the body on Tenedos, where the inhabitants erected an altar to Melikertes; *Aitia*, Bk. IV, frag. 91 (ed. Pfeiffer). Early inhabitants, the Lelegas, were reputed to have sacrificed children on his altar, a story echoed in the epithet βρεφόκτονος in Lykophron, *Alex.* 229. The scholiast on the passage, who imagines Melikertes watching the sacrifice, identifies him as the son of Ino and a μάντις; see Tzetzes on the passage. See also Frazer, *Alexandria,* 728–29; Farnell, *Greek Hero Cults,* 40–41; and Gantz, *Early Greek Myths,* 591–92.

[16]Ino-Leukothea: S. Eitrem, "Leukothea 6," PW 12 (1925) cols. 2294–95; Lewis R. Farnell, "Ino-Leucothea," *JHS* 36 (1916) 36–44; Will, *Korinthiaka,* 169–76. For her identification with the Goddess of Pyrgi = Mater Matuta, see Iadwiga Krauskopf, "Leukothea nach den antiken Quellen," in *Akten des Kolloquiums zum Thema die Göttin von Pyrgi: archäologische, linguistische und religionsgeschichtliche Aspekte (Tübingen, 16–17 Januar 1979)* (ed. Aldo Neppi Modona and Friedhelm Prayon; Firenze: Olschki, 1981) 137–48. Bonnet ("Culte de Leucothéa") surveys the geographical range of her cult.

[17]Apotheosis and change of form/name in the sea: compare Britomartis-Diktynna and Glaukos Pontios. See S. Eitrem, "A Purification Rite and some Allied 'rites de passages'," *Symbolae Osloenses* 25 (1947) 36–53; Farnell, "Ino-Leucothea," 39; Burkert, *Homo Necans,* 204–5; and M. Mertens-Horn, "Herakles, Leukothea e Palaimon sul tempio arcaico del Foro Boario," in *Deliciae Fictiles II. Proceedings of the Second International Conference on Archaic Architectural Terracottas from Italy Held at the Netherlands Institute in Rome, 12–13 June 1996* (ed. P. S. Lulof and E. M. Moormann; Amsterdam: Nederlands Instituut te Rome, 1997) 147. Glaukos is sometimes linked to Melikertes as his lover or by taking the name Melikertes: Athenaeus 7.296a–297c; Ovid, *Met.* 13.900–68; and Gantz, *Early Greek Myths,* 732–33. Apotheosis in the sea: D. Warland, "Tentative d'exégèse des fresques de la tombe 'du Plongeur' de Poseidonia," *Latomus* 57 (1957) 261–91. The names "Melikertes" and "Palaimon" are inconsistently used in the sources to indicate the god and the hero. Likewise, his age and form shift between infant in arms, child, and youth according to the authors' or artists' imagination and the context. Both names are used interchangeably in this paper.

[18]The plaques are incomplete and lack an inscription to ensure the identification; see *LIMC* 6/2, s.v. "Melikertes," nos. 15–18, 20 (dolphin). A similar image appears on Corinthian coins of Lucius Verus (161–169 C.E.). For bibliography on dolphin-riders in myth and art, see Wolfgang Fischer-Bossert, *Chronologie der Didrachmenprägung von Tarent. 510–280 v. Chr.* (Berlin: de Gruyter, 1999) 420, nn. 99–100; and H. A. Shapiro, *Art and Cult under the Tyrants* (Mainz: Philipp von Zabern, 1989) 60–61. I thank Alan Shapiro for calling my attention to his

century B.C.E. is confirmed by the prayer addressed to him as protector of ships in Euripides' *Iphegeneia in Tauros* (lines 270–71).[19] He first appears in Latin literature as a comrade of Poseidon in Plautus's *Rudens*,[20] a play based on a work of the fourth-century B.C.E. dramatist, Diphilos.[21] The Greek poet Parthenius, influential at Rome in the mid-first century B.C.E., grouped him with the marine deities Glaukos Pontios and Nereus; Vergil imitated the line, imagining a shrine on the shore visited by grateful sailors.[22] A connection between Melikertes and the Phoenician god Melqart, a figure closer in character to Heracles than the youthful dolphin-rider, has been suggested, but no persuasive evidence has yet been found to support it.[23]

---

discussion. Other dolphin-riding heroes include Phalanthos of Tarentum, Telemachos of Zakynthos, Koiranos of Paros, Enalos of Lesbos, Eikadios of Crete, and Arion of Methymna.

[19]ὦ ποντίας παῖ Λευκοθέας, νεῶν φύλαξ, / δέσποτα Παλαῖμον· ἵλεως ἡμῖν γενοῦ. ("O child of Leukothea of the sea, guardian of ships, / Lord Palaimon, be gracious to us.") The identification of Palaimon as child of Leukothea assures his connection with Melikertes.

[20]*Sed O Palaemon, sancte Neptuni comes, / † Qui Herculis socius esse diceris, † / Quod facinu' uidea?* (*Rudens* 160–62). The obelized line raises the possibility that Palaimon is used here as an epithet of Hercules, but that is unlikely since the passage concerns a shipwreck and Palaimon the sea-deity would be more appropriate to the sense. J. D. Craig looks for a connection with Melqart ("Plautus, *Rudens* 160–162," *CR* 40 [1926] 152–53); von Geisau sees an epithet of Hercules ("Palaimon" PW Suppl. 9 [1962] col. 514). If a reference to the Corinthian Palaimon is accepted for this passage, it places him in a Roman literary world that drew heavily on Hellenistic Greek poetry. In other contexts the name Palaimon is used as an epithet of Heracles and is unrelated to the Corinthian marine deity.

[21]Diphilos, a contemporary of Menander, would have known the oracular shrine of Leukothea in his native Sinope, a Milesian colony on the Black Sea (Strabo 498), and at Miletus there was a contest of boys in her honor (Konon 33). Palaimon, closely connected to his mother in myth, may well have been honored with her in Asia Minor; see Farnell, "Ino-Leucothea," 37–38.

[22]Parthenius, frag. 36: Γλαύκῳ καὶ Νηρῆι καὶ εἰναλίῳ Μελικέρτη; Virgil, *Georg.* 436–37: *votaque servati solvent in litore nautae / Glauco et Panopeae et Inoo Melikertae.* Compare *Aen.* 5.823. For analysis of Parthenius's influence at Rome, see J. L. Lightfoot, *Parthenius of Nicaea* (Oxford: Clarendon, 1999) 50–76; and 194–95, frag. 36.

[23]See von Geisau, "Palaimon," cols. 514–16. In Athens Palaimon is again associated with Heracles in the healing cult of Pankrates on the Ilissos River, but in the form of an old man with a cornucopiae, scepter or phiale; see Vikela and Vollkommer, "Melikertes" *LIMC* (1982) 6/1: 437–38; 6/2:227–28, nos. 50, 52, 58, 59; and Eugenia Vikela, *Die Weihreliefs aus dem Athener Pankrates-Heiligtum am Ilissos: Religionsgeschichtliche Bedeutung und Typologie* (Mitteilungen des deutschen archäologischen Instituts, Athenische Abteilung, Beiheft 16; Berlin: Gebr. Mann, 1994) 81–108. The association of Melikertes and Phoenician Melqart probably owes more to the similarity of names and some characteristics shared by Heracles and Melqart than to a cultic identity; see M. L. West, *The East Face of Helicon* (Oxford: Clarendon, 1997) 58; and E. Maass, *Griechen und Semiten auf dem Isthmos von Korinth* (Berlin: G. Reimer, 1903). For Melqart: W. Kroll, "Melqart," PW Suppl. 6 (1935) cols. 293–97. Recent attempts (e.g., Michael G. Astour, *Hellenosemitica* [2nd ed.; Leiden: Brill, 1967] 209–12) to revive the connection are unconvincing.

Ovid presents a new version of the legend, locating the apotheosis of mother and son at Rome and identifying them with Mater Matuta and Portunus (*Fast.* 6.538–52 and *Met.* 4.416–542). It is difficult to know whether the poet is reflecting a cultic reality or simply telling a story.[24] Madeleine Mertens-Horn recently proposed that a statue from the archaic temple of Mater Matuta in the Forum Boarium represents Leukothea and Palaimon, although the fragmentary condition of the piece leaves the identification open to question.[25] Marcel Piérart, for his part, accepts a cult of Palaimon-Portunus at Rome and suggests that the colonists brought it with them to Corinth, where they made Palaimon a protector of harbors and of the games.[26] On the other hand, a Greek source for Ovid's knowledge of Melikertes and Ino is equally possible. Albert Schachter has argued that Ovid, while a student in Athens, became familiar with Theban lore through families with connections in Boeotia.[27] Italian business men, who seem to have had interests in the Corinthia before the colony was founded, may have passed on stories of old Corinth to visitors such as the young Cicero and to the colonists after 44 B.C.E.[28] It seems to me that the relationship between Ovid's accounts and the

[24]On differences in treatment between the two versions, see Franz Bömer's analysis of the sea-leap (*P. Ovidius Naso. Metamorphosen Buch IV–V* [Heidelberg: C. Winter, 1976] 139–40). For the narrative structure of the *Fasti* and the Roman interpretation of Ino, see E. Salvadori, "La struttura narrativa dei Matralia: Ovidio, *Fasti* vi 473–550," *Sandalion* 5 (1982) 208–21. E. Fantham argues that Ovid invented the story ("The Role of Evander in Ovid's *Fasti*," *Arethusa* 25 (1992) 155–71); this is disputed by H. C. Parker ("The Romanization of Ino [*Fasti* 6, 475–550]," *Latomus* 58 [1999] 336–47); see also Carol Newlands, *Playing with Time: Ovid and the* Fasti (Ithaca, N.Y.: Cornell University Press, 1995); and Christopher Smith, "Worshipping Mater Matuta: Ritual and Context," in *Religion in Archaic and Republican Rome and Italy* (ed. Edward Bispham and Christopher Smith; Edinburgh, Edinburgh University Press, 2001) 136–55. For a connection between her cult at Chaeroneia and Rome, see Plutarch, *Quaest. rom.* 16 (267d), and n. 14, above.

[25]"Herakles, Leukothea e Palaimon," 143–48.

[26]"Panthéon et hellénisation," 104–9.

[27]"Ovid and Boeotia," in *Studies in the History, Topography, and Culture of Boiotia* (ed. Albert Schachter; Teiresias Supplement 3; Montreal: McGill University, Department of Classics, 1990) 103–9. Italian *negotiatores* had been active in Boeotia since the second century B.C.E.

[28]Elizabeth R. Gebhard and M. W. Dickie, "The View from the Isthmus: ca. 200–44 B.C.," in *Corinth: The Centenary, 1896–1996* (ed. Charles K. Williams II and Nancy Bookidis; Corinth XX; Princeton, N.J.: ASCSA, 2003) 277; cf. A. J. S. Spawforth, "Roman Corinth: The Formation of a Colonial Elite," in *Roman Onomastics in the Greek East: Social and Political Aspects* (ed. A. D. Rizakis; Μελετήματα 21; Athens: Research Center for Greek and Roman Antiquity; Paris: de Boccard, 1996) 171–73. James Wiseman ("Corinth and Rome I: 228 B.C.–A.D. 267," *ANRW* II.17.1 [1979] 493–96) suggests that local inhabitants passed on knowledge of cult practice to the colonists; Piérart ("Panthéon et hellénisation," 87) doubts that they had much influence in the new city.

cults of Melikertes-Palaimon in Roman Corinth is unclear, and that the rites celebrated for him at the Isthmus before 146 B.C.E. may well have influenced those instituted by the colonists. Some of the arguments are presented in this essay, but the topic requires a fuller treatment.

To return to the dual nature of Melikertes, it has been suggested that the hero and the god were originally separate deities rather than a divine being that was worshipped under different aspects.[29] While it is not impossible that this was the case in the distant past, for the historical period the theory lacks support in the extant sources. From the time of Hesiod and Homer, Ino is portrayed as a mortal woman who became divine in the sea and, while not specifically mentioned, Melikertes was very likely imagined to have shared her fate.[30] Their tombs and cults are spread throughout the eastern Mediterranean.[31] In antiquity, the question of what rites were appropriate for figures of a dual nature was not easily solved. Xenophanes is reported to have replied to the Eleans who asked if they ought to sacrifice and sing dirges to Leukothea: "If they believed her to be a goddess, they should not sing dirges to her; but if a mortal, they should not sacrifice to her" (Aristotle, *Rhet.* 1400b5–8).[32] Cicero groups mother and son with others who received rites as gods and heroes: Hercules, Aesculapius, and the Dioscuri. "Even in Greece they worship a number of deified human beings in the whole of the country," he writes, but he omits mention of their heroic aspects (*Nat. d.* 3.15.39).[33] In summary: the

[29]Maass, *Griechen und Semiten,* 112–14; Will, *Korinthiaka,* 174–75; Vikela, *Die Weihreliefs,* 84–87; contra Farnell, "Ino-Leucothea," 39–40. Schachter (*Cults of Boiotia* 2:62; and "Kadmos and the Implications of the Tradition for Boiotian History," in *La Béotie antique: Colloques internationaux du Centre de la recherche scientifique (Lyon-Saint-Étienne, 16–20 mai 1983)* [ed. Gilbert Argoud and Paul Roesch; Paris: Éditions du Centre National de la Recherche Scientifique, 1985] 153) separates the Theban Ino-Leukothea from the sea-goddess Leukothea.

[30]For the sea-leap as a path to re-birth: Eitrem, "Purification Rite"; and M. B. Hatzopoulos, *Cultes et rites de passage en Macédoine* (Μελετήματα 19; Athens: Research Center for Greek and Roman Antiquity; Paris: de Boccard, 1994). As a rite of initiation: Will, *Korinthiaka,* 172–76; Warland, "Tentative d'exégèse," 278–80; and see n. 17, above. Compare the pursuit and sea-leap of Dionysos and his rescue by Thetis (*Il.* 6.130–35).

[31]See Bonnet, "Culte de Leucothéa."

[32]Plutarch puts the same story in the mouth of Lycurgus speaking to the Thebans (*Quest. lac.* 16.228 E).

[33]On Thasos they sacrificed (θύειν) to Heracles as a god and burned a holocaust (ἐναγίζειν) to him as a hero (Herodotus 2.44). Pausanias reports the same practice in his cult at Sicyon (2.10.1). Birgitta Bergquist found evidence for both rites in his Thasian shrine (*Heracles on Thasos* [Boreas 5; Uppsala: University of Uppsala, 1973]), although analysis of the bones shows that the sacrificed animals must have been eaten. See J. Des Courtiles, A. Gardeisen, and A. Pariente, "Sacrifices d'animaux à Hérakleion de Thasos," *BCH* 129

dual aspect of Ino and Melikertes was well established in myth and cult before Roman Corinth was founded, and there were several avenues by which knowledge of Melikertes-Palaimon could have reached the colonists.

THE CULT OF MELIKERTES-PALAIMON

The rites celebrated for the hero on the Isthmus before the destruction of Corinth, as well as what rituals appear to have been continued by the Roman colonists when they re-established his cult, are the next topic. Euphorion, writing in the 3rd century B.C.E., gives us a glimpse of a ceremony for the hero connected with the Isthmian Festival. The poem, of which only a few lines survive, belongs to a class of learned poetry concerned with the Panhellenic games and their customs, especially the victors' wreaths.[34] Its theme is the origin of the Isthmian pine crown before it was changed to celery (*selina*) in emulation of the wreath at Nemea:

> Κλαίοντες δέ τε κοῦρον ἐπ' † αιλισι † πιτύεσσι
> κάτθεσαν, ὁκκότε δὴ στέφανον ἄθλοις φορέονται
> οὐ γάρ πω τρηχεῖα λαβὴ κατεμήσατο χειρῶν

(1996) 799–800; discussed by Gunnel Ekroth, *The Sacrificial Rituals of Greek Hero-Cults in the Archaic to Early Hellenistic Periods* (Stockholm: University of Stockholm, 1999) 105, 192–93, 205–6. Ekroth concludes that he was mainly worshipped as a god (205 with n. 933). The similarity between rites to Heracles and to Achilles at his tomb (Philostratus, *Her.* 53.8–15), probably deriving from the fact that they were both mortals who became gods, is noteworthy (Ekroth, *Sacrificial Rituals*, 105–6). Achilles was honored as hero at Troy and in Greece, Southern Italy, and Asia Minor, and as a god on the island of Leuke in the Black Sea (G. Hedreen, "The Cult of Achilles in the Euxine," *Hesperia* 60 [1991] 313–30); Walter Burkert notes the role of his goddess mother in his achieving divine status (*Greek Religion* [Cambridge, Mass.: Harvard University Press, 1985] 172, n. 30; 205). Ino-Leukothea perhaps had a similar part in Melikertes-Palaimon's deification. Pausanias includes Amphiaraus, Protesilaus, and Trophonios among such men of old who became immortal (1.34.2; cf. *Il.* 2.695–702; and Herodotus 9.120–23). For Asclepius as god and hero, see J. Riethmueller, "*Bothros* and Tetrastyle: The *Heröon* of Asclepius in Athens," in *Ancient Greek Hero Cult* (ed. R. Hägg; Stockholm: Svenska Institutet i Athen, 1999) 123–43; contra Ekroth, *Sacrificial Rituals*, 198 and n. 900. Ekroth's analysis of sacrificial terminology leads her to see a broadening of ἐναγίζειν to include divine recipients and the rites of heroes to equal those of the gods (86–89; 205 n. 931). Aristotle and Plutarch reflect a different view. On holocausts, see Burkert, *Greek Religion*, 63.

[34] Compare Callimachus (*Aetia* 3, frag. 59; ed. Pfeiffer). Ovid (*Met.* 1. 445–51), writing in the same tradition, proposed a change in the Pythian wreath from oak to laurel; see A. C. Hollis, "Ovid, Metamorphoses 1,445ff: Apollo, Daphne and the Pythian Crown," *ZPE* 112 (1996) 69–71. Callimachus wrote a prose Περὶ Ἀγώνων (frag. 403; ed. Pffeifer) and Euphorion a Περὶ Ἰσθμίων (frag. 180; ed. Groningen). See also Nicander (*Alexipharmaca* 604–6).

Μῆνις παῖδα χάρωνα παρ' Ἀσωποῦ γενετείρη
ἐξότε πυκνὰ σέλινα κατὰ κροτάφων ἐβάλοντο.[35]

Weeping they laid the youth by [the shore] on boughs of pine,
When still they bore them as the victor's crown.
Not yet had savage grip of hands brought down
Menē's fierce-eyed son by Asopus' daughter's side.
But ever since they've put full wreaths of celery on their brows.[36]

The corrupt text raises questions of interpretation, but the general sense of lines 1 and 2 is clear: two or more men are lamenting as they place the body of a youth, surely Melikertes, on a mass of pine boughs, in the place where boughs for the crowns of the victors at the games are gathered.[37] The poem probably included the death and funeral of Melikertes and the founding of the Isthmian Games, topics the poet would have treated in his prose work on the Isthmian Games.[38]

Euphorion seems to have thought that the rites for Melikertes were celebrated at the time of the games, since he links the act of placing the body on pine boughs with the crown worn by victors. A scholiast (ad Lycophron, *Alex.* 107) gives further details: the youths are named Amphimachos and Donakinos, and they find the body at Schoinountia (= Schoinous,[39] the eastern harbor of

[35]Euphorion (frag. 84; ed. Powell = frag. 89; ed. Groningen). The text is that of van Groningen, *Euphorion* (Amsterdam: Hakkert, 1977) 153; the poem is quoted in Plutarch, *Quest. conv.* 5.3 (677A); also in Byzantine scholiasts at AP of the cod. *Paris. suppl. Gr.* 316; see A. C. Lolos, "Antike Scholien zur Antologie Graeca-Palatina," *Hellenika* 33 (1981) 374–81. Text is lacunose.

[36]The reference is to Heracles' killing of the Nemean lion and the institution of the Nemean Games, at which the victors' crown was made of *selina*; Plutarch, *Quaest. conv.* 5.3, trans. P. A. Clement and H. B. Hoffleit in *Plutarch's Moralia* (LCL; Cambridge, Mass.: Harvard University Press, 1969). Hoffleit reads ἐπ' ἀγχιάλοις for the crux in the first line, as do Meinke, Scheid, and Powell. In the second line he follows Bernardakis, reading στεφάνωμ' for codd. στέφανον.

[37]Van Groningen (*Euphorion*, 155) reviews possible readings for ὁκκότε: 1) = ὁτε, adverb of time, "quand aux jeux, on remporte les couronnes." In this sense the line would mean that the games, and more especially the crowning of the victor, take place at the time of the year when formerly the funeral rites of Melikertes were held. Preferably, 2) = ὁκκόθι, adverb of place. They laid Melikertes on a bed of pines in the same place where they in fact obtained pines for the crowns. E. Magnelli ("Miscellanea critica," *Eikasmos* 10 [1999] 106–7) interprets the action as putting the body of Melikertes on a pyre made of pine branches, and suggests αὐαλέαις for the crux in line 1. My thanks to Hugh Lloyd-Jones for bringing Magnelli's article to my attention.

[38]Van Groningen, *Euphorion*, 156, 230.

[39]George Huxley (personal communication) pointed out the "marshy" connotations of the names: Σχοίνους, "place where reeds grow"; and Donakinos, diminutive of δόναξ, "reed," which may reflect the nature of the place.

the Isthmus).[40] In this version, Ino's corpse is found with that of Melikertes, and both are taken to Corinth where Sisyphos establishes an annual contest and sacrifice. The scholiast evidently knew of a tomb and cult of Ino on the Isthmus and associated it with that of her son.[41] It is apparent that the ceremony took place at the time of the Isthmian games, and, although only two youths are mentioned, the participants were very likely the young men of Corinth. The action may have gone something like this: Two young Corinthians, representing the legendary figures of Amphimachos and Donakinos, placed an image of the hero on a bed of pine branches at the place by the shore where tradition held that his body had been found. They then led their companions in the traditional dirge or *thrēnos* that was customary for his burial rites.[42] The formal chant, sung antiphonally during the laying out of the body or at the tomb of a hero,[43] seems to have been a characteristic feature of the Melikertes-Palaimon cult on the Isthmus. Euphorion gives it prominence by placing the participle κλαίοντες at the beginning of the line, and later authors mention the *thrēnos* when referring to his rites.[44] The song would have belonged to a genre of lyric *thrēnoi* that had been established by the 6th century B.C.E. for performance at wakes.[45] Several examples are included in the Pindaric corpus, although it is unclear for whom they were composed.[46] In one piece the poet

---

[40][Ino] πεσοῦσα μετὰ τοῦ παιδὸς αὐτῆς Παλαίμονος εἰς τὴν θάλασσαν διὰ τὸ διώκεσθαι ὑπ' Ἀθάμαντος ἀπεπνίγη. ἐξήχθη δὲ ὑπὸ Κόρινθον περὶ Σχοινουντίαν ὑπὸ δελφῖνος. Ἀντίμαχος δὲ καὶ Δονακῖνος ἀνελόμενοι τὰ σώματα ἄγουσιν εἰς Κόρινθον. Σίσυφος δὲ ἀδελφὸς Ἀθάμαντος βασιλεύων Κορίνθου ἀγῶνα καί θυσίαν ἐπ' αὐτοῖς ἐτησέως ἐκελεύσε γενέσθαι. Compare Pindar, *Isthm.* hyp. b; and van Groningen, *Euphorion*, 153–56.

[41]See n. 14, above.

[42]Thus van Groningen, *Euphorion*, 155. In *Od.* 24.65, κλαίομεν refers to all the dirges sung for Achilles. The mourning song or θρῆνος belonged to a rite over the body of the deceased, here replaced by an image. Compare the rites for Adonis, in which an image placed on a bier was the center for lamentations before being thrown into the sea: Aristophanes, *Lys.* 387–98; Theocritus, *Id.* 15.100–44. See Margaret Alexiou, *The Ritual Lament in Greek Tradition* (Cambridge: Cambridge University Press, 1974) 55–58; Eugen Reiner, *Die rituelle Totenklage der Griechen* (Berlin: W. Kohlhammer, 1938) 41; and Neil Hopkinson, ed., *A Hellenistic Anthology* (Cambridge: Cambridge University Press, 1998) 217–19.

[43]Compare the laments for Hektor (*Il.* 24.720–22) and Achilles (*Od.* 24.58–61). For laments in general, see Reiner, *Rituelle Totenklage*; and Ernesto de Martino, *Morte e pianto rituale nel mondo antico* (Torino: Edizioni scientifiche Einaudi, 1958). For laments for gods and heroes, see Alexiou, *Ritual lament*, 55–62; and Katharine Derderian, *Leaving Words to Remember: Greek Mourning and the Advent of Literacy* (Leiden: Brill, 2001) 117–27.

[44]Statius, *Theb.* 6.10–14; 9.401-3; compare Opheltes (ibid., 6.118–25; 135–92); see also Philostratus, *Her.* 53.4.

[45]Hopkinson, *Hellenistic Anthology*, 218.

[46]Derderian (*Leaving Words to Remember*, 122–26) sees the Pindaric *thrēnos* as being performed orally and functioning as a memorial to the human dead on a par with athletic

mentions Ino in a context suggesting the myth of Melikertes.[47] It would be attractive to suggest that the song was commissioned for the festival, but there is no evidence to support the connection. It was perhaps such a *thrēnos* that the Eleans were singing for Leukothea when they asked Xenophanes' advice on adding a sacrifice to the rites, as mentioned above. In Corinth, laments were performed for Medea's children in the Sanctuary of Hera at Perachora, where it is said that a chorus of fourteen youths and maidens spent a year appeasing the goddess.[48]

The ritual, if it followed the usual pattern for heroic cult, would have taken place at night. The priest would have begun with a prayer inviting the hero to join the feast and blood-offering, the dirge would have followed, and the image of the hero on its bier of pines would have been carried to the place

---

contests and the victor's crown. It bridged the space between the participants and the under-world, elevating the ordinary dead to the rank of heroes through the pleasures of the afterlife that they enjoy as initiates (ὄλβιοι) in the mysteries. Detailed commentary: M. Cannatà Fera, *Pindarus: Threnorum Fragmenta* (Rome: Athenaei, 1990).

[47]Pindar, *Thrēnoi* frag. 4a = 128d (ed. Snell, 107), begins:

]α[ ] . [ ]. [
Ἰ]νὼ δ' ἐκ πυ[ρ
ἁρπά]ξαισα [παῖδ' ἔρ]ρ{ε}ιψεν ε . [
]ἀγ' λαοκ[όλπου] Δωρίδος
πε]ντήκο[ντα κο]ύραις
]λελευθ[. . . .]γεων καια[
]ερθενε [. . . .]νθησεμεγ[

Ino, snatching [the boy] from the fire, threw (herself?) . . .
Fifty daughters of shining-bosomed Doris . . .
[coming?] from their [ ] caverns (καια[τῶν]).

In the remainder of the fragment there is mention of hereditary customs (πατ[ρ]ῶι') friendly welcomes (φιλοφ[ρ]οσύναι), festivals that last ([ἑ]ορταὶ ἔμπεδο[ν]), honest councils (ὀρθαι τε β[ουλ]αι), and ever-flowing springs (κράνας ο[υ' π]ρολε̣ί̣πει[. . . / ὕ]δωρ). The poet is following the version in which Ino snatched Melikertes from a cauldron of boiling water before her sea-leap. She was welcomed by the Nereids, the fifty daughters of Doris and Nereus: Pindar, *Isthm.* hyp. a, d; schol. ad Lycophron, *Alex.* 229; Apollodorus 3.4.3.

[48]Parmeniskos, apud schol. ad Euripides, *Med.* 264; Pausanias 2.3.7; Philostratus, *Her.* 53.4. Martin P. Nilsson, *Griechische Feste von religiöser Bedeutung* (Leipzig: B. Teubner, 1906) 57–60. Initiatory role of the cult: Angelo Brelich, *Paides e Parthenoi* (Rome: Edizioni dell'Ateneo, 1969) 355–65; and Fritz Graf, "Medea, the Enchantress from Afar: Remarks on a Well-Known Myth," in *Medea: Essays on Medea in Myth, Literature, Philosophy, and Art* (ed. James J. Clauss and Sarah Iles Johnston; Princeton, N.J.: Princeton University Press, 1997) 39–40. Cult of Hera Akraia: Sarah Iles Johnston, "Corinthian Medea and the Cult of Hera Akraia," in ibid., 46–55. Corinthian cult of dead children with tomb in the sanctuary of Hera Akraia, and Medea as a Corinthian goddess: West, "Eumelos," 123–24.

of sacrifice. After offering a black bull, the participants would have dined.[49] The ceremony may have begun at Melikertes' altar, which marked the place where his body was found on the shore (Pausanias 2.1.3). As mentioned above, such an altar is represented on coins of Roman Corinth (fig. 6.1a).[50] Philostratus appears to have known of a tomb (*taphos*) of Melikertes, which he mentions in the same terms as the tomb of Pelops at Olympia (*V.A.* 3.31), but no monument comparable to the Pelopion has been found on the Isthmus. For rites connected with the games, we might expect an altar/tomb near the altar of Poseidon.[51]

This much can be restored or suggested for Melikertes' rites at the Isthmus before 146 B.C.E. The next point to examine is evidence for the same or similar ceremonies celebrated for him by the Roman colonists. The main feature is the *thrēnos* that is emphasized in connection with his cult in several works of the Roman period. Most extensive is Statius's treatment in the *Thebaid* (written under the Flavians), a parallel for the death and funeral of the infant Opheltes at Nemea that occupy a central place in the narrative. Palaimon and his mother appear frequently throughout the poem, but of most interest here is the passage at the beginning of Book 6, where Leukothea, mourning her son, is introduced as a foil to the laments of Opheltes' mother and nurse. That the poet has an explicit ritual of Palaimon in mind rather than a mythological reminiscence is evident in the mention of the boy's "sad altars" (*aras tristes*) and rites to him that are characterized as a "black superstition" (*nigra superstitio*). Leukothea is the chief mourner, but in place of the usual antiphonal *threnos*, the Isthmus itself joins the lament and is answered by the weeping city of Thebes across the gulf.[52] It is a bold geographical image that extends the scope and intensity of the lament by imagining it filling the

---

[49]Compare the rites for the heroes at Plataea (during the day, Plutarch, *Arist.* 21.2–5); for Pelops at Olympia (Pindar, *Ol.* 1.90–93; and W. J. Slater, "Pelops at Olympia," *GRBS* 30 [1989] 485–501); for Herakles and the sons of Herakles at Thebes (Pindar, *Isthm.* 4.61–73; and Schachter, *Cults of Boiotia*, 2:25–30). For heroes without tombs or whose burial places are secret, see F. M. Dunn ("Euripides and the Rites of Hera Akraia," *GRBS* 35 [1995] 109–11) on the children of Medea at Corinth, whose tomb, he argues, was a late addition to the story.

[50]Pausanias's guides were well informed about traditional lore. The monument with its pine tree may have been ancient; equally likely it could have been a replacement for something that had been or was reported to have been there. Praxiteles, who appears at two of Plutarch's Corinthian symposia, gives learned discussions on agonistic symbols; see Christopher P. Jones, "Pausanias and His Guides," in *Pausanias: Travel and Memory in Roman Greece* (ed. Susan E. Alcock, John F. Cherry, and J. Elsner; Oxford: Oxford University Press, 2001) 38.

[51]Tomb and altar as one: Aiakos on Aegina (Pausanias 1.39.6).

[52]*mox circum tristes servata Palaemonis aras/nigra superstitio, quotiens animosa resumit/Leukothea gemitus et amica ad litora festa/tempestate venit: planctu conclamat*

country in which the boy died and awakening a response in his mother's homeland. Statius's literary background and the Hellenic atmosphere of his home city of Naples make it likely that his knowledge of the cult was based on traditional accounts, which would explain his emphasis on the dirge that was a familiar rite for the child-hero. His introduction of the black superstition observed on Palaimon's sad altars suggests that the cult included mysteries of some sort.[53]

The same question of traditional versus contemporary rites arises with respect to a reference to Melikertes' cult in Plutarch's *Life of Theseus*, written shortly after Statius's *Thebaid*. Plutarch credits Theseus with the founding of the Isthmian Games, passing over Melikertes by saying that his rites were noctural *teletai*, in pointed contrast to the Panhellenic festival of Poseidon (*Thes.* 25.4). The *teletai* seem likely to have been mysteries, but it is difficult to know whether they were introduced in the first century C.E. or had existed before the sack of Corinth. In view of Plutarch's familiarity with the Isthmus, its deities, and its festivals, his reference to the rites should reflect a contemporary reality, while in regard to Theseus as founder of the Isthmian Games he is probably following Hellanicus (late fifth century B.C.E.).[54]

Both dirge and *teletai* appear in Philostratus's mention of Melikertes' rites in the *Heroikos,* where he draws a comparison with the rites that the Thessalians used to offer every year to Achilles at his tomb in the Troad (52.3):[55] "Achilles also received hymns from Thessaly, which they sang at night, coming each year

---

uterque / Isthmos, Echioniae responsant flebile Thebae; "Then black superstition is celebrated around the sad altars of Palaimon, and so often (as the rites are held) brave Leukothea renews her groans and at the time of the festival comes to the friendly shores. From end to end the Isthmus resounds with weeping and Echionian Thebes responds" (*Theb.* 6.10–14).

[53]Statius belonged to a literary family in Naples, and his father, a *grammaticus*, had won competitions at the Pythian, Nemean, and Isthmian Games (*Sil.* 5.3.141–45). Statius's Greek background: Alex Hardie, *Statius and the Silvae* (Liverpool: F. Cairns, 1983) 7, 57–59, 67; and Michael Dewar, ed., *Statius, Thebaid IX* (Oxford: Clarendon, 1991) xv–xxxvii; Charles McNelis, "Greek Grammarians and Roman Society during the Early Empire: Statius' Father and His Contemporaries," *Classical Antiquity* 21 (2002) 67–94. Betsey Robinson suggests that he visited Corinth on the basis of his reference to the covered Lechaion Way in *Sil.* 2.2.30–35 ("Fountains and the Culture of Water at Roman Corinth" [Ph.D. diss., University of Pennsylvania, 2001] 184).

[54]For the use of *teletai* in the sense of both festival and mysteries in Greek and Roman terminology, with a preference for mysteries in the later sources while not excluding festival, see now Kevin Clinton, "Stages of Initiation in the Eleusinian and Samothracian Mysteries," in *Greek Mysteries: The Archaeology and Ritual of Ancient Greek Secret Cults* (ed. M. B. Cosmopoulos; London: Routledge, 2003) 50–60. For discussion of the Isthmian founding legends, see Gebhard, "Beginnings," 26, table 2.

[55]On contemporary belief in heroes and in the rites as described by Philostratus: Christopher P. Jones, "Philostratus' *Heroikos* and Its Setting in Reality," *JHS* 121 (2001) 147–48.

to his grave and mingling some kind of mystery rite (τελέτη) with the offerings to the dead (ἐναγίσματα), as do the Lemnians and the Peloponnesians descended from Sisyphus."[56] Regarding Melikertes' rites and those for Medea's children, he remarks, "[The rites] resemble a θρῆνος that is both τελεστικός and ἔνθεος, for they [Corinthians] propitiate the children and sing hymns to Melikertes." (53.4)[57]

His description of Corinthians as those descended from Sisyphus might be construed as a reference to practices before 146 B.C.E., but, considering the current state of the evidence, a firm line probably cannot be drawn between what happened in Greek Corinth and what was done by the Roman colonists.[58] Philostratus may have known of mourning songs and sacrifices for the dead that were said to go back to early Corinth but were current in his day. His description of the *thrēnos* as *telestikos* and *entheos* has the same flavor of mystery cult that we saw in Plutarch's brief mention of the cult.

Although in myth Melikertes' fate is closely tied to that of Dionysos, it is not clear to what extent, if any, his early rites included Dionysiac-type mysteries.[59] Ovid's portrayal of the story (*Met.* 4.481–530), drawing on Hellenistic traditions, has a strong Dionysiac flavor, but that aspect is not necessarily significant for cult practice.[60] The first iconographic evidence of Melikertes' association with Dionysos is the image of the young dolphin rider waving a thyrsus on coins of 32/33 or 33/34 C.E. (fig. 6.2).[61] His cult as revived by the Roman colonists evidently involved mysteries: for Philostratus, even

---

[56]Text and translation: Ellen Aitken and Jennifer Berenson Maclean, eds., *Flavius Philostratus: Heroikos* (Atlanta, Ga.: Society of Biblical Literature, 2001).

[57]καὶ μὴν καὶ ὕμνων ἐκ Θετταλίας ὁ Ἀχιλλεὺς ἔτυχεν, οὓς ἀνὰ πᾶν ἔτος ἐπὶ τὸ σῆμα φοιτῶντες ᾖδον ἐν νυκτί, τελετῆς τι ἐγκαταμιγνύντες τοῖς ἐναγίσμασιν, ὡς Λήμνιοί τε νομίζουσιν καὶ Πελοποννησίων οἱ ἀπὸ Σισύφου (52.3). . . . τὰ μὲν γὰρ Κορινθίων ἐπὶ Μελικέρτῃ (τούτους γὰρ δὴ τοὺς ἀπὸ Σισύφου εἶπον), καὶ ὁπόσα οἱ αὐτοὶ δρῶσιν ἐπὶ τοῖς τῆς Μηδείας παισίν, οὓς ὑπὲρ τῆς Γλαύκης ἀπέκτειναν, θρήνῳ εἴκασται τελεστικῷ τε καὶ ἐνθέῳ· τοὺς μὲν γὰρ μειλίσσονται, τὸν δὲ ὑμνοῦσιν (53.4).

[58]Pausanias 2.3.6–7; see n. 48, above.

[59]Salvador Lavecchia (*Pindari Dithyramborum Fragmenta* [Rome and Pisa: Edizioni dell'Ateneo, 2000] 219–28) understands a reference to Corinth and the Isthmus in a fragmentary Pindaric dithyramb that he imagines was performed at a Corinthian festival of Dionysos, but the connection seems unlikely.

[60]Seelinger ("Dionysiac Context") reviews the evidence. J. Fontenrose sees a parallel between Ino's sea-leap with Melikertes and that of Dionysos fleeing Lycurgus ("The Sorrows of Ino and Procne," *TAPA* 79 [1948] 163–67); see n. 30, above. For the protodionysiac character of his cult, see Will, *Korinthiaka*, 216–21.

[61]Michel Amandry, *Le monnayage des duovirs corinthiennes* (BCHSup 15; Paris: de Boccard, 1988) 59–66, 78–79, cat. nos. XVI 47, XVI, 51, XVI 54, XVI 58, XVI, 60, plate XXIV: B.I (Da). For attribution of this anonymous series to L. Arrius Peregrinus and L. Furrius Labeo, Corinthian duoviri in 32/33 or 33/34 C.E., see ibid., 62–63. Isthmian imagery predominates in the series.

Fig. 6.2 Melikertes riding dolphin with thyrsus over
left shoulder (Corinth coin: 1936-414). Scale 8:1.

the traditional dirge is *telestikos* and *entheos* ("ecstatic, inspired by god").[62]
Nonnos presents Melikertes as Dionysos's first initiate (9.97).

Granted that certain features of the Greek hero cult on the Isthmus were
re-established in the Roman colony, what are the possible means of transmission?[63] The answer may lie, for the most part, with the Sikyonians who
assumed sponsorship of the Isthmian festival immediately after 146 B.C.E.
and presumably moved the events to Sikyon. The altar to Isthmian Poseidon
that Pausanias saw in the heart of that city probably belongs to this period
(2.9.6), and it may well have been shared by Melikertes (Nonnos 9.88–90).
The other towns of the Corinthia that escaped Corinth's fate, such as Tenea,
may also have continued some observance of the hero's cult.[64]

---

[62]τελιστικός, connected with mystic rites; see Plato, *Phaedr.* 265b, where it is used of
mystic rites inspired by Dionysos. ἔνθεος, "full of the god, inspired, possessed" (LSJ⁹); used
of Bacchants possessed by Dionysos (Sophocles, *Ant.* 964: ἔνθεοι γυναῖκες).

[63]Compare the rites for the heroes at Plataiai that Plutarch reports as continuing in his day,
an example of the *longue durée* of religious observance that was possible in a place without
the political disruption and ethnic discontinuities experienced by Corinth. For changes, see
Albert Schachter, *Cults of Boiotia*, 3:129–32, 137–38. Robert Parker (*Athenian Religion:
A History* [Oxford: Clarendon Press, 1996] 137 n. 57) points out that the sources for the cult
are not early and that the Panhellenic *Eleutheria* festival is post-Classical.

[64]See n. 28, above. Information about the cult was available in literary works, as discussed
above, and in later times Pausanias's guides as well as Plutarch's friends were well informed
on ancient religious customs (Jones, "Pausanias," 38).

THE GAMES RETURN TO CORINTH

The administration of the Panhellenic Isthmian festival and the cults associated with it restored to the new city significant elements from its Hellenic past, including the date at which the festival took place, since the games belonged to the Olympic *periodos* which continued to be administered in the traditional manner.[65] From the prevalence of Isthmian imagery on the early coinage, the *duoviri* and their colleagues seem to have eagerly embraced their role as sponsors of the ancient games. Already, as Favorinus would remind them a century and a half later, the Corinthians were Romans who would like to appear Greek.[66]

The new city seems not to have delayed in bringing the games back from Sikyon.[67] Its resources would have been stretched to administer a Panhellenic festival as early as 42 B.C.E.,[68] but Isthmian Poseidon is prominently displayed on the coinage (fig. 6.3).[69] Further reference to the Isthmus occurs in the next series, in which the obverse shows a wreath or crown (possibly of pine) and the reverse bears a dolphin with trident in a design that suggests an emblem (figs. 6.4a–b, p. 184).[70] Specifically athletic imagery appears on

[65]On the administration of the Isthmian Games according to Greek custom, see Daniel J. Geagan, "Notes on the Agonistic Festivals of Roman Corinth," *GRBS* 9 (1968) 69–80.

[66]See Jason König, "Favorinus," 141–44; and the essay of L. Michael White in this volume (pp. 61–110).

[67]The last games under Corinthian administration would have been in the spring of 146 B.C.E.; the sack of Corinth took place that summer, and the festival in 144 B.C.E. was presumably administered by Sikyon (Pausanias 2.2.2).

[68]Amandry (*Le monnayage*, 28–30) places the first duovirs in 43 or 42 B.C.E. Mary E. Hoskins Walbank ("The Foundation and Planning of Early Roman Corinth," *JRA* 10 [1997] 98–99) suggests that the colonists probably arrived by October of 44 B.C.E. or in the following spring. For the procedures followed, compare the foundation charter of Urso; see M. H. Crawford, ed., *Roman Statutes* (2 vols.; BICSSup 64; London: University of London, 1996) 1:393–454.

[69]Amandry, *Le monnayage*, duoviral Class II, 43 or 42 B.C.E., 32–33, 123–24, plates II–III; *NCP* 16, no. 10, plate D.LII. Compare Zeus and Athena on the coins of Class III dated to 42 or 41, B.C.E. (ibid., 33, plate III). It seems unlikely that a major statue of Poseidon would have escaped the ravages of Mummius and then the pirates who followed him in plundering the area. The figure should thus be taken not as a Corinthian statue but as a representative image of Isthmian Poseidon. The same male figure seated on a rock is used to personify the Isthmus, a type peculiar to Corinth and used interchangeably with Poseidon; *LIMC* 5/2, s.v. "Isthmos," nos. 2, 3a, 4, 5.

[70]Corinth coin: 2002-94; Amandry, *Le monnayage*, duoviral Class III, plate IV:c (D1 with R1 or R2). The dolphin with trident behind was the identifying stamp on roof tiles for the sanctuary; see Elizabeth R. Gebhard, *The Theater at Isthmia* (Chicago: University of Chicago Press, 1973) 108 and 151, fig. 58. Michael Mills is preparing a full publication of the stamped tiles.

Fig 6.3 Poseidon seated on a rock (Corinth coin: Theater 1929-322). Scale 4:1.

the first quinquennial issue in 40 B.C.E.: a hydria on the obverse, while the reverse shows the pine crown of the Isthmian victor.[71] Since it seems unlikely that the Corinthian duovirs were advertising a festival held in Sikyon, the Isthmia of 40 B.C.E. were probably managed by the Corinthians. Images of Poseidon with a pine crown on the reverse continue on coins of P. Aebutius and C. Pinnius issued between 39 and 36, perhaps for the games of 38 B.C.E.[72]

[71]Corinth coin: Agora SE, IV-15-1933 (6-33); Amandry, *Le monnayage*, 39–41, Class III, plate IVc (D1 with R1 or R2). Pine needles appear between the long ovals on the wreath. For the hydria in an athletic context, see Gebhard, "Isthmian Games," 81 and n. 15; on the Isthmian wreath, see Oscar Broneer, "The Isthmian Victory Crown," *AJA* 66 (1962) 259–63, plates 67–68.

[72]Corinth coin: S. of Museum, XI-27-1915 (21). Amandry, *Le monnayage*, 36–38; plate VI: c (D13 with R1–8). The head of Poseidon on the obverse is based on a Classical type, and the pine crown enclosing the magistrates' names is fully rendered on the reverse.

Fig. 6.4a Wreath (obv. Corinth coin: 2002-94). Scale 4:1.

Fig. 6.4b Dolphin with trident (rev. Corinth coin: 2002-94). Scale 4:1.

Thus, on the basis of coins minted in the first years of the colony, it is evident that the Isthmian cult and games occupied a place of importance in the minds of the Corinthian administration as soon as the colony was established. The economic benefits deriving from a Panhellenic festival would have been as important as the prestige.[73] After Actium, Caesarea were initiated in honor of the imperial house and held at the same time as the Isthmian festival under the jurisdiction of the same *agōnothetēs*.[74] Although it may have been a profitable enterprise, it should be kept in mind that the new colony would have borne a heavy administrative burden in undertaking to host such festivals; too little is known about the period to say how the arrangements were handled in those early years.

The location of the contests is another question. They were almost certainly held in Corinth, although an appropriate venue has yet to be found for them. The sanctuary on the Isthmus, while not completely deserted after the sack of 146 B.C.E., had been abandoned as a place for festivals and active cult practice. The long altar was demolished, and carts regularly traveled through the sacred area; the temple was in ruins, the theater despoiled of its seats, and in general the place was in disrepair. Signs of renewed activity do not appear until the middle years of the first century, and at that time the festival seems to have resumed its traditional place on the Isthmus.[75] On epigraphic grounds, Mika Kajava has recently proposed that the games of 43 B.C.E. marked the return.[76] In preceding years, both the Isthmia and Caesarea were almost certainly held in Corinth.

[73]A. J. S. Spawforth ("Agonistic Festivals in Roman Greece," in *The Greek Renaissance in the Roman Empire: Papers from the Tenth British Museum Classical Colloquium* [ed. Susan Walker and Averil Cameron; BICSSup 55; London: University of London, 1989] 197) quotes Dio of Prusa (*Or.* 35.15–16): "wherever the greatest crowd of people gathers together, there we are bound to find the most money." See also Gebhard, "Isthmian Games," 79–82.

[74]Geagan, "Agonistic Festivals," 69–76.

[75]On the history of the question: Gebhard, "Isthmian Games," 79–89; archaeological evidence: Gebhard et al., "Isthmia, 1989: III," 416–33; interval period: Gebhard and Dickie, "View from the Isthmus."

[76]The first reference to the games being regularly celebrated at the Isthmus is found in an honorary inscription erected by Regulus in honor of his father's service as *agōnothetēs* of the Isthmia and Caesarea (J. H. Kent, *The Inscriptions, 1926–1950* [Corinth VIII.3; Princeton, N.J.: ASCSA, 1966] no. 153. For the return in 43 C.E.: Mika Kajava, "When Did the Isthmian Games Return to the Isthmus? (Re-Reading *Corinth* VIII.3, no. 153)," *CP* 97 (2002) 171–76. For the return of the games in 55 or 57 C.E.: Gebhard, "Isthmian Games," 87–88. The archaeological context cannot be dated more precisely than the middle of the first century C.E.; see Gebhard, Hemans, and Hayes, "Isthmia, 1989: III," 425–26; Macadem Floor Construction, I: deposits 1–7.

In the city of Corinth, future excavations will perhaps uncover extensive athletic facilities, possibly in the area of the Greek gymnasium near the Asclepieion.[77] At present only one racecourse has been cleared, and it lies in the Lechaion Valley, where the colony laid out its forum. The track in its final phase belongs to the Hellenistic period and, although cart roads crossed the surface during the interval, it would have been available with some repairs for use in the first century B.C.E.[78] On the other hand, the *dromos* had neither the length of a canonical stadium nor a standard starting platform. Perhaps under the economic pressures of the early years the colonists made use of it. In any case, the area continued to attract monuments for victories in the games as it had in the past, and an early Roman tripod joined the line of Greek commemorative bases near the racecourse.[79] For the musical events of the Isthmian program, the old theater could have been pressed into service.[80] The end of competitions in the forum, if indeed they were held there, came when Cn. Babbius Philinus built an ornamental fountain over the west end of the

[77]Excavations in the gymnasium area: J. R. Wiseman, "Excavations at Corinth, The Gymnasium Area, 1966," *Hesperia* 36 (1967) 402–28; idem, "Excavations in Corinth, The Gymnasium Area, 1967–1968," *Hesperia* 38 (1969) 64–106; idem, "Excavations in the Gymnasium Area, 1969–1970," *Hesperia* 41 (1972) 1–42.

[78]The surface was not buried until well into the first century C.E. Stratigraphy above the track: Charles K. Williams II, "Corinth, 1969: Forum Area," *Hesperia* 39 (1970) fig. 1; idem and J. E. Fisher, "Corinth, 1970: Forum Area," *Hesperia* 40 (1971) 22; Corinth Notebook 440; Lots 5805, 5806, 5808, 5811, 5612, and Basket 44, restudied by Williams in 1984. The upper layer contained large stones that served as a bedding for the forum pavement. The soils below held material belonging to at least the first half of the first century. No use-level or chronologically defined horizons were encountered above the racecourse, nor were there signs of a Mummian destruction layer. Robert L. Scranton (*Monuments in the Lower Agora and North of the Archaic Temple* [Corinth I.3; Princeton, N.J.: ASCSA, 1951] 135–36, 148–49) posits two floors predating the laying of the marble pavement, which he dates to the end of the first century. On Roman alterations to the valley, see Charles K. Williams II and P. Russell, "Corinth: Excavations of 1980," *Hesperia* 50 (1981) 1–2; and Walbank, "Foundation and Planning," 117–18.

[79]Williams, "Corinth, 1969," 29–30; and idem, "Pre-Roman Cults in the Area of the Forum of Ancient Corinth" (Ph.D. diss., University of Pennsylvania, 1978) 130, 146. Robinson ("Fountains," 237) prefers a date for the tripod base before 146 B.C.E., since a late date would suggest that the cult of the Sacred Spring continued during or after the interim period. In any case the wall along the spring, where similar monuments had been erected in old Corinth, remained open during the interval since a road cut into its upper surface; see David Romano, "A Tale of Two Cities: Roman Colonies at Corinth," in *Romanization and the City* (ed. Elizabeth Fentress; JRASup 38; Portsmouth, N.H.: Journal of Roman Archaeology, 2000) 91, fig. 6; contra Robinson, "Fountains," 236.

[80]Stillwell (*The Theatre* [Corinth II; Princeton, N.J.: ASCSA, 1952] 79–81) suggests that in the first period of the colony the theater was used in its Greek form with the addition of a low wooden stage.

racetrack.[81] He dedicated the monument to Poseidon, and it is tempting to see some connection with the Isthmian deities. The idea finds support in the two dolphins that flanked the fountain, one of which was found near the monument together with its base, inscribed *Cn. Babbius Philinus Neptuno Sacr.*[82] That the dolphin had borne a rider was noticed recently by Betsey Robinson, who saw a roughly picked surface along the back of the dolphin and running down the right side and, in a smaller line, to the nose. She interpreted the cuttings as the remains of a figure, perhaps Palaimon or a Nereid, that had been sculpted in one piece with the dolphin and later chiseled away.[83] The rider was lying on the dolphin, probably with one arm towards the head, as Palaimon on coins of 32/33 C.E. (fig. 6.5, p. 188),[84] or on the two dolphins represented in a small marble statue (fig. 6.6, p. 188).[85] We have seen that Palaimon had long been the companion of Isthmian Poseidon, and, if the fountain did indeed make a visual reference to the Isthmian festival by being placed at the end of a racecourse used for the contests, images of the hero on his dolphin would have emphasized the connection. The ensemble is the earliest monument at the west end of the forum, and it must have been a notable sight in the early colonial city.[86] It was surely a dedication to Poseidon,

[81]Scranton, *Monuments,* 32–36, plate 13. For a new restoration, see Charles K. Williams II, "A Re-Evaluation of Temple E and the West End of the Forum of Corinth," in *The Greek Renaissance in the Roman Empire: Papers from the Tenth British Museum Classical Colloquium* (ed. Susan Walker and Averil Cameron; BICSSup 55; London: University of London, 1989) 158–59, 161 n. 14, plates 60–61. Williams places the construction early in Babbius's career, before he became a duovir (between 7/8 and 12/13 C.E.; Kent, *Inscriptions,* 25); see now Robinson, "Fountains," 247–63, figs. 6.1–6.5.

[82]Bases: A. B. West, *Latin Inscriptions, 1896–1926* (Corinth VIII.2; Cambridge, Mass.: ASCSA, 1931) 5–6, nos. 2–3 (I-438, I-794). Dolphin: Franklin P. Johnson, *Sculpture, 1896–1923* (Corinth IX; Cambridge, Mass.: ASCSA, 1931) no. 204 (S-316, S-316a); Scranton, *Monuments,* plate 15.1, shows statue and base together.

[83]"Fountains," 254 n. 38. I am grateful to Nancy Bookidis for examining the dolphin with me and confirming Robinson's observation that it had carried a figure.

[84]Corinth coin: Road N. of St. John's, III-10-1933 (6), minted under L. Arrius Peregrinus and L. Furius Labeo; Amandry, *Le monnayage,* catalogue 179–80, plate XXIV: B.I (Re1, Re2, Re17, Re18, Re19), chronology, 59–66; *LIMC* 5/2, s.v. "Melikertes," no. 34; and *NCP,* plate B viii.

[85]Johnson, *Sculpture,* 55, no. 72 (S-760), from the same area as the fountain. Its scale (preserved length 0.45 m) and style of workmanship preclude it from having had a place on Babbius's fountain. The Palaimon-on-double-dolphin motif occurs on a coin of L. Paconius Flaminus and Cn. Publicius Regulus, duovirs in 50/51; see Amandry, *Le monnayage,* 21, 64, 74, 200; Em. XXI, plate xxx; and *LIMC* 5/2, s.v. "Melikertes," no. 47.

[86]For the effect, see Robinson, "Fountains," 255–59. On the date of the ensemble, see Charles K. Williams II and Orestes H. Zervos, "Excavations at Corinth, 1989: The Temenos of Temple E," *Hesperia* 59 (1990) 353, fig. 5.

Fig. 6.5 Melikertes guiding the dolphin (Corinth coin: Road north of St. John's, III-10-1933, no. 6). Scale 4:1.

Fig. 6.6 Marble statue of Melikertes on two dolphins (S-760).

but the absence of any sign of an altar makes it difficult to imagine it as a place for offerings. The altar of Isthmian Poseidon, probably associated with Melikertes, may have stood elsewhere.

THE ISTHMIAN PALAIMONION

The first shrine for Melikertes-Palaimon to be discovered was built at the Isthmian sanctuary some time around the mid-first century C.E. The sanctuary was uncovered and published by Oscar Broneer between 1955 and 1973, and further excavations were carried out in 1989; a new study designed to integrate the archaeological and literary evidence for the cult is underway.[87] The present discussion, however, is largely confined to the initial phase of the shrine, which began when athletic festivals returned to the Isthmus.

The sanctuary is located at the southeast corner of the temenos of Poseidon, over one end of the Classical Stadium and incorporating an underground reservoir that had supplied the stadium with water (figs. 6.7a–b, pp. 190–91). Despite extensive excavation, no evidence for earlier cult activity has been found in the area, and it must be concluded that the location of the shrine depended on some aspect of the site important to the Roman colonists and not on the re-establishment of a pre-Roman cult. Piérart has suggested that it was the chance discovery of the subterranean reservoir and its mythological identification as the holy place of Palaimon that led the colonists to establish his shrine in this place.[88] The eastern manhole leading to the reservoir appears to have been a focus of cult activity, as discussed below. Nearby there was a rectangular pit (A) for sacrifices (fig. 6.8, p. 192). A new pit (B) was opened and the precinct enlarged in the later first century (Phase II), and

[87]Oscar Broneer, *Isthmia, Topography and Architecture* (Isthmia II; Princeton, N.J.: ASCSA, 1973) 99–112; and Gebhard et al., "Isthmia, 1989: III," 428–54.

[88]See Piérart, "Panthéon et hellénisation," 103–5. The stadium was no longer visible since it had been abandoned and covered in the early years of the third century B.C.E.; see Broneer, *Topography and Architecture,* 47–66; and Elizabeth R. Gebhard and F. P. Hemans, "University of Chicago Excavations at Isthmia, 1989: II," *Hesperia* 67 (1998) 33–40 and fig. 15 (plan). For a selection of the Hellenistic fills that were brought to level the area after the Classical Stadium went out of use, see Catherine Morgan, *The Late Bronze Age Settlement and Early Iron Age Sanctuary* (Isthmia 8; Princeton, N.J.: ASCSA, 1999) appendix III, 458. The reservoir for the stadium water supply was fed by Water Channel III coming from a source west of the sanctuary (Broneer, *Topography and Architecture,* 26–27; plan iv shows water channels for the central sanctuary). The water supply was cut off and the channel abandoned with the Classical Stadium.

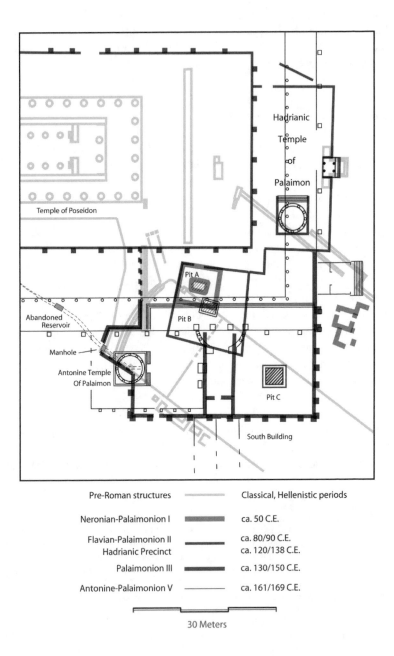

Fig 6.7a Restored plan of the Palaimon, all phases.

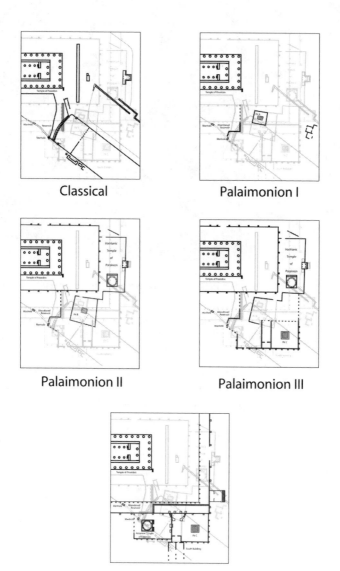

Fig. 6.7b Key to the plan of the Palaimon, highlighting phases.

Fig. 6.8 Restored view of Palaimonion, phase I, looking west. (P. Sanders)

in the second century a small temple to Palaimon was built within its own
enclosure at the east side of the Temple of Poseidon (Phase III; fig. 6.7a–b).
The entire shrine was expanded with the addition of a third pit (C) and two
further precincts circa 130–150 C.E. (fig. 6.11, p. 198). Subsequently, when
Poseidon's temenos was enlarged, Palaimon's temple was moved to the
southwest precinct. A passageway through the podium gave access to the
underground reservoir (Phase V; fig. 6.7a–b).

Originally Pit A was rather small.[89] A low wall surrounded it, leaving a
space of 2 to 3 m at the sides (fig. 6.8). Its function is not in doubt. When
discovered, the cavity was filled to the top with heavily charred bones of
young cattle representing all parts of the skeleton. Mixed with the bones
were wood ash, carbonized remains of bread/hard wheat, fig seeds,
pomegranate seeds, and a date pit, as well as fragments of phialai, cups,
mugs, and jugs.[90] The animal was evidently whole when it was placed

[89]Broneer, *Topography and Architecture,* 100, plate 37d; and Gebhard et al., "Isthmia,
1998: III," 428–33, fig. 12, plate 73b–c. The pit, 2.30 x 1.40 m and ca. 1.60 m deep, was
later enlarged to 3.50 x 2.30 m.

[90]A portion of fill in the pit left by Broneer was excavated in 1989 (ibid., 430–31; vessels:
448–49, nos. 18–23).

on a pyre[91] and consumed by fire.[92] After the blaze died away, the worshippers consigned their cups and bowls to the pit. The cavity resembles a *bothros*, although larger than most examples used to hold libations or the refuse from sacrifices. It could have been imagined as establishing contact with the underworld.[93] The name given to the Isthmian pits is preserved in a list of benefactions made to the sanctuary by one P. Lucinius Priscus Iuventianus in the second century (IG IV 203.9), where it is called ἐναγιστήριον.[94] The word, derived from ἐναγίζειν ("to offer sacrifices to heroes and the human dead"), must refer to the place where such sacrifices were made. In her study of sacrificial terminology, Gunnel Ekroth concludes that ἐναγίζειν may have been in contemporary use with reference to the rites for Palaimon that were carried out in and around the pit.[95] Philostratus, in his description of sacrifices

---

[91]Funeral pyres: Donna Kurtz and John Boardman, *Greek Burial Customs* (London: Thames and Hudson, 1971) 73–74 (Archaic Attica), 195 (Classical Thera, Eretria). An Attic red-figure vase shows Croesus on his pyre, ca. 500 B.C.E. (John Boardman, *Athenian Red Figure Vases: The Archaic Period* [London: Thames and Hudson, 1975] 112, fig. 171). Literary sources: Homer on the pyre for Achilles (*Il.* 23.110–126; pyre did not burn, 23.192–225); and Statius on the pyre for Opheltes (*Theb.* 6.54–83, construction; 6.202–12, fire). It is not impossible that those who instituted the sacrifices for Melikertes-Palaimon in the Roman sanctuary were inspired by poetic descriptions, as Piérart suggested ("Panthéon et hellénisation," 85–109).

[92]The bones were of young cattle, weighing 22.35 kg in a cavity of 5.92 m^3. One individual 1–1.5 years old and another at least 3.5–4 years old could be identified. The density of the ash and bone and the fact that three separate layers were present within the pit show that more than one sacrifice is represented. The pit would have been cleaned out during its period of use. Further faunal analysis: Gebhard and Reese, "Sacrifices." For the rarity of holocaustic sacrifices, see Ekroth, "Altars in Greek Hero-Cults," esp. 129; and, for a more detailed discussion, idem, *Sacrificial Rituals,* esp. 102–7 and n. 453; table 9 charts the frequency of the term. Compare the holocaust in the festival of Herakles on Mt. Oitia (Burkert, *Greek Religion*, 63).

[93]For the range of functions attached to *bothroi* and the rituals related to them, see Ekroth, "Sacrificial Rituals," 43–56. For some examples, a certain size is implied by the context, e.g., at Lebadeia where the *bothros* was large enough for Pausanias to disappear into its depths (Pausanias 9.39.6).

[94]Daniel J. Geagan, "The Isthmian Dossier of P. Licinius Priscus Juventianus," *Hesperia* 58 (1989) 350; and Ekroth, "Altars in Greek Hero-Cults," 62–64. Ekroth points to an analogy with θυσιαστήριον, "altar," derived from θυσιάζειν (63 n. 284), and suggests that *enagizein* sacrifices were part of the cult practices established for Palaimon in Roman times; similarly, Piérart, "Panthéon et hellénisation," 106–9.

[95]Ekroth, *Sacrificial Rituals*, 65–107. In Greek contexts, especially as used by Pausanias, the term represents sacrifice at the tomb of a hero; see also Philostratus, *Her.* 52.3; 53.11–13, referring to rites for Achilles at his tomb at Troy; and Plutarch, *Arist.* 21.2, referring to the tombs of the Plataean heroes. Arthur Darby Nock ("The Cult of Heroes," in *Essays on Religion and the Ancient World* [ed. Zeph Stewart; Oxford: Clarendon, 1972] 590–93) examined the significance of the aspect of the deity in regard to a sacrifice (*thyein*) or holocaust (*enagismos*); see also Burkert, *Greek Religion*, 205.

at the tomb of Achilles at Troy, recounts that "they dug offering pits (βόθροι) on it [the tomb mound] and then slaughtered the black bull as to one who is dead."[96] They then went to the shore, sacrificed another bull to Achilles as to a god, and ate the entrails. This dual aspect of Achilles recalls the similarly double nature of god and hero discussed above with respect to Melikertes-Palaimon and his mother. Note Melikertes' altar by the shore (fig. 6.1a).

The presence of dining and cooking wares in all three Palaimonion pits (A–C) supports the suggestion that the worshippers feasted as well as sacrificed. At Troy the meal was held on the shore after the sacrifice of a second bull, although Achilles and Patroclus were called upon to join the feast before the first offering at his tomb (Philostratus, *Her.* 53.11). So too in rites for the heroes at Plateaea (Plutarch, *Arist.* 21.2). The feast of the participants in honor of the hero was an important element in hero cult.[97] Gunnel Ekroth argues that the feast and blood-offering to which the dead were invited were symbolic and not shared with mortals.[98] On the other hand, as noted above, recent analysis of the sacrificial debris from the Sanctuary of Heracles on Thasos revealed that some portion of the animal had been eaten. For Palaimon the presence in the pit of cooking pots and dining vessels makes it likely that the meal was consumed in the immediate vicinity of the sacrifice (figs. 6.9a–b).[99]

That the rites took place at night is amply attested by the quantity of lamps found in all areas of the shrine, and especially in the western precinct of Phases III and V (figs. 6.10a–b, p. 196).[100] The archaeological remains are in keeping with what we would expect for a hero cult.

[96]*Her.* 53.11, trans. Aitken and Maclean. Tomb and altar (*bōmos*) are combined in the case of Aiakos on Aegina. The altar was not much raised above the ground and its identity as his tomb was kept secret (Pausanias 1.39.6). No tumulus seems to have been present in the Roman Palaimonion.

[97]On the feast for Pelops, see Slater, "Pelops," 1989. In general, see Burkert, *Greek Religion*, 205. Nock ("Cult of Heroes," 577–78, 582–89) emphasizes the importance of the cult feast for the hero and the lack of clear demarcation between chthonic and celestial rites to beings such as Heracles, Melampus, Amphiareus, the Dioscuri, Hyacinthus, Throphonius, and Theseus. See now Hägg, ed., *Greek Sacrificial Ritual*.

[98]This would be a nonparticipatory sacrifice, which in some contexts is explicitly contrasted with θύειν (Ekroth, "Altars in Greek Hero-Cults," 80–82; contra: Slater, "Pelops").

[99]The slip-coated phialai excavated in 1989 amounted to ca. 3,800 g, the mugs ca. 1,130 g, and the gray jugs ca. 1,000 g (Gebhard et al., "Isthmia, 1998: III," 441–43; Pal I dep 1.2). The phialai may be interpreted as votives, but the mugs and jars are equally at home in the context of a feast.

[100]More than 58% of all the lamps from Isthmia came from the Palaimonion area (Oscar Broneer, *Terracotta Lamps* [Isthmia 3; Princeton, N.J.: ASCSA, 1977] 89). Most lamps are of the small Broneer type 16, although a new, much larger type made specifically for the cult came into use before the end of Pit A (ibid., 35–52; and Gebhard et al., "Isthmia, 1998: III," 445, fig. 16.52).

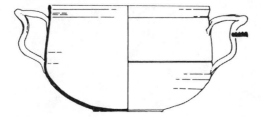

Fig. 6.9a Cup from Pit A (IP 8195). Scale 1:3.

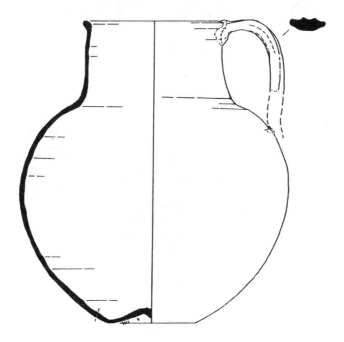

Fig 6.9b Utility vessel from Pit A (IP 8227). Scale 1:3.

Fig. 6.10a View of lamps (Palaimonion and Broneer Type 16) as found in the western precinct of the shrine, 1956.

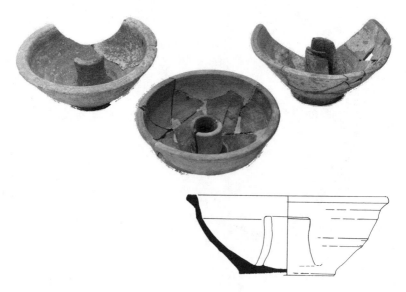

Fig. 6.10b Palaimonion lamps, Type A (IP 7663, 648, 6644; drawing, IP 648). Scale of drawing 1:3.

The other element of Palaimon's shrine was an underground chamber that belonged to an abandoned reservoir. Its name is given by Pausanias, who says: "There is also another thing called an *adyton*, and an underground descent to it, where they say Palaimon is concealed" (2.2.1).[101] He has just described the Temple of Palaimon with its statues, probably the first temple at the east side of Poseidon's temenos. His first words, ἔστι δὲ καὶ ἄλλο, make it clear that the *adyton* is separate from the temple. This is contrary to what Broneer believed, but in the other instances where Pausanias uses the same phrase, the reference is always to another object, separate and distinct from the one previously mentioned. The sense is additive, as in a list of places.[102]

Thus, at the time of Pausanias's visit there was a holy place reached by an underground descent, unconnected with the Temple of Palaimon. The chamber was embedded in the mythology of the place, its creation attributed by one author to Poseidon himself who split open the earth to provide an *adyton* for the hero.[103]

The first temple stood alone in the eastern precinct where its podium can still be seen (fig. 6.11); its superstructure is depicted on Corinthian coins issued under Hadrian.[104] With construction of stoas around the temenos of Poseidon, the monument was rebuilt on a new podium in the western enclosure of the Palaimonion (fig. 6.7, Phase V). A passage through the foundation

[101]ἔστι δὲ καὶ ἄλλο ἄδυτον καλούμενον κάθοδος δὲ εἰς αὐτὸ ὑπόγεως. ἔνθα δὴ τὸν Παλαίμονα κεκρύφθαι φασίν.

[102]Examples include one harbor and then another (1.1.4), a statue of Apollo and then a further Temple of Apollo (1.19.1), another tomb of Laïs (2.2.5), another temple (3.15.6). Such a meaning was understood before Broneer's excavations: see J. G. Frazer, ed., *Pausanias's Description of Greece* (6 vols.; 1897; repr., New York: Biblo and Tannen, 1965) 3:14–15. For *adyton* as an underground chamber, see Pausanias 7.27.2; 9.39.10–13; 10.32.13–18; as a chamber of uncertain location: 5.1.5; 10.33.11. See also Will, *Korinthiaka*, 177–80, 184–87; and Domenico Musti and Mario Torelli, eds., *Pausania: Guida della Grecia II* (Milan: Fondazione Lorenzo Valla/Mondadori, 1986) 17, 212. Broneer interpreted the passage in relation to the Temple of Palaimon that he uncovered and found connected by a passage to an underground cavity (*Topography and Architecture* 99, 109–12). See also fig. 6.7, Phase V, above).

[103]Philostratus, *Imag.* 2.16.

[104]See K. M. Edwards, *Coins, 1896–1929* (Corinth VI; Cambridge, Mass.: ASCSA, 1933) no. 111 and other examples listed in Gebhard, "Isthmian Games," 93 n. 6. Most examples show the boy lying on the dolphin within, but some versions have a seated statue of Poseidon (Corinth coin: Agora SE, V-29-1933) or a similarly posed figure of Isthmus (*NCP* plate FF, suppl. 1, v = Paris 1005). I thank Mary Walbank for calling my attention to the issue with Poseidon. For stratigraphic and architectural reasons, the temple on the Hadrianic coins is unlikely to be the same building as the one that was excavated by Broneer. For the archaeological evidence, see Gebhard, "Isthmian Games," 89–93; and Gebhard et al., "Isthmia, 1998: III," 438–41. Contra: Piérart ("Panthéon et hellénisation," 97), who is confused about the archaeology and thus the architectural sequence of the shrine's development.

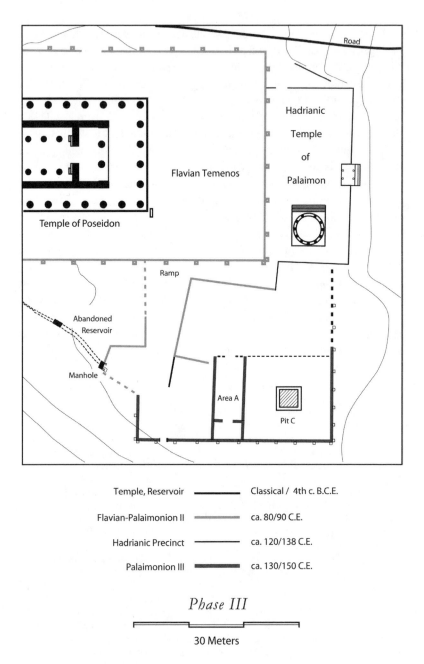

Fig. 6.11 Restored plan of Palaimonion, phase III.

Fig. 6.12 Classical Stadium reservoir, northwest end, after construction of the south stoa.

provided access to the underground chamber, replacing the manhole (the "underground descent" of Pausanias).

When the reservoir was discovered by Roman colonists, as suggested by Piérart,[105] they would have seen a long, narrow cavity cut from the native marl of the Isthmian plateau, its uneven sides covered with waterproof cement, the roof arched (fig. 6.12).[106] Long abandoned, it would have appeared in the dark as a secret, hidden place, its stuccoed sides suggesting that once there

---

[105]Piérart, "Panthéon et hellénisation," 103–5; see p. 189, above.

[106]Over 17 m long and 0.45–0.75 m in width, with a maximum height of 1.20 m (Broneer, *Topography and Architecture*, 27, plate 13a).

had been water there, conjuring a suitably aquatic environment for a marine divinity.[107] The descent through one of of the manholes would have given them the impression of penetrating the depths of the earth and sea.[108]

A ramp connected Pit A with the eastern manhole. Along its west side ran a rubble wall that Broneer removed in the course of the early excavations in order to clear the stadium below it (no. 1 in figs. 6.13 and 6.14, p. 202). The wall as preserved at the time of the excavation appears in photographs and on the actual state plan.[109] Beginning at the north end, segment 1 ran north-south for ca. 5 m. It was bedded on a layer of soil slightly west of and above the ashlar foundation for an earlier terrace wall.[110] A second segment of the wall (2), beginning after a gap made by the south wall of the south stoa, turned westward for ca. 7.20 m. It rested on a layer of soil and stones about 0.17 m above the stadium floor.[111] A short third segment (3) turned southward again, following the empty footing trench for the Classical temenos wall, and it came to an end at the eastern manhole (figs. 6.7, Phases I–III, and 6.13). The type of masonry, as described in the field notebooks and documented in

[107]Until the natural surface was lowered for construction of the south stoa in the latter years of the second century (fig. 6.7, Phase V), the reservoir would have been completely underground, reached only through the two manholes; see fig. 6.13, opposite. The western manhole gave access to the main reservoir, while the east end was closed by a stone partition. The eastern manhole lay to the east of the partition, where water had collected before issuing into the stadium channels.

[108]Broneer, *Topography and Architecture*, 110, plate 41c, plan VIII. The area was much altered with construction of the second Temple of Palaimon (ibid., 109–12; facade: plate 42b).

[109]James Hanges, during his study of excavation records concerning the Palaimonion, realized that the three segments of the wall that had been removed were related to the early period of the Palaimonion because their elevation was well below the surface in use in the final period of the shrine (Phase V). They are recorded in Notebook 9, pp. 50, 89; Notebook 11, pp. 124–25. Broneer does not mention them in his published work. Actual state plan: *Topography and Architecture*, plan II. A portion of the plan is reproduced in fig. 6.13, opposite.

[110]Broneer (*Topography and Architecture*, "Lower Terrace Wall," 68–69) thought the ashlar terrace wall was Roman, contemporary with Palaimonion I and II, and apparently dismissed the upper wall as belonging to the post-sanctuary period. The terrace wall, composed of reused ashlar blocks, cannot be dated contextually, but it has no parallels in constructions associated with the Early Roman period; it would be more at home in the third century B.C.E., when it would have formed part of the landscaping in the area after the stadium was abandoned. The wall (1) at a higher level, which we associate with the early Palaimonion, was composed largely of field stones with the addition of two reused ashlar blocks. It was bedded on a layer of stones and soil that reached down to the floor of the stadium. The upper part of segment 1 had a thickness of ca. 0.85 m (Notebook 11, pp. 124–25).

[111]Notebook 9, pp. 38, 50, 89, 91 (referred to as Wall 4). Composed of courses of fairly large field stones and one stone that was noted as a boulder, the wall was preserved to a height of 1.15 m at its east end. The rear wall of the south stoa ran along its northern side.

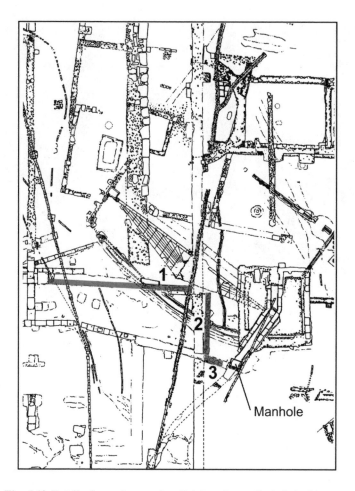

Fig. 6.13 Detail of actual state plan, Palaimonion walls 1–3, looking east. Wall 1 probably extended farther north; compare figs. 6.11 and 6.14, p. 202.

contemporary photographs, is similar to the precinct walls of Pits A and B. Furthermore, the wall's bedding is comparable in depth to the soil beneath the precinct walls. While the first stretch of wall (no. 1 in fig. 6.13) bordered the ramp along the west side of Pit A, segments 2 and 3 extended the wall farther to the west and south, defining an area in front of the manhole (figs. 6.7a–b). A fourth section of the wall probably stood along the south side of the area, forming a three-sided niche or enclosure. The enclosure was open for a width of ca. 8 m at the east side and it had a depth (east-west) of ca.

Fig. 6.14 View of excavations in west end of the Palaimonion, 1956, looking east. Walls 1, 2, and 3 are in the central foreground and at right. Compare Fig. 6.13.

7 m (figs. 6.7 and 6.8). The steep slope leading up to the manhole had a rise of 1:3.5, which gave added emphasis to the spot imagined as the tomb of the hero.

What evidence is there of the area's function? The most conspicuous remains are the lamps. Figure 6.10a shows a cluster of these lamps during excavation, and many such groups are described in the excavation records. Some are the small, handheld lamps of Broneer Type 16 (one is on the left in fig. 10a), but most are the larger lamps created for the Palaimonion. These must have been set on the ground, and they held enough oil in the bowl-shaped body to burn throughout the night (fig. 6.10b).[112]

Discussion of the possible nature of the rites performed in front of the god's underground *adyton* is beyond the scope of this paper. Suffice it to say they took place at night. In that respect we may recall Plutarch's comment that the ceremony for Melikertes was held at night and had the form of a

[112]Palaimonion lamps: Broneer, *Terracotta Lamps*, 35–52. Hayes brings the date of the first Palaimonion lamps into the final period of Pit A, before ca. 80 C.E. (Gebhard et al., "Isthmia, 1998: III," 445–46). The small Type 16 lamps were used in the initial period and continued in later times.

τελετή (*Vit. Thes.* 25.4). Aelius Aristides comments that "it is good . . . to speak his name and take his oath and to participate in his rite (τελετή) and celebration (ὀργανισμός)" (*Or.* 46.40). For Statius they were a black superstition, implying something out of the ordinary, excessive, and sinister.[113] What precisely the *adyton* symbolized is unclear. Pausanias's wording (ἔνθα δὴ τὸν Παλαίμονα κεκρύφθαι) shows that for him it was Palaimon's tomb. On the other hand, the possibility of other interpretations arises from the fact that the chamber became easily accessible in Phase V. The manhole was replaced by a passage that led from a door in the front of the temple podium, into the main cavity of the reservoir. An underwater environment inside the chamber was created by painting the interior blue as well as by extending the waterproofing of the old reservoir to cover the new extension through the podium so that the entire chamber could have held water. It is not impossible that the rites included an illusory descent beneath the sea to visit Palaimon, but other interpretations are possible.

In conclusion, we have seen that Melikertes, the legendary hero for whom the Isthmian Games were instituted, was honored at the time of the festival with funeral rites that appear to have included a re-enactment of the discovery of his body at the shore, a memorial *thrēnos* performed over the body, and a procession to his tomb. In re-establishing their right to the Isthmian festival, the colonists of Roman Corinth apparently continued the traditional mourning song for Melikertes-Palaimon. On the other hand, they developed a new sanctuary for his cult, which had as its focus a subterranean chamber (formerly the reservoir for the Classical Stadium) that they understood as his *adyton* or tomb. A pit was opened nearby for the holocaustic sacrifice of a bull, and in its vicinity the participants shared a meal in his honor. There was thus both continuity and change in cult practice between the rites observed in Greek Corinth and in the Roman colony, but the debt to tradition seems to have been greater than previously supposed.

---

[113]On *superstitio*, see D. Grodzynski, "*Superstitio*," *REA* 76 (1974) 36–60.

CHAPTER SEVEN

The Stones Don't Speak and the Texts Tell Lies: Sacred Sex at Corinth

John R. Lanci

> Corinth is called "wealthy" because of its commerce, since it is situated on the Isthmus and is master of two harbours. . . . The temple of Aphrodite was so rich that it owned more than a thousand temple-slaves (ἱεροδούλους), courtesans (ἑταίρας), whom both men and women had dedicated to the goddess. And therefore it was also on account of these women that the city was crowded with people and grew rich; for instance, the ship-captains freely squandered their money, and hence the proverb, "Not for every man is the voyage to Corinth."
>
> Strabo, Geography 8.6.20

No archaeological evidence suggests that rituals of sacred sex were practiced at Corinth, and textual scholars have for some time questioned the reliability of Strabo and Athenaeus, the two primary sources "documenting" the existence of Corinthian cultic prostitution.[1] Nonetheless, Aphrodite's thousand Corinthian temple prostitutes continue to dance through the footnotes of scholarly research—archaeological, historical, and religious. Strange indeed

---

[1]The epigraph was translated by Horace L. Jones, *The Geography of Strabo* (LCL; 8 vols.; Cambridge: Harvard University Press, 1917–1933) 4:189–91. See Hans Conzelmann, "Korinth und die Mädchen der Aphrodite," *Nachrichten der Akademie der Wissenschaften in Göttingen* 8 (1967) 247–61; and H. D. Saffrey, "Aphrodite à Corinthe: réflexions sur une idée reçue," *RB* 92 (1985) 359–74. For a readily accessible survey of the situation, see Jerome Murphy-O'Connor, *St. Paul's Corinth: Texts and Archaeology* (3d ed.; Minneapolis: Liturgical Press, 2002) 55–58, 144–47.

is this notion of ritual prostitution flourishing in a Greek city: the practice is so anomalous, so oddly placed within the matrix of religious life in the surrounding region, that it cannot help but intrigue and at the same time disturb a student of religion. Received wisdom suggests a connection between Corinthian Aphrodite and the fertility cults of the ancient Near East.

In the course of conversation over lunch one day, I mentioned to a specialist in Near Eastern languages this postulated connection, and asked for a quick overview of the religious context of ritual prostitution in the ancient Near East. Our conversation went something like this:

"What ritual prostitution?" she asked. "There's virtually no evidence for ritual prostitution *anywhere* in the Near East."

"Um, you know what I mean," I said. "The religious rituals associated with the fertility goddesses."

"What fertility goddesses?" she responded.

"Uh, Inanna, Asherah, Ishtar," I said. "You know, the goddesses of the ancient fertility cults."

"What fertility cults?" she asked me. "There were no fertility religions in the ancient Near East."

That was news to me.

And relevant news at that. My colleague had reminded me that we must be very cautious when we traverse the distance between one scholarly discipline and another. For many, such a venture is too fraught with interpretive danger to attempt. To those laboring in the fields of archaeology and religion who are willing to take the risk, I offer some reflections on the kinds of problems we will continue to confront: problems concerning the translation of ancient religious terminology and the rhetorical nature of our textual sources, and the difficulties we all have in understanding ancient worship practices. The Greek city's alleged worship of Aphrodite will serve as a platform for the discussion that follows; no one claims there were sacred prostitutes in Corinth's Roman incarnation. But the concerns and questions raised will, I trust, be relevant to those working on material from any period of Corinthian history.[2]

PROBLEM ONE: THE TERMINOLOGY OF SACRED SEX

When my lunch partner, Beth LaRocca-Pitts, reacted with bewilderment to my attempt to entice her into a discussion of ancient fertility cults, she

[2]Note that I come to this conversation a religious specialist whose field may be broadly identified as "religious studies," rather than the more restrictive Judeo-Christian term "theology."

was signaling a problem concerning translation.[3] Specialists in ancient Near Eastern studies question the traditional translation of derivatives of one root in particular and suggest that the entire notion of ancient rituals of sacred sex is a canard, however unintentional.

Almost three decades ago, Eugene Fisher pointed out problems with the received understanding of the presence of "widespread cultic prostitution" in the ancient Near East.[4] Focusing on the Code of Hammurabi, he studied four types of "sacred women," one of which was the *qadištu*, a word which literally means "holy one" but has been translated as "sacred prostitute." Fisher indicated that the Code of Hammurabi never refers to any of the four types of women in the context of sexual activity, and certainly does not associate them with a situation that we would identify as prostitution. Read on its own, the code indicates the existence of groups of women who, Fisher suggested, formed priestly classes or guilds. There are no references to the sexual behavior of the women, and Fisher concluded that there is no evidence for the institution of sacred prostitution.

In 1989, Joan Goodnick Westenholz took advantage of a continuing stream of new texts to re-examine the term *qadištu* in the context of Mesopotamia and the Hebrew Bible.[5] In her work, she demonstrates in great detail that in Ugaritic and Akkadian texts from Ugarit, nominal forms derived from the root *qdš* refer to "a group of people connected with the temple and its cult whose status was inheritable."[6] She then proceeds to Akkadian texts from Mesopotamia, in which *qadištu* and related nouns refer to women of special status. Their exact function is hard to pin down; as Westenholz points out, religious symbols and titles undergo continual change in status and function.[7]

Westenholz examines the meaning of *qadištu* in Old Babylonian legal texts, documents roughly contemporary to the Code of Hammurabi, establishing that the *qadištu* was in some way devoted to the rituals of a male deity. A passage from the Atra-ḫasis myth suggests that the *qadištu* was associated with childbirth. Only rarely do texts indicate that a *qadištu* served as

[3]I am indebted to LaRocca-Pitts, a professor of Hebrew Bible at Duke University, for her "heads up" concerning this problem. While I am conversant with Biblical Hebrew, I must admit to a lack of training in Ugaritic, Akkadian, and Sumerian. Thus, in what follows I rely on secondary sources, and the reader should consider this section's survey to be an extension of LaRocca-Pitts's warning of the need for further research.

[4]Eugene J. Fisher, "Cultic Prostitution in the Ancient Near East? A Reassessment," *BTB* 6 (1976) 225–36.

[5]Joan Goodnick Westenholz, "Tamar, *Qĕdēšā, Qadištu*, and Sacred Prostitution in Mesopotamia," *HTR* 82 (1989) 245–65.

[6]Ibid., 250.

[7]Ibid., 251.

a votary of a god (namely Adad, at Kish and Sippar) or goddess (Annunītu, at Mari).[8] Westenholz continues her examination of the *qadištu*-woman in Middle Babylonian, Assyrian, and Sumerian texts, and while the *qadištu* seems to be associated with a wide variety of cultic practices—everything from childbirth and ritual purification to witchcraft and ritual exorcism—Westenholz finds nothing to connect these women with prostitution, sacred or otherwise. On the contrary, various texts indicate that sexual activity within the sacred sphere was prohibited, and that offenders were believed to be punished by physical ailments.[9]

How would one define "sacred prostitution," anyway? Westenholz cites the *Oxford English Dictionary*, which indicates that the word "prostitution" comes from the Latin *prostituere*, "to place before, to expose publicly, to offer for sale." Sacred prostitution, she concludes, would be "the act of offering the body to indiscriminate lewdness for hire in the sacred sphere, ritual, or place," and for this kind of activity there is not a shred of evidence from the ancient Near Eastern texts.[10] Indeed, as Phyllis Bird has noted, ancient Semitic cultures had words for prostitutes and they had terminology for female cultic functionaries, but "terms used in the indigenous languages to describe the two classes never connect the sacred sphere with prostitution or prostitution with the cult." Except, she adds, in the Hebrew Bible.[11]

When we move to biblical studies, recent consensus suggests that the idea of cultic prostitution is as problematic with respect to the Hebrew Bible as it is in other ancient Near Eastern texts. I will not explore the biblical evidence in detail; rather, I want to touch briefly on two ways in which traditional interpreters have apparently misunderstood the evidence and as a result "discovered" in the Hebrew Bible evidence for the existence of ancient "pagan" Canaanite rituals of sacred prostitution associated with fertility.

The first misunderstanding results from the blurring of the distinction between biblical metaphor and historical fact. When Israelite prophets wanted to warn against idolatry, they spoke in metaphors: apostasy against God is often condemned as a behavior analogous to marital infidelity, sexual license, or prostitution. They used such metaphors, as Jo Ann Hackett points out, "for drawing boundaries between the good guys and the bad guys."[12]

[8]Ibid., 251–53.

[9]Ibid., 263.

[10]Ibid., 261–62.

[11]Phyllis Bird, " 'To Play the Harlot': An Inquiry into an Old Testament Metaphor," in *Gender and Difference in Ancient Israel* (ed. Peggy L. Day; Minneapolis: Fortress, 1989) 76.

[12]Jo Ann Hackett, "Can a Sexist Model Liberate Us? Ancient Near Eastern 'Fertility' Goddesses," *Journal of Feminist Studies in Religion* 5 (1989) 73.

Phyllis Bird points to the book of the prophet Hosea as a prime source for "proof" of the existence of ancient sacred prostitution. With its famous call to the prophet to take a whore for his wife, it contains "the birth of a metaphor"; that is, the language of prostitution is a metaphor for Israel's straying from God to idolatry. The problem according to the text is the "perverted worship" of Israelite men. But Israelite women are also condemned: not for the first time in antiquity, they are accused of sexual impropriety.[13] According to Bird, the two condemnations (against male idolatry and female sexual profligacy) are never conflated in Hosea, but the distinctions do get clouded in later interpretations. This confusion of metaphor with fact probably began in antiquity. But as Robert Oden and others have shown, the history of misinterpretation continues into the modern period.[14]

Without delving further into these complicated and nuanced issues of interpretation, I advance to a second misunderstanding, which concerns the "sacred marriage," the *hieros gamos* that scholars have traditionally pointed to as an important source of Near Eastern sexual rituals associated with fertility. As the ritual is typically described, the king engages in sexual intercourse with a priestess who represents the goddess, thus ensuring fertility and prosperity for all in the kingdom. Once again, however, the evidence for such ritual actions is problematic. Some Mesopotamian art does appear to depict what could be construed as sacred marriage rituals. But no artifacts bearing inscriptions have survived, and without some textual vocalization, the stones don't speak. How can we know that what is represented was in fact a sacred ritual?[15] Hackett argues that the idea that the *hieros gamos* was literally acted out is a reconstruction found only in the secondary literature. What textual references there are to sacred marriage in the Mesopotamian material never claim that the ritual was actually performed.[16]

Of course, this does not mean that the religious systems of the ancient Near East were unconcerned with fertility. Hackett observes that fertility religion existed everywhere in the Near East: everywhere, including in the Hebrew Bible, we find rituals associated with birth and the growth of crops

---

[13]Bird, " 'To Play the Harlot,' " 80–89.

[14]Robert A. Oden, *The Bible without Theology* (Urbana: University of Illinois Press, 1987), esp. 135–40.

[15]Ibid., 151.

[16]Hackett, "Sexist Model," 70. Moreover, as Dale Martin pointed out in a discussion at the "Urban Religion in Roman Corinth" conference in January 2002, even if it was acted out, we cannot assume without evidence that the ritual involved sex between the king and an actual woman. Human religious imagination would not require a physical stand-in for the ritual of sacred marriage to have its powerful effect.

and cattle. But were there religions—or, for that matter, deities—that had the promotion of fertility as their primary purpose? For such religions or deities there is no supporting evidence.

Of course, the possibility that ritual sex occurred in the context of ancient Near Eastern cultures cannot be ruled out. But when the literary evidence is evaluated apart from the presuppositions of the scholarly literature, we find no indisputable evidence for religions centered on fertility, or fertility goddesses, or the ritual enactment of sacred marriages, and no ritual prostitution can be documented with any certainty. These notions, when they do crop up in ancient sources, seem to be accusations rather than statements of fact.[17] In the words of Westenholz, the idea of Near Eastern sacred prostitution "is an amalgam of misconceptions, presuppositions, and inaccuracies."[18] Sacred prostitution would appear to be the product of modern scholarly circular reasoning.[19]

Problem Two: The Texts Tell Lies

Linguistic ambiguities surrounding the terminology of sex, slavery, and religious ritual are not limited to the study of the ancient Near East. The Greek written sources provide ample opportunity for befuddlement concerning sacred prostitution. Classical scholars and biblical text critics alike generally confuse, conflate, or create references to ἑταίραι and ἱερόδουλοι. The role and meaning of the *hetaira* in Greek society seems particularly problematic; these "courtesans"—literally, "companions"— show up everywhere in the literature and would appear to be significantly different from prostitutes (πόρνη), but the term's origins are unclear,[20] and it carries different meanings depending on the contextual nuances. The word *hierodoulē* was etymologically more precise—it clearly signified "sacred slave"—and identified someone as the property of a deity or temple complex. Some *hierodouloi* (the masculine form of the word denoted sacred slaves of both genders) worked in towns and villages dedicated to a god as "serfs of the divinity," while others were donated to a deity as sacred maintenance staff, serving as public slaves of the temple.[21]

---

[17]Oden, *The Bible*, 132.

[18]Westenholz, "Tamar," 263.

[19]Fisher, "Cultic Prostitution," 228.

[20]Leslie Kurke has suggested that the *hetaira* was "invented" by participants in the Greek symposium; see her "Inventing the *Hetaira*: Sex, Politics, and Discursive Conflict in Archaic Greece," *Classical Antiquity* 16 (1997) 106–50.

[21]*OCD*[3], 705.

Despite the apparent simplicity of the concept, interpreters of ancient sources assume with little or no citation of evidence that the *hierodouloi* participated in rituals of sacred prostitution or some other form of sacred sexual intercourse.[22] For instance, in his widely cited study of the "meaning of Aphrodite," Paul Friedrich asserts with respect to the *hierodouloi* associated with Aphrodite's worship at Cythera, Corinth, and Eryx, that "in all such cases the hierodule *represented or incarnated the goddess*."[23]

The processes by which scholars put a sexual spin on the language of sacred slavery are as convoluted as those we have seen with respect to the terminology of the ancient Near East. Permit me to illustrate the lay of the linguistic land by referring to a single incident from the history of Corinth.

According to a number of ancient sources, in 480 B.C.E. the women of Corinth prayed to Aphrodite to enflame their menfolk with a desire for battle against the invading Persians. Such public piety on the part of these women was a big deal for the ancients, apparently; the author of the *De Herodoti malignitate* proclaims that they were the only women in Greece to offer such spirited prayer,[24] and the short poem that Simonides wrote in their honor survives in four or five different sources.

But who were these women? What was their status?

The Simonides fragment simply refers to them with the feminine plural article αἱ ("the [women]"). The contexts in which the fragment is preserved, however, usually interpret this article. Thus, the author of the *De Herodoti malignitate* identifies them as generic women / wives of the city (γυναῖκες) praying to Aphrodite to fire up their menfolk / husbands (ἄνδρες). That their status is respectable is implied by the context of the author's argument: in the middle of excoriating Herodotus for his anti-Corinthian bias, he mentions the piety and bravery of the women of Corinth, noting also that it is odd that Herodotus makes no mention of an incident so famous that even the country bumpkins of Caria must know about it.[25]

---

[22]"Contemporary scholarship uses the expression *sacred prostitution* to refer to a sexual rite practiced in the ancient Near East . . . [in] the temples of Ishtar, Astarte, Mâ, Anāhitā, and Aphrodite." So begins Frédérique Apffel Marglin in her survey of "Hierodoulia" in the *Encyclopedia of Religion* (ed. Mircea Eliade; New York: Macmillan, 1987) 6:309.

[23]Paul Friedrich, *The Meaning of Aphrodite* (Chicago: University of Chicago Press, 1978) 22; emphasis in original. As far as I can see, he presents no actual evidence for his incarnational conclusions.

[24]Plutarch, *Mor.* 871a. Plutarch's authorship of this section of the *Moralia* is disputed.

[25]Ibid., 871b.

Athenaeus, however, sees things differently. According to his source, Chamaeleon of Heracleia, this incident fits a pattern of curious Corinthian piety. The people of Corinth, he writes, had an ancient custom:

> Whenever the city prays to Aphrodite in matters of grave importance, [they] invite as many prostitutes (ἑταίρας) as possible to join in their petitions, and these women add their supplications to the goddess and later are present at the sacrifices.[26]

Thus, it was the *hetairai*, the "companions" of Corinth, who were memorialized in Simonides' poem, and both the author of *De Herodoti malignitate* and Athenaeus agree that the poem was composed on the occasion of a dedication in the sanctuary of Aphrodite when the women's prayers were answered.

But who were these *hetairai*? Were they prostitutes? Were they cultic functionaries? And what exactly was dedicated to the goddess?

Here is where interpretation becomes complicated. If we adhere to his text, Athenaeus states that it was customary to invite the "companions" of Corinth to join in the prayers to Aphrodite in times of special need. Once the Persians were repelled, a grateful city erected an inscription (πίναξ) with the name of each separate *hetaira* engraved on it. This memorial, according to Athenaeus, was what was dedicated to the goddess. The author of the *De Herodoti malignitate* diverges a bit here, recording that statues of the women were erected and dedicated in the sanctuary.[27] Yet while the *De Herodoti malignitate* and Athenaeus differ as to the social status of the women involved (married women versus "companions"), neither text refers to the women as prostitutes (though modern translators render Athenaeus's *hetairai* as such)[28] and neither one associates the women with the cult of the goddess in any official capacity, which we would expect if they were recording an instance of liturgical rituals of sacred prostitution.

From our modern vantage point, we can, I suppose, understand why "companions" might be summoned to pray to Aphrodite; after all, we understand her to have been the "goddess of love" (I return to this issue in the final section of this essay). However, it is important to note that the women, even if they *were* courtesans, prayed that the men of the city would become

---

[26]Athenaeus, *Deipn.* 13.573; trans. Charles B. Gulick, *The Deipnosophists* (7 vols.; LCL; Cambridge, Mass.: Harvard University Press, 1927–1941) 6:96–97.

[27]Thus, Simonides is construed as referring to the statues, not the women, when he begins his poem, "These women were set up/dedicated (ἔσταθεν)."

[28]See, e.g., Charles Burton Gulick's translation in the LCL, which renders ἑταίρα as "harlot," "companion," and "prostitute."

fired up to make war, not love; could this indicate that they were praying not to a love-goddess but to the city's protector, Aphrodite Armed, or Aphrodite in her guise of Οὐρανία, i.e., Queen of Heaven? So, who were the women? It is impossible to say for sure, since both ancient sources (as well as Strabo, who does not mention this incident but does expand on the idea of *hierodouloi* at Corinth)[29] composed their accounts hundreds of years after the fact. But if we read the texts we have, one thing appears certain: the women honored for the efficacy of their prayer and memorialized by Simonides' epigram were not identified as sacred prostitutes dedicated to Aphrodite; what was dedicated was a tablet with their names on it, or perhaps statues depicting them. To find in these sources the presence of slaves dedicated to the sexual service of the goddess of love, one has to read into the accounts something that is not there.[30]

Now, this is not to say that modern interpreters have created sex slaves for Corinthian Aphrodite out of the whole cloth of scholarly inference. Strabo reports that Aphrodite's temple possessed more than a thousand sacred slaves (*hierodouloi*) in the Greek period. He identifies the hierodules as *hetairai* dedicated by both men and women and clearly associates them with the city's reputation for sexual license.[31] What is unclear (unknown, actually) is where Strabo got his information, which would have been circulating for five hundred years before he came upon it.

Herodotus, too, reports the existence of sacred prostitution with respect to the worship of Aphrodite, though among the Babylonians, not the Corinthians:

> Every woman who lives in that country must once in her lifetime go to the temple of Aphrodite and sit there and be lain with by a strange man. . . . When once a woman has taken her seat there, she may not go home again until one of the strangers throws a piece of silver into her lap and lies with her, outside the temple. . . . Once she has lain with him, she has fulfilled her obligation to the goddess and gets gone to her home.[32]

[29]See Strabo, *Geogr.* 8.6.20, cited at the opening of this essay.

[30]So, for example, Christopher Brown, in his close study of the epigram of Simonides ("The Prayers of the Corinthian Women," *GRBS* 32 [1991] 5–14). Despite the ancient texts that identify the women as wives, Brown sees it as plausible that they are courtesans. He does this by citing a modern interpreter who identifies the *hetairai* of Athenaeus with the *hierodouloi* of Strabo (*Geogr.* 8.6.20) and assumes that these temple slaves are sacred prostitutes (ibid., 8).

[31]*Geogr.* 8.6.21.

[32]*Hist.* 1.199, translated by David Grene, *Herodotus: The History* (Chicago: University of Chicago Press, 1987) 124.

Concerning the factual accuracy of Herodotus, I need say little. Considered by Cicero to be the "Father of History," he was also characterized in antiquity as *fabulosus*—in modern parlance, the "mother of all liars."[33] "Greeks and Romans were not apt to kneel in silent adoration before their own classical writers," Arnaldo Momigliano observes dryly. "But no other writer was so severely criticized as Herodotus."[34]

Criticized, yes, but the ancients mined him for information nonetheless. Strabo read him and used him as a source for his account of Babylonian sacred sex rituals.[35] Most—perhaps all—ancient reporters of sacred rituals of prostitution relied on Herodotus,[36] and many modern scholars have used both Strabo and Herodotus uncritically as well.[37] Thus, we confront another interpretive circle game: the accuracy of Herodotus has not been questioned because scholars have assumed that even if he didn't get the facts completely straight, he was referring to rituals whose existence is attested in other ancient sources. But as far as we can tell, those other ancient sources were relying on Herodotus.[38]

When I teach the New Testament to college sophomores, I introduce them to a disturbing problem we face when reading ancient texts: their authors did not understand their job to be reporters of historically accurate facts. The students' initial response is often, "Oh, so these books, the Gospels and stuff, they're full of lies." It takes a while, but they get it eventually: ancient texts must be read in their context and with attention to their genre and purpose. In other words, they must be read critically; if you approach the Gospel of Matthew (as astronomers and astrophysicists do just about every Christmas) with the intention of explaining how a star could guide the Magi to Bethlehem, you are missing the point of the text. Here, I suppose I am preaching to the

---

[33]See *Leg.* 1.5 and *Div.* 2.116.

[34]Arnaldo Momigliano, "The Place of Herodotus in the History of Historiography," *History* 43 (1958) 2.

[35]*Hist.* 16.1.20. Strabo's familiarity with Herodotus's material on Babylon may have made it all the easier for him to accept (or invent) the presence of a thousand temple prostitutes in Corinth.

[36]Oden (*The Bible*, 144–47) claims that virtually all of the non-Christian sources for sacred prostitution in antiquity are dependent directly or indirectly on Herodotus.

[37]See, for example, the work of three authors pertinent to this study: Donald Engels, *Roman Corinth: An Alternative Model for the Classical City* (Chicago: University of Chicago Press, 1990) 97–98; Friedrich, *Aphrodite*, 21–22; and Bonnie MacLachlan, "Sacred Prostitution and Aphrodite," *SR* 2 (1992) 145–62.

[38]Mary Beard and John Henderson, "With This Body I Thee Worship: Sacred Prostitution in Antiquity," in *Gender and Body in the Ancient Mediterranean* (ed. Maria Wyke; Malden, Mass.: Blackwell, 1998) 59.

choir; few of us would uncritically cite a religious text to support a historical argument. But why do so many historians, archaeologists, and scholars of religion check their critical faculties at the door when they read Strabo? Or Pausanias? Or Athenaeus?

If these writers were not as concerned as the Cable News Network or the contemporary scholarly community with "what actually happened," why did they write these texts? The ancient sources, including those containing accusations of sacred prostitution, are not travel guides objectively pointing out four-star attractions not to be missed. They are rhetorical texts; they are making arguments—about Corinth (often in relation to Athens), or about what it is to be a Greek or a barbarian.[39] Oftentimes, the authors are engaged in boundary formation and cultural self-definition.[40] To accept the accuracy of Strabo's account of a thousand Corinthian temple prostitutes is just as inadequate a reading as an astronomer's physical, literal explanation of the migrating star of the Magi.

François Hartog writes of the "rhetoric of Otherness" with respect to Herodotus.[41] The idea of the Other, and the way the Other functions in a society, would be a fruitful field for us to till more extensively with respect to Corinth. The only study I have seen in this regard is that of Mary Beard and John Henderson, who argue that the accounts of sacred prostitution were a response to what they call Corinth's unique identity within Greece as an "Orientalizing Other."[42] The thesis as they present it is not compelling. But it is a good question to ponder: To what degree was Corinth considered the Other within Greece or within the eastern Roman empire? Is that why

[39]As George Kennedy writes (*The Art of Persuasion in Greece* [Princeton, N.J.: Princeton University Press, 1963] 44), "Beginning with [Herodotus], history is second only to oratory as a genre influenced by rhetoric."

[40]The role that Greek theater played in Athenian self-definition has been thoroughly studied; see Josiah Ober and Barry Strauss, "Drama, Political Rhetoric, and the Discourse of Athenian Democracy," in *Nothing to Do with Dionysos?* (ed. John J. Winkler and Froma I. Zeitlin; Princeton, N.J.: Princeton University Press, 1990) 237–70; and the articles in Gregory W. Dobrov, ed., *The City as Comedy: Society and Representation in Athenian Drama* (Chapel Hill: University of North Carolina Press, 1997).

[41]François Hartog, *The Mirror of Herodotus: The Representation of the Other in the Writing of History* (Berkeley: University of California Press, 1988); see also Vivienne Gray, "Herodotus and the Rhetoric of Otherness," *AJP* 116 (1995) 185–211; Donald Lateiner, *The Historical Method of Herodotus* (Toronto: University of Toronto Press, 1989) 25; and Paul Cartledge, "Herodotus and 'the Other': A Meditation on Empire," *Échos du Monde Classique/Classical Views* 34 = n.s. 9 (1990) 27–40.

[42]"The rest of Greece saw Corinth as a foreign city within their midst, an Orientalizing Other. Corinthians embraced this image, not merely colluding in but celebrating their city's image as Greece's internal Other" (Beard and Henderson, "With This Body," 57).

Aristophanes and other Athenian writers zeroed in on this particular port city's sexual practices?

Perhaps it is not Corinth itself that was the Other. Perhaps in this instance (as is so often the case), what is involved here is the question of gender. A number of thinkers have challenged us to focus on "how gendered bodies and sexual difference are communicated visually and symbolically in the art and artifacts" of the ancient world;[43] some have explored the "otherness" of specific groups of females, such as *hetairai*, maenads,[44] and, most extensively, Amazons.[45]

PROBLEM THREE: RECOVERING THE MEANING OF RELIGIOUS WORSHIP

Probably the most formidable problem with the posited presence of sacred prostitution in Greek Corinth has nothing to do with how material and textual evidence has been interpreted. This problem—actually an interrelated collection of difficulties—has to do with the nature of religion in general and our perception of ancient religions in particular.

Religion in premodern cultures is embedded in every aspect of human activity. In traditional communities, religion is a prominent agent in the process of discovering meaning and making sense of life in the world; there is "no religious sphere separate from that of politics or warfare or private life."[46] And yet, how often do we encounter works of history or archaeology

---

[43]Ann Olga Koloski-Ostrow and Claire D. Lyons, "Naked Truths about Classical Art: An Introduction," in *Naked Truths. Women, Sexuality and Gender in Classical Art and Archaeology* (ed. eaedem; New York: Routledge, 1997) 1; see also Marie L. S. Sorensen, *Gender Archaeology* (Cambridge: Polity Press, 2000); Bonnie E. Smith, *The Gender of History* (Cambridge, Mass.: Harvard University Press, 1998); Gail Corrington Streete, *The Strange Woman: Power and Sex in the Bible* (Louisville, Ky.: Westminster/John Knox, 1997), esp. 43–74; and Judith P. Hallett, "Women as *Same* and *Other* in Classical Roman Elite," *Helios* 16 (1989) 59–78.

[44]Jenifer Neils, "Others Within the Other: An Intimate Look at Hetairai and Maenads," in *Not the Classical Ideal: Athens and the Construction of the Other in Greek Art* (ed. Beth Cohen; Leiden: Brill, 2000) 203–26.

[45]See Marilyn Goldberg, "The Amazon Myth and Gender Studies," in *ΣΤΕΦΑΝΟΣ* (ed. Kim J. Hartswicke and Mary C. Sturgeon; Philadelphia: University of Pennsylvania, 1998) 89–100; Andrew Stewart, "Imag(in)ing the Other: Amazons and Ethnicity in Fifth-Century Athens," *Poetics Today* 16 (1995) 571–97; John Henderson, "*Timeo Danaos*: Amazons in Early Greek Art and Pottery," in *Art and Text in Ancient Greek Culture* (ed. Simon Goldhill and Robin Osborne; Cambridge: Cambridge University Press, 1994) 85–137; and Josine H. Blok, *The Early Amazons* (Leiden: Brill, 1995).

[46]Simon R. F. Price, *Religions of the Ancient Greeks* (Cambridge: Cambridge University Press, 1999) 3.

in which religious materials are passed over in silence or confined to a single chapter or even a footnote?

One cannot blame historians or archaeologists for shying away from the complex questions that religious activity raises. With respect to the ritual at hand, how can we evaluate the textual evidence for sacred prostitution without clarifying what such a ritual might have signified to the participants?[47] How do we discern the import of *any* ritual to people who have been dead for millennia and did not favor us with written accounts of their thoughts? If religious rituals involving sexual activity did exist, it is very unlikely that those who practiced them would have understood what they did to be prostitution, a practice marked by indiscriminate activity and emotional indifference. Ancient worshippers, were they available for interviews, might articulate a theology closer to that of religious consecration or sacrament.

Despite the difficulties inherent in such analysis, to incorporate religious practice into historical and archaeological reconstructions of Corinth—in either the Greek or Roman period—we have to study more closely the wider matrix of religious rituals in the Corinthia. The idea of sacred prostitution at Corinth lacks any credibility from a religious point of view until it has been situated within the ritual, liturgical context of the city around it. As Beard and Henderson note, none of the ancient sources place sacred prostitution into "a narrative of any encounter within the institution that it envisages." "What story," they ask, "would fit this practice?"[48] Greek religion, like any religious system, must be understood not as a scrambled puzzle of myths for us to decode, but as a way of interpreting the world.[49] Groups of worshippers shape the way they characterize the gods. According to Christiane Sourvinou-Inwood, the Greeks developed local pantheons, each "an articulated religious system within which divine beings . . . [were] associated and differentiated."[50] The questions we religionists ask of rituals—How is this practice construed as worship? What do the rituals signify? How do they relate to the underlying mythic meanings?—are tough to answer even when we can pull up a chair and engage the participants in discussion. At

---

[47]We know, as an example, that prostitutes had a recognized part to play in the *Ludi Florales* in republican Rome. Would the Romans have understood this as a cultic ritual involving prostitution? See T. P. Wiseman, "The Games of Flora," in *The Art of Ancient Spectacle* (ed. Bettina Bergmann and Christine Kondoleon; Washington, D.C.: National Gallery of Art, 1999) 197. I thank Christine Kondoleon for this reference.

[48]Beard and Henderson, "With This Body," 58.

[49]Greek religion was "a response to life as lived by ancient Greeks" (John Gould, "On Making Sense of Greek Religion," in *Greek Religion and Society* [ed. P. E. Easterling and J. V. Muir; Cambridge: Cambridge University Press, 1985] 5).

[50]Christiane Sourvinou-Inwood, "Persephone and Aphrodite at Locri: A Model for Personality Definitions in Greek Religion," *JHS* 98 (1978) 101.

this far remove, they may never yield indisputable information, but I wonder what specialists in ritual studies might have to say. Until someone can hazard a good guess about not only how ritual sex might have arrived in Greece, but why it took root there, and how this atypical form of worship fit into the wider religious life of the city, Robert Oden's assertion—that sacred prostitution in antiquity was an accusation, not a reality—is difficult to refute.

Conclusion: There's Something about Aphrodite

Let me close with a final thought concerning the Queen of Heaven herself. The religionist in me feels a vague sense of unease about Aphrodite, or at least about how we have come to "understand" her.

Of her origins, we know little. In the earliest Greek traditions, she is born from the world of the Titans amid sexual violence, castration, and the restless froth of the sea. Aphrodite was not a god of the civilized and the urban, she was a force—*the* force—of nature "controlling the life of the earth and the waters of the sea, and . . . ruling in the shadowy land of the dead."[51]

But over time she acquired a new birth-story as a child of Zeus conceived in a more conventional way. At no point in her development can Aphrodite be stereotyped or easily categorized, since "she" was probably an ongoing, rolling conflation of regional goddesses who never lost all of the aspects of their local affiliations.[52] But we observe a tendency, at least in literary texts, to situate her within the realm of fertility and love. Jo Ann Hackett detects a similar movement in the ancient Near East. Restricted to the sphere of fecundity and the feminine, the power of ancient goddesses was diffused and trivialized. By creating the category of "fertility goddesses," the Israelites (and modern scholars) developed a version of the divine that is "comforting and non-threatening" and not quite so complex.[53] Bruce Thornton notes that by the time we meet her in the *Argonautica*, when Hera and Athena come calling to borrow Eros, Aphrodite "comes off rather like some Hellenistic middle-class housewife, idly combing her hair while hubby Hephaistos is off

---

[51]Lewis R. Farnell, *The Cults of the Greek States* (5 vols.; Oxford: Clarendon Press, 1896–1909) 2:668.

[52]In any case, as Sourvinou-Inwood points out ("Persephone and Aphrodite," 102), we should not "extrapolate from one local cult [of a deity] to another and attempt to interpret an aspect found in one place through another found elsewhere."

[53]Hackett, "Sexist Model," 74–75. Bruce Thornton (*Eros: The Myth of Ancient Greek Sexuality* [Boulder, Colo.: Westview Press, 1997] 54) asserts that the Greeks tamed the goddess through "the technology of ritual."

at work." She has become, Thornton observes, "one of those sophisticated eternal hedonists living the good life on the peaks of snowy Olympus," one of the "younger, anthropomorphic culture-gods who supersede the monstrous, more nature-oriented pre-Olympians."[54] And yet, she is never really that far away from her earlier cosmic power, and even as a housewife she can still wreak havoc, as Jason and his Argonauts discover.

Herein lies the source of my Aphrodisian anxiety. For the Greeks, even those who produced our literary sources, the gods did not merely signify ideas or archetypes ("god of wine," "goddess of love"); these are later categories.[55] And the Greek goddesses were not by nature *women*.[56] For all their similarities to you and me, the gods in the piety of the Greeks were, in essence, not human, and they were not tamed by the Greek imagination for very long.

In my imagination, I look at Acrocorinth and I recall Vincent Scully's words about the goddess and the location of her shrines: in their most characteristic form, they "express a nature which seems, like Artemis, to go beyond the reach of reason or control." Her holy ground often has "the appearance of unexpected and irresistible forces, expressing a nature at once aggressive and triumphant."[57] These are sites worthy of an Ouranian Aphrodite, "the power that causes the love that is in heaven and earth, the love that works in the rain, and brings forth cattle and herbs" for the human community.[58]

I look at Acrocorinth and I wonder: Have we been a bit too quick to assume the domestication of this divine force of nature? Are we misled by the likes of Praxiteles—the first, we are told, to depict the goddess nude and vulnerable?[59]

---

[54]Ibid., 65, 54.

[55]Nicole Loraux, "What Is a Goddess?" in *A History of Women in the West* (ed. Pauline S. Pantel; Cambridge, Mass.: Harvard University Press, 1992) 17; and Sourvinou-Inwood, "Persephone and Aphrodite," 101–2.

[56]Loraux ("What Is a Goddess?" 16–17) observes that "*thea* can always be replaced by *theos*" and that "*he theos* denotes a divine being who happens to be marked by a feminine sign."

[57]Vincent Scully, *The Earth, the Temple, and the Gods* (New Haven, Conn.: Yale University Press, 1979) 93–95.

[58]Farnell, *Cults of the Greek States*, 2:669.

[59]It has been suggested that Praxiteles' statue inaugurates a mode of representation that signals a change in attitude toward the female body (Nanette Salomon, "Making a World of Difference," in *Naked Truths: Women, Sexuality and Gender in Classical Art and Archaeology* [ed. Ann Olga Koloski-Ostrow and Claire D. Lyons; New York: Routledge, 1997] 203). More to my point, Lesley Beaumont asserts that Praxiteles' Knidian statue depicts a change in attitude toward Aphrodite herself ("Born Old or Never Young? Femininity, Childhood, and the Goddesses of Ancient Greece," in *The Sacred and the Feminine in Ancient Greece* [ed. Sue Blundell and Margaret Williamson; New York: Routledge, 1998] 91). What we need, but do not yet have, as far as I know, is a rigorous treatment of the religious understanding behind this statue and its influence on the later worship of the goddess.

If so, even Walter Burkert, whose opinion has of late become something of a gold standard in matters of Greek religion, has been hoodwinked, going all soft and cuddly over Aphrodite's association with "the joyous consummation of sexuality" and soft-pedaling her more horrific attributes.[60] I suspect that the accusations concerning sacred sex in Corinth have something to do with controlling the power of this great, terrifying, and, in the end, untamable divine force, and perhaps in controlling her women as well.

The port city of Corinth had a reputation for its prostitutes and courtesans. Prostitutes and courtesans were two categories of women not contained or controlled by custom and law to the degree that others were. Is there a connection between the power of uncontrolled sexually active women in Corinth and their untamable goddess?[61]

It was not for tips about lovemaking and cosmetics that the women of Corinth climbed haunting Acrocorinth in 480 B.C.E. They petitioned their goddess, but not to grant fertility to the land. No, they begged a great and terrifying divine force to inspire their warriors to overwhelm the horrifying, destructive power of war.

The ancient sources may spin the story to the Corinthians' disadvantage and call into question the status or virtue of the women involved. But the ancient sources never deny the wisdom of that journey.

[60]Walter Burkert, *Greek Religion* (trans. Peter Bing; Cambridge, Mass.: Harvard University Press, 1985) 154–55.

[61]For an example of women whose sacrifices play a part in taming the divine, see Susan Guettel Cole, "Domesticating Artemis," in *The Sacred and the Feminine in Ancient Greece* (ed. Sue Blundell and Margaret Williamson; New York: Routledge, 1998) 27–43.

Chapter Eight

Roman Corinth: The Final Years of Pagan Cult Facilities along East Theater Street

Charles K. Williams II

This essay examines the religion of the common people in an everyday place at the interface between pagan and Christian culture. The specific location for this interface is immediately east of the ancient theater in Roman Corinth. The remains that have generated the discussion are the architecture and artifacts that have been excavated by the American School of Classical Studies in Athens between 1982 and 1989.

The topographical focus of this essay is the eastern flank of the theater of Corinth, in which the Romans presented dramatic and comic productions, elaborate official celebrations and spectacles, and, later, gladiatorial games, animal hunts, and aquatic games. Here beside the street that flanked the Roman theater stood a row of structures numbered 1, 3, 5, and 7 (fig. 8.1, p. 222). This incompletely excavated series continues from the northeast corner of the cavea southward up the east side of East Theater Street toward the Fountain of Glauke and the Roman forum. Structures that continue southward past Building 7 are part of an earlier investigation and, because of the lack of detailed excavation records, are not considered in the present discussion.

Fig. 8.1 General view of Buildings 1, 3, 5 and 7 from the west. East Theater Street passes across the middle of the photograph.

Building 1 and 3 and Environs

Buildings 1 and 3 at the foot of the street appear to have been erected specifically to cater food to theatergoers attending performances. Not only do the north rooms of both buildings contain large domed ovens, but the number of bones found in Building 3, especially in its south room, indicate that large amounts of meat were served there (fig. 8.2, p. 224). These two adjoining structures were erected in the first century C.E. and were destroyed in an earthquake in the second quarter of the second century C.E. Only the northern room of Building 1 survived into the last quarter of the third century, or the early fourth century, but it did not necessarily function at that late date as a public kitchen. Dividing Buildings 1 and 3 from the row of buildings farther up the slope is a buttressed terrace wall, the west end of which stops at East Theater Street. Building 5 stands upon the terrace supported by this wall, with its south end abutting Building 7.

Before turning to the cultic aspects of Buildings 5 and 7, which are the main theme of this essay, certain random finds from the neighborhood of East Theater Street that are probably related to cult activity in the area should be cited here. Of the scattered and fragmentary terracotta figurines recovered from the Roman period, the greatest number represent Aphrodite. Thirteen such unstratified figurines of the goddess have been found.[1] Except for one of the Fréjus type, all are naked or have a robe wrapped only around the legs. At least two are bedecked with necklaces or bracelets on the upper arm.[2]

A fragment of a small inscribed column—either part of an altar, or possibly a statue base because it has a socket on its top in which a statue could have been secured—was recovered from a modern wall over the upper east side of the cavea of the theater, west of Buildings 5 and 7. Its importance here is the inscription that it carries, a dedication to Isis and Sarapis.[3] Other stray objects from east of the theater that are related to this Egyptian cult include a fragmentary marble statuette of a devotee of Isis, identifiable by her dress; a terracotta figurine of Harpocrates; a Bes; and three boat lamps.[4]

---

[1]MF-1981-1, MF-1981-51, MF-1983-27, MF-1983-55 (Fréjus type), MF-1984-70, MF-1985-3, MF-1985-27, MF-1985-74, MF-1985-75, MF-1987-26, MF-1987-28, and MF-2002-26.

[2]MF-1984-4 and MF-1981-51. An Aphrodite from the intermediate occupation debris of Building 5, MF-1985-25, also wears this type of jewelry.

[3]I-3609, J. H. Kent, *The Inscriptions, 1926–1950* (Corinth VIII.3; Princeton, N.J.: ASCSA, 1966) 33, no. 57, plate 8.

[4]Marble statuette of devotee, S-3602. Harpocrates, T-528; Bes, C-1987-50A-C; ship-shaped lamp with bust of Serapis in front of handle, L-1993-13. The second ship-shaped lamp, L-1174, is is a random find from the area of the odeum, southwest of Building 7, published

Fig. 8.2 Building 3 of East Theater Street, from the south, showing its north room with ovens at top and storeroom at bottom.

The lamps are very fragmentary; one, however, preserves the head of Sarapis in the panel immediately under its handle, another probably the head of Isis. Important within this group is a fragmentary Osiris hydreios jar, a cult vessel that was supposed to contain Nile water, the lifeblood of Osiris. The body of the jar is decorated with Egyptian gods carved in low relief, its shoulder with the customary necklace. The Osiris head that once crowned the jar is now missing. This last find was recovered from a stratified context—albeit fill of the fifth century C.E.—which originally had contained wall blocks of the western façade of Building 7.

Finds recovered from insignificant contexts but related to the cult of Cybele and Matrona comprise the two next most common groupings. One should include here a fragmentary marble votive relief of Cybele enthroned in a niche, a possible terracotta head of Attis, and a very fragmentary terracotta figurine, probably representing the tympanum of a devotee of Cybele.[5] Matrona, with a writing tablet on her lap, or with a scroll in hand, is represented only in three fragments.[6] There are other fragmentary objects from the area that could suggest cult activities, but at the moment they are single pieces that cannot bear the weight of commentary.

Other unstratified figurines do not represent gods or goddess and are more raw in their subject matter.[7] Among the most bizarre is a category of grotesques. This type of overweight female figure may have first appeared in the Late Classical period; the earliest such figure of Roman date from a stratified context around the theater is Hadrianic.[8] The latest such figurines, datable by context within the fourth and fifth centuries C.E., are the largest; if

---

by Oscar Broneer in *Terracotta Lamps* (Corinth IV.2; Cambridge, Mass.: ASCSA, 1930) 284, no. 1448, plate XXI. The figure on its disc holds a palm branch; the head is probably that of Isis. The third ship-shaped lamp, L-2002-4, is from a road surface of East Theater Street. It preserves only a fragmentary underside. A fourth ship-shaped lamp, L-1984-12, was found stratified within Building 5. Its top panel is decorated with a person holding garlands in upraised hands, standing on the back of a lion(?); a frog is seated behind the spout of the lamp. See Charles K. Williams II and Orestes H. Zervos, "Corinth, 1985: East of the Theater," *Hesperia* 55 (1986) 157, no. 24, plate 35.

[5]Marble statuette of enthroned Cybele, S-3490; terracotta head of Attis(?), MF-1981-39; fragmentary figurine of devotee of Cybele with tympanum, MF-1983-42.

[6]Head, MF-1985-6; tablet in lap, MF-1984-23; scroll at lap, MF-1985-22.

[7]MF-1988-6, erotic group, found in leveling fill near cavea wall of theater, Charles K. Williams II and Orestes H. Zervos, "Corinth, 1986: Temple E and East of the Theater," *Hesperia* 58 (1987) 20, no. 21, plate 7.

[8]MF-1984-15, from above working chips after destruction of Building 3.

Fig. 8.3 Grotesque, fragment
of female torso (MF-13501).

fully restored, they probably stood ca. 0.26 m tall.[9] They come in two types, one with and one without white slip and red and brown paint. Grandjouan suggests that these are tattooed women, with an Egyptian origin. I suggest an alternative explanation, that the decoration is a complicated costume of red ribbons and black netting.[10] The question is not, however, the type of decoration so much as the type of cult to which they can be assigned. Note that the clay in the area between the legs is pierced with a knife to emphasize the

[9]The fragmentary female grotesques found in the vicinity of the east side of the theater are: MF-8357, MF-1981-25, MF-1982-75, MF-1983-49, and MF-1985-73. From around Temple E come MF-86-3 and MF-1989-27. Others from the Corinth collection, but without provenience, are: MF-271, MF-4745, MF-6506, and MF-13501. Nos. MF-6506 and MF-13501 are especially close to C. Grandjouan, *Terracottas and Plastic Lamps of the Roman Period* (Agora 6; Princeton, N.J.: ASCSA, 1961) no. 620. MF-2001-16, an arm, comes from new excavations southeast of the Corinthian forum; for a reasonable parallel from Athens, see Grandjouan, *Terracottas and Plastic Lamps*, 24, 62–63, no. 619, dated late fourth to fifth century c.e. In Grandjouan's discussion of this type of grotesque, which she identifies as Baubo or Kotyto, she is "tempted to associate the figurines with the orgiastic cult of Kotytto [*sic*]. . . . The coroplastic type is of great antiquity in Athens and also resembles certain female temple attendants in Egypt."

[10]In support of the theory that the decoration represents clothing, see Paul Perdrizet, *Les terres cuites grecques d'Égypte de la collection Fouquet* (Nancy: Berger-Levrault, 1921) 122, plate 82, far right: a terracotta female grotesque from Egypt, clearly wearing a patterned shirt or shift, lifted above the stomach.

gender (fig. 8.3). I would consider this type of figurine to be a birth goddess in the form of a pregnant female rather than a temple prostitute or Baubo, although scholars hold varying opinions.[11]

Building 5

I now turn to the in situ evidence for domestic or private cult within Building 5, and then within Building 7 just to its south. Buildings 1 and 3 appear to have been constructed as a single architectural project, if one is to judge from their homogeneous western façade and their similarity in plan (fig 8.4, p. 228). For the same reason one can hypothesize that Buildings 5 and 7 are the result of a similar project. The two buildings were constructed within parallel eastern and western façades between which ran parallel east-west walls that formed corridor-like spaces. Partition walls subdivide each of the parallel corridor-like spaces into two or three rooms. Building 5 preserves evidence of a destruction, a rebuilding thereafter, a single refurbishing of the floor, and then the final destruction, all with little noticeable change of floor plan.

The first destruction probably was the result of an earthquake of the second quarter of the second century.[12] Artifacts and pottery weighing over 123.6 kg have been recovered from between the floor of the room destroyed in the quake and the floor of its reconstruction or final occupation.[13] This assemblage contained much kitchen ware, including stewpots and a baking dish, as well as table ware, of which a pitcher, four mugs, and bowls and plates were inventoried. The deposit also included storage vessels, such as amphoras, and a goodly range of household wares, such as a bone spoon, fragmentary terracotta theatrical masks, and fragmentary milky green wall plaster. Three pieces of the wall plaster were scratched by at least two different hands writing in Greek. One fresco fragment was scratched with uppercase letters in a practiced style; the other two were written in a more cursive style (figs. 8.5a and 8.5b, p. 229). Two of the fragments, although small, preserve two lines

[11]Perdrizet classifies this group under "la soi-disant Baubo," suggesting, however, that this type may represent a birth goddess. D. B. Thompson ("Three Centuries of Hellenistic Terracottas, I, B and C," *Hesperia* 23 [1954] 90 n. 9; see also plate 21) suggests that the Greek Hellenistic examples were caricatures of sacred hetairai.

[12]Williams and Zervos, "Corinth 1985," 155–58.

[13]Pottery lots 1984-43, 1985-22, and 1985-100.

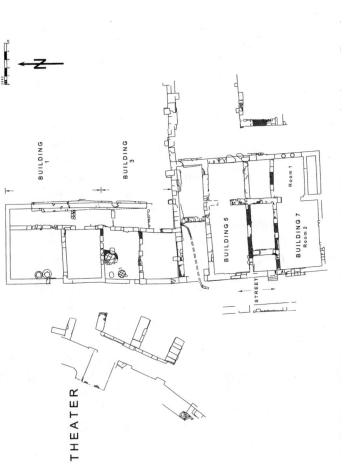

Fig 8.4 Plan of Buildings 1, 3, 5, and 7 along east side of theater; second or intermediate phase.

a

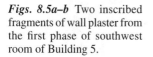

Figs. 8.5a–b Two inscribed fragments of wall plaster from the first phase of southwest room of Building 5.

b

of Greek, the third only the bottom of a single line.[14] Unfortunately, because the fragments are so small, any comment on the content would be guesswork. They are not, however, childish or frivolous doodlings.

A number of figurines also came from the destruction debris between floor levels: an Aphrodite with a draped Pan at her side (fig. 8.6a, p. 230); an Aphrodite of the Knidian type (fig. 8.6b, p. 230); the torso of a third Aphrodite, naked to the hips; a hunting Artemis; and a draped female figurine.[15]

---

[14]Williams and Zervos, "Corinth 1985," 158, plates 33–34. From the final destruction debris within the southwest room of Building 5 comes a fragment of heavy wall plaster, A-1985-5, frescoed yellow, scratched in a not very practiced hand with two lines: EION/B; the surface quality of this fresco, however, is not similar to that of the fresco of the panels decorated with birds, which had fallen into Building 3 after its destruction by earthquake.

[15]MF-1985-12, Aphrodite and draped Pan. See Williams and Zervos, "Corinth 1985," 156–57, no. 21, plate 34; in the original catalog entry the Pan is identified as Priapus. Numerous small bubbles are visible in the clay, the result of forming the figurine in a plaster mold. Aphrodite's hair, parted at the middle, falls in four braids or ringlets of curls with one coil of curls behind each ear, falling vertically to her shoulder. Style of hair reflects first half of second century. Hand-made crown of rolled clay, added pellets, perhaps wreath with flowers; crown painted yellow-ochre sits on back of head, behind braids or curls. For type, see Grandjouan, *Terracottas and Plastic Lamps*, no. 338, fig. 1, plate 8. Other examples include the following: MF-1985-25, Aphrodite, Knidian type, a coiled ankle bracelet on each ankle, wearing basically the same hair style as preceding figurine (MF-1985-12); published in Williams and Zervos, "Corinth 1985," 157, no. 22, plate 34. MF-1985-13, torso of semi-draped Aphrodite. MF-1985-14, plaque of hunting Artemis, in ibid., 157. MF-1985-15, draped female. L-1985-12, boat lamp, no. 24 in ibid., 157, plate 35. Other lamps include L-1984-73, L-1985-2, L-1985-11, L-1985-15, L-1985-19, and L-1985-25.

Fig. 8.6a Aphrodite/Venus with standing Pan (MF-1985-12).

Fig. 8.6b Aphrodite/Venus, Knidian type (MF-1985-25), from first occupational phase of Building 5.

The three largest figurines range in height from 0.24 to 0.347 m. Also included within this fill are seven lamps, one of which is in the form of a boat—a type of lamp usually associated with Isis Pelasgia.[16] The boat lamp here may possibly have been associated with a conflation of Aphrodite and Isis.

On the final floor of this same room was found a heavy concentration of pebble and ash, apparently a hearth without surrounding curb or raised floor, that was buried directly beneath the final destruction debris of the building. Roof tiles were found piled on the earth floor where they had cascaded to the bottom of the south wall when the roof timbers had been pulled loose from their sockets, apparently in an earthquake. Of interest are the finds that were recovered from within this debris around the hearth and the south wall of this room. Most telling are five mold-made terracotta figurines recovered from

[16]L-1984-12. See n. 4, above.

the debris of pisé walls. Two of the figurines depict Aphrodite or Venus (fig. 8.7, p. 232), two depict seated dogs (figs. 8.8a and 8.8b, p. 232), and one is a bust of Athena (fig. 8.9, p. 233). One figurine of Venus and one of a dog were found complete and unbroken, their hollow interiors still containing pebbles.[17] The five terracottas had served as rattles, at least in one of their functions. Eight lamps and a fragmentary incense burner in the form of a large lamp, the discus of which is decorated with a representation of Cybele,[18] are also part of the assemblage. Cybele is represented seated, wearing a mural crown, with her right elbow over a tympanum and her left hand holding a scepter (fig. 8.10, p. 233). It is appropriate to group her with the Aphrodite figurines, for she and Venus Genetrix were from an early date coupled on the Palatine in Rome as goddesses who shared a history in Asia Minor.[19] From the tile debris above the floor were also recovered two Corinthian mold-made bowls with Dionysiac scenes in relief around their exterior.[20] The total assemblage of frescoes, figurines, two molded bowls with cult scenes, lamps, and an incense burner from the final occupation level of Building 5 suggests that a cult area, perhaps a private shrine, had been maintained within this room at the time of its destruction.

The objects listed above suggest a definite focus for the religious overtones of this room. The presence of the three terracotta figurines of Aphrodite, two rather larger in scale than the rest, above the original floor, as well as two other later figurines of Aphrodite within the final destruction debris, indicates that the goddess was honored within the room throughout its lifetime.

Frescoed wall decoration in fragmentary condition was recovered from amidst the architectural debris along the south wall of this room. The overall large-scale design was painted upon a single thin coat of white wall plaster, which served as the background for verticals from which hang heavy swags of greenery and fruit, tied with ochre and red rope and ribbon. In the same debris were found fragments that, at first glance, do not appear to fit into the

---

[17]MF-1985-49, intact terracotta rattle in the form of a seated dog; MF-1985-47, intact terracotta rattle in the form of Aphrodite drying her hair beside pedestal basin; MF-1985-50, broken terracotta rattle in form of a seated dog; MF-1985-48, broken terracotta rattle in form of Aphrodite drying her hair beside pedestal basin; MF-1983-41, broken terracotta rattle(?) in form of bust of Athena.

[18]Thymiaterion, L-1984-1a, b. Ibid., no. 18a–b, plate 10.

[19]A. Bartoli, "Il culto della Mater Deum Magna Idaea e di Venere Genitrice," *Atti della Pontificia Accademia Romana di Archeologia* 6 (1947) 229.

[20]C-1984-1 and C-1984-2; Charles K. Williams II and Orestes H. Zervos, "Corinth, 1984: East of the Theater," *Hesperia* 54 (1985) 61, no. 13, fig. 2, plate 10; and 62, no. 14, fig. 2, plate 10.

Fig. 8.7 Terracotta Aphrodite/Venus figurine-rattle (MF-1985-48), from last occupational phase of Building 5.

Fig. 8.8a Dog figurine-rattle (MF-1985-49), from last occupational phase of Building 5.

Fig. 8.8b Dog figurine-rattle (MF-1985-50), from last occupational phase of Building 5.

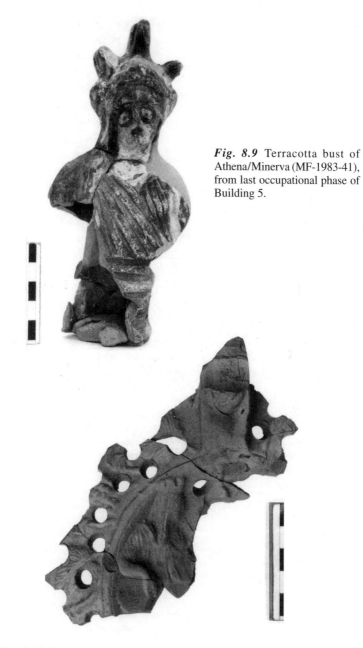

Fig. 8.9 Terracotta bust of Athena/Minerva (MF-1983-41), from last occupational phase of Building 5.

Fig. 8.10 Thymiaterion with Cybele on disc (L-1984-1a, b), from last occupational phase of Building 5.

design of large-scale swags. First of all, this second, much less numerous, group of fragments had a yellow ground, not white. Second, upon these fragments are figures painted at a very small scale.[21] They are, in one case, the head of a figure wreathed with green leaves, without much doubt a lar, and in the other case, legs with winged feet, probably belonging to Hermes, possibly coming from a lararium that had been painted on the wall.

The question of whether the northwest room of Building 5 contained a single lararium, however, is complicated by the discovery of a small marble capital within the destruction debris over the floor of that room.[22] It is of Aeolic type and of a scale and style that could be appropriately used in a columnar frame, a design that falls into the category of the pseudo-aedicula. It can be paralleled by a pedimental wall shrine with free-standing Corinthian columns flanking the niche dedicated to Fortuna Santa within the latrine in the Casarma dei Vigili at Ostia.[23] The marble column capitals there are the size of the Corinthian example. Lararia at Ostia supply other parallels.[24]

If one restores the capital in question to the architectural frame of a niche in Building 5, one might follow parallels from Pompeiian research and restore two shrines to the room rather than one shrine.[25] Some buildings in Pompeii shelter more than one shrine, but the shrines are found in different areas and serve different strata of the household. It appears that painted lararia were used by a lower level of occupants than those who worshipped at a built niche, which would contain figurines in the round. Painted lararia are

---

[21]The preliminary publication of this wall is by Laura M. Gadbery, "Roman Wall Painting at Corinth: New Evidence from East of the Theater in the Roman Period," in *The Corinthia in the Roman Period* (ed. Timothy E. Gregory; JRASup 8; Ann Arbor, Mich.: Journal of Roman Archaeology, 1993) 54–55, fig. 5. For the Farnesina parallel, see Marina Sapelli, *Guide: The National Roman Museum, Palazzo Massimo alle Terme* (Rome: Soprintendenza Archeologica di Roma, 1999) 56–57.

[22]A-1986-5, bottom diameter ca. 0.05 m, width of abacus 0.057 m. A second, more fragmentary and slightly smaller capital, A-1988-2, bottom diameter 0.045 m, was found in the overburden of Building 7.

[23]For lararia and figures associated with them, see George K. Boyce, *Corpus of the Lararia of Pompeii* (MAAR 4; Rome: American Academy in Rome, 1937), esp. 10, where lararia are divided into three types: the niche, the aedicula, and the painting. D. G. Orr ("Roman Domestic Religion: A Study of the Roman Household Deities and Their Shrines at Pompeii and Herculaneum" [Ph.D. diss., University of Maryland, 1972] 85–86) shows that a three-type division is a bit simplistic.

[24]In the Casa del Larario at Ostia, for example, the maximum width of the niche is 1.04 m. Its floor is ca. 2 m above the floor of the court. Two flat pilasters of the Corinthian order, supporting a triangular pediment, frame the niche.

[25]R. A. Tybout, "Domestic Shrines and 'Popular Painting': Style and Social Content," *JRA* 9 (1996) 358–74. For stratification, see ibid., 366–70.

generally found in service areas or shops and, apparently, accommodated slaves and freedpersons. Niches and pseudo-aediculae are found in the better quarters and were reserved for members of the family. In this Corinthian case, we have fresco fragments of a Mercury and a lar. Both are appropriate to a frescoed lararium that belongs in a shop or service area. On the other hand, a series of figures such as these could possibly have been central figures in a decorative program of panels along the length of the wall of the room, as in the western room of Building 7 (see pp. 236–42 and fig. 8.11, below).

Thus, a lararium in the form of a pseudo-aedicula might possibly be restored to a place high in the south wall of this room in both phases of Building 5, on the basis of a parallel with a niche in Building 7; then the northwest room of Building 5 would have contained two lararia. Yet the evidence for such a niche with architectural frame in Building 5 is only the small Aeolic capital; one can alternatively restore that capital to a column in a small window or to furniture, leaving only the single painted lararium as the cult area in the southwest room of Building 5.

No altar was found in the ruins. A low table may have been set in front of the lararium, if one did exist here, or to its side, and reserved for a thymia-terion and the terracotta rattle figurines;[26] if those rattles were to be handled by worshippers, storing them in a niche ca. 2.20 m above the floor would have been extremely inconvenient for everyday use. The figurines must have been placed more conveniently for use in a service, closer to floor level.[27]

It is quite obvious by a comparison of the terracottas recovered from the earlier and later deposits of Building 5 that the quality of the minor religious objects drops in the third century C.E. For example, new figurine molds were not being made; rather, the age-old molds, although heavily worn, were be-ing reworked and the products from them were being sold, with the result that objects of lower quality were being recirculated and accepted by the public for cult use. This lack of interest in the quality of the religious object may be an expression of the lack of vibrancy of an age-old religion; it may also, in some part, be a reflection of Second Sophistic philosophy, in which cult statues and, I assume, associated cult objects are considered mundane, conventional, and unrelated to the gods themselves.[28]

[26]See Grandjouan, *Terracottas and Plastic Lamps*, 26–28, nos. 739, 1086, for seated Maltese dogs.

[27]It seems that tables were rare in their replacement of, or supplement to, altars. See Boyce, *Lararia of Pompeii*, 15–16. In the specific case of the northwest room of Building 5, the hearth on the floor may possibly have served for sacrificing, or we are missing from the full assemblage of this room a portable altar. See August Hug, "Mensa," *PW* 15 (1932) 946–48.

[28]Lucian, *Sacr.* 11–14; *Pro imag.* 8; *Gall.* 24.

BUILDING 7

Three distinct architectural phases can be distinguished in Building 7. The original design of the structure was much obscured by later alteration and repair. Little can be said about it, except that the building was entered through an eastern façade, and not from East Theater Street, which was the route used by the persons who were going to the theater and heading for the less prestigious seats in the upper cavea. In this first period, the room by which one entered the building had a doorway opening through its north wall to an adjacent room and a bench along its south wall. One would, however, have continued to the west through a wide doorway into a larger room. This western room had one door each in its north and south walls; these gave access to the adjacent rows of rooms north and south.

In its intermediate period of occupation, generally datable within the second century C.E., Building 7 was subdivided into three rows of independent suites; the central one comprised the entrance hall (Room 1; see fig. 8.4) and the larger room to its west (Room 2). Together the two rooms occupied the full east-west width of the building. The nearly square eastern room, measuring 5.39 m east-west and 5.41 m north-south, was now entered through a two-columned eastern façade. The bench along its south wall was retained, but the doorway in the north wall was blocked and plastered over. The wide doorway in the west wall was maintained for access into Room 2 and probably at this time given a niche, the bottom of which is set at 2.20 m above the floor of the room. That niche is roundheaded and partially cut into the north jamb and partially into the wall north of the jamb. It was plastered white and decorated with pink four-leafed roses tied by ribbons. The roses may be a significant decoration, for in Cyprus blood offerings were prohibited on the altar of Aphrodite; the goddess asked only for incense and flowers.[29] At Eryx her cult is similar in this respect. Legend has it that, there at night, she replaced the blood offerings that had been placed on the altar, so that in the morning the altar was covered with roses and new herbs.[30]

The larger, western room, Room 2, measures 8.30 m east-west by 5.36 m north-south. Its north, south, and eastern walls are still preserved to a height of between 1.76 and 1.90 m.[31] The doorways in the north and south walls of

---

[29]See Robert Schilling, *La religion romaine de Vénus, depuis les origines jusqu'au temps d'Auguste* (2d ed.; Paris: de Boccard, 1982) 237, esp. n. 6; and 352.

[30]Aelian, *Nat. an.* 10.50; see also Schilling, "Le sanctuaire de Venus près de Casinum," in *Perennitas: Studi in onore di Angelo Brelich* (Rome: Edizioni dell'Ateneo, 1980) 237 n. 6.

[31]The northern door jamb of the eastern wall is preserved, however, to a maximum height of 2.72 m above the original floor of the room.

this room now are blocked. The walls are plastered, and then divided into panels, each panel frescoed with a standing figure at its center. The figures are generally ca. 0.40 m tall (fig. 8.11, p. 238). At the west end of the north wall is a naked Herakles, holding his club in his right hand and with the lion skin over his right shoulder. Next to him stands Hera, then Zeus, who, like Herakles, is represented naked. A helmeted Athena decorates the east end of the north wall (fig. 8.12, p. 239). The doorway from the eastern room is off-center, leaving the section of the eastern wall north of the doorway too narrow to carry a panel with a human figure. It was decorated instead with Hera's peacock. The corresponding section of the eastern wall to the south of the doorway is wider and carries an immature male figure, probably Eros. The identification of the figure as Anteros is suggested, however, by the graffito "Anteros" scratched under the figure by someone who preferred that to Eros. Next to Eros, but also the first figure on the south wall of the room, is Aphrodite admiring her reflection in the shield of Ares, which she holds at one side (fig. 8.13, p. 239). One of the other fragments from the south wall, preserved only in fallen fresco fragments, is a hunting Artemis.[32]

It should be noted that the figures had been applied directly to a fine surface layer of white wall plaster, but the decoration was not meant to be inexpensive. Aphrodite had parts of her flesh accented in gold leaf, a rarity that suggests the importance of this frescoed figure within the decorative scheme.[33] The pose and shield that she holds identify her as Hoplismene, or Armed Aphrodite. This is verifiable by comparison with representations of

---

[32]The frescoed Artemis may be a free version of S-2392 / S-1997-1, a Corinthian statue of hunting Artemis that was found in the southwest quadrant of the Corinthian forum. That statue appears to have had some cultic importance to the pagan population of Corinth, for efforts were made to protect the statue in later times, or to counter its pagan powers, by the incision of a Christian cross on its side. Compare the Artemis in fresco to the marble torso: legs are spread in the same pacing stance, although the bow under the breasts is more pronounced and color is added to the frescoed version. In the frescoed versions both of Artemis and of Aphrodite/Venus, all subsidiary figures have been removed from the composition. For S-239/S-1977-1, with the back of her hunting dog against her left leg, see plate 49 of Charles K. Williams II, L. M. Snyder, E. Barnes, and Orestes H. Zervos, "Frankish Corinth, 1997," *Hesperia* 67 (1998). For the fresco fragment, see fig. 12, top left, in Gadbery, "Roman Wall Painting," 62.

[33]Ibid., 63: "Tiny particles of gold leaf still adhere to her face . . . , to her voluptuous breasts, to her groin, and to bracelets on her upper and lower left arm. Gold leaf was also applied to the bracelet on her upper right arm." For a parallel use of gold leaf to accent frescoed figures in a sacello, this one at Ostia, see J. T. Bakker, *Living and Working with the Gods: Studies of Evidence for Private Religion and Its Material Environment in the City of Ostia (100–500 AD)* (Dutch Monographs on Ancient History and Archaeology 12; Amsterdam: J. C. Gieben, 1994) 259.

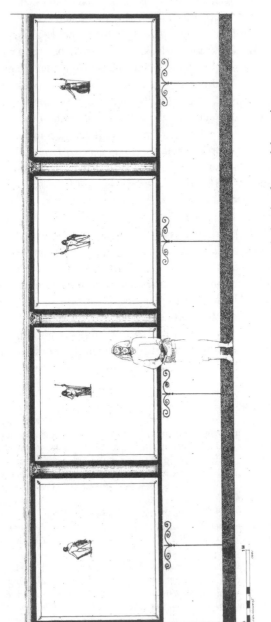

Fig. 8.11 Drawing of north wall of room 2, Building 7, restored, showing frescoed decoration.

Fig. 8.12 Head of Athena/Minerva, wall fresco, Building 7, north wall of room 2.

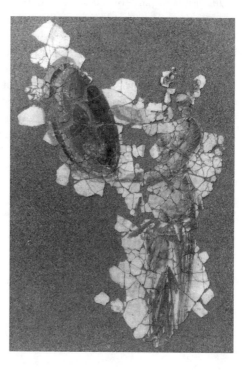

Fig. 8.13 Aphrodite/Venus, wall fresco, Building 7, north wall of room 2.

the Roman cult image from her temple on Acrocorinth on Corinthian coins of the Roman period, and as mentioned by Pausanias (2.5.1).[34] Pausanias also observed that a statue of Eros was associated with her within that temple. This two-room shrine was subdivided in the third and final architectural phase of Building 7. The doorway that had connected Room 1 and Room 2 was blocked with rubble and mud mortar, dividing the suite into two independent units (fig. 8.4 shows the unblocked doorway, during the second phase). The cult area now was minimized and contained within the eastern room. The eastern entrance through the columned façade was maintained, although altered somewhat. Apparently a door, or doors, was added within the columned entrance, because on the floor of the eastern room and under the final destruction debris of the building were found window glass and a framework of wood, enough evidence to indicate that a wooden door had been constructed within at least one of the original intercolumniations of the room that had earlier served as the vestibule.

The stones, tiles, and mud mortar that now blocked the doorway that had served in the two-room suite were left exposed. No new coat of plaster was applied and the eastern room was not redecorated. But apparently the niche in the northern jamb of the blocked doorway in the room's western wall continued to be used until Building 7 was destroyed, for in the final destruction debris on the floor below that niche was found a rattle in the form of a dog similar to the two recovered from the same chronological stratum within Building 5 (fig. 8.14).[35] These rattles in the form of a dog may be of little significance, except that in Greco-Roman astronomy in Egypt, as Török states, "Sirius belongs to the constellation Canus Maior and was hence represented in the form of a dog. Terracottas representing dog figurines may thus be associated with the notion of fertility and abundance."[36] Sirius announces the inundation of the Nile.

Once the two-room suite was subdivided, Room 2 was pressed into use as a commercial establishment, with its own entrance from East Theater Street (fig. 8.15). The wall frescoes that in the earlier phase had covered the walls of this room were left intact except where modification demanded covering or

---

[34]Corinthian bronze coins of the Roman period clearly show the representation of this cult statue on Acrocorinth.

[35]MF-1988-22.

[36]Laszlo Török, *Hellenistic and Roman Terracottas from Egypt* (Bibliotheca Archaeologica 15; Monumenta Antiquitatis extra fines Hungariae reperta 4; Rome: "L'Erma" di Bretschneider, 1995) 172–73.

Fig. 8.14 Dog figurine-rattle (MF-1988-22), room 1 of Building 7, last phase.

Fig. 8.15 View of room 2, Building 7, last phase, frescoes removed for preservation, showing blocked door in east wall and dolium used in final phase.

cutting into the figures for functional reasons. The figures were not defaced, however; not even the faces were altered or mutilated. During this remodeling a closet was constructed in the southwest corner of the room, defined by a tile partition that rose, apparently, to 1.23 m above a newly spread marl. The closet opened toward the north with a press placed at its back. The waste was squeezed onto a tile floor surrounded by low barriers. From there a drain carried the fluid off through the western façade into East Theater Street.

Into the floor to the east of the partition was set a wide-mouthed table amphora of less than half a meter in height. Five larger containers were set, however, along the north wall. The container at the northeast corner of the room definitely was a large pithos or dolium (fig. 8.15). It was placed so that it almost touched the frescoed wall and blocked most of the frescoed figure of Athena from sight. The dolium served there until the final days of Building 7, but the adjacent storage jar was cut off at floor level and buried under a new earth floor. The three containers farther west were also removed during this alteration, and the depressions were packed with sherds that, when mended, became complete or largely complete amphoras. It can be said, rather safely, that in the third occupational phase of the building, the room lost all its cultic significance. The physical remains indicate that the room had become an industrial establishment or shop. The change in type of occupation could also suggest a change in ownership.

Judging from the two latest earth floors within the western room, both to be associated with the final phase of occupation of Building 7, the alterations after the initial conversion were minor. Possibly the removal of the storage jars and the filling of the pits with amphora sherds is the result of a minor disaster such as a low-register earthquake, but not necessarily. The walls show no evidence of structural repair, although some fresco may have flaked off at this time. The changes within the room have to do with function, i.e., the discarding of all the storage jars along the north wall except for the pithos at the northeast corner. That remained in situ and was reused. There is, however, still no sign of replastering, repair, or defacing of frescoes that adhered to the wall.

The final occupation of this industrial establishment or shop was brought to an end by what must have been a very serious earthquake. The building collapsed westward, as attested by the position of the one column of the eastern façade that was preserved where it fell (fig. 8.15). Blocks from the top of the walls, at least one with fresco still clinging to one of its sides, were recovered from high up in the mud fill that, together with the wall blocks, had buried the two rooms.

Aphrodite in East Theater Street

Apparently, once the damage done by this major earthquake was assessed, Buildings 5 and 7 were abandoned. In fact, it appears that the whole site east of the theater was abandoned at this time except for East Theater Street itself, which continued to be used into the mid-fifth century. In the restitution of the street for traffic after the earthquake, a heavy wall was constructed along the west side of the street northward to the vomitorium of the theater. This wall and, on the other side of the street, the remains of the western façade of Buildings 5 and 7 kept the roadway free of wash and piled destruction debris. The wall blocks of the façade of Buildings 5 and 7 were removed for reuse down to socle level only when East Theater Street went out of use in the middle or second half of the fifth century. Luckily a segment of the west façade wall along East Theater Street, where the façade of Buildings 5 and 7 had been repaired, preserved the lower torso of an over life-sized Aphrodite statue in white marble, lying where it had been reused as building material.[37] The torso was sawn vertically into two pieces down the center line of the stomach and groin (figs. 8.16a and 8.16b, p. 244). It was then hacked apart from the front by a pick applied at the navel, apparently less to facilitate the use of the marble as building material than to prohibit future appreciation of the statue. Broken and mutilated as the torso is, the two pieces are heavy and, without the efforts of two or three people, probably would not have moved far from the site of the statue's original position. The two fragments were found side by side on the original ashlars of the lower wall as part of the base of a new rubble upper wall. It is possible, and I consider it likely, that this Aphrodite, before having been dealt with in this most unsympathetic manner, had stood at the west wall of the frescoed room of Building 7, where, during the second architectural phase, it could be appreciated through the columns of the east façade of the building by anyone entering the two-room suite.

At this point a single digression is in order. From the evidence that is presented here, one can deduce that Aphrodite was an important presence in the area east of the theater in the first and second centuries c.e. In the fresco of her in the cult room of Building 7, she is represented as Aphrodite Hoplismene, whose pre-Roman cult in mainland Greece was limited to Corinth and was associated with the protection of the city and, in early times, temple prostitution.[38] One must be careful, however, if one takes what might seem to be

---

[37]S-1984-5.

[38]For a discussion of the cult of Aphrodite Hoplismene on Acrocorinth, see Charles K. Williams II, "Corinth and the Cult of Aphrodite," in *Corinthiaca: Studies in Honor of Dar-*

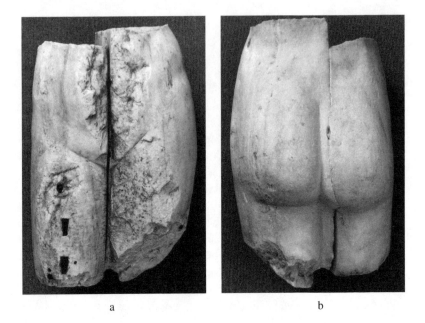

a   b

Figs. 8.16a–b Marble torso, Aphrodite/Venus (S-1984-5): (a) front and (b) back.

the next logical step indicated by the archaeological evidence of the Roman period: that the area around the theater was a fertile place for prostitution and lay under the protection of Aphrodite.

With the above facts in hand, one must consider two points before coming to such a conclusion. First, no part either of Building 5 or of Building 7 ever had the form of a Roman house of prostitution. Neither Corinthian building is divided into cells or small rooms, such as those found in Pompeii, nor is there evidence for stairs to a second floor where one might restore such spaces.[39] Nor does either building have the form of an inn. Second, although

---

rell A. Amyx (ed. Mario A. Del Chiaro; Columbia, Mo.: University of Missouri Press, 1986) 12–24; and the essay by John R. Lanci in this volume (pp. 205–20).

[39]See Lupanar, VII 12,18. E. La Rocca, M. de Vos, and A. de Vos, *Guida archeologica di Pompei* (Verona: A. Mondadori, 1976) 302–4. Interestingly, although there are about twenty-five identified bordellos in Pompeii, not one has been positively identified in Ostia, even though it was an international port; see Russell Meiggs, *Roman Ostia* (2d ed; Oxford: Clarendon, 1973) 229. Second-floor rooms of inns may have served such a function.

prostitution is associated with the cult of Aphrodite on Acrocorinth in the pre-Roman period, probably meant originally to stimulate procreation and thus maintain the supply of labor for the well-being and defense of the city, there is no evidence that this particular cultic practice was re-established by the Romans after 44 B.C.E. Although the Romans did re-establish many Greek sanctuaries on their original sites in and around the city of Corinth after 44 B.C.E., those that served as state cults were, without doubt, carefully controlled by the Roman authorities, even if initially their officiating priests may not have been directly imported from Rome. The cult of Aphrodite Hoplismene must have achieved state sponsorship early after resettlement, as suggested by the number of depictions of her cult statue and temple on Acrocorinth that appear on Corinthian bronze coins of the second century C.E. It seems highly unlikely that institutionalized prostitution would have been included as part of the state cult of a Venus who was primogenitor of the tribe of Julius Caesar, and of a man who, in his turn, was the founder of Roman Corinth.[40]

This does not mean, however, that a neighborhood cult of Venus that existed near the theater would have operated according to the requirements of the state cult, such as those of Venus Genetrix or Venus Hoplismene in the center of the city or on Acrocorinth. Representations of Venus in figurines, frescoes, and sculpture that have been found around the theater are largely those of a goddess of love and beauty, naked to the waist, finishing her bath or wringing out her hair. In conjunction with this point, evidence from Egypt should be cited. There Aphrodite Anadyomene was called upon in the second and third centuries C.E. to bring conjugal happiness to the young wife. Statues of Aphrodite are mentioned there as items of the dowry, carefully packed in cases, which were later set up as part of the domestic cult. The archaeological material that has been recovered from east of the theater might be interpreted today as bawdy or suggestive of attractions beyond the family circle. It should be remembered, however, that in the inventory of lararia and figurines associated with lararia at Pompeii, Aphrodite has been attested in at

---

[40]Schilling, *La religion romaine de Vénus*, 435, no. 7, plate 31. Of interest in this case is the head of Augustus, obverse, with reverse of a variant of Armed Venus, half nude, leaning on colonnette, helmet in right hand, javelin in left, shield also resting against small column, with inscription: R. CAESAR DIVI F; Derier, 3128. Compare Ernest Babelon, *Description historique et chronologique des monnaies de la République romaine vulgairement appelées monnaies consulaires* (2 vols.; Paris: Rollin et Feuardent, 1885–1886) 2:50, no. 109; Babelon sees a scepter in the left hand, not a javelin.

least twenty-one cases.[41] I would thus maintain that the figurines as well as the over life-size marble statue of Venus, probably a cult object, had denoted in their pagan context familial duties and pleasures, children, and the support of the wife in her role within her household. The statue's maltreatment and conversion into building material was probably, at least in part, the result of the Christians' frustration with what seemed to them the misrepresentation or perversion by the pagan cult of some basic precepts of life.

This theory can be tested by a second cult object recovered from the East Theater Street wall into which the Aphrodite/Venus had been built. This is an Osiris hydreia jar of the type that had been venerated because it was supposed to contain the Nile water gathered at flood time. That Nile water was the blood of Osiris, a sign of rebirth and new life.[42] The Corinth hydreia jar, made of black steatite, is badly mutilated, split in half, and its head had been removed long before the jar was recovered by excavation. The relief figures of cult significance that originally had decorated the body have been purposely defaced by chisel to the point that the images are now barely recognizable. This cult object, like the torso of Aphrodite/Venus, definitely was not damaged accidentally in an earthquake.

The evidence reviewed in this essay suggests that the private and semi-private religion of the Roman Corinthians started to lose ground, but slowly and gently, toward the end of the second century. It seems that it is only in a later period, and well after the second quarter of the third century, that the reaction to paganism started to turn militant. From a Judeo-Christian frame of reference, the pagan worship of Aphrodite may seem immodest, ridden with superstition or worse, but the pagan artifacts should be evaluated from their own points of reference. The birth goddess is an expression of fecundity[43] and, perhaps, even displays an element of pain. Certainly she embodies support for the woman or women of the household. The Venus Anadyomene is easily associated with ritual lustrations before marriage. The nakedness of the goddess, then, is in fact a necessary feature in the practices of the cult of Venus. The introduction of foreign elements as well as the introduction of dog rattles may well indicate a widened focus of the cult or deity, although

---

[41]Boyce, *Lararia of Pompeii*. When using this statistic it should be remembered that fleeing Pompeiians in many cases removed the freestanding statuettes when they made their escape.

[42]S-1984-2. See Williams and Zervos, "Corinth, 1984," 80, no. 49, plate 17. This jar has a solid body and could contain no substance of any sort. It apparently had served a purely symbolic or ritualistic function within the cult of Isis.

[43]Lucan, *Civil Wars* 10.209: "Ad fecunda Venus cunctarum semina rerum possidet."

today, layers of meaning undoubtedly lie unrecognized, or remain unclear or misinterpreted. For example, the image of a dog may refer to the constellation of Canus Maior and indicate the connection of ancient astronomy or astrology to the cult.[44] The new moral tone of a rising Christian society certainly has impaired our ability to understand the earlier beliefs. It is hoped, however, that impartial archaeological research can aid in presenting a lucid view of the pagan idiom and the basic needs that it had tried to satisfy.

[44]Ibid., 10.211–37.

Chapter Nine

Unquiet Graves: Burial Practices of the Roman Corinthians

Mary E. Hoskins Walbank

Introduction

It is the living who perform the funerary rites for the dead, and in studying burial practices we are attempting not only to document rituals but also to interpret the beliefs of a society. Personal or private religious beliefs are by their very nature elusive. This is particularly the case in a colony such as Corinth where, to begin with, Roman citizens, intimately involved in the practice of traditional Roman cults, were living side by side with the local population, who may well have maintained their own long-standing religious practices. When and how the beliefs of the old and new inhabitants coalesced, it is impossible to say for certain. There is much literary and documentary evidence for burial practices in the Greco-Roman world, but very little that can be related specifically to Corinth; the evidence at this site is almost entirely archaeological.

In the early 1960s, several chamber tombs and a number of single graves of the Roman period were excavated to the northeast of the city of ancient Corinth. They came to light when an irrigation channel was being cut below the lower of the two plateaus on which the city is sited. Further to the west, opposite the hill of Cheliotomylos and about 100 m east of the area where several tombs had been excavated in the 1930s, another large chamber tomb was exposed. In all, seven chamber tombs and about sixty-five single graves were excavated, some of which had been damaged by the construction crew, while others were more or less intact. Because excavation followed the line of the channel, rather than being concentrated on one cemetery area, it resulted in a genuine cross section of burials, which range in date from the time of the early colony to the beginning of the sixth century C.E. Together these excavations provide material for the first detailed examination of the burial practices of the Roman Corinthians.[1]

The Roman colony of *Laus Iulia Corinthiensis* was founded in 44/43 B.C.E. on the site of the Greek city destroyed by Mummius a century earlier. For the Romans, the division between the living and dead was fundamental, and it was written into the founding charters of colonies such as Corinth.[2] To avoid pollution, the urban cemeteries had to be outside the *pomerium*, the legal and religious boundary of the city. This prohibition against burial within the city held until at least the mid-fourth century C.E., when it began to crumble under the impact of Christianity and the preference of Christians for burying near their place of worship. At Corinth, the *pomerium* was well within the Greek city wall, on the approximate line of the Late Roman fortification, which was built in the early fifth century C.E.[3] Single graves and elaborate built tombs have been found outside the wall and lining the main roads going north from the city to the coast and Lechaion, as well as along the routes leading west in the direction of Sikyon, east to Hexamilia and the Isthmian sanctuary, and to Kenchreai on the Saronic Gulf. In the immediate vicinity of the city, the most important cemetery is in the plain to the north of the city; it is through this area, on the sloping terrain just below the Greek city wall, that the modern irrigation channel was constructed (fig. 9.1).

[1]This brief account is part of a larger study to be published in the Corinth Excavations series. It is a collaborative undertaking between myself and Kathleen W. Slane, with an important contribution on the skeletal remains by Ethne Barnes. The excavation was directed by Henry S. Robinson, then Director of the American School of Classical Studies at Athens, at the request of the Greek Archaeological Service. I am grateful to him and to the succeeding directors of Corinth Excavations, Charles K. Williams II and G. D. R. Sanders, for their advice and support.

[2]See the *Lex Coloniae Genetivae Iuliae Ursonensis* (*ILS* 6087) and commentary in Michael H. Crawford, ed., *Roman Statutes* (BICSSup 64; London: University of London, 1996) 393–454. Urso was planned at the same time as Corinth.

[3]On the *pomerium* and location of the urban cemeteries, see Mary E. Hoskins Walbank, "The Foundation and Planning of Early Roman Corinth," *JRA* 10 (1997) 95–130.

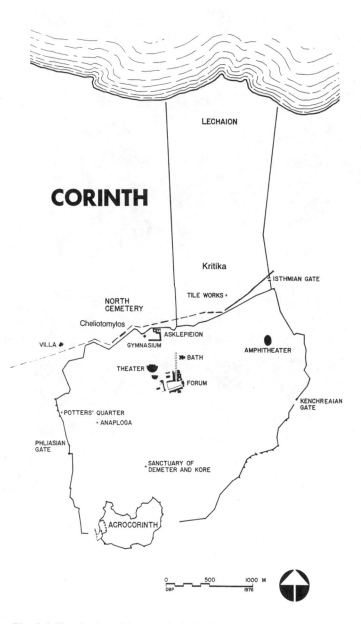

Fig. 9.1 Sketch plan of Roman Corinth. The dashed line indicates the modern irrigation channel; the solid line marks the sites of the excavations.

Fig. 9.2a Sarcophagus unopened.

Fig. 9.2b Sarcophagus opened.

THE SINGLE GRAVES AND DEPOSITS

Of the sixty or more single graves, eighteen were recycled Greek sarcophagi—a reminder that this whole area had previously been a cemetery. In one instance, the end of a sarcophagus had been broken and lengthened, with small

Fig. 9.3 Tile grave cut into earlier grave.

blocks and tile fragments set in mortar, to take two adult corpses. Figures 9.2a and 9.2b show an intact sarcophagus containing a single adult male skeleton. He was in a fully extended position with his head to the east and arms at his sides. Unguentaria had been placed on either side of his head at the time of burial. At his feet were a second skull and two cremation urns, which belong in the second half of the first century C.E. One urn contained the cremated remains of a woman and the other an adult (of unknown sex) and a child. The cover slab had been broken, presumably to put the urns into the sarcophagus after the first interment, which suggests that they were members of a single family. The grave offerings are characteristically simple: another unguentarium on the cover slab, and a jug and lamp at the southeast corner.

Tile graves are more numerous than sarcophagi and were used in all periods. The construction is simple. In this typical grave (fig. 9.3), dated to the fourth century C.E. and cut into an earlier grave, two curved tiles have been placed on either side of the corpse and one end closed with a tile fragment. The other end, where the head was, was left open, perhaps in order that libations could be made. The grave contained the skeleton of a woman in her twenties or thirties. The body had been placed in the usual extended position on its back, but the head had been turned to the side, rather than facing upwards. The grave is also unusual in that tile fragments had been piled on top of the basic tile covering, and grave offerings were placed against the tiles outside the grave at the head, middle, and feet at the time of burial.

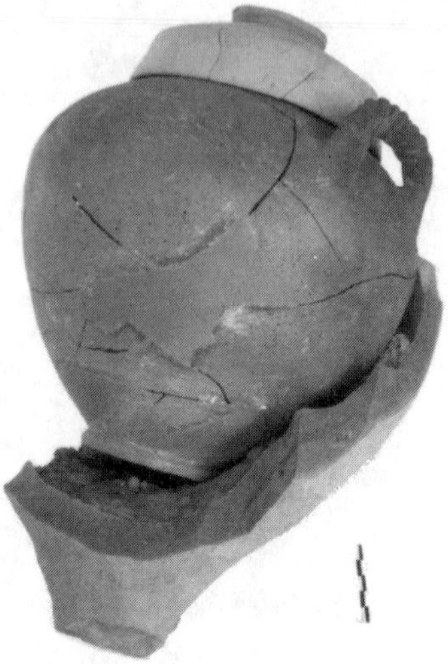

Fig. 9.4 Cremation urn
placed in amphora over
pillaged sarcophagus.

Another, very simple form of burial was to put the cremation urn inside a
complete amphora, which in one case had then been placed over a pillaged
sarcophagus (fig. 9.4). It is probable, from evidence elsewhere in Corinth, that
this simple form of burial, with the container sunk directly into the ground,
was frequently used. In one chamber tomb, amphorae were also used in place
of special cremation urns, and there are instances of infants being buried in
amphorae. There were also a few deposits of unguentaria—in one instance there
was also an iron strigil—which were sometimes found in association with ash
or iron nails. These are probably the remains of cremations, for which the body
had been placed on a bier and burned on the site of the burial. According to the
Roman *agrimensores*, public areas on the outskirts of a city had to be reserved
for the funerals of the poor.[4] It is possible that some of these deposits, which
were grouped together, are the remains of such funerals, but other deposits
were found interspersed with the chamber tombs and graves along the line of
the irrigation channel. There does not seem to have been any orderly development or alignment of the tombs in this area, unlike some other cemeteries
where important chamber tombs lined the road and the graves of the poor were
confined to the rear. Perhaps it was because the steep slope and distance from
the main roads to the coast meant that this was not a prime location.[5]

---

[4]*De controversiis* (ed. Thulin 65.2 = ed. Lachmann 19.12).

[5]The area was not used to capacity. Several Greek tile graves were not reused nor were two
cists at the far end of the line of excavation beyond the East Long Wall: one still contained

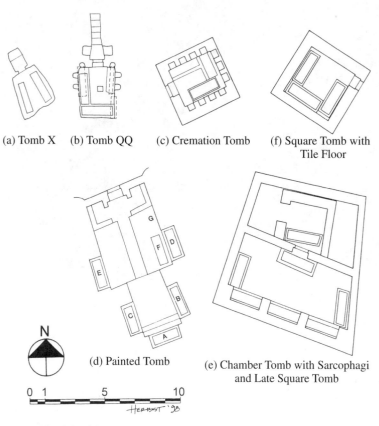

(a) Tomb X   (b) Tomb QQ   (c) Cremation Tomb   (f) Square Tomb with
Tile Floor

(d) Painted Tomb   (e) Chamber Tomb with Sarcophagi
and Late Square Tomb

N

0 1   5   10

Fig. 9.5a–f Chamber tombs excavated along the irrigation channel.

THE CHAMBER TOMBS

Here, as elsewhere in Corinth, the Romans cut chamber tombs into the soft
limestone of the scarp. The earliest and simplest tomb (fig. 9.5a) had a vertical
shaft entrance with a single cover slab giving access to a tiny antechamber
and the doorway of the actual chamber. A neighboring tomb had a similar
but more elaborate plan (fig. 9.5b) with a stepped passageway that widened

---

vessels of the fourth and early third century B.C.E.; the other had been pillaged in antiquity.
There must have been a road to provide east-west communication below the lower plateau,
but it probably lay farther to the north on more level ground.

Fig. 9.6 Cremation Tomb with a single reused sarcophagus
in foreground. The line of the irrigation channel is on the right.

out before the doorway. In the chamber there were niches in the walls for
cremation urns, and brick-built sarcophagi and a bench around the walls;
under the sarcophagi there were more cremation burials. A limestone altar
or offering table had been placed in the center of the chamber. The tomb
was probably built in the mid-first century c.e. and used as late as the fourth
century, but it is not clear whether the use was continuous. Unfortunately, it
had been disturbed in antiquity.

Other tombs had been partially cut into the cliff with built façades and
roofs. One of them had been designed primarily for cremation burials, with
niches for the urns (figs. 9.5c and 9.6). There are pinholes above some of
the niches for garlands or nameplates. The sarcophagus along the south side
may have been a feature of the original construction, but the central area was
later divided to provide two extra sarcophagi for bodies or for urns. It was
built in the mid-first century c.e. and used until the mid-third century. This
tomb had also been ransacked in antiquity. Several tombs of this plan have
been found elsewhere at Corinth, and at least two of them still had cremation
urns in situ either set on or sunk into the floor of the niches.

Fig. 9.7 Tomb X: cover slab of west grave with libation hole.

Chamber Tomb X

It is worth looking in more detail at the burial arrangements in two of the chamber tombs. The small Tomb X referred to earlier (fig. 9.5a) was built in the early first century C.E. The tiny chamber—too low to stand up in—was cut irregularly into layers of bedrock. Two narrow graves had been let into the floor, and the interior of both graves had been built up to form a pillow at the south end. The east grave contained two skeletons and the west grave the lower part of one skeleton; neither grave appeared to have been disturbed, although there were no offerings clearly associated with them. In the cover slab on the west grave, directly over the place where the skull would have been placed on the pillow, there was a hole for libations (fig. 9.7). Pouring food and drink onto the bones of the dead in the expectation of nourishing the spirit was a common, albeit illogical, practice in the ancient world, but this is the only example of a hole for such libations found so far at Corinth.[6]

[6]A similar hole was found in the cover slab of a grave in a chamber in the Kerameikos in Athens, used from the end of the first into the second century C.E. The grave had been reused and contained the skeletal remains of six corpses (Jutta Stroszeck, with contributions from Klaus Hallof and Anna Lagia, "Kerameikosgrabung 1999," *AA* [2000] 472–73). A third-century C.E. tile grave excavated at Brauron had a terracotta libation pipe (Kleopatra Eustratiou, "Chronika," *ArchDelt* 44 [1989] 76 and plate 56). The practice was common in Roman cemeteries, for instance, in the necropolis below St. Peter's Basilica, at Isola Sacra, and as distant as Caerleon in Roman Britain; see Jocelyn M. Toynbee, *Death and Burial in the Roman World* (London: Thames and Hudson, 1971) 51–52.

More interments had been made directly on the floor of the tomb, and six cremation urns were also found against the wall. A deposit of bones of an adult male and a young child were placed over the east grave, with the adult skull to the south and an incense burner beside it. The fragmentary remains of two more adults were crowded together across the south end of the chamber. The fact that the larger bones had been laid out east-west suggests that they had been rearranged within the tomb, together with grave gifts and personal possessions. The offerings in the southwest corner were more numerous and of a higher quality than those found elsewhere in this excavation. They included four lamps, two of local Corinthian and two of Italian manufacture; one of the latter was decorated with a peacock sitting on a pomegranate branch. All of the lamps had been used. There were two painted incense burners, as well as several nice glass unguentaria, which would have contained oils or perfume. It is likely that the vessels lying on the cover slabs of the west grave were also funerary offerings. The combination of three small amphorae,[7] a bowl, and a shallow two-handled cup suggests that food and drink had been provided for the dead.

Also found in the southwest corner and to be associated with the second deposit were a number of figurines, which may have been personal possessions or gifts from mourners. There were eight figurines in all, and there is no obvious explanation for the choice of subject. Four are human figures, which include the seated figure of a young girl looking down modestly, with her hands folded demurely in her lap (fig. 9.8a), and a young boy (fig. 9.8b). The latter is particularly interesting because he is wearing a *bulla*, the amulet which was only worn by a freeborn Roman boy until he reached the age of fourteen, when he assumed the *toga virilis* and was regarded as an adult. Three composite figurines have mythological or religious connotations: one represents a chubby Eros embracing Psyche, and another shows Eros mounted on a horse (fig. 9.8c). Figurines of Eros are often associated with children.[8] The third composite figurine shows Aphrodite wrapped in a cloak and seated on a billy goat (fig. 9.8d). It is not surprising to find Aphrodite, who was immensely popular in both Greek and Roman Corinth as a civic goddess, but she also had a chthonic role, hence her title "Melainis"; she watched over marriage and children and, for the Romans, she could also

---

[7]Two table amphorae plus a third, identified by Kathleen Slane as the kind that would have held dates.

[8]At Cheliotomylos, another example of this figurine of Eros on horseback was found just outside a tile grave (unpublished); a different figurine of Eros was found together with a rattle in a child-sized sarcophagus (T. Leslie Shear, "Excavations in the North Cemetery at Corinth in 1930," *AJA* 34 [1930] 428–29).

Fig. 9.8a–d Tomb X: figurines found in SW corner.

Fig. 9.9 Tomb X: cremation urn in doorway.

represent the spirit of regeneration. Any of these roles would be applicable in a funerary context. While similar figurines have been found elsewhere at Corinth, this is the largest collection recovered from a single grave.[9]

At some point there was a rock fall within the chamber, after which the debris and remains of cremations were packed into the walls, but it is impossible to say whether the cremations were contemporary with the inhumations or later. Subsequently, the floor of the antechamber was covered with a layer of mud, perhaps caused by seepage of water or possibly the result of an earthquake.[10] This was followed by another period of use when a number of cremation urns were placed on the mud layer. The earliest of these urns was placed just within the chamber, together with an unusual green-glazed lamp; five more urns blocked the doorway and antechamber (fig. 9.9). These must have been the last interments. Possibly the roof collapsed to such an extent that it became impossible to continue using the chamber.

[9]Aphrodite seated on a goat may be Aphrodite Epitragia or Pandemos (*LIMC* 2/1:99, no. 950). Pausanias (2.4) refers to a sanctuary of Aphrodite Melainis in Kraneion to the east of the city. Other literary references are collected in Lewis R. Farnell, *The Cults of the Greek States* (5 vols.; Oxford: Clarendon Press, 1896–1909; repr., Chicago: Aegean Press, 1971) 2:652–56. A single sarcophagus on the line of the irrigation channel contained four figurines, including another example of the figurine of Eros and Psyche, a fragmentary Aphrodite, and an unidentified seated goddess.

[10]The geology of the area means that flash floods and rock falls were a constant hazard.

From the finds, we can establish that the tomb was in use from the early first to the early second century C.E.[11] It held the remains of eleven individuals, two of whom were children.[12] Although some of the remains, with their burial goods, had been disturbed, they had been carefully handled. This is the only tomb where we concluded that different generations of a single family were interred sequentially. The cremation burials may represent a change in burial rite; some of them may also represent inferior status within the family group, as has been observed elsewhere.[13] They could also have been slaves or freed members of the family.

There is an unusual feature associated with this tomb. On the surface of the scarp, directly above the underground chamber, the excavator recorded rubble walls that were aligned with the walls of the tomb below. The earth above the tomb was sterile. This suggests that there was an enclosure above the chamber tomb which would have served to mark off the ground, and the tomb below, as belonging to a particular family, and therefore subject to the normal protection of Roman law. This may account for the fact that this is one of the very few chamber tombs that was never used again. The preservation of the tomb, as well as the figurine of the boy wearing a *bulla*, suggests that it may have belonged to a freeborn Roman family. Corinth was notorious for its freedman antecedents well into the first century C.E. and, in such circumstances, it is not unreasonable to think that a freeborn family would wish to emphasize its socially superior status.

The Painted Tomb

The second chamber tomb I wish to discuss is considerably larger and more elaborate (fig. 9.5d). It was an isolated discovery, to the west of the main excavations, and is known as the Painted Tomb on account of the frescoes decorating the interior.[14] The tomb was partially cut into the hillside with what must have been a handsome built entrance; unfortunately, the doorway and

---

[11]The only coin, much corroded, was minted in 2/1 B.C.E.; it was found in the clay packing under a rocky projection in the back wall together with a gold earring and a small pot. The lamps found with the exposed bodies belong in the middle or second half of the first century C.E. At least one of the cremation urns from the entrance has been dated in the late first or early second century.

[12]Not counting cremation burials packed into walls.

[13]Toynbee (*Death and Burial*, 134–36) summarizes the evidence from Isola Sacra and the necropolis below St. Peter's Basilica.

[14]Reported briefly in "Chronika," *ArchDelt* 18 (1963) 77; and "Chronique des fouilles," *BCH* 87 (1963) 723–24, where an Augustan date was suggested.

Fig. 9.10 Painted Tomb: antechamber and passage to inner chamber.

Fig. 9.11 Painted Tomb: arcosolium A showing "pillow" and cover slabs over cist.

most of the antechamber had been destroyed by the bulldozer. The original tomb, which was built in the first half of the second century C.E., consisted of one large open-plan chamber, which was subdivided into three separate areas. A passage sunk between two rock-cut platforms led from the antechamber into the inner chamber (fig. 9.10). It is not clear how high the original ceiling was because of a partial collapse in antiquity. The tomb was designed for inhumations, with no provision for accompanying cremation burials. The focus of the tomb was the arcosolium (A), which was cut into the back wall of the inner chamber, directly in line with the entrance and approached by two steps; a rectangular cist was sunk into the floor (fig. 9.11). Similar, slightly smaller arcosolia (B and C), each with a cist, were cut into the east and west walls of the inner chamber and also in the walls of the outer chamber (D and E) above the level of the platforms. In the interior of each of the cists, a pillow had been carved at the south end (in the case of cist A, at the east end). All but cist B were covered with stone slabs or roof tiles and sealed.[15]

With the exception of cist B, which may never have been used, the cists contained multiple burials. A large number of vessels for food and drink, together with lamps, had been carefully placed on the step below arcosolium A at the rear of the inner chamber or stored on the floor in the northwest corner. With these vessels and lamps is associated a thin layer of burnt matter, spread over the floor with a heavier concentration in the center, for which sacrificial meals are the obvious explanation.

When the tomb was built, the whole of the interior was carefully plastered and elaborately painted, but only the frescoes along the walls of the passage have survived in a comprehensible form. The attractive Nilotic scenes, divided by stylized lotus flowers and reeds, show small figures going about daily tasks, such as hauling nets and catching fish (fig. 9.12a, p. 264). Such scenes are, of course, often found in a funerary context as a reminder of the pleasures of the life to come, and the theme of a journey over water to the afterlife is familiar from wall paintings elsewhere; it is also frequently found on sarcophagi. However, the position of these river scenes along the passage, where they would be difficult to see—and awkward to paint in the confined space—is interesting. The dead may have been laid out temporarily on the platform above the frescoes, and the placing of the Nilotic scenes below would imply a journey across the water to life beyond the grave. Or the intention may have been to emphasize the importance of the burials in the inner chamber, since the body would actually pass between the watery scenes to the final resting place.

[15]There were very large pieces of painted plaster from the collapsed roof at the bottom of the cist.

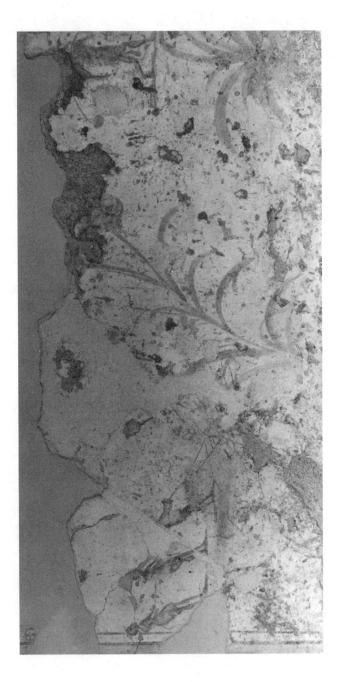

Fig. 9.12a Painted Tomb: detail of fresco on east wall of passage.

Fig. 9.12b Painted Tomb: detail of fresco in center of east wall of passage.

For mourners and family members gathering at the tomb on later occasions, perhaps placing offerings on the benches in the antechamber, the paintings would be just visible in the passage leading to the inner chamber.

One particular scene, placed in the center of the wall painting on the left as one entered the chamber, may have further significance (fig. 9.12b). A pygmy is standing in a boat with two crossed sticks held in each hand. He could simply be a fisherman holding throwing sticks, but his left arm is raised high in front and his right arm behind so that the four sticks point in all directions and can thus ward off the Evil Eye.[16] If this interpretation is correct, it is worth noting that the pygmy is facing inwards, which is a reminder not only that the burial place should remain undisturbed, but also that the dead were considered to be a source of supernatural, and often malign, influences from which the living had to be protected.

[16]See the discussion in Doro Levi, *Antioch Mosaic Pavements* (Princeton, N.J.: Princeton University Press, 1947) 32–33. I am grateful to Elizabeth Gebhard for pointing this possibility out to me at the symposium and to Matthew Dickie for a later discussion.

The tomb remained in use until about 300 C.E., when the roof collapsed, covering the vessels and lamps with debris. There appear to have been two subsequent renovations, in the course of which the passage was filled in and the floor of the inner chamber raised to the level of the platforms. This must have made access to the inner chamber much more difficult. The additional cist F, which spoils the symmetry of the outer chamber, may have been cut into the floor of the platform during the first period of use, or it could have been made after the passage had been filled in.[17] Another late burial (G) was made in the debris of a second rock fall in the outer chamber.

The use and reuse of the individual cists varied. In the inner chamber, the remains of at least nine individuals had been interred at different times in cist A.[18] A coin of Arcadius (383–392 C.E.) found with the bones was in fair condition, and therefore it was probably deposited with one of the burials at the end of the fourth century or beginning of the fifth century. There were no other grave goods, which suggests that the cist had been cleared out before being reused in the last phase. Cist C had been used repeatedly; the burials were in three layers. Three adult males and an infant were at the lowest level, placed there at different times. Two adult males came next, followed by an adolescent female. In the top layer were three infants, each buried at a different time. There were ten individuals in all.[19] With the top layer was a thin glass cup of the late fourth or fifth century. In the outer chamber, cist D contained the disturbed remains of at least seven individuals, six adults and one adolescent; finds at the lowest levels were dated in the late first and second centuries. Cist E also contained seven individuals. A bowl dated in the mid-second century was found with the bones at the lowest level, and a bowl and jug, together with a coin of Gallienus (264–266 C.E.) in good condition, had been placed at the upper level. The later corpses and associated grave goods had been deposited on top of the existing remains.[20] It is likely that neither cist was reused after 300 C.E.

Later still, low rubble walls were built across several of the arcosolia, which suggests that the recesses were used again in the final stage after bodies

---

[17]The first interments certainly took place after the tomb was first painted, since the cover slab covered the original decoration. It contained the remains of four adults and one child deposited at different times.

[18]Five adults, three children, and one infant.

[19]Thanks are due to Art Rohn for his work in establishing the order of burial.

[20]Cist D contained six adults and one adolescent; cist E contained two adult females, one male, two children, and two infants, one a newborn. Quantities of painted wall plaster had fallen round the sealed cover of cist E, showing that the latest burials had taken place before the roof collapsed.

had been deposited in the cists. They may be represented by a few bones from five adult skeletons that were found in the fill of the inner chamber. The tradition of placing a lamp and coin with a burial, although not necessarily in direct contact with the body, continued. The latest coin to be deposited was a small, very worn coin of Theodosius I (379–395 C.E.), which must have been in circulation for a considerable time before being deposited, together with a lamp of the late fourth century, on the cover slab of cist C. A pitcher reused as a cremation urn had been placed in the east arcosolium (B) of the inner chamber with a late lamp.[21] There may have been another very late burial in the outer chamber opposite grave G, where a few bones with a lamp, dating from the mid-fifth to the sixth century, were found in the fill. The tomb was evidently used until the late fourth century and probably up to the mid-fifth century, but not for long after that.

When the floor of the inner chamber was raised, it was partially paved with materials brought in from outside, which included a gravestone inscribed ΘΕΟΝΑΣ ΠΡΕΙΜΑ ΧΑΙΡΕ. The lettering dates the inscription between 150 and 250, probably nearer the latter, and the salutation ΧΑΙΡΕ indicates that she was pagan. From its condition, the stele must have stood upright over her grave in the open for a considerable time before being reused in the floor. It probably came from nearby. With this one exception, we have no inscriptions in this or any other of our tombs that would help in interpreting the finds.

However, analysis of the skeletal remains has provided useful information about the people buried in this tomb. At least forty-two people were interred in the cists and graves, of whom seven were children and seven were infants; in addition to these are the five adults whose remains were found in the fill in the chamber.[22] Some genetic similarities suggest that most of the dead came from the same genetic population, presumably from Corinth or the vicinity. That is not particularly surprising, but when one examines the contents of the individual cists there are some interesting findings. In cist C, many individuals had similar genetic traits indicative of family ties.[23] In contrast, the seven individuals in cist D had the most dissimilar genetic traits. One adult from cist D, however, had a similar skull shape to three individuals in cist C, indicating that the four were from the same genetic population. Thus, in one grave

---

[21]This is the only cremation burial in the tomb and the remains were minimal: two small adult bone fragments.

[22]The given number of individuals represented is always the minimum.

[23]There is a gender imbalance in cist C: the ten occupants comprise five adult males and four infants aged between three and thirty months, but only one female aged between seventeen and eighteen. This raises some intriguing questions.

the dead were closely related while in another there was little or no family connection, although there was a single link between the two graves.

Analysis of the bone data also showed functional stress in both men and women in most of the tombs. In the Painted Tomb, the adult males in cists A and C had occupations that required strenuous physical activity. There had been overuse of the shoulders, arms, and lower back caused by lifting heavy loads, pulling, and carrying, but there was also occupational stress affecting the wrists and hands. This suggests that they were craftsmen, such as weavers or potters, or perhaps members of the building trades, rather than unskilled laborers.[24] The routines of ordinary domestic life would, of course, have taken a far greater toll on the body than they do today in western civilization. Even so, it seems likely that these were people of the artisan class who would have been unable to afford their own chamber tomb, but who were able to pay for a place in a communal tomb. They could have been members of an extended family, or they may have acquired burial rights through marriage. Perhaps, in the case of cist D, they belonged to a trade association or burial club. Such a provision for burial was common in the Greco-Roman world, and the clubs were open to slaves and freedmen as well as to the ordinary working class. The club or association might perform the funerary rites as well.[25]

It is unlikely that the Painted Tomb was a single-family tomb.[26] It could have been a collective tomb commissioned by a group of individuals. Or, it may have been originally intended to house the family and dependents of the builder, who was someone with fairly sophisticated taste, to judge by the tomb's decoration. He would presumably have kept the most prominent burial space, arcosolium A, for himself, but given or sold off some of the other arcosolia to people who may or may not have been relatives. In either case each arcosolium becomes a separate burial site. This might account for the fact that arcosolium B

[24]For example, repeated overuse from extending, raising, and rotating the arm overhead and inward is consonant with the use of an upright loom. The long-term production of large pots (though not small ones) would produce the functional stress noted on the forearms, wrists, and especially the thumbs, while repetitive overuse from flexing the thigh could be caused by long-term use of the kick wheel. I owe the second of these observations to Walter Dexter, a middle-aged professional potter.

[25]On funerary activities of professional associations, see Onno M. van Nijf, *The Civic World of Professional Associations in the Roman East* (Amsterdam: J. C. Gieben, 1997) 31–69, esp. 45–49 on communal tombs. See also Keith Hopkins, *Death and Renewal* (Cambridge: Cambridge University Press, 1983) 211–12.

[26]The names of the occupants may have been attached to the entrance, which had been torn away. A chamber tomb of similar plan excavated at Cheliotomylos (T. Leslie Shear, "Excavations in the North Cemetery at Corinth in 1931," *AJA* 35 [1931] 429–36) had cuttings on the lintel for the insertion of name plaques.

in the Painted Tomb—a desirable location in the inner chamber—was never occupied, although it may have been bought or reserved.

One might turn to Roman sepulchral law for some guidance on this question, but that body of law is complex and sometimes contradictory.[27] On the one hand, a tomb or grave was considered *locus religiosus*, subject to divine law, and therefore it could not be sold or used for any other purpose. On the other hand, there is ample epigraphic evidence that people sold or bequeathed space in tombs for inhumations or for cremation urns.[28] Tombs could even be seized for nonpayment of debt. An additional complication with regard to our Corinthian tombs is that, strictly speaking, land in the provinces did not come under the same religious rules as Roman soil. However, Corinth was a Roman colony, and its official religious institutions were based on those of Rome. It is reasonable, therefore, to assume that in the private sphere the same religious rules would have applied as at Rome.[29] Chamber tombs fell into two distinct categories.[30] They could be *sepulchra familiaria*, built by the head of the family for his immediate relatives, freed members of the family, and their descendants, all bearing the family name and responsible for maintaining the tomb. Alienation of these tombs was usually prohibited. Inscriptions referring to such tombs have been found at Corinth, although none of them can be attached to a particular tomb.[31] The other category of tomb, *sepulchra hereditaria*, could be inherited either within the family or by someone outside it. In the latter case, the whole tomb or shares in it could be transferred or sold by the new owner. I think that the majority of the chamber tombs along the irrigation channel come into this category because of their size and the length of time they remained in use, although we cannot be certain, given the lack of epigraphic evidence.

---

[27]The most detailed discussion of sepulchral law is Ferdinand de Visscher, *Le droit des tombeaux romains* (Milan: Giuffré, 1963); for a succinct account, see John A. Crook, *Law and Life in Ancient Rome* (London: Thames and Hudson; Ithaca, N.Y.: Cornell University Press, 1967) 133–38.

[28]See Toynbee, *Death and Burial*, 73–79 and nn. 269–90.

[29]When Pliny (*Ep.* 10.68–69), as governor of Bithynia, asked Trajan whether people could move the remains of their deceased relatives because their tombs had fallen into disrepair or been disturbed by erosion of the river, the emperor said that it was unreasonable for them to have to get permission from the *pontifex maximus* in Rome and that Pliny should decide, as had previous governors, on the merits of the case. The underlying assumption is that Roman custom should be followed.

[30]Gaius, apud *Digesta* 11.7.5: "Familiaria sepulchra dicuntur, quae quis sibi familiaeque suae constituit, hereditaria autem, quae quis sibi heredibusque suis constituit."

[31]See, e.g., John Harvey Kent, *The Inscriptions 1926–1950* (Corinth VIII.3; Princeton, N.J.: ASCSA, 1966) nos. 280, 284–87. Hopkins (*Death and Renewal*, 205–6) notes that in Italy it was apparently rare for tombs to hold the remains of several generations of family members.

Burial Practices

What can we say about the burial practices of the people buried in this particular area? First, the practices of inhumation and cremation coexisted during the first and early second centuries both with regard to single graves and in the chamber tombs, where specific provision was sometimes made for both rites. It is often said that cremation was the customary Roman practice and that inhumation was preferred in the Greek world, although neither rite was used exclusively.[32] The cremation burials may reflect the preference of the Roman colonists. On the other hand, cremation can also imply a lower status within the family group. That is, the most important members of the family were inhumed, while other members and dependents were cremated. Or it may simply have been a matter of personal choice. A well-known example of the latter is not from Corinth but from the Vatican cemetery. In the second century, Marcus Tullius Hermadion had himself cremated and prepared the marble ash chest during his lifetime, but he buried his son according to the more progressive rite of inhumation.[33] A similar choice was evidently available to the Roman Corinthians, although eventually cremation burial did die out. There is no provision for cremations in the Painted Tomb, which was constructed by the mid-second century, nor in the large Tomb with Sarcophagi, which dates from about 100 C.E.

Some chamber tombs were built at Corinth during the Classical and Hellenistic periods, although the preference was for burial in single sarcophagi. In the Roman period, chamber tombs become very common and they were reused extensively. However, the prevalence of multiple burials in the tombs along the irrigation channel was an unexpected finding. All four of the chamber tombs used into the fifth century contained multiple burials, sometimes seventeen or eighteen in one sarcophagus.

[32]See, for example, Ian Morris, *Death-Ritual and Social Structure in Classical Antiquity* (Cambridge: Cambridge University Press, 1992) 52: "By A.D. 60, when Petronius (111.2) called inhumation a 'Greek custom', the empire can be roughly divided into a western/cremating/Latin part and an eastern/inhuming/Greek part. Even where Romans established colonies in the East, inhumation continued. Twenty-eight graves in the North Cemetery at Corinth date between its refoundation as a *colonia* in 44 B.C. and c. A.D. 100; only four are cremations." His statement is true of that part of the North Cemetery that has been published, but it is misleading with regard to the larger picture at Corinth. It has also been noted that the practice of cremation in Asia was widespread: see Marcello Spanu, "Burial in Asia Minor during the Imperial Period with Particular Reference to Cilicia and Cappadocia," in *Burial, Society and Context in the Roman World* (ed. John Pearce, Martin Millett, and Manuela Struck; Oxford: Oxbow Books, 2000) 169–77, esp. 174.

[33]Jocelyn M. Toynbee and John Ward-Perkins, *The Shrine of St. Peter* (London: Longmans, Green, 1956) 46. The Tomb of the Caetennii was designed originally for cremations and then invaded at ground level by inhumations.

The Tomb with Sarcophagi (fig. 9.5e) consisted of a chamber and a large open courtyard, which had a well in the southeast corner. It was remodeled more than once and also cleaned out, perhaps when new owners took over; at a late stage, another, square tomb was built in the courtyard. There were at least ninety-eight interments in the sarcophagi and in the floor of the chamber, and eventually in the courtyard as well. Within the sarcophagi, earlier bones were either pushed aside to make room for the latest burial or else the corpse was simply laid on top. Some of the skulls were repositioned to make more space. Only one sarcophagus did not hold multiple burials, but simply the fragmentary bones of an adolescent (age unknown) and fragments of a small child's skull. Two curse tablets were found with the bones, and this may account for the fact that the sarcophagus was not reused.

Another unexpected finding was the large number of infants and newborns who were interred. Conventional wisdom is that in the Greco-Roman world they were not normally accorded full burial, and there are certainly instances at Corinth of a newborn being buried in a domestic context. However, the remains of infants and newborns, as well as children, were found in all our chamber tombs and in some cremation burials. Sometimes the burials can be explained as a mother and child who died at the same time, but it is less easy to account for the figures from the Tomb with Sarcophagi. The overall ratio of adult males to females is about equal (total forty-one), whereas there are twenty-five children and twenty-nine infants, including sixteen newborns. It seems that the occupants of this particular tomb, as well as their neighbors, felt that even their tiny babies should be accorded the same burial rights as other members of the community.[34]

Primary multiple burials of small numbers are found in sarcophagi from the first and second centuries onwards. We cannot be sure when the multiple burial of large numbers was introduced at Corinth, but the practice was well established by the end of the third century. The various phases in the tombs suggest that multiple burials may have taken place for a period, after which there was a wholesale clearing out before occupation began again. Perhaps one can see in this the use of a tomb by one family, which eventually died out—or maybe the cists were emptied when they became too full. This raises the possibility of multiple secondary burial. Not far from the Tomb with

---

[34]Jean-Pierre Néraudau, "La loi, la coutume et le chagrin: réflexions sur la mort des enfants," in *La mort, les morts et l'au-delà dans le monde romain* (ed. François Hinard; Caen: Université de Caen, 1987). Current research on the family and attitudes towards infant mortality is summarized by Margaret King, "Commemoration of Infants on Roman Funerary Inscriptions," in *The Epigraphy of Death* (ed. Graham Oliver; Liverpool: Liverpool University Press, 2000) 117–54.

Sarcophagi, half of a stone sarcophagus had been deliberately tipped up on its end and sunk into the ground to form a pit. It contained the jumbled remains of twelve adults, two adolescents, two children, and two infants. A small third-century pitcher and a mid-fourth-century coin of Constantius II found in the pit suggest that the bones had been originally deposited between ca. 250 and 400. These remains may represent secondary burial or they could have been simply cleaned out. However, the reburial, or at least the rearrangement of bones, is very clear in one of the tombs on Cheliotomylos. In one corner of the inner chamber, but not in a grave, there was a mass of dry, clean, well-preserved bones including six skulls, and below them were layers of older bones; each layer had been carefully covered with earth before the next layer was deposited. This certainly suggests secondary burial.[35]

GRAVE OFFERINGS

Interments in single graves and in the chamber tombs were almost always accompanied by, at the least, a dish and drinking cup; providing sustenance for the dead was part of the burial ritual. In two of the Painted Tomb graves, round-mouth pitchers that would have held liquids were buried above the body, which suggests that they were used at the time of burial, probably for libations, and then interred with the bodies.[36] There is additional evidence for funerary meals. This is most apparent in the Painted Tomb, where vessels suitable for both cooking and serving a meal had been stored. The chamber tombs also preserve evidence for a commemorative cult of the dead. There was a stone altar in the centre of Tomb QQ, and the bench and sarcophagi would have provided seating around the chamber (figs. 9.5b and 9.13). The tomb had been disturbed and there is no record of associated finds, but in another chamber tomb on the hill of Cheliotomylos, the stone altar at the far end of the inner chamber still had charred embers and fragments of a lamp on it when excavated. The Tomb with Sarcophagi (fig. 9.5e) was built with a spacious precinct; it must surely have been used for some communal

---

[35]On secondary burial in Asia Minor in small stone or marble chests (*ostothēkai*), see Spanu, "Burial in Asia Minor," 172, as well as the essay by Christine Thomas in this volume (pp. 281–304).

[36]The contents of the cremation urns have not been analyzed, but it is worth noting that when chemical analysis was done on three urns at Pompeii, water, wine, and oil were found to have been mixed with the ashes and bone fragments. The urns were glass and had been placed in lead containers. See August Mau, *Pompeii, Its Life and Art* (rev. ed., 1902; trans. Francis W. Kelsey; repr., New Rochelle, N.Y.: Caratzas Bros., 1982) 424.

Fig. 9.13 Tomb QQ: stone altar or offering table.

purpose, and commemorative meals are one obvious answer. The fact that the well in the precinct predates the construction of the tomb around it shows that the provision of water was considered important. All this is reminiscent of the kitchen facilities in the tombs at Isola Sacra. [37] The importance of the funerary meal is evident in the name—*culina*—given to the area reserved on the outskirts of the town for the funerals of the very poor that I mentioned earlier.[38] There is no epigraphic or literary evidence referring to commemoration of the dead at Corinth, but festivals such as the Parentalia and the Rosalia are mentioned in inscriptions all over the Mediterranean as times for making offerings to dead relatives and friends. There must have been other private family occasions as well, such as anniversaries. These meals expressed the sense of community between the living and the dead. They should not be confused with the communion meals of the personal or mystery religions.

[37]The tomb at Cheliotomylos referred to earlier (Shear, "Excavations 1931") had a well in the center of the chamber. For Isola Sacra, see Guido Calza, *La Necropoli del porta di Roma nell'Isola Sacra* (Rome: Instituto di Archeologia e Storia dell'Arte, 1940) 56. The literary evidence has been collected by Hugh Lindsay, "Eating with the Dead: The Roman Funerary Banquet," in *Meals in a Social Context: Aspects of the Communal Meal in the Hellenistic and Roman World* (ed. Inge Nielsen and Hanne Nielsen; Aarhus: Aarhus University Press, 1998) 67–79.

[38]Also Paulus (ca. 200 C.E.) quoting Festus: *Culina vocatur locus, in quo epulae in funere comburuntur*, "The place where they burn the funeral meals is called the kitchen" (*Sent. recep.* 65.12). It is interesting that this area was regarded as *locus publicus*, not *religiosus*.

The undisturbed single burials allow us to make some observations with regard to the treatment of the corpse. The body was laid out on its back in the extended position, the arms at the sides, the head usually facing upwards, but sometimes to the side, and resting on a pillow built up on the floor of the sarcophagus or cist. In the chamber tombs, the head is always placed away from the door. The body was probably carried on a bier, of which only the nails survive in some cases (see also n. 46, below). A collection of large bone pins found in the Painted Tomb may have been used to fasten a covering or shroud over the body. It is reasonable to think that a bier and covering were used when carrying the corpse to the burial ground. No traces of clothing have survived and there were only a few items of personal jewelry. Several pairs of gold loop earrings were found in the Painted Tomb; since they were for pierced ears, they must have been left on the corpse when it was interred. Other jewelry is simple: a bronze bangle, beads, and an iron ring set with a carved gem. Two small silver coins of the fourth century B.C.E., which may have been jewelry or possibly keepsakes, were also found in one of the Painted Tomb cists. Often a bronze coin had been placed in the mouth or sometimes in the hand. In some cases, all that remains is a cupric stain on the bones where the coin disintegrated. Charon's fee—to ensure safe passage to the afterlife—is well known in Roman contexts, but it was by no means a universal custom in Greece.[39] These coins are often very worn, and it was obviously the thought, and not the value of the coin, that counted.

Unguentaria were found in many of the graves (fig. 9.14). In some instances they were placed one on either side of the head, but they were also found at the feet or between the legs. They probably held oils or other substances used in preparing the body for burial and to help in preserving the body—or at least to disguise the smell. Decomposition must always have been a problem. In two instances, unguentaria were found above the cover over the head of the corpse, which suggests that the contents were poured as a libation at the end of the ceremony. Some of the unguentaria were glass, but the majority were made of clay.[40] Thymiateria or incense burners (fig. 9.15) probably served the same purpose. They may have been brought from the place where the deceased was originally laid out, or they could have been used at the time of burial.

---

[39]Robert Garland, *The Greek Way of Death* (2d ed.; London: Duckworth, 2001) 23; Morris, *Death-Ritual*, 105–6. In the North Cemetery, coins were found in only sixteen graves, two of which were Roman in date.

[40]This may have been a question of expense, since most of the clay unguentaria were found with open deposits, but they were also used in Tomb X. It could also have been a matter of fashion.

Fig. 9.14 Clay unguentaria.

Fig. 9.15 Thymiateria.

Lamps were found in large numbers in the chamber tombs; the Painted Tomb and Tomb QQ produced fifty-two and thirty-nine respectively. Only three lamps were recovered from the individual graves. It may be that they were normally placed outside the grave and have not survived, whereas those in the tombs did. All the lamps had been used. There is no reason to think that funerals took place at night in the period we are dealing with, but lamps would certainly have been needed inside the chamber tombs to provide lighting when the body was being interred. In the funeral context, lighted lamps are generally regarded as having had a purifying or apotropaic function, but their use may also have become traditional, a mark of respect on the part of the mourners similar to that expressed by the lighting of a candle today. On the figured lamps, there is a variety of designs; the choice may or may not be significant. The peacock and pomegranate (on a lamp in Tomb X) are well-known funerary symbols. There are several lamps with gladiatorial scenes that may have been thought suitable because gladiators were courageous and did not fear death. In the Tomb with Sarcophagi there were a few lamps with Christian symbols (see below). On the other hand, the designs could have been the personal choice of participants in the ceremony or simply types popular at Corinth. What is abundantly clear is that the custom of placing a lamp and coin either over or near the grave persisted into the late fifth and even the sixth centuries in the absence of all other offerings.[41]

Grave offerings apart from those already mentioned were notably sparse. It was a surprise, therefore, to find several of the thin gold disks known as *bracteates* or "ghost money" among the multiple burials in two of the late tombs (fig. 9.16). They must have been deposited in the sarcophagi between 300 and 450. The disks were made in a rather amateurish fashion by pressing gold foil over Sikyonian coins with a dove, dated in the Late Classical or Hellenistic period. They are frequently found elsewhere in the Peloponnese and Magna Graecia and until now have always been regarded as belonging in the Hellenistic period, and as the equivalent of coins for Charon's fee.[42] The context for our gold disks, however, is certainly Late Roman. Similar disks have been found in other Roman graves at Corinth where it is apparent from their location and the presence of actual coins or of cupric stains on the skeleton that they were not being used as substitutes for coins. The impressions are easy to make and they were probably the work of someone connected with the burial rather than a craftsman. They are too fragile to have been used as jewelry. They may have been fastened lightly in some way to clothing or a cover, but it is more likely that gold disks were simply put into the grave as part of the burial rite. I concluded that they were talismans intended to protect the dead from harm.[43]

The talismanic power of the gold may have been of primary importance, but I think that the image was also significant. By far the most popular type, not simply at Corinth and Sikyon, but elsewhere, is the Sikyonian dove. The preference is easy to understand. For both Greeks and Romans the dove was a symbol of marital affection and constancy; it appears frequently with the dead on Roman tombstones.[44] The dove was also sacred to Aphrodite and to Demeter, both of whom were particularly venerated at Corinth, so it would have been especially appropriate here. Although the dove was not a common symbol for

---

[41]Over one late grave at Cheliotomylos, six coins had been placed with one lamp. There were six skulls below—one coin per head.

[42]Donna Kurtz and John Boardman, *Greek Burial Customs* (London: Thames and Hudson, 1971) 211, 363; Garland, *Greek Way of Death*, 23.

[43]Coins, particularly gold coins (and other gold objects), have often been used as talismans or in exorcisms and religious rites. In such cases the special virtue is attributed to the metal rather than to the actual coin. The substitution of a gold foil impression for a real gold coin would not damage the efficacy of the offering.

[44]Trimalchio (Petronius, *Sat.* 71) was following fashion, as always, when he wanted a sculpture of his wife Fortunata holding a dove outside his tomb.

Fig. 9.16 Gold foil disks from Tomb with Sarcophagi and Square Tomb with Tile Floor.

the early Christians, the later portrayal of the soul as a dove would have made the Sikyonian coins acceptable to Christians as well as to pagans.

Religion and magic go hand in hand in the ancient world. There was a renewed interest in magical beliefs and in apparitions from the second century c.e. onwards.[45] Charms to ward off evil were very popular, and some of the items in the graves are best regarded as apotropaic. In several graves there was an iron nail, which was regarded as a means of protection against the supernatural. In the single grave of a child aged four or five years in the Tomb with Sarcophagi, eggshell fragments and a large animal tooth were found mixed with the child's bones.[46] A bronze bell was found in the same sarcophagus as two of the gold disks. The need to ward off evil and also perhaps to prevent the dead from harming the living is evident and persistent.[47] In the same tomb in which two of the gold disks were found, but in a different sarcophagus, lead curse tablets had been placed. One is a

[45]Lucian (*Philops.* 30–31), writing in the second half of the second century, gives a satirical account of a haunted house at Corinth and its exorcism. When buried with the appropriate funeral rites, the ghost ceased to haunt the house.

[46]If there are several nails, with fragments of wood adhering or a stain in the earth, they may have been part of a bier or box; otherwise they are likely to have been apotropaic in function. Nails may be found in the hand or placed on the skull, but sometimes they were just put in the grave. Eggshells were found in thirty-seven graves and one deposit of the fifth and fourth centries b.c.e. in the North Cemetery.

[47]Such superstitions, including the use of coins on account of their types, lasted well into the Christian era. At the end of the fourth century, John Chrysostom was inveighing against Christians who bound bronze coins bearing the head of Alexander the Great to their heads and feet in the hope of salvation (*Catech. illum.* = *PG* 49.239). In general, see Valerie Flint, "The Demonisation of Magic and Sorcery in Late Antiquity: Christian Redefinitions of Pagan Religions," in *Witchcraft and Magic in Europe, Ancient Greece and Rome* (ed. Bengt Ankarloo and Stuart Clark; Philadelphia: University of Pennsylvania Press, 1999).

plea for justice rather than a curse.[48] The date of the tablets is unknown, but it is interesting that, unlike the other sarcophagi which held large multiple burials, this one contained only the remains of an adolescent (of unknown sex) and a young child.

The paucity of funerary offerings can be interpreted in various ways. Perhaps it was a desire for simplicity. This could be symptomatic of the general attitude of the Corinthians. It is noticeable, for example, that in the chamber tombs there are none of the elaborate ash chests or marble funerary altars found elsewhere. With the exception of a glass cinerary urn, all the cremation containers found so far at Corinth are lead or earthenware.[49] The growing scarcity of grave goods could also be connected with a change in ritual, with the emphasis on burial rites rather than the display of gifts. However, I am inclined to think that this scarcity is explained by my conclusion that the people who buried here belonged to the artisan, working class, and that the absence of gifts is a reflection of their restricted social circle. Other graves at Corinth contain richer and more numerous gifts; so do graves of the Roman period at Patrae.

CONCLUSIONS

To put our findings into context, this is an area where the ordinary working class of Roman Corinth buried its dead for five hundred years. Burial practice is by its very nature conservative. But it is also subject to outside influences. Here we have seen it evolve over time: cremation eventually disappears; the spatial organization of the tombs changes; grave goods become increasingly rare; and the popularity of multiple burial grows. The consistent factor would seem to be a sense of communality both among the living and between the living and the dead.

During that same time, a major change was taking place in the religious beliefs of the Greco-Roman world, as we know in retrospect. There is little

[48]Personal communication from David Jordan, who is studying the tablets. The preference was to put curse tablets with a corpse, preferably a young one, since it was thought to make for a quicker transition to the underworld, but the curse did not necessarily relate to the body.

[49]For the glass urn, see James Wiseman, "Excavations in Corinth, The Gymnasium Area, 1967–1968," *Hesperia* 38 (1969) 86–87. The cremation urn in the North Cemetery (Grave 516) that contained twenty-seven gold leaves mixed with the bones was made of lead. The choice of material may, of course, have something to do with the shortage of good marble at Corinth.

indication of any sect or cult in our excavations (save perhaps for the choice of figurines deposited in the graves), although Corinth was a cosmopolitan city with a number of flourishing foreign cults. Nor did we find in these burials any clear evidence of Christianity. Elsewhere in Corinth there is indisputable evidence of Christian burials.[50] Our tombs are more difficult to assess, partly because Christians did not necessarily draw attention to themselves and often used existing cemeteries; and also because some non-Christian burial rites, such as communal meals, were retained, but given a different interpretation. A few of the late lamps deposited in the Tomb with Sarcophagi do have Christian symbols, and this suggests that Christians were among the last people to use the tomb, in the second half of the fifth century. It depends, too, how much weight one puts on the evidence of multiple burial, which was certainly favored by the early Christians, although not exclusively—there are numerous single Christian graves. I have less confidence that burial with the head to the west is conclusive. Several very late burials in the chamber tombs do have this orientation, but it may have been simply a practical matter of fitting them in. It was not, in any case, a primary Christian belief, but rather adopted from the common pagan practice of facing the rising sun, and the literary evidence is much later. The east-west alignment did eventually become standard practice, but the exact date cannot be determined, nor can one assume that those not buried with their heads to the west were not Christian.

I have been discussing the ordinary graves of very ordinary people. Interpretation demands comparative information, and there are other cemeteries in and around Corinth that have yet to be studied in the same detail. Nor should I leave the impression that the graves along the irrigation channel are typical of Roman Corinth. They are only a small part of the important Kritika cemetery in the plain to the north of the city. Conspicuous display for the benefit of passersby was one of the features of burial in the Greco-Roman world, and early reports in Greek journals describe monumental tombs lining the roads leading from the coast through this cemetery. One of the earliest chance discoveries was the impressive marble sarcophagus depicting the departure of the Seven against Thebes and the death of Opheltes.[51] Sarcophagi of the Roman period are rare at Corinth and nearly always come from Kritika.

---

[50]For example, in Lerna Hollow: "The crosses found on tombstones and terracotta lamps or scratched onto the graves themselves provide ample evidence" (Wiseman, "Excavations 1967–1968," 79–86).

[51]Franklin P. Johnson, *Sculpture, 1896–1923* (Corinth IX; Cambridge, Mass.: ASCSA, 1931) 114–18, no. 241.

During the construction of the Corinth/Patras highway, archaeologists of the Greek Service found a row of built tombs with party walls fronting directly onto the road.[52] There were also single graves similar to ours, but with much richer grave goods. The site where these finds were made is farther into the plain—a more desirable and, no doubt, a more expensive location. I have referred several times to the chamber tombs in the Cheliotomylos area; more than a hundred single graves, some in family groups, were excavated there as well.[53] When all this material has been studied, we shall be able to fill out the picture of burial practices at Roman Corinth.

[52]Evangelia Protonotariou-Deilaki, "Chronica," *ArchDelt* 24 (1969) 102 and plates 78–79. One of the sarcophagi had an attractive marble lid decorated with a putto holding up garlands of fruit and flowers.

[53]This material is currently being prepared for publication and the chamber tombs published in 1931 are being restudied. The dates for the latter given by Shear are subject to revision.

CHAPTER TEN

Placing the Dead: Funerary Practice and Social Stratification in the Early Roman Period at Corinth and Ephesos

Christine M. Thomas

INTRODUCTION: PATTERNS OF CHANGE IN FUNERARY PRACTICE

Graves appear everywhere in archaeological digs, but are ironically often overlooked in historical reconstruction. They give archaeologists more representative evidence of human societies across class, gender, and ethnic groups than any other single type of artifact, simply because nearly every human individual is disposed of in some deliberate manner after death.[1] Thus, graves should be uniquely able to inform us about social structure and cultural change. It has become a commonplace to observe that graves tell us not about the dead, but about their survivors, who perform the rituals and commission the monuments: funerary activities are spectacles and displays performed by the living.[2]

---

[1] I would like to thank the archaeologists of Corinth who participated in this conference, especially Mary Walbank, Kathleen Slane, Betsy Gebhard, and Charles K. Williams II, all of whom made valuable comments on the conference version of this paper, especially with regard to the Corinthian materials.

[2] Recent studies of funerary rituals as indicators of social and political structures in antiquity include Keith Hopkins, *Death and Renewal* (Cambridge: Cambridge University Press, 1983); Ian Morris, *Death-Ritual and Social Structure in Classical Antiquity* (Cambridge: Cambridge University Press, 1992); Harriet I. Flower, *Ancestor Masks and Aristocratic Power in Roman*

A further corollary developed in recent research is that it is not the religious or ideological content of the funerary rituals and monuments themselves, but rather the patterns of change in their use that are the meaningful feature.[3] Historians of religion have long realized that ritual does not carry its own explanation. Ritual action is "primary" or "absolute" in the sense that the action operates in the absence of fixed meaning. The meanings attached to ritual are context specific and can change over time. Argument about the meaning of the same ritual is often a means of defining group boundaries. Catholics and Protestants during the Reformation were performing the selfsame Eucharist ritual; but whether one believed the ritual action was a mere memorial of Christ's death, or a supernatural process by which the bread was transformed into Christ's body, determined the group to which one belonged.

In order to employ these theoretical insights, a certain prefiguring of the archaeological record is necessary. Although careful primary recording and description are the indispensable foundation of any analysis of archaeological materials, a dataset can only answer historical questions of social structure or cultural processes when arranged by means of specific analytic categories. As the New Archaeologists recognized long ago, the data do not speak; archaeologists must pose the questions. But as postprocessualists have pointed out, these questions not only prefigure the data, but also guide what one sees in the archaeological record when one makes the selection of relevant data.[4] Instead of viewing this theoretical situation as the end of objectivity, one can view it as a perspective that opens up new ways in which the data can answer our questions.

Among historians of religion, specialists in early Christianity have been particularly engaged with the question of the effect of Roman contact upon the various cultural units of the Eastern Mediterranean during the Late Republic and Early Empire. The nascent Christian movement enters this matrix as a change, a *novum*; even its contemporaries viewed it as an innovation, as did some of its

---

Culture (Oxford: Clarendon, 1996); Carlin Barton, *The Sorrows of the Ancient Romans: The Gladiator and the Monster* (Princeton, N.J.: Princeton University Press, 1993) 11–46; and Donald G. Kyle, *Spectacles of Death in Ancient Rome* (London: Routledge, 2001).

[3]Developed most explicitly in Morris, *Death-Ritual*, 1–30. For further suggestions on the use of funerary materials, see Rick Jones, "A Quantitative Approach to Roman Burial," in *Burial in the Roman World* (ed. Richard Reece; London: Council for British Archaeology, 1977) 20–25.

[4]Representative introduction in Ian Hodder, *The Archaeological Process* (London: Blackwell, 1999), esp. 1–19, 30–65, 80–104; see also idem, *Reading the Past* (2d ed.; Cambridge: Cambridge University Press, 1991) 156–93.

practitioners.[5] Understanding how this movement took its place alongside other factors of cultural change may answer the question of the otherwise unexpected appeal of the new religion and its success in gaining adherents. Funerary materials can assist in sketching out the effects of Roman contact on the eastern provinces. As observed, the point of such a study would not be merely to investigate the degree to which the coming of Roman settlers to the East affected indigenous funerary cult, but rather to focus on the processes of change that become evident in the arena of funerary practice. Along these lines of analysis, lack of change also becomes meaningful, a positive indicator rather than a dearth of signification.

This essay is a limited comparative study of burial practices in Corinth and Ephesos during the Late Republic and Early Roman periods. One should expect slightly different pictures, for the two cities diverged considerably in their relationship to Rome. Corinth was refounded as the Roman colony *Laus Iulia Corinthiensis* in 44/43 B.C.E.,[6] about a hundred years after it was destroyed by the Roman general Mummius. Although recent studies suggest that considerable continuity existed between Greek and Roman Corinth,[7] and that the area continued to be populated in the interim,[8] the relative position of Roman citizens in Corinth was different from that held in other provincial cities. Ephesos is an apposite example. Its direct contact with Rome was quite early, for it became the provincial capital in 29 B.C.E. under the Roman

[5]This statement is so general as to require much more extensive documentation. Although apologists in the second century, such as Justin Martyr (*1 Apol.* 53; *Dial.*, passim), are careful to stress the continuity of Christianity with Judaism, the legal basis of persecution was that the Christian cult was not a religion with an ancient pedigree but an innovation—hence the Christian attempts to address the issue of innovation (Justin, *1 Apol.* 1; *Diogn.* 1). Celsus similarly judged the Christians as innovators (Origen, *Cels.* 1.14; 2.4; 5.33). The apocalyptic stream of early Christianity represented by Paul also stressed the newness of the Christian revelation, although Paul clearly believed that he was part of the Jewish tradition and that his activity was located in its last phase (e.g. Rom 9–11; Gal 3:23–4:7). On the legal basis of the persecution of the Christians, see briefly but clearly Mary Beard, John North, and Simon Price, *Religions of Rome* (2 vols.; Cambridge: Cambridge University Press, 1998) 1:225–27; classic treatment in A. N. Sherwin-White, *The Letters of Pliny: A Historical and Social Commentary* (Oxford: Clarendon Press, 1966) 691–712, 772–87. Part of Sherwin-White's treatment appeared earlier in idem, "Early Persecutions and Roman Law Again," *JTS* n.s. 3 (1952) 199–213.

[6]On the date, see Mary E. Hoskins Walbank, "The Foundation and Planning of Early Roman Corinth," *JRA* 10 (1997) 95–130, esp. 97–99; for a general survey of Hellenistic and Roman Corinth, see James Wiseman, "Corinth and Rome I: 228 B.C.–A.D. 267," *ANRW* II.17.1 (1979) 438–548.

[7]See the remarks in Walbank, "Foundation and Planning," 95–96.

[8]I. B. Romano, "A Hellenistic Deposit from Corinth: Evidence for Interim Period Activity," *Hesperia* 63 (1994) 57–104; and Walbank, "Foundation and Planning," 103–7.

Senate, a situation that remained unchanged under Augustus. But the Roman political and economic functionaries interacted with a provincial elite of considerable power and organization, who maintained their traditional practices and cults even at those points when they most directly incorporated Roman cultural expressions.[9]

The record of funerary practices for both locations is incomplete. Despite the careful publication of the North Cemetery,[10] study of burial practice in Roman Corinth is far from systematic. The materials are scattered among numerous journals as publications of individual items or brief notes in annual excavation reports.[11] The situation at Ephesos, if anything, is worse still. The published record includes no analogue to the North Cemetery of Corinth. Burials at Ephesos have only recently begun to be published in any systematic fashion,[12] and large bodies of material that would provide quantifiable data for the Roman period are lacking. This study will thus be provisional, as indeed all archaeological work is, and subject to reversal by new finds.

CREMATION AND SARCOPHAGUS INHUMATION AT CORINTH

Many graveyards with Roman burials have been uncovered at Corinth over the past century. There is a large concentration in the North Cemetery,[13] and

---

[9]Guy Rogers, *The Sacred Identity of Ephesos: Foundation Myths of a Roman City* (London: Routledge, 1991) 80–151.

[10]Carl Blegen, Rodney Young, and Hazel Palmer, *The North Cemetery* (Corinth XIII; Princeton, N.J.: ASCSA, 1964).

[11]An important exception is the systematic study of the Corinthian materials in the unpublished dissertation of Joseph Rife (available through UMI): "Death, Ritual, and Memory in Greek Society During the Early and Middle Roman Empire" (Ph.D. diss., University of Michigan, 1999) 199–332. In addition to its careful collection of relevant data, it offers an integration of the relevant publications in modern Greek.

[12]The Sacred Way around Panayırdağ has produced numerous grave monuments that have been carefully excavated and published: Dieter Knibbe and Gerhard Langmann, *Via Sacra Ephesiaca I* (BerMatÖAI 3; Vienna: Schindler, 1993) 9–13, 36–54, plates 13–24, 27–29, 37, figs. 19–21; Dieter Knibbe and Hilke Thür, *Via Sacra Ephesiaca II* (BerMatÖAI 6; Vienna: Schindler, 1995) 33–46, 49–58, 62–83. The well-known tombs in the area of the Cave of the Seven Sleepers are part of the same necropolis, though chiefly used in Late Antiquity (*Das Cömeterium der sieben Schläfer* [FiE 4.2; Vienna: Österreichisches Archäologisches Institut, 1937]). For a general overview, see Wolfgang Pietsch, "Außerstädtische Grabanlagen von Ephesos," in *100 Jahre österreichischen Forschungen in Ephesos: Akten des Symposions Wien 1995* (ed. Herwig Friesinger and Friedrich Krinzinger; Vienna: Österreichische Akademie der Wissenschaften, 1999) 455–60.

[13]Blegen et al., *North Cemetery*.

some individual and chamber graves in the nearby Cheliotomylos area;[14] a graveyard containing some Roman graves is located near the amphitheater,[15] a small cemetery in the Anaploga district was found by Robinson,[16] some funerary monuments have turned up in Craneum,[17] and a few imperial graves were found near the Phliasian gate.[18] Mary E. Hoskins Walbank, in her contribution to this volume, reports on research in an area of Roman burials northeast of the ancient city, and another large chamber tomb in the Cheliotomylos area.[19] She has pointed out elsewhere that the placement of these cemeteries should be seen in relationship to urban development in Roman Corinth: since it was customary for the dead to be interred outside the city, the cemeteries provide an indication of the limits of settlement in early Roman Corinth.[20]

The largest published body of tombs at Corinth remains those of the North Cemetery. From 1928 to 1930, a campaign led in the first year by T. Leslie Shear and in the second and third years by Josephine Platner uncovered a total of 468 graves. Only 28 of these are Roman period, a rather small percentage in a graveyard dominated by Archaic and Classical burials; the Roman presence

---

[14]For inhumation burials from various Roman periods, in chamber tombs, tile graves, sarcophagi, and rock-cut tombs, see T. Leslie Shear, "Excavations in the North Cemetery at Corinth in 1930," *AJA* 34 (1930) 403–31, esp. 428–30; for inhumation burials from the first to fourth century C.E. in a chamber tomb, see idem, "The Excavation of Roman Chamber Tombs at Corinth in 1931," *AJA* 35 (1931) 424–41. A chamber tomb with inhumations and columbaria for cremation burials dating from the first to third centuries C.E. was found "north of the city wall and east of the 'Tile Works'"; see Henry S. Robinson, "Excavations at Corinth" (Chronika B1), *ArchDelt* 18 (1963) 77.

[15]T. Leslie Shear, "Excavations in the Theatre District and Tombs of Corinth in 1929," *AJA* 33 (1929) 536–38.

[16]For Late Roman interments enclosed by a peribolos wall, see Robinson, "Excavations," 79; for Hellenistic graves at Anaploga, see Elizabeth G. Pemberton, "Ten Hellenistic Graves in Ancient Corinth," *Hesperia* 54 (1985) 271–307; and for classical graves at Anaploga, see Henry S. Robinson, "A Sanctuary and Cemetery in Western Corinth," *Hesperia* 38 (1969) 1–35, esp. 34–35.

[17]M. Šašel Kos, "A Latin Epitaph of a Roman Legionary from Corinth," *JRS* 68 (1978) 22–25.

[18]Rhys Carpenter and Antoine Bon, *The Defenses of Acrocorinth and the Lower Town* (Corinth III.2; Cambridge, Mass.: ASCSA, 1936) 75.

[19]See pp. 249–80, above. The essay is part of a larger work, in collaboration with Kathleen Slane and with an archaeoanthropological contribution from Ethne Barnes, to be published in the Corinth series. One of the gravesites, the large painted chamber tomb about a hundred meters east of the Cheliotomylos hill, is briefly published in Robinson ("Excavations," 77), and is also reported in Georges Daux, "Chronique de fouilles et découvertes archéologiques en Grèce en 1962," *BCH* 87 (1963) 689–878, esp. 722, 724.

[20]Walbank, "Foundation and Planning," 107–11.

represents a reoccupation of a graveyard that had ceased to be used after the fourth century B.C.E.[21] Most of these Roman tombs are inhumations in tile graves or reused early Corinthian sarcophagi.[22] Interestingly, however, there are four cremations in this cemetery dating to the early Roman period, for all the Roman graves in general should be assigned to a period from shortly after 44 B.C.E. until the end of the first century C.E. The Roman cremations are, moreover, the only cremations in this extensive cemetery, which contains graves dating from the Middle Helladic and Geometric periods as well as the Archaic and Classical periods. Palmer writes that the cremations are to be attributed to Roman colonists, who took their place in the graveyard alongside their inhuming Greek neighbors.[23] This has been confirmed by the more systematic study of Joseph Rife, who finds no archaeological evidence for cremation before the founding of the Roman colony.[24] Even more striking than the sudden appearance of the rite during the Roman period is its domination of burial practice during that period. It is the single most prevalent burial rite, accounting for 43% of the burials in Rife's study. The remaining 57% of the burials are divided among the various sorts of inhumation: tile graves, chamber tombs, sarcophagi, cist graves, and vessel graves.[25]

Similarly, Walbank has found a notable if not overwhelming presence of cremation graves among the Roman graves she has investigated. Her data can be dated securely enough to attest that the practice of cremation in these tombs is not in evidence after the mid-second century C.E. By this time, the graves in this area show only inhumation, often in the sarcophagi and arcosolia that become so common in Late Antiquity.

Thus, the coming of Rome to Corinth is accompanied by the introduction of a completely different mode of disposing of the body. This is unremarkable.

[21]Hazel Palmer, "The Classical and Roman Periods," in *The North Cemetery* (ed. Carl William Blegen, Hazel Palmer, and Rodney S. Young; Corinth XIII; Princeton, N.J.: ASCSA, 1964) 65, 70.

[22]For further evidence of the reuse of Greek graves by Romans, see Shear, "Theatre District," 544–55. The prevalent reuse of graves of the Classical and Hellenistic periods at Corinth probably indicates some lack of continuity between the early inhabitants of Corinth and the later Roman settlers. Rife believes this to be instead an indication of an attempt by the later settlers to establish an identity with the Greek past ("Death, Ritual, and Memory," 253, 267–68, 272–73, 327–28), but I view this as unlikely because reuse of grave sites, though frequently practiced, was widely considered to be unacceptable behavior in antiquity. The care shown toward previous remains and grave gifts that Rife notes may have expressed no more than respect toward the dead and fear of disturbing them.

[23]Palmer, "Classical and Roman Periods," 70–71.

[24]Rife, "Death, Ritual, and Memory," 255.

[25]Ibid., 260.

With the exception of isolated sarcophagus burials in Roman aristocratic families until about the second century B.C.E., cremation was the customary mode of interment at Rome from about the fourth century B.C.E. onward for all but the lowest classes,[26] who may not have been able to spare the fuel necessary to dispose of a corpse. Cremation would have been the norm for the Romans who settled in Corinth, to the extent that they were wealthy enough to carry it out.

Burial practice in the Greek world varied greatly according to location and period; whereas Rome was a single city, the Greek East comprised a vast conglomeration of cities and cultures that was not centrally organized. Although cremation burial had been practiced in the Greek world since the so-called Dark Ages, cremation was nevertheless never as common there during the Roman period as it was in the capital.[27] Generally during the Roman period, people in the eastern provinces inhumed their dead in shaft or chamber burials, in sarcophagi or larnaxes, or in rock-cut tombs. Corinth in particular has a very early series of sarcophagus burials dating from the Geometric and Archaic periods, owing to the plentiful presence of poros, a soft and easily cut local limestone.[28] Gradually, from about 100 to 200 C.E., even Rome and the Western territories adopted inhumation, in particular sarcophagus inhumation, which then became the norm for the rest of Late Antiquity.[29]

---

[26]Overview in Arthur Darby Nock, "Cremation and Burial in the Roman Empire," *HTR* 25 (1932) 321–59, esp. 321–31; see also Morris, *Death-Ritual*, 42–67; and Jocelyn M. C. Toynbee, *Death and Burial in the Roman World* (Ithaca, N.Y.: Cornell University Press, 1971) 14–17, 39–42. On cremation in Italy before Augustus, see Glenys Davies, "Burial in Italy up to Augustus," in *Burial in the Roman World* (ed. Richard Reece; London: Council for British Archaeology, 1977) 13–19.

[27]Evidence of occasional cremation in Asia Minor is cited by Marcello Spanu, "Burial in Asia Minor during the Imperial Period, with Particular Reference to Cilicia and Cappadocia," in *Burial, Society and Context in the Roman World* (ed. John Pearce, Martin Millett, and Manuela Struck; London: Oxbow, 2000) 169–77, esp. 174. Donna Kurtz and John Boardman note the preference for inhumation in the East by the Hellenistic period even in locations that had a long prior tradition of cremation (*Greek Burial Customs* [Ithaca, N.Y.: Cornell, 1971] 162–64). Sara Cormack argues that Roman influence in the eastern provinces was more evident in the external funerary monuments than in actual practice ("Funerary Monuments and Mortuary Practice in Roman Asia Minor," in *The Early Roman Empire in the East* [ed. Susan Alcock; Oxford: Oxbow, 1997] 137–56, esp. 152–54).

[28]Rodney S. Young, "The Geometric Period," in *The North Cemetery* (ed. Carl W. Blegen, Hazel Palmer, and Rodney S. Young; Corinth XIII; Princeton, N.J.: ASCSA, 1964) 18–20; and idem, "The Protocorinthian Period," in ibid., 50–52.

[29]Toynbee, *Death and Burial*, 39–42; Morris, *Death-Ritual*, 52–69; and Guntram Koch and Hellmut Sichtermann, *Römische Sarkophage* (Munich: C. H. Beck, 1982) 23–30.

Attempts have been made to account for changes in burial practice with intellectualist explanations. The rather striking switch from cremation to sarcophagus inhumation in Rome and the western provinces has been attributed to the increasing popularity of mystery religions, including Christianity, and other ideologies that offered a more definite perception of the afterlife and would seem to have placed value on preservation of the body for this purpose.[30] If this is so, then the converse would presumably have been true for the practice of cremation: the rite would have expressed a lack of interest in the perdurance of the individual in the afterlife.

Our ancient sources, however, indicate just the opposite. Cremation seems to be the rite more often associated with the liberation of the soul for a happy afterlife. Inhumation, on the other hand, tends to express more traditional attitudes toward death. The literary sources in this period overwhelmingly testify that a strong and confidently expressed belief in a happy afterlife is the exception, rather than the rule, for both Greek and Roman cult. The dictum "I was not, I was, I am not, I care not" was so common a sentiment as sometimes to have been abbreviated *n f f n s n c*.[31] Indeed, far more common in the Imperial period in both East and West, and earlier in the Republican, Hellenistic, and Classical periods, was a tentative oscillation between two beliefs: the first, that the spirit is somehow set free from the body at death so that it continues to live; and the second, that the dead are still resident in their graves.

Roman death cult gives the best examples of the tomb as permanent dwelling place, with its annual banquets at the tombs of the dead on their birthdays (*dies natalis*); at the Rosalia in May, which was not specifically a festival of the dead; and at the Parentalia in February, which was.[32] Romans often made provisions in their wills for a foundation to finance these annual dinners, and sometimes for even more frequent offerings on the kalends of every month.[33] They specify the types of foods that were to be bought and

---

[30]Franz Cumont, *Recherches sur le symbolisme funéraire des Romains* (Paris: P. Geuthner, 1942) 363, 380–81; idem, *Lux Perpetua* (Paris: P. Geuthner, 1949) 387–90; Robert Turcan, "Origines et sens de l'inhumation à l'époque impériale," *REA* 60 (1958) 323–47; A. Audin, "Inhumation et incinération," *Latomus* 19 (1960) 312–22, 518–32; Fernand de Visscher, *Le droit des tombeaux romains* (Milan: Giuffré, 1963) 39–42; and Toynbee, *Death and Burial*, 41.

[31]*Non fui, fui, non sum, non curo*; *CIL* 5/1 no. 2893. See Richmond Lattimore, *Themes in Greek and Latin Epitaphs* (Urbana: University of Illinois, 1962) 84–85 with n. 473.

[32]For the Rosalia, see Lattimore, *Themes*, 137–40. For the Rosalia and Parentalia, see Toynbee, *Death and Burial*, 63–64; and Beard et al., *Religions of Rome*, 1:31, 50. Compare Ovid, *Fast*. 2.533–616 (Feralia).

[33]Toynbee, *Death and Burial*, 61–62.

served (sausages are frequently mentioned) and the types of flowers to be displayed, often violets and roses.[34] The Corinthian evidence also gives clear testimony of these two types of beliefs in the pre-Roman period. In the Classical period, from the fifth century on, it was normative practice to leave for the dead in their tombs both a pitcher, often an *oinochoē*, and a cup from which to drink.[35] Such practice suggests that the dead are indeed resident in their tombs, and Walbank and her colleagues have documented the practice of funerary meals at the tombs they are publishing.[36] This evidence resembles Greek practice elsewhere, with the distinction that at some other sites food and pots would be "killed" —that is, burnt or broken—at a funeral or other observance so that they could reach the dead person for their use.[37] According to Herodotus, the deceased wife of Periander appeared as a shade to her husband and complained that she was cold because he did not burn any clothing for her at her funeral (5.92). Thus, while the Greeks clearly conceived of the dead person as being somewhere else, in a realm of the dead where only "killed" food or clothing could reach them, offerings would nevertheless be made at the tomb. The festival calendar of many Greek cities provided, like Athens, for an annual festival of the ancestors, during which they would be fed at their graves and the untended dead would also be propitiated.[38] The Roman version of this, the Lemuria, which took place in May, effected this propitiation by enjoining the living to throw black beans over their shoulder nine times.[39]

Early Corinthian sarcophagus burials, especially from the Archaic period onward, witness the care taken to protect the corpse from decay. The monolithic sarcophagi are not only proof against dirt and disturbance; their interiors are also carefully stuccoed to prevent the intrusion of moisture: the makers of these graves were concerned to preserve these bodies to the best of their ability.[40] Given the other gravesite rituals, however, the motive may

[34]For an example from Asia Minor, see the inscription in Peter Herrmann and Kemal Ziya Polatkan, "Das Testament des Epikrates und andere neue Inschriften aus dem Museum von Manisa," *SÖAW* 265.1 (1969) 1–64, esp. 1–36.

[35]Palmer, "Classical and Roman Periods," 78–82.

[36]Particularly in the chamber tomb known as the Painted Tomb (first published in Robinson, "Excavations," 77), where vessels for food and drink were stored inside the tomb and are associated with a thin layer of ash, probably from the preparation of funerary meals.

[37]Kurtz and Boardman, *Greek Burial Customs*, 215–16.

[38]The festival of the Genesia at Athens was a public recognition of the dead; see H. W. Parke, *Festivals of the Athenians* (Ithaca, N.Y.: Cornell University Press, 1977) 53–55.

[39]See Ovid, *Fast.* 5.419–92; Toynbee, *Death and Burial*, 64; and recently R. J. Littlewood, "Ovid among the Family Dead," *Latomus* 60 (2001) 916–35.

[40]Young, "Protocorinthian Period," 51; and Palmer, "Classical and Roman Periods," 72.

not have been to preserve the body for some resurrection in the afterlife, but to preserve the body precisely where it was at the grave site, so that it could continue to be tended in its new "home" in the cemetery, the city of the dead on the outskirts of the city of the living. One must take grave gifts seriously as offerings to the dead: the dead remain in some sense in their tomb, or the tomb is at least the most important spatial link between them and their living survivors. Otherwise the placement of the gifts there and the continued annual offerings and meals at the gravesite lack justification. Because of the belief in the continued existence of an individual at his grave site, Greek epitaphs in particular show great concern that a grave not be disturbed and reused.[41]

The Romans shared this concept and expressed it quite clearly: upon death, the dead would join in with the undifferentiated *manes*, the ancestral spirits that aid humankind if honored but trouble them if neglected. The *manes* were thought to live in the ground, near the burial place or in the tomb, which was often house-like, as were those of the ancient Etruscans.[42] Feeding tubes brought food and wine into direct contact with the bones or ashes of the deceased and were thought to be able to nourish the dead person, not only at Rome but throughout the empire in this period.[43] Many Roman texts emphasize the consubstantiality of the corpse with mother earth; a Roman epitaph for a child Optatus records a prayer that the earth, who is his mother

---

[41]There is one Corinthian example known to me of a curse formula threatening those who would disturb the grave with subsequent burials: "If others should bring another corpse . . . , may their offspring not remain on earth." (['Εὰν δ]ὲ ἄλλ[οι ἄ]- / γνωσιν βουλό- / μενοι σὺν ἐμοὶ / θάπτ(ε)ιν ἄλλον νε- / κρόν, ἐ(ν)θάδ᾽ ἄγοντες, / μήτ᾽ ἐκείνων ἐπὶ γέ- / ης ἔκγονα ἐνκαταμεί- / νη(ι); text in Benjamin Dean Meritt, *Greek Inscriptions, 1896–1927* [Corinth VIII.1; Cambridge, Mass.: ASCSA, 1931] no. 135). I follow Nikos A. Bees (*Corpus der griechisch christlichen Inschriften von Hellas: Inschriften von Peloponnes: Bd. 1, Isthmos-Korinthos* [vol. 1 of *Inscriptiones graecae christianae veteres et byzantinae*; Chicago: Ares, 1978] 35–37, no. 16) in restoring ἄλλ[οι] rather than Merritt's ἄλλ[ον]. Bees dates the inscription to the fourth century C.E. chiefly on the basis of its orthography, though there are solid palaeographic reasons for this dating as well. Despite its inclusion in this corpus, there is nothing Christian about this inscription, which alludes to Greek epic. On curse formulas as a theme in epitaphs, see Lattimore, *Themes,* 108–18. Lattimore correctly notes that such curse formulas are not only almost exclusively Greek, but are concentrated especially in Asia Minor, above all in Phrygia.

[42]The classic study is Walter Friedrich Otto, *Die Manen* (Berlin: J. Springer, 1923); see also Toynbee, *Death and Burial,* 35, 37; and Beard et al., *Religion of the Romans,* 1:30. For the *manes* in epitaphs, see Lattimore, *Themes,* 90–95.

[43]For examples in Rome, Italy, and Great Britain, see Toynbee, *Death and Burial,* 51–52; in Italy, see de Visscher, *Droit des tombeaux,* 28. Walbank (in this volume) cites an example of a hole for a feeding tube at Corinth in one of the chamber tombs she publishes, Tomb X (see pp. 257–61, above; the hole is illustrated in fig. 9.7).

now, will turn his ashes into roses and violets.[44] One text even associates a sort of personal immortality with the return to the bosom of the earth: *cinis sum, cinis terra est, terra dea est, ergo ego mortua non sum* ("I am ashes, ashes are earth, earth is a goddess; thus, I am not dead").[45] More often, however, the decay of the corpse is viewed not so much as a sign of immortality but as a metamorphosis, a change in state to another form of life, as in the inscription of Optatus.

Cremation, on the other hand, is often associated in ancient sources with the idea of immortality, that the soul is freed from the body upon death and flies upward into the heavens, where it enjoys a truly otherworldly existence among the stars of the Milky Way, an astral apotheosis. At imperial funerals, an eagle was released to suggest the emperor's apotheosis, as his immortal spirit flew up from the corpse on the pyre.[46] Other examples show that such a celestial afterlife was not just the hope of the emperor: Scipio Africanus is depicted as dwelling among the stars in the "Dream of Scipio."[47] In the background of this belief is a Middle Platonic conception of the human being, in which the body is a hindrance to the soul's progress in virtue and is left behind at death, like an old garment, as the soul continues its heavenward journey to its true home.[48] How different these conceptions are from modern Christianized notions of cremation, which was until recently only the province of atheists and freethinkers!

Cremation and inhumation, which appeared side by side in Greece and Imperial Rome, are thus in many ways ritual analogues that manifest the same conception of the afterlife. Grave goods are present in both forms of burial. In Rome, feeding tubes have been attested for both.[49] Ashes have been found interred inside sarcophagi.[50] To understand cremation at Corinth and at Ephesos, then, one should move beyond the mere appearance of the ritual to analyze how the ritual appears within the patterns of change and continuity during the early Roman period in funerary ritual at both sites.

[44]*CIL* 9 no. 3184; see other examples in Lattimore, *Themes*, 130–31, 136.

[45]*CIL* 6/4 no. 29609, cited in Toynbee, *Death and Burial*, 37.

[46]Javier Arce, *Funus Imperatorum: los funerales de los emperadores imperiales* (Madrid: Alianza, 1988) 131–40; Simon R. F. Price, "From Noble Funerals to Divine Cult: The Consecration of Roman Emperors," in *Rituals of Royalty: Power and Ceremonial in Traditional Societies* (ed. David Cannadine and Simon Price; Cambridge: Cambridge University Press, 1987) 56–105, esp. 94–95; Toynbee, *Death and Burial*, 59; Morris, *Death-Ritual*, 54–56.

[47]Cicero, *Resp.* 6.15–18.

[48]Albinus, *Epit.* 16.2; Cicero, *Resp.* 6.15–16.

[49]Toynbee, *Death and Burial*, 51–52.

[50]Nock, "Cremation and Burial," 327 with n. 34, 333–34 with n. 61.

Roman influence is apparent in the attestation of a particularly Roman form of burial at Corinth. It is important, however, not to stop the analysis with this observation. A more salient feature is that the Roman graves at Corinth, at least initially, do not seem to be particularly rich or ostentatious, on the evidence of the North Cemetery and the graves that are being published by Walbank.[51] Wealth in graves, or its absence, is a critical marker of change, but again, this is meaningful contextually rather than as an absolute quantity. Wealth in graves does not indicate a particularly wealthy society; similarly, the individuals who have the wealthiest graves were usually not the wealthiest in life. Anthropological studies have shown that stable societies tend to have graves that become slightly more modest over time, and that graves are richer during periods of social stress. Very rich burials show the instability of the elite and their need to legitimate themselves vis-à-vis other classes that might aspire to power.[52] The relative absence of wealth in the Corinthian cremation burials would not necessarily suggest poverty, but rather that those Romans who performed the burials were in a relatively stable position within their society.

Ephesos: A "Style War" of Burial Containers

This possibility comes into stronger relief when compared to the evidence from Ephesos. As in Corinth, Roman contact at Ephesos led to the appearance of cremation burials, attested by a series of about 180 burial containers and fragments[53] produced from the first century B.C.E. to the

---

[51]Palmer, "Classical and Roman Periods," 78–79, 82; Walbank, "Unquiet Graves."

[52]M. Parker Pearson, "Economic and Ideological Change: Cyclical Growth in the Pre-State Societies of Jutland," in *Ideology, Power, and Prehistory* (ed. Daniel Miller and Christopher Tilley; Cambridge: Cambridge University Press, 1984) 69–92; and Vere Gordon Childe, "Directional Changes in Funerary Practices during 50,000 Years," *Man* 45 (1945) 13–19.

[53]I am preparing a catalog of these containers for publication with the collaboration of archaeologist Cengiz İçten of the Efes Müzesi in Selçuk, Turkey. The series includes eighty-seven complete *ostothēkai* and forty-three fragments from Ephesos and its environs, located in the various museum and excavation depots in Selçuk, on the site of Ephesos, and at St. John's Basilica. At least fifty other recognizable fragments of *ostothēkai* remain uncataloged on the shelves in these depots. Within the parameters of this project, only fragments with inscriptions or significant stylistic value were recorded. I thank Selahattin Erdemgil, former director of the Efes Müzesi, Selçuk, both for permission to cite these materials in this article and, more generally, for every assistance he lent in preparing a catalog of these items; Dr. Helmut Engelmann of the Institut für Altertumskunde in Cologne for his assistance with the inscriptions; and Ulrike Outschar, Hilke Thür, and the late Klaus Tuchelt for their comments and advice.

first century C.E.[54] It was truly the introduction of a new rite; cremation is attested elsewhere at Ephesos, but only later than this early series of burial containers.[55] At Ephesos, however, the introduction of cremation led to the opposite of what one finds at Corinth. Instead of a stable collection of modest receptacles, cremation at Ephesos led to a cycle of increasing ostentation in burial containers, a "style war" between the Roman settlers and the provincials. Thus, the same burial practice shows diametrically opposite patterns of use at Corinth and at Ephesos. This divergence correlates with the radically different social location of the Roman settlers at Corinth and at Ephesos.

When the Ephesian ash chests, or *ostothēkai* as they are termed in Asia Minor,[56] are arranged stylistically and chronologically, they document a radical change in funerary iconography for these items during the

[54]Some of the *ostothēkai* have been published in Nuşin Asgari, "Die Halbfabrikate kleinasiatischer Girlandensarkophage und ihre Herkunft," *AA* (1977) 329–80, esp. 373 (inv. 806, 451, 452). Inv. 452 is published along with another *ostothēkē* (inv. 1847) in S. Erdemgil et al., *Ephesus Museum Catalogue* (Istanbul: n.p., 1989) 107–8; and idem, *Ephesus Museum* (Istanbul: Dogü Publications, 1999) 87–88. Asgari's unpublished 1965 doctoral thesis catalogs numerous *ostothēkai* from Asia Minor, of which thirty-one are from Ephesos (eadem, "Helenistik ve Roma Çağlarında Anadolu Ostotekleri" [Ph.D. diss., Istanbul University, 1965] 75–92). For a general overview, see Christine Thomas and Cengiz İçten, "The Ephesian Ossuaries and Roman Influence on the Production of Burial Containers," in *100 Jahre österreichische Forschungen in Ephesos: Akten des Symposions Wien 1995* [ed. Herwig Friesinger and Friedrich Krinzinger; Vienna: Österreichischen Akademie der Wissenschaften, 1999] 549–54, plates 131.3–4; 132.1–4.

[55]Wolfgang Pietsch and Elisabeth Trinkl, "Der Grabungsbericht der Kampagnen 1992–93," in Knibbe and Thür, eds., *Via Sacra II*, 33–42; and Susanne Fabrizii-Reuer and Egon Reuer, "Die Ergebnisse der anthropologischen Untersuchung von 18 kg Leichenbrand aus der Ringnekropole von Ephesos," in ibid., 62–66.

[56]*Ostothēkai* are analogous in function to Roman *cineraria*, which are widely published in scattered journals; for a large collection, see Friederike Sinn, *Stadtrömische Marmorurnen* (Mainz: von Zabern, 1987). The items from Asia Minor are stylistically distinct from the Roman *cineraria* in form, iconography, and development, and thus are usually designated by the term *ostothēkai* in modern scholarship. The Roman *cinerarium* is usually labeled *ossuarium marmoreum*, *arca*, or *ara* in the inscriptions on the objects themselves. In literature, the *cinerarium* is usually referred to as an *olla*; other names are *olla ossuaria*, *urna*, *urnula*, *hydria*, *vascellum*, *testa*, and *urceus* (see Sinn, *Marmorurnen*, 6). *Ostothēkē* is the usual self-designation of the Ephesian objects, which appears in eight of the inscriptions. The only other terms employed in the inscriptions on the Ephesian objects are the less specific τὸ μνημεῖον (once) and τὸ ἡρῷον (once). The term *ostothēkē* is attested in west and west-central Anatolia: Bithynia, Ionia, Caria, Galatia, Pisidia, Lykia, Cilicia, and Isauria; see J. Kubinska, "Les ostothèques dans les inscriptions grecques de l'Asie Mineure," *Études d'archéologie classique* 9 (1997) 7–58; eadem, *Les monuments funéraires dans les inscriptions grecques de l'Asie Mineure* (Warsaw: Éditions scientifiques de Pologne, 1968) 64–67.

Fig. 10.1 Plain *ostothēkē* of Εἰκάδιος Τυσκλᾶνος. Medium-grained bluish white marble. Chest H 31 cm x W 44.5–45.5 cm x D 37 cm; wall thickness 5 cm. Letter height 1.5 cm. Lid in photograph does not pertain to chest. Efes Müzesi inv. no. 10-3-89. Published in Thomas and İçten, "Ephesian Ossuaries." For the inscription, see Helmut Engelmann and Cengiz İçten, *Zeitschrift für Papyrologie und Epigraphik* 91 (1992) 288 no. 11.

Augustan period. In the Late Republican period at Ephesos, as elsewhere in the Greek East including Corinth, ash chests used for cremation burial bore simple, undecorated faces. Their only adornment would have been a carved or painted inscription (fig. 10.1). Around the turn of the millennium, in the Augustan period, these simple chests quickly gave way to models with carved garlands, a style both more ostentatious and labor-intensive (fig. 10.2). The change from plain to garland *ostothēkai* between the last half of the first century B.C.E. and the first half of the first century C.E. is dramatic (fig. 10.3). The garland *ostothēkē* nearly completely displaces the plain *ostothēkē* in the Augustan period. The plain containers stop being produced in the early first century of the common era; there are only two examples of plain *ostothēkai* that may date after the turn of the millenium.

The basic trend in funerary iconography at Ephesos is one of greater ostentation over time, as the simple chests are replaced by chests with garlands. This is continued at the other chronological end of the series by the garland sarcophagus, which comes into use just as the garland *ostothēkē* stops being

Fig. 10.2 Garland *ostothēkē* of Φιλεῖνος Νεικίου and Νικέας Νικίου. Coarse-grained bluish white marble. Chest H 35 cm x W 53.5 cm x D 39.5 cm; wall thickness 5.5 cm. Letter height first inscription, 2.5 cm; second inscription, 3 cm. For the inscriptions, see *Inschriften von Ephesos*, 6.2300b. Efes Müzesi inv. no. 1847. Published in Thomas and İçten, "Ephesian Ossuaries."

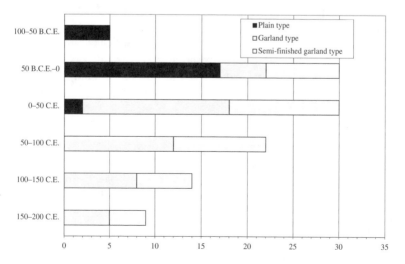

Fig. 10.3 Distribution of the three types of Ephesian *ostothēkai* over time.

produced, during the first half of the second century C.E.;[57] though closely related in style and production technique to the garland *ostothēkē*, the sarcophagus is clearly much more expensive to produce.

Moreover, the pattern of greater ostentation in funerary container is associated with rapid changes in style at Ephesos. The alteration from the plain to the garland *ostothēkē* takes place within about fifty years; from the garland *ostothēkē* to the garland sarcophagus is another fifty to one hundred years. Anthropological studies show that such "style wars" occur when there is pressure upon a group's identity and boundaries: the more pressure there is on a group, the more its members mark themselves off symbolically from their neighbors.[58]

The pattern of ostentation and rapid change begins to make more sense when we recognize that the carriers of change in these Ephesian burial containers were Roman citizens. The inscriptions demonstrate that they were the major consumers of both the plain and the garland *ostothēkai*. On the plain *ostothēkai*, the names of Roman citizens appear in more than half the primary inscriptions (nine of fifteen); the others are simple Greek names. Roman citizens are even more numerous as dedicators of the garland *ostothēkai*, appearing in more than three quarters of the primary inscriptions dating before about 150 C.E. (thirty-six out of forty-six total). More than half of the Roman names have Greek cognomina and thus probably identify freedmen (58%, or twenty-six of forty-five, of the Roman names on plain and garland *ostothēkai*).[59] The number of freedmen in this sample is most likely even higher than indicated by these figures, since most of the fragments are not long enough to preserve the cognomen.[60]

The freedmen in these inscriptions were not primarily imperial freedmen. Only three of twenty-six carry imperial *gentilicia* (Iulius and Claudius). One of the Iulii was not a freedman, but a slave of the family of Caesar, Eutychus Caesaris, who indicated his profession as *dispensator*, custodian of

---

[57]The earliest datable garland sarcophagus at Ephesos is that of Celsus, ca. 107–114 C.E.; see the discussion in n. 66, below.

[58]See Ian Hodder, "Economic and Social Stress and Material Culture Patterning," *American Antiquity* 44 (1979) 446–54; on variability and emulation, see Daniel Miller, *Artefacts as Categories: A Study of Ceramic Variability in Central India* (Cambridge: Cambridge University Press, 1985) 141–205, esp. 184–96.

[59]At this early date, Roman citizens with Greek cognomina are more likely to be freed slaves than free provincials who have attained Roman citizenship.

[60]In the case of fragments in which part of the name is broken off, Roman citizenship is assumed if Roman gentilicia or praenomina are present.

the imperial payroll.[61] *Dispensatores* often were granted citizenship later in their careers than other imperial slaves, because they handled large amounts of money.[62] The fine workmanship of his *ostothēkē* suggests that Eutychus was quite wealthy, which is hardly surprising.

Additionally, a number of these freedmen were not from the city of Rome, but rather from the towns of Italy.[63] The unusual Italian *gentilicia* attested among them, such as Freganius, Audius, and Carustanius, illustrate some of the Roman families to whom slaves and freedmen in early imperial Asia Minor would have been attached: the less prominent Roman citizens who, for purposes of career advancement, or as a result of happenstance, landed in the provinces. There were, of course, also many cases of freedmen appearing in the provinces as agents and employees of the more illustrious Romans who stayed in their native city.[64] In Corinth, the ruling class of the young colony from Augustus to Nero was primarily composed either of freedmen from prominent Roman families, or Roman businessmen from less prominent families and their freedmen associates. Almost none of the duovirs during this period came from the veteran stock that was said to have formed a large body of the original colonists.[65]

After 150 C.E., the primary inscriptions on the Ephesian *ostothēkai* contain mainly simple Greek names; only two of eleven examples contain Roman *gentilicia*. The figures for the secondary and tertiary use of *ostothēkai* are about the same; of the twelve names from secondary or tertiary inscriptions—many of which date to the second and third century C.E., when citizenship among provincials was more common—only three designate Roman citizens. Roman citizens at this point were no longer employing the *ostothēkai* as burial containers. This shift is synchronous with the onset of sarcophagus production

---

[61]Inscription published in *IvE* 6.2255a.

[62]Michel Christol and Thomas Drew-Bear, "Documents latins de Phrygie," *Tyche* 1 (1986) 41–87, esp. 60–61.

[63]For full treatment and citations, see Christine M. Thomas and Cengiz İçten, "The *Ostothēkai* of Ephesos and the Rise of Sarcophagus Inhumation: Death, Conspicuous Consumption, and the Roman Freedmen," in *Akten des Symposiums des Sarkophag-Korpus 2001* (ed. Guntram Koch; Sarkophag-Studien; Mainz: Zabern, 2005).

[64]Susan Treggiari, *Roman Freedmen during the Late Republic* (Oxford: Clarendon Press, 1969) 102–6.

[65]See A. J. S. Spawforth, "Roman Corinth: The Formation of a Colonial Elite," in *Roman Onomastics in the Greek East: Social and Political Aspects* (ed. A. D. Rizakis; Μελετήματα 21; Athens: Research Center for Greek and Roman Antiquity; Paris: de Boccard, 1996) 167–82. Spawforth's work is based on the duovir lists of Michel Amandry, *Le monnayage des duovirs corinthiens* (BCH Sup 15; Paris: de Boccard, 1988).

at Ephesos. The first datable garland sarcophagus at Ephesos is that of Celsus Polemaeanus from ca. 110 C.E.,[66] preserved in the Celsus library.

The rapid change in funerary iconography in Ephesos, and the increasing ostentation in the burial containers, is a smoking gun for the political and social instability caused by the advent of Roman freedmen on the provincial scene in Ephesos. The people who were the primary purchasers of the garland *ostothēkai* were individuals who were marginal in Roman society as a whole. Since they were freed slaves, they did not have the noble breeding so important in the traditional Roman hierarchy.[67] On the other hand, freedmen were often extremely wealthy, since they held official positions in which they came in contact with large sums of money, or worked as merchants or enterpreneurs—something nobles would never do.[68] Yet, although they were only recently slaves, they had a precious commodity that, in the late republic and the first century of the empire, very few provincials had: Roman citizenship. When they moved to the provinces, then, they experienced a relative rise in status vis-à-vis the provincials. Being in the provinces exacerbated the status inconsistency that they already experienced in Rome as sometimes quite wealthy and influential individuals who nevertheless came from obscure families of no social standing.

The increase in ostentation in burial containers, that is, the display of wealth and power, was a ritual strategy on the part of freedmen that legitimated their power against the other contenders for power, the provincial elite, the hereditary rulers of Ephesos. The rapid changes in funerary fashions over the course of the first century C.E. were an attempt by the freedmen to maintain a distinctive group identity in their burial choice, since the provincials followed their stylistic lead at each juncture.

This process of rapid change, however, eventually stopped with the rise of the sarcophagus. Clearly social factors accounted for the greater homogeneity and stability represented by a burial practice that became standard throughout

[66]Epigraphic evidence shows that Celsus must have died between 107 and 117 C.E., but probably before 114 C.E.; Josef Keil, *Die Bibliothek* (FiE 5.1; Vienna: Österreichisches Archäologisches Institut, 1944) 61–63, 83. Volker Michael Strocka ("Zur Datierung der Celsusbibliothek," in *The Proceedings of the Xth International Congress of Classical Archaeology, Ankara-Izmir 23–30 September 1973* [ed. Ekrem Akurgal; Ankara: Türk Tarih Kurumu, 1978] 893–99) would date the beginning of construction of the library, which most likely followed immediately on the death of Celsus, to ca. 112/13 C.E. on the basis of stylistic comparison with regional architecture and its relative place in the building program of Ephesos.

[67]Treggiari, *Roman Freedmen*, 1–11; A. M. Duff, *Freedmen in the Early Roman Empire* (Oxford: Oxford University Press, 1928) 1–11.

[68]Treggiari, *Roman Freedmen,* 87–106; Duff, *Freedmen,* 91–93.

the empire. Around the beginning of the second century C.E., Roman citizenship among provincials had become more common, and under Trajan they even began to enter the Senate in significant numbers.[69] Thus Roman freedmen and the provincial elite experienced a rapprochement as the provincial elite achieved Roman citizenship and came to be more active in the process of Romanization in the provinces. By the time Caracalla granted citizenship to all the free inhabitants of the Roman empire in 212 C.E., burial practice was well on the way to homogenization throughout the empire.

FUNERARY PRACTICE AND SOCIAL STATUS

If it is true that the Roman graves at Corinth are only as rich, or not quite as rich, as the graves of the Hellenistic or Classical periods, this pattern is meaningful and contrasts significantly with the Ephesian example. It is indeed difficult to make generalizations on the basis of the North Cemetery alone, which has a disproportionately small number of Roman graves. Yet the evidence is striking: 10 of the 28 graves have no gifts at all, and the rest have an average of 3.5 pots, compared with the average of 5.7 pots in fifth-century B.C.E. burials.[70] Grave goods that become slightly less ostentatious over time indicate a stable society in which the elite do not have to legitimate their position.[71]

The location and prevalence of wealth in Roman graves at Corinth can only be given in outline. Only the North Cemetery has been extensively published. Detailed records from the Cheliotomylos cemetery are lacking.[72] Most critically, the early reports of sumptuous graves on the roads leading out of the city have not been systematically published.[73] It is likely that one would have found the most wealthy graves here, and that the North Cemetery and the graves published by Walbank simply represent more modest burials. No dates have been published for these graves on the roads leading out of the city,

[69]A. N. Sherwin-White, *The Roman Citizenship* (Oxford: Clarendon Press, 1980) 259–60, 306–13; the case of Athens is treated in Michael Woloch, *Roman Citizenship and the Athenian Elite A.D. 96–161: Two Prosopographical Catalogues* (Amsterdam: Hakkert, 1989).

[70]Palmer, "Classical and Roman Periods," 78–79, 82; Walbank notes a general paucity of grave goods among the Roman tombs that she is publishing.

[71]Pearson, "Ideological Change"; Childe, "Directional Changes."

[72]Shear, "North Cemetery," 428–30; idem, "Chamber Tombs," 424–41.

[73]P. Monceaux, "Fouilles et recherches archéologiques au sanctuaire des jeux isthmiques IV: Ruines d'Ephyra, le diolcos, la nécropole de Corinthe," *Gazette Archéologique* 1885, 402–12. On the road toward Lechaion, built tombs were found alongside the ancient road; several sarcophagi were found within them, one with a garland lid from the Roman period (Evangelia Protonotariou-Deilaki, "Chronika," *ArchDelt* 24 [1969] 102–3 and plates 78–79).

but it is likely that these are Roman-period sarcophagi.[74] If they are datable to the second or third century, they fall into the general pattern of inhumation burial across the empire, and do not tell us anything specifically about Corinth in the critical period before the rise of sarcophagus inhumation. They do, however, show that Corinth was home to much more ostentatious burials than those documented in the chamber tombs or the North Cemetery.

On the other hand, had Corinth produced in any number the highly decorated ash chests that one finds among the Roman citizens of freedman status at Rome or at Ephesos, it is likely that we would have some trace of them. These are portable objects that, at least in Asia Minor, are not usually found in primary context, but often in secondary use elsewhere. At Rome and at Ephesos, the lavishly decorated *ostothēkai* are typically used as fountain basins or wall stones. So, although a complete analysis of wealth in graves cannot be performed at Corinth—nor at Ephesos—the known typologies of receptacles for cremation burial for both locations is probably relatively representative.

The data are prevalent enough to suggest, however, that both at Corinth and at Ephesos, the cremation burials represented burials that were relatively less lavish and less wealthy than other contemporaneous burials. The graves published by Walbank, which are located in chambers and have been found in primary context, neatly show cremation burials alongside contemporaneous inhumation burials, which generally have better grave gifts and more elaborate receptacles. At Ephesos, it is clear that the wealthier and more prominent graves in the Late Republican and Roman Imperial periods were located along a processional street leading from the city center to the Artemision.[75]

---

[74]The sarcophagus portraying the Seven against Thebes, which was not found in primary context, may be one of these sarcophagi from along the roads leading out of Corinth. The editor dates it to the second century c.e.: Franklin P. Johnson, *Sculpture, 1896–1923* (Corinth IX.1; Cambridge, Mass.: ASCSA, 1931) 114–20. Another elaborate Roman tomb, this one from Isthmia to Kenchreai and dated to the first century c.e., is published in W. Willson Cummer, "A Roman Tomb at Corinthian Kenchreai," *Hesperia* (1971) 205–31. Since the monument had been partially destroyed and was empty within, it is impossible to know whether this was an inhumation or cremation burial; the inner chamber is in any case large enough for a sarcophagus.

[75]Knibbe and Langmann, *Via Sacra I*; Knibbe and Thür, *Via Sacra II*; Hilke Thür, "The Processional Way in Ephesos as a Place of Cult and Burial," in *Ephesos, Metropolis of Asia* (ed. Helmut Koester; HTS 41; Philadelphia: Trinity, 1995) 157–200; eadem, " 'Via Sacra Ephesiaka': Vor der Stadt und in der Stadt," in *Steine und Wege: Festschrift für Dieter Knibbe* (ed. Peter Scherrer, Hans Taueber, and Hilke Thür; Sonderschriften 32; Vienna: Österreichisches Archäologisches Institut, 1999) 163–72; and Dieter Knibbe, "Via Sacra Ephesiaka," in *100 Jahre österreichische Forschungen in Ephesos: Akten des Symposions Wien 1995* (ed. Herwig Friesinger and Friedrich Krinzinger; Vienna: Österreichischen Akademie der Wissenschaften, 1999) 449–54.

These have not yielded cremation interments, with a single exception: two pithoi with multiple cremation burials that suggest a much lower social class than do the *ostothēkai*.[76]

Thus, the data at Ephesos and Corinth follow a pattern well known in Rome, that cremation initially indicated lower social status and first took hold among the lower, nonsenatorial classes. This is confirmed by the nature of the cremation containers detailed both in Walbank's study and in the extensive publication of the North Cemetery. The containers are largely plain and of local materials, sometimes even earthenware.[77] Moreover, literary, epigraphic, and numismatic evidence demonstrates that the early Roman inhabitants of Corinth were usually the free urban poor of Rome, freedmen, or veterans. Their rulers and magistrates were also Roman citizens, who differed from the other inhabitants only in being more wealthy; *negotiatores* and wealthy freedmen attached to prominent Roman families dominated the duovirs from Augustus to Nero.[78]

These earthenware containers, with their plain undecorated sides, form a parallel to the early plain *ostothēkai* at Ephesos. Though the Ephesian objects are inherently more valuable because they are marble, at Ephesos this would not necessarily have been an indication of extensive wealth, since marble is plentiful in the region, although it is not of particularly high quality. The environs of Ephesos housed several quarries; the city was a center of the early production of garland sarcophagi, though it paled in comparison to Prokonessos or Dokimeion, which produced marble of much higher quality. Among the Ephesian *ostothēkai*, the bluish-white marble of the Belevi quarry is fairly common.

In the case of both Ephesos and Corinth, the advent of Rome represents the introduction of the rite of cremation. At both locations, this results in some instability in burial customs. At Corinth, as Rife has noted, the early cinerary urns lack standardization, as do in fact all forms of burial during the early Roman period; the large variety of grave types represents instability and stylistic experimentation that eventually resolved itself in the regularized forms one finds in the second century c.e.[79] What is different at Ephesos is that

---

[76]Fabrizii-Reuer and Reuer, "Ergebnisse."

[77]Two exceptional cases are the urn of blue glass (mid to late first century c.e.; James Wiseman, "Excavations in Corinth, the Gymnasium Area, 1967–68," *Hesperia* 38 [1969] 64–106, esp. 86–87); and a lead urn containing twenty-seven gold leaves from a wreath, as well as seven unguentaria, carefully interred in a pit lined with steles (first century c.e.; Blegen, *North Cemetery*, 198, no. 516).

[78]Spawforth, "Colonial Elite."

[79]Rife, "Death, Ritual, and Memory," 221–22, 254.

the *ostothēkai* became a vehicle for ostentatious display, unlike the situation at Corinth. At Ephesos, as I have suggested, the lines of differentiation seem to have been drawn between freedmen and Greek citizens without Roman citizenship. Thus, a container that had formerly been evidence of a lower status in Rome meant something different at Ephesos. Because of the relative scarcity both of freeborn Romans and of Roman citizenship, the *démodé* burial fashions of the freedmen inspired imitation at Ephesos among those who did not have Roman citizenship but wished to pretend to the Roman way of life. The same situation did not obtain at Corinth, where Roman citizenship was relatively common. There was no class of wealthy and influential provincials without Roman citizenship.

Although this is not a study of burial practices in the city of Rome, it must be noted here that the matter of cremation burial there was extraordinarily complex, and forms a shifting background against which to view the Ephesian and Corinthian data. Although cremation seems to have taken hold first among the lower classes at Rome, in the course of the first century B.C.E. it moved up the social ranks until, for much of the imperial period, an imperial funeral was typically a cremation ceremony.[80] To understand this shift, it is necessary to look at cremation as a total phenomenon. If one views cremation and inhumation as methods of funerary display, rather than as techniques of corpse disposal, then cremation is by far the more spectacular. Augustus's funeral pyre burned for five days, throughout which Livia remained mourning by its side.[81] The spectacle of the cremation was the point of the procedure, rather than the mere disposal of the corpse. Septimius Severus died in York, and according to Herodian was cremated there. The urn was duly deposited in the mausoleum upon its return to Rome. However, the imperial family additionally had a wax image of the deceased emperor made, which was then left lying in the palace; doctors visited for seven days, proclaiming that their "patient" was faring worse each day. Finally, the effigy was proclaimed dead and given the usual pomp of an imperial funeral, including a presentation in the forum, a huge funerary pyre on which the effigy was burned, and the release of an eagle.[82] This was far more ostentatious than the usual Greek *ekphora*, which at Athens, after the

---

[80]It seems that the emperors continued to be cremated longer than the rest of the elite population, who seem to have turned earlier to sarcophagus burial, though this is a matter of dispute; see Morris, *Death-Ritual*, 54–56; Arce, *Funus*, 130–31; and Price, "Noble Funerals," 95–97. On the spread of cremation in Italy, see Davies, "Burial in Italy."

[81]For the accounts, see Tacitus, *Ann.* 1.8, 16, 50; Suetonius, *Aug.* 100; and Dio Cassius 44.35–51.

[82]See Toynbee's discussion (*Death and Burial*, 59–60) of the account in SHA *Severus* 24.

sumptuary laws of Demetrios of Phaleron in 317 B.C.E., was conducted before dawn, and through side streets rather than the main thoroughfares.[83] Cremation as a method of disposal was also potentially more expensive. Although it was generally used, at Rome, by individuals of lesser wealth and status, the very poorest of the Romans could not have afforded the outlay of fuel to burn the corpse. Burials of partial cremations have been found at Nauplion and Tiryns,[84] and also recently at Ephesos.[85] Such partial cremations were probably not intentional, but rather resulted when the family did not have enough fuel to maintain the funeral pyre at a sufficient heat to carbonize the corpse completely.

The use of cremation increased in the later years of the republic, which were extraordinarily unstable for the senatorial elite. Others have written about how funerary ostentation served the purposes of family political strategies in Rome.[86] There was a conscious adoption of the cultural modes of the lower classes in order to produce a spectacle. Such an adoption may be compared with Carlin Barton's studies of senators and equestrians during the Late Republic and Early Empire who willingly trained to be gladiators, thus achieving the spectacular and honorable death in combat that was increasingly unavailable to them as the empire consolidated, excluding them from their traditional roles in the practice of politics and war.[87]

The Corinthian data agree with the data from Ephesos in suggesting the gradual disappearance of cremation in the second century C.E. This trend in itself is fascinating, because it shows that the second-century homogenization of burial practice took place not only in a provincial city such as Ephesos, but also in a Roman colony, which did not have the predominance of Greek citizens known in other cities in the Roman East.[88] This suggests that the eventual implementation of sarcophagus inhumation had less to do with the imposition of Greek mores upon Rome and more to do with the changing

---

[83]Kurtz and Boardman, *Greek Burial Customs*, 166.

[84]Ibid., 180.

[85]Fabrizii-Reuer and Reuer, "Ergebnisse."

[86]Hopkins, *Death and Renewal*; Flower, *Ancestor Masks*; and Kyle, *Spectacles of Death*.

[87]Carlin Barton, "Savage Miracles: Redemption of Lost Honor in Roman Society and the Sacrament of the Gladiator and the Martyr," *Representations* 45 (1994) 41–71; idem, "The Scandal of the Arena," *Representations* 27 (1989) 1–36.

[88]Likely there were Greek inhabitants at the time of the foundation of the colony; these would not automatically have received Roman citizenship, though they may have been incorporated early (see the discussion in Walbank, "Foundation and Planning," 99; and Rife, "Death, Ritual, and Memory," 204–6). These individuals, however, were not members of a power elite as in other provincial cities.

value of Roman citizenship around the empire and its effect on social distinctions. Sarcophagus inhumation, when it was taken up in the second century, accorded well with more ancient Roman practices and attitudes to the dead and their existence in the tomb. Cremation seems to have increased at Rome because of social instability and the need for ostentatious spectacle during the Republican period. Sarcophagus inhumation expressed an empire-wide cultural fusion and stasis: the practice spread during the second century, when provincials were increasingly gaining citizenship. In 212 C.E., Caracalla's grant of citizenship to the free population of the empire abolished the distinction between Roman citizens and freeborn provincials.

It is only within the brief window of the first century C.E. that one finds a significant difference in the place of cremation at Ephesos and at Corinth. This seems to be directly related to the relative position of Roman citizens within these two cities. Although the Roman settlers of Corinth may well have been freedmen, and hardly elite, Corinth was a new foundation, a colony. The position of Roman settlers within the polity was not in question. Ephesos, on the other hand, became a provincial capital and yet maintained a degree of autonomy in its local government and its civic religious life, in which the provincial elite still played an important role. It seems that the missing element at Corinth was a provincial elite such as one finds at Ephesos, an elite that would serve as the guardian of a continuing cultural and civic heritage, and that not only desired to emulate the Roman settlers but was also financially able to do so. Because of its differing polity, the wealthy and powerful provincial elite at Ephesos developed specific ritual strategies for their inclusion into the new Roman identity. Their emulation of Roman styles in turn motivated Roman freedmen and citizens to attempt to differentiate themselves from the provincials in their funerary practices. These strategies continued until a point in time when the real differences between Roman and provincial had faded away.

Fig. 11.1 Paul carrying scrolls of his letters, in a mosaic
from the Arian baptistery in Ravenna, fifth-sixth century C.E.

Chapter Eleven

Paul's Letters to Corinth: The Interpretive Intertwining of Literary and Historical Reconstruction

Margaret M. Mitchell

Introduction: The Earliest Evidence for Christianity at Corinth

It took several hundred years for Christians to leave any impact on the archaeological record of ancient Corinth.[1] But because of the remarkable epistolary archive preserved in canonical 1 and 2 Corinthians, we are able to go a long way toward reconstructing the early history of the Pauline Christian religious cells which began to emerge around the Mediterranean in the late 40s and 50s of the Common Era. Paul claims that he was the first to bring the Christian cult to Corinth (1 Cor 3:6; 2 Cor 10:14), the inaugural missionary to this key urban multi-ethnic and religiously plural setting[2] in which Christianity was to gain a foothold and flourish continuously thereafter up to modern times.[3] The two letters known in their present form as 1 and

---

[1]See the essays by Guy Sanders (pp. 419–42) and Vasiliki Limberis (pp. 443–57) in this volume.

[2]As indicated in Paul's statement to the Corinthians of the self-evident fact that εἰσὶν θεοὶ πολλοὶ καὶ κύριοι πολλοί ("there are many gods and many lords," 1 Cor 8:5).

[3]After the devastating earthquake of 1858, the modern city of Corinth was moved northeast, onto the gulf.

2 Corinthians include such invaluable information as the tradition from the Jerusalem church of the witnesses of the resurrection of Jesus (viewed as an event of crucial proportion requiring and receiving thorough documentation [1 Cor 15:3–8]); the early liturgical libretto, or part of it, for the cult meal they call the κυριακὸν δεῖπνον ("lordly supper," 1 Cor 11:23–27); descriptions of the worship service held when the community συνέρχεσθαι ἐπὶ τὸ αὐτό (" 'comes together' at the same place") and its various speaking parts (1 Corinthians 14); quoted words of the central religious figure the group proclaimed, a certain Jesus Messiah (1 Cor 7:10; 9:14); some of the earliest confessions of faith to which the Pauline Christians adhered (in addition to 1 Cor 15:3–8, see 8:6; 12:3; 16:22; 2 Cor 5:14–15; 8:9); a recorded judicial decision to expel one member from the assembly (1 Cor 5:1–13); debates over such important lifestyle issues as marriage, sexual behavior, eating habits, and deportment (including a reference to the real possibility mentioned in 1 Cor 8:10: ἐν εἰδωλείῳ κατακείμενος, "sitting in an idol shrine"); and abundant information about the financial arrangements of this early religious community (1 Cor 16:1–4; 2 Corinthians 8, 9). The letters also contain—albeit in metaphorical and polemical form, and by the hand of its chief provocateur—a most remarkable record of the early history of the Corinthian ἐκκλησία ("assembly/church") itself.

Paul sketches the history at an early point as follows: ἐγὼ ἐφύτευσα, Ἀπολλῶς ἐπότισεν, ἀλλὰ ὁ θεὸς ηὔξανεν ("I planted, Apollos watered, but God caused it to grow," 1 Cor 3:6). The letter provides more information by which we may unpack Paul's metaphorical foundation role of "planting."[4] In 1 Cor 2:1–5 and 3:10, Paul insists that what he did when he came to Corinth was engage in a preaching ministry (κηρύσσειν) that was focused self-consciously and monoptically on "Jesus Christ crucified" (1 Cor 2:2). In what may be the single most important passage in early Christian literature, 1 Cor 15:1–11, Paul recounts the content of this εὐαγγέλιον ("good news") which he handed on (παραδιδόναι) to the Corinthians who joined his movement through baptism and some type of confession of faith (15:11):[5]

ὅτι Χριστὸς ἀπέθανεν ὑπὲρ τῶν ἁμαρτιῶν ἡμῶν κατὰ τὰς γραφὰς
καὶ ὅτι ἐτάφη καὶ ὅτι ἐγήγερται τῇ ἡμέρᾳ τῇ τρίτῃ κατὰ τὰς γραφὰς
καὶ ὅτι ὤφθη Κηφᾷ εἶτα τοῖς δώεκα· ἔπειτα ὤφθη ἐπάνω πεντακο-
σίοις ἀδελφοῖς ἐφάπαξ, ἐξ ὧν πλείονες μένουσιν ἕως ἄρτι, τινὲς

---

[4]By ca. 170 C.E., Dionysios, bishop of Corinth, will apply the planting metaphor to the activities of *both* Peter and Paul in his city (Eusebius, *Hist. eccl.* 2.25.8).

[5]On baptism and confession as initiating moments, see 1 Cor 12:3, 13; compare 6:11.

δὲ ἐκοιμήθησαν· ἔπειτα ὤφθη Ἰακώβῳ εἶτα τοῖς ἀποστόλοις πᾶσιν· ἔσχατον δὲ πάντων ὡσπερεὶ τῷ ἐκτρώματι ὤφθη κἀμοί.

that Christ died on behalf of our sins according to the Scriptures, that he was buried, that he has been raised on the third day according to the Scriptures, and that he appeared to Cephas, and then to the twelve; then he appeared to more than five hundred brothers and sisters all at once, of whom many remain even until now, although the majority have gone to sleep; then he appeared to James, then to all the apostles. And last of all, as though to one born out of season, he appeared also to me. (15:3–8)

Paul's "gospel," as this passage shows, was a story with a set plot—here in four major scenes—that could be expanded accordion-like to embrace the wider canvas from creation to the eschaton or contracted by synecdochical reference to one of its constituent events,[6] such as the crucifixion of Jesus (as in ὁ λόγος τοῦ σταυροῦ, "the word of the cross," in 1 Cor 1:18). The latter was Paul's chosen shorthand reference to his inaugural missionary proclamation from a later perspective, when he deemed the resurrection too problematic to serve that function (see especially 1 Cor 2:2: οὐ γὰρ ἔκρινά τι εἰδέναι ἐν ὑμῖν εἰ μὴ Ἰησοῦν Χριστὸν καὶ τοῦτον ἐσταυρωμένον, "for I decided to know nothing among you except Jesus Christ, and him crucified").

What Paul recounts of these Corinthians' response to his message is likewise telling, for the key character in the story (who, interestingly enough, does not explicitly appear in the compact formulation of 1 Corinthians 15:3–8) is a θεός who is the God of Israel. Ἡμῖν εἷς θεὸς ὁ πατήρ ("for us there is one God, the father"), Paul states in 1 Cor 8:6, with clear reference to the Shema of Deut 6:4, which in the Septuagint reads: Ἄκουε, Ἰσραηλ· κύριος ὁ θεὸς ἡμῶν κύριος εἷς ἐστιν ("Hear, Israel: the Lord our God is one Lord"). Hence the first step for Corinthian would-be Christians joining Paul's group of self-styled "holy ones," "called ones" (ἅγιοι, κλητοί),[7] or "brothers and sisters" (ἀδελφοί),[8] was the rejection of "the dumb idols" (τὰ εἴδωλα τὰ ἄφωνα) by whom they had earlier "been carried off" (ὡς ἂν ἤγεσθε ἀπαγόμενοι, 1 Cor 12:2). This vituperative catchphrase ("dumb idols") presumably

---

[6]For a fuller exposition of this hermeneutical technique, see Margaret M. Mitchell, "Rhetorical Shorthand in Pauline Argumentation: The Functions of 'The Gospel' in the Corinthian Correspondence," in *Gospel in Paul: Studies on Corinthians, Galatians, and Romans for Richard N. Longenecker* (ed. L. A. Jervis and P. Richardson; Sheffield: Sheffield Academic Press, 1994) 63–88.

[7]κλητοὶ ἅγιοι ("called saints") in 1 Cor 1:2; ἅγιοι alone ("saints") in 1 Cor 6:1, 2; 14:33; 16:15; 2 Cor 1:1; 13:12; κλητοί ("called ones") in 1 Cor 1:24.

[8]See, e.g., 1 Cor 1:10, 11, 26; 2:1; 3:1; 4:6; 5:11; 6:5, 6, 8; 7:12, 14, 15, 24, 29; 8:11, 12, 13; 9:5; 10:1; 11:33; 12:1; 14:6, 20, 26, 39; 15:1, 6, 50, 58; 16:15, 20; 2 Cor 1:8; 8:1; 13:11.

encompasses all the gods and goddesses worshipped at Corinth—i.e., the occupants of the temples ringing the forum and found elsewhere within the archaeological site of ancient Roman Corinth (as well as the sanctuaries at the neighboring port of Cenchreae and at Isthmia),[9] including Apollo, Athena, Poseidon, Aphrodite, Tyche, Hera, Asklepios, Demeter and Kore, and Isis and Serapis, as well as the Roman imperial cult. In this "boom town" of resurgent Roman Corinth, Paul claimed also to have, "like a wise construction engineer, laid a foundation" (ὡς σοφὸς ἀρχιτέκτων θεμέλιον ἔθηκα, 3:10), as though for a new temple in or around the forum, a spiritual edifice he calls θεοῦ οἰκοδομή or ναὸς θεοῦ ("God's edifice" or "God's temple"), which houses a divine occupant he terms τὸ πνεῦμα τοῦ θεοῦ ("the spirit of God," 3:9–17).

The shift in religious orientation away from "dumb idols" that Paul celebrates was not solely a cognitive decision to adopt philosophical monotheism on the part of those whom Paul convinced to join his conventicles and to worship a God capable of speech (ὁ θεὸς ὁ εἰπών· ἐκ σκότους φῶς λάμψει, "God is the one who said: 'from darkness light will shine,'" 2 Cor 4:6). It was also a distinctly sociocultural phenomenon, for it signaled the incorporation of the new convert into the story, promises, and election of Israel (πιστὸς ὁ θεός, δι' οὗ ἐκλήθητε εἰς κοινωνίαν τοῦ υἱοῦ αὐτοῦ Ἰησοῦ Χριστοῦ τοῦ κυρίου ἡμῶν, "faithful is God, through whom you were called into communion with his son Jesus Christ our Lord," 1 Cor 1:9). τὰ ἔθνη ("the nations/Gentiles") for them now referred to *outsiders* with all their smackings of immorality (1 Cor 5:1), and, in turn, the Scriptures of Israel, αἱ γραφαί, were now taken as *our* national story, such that the patriarchal figures are οἱ πατέρες ἡμῶν ("our fathers"), the biblical texts now *our* destined literary deposit (ταῦτα δὲ τυπικῶς συνέβαινεν ἐκείνοις, ἐγράφη δὲ πρὸς νουθεσίαν ἡμῶν, εἰς οὓς τὰ τέλη τῶν αἰώνιων κατήντηκεν, "These things happened to them typologically, but they were written for our admonition, we upon whom the ends of the ages have come," 1 Cor 10:11), texts which only "we" can read with full insight (2 Cor 3:14–18). The effect of Paul's gospel was to present to a small number of Corinthian individuals and households a narrative of salvation history that, through their ritual acceptance and incorporation into the present

[9]See James R. Wiseman, "Corinth and Rome I: 228 B.C.–A.D. 267," *ANRW* II.7.1 (1979) 438–548, esp. 509–21, and fig. 12; the discussion in Victor Paul Furnish, *II Corinthians* (AB 32A; Garden City, N.Y.: Doubleday, 1984) 10–22; and more recently Nancy Bookidis and Ronald S. Stroud, *Demeter and Persephone in Ancient Corinth* (American Excavations in Old Corinth, Corinth Notes 2; Princeton, N.J.: ASCSA, 1987).

religious assembly (termed ἐκκλησία τοῦ θεοῦ, "the assembly/church of God"), would allow them to take their lawful places as οἱ σῳζόμενοι ("the saved ones," 1 Cor 1:18; 15:2) in the unfolding events of the final days of the "form of this world [which] is passing away" (παράγει ... τὸ σχῆμα τοῦ κόσμου τούτου, 1 Cor 7:31). The process of identity-transfer Paul's gospel offered entailed also dramatic ethical consequences. After a long list of vices, Paul contrasts his believers' past with their new living reality: καὶ ταῦτά τινες ἦτε· ἀλλὰ ἀπελούσασθε, ἀλλὰ ἡγιάσθητε, ἀλλὰ ἐδικαιώθητε ἐν τῷ ὀνόματι τοῦ κυρίου Ἰησοῦ Χριστοῦ καὶ ἐν τῷ πνεύματι τοῦ θεοῦ ἡμῶν ("and these things some of you were; but you were washed off, but you were sanctified, but you were justified in the name of the Lord Jesus Christ and in the spirit of our God," 1 Cor 6:11). What he is referring to is the baptismal rite of initiation: the "name" of Christ is what they became united with, and the ritual was thought to involve the bestowal of the divine spirit on the convert and the entire group of believers who become the σῶμα Χριστοῦ ("body of Christ"). The group also engaged in a special meal intended to reify and re-present this cultic unity.[10] Later Paul confidently proclaims the success of his original preaching to this group of people: οὕτως κηρύσσομεν καὶ οὕτως ἐπιστεύσατε ("thus we preach and thus you believed," 15:11).

It seems that after Paul founded various cells of "those who call upon the name of our Lord Jesus Christ" in Corinth and Cenchreae,[11] who met in the houses of wealthy Corinthians such as Gaius (Rom 16:23), he continued on his way as an itinerant or semi-itinerant missionary, on to Ephesos. From Ephesos he wrote a letter back to the Corinthians[12] to respond to the multiplicity of contacts he had received from them (during an unknown interval of time), which included visits from what appear to be two separate delegations ("Chloe's people," 1 Cor 1:11; and Stephanas, Fortunatus, and Achaicus, 1 Cor 16:17); a letter from some of the Corinthians containing

---

[10]1 Cor 11:17–34; and, especially, 10:16–17: Τὸ ποτήριον τῆς εὐλογίας ὃ εὐλογοῦμεν, οὐχὶ κοινωνία ἐστὶν τοῦ αἵματος τοῦ Χριστοῦ; τὸν ἄρτον ὃν κλῶμεν, οὐχὶ κοινωνία τοῦ σώματος τοῦ Χριστοῦ ἐστίν; ὅτι εἷς ἄρτος, ἓν σῶμα οἱ πολλοί ἐσμεν, οἱ γὰρ πάντες ἐκ τοῦ ἑνὸς ἄρτου μετέχομεν ("The cup of blessing which we bless—is it not a communion of the blood of Christ? The bread which we break—is it not a communion of the body of Christ? Because one bread, one body, we the many are. For we all partake from the one bread").

[11]See Rom 16:1–2 on Phoebe, whose close association with Paul makes it likely that he had a major role in the foundation of a Christian ἐκκλησία ("assembly/church") in the eastern port.

[12]Paul also wrote an earlier letter, from an unknown location, to which he refers in 1 Cor 5:9. That letter is lost (see p. 324, below).

questions about ethical and sexual matters (1 Cor 7:1); and oral reports that may go beyond the delegations (5:1; 11:18). That is the situation we can see readily in the letter we call 1 Corinthians, largely confirmed also by the much later narrative of Acts 18, though there the initially important role of Jewish converts, as is often the case with Luke, is emphasized much more.[13] By contrast, scholars have thought that 2 Corinthians seen as a whole presumes a different scenario and focal point for Paul's epistolary interventions into this ἐκκλησία. In that document, inner-Corinthian divisions are no longer in view; rather, the Corinthian Christians seem to be united in suspicion of and opposition to Paul, in varying stages of intensification and resolution of conflict. Paul is thought to be inferior to other missionaries, lacking in letters of recommendation and an authenticating personal presence, and is rumored by some to be seeking to fleece the church by organizing an ersatz collection for the saints in Jerusalem which is actually designed to line his own pocket. It has remained a vexing problem for Pauline scholars to account for what they perceive as this dramatic shift in the situation at Corinth.[14]

RECENT RESEARCH ON THE CORINTHIAN EPISTOLARY ARCHIVE

History-of-religions investigations of the Corinthian correspondence have traditionally focused on the identity, background, and rationale of the "opponents" Paul faced at Corinth. Because of their apparent emphasis on the buzz-word γνῶσις (gnōsis; 1 Cor 8:1), in the 1960s and 70s the German scholar Walter Schmithals and others argued that the Corinthians were Gnostics whose docetic Christology and libertinist behavior Paul was forced to combat.[15] This position has fallen into disfavor in the last few decades, both because its appropriation of second-century Christian heresiological designations of "Gnostics" for a mid-first-century Christian group was deemed

---

[13]We may note here that in terms of architectural realia Luke and Paul each mention three edifices at Corinth, but not the same three. Luke tells of a συναγωγή, βῆμα, and οἰκία Τιτίου Ἰούστου ("synagogue," bēma, and "house of Titius Justus"; Acts 18:4, 12, and 7, respectively) and Paul of οἰκίαι, εἰδωλεῖον and (his metaphorical counterconstruction) ὁ ναὸς τοῦ θεοῦ ("houses," eidōleion, and "the temple of God"; 1 Cor 11:22; 8:10; and 3:16).

[14]Or in Paul's perception of that reality from a distance, or (most likely) some combination of both.

[15]Walter Schmithals, Gnosticism at Corinth (trans. J. E. Steely; Nashville, Tenn.: Abingdon, 1971); earlier, Ulrich Wilckens, Weisheit und Torheit (BHT 26; Tübingen: Mohr Siebeck, 1959).

anachronistic,[16] and because of the problematization of the category "Gnosticism" itself,[17] and the debates over terminological distinctions between "gnosis" and "Gnosticism,"[18] as well as doubts about the existence of "pre-Christian" gnosticism.[19] Now one hears more often not of Corinthian "gnostics" but of "enthusiasts,"[20] or "spirit-people,"[21] a fluidly ambiguous term meant to denote their charismatic sensibilities, fondness for ecstatic speech, and tendency to go overboard with the Pauline gospel of freedom from conventional norms. This position has also often depended upon an exegetical decision, that the position held by ἐν ὑμῖν τινες ("some of you"), that ἀνάστασις νεκρῶν οὐκ ἔστιν ("there is no resurrection of the dead," 1 Cor 15:12), is identical to that attributed to the "heretics" Hymenaeus and Philetus in 2 Tim 2:17–18 who say τὴν ἀνάστασιν ἤδη γεγονέναι ("the resurrection has already happened"). That argument, that the Corinthians were afflicted by a kind of realized eschatology, was nicely challenged by David W. Kuck,[22] but it nonetheless continues to influence scholarship, as we can see, for instance, in Antoinette Clark Wire's *The Corinthian Women Prophets.*[23]

[16]See the overall assessment in Pheme Perkins, *Gnosticism and the New Testament* (Minneapolis: Fortress, 1993) 74–92.

[17]Michael Allen Williams, *Rethinking "Gnosticism": An Argument for Dismantling a Dubious Category* (Princeton, N.J.: Princeton University Press, 1996). For updates of this research, see Karen L. King, *What is Gnosticism?* (Cambridge, Mass.: Harvard University Press, 2003) and Christoph Markschies, *Gnosis: An Introduction* (trans. John Bowden; New York: T&T Clark, 2003).

[18]See Birger A. Pearson, "Philo, Gnosis, and the New Testament," in idem, *Gnosticism, Judaism, and Egyptian Christianity* (Studies in Antiquity and Christianity; Philadelphia: Fortress, 1990) 165–82, with important bibliography on these terminological distinctions; and Wolfgang Schrage's list of currently debated designations: "die meisten heute vorsichtiger auch bei den Korinthern von Prae-Gnosis oder Proto-Gnosis sprechen, von Gnosis *in status nascendi*, von Frühgnosis oder Frühstufe der Gnosis oder, wohl am besten, von 'gnostisierenden' Pneumatikern oder Tendenzen" (*Der erste Brief an die Korinther* [4 vols.; EKK 7; Zürich: Benziger; Neukirchen-Vluyn: Neukirchener Verlag, 1991–2001] 1:52).

[19]See the classic study of Kurt Rudolph, *Gnosis: The Nature and History of Gnosticism* (San Francisco: Harper & Row, 1983); Perkins, *Gnosticism and the New Testament*, 1–50; and Pearson, "Frieländer Revisited: Alexandrian Judaism and Gnostic Origins," in idem, *Gnosticism, Judaism, and Egyptian Christianity*, esp. 10–28.

[20]Thus Andreas Lindemann (*Der Erste Korintherbrief* [HNT 9/1; Tübingen: Mohr Siebeck, 2000] 14): "Dabei läßt es sich aus dem Gesamtzusammenhang des Briefes wahrscheinlich machen, daß die Ursachen für diese Position in einem religiösen Enthusiasmus liegen."

[21]Jerome Murphy-O'Connor, *The Theology of the Second Letter to the Corinthians* (New Testament Theology; Cambridge: Cambridge University Press, 1991) 12–15, and passim.

[22]David W. Kuck, *Judgment and Community Conflict: Paul's Use of Apocalyptic Judgment Language in 1 Corinthians 3:5–4:5* (NovTSup 66; Leiden: Brill, 1992).

[23]Antoinette Clark Wire, *The Corinthian Women Prophets: A Reconstruction through Paul's Rhetoric* (Minneapolis: Fortress, 1990).

Other scholars, such as Gerhard Sellin, have focused on the relationship between Alexandrian anthropological hermeneutics as exemplified by Philo, for instance, and the Corinthian position about resurrected bodies.[24] The tide of research that has sought to identify the religious makeup or background of the Corinthian opponents of Paul has, however, been challenged, both by the inconclusiveness and speculative nature of much twentieth-century scholarship,[25] and by the insistence in later studies that this approach, largely imported from the study of Galatians, is inappropriate for 1 Corinthians, at least because here Paul does not face a unified body of "opponents," but rather a church which is divided within itself over various issues of Christian life, ritual practice, and thought.[26]

But 2 Corinthians has been treated as a different matter, for there the inner-Corinthian conflicts have, in the eyes of many commentators, receded in favor of Paul's emphasis upon outsiders whom he vilifies as ψευδαπόστολοι, οἱ διάκονοι σατανᾶ ("false-apostles," "the ministers of satan," 2 Cor 11:13–15). The most influential work here has been Dieter Georgi's *The Opponents of Paul in 2 Corinthians*,[27] which argued that the encroaching missionaries were Hellenistic-Jewish itinerant wisdom teachers who championed Moses as a divine man (and whom Paul confronts directly, therefore, in 2 Corinthians 3). Others, like Jerome Murphy-O'Connor, have taken a similar line and argued that the opponents were "spiritual people" influenced by Apollos and his Alexandrian stream of exegetically erudite Hellenistic Judaism.[28]

---

[24]Gerhard Sellin, *Der Streit um die Auferstehung der Toten: eine religionsgeschichtliche und exegetische Untersuchung von 1 Korinther* (FRLANT 138; Göttingen: Vandenhoeck & Ruprecht, 1986).

[25]The decline in scholarly interest or confidence in constructing a comprehensive picture of the history-of-religions background to the Corinthian conflicts may be illustrated by the judgment of one of the most recent critical commentaries on 1 Corinthians: "Der Versuch einer systematischen Rekonstruktion der in Korinth vertretenen religiösen Haltungen ist mit großen Unsicherheiten behaftet; alle Versuche, das Denken der korinthischen Christen von religionsgeschichtlich auch sonst bekannten Phänomenen her deuten zu wollen, müssen überaus vage bleiben" (Lindemann, *Der Erste Korintherbrief*, 14).

[26]Margaret M. Mitchell, *Paul and the Rhetoric of Reconciliation: An Exegetical Investigation of the Language and Composition of 1 Corinthians* (HUT 28; Tübingen: Mohr Siebeck, 1991; Louisville, Ky.: Westminster/John Knox, 1993). In his monumental commentary, Schrage has insisted that at Corinth Paul faced not so much "Irrlehrer" as "Irrpraktiker" (*Der erste Brief an die Korinther*, esp. 1:62).

[27]Dieter Georgi, *The Opponents of Paul in 2 Corinthians* (Philadelphia: Fortress, 1986).

[28]Murphy-O'Connor, *The Theology of the Second Letter to the Corinthians*, 13–15 and passim.

All such theories are unstable due to the fact that Paul's letters, because of their allusively abusive references to his opponents, render precise historical reconstruction very difficult. For instance, we cannot even be sure if those whom he refers to in his varied lexicon of contempt are all the same people. Are the ψευδαπόστολοι ("false-apostles") of 2 Cor 11:13 the same as οἱ ὑπερλίαν ἀπόστολοι ("the super-duper apostles") he mentioned eight verses earlier?[29]

More successful, perhaps, than these theories about the "opponents" in 2 Corinthians have been history-of-culture and rhetorical investigations into Paul's own language and argumentation in parts of 2 Corinthians, such as Hans Dieter Betz's *Der Apostel Paulus und die sokratische Tradition*,[30] which places Paul's polemic in the tradition of ancient apologetic rhetoric used by philosophical teachers against detractors; Ronald Hock's work on Paul's refusal of payment for his preaching and the abundant discussion among philosophers on this topic;[31] Dale Martin's first book *Slavery as Salvation*,[32] which sought the larger resonances of Paul's words that he had "enslaved himself to all" in ancient *topoi* about the self-enslaved leader; Martin's second book, on the role of somatic ideologies in the conflicts;[33] and Paul Duff's work on the role of ancient cultic processions in Paul's own argumentation in 2 Cor 2:14–7:4.[34] In recent years, important investigations have been made into popular philosophical notions known to Paul and his readers, such as Abraham Malherbe's study on freedom in 1 Corinthians 9 and contemporary

[29]The literature on this topic is considerable. See, for instance, C. K. Barrett, "Paul's Opponents in 2 Corinthians," in *Essays on Paul* (Philadelphia: Westminster, 1982) 60–86; Furnish, *II Corinthians*, 48–54; Margaret E. Thrall, *A Critical and Exegetical Commentary on the Second Epistle to the Corinthians* (ICC; 2 vols.; Edinburgh: T&T Clark, 1994, 2000) 2:671–76.

[30]Hans Dieter Betz, *Der Apostel Paulus und die sokratische Tradition: Eine exegetische Untersuchung zu seiner 'Apologie' 2 Kor 10–13* (BHT 45; Tübingen: Mohr Siebeck, 1972).

[31]Ronald F. Hock, *The Social Context of Paul's Ministry: Tentmaking and Apostleship* (Philadelphia: Fortress, 1980).

[32]Dale B. Martin, *Slavery as Salvation: The Metaphor of Slavery in Pauline Christianity* (New Haven, Conn.: Yale University Press, 1990).

[33]Idem, *The Corinthian Body* (New Haven, Conn.: Yale University Press, 1995); see my review in *JR* 77 (1997) 290–92.

[34]Paul B. Duff, "The Transformation of the Spectator: Power, Perception, and the Day of Salvation," *SBLSP* 26 (1987) 233–43; idem, "Metaphor, Motif, and Meaning: The Rhetorical Strategy Behind the Image 'Led in Triumph' in 2 Cor 2:14," *CBQ* 53 (1991) 79–92; idem, "Apostolic Suffering and the Language of Processions in 2 Corinthians 4.7–10," *BTB* 21 (1991) 158–65; and idem, "The Mind of the Redactor: 2 Cor 6:14–7:1 in Its Secondary Context," *NT* 35 (1993) 160–80.

philosophical arguments,[35] Samuel Vollenweider's careful treatment of Cynic and Stoic arguments about freedom in relation to 1 Corinthians 9,[36] Clarence Glad's investigation of Epicurean-like community ethical instruction and psychagogy in 1 Corinthians,[37] and the latest book to come from Robert M. Grant's pen, *Paul in the Roman World*.[38] But aspects of Corinthian Christian religious life have also been compared for affinities, broadly speaking, with Greco-Roman religious cults, such as Hans-Josef Klauck's comprehensive study on cult meals and Gerhard Dautzenberg's on prophecy and glossolalia.[39]

The two other areas where the greatest attention and advances have been made in scholarship on Paul's Corinthian letters in the last two decades have been social history and literary analysis. It is no coincidence that in the pioneering works of sociological analysis of early Pauline communities by Gerd Theissen and Wayne Meeks, 1 Corinthians played a major role, far greater than any other Pauline letter.[40] This is because of that letter's explicit attention to the very issues of interest to sociological research: group formation, demographics, community life, self-regulation, etc. Theissen noted that we have the names of more Christians from Corinth than from any other ἐκκλησία ("local Christian assembly") by far, with the possible exception of Rome (assuming Romans 16 to be authentic).[41] By contrast, Paul mentions no Thessalonian Christian by name, and only two from Philippi.[42] The quest for the social history of early

[35]Abraham J. Malherbe, "Determinism and Free Will in Paul: The Argument of 1 Corinthians 8 and 9," in *Paul in His Hellenistic Context* (ed. Troels Engberg-Pedersen; Minneapolis: Fortress, 1995) 231–55.

[36]Samuel Vollenweider, *Freiheit als neue Schöpfung. Eine Untersuchung zur Eleutheria bei Paulus und in seiner Umwelt* (FRLANT 147; Göttingen: Vandenhoeck & Ruprecht, 1989).

[37]Clarence E. Glad, *Paul and Philodemus: Adaptability in Epicurean and Early Christian Psychagogy* (NovTSup 81; Leiden: Brill, 1995).

[38]Robert M. Grant, *Paul in the Roman World: The Conflict at Corinth* (Louisville, Ky.: Westminster/John Knox, 2001).

[39]Hans-Josef Klauck, *Herrenmahl und Hellenistischer Kult. Eine religionsgeschichtliche Untersuchung zum ersten Korintherbrief* (NTAbh n.s. 15; Münster: Aschendorff, 1982); Gerhard Dautzenberg, *Urchristliche Prophetie: Ihre Erforschung, ihre Voraussetzung im Judentum und ihre Struktur im ersten Korintherbrief* (BWANT 104; Stuttgart: Kohlhammer, 1975).

[40]Gerd Theissen, *The Social Setting of Pauline Christianity: Essays on Corinth* (ed. and trans. J. H. Schütz; Philadelphia: Fortress, 1982); and Wayne Meeks, *The First Urban Christians: The Social World of the Apostle Paul* (New Haven, Conn.: Yale University Press, 1983).

[41]Theissen (*Social Setting of Pauline Christianity*, 94–95) lists sixteen named Corinthians.

[42]Euodia and Syntyche in Phil 4:2. Luke offers the names of three apparently Thessalonian Christians: Jason, Aristarchus, and Secundus (Acts 17:7; 20:4; 27:2). For a thorough discussion of the demographics in the Pauline communities, see the essay by Steven J. Friesen in this volume (pp. 351–70).

Christians has led to a view of the Corinthian conflicts as rooted not solely in divergence of theological opinion, but also in some basic facts on the ground within the Corinthian communities. But rhetorically embedded statements such as 1 Cor 1:26—'not many (of you) are wise according to the flesh, not many powerful, not many of noble birth"—cannot just be plucked from the text and statistically applied to demographic and social-historical questions. Is this statement ironic or literal, to be construed as universally or only partially applicable? The meaning of these documents, in whole and in part, is always determined by context—in this case by the intersection of two fundamental spheres of context: the literary and the historical.

In the last three decades a great deal of research has gone into investigating the composition of the Corinthian epistolary archive, which involves a most complicated set of questions. The two canonical letters, especially the second, contain references to other letters (1 Cor 5:9; 2 Cor 2:3–9; 7:8–12; 10:10) and to a bewildering array of visits promised, delayed, and actualized (1 Cor 4:19–21; 11:34; 16:5–9; 2 Cor 1:15–2:1; 2:12–13; 7:5; 12:21; 13:1–2), as well as literary breaks, astonishing shifts in tone (such as at 2 Cor 10:1) and in content (conciliation, castigation, self-defense, financial appeals), repetitions (such as chapters 8 and 9 of 2 Corinthians), and inconsistency in the nature of the relationship between the epistolary partners (contrast 2 Cor 1:24 and 13:5, for example), all of which strongly suggests that more than one letter has been combined in forming 2 Corinthians. Although a minority of scholars still hold out for the unity of the epistle,[43] most Pauline scholars affirm some partition theory of the letter—meaning that they think the letter in its published form was compiled from as few as two to as many as five different letters or letter fragments (or six, if one counts 6:14–7:1 as a separate fragment).[44] We can enumerate the main proposals[45] as follows:

[43]The most serious attempts are those of Frances M. Young and David F. Ford, *Meaning and Truth in 2 Corinthians* (Grand Rapids, Mich.: Eerdmans, 1988); and Reimund Bieringer and Jan Lambrecht, *Studies on 2 Corinthians* (BETL 112; Leuven: Leuven University Press, 1994), on which see my review in *ThLz* 121 (1996) 354–56.

[44]For the options about this passage, and the now-considerable bibliography, see Thrall, *Second Epistle to the Corinthians*, 1:25–36. I regard the passage as an interpolation, but will not here engage in the debates about its authorship.

[45]There are other options, including those who combine parts of both 1 and 2 Corinthians, but they have not achieved any measure of support. See in particular Walter Schmithals, "Die Korintherbriefe als Briefsammlung," *ZNW* 64 (1973) 263–88; idem, *Gnosticism at Corinth*; idem, *Die Briefe des Paulus in ihrer ursprünglichen Form* (Zurich: Theologischer Verlag, 1984); and Robert Jewett, "The Redaction of 1 Corinthians and the Trajectory of the Pauline School," *JAARSup* 46 (1978) 389–444. A full overview of the major hypotheses may be

A. Two Letters (in two different chronological arrangements)

  1) 2 Corinthians 1–9 precedes 2 Corinthians 10–13 (Barrett, Furnish)[46]
  2) 2 Corinthians 10–13 precedes 2 Corinthians 1–9 (Kennedy, Watson)[47]

B. Three Letters (Windisch, Thrall, Quesnel)[48]

  2 Corinthians 1–8
  2 Corinthians 9
  2 Corinthians 10–13

C. Five Letters (Bornkamm, Betz)[49]

  2 Corinthians 2:14–7:4 (minus 6:14–7:1)
  2 Corinthians 10:1–13:10
  2 Corinthians 1:1–2:13; 7:5–16; 13:11–13
  2 Corinthians 8
  2 Corinthians 9

---

found in Gerhard Sellin, "Hauptprobleme des Ersten Korintherbriefes," *ANRW* II.25.4 (1987) 2940–3044, particularly 2964–86; especially valuable on the historical roots of this research, which go back to Johann Salomo Semler in 1776, are Hans Dieter Betz, *2 Corinthians 8 and 9: A Commentary on Two Administrative Letters of the Apostle Paul* (Philadelphia: Fortress, 1985) 3–36; and Thrall, *Second Epistle to the Corinthians* 1:1–49.

[46]C. K. Barrett, *The Second Epistle to the Corinthians* (HNTC; New York: Harper & Row, 1973) 21; and Furnish, *II Corinthians*, 35–48. For a list of other scholars holding to this hypothesis, see Thrall, *Second Epistle to the Corinthians*, 1:49.

[47]James Houghton Kennedy, *The Second and Third Epistles of St. Paul to the Corinthians, with Some Proofs of Their Independence and Mutual Relation* (London: Methuen, 1900); and Francis Watson, "2 Cor. x–xiii and Paul's Painful Letter to the Corinthians," *JTS* 35 (1984) 324–46. For a complete list of adherents to this hypothesis, see Thrall, *Second Epistle to the Corinthians*, 1:49.

[48]Hans Windisch, *Der zweite Korintherbrief* (KEK 6; Göttingen: Vandenhoeck & Ruprecht, 1924) 5–31; Thrall, *Second Epistle to the Corinthians*, 1:1–49 and passim; and Michel Quesnel, "Circonstances de composition de la seconde épître aux Corinthiens," *NTS* 43 (1997) 256–67.

[49]Günther Bornkamm, "Die Vorgeschichte des sogennanten zweiten Korinterbriefes," in *Sitzungsberichte der Heidelberger Akademie der Wissenschaften, Philologisch-historische Klasse* (Heidelberg: Winter, 1961) 7–36 (I cite the original pagination; this essay was twice republished: in Bornkamm's *Gesammelte Aufsätze*, vol. 4 = *Geschichte und Glaube, Zweiter Teil* [BEvT 53; Munich: Kaiser, 1971] 162–90, with a *Nachtrag* on pp. 190–94; and in an abbreviated English version, "The History of the Origin of the So-Called Second Letter to the Corinthians," *NTS* 8 [1962] 258–63); and Betz, *2 Corinthians 8 and 9*. Both Bornkamm and Betz build upon important arguments made earlier by Johannes Weiss in *Earliest Christianity* (trans. F. C. Grant et al.; 2 vols.; New York: Harper, 1959) 1:344–57; trans. of *Das Urchristentum* (Göttingen: Vandenhoeck & Ruprecht, 1914–1917). A recent variation on Bornkamm's thesis has been proposed by N. H. Taylor ("The Composition and Chronology of Second Corinthians," *JSNT* 44 [1991] 67–87), who moves the letter in 2 Corinthians 10–13 up before 2:14–7:4. For a critique of this proposal, see n. 65, below.

Each of these hypotheses has its strengths and weaknesses, both real and apparent. As an example of the latter, proponents of both A.1 and B argue that their hypotheses are more compelling because the canonical order follows the (putative) historical order in which the letters were sent.[50] Although at first glance this seems reasonable, it is in fact a claim that essentially begs the question of what principle of editorial arrangement was employed in the formation of canonical 2 Corinthians, so it dissolves as a definitive argument. On the other hand, the real strength of proposals A.1 and B is that they take seriously the definitive break in tone, style, and content between 9:15 and 10:1, and have accurately perceived the enormous difference in historical situation in the two contexts (a confident fundraising appeal versus a bitter defense against personal insult). Many of these scholars have also rightly observed that 2 Cor 12:18 seems to be an almost literal, retrospective reference to a "sending" of Titus and a brother that can hardly be different than what Paul does in 2 Corinthians 8, and they have made this a key argument in the chronological relationship of the two parts. But this decision requires that the "letter of tears" mentioned in 2 Cor 2:4 be lost somewhere in the void between 1 Corinthians and 2 Corinthians.[51]

The proponents of option A.2, which has been vigorously revived most recently by Francis Watson,[52] are able to point to considerable and remarkable exegetical connections between Paul's exegesis of the "painful letter" in 2:3–9 and the text of 2 Corinthians 10–13, and thus to argue that the letter in question is in fact not lost, but has been appended to the later missive (hence in reverse chronological order). "The letter of tears" should be identified with 2 Corinthians 10–13 which, necessarily, was sent *before* chapters 1–9, which make reference to it. But in making this argument, which I find quite convincing,[53] Watson must work strenuously to deny (against evidence equally as

---

[50]Thrall, *Second Epistle to the Corinthians*, 1:46. See also Quesnel ("Circonstances," 267), who appeals to usual Pauline practice: "[Une telle façon de faire] correspond à la façon la plus normale de procéder." But we have no evidence to support such an assumption of a "normal" epistolary practice in this regard.

[51]Barrett, *The Second Epistle to the Corinthians*, 23, 88; and Furnish, *II Corinthians*, 41.

[52]"Paul's Painful Letter."

[53]Retrospective allusions in 2 Corinthians 1–2 to parts of 2 Corinthians 10–13 that were perceived already by Kennedy (*Second and Third Epistles of St. Paul*, 80–86) and Kirsopp Lake (*The Earlier Epistles of St. Paul: Their Motive and Origin* [London: Rivingtons, 1911]) 57–58 are 13:10 // 2:3; 13:2 // 1:23; and 10:6 // 2:9. Watson ("Paul's Painful Letter," 339) has added to those arguments strong evidence that "2 Cor. x–xiii *as a whole* fits the description of the painful letter." I would sharpen both sets of arguments by literary-rhetorical evidence. In 2 Cor 2:4 and 9, Paul characterizes his purpose in the "letter which caused grief" with three key terms, each of which is prominent in 2 Corinthians 10–13: δοκιμή

plausible as that which he uses for chapters 10–13) the identification of the money-related dispatch of Titus and an unnamed brother in 2 Cor 12:18 with that precise action as carried out in 8:16–17, having to go to great lengths to speculate that there must have been some other, unreported visit to which 12:18 refers.[54]

Thus we see that proponents of the two-letter division hypothesis have had to choose between the two most clearly retrospective references within 2 Corinthians: to Titus's visit and to "the letter of tears." The same is true of option B, though it does have the salutary advantage over both versions of option A of responding to the serious difficulty posed by the collection appeal in 2 Corinthians 9, which is literarily redundant after chapter 8, while simultaneously chronologically inconsistent with it.[55] Option C, the five-letter division hypothesis, takes seriously the literary linkage between 2:12–13 and 7:5, as well as the unified argumentation in the section, which even the proponents of the other theories must grant.[56] This theory also, in Betz's revised version of Bornkamm's, does justice to the literary integrity within 2 Corinthians 8 and

---

("attestation," 2 Cor 2:9; compare 13:3, 5–7), ὑπακοή ("obedience," 2 Cor 2:9; 10:5–6), and ἀγάπη ("love," 2 Cor 2:4; compare 11:11; 12:15). Since these terms are used (retrospectively) to characterize the rhetorical purpose of the earlier missive, a further, decisive argument in favor of the identification is the fact that the two key terms ὑπακοή and δοκιμή ("obedience" and "attestation") do not just appear somewhere in the midst of chapters 10–13, but figure prominently in the προοίμιον (prooimion) on the one hand (10:5–6), and in the ἐπίλογος (epilogos) on the other (13:5–10; compare 13:3), where rhetorically one expects the major point of an argument to be stated and recapitulated. As for ἀγάπη ("love"), although the exact term does not appear in either the prooimion or the epilogos to 2 Corinthians 10–13, οἰκοδομή ("upbuilding"), with which Paul had already syllogistically equated ἀγάπη ("love") in an earlier letter to them (1 Cor 8:1: ἡ δὲ ἀγάπη οἰκοδομεῖ, "but love builds up"), does appear (2 Cor 10:8; 13:10; see also in the proof, at 12:19), and hence forms an inclusio that highlights this described purpose of the entire missive.

[54]This argument is forced on Watson because he is trying to place chs. 10–13 in chronological relation to the entirety of chs. 1–9 ("Paul's Painful Letter," 328–29, 332–33; so also Thrall, Second Epistle to the Corinthians, 1:15, on the grounds that 2 Cor 12:18 refers to one brother, whereas ch. 8 mentions two [8:18, 22], but this is to underestimate the fact that in ch. 8 each brother is sent separately, and on a different authorization [as argued by Barrett, Second Epistle to the Corinthians, 325]). In order to deny the remarkable correspondence between 2 Cor 12:18 and 8:6, 18, Thrall and Watson ("Paul's Painful Letter," 333) must unduly emphasize a minor difference between the passages (one that in fact reflects an actual distinction between brothers made in 2 Corinthians 8!) and greatly underplay the considerable evidence of congruity.

[55]Compare the temporal referent ἀπὸ πέρυσι ("from a year ago") in 2 Cor 8:10 (when they began, but emphatically did not complete, the collection) with 2 Cor 9:2 (how long they have been ready).

[56]Furnish, II Corinthians, 35 ("functionally distinct"); Thrall, Second Epistle to the Corinthians, 1:188 ("thematically . . . a self-contained whole").

2 Corinthians 9 as recognizable ancient administrative letters, which renders problematic either their original conjunction with one another, or with chapters 1–7. But proponents of the five-letter division hypothesis have not fared as well when it comes to the cross-references among the texts; in particular, Bornkamm's and Betz's placement of 2 Corinthians 8 as the penultimate piece of the correspondence prohibits any connection with 2 Cor 12:18, which, according to their scenario, must have been a prior communication in reference to some other (but unrecorded) postulated sending of Titus. This brief survey of research leaves us with the question: Is there any way to integrate all of these observations—both literary and historical—into a coherent picture of the history of the Corinthian correspondence?

2 Corinthians 8 and the Literary History of the Corinthian Correspondence

I propose a version of the five-letter hypothesis that allows for each of the salient observations just rehearsed and better accounts for the chain of events from 1 Corinthians through the collection of letters preserved in 2 Corinthians. My proposal is based upon an insistence on the imperative of intertwining the literary and the historical in working with the Corinthian letters. Despite many wise pleas to keep the two aspects in play, Pauline scholars have continued to think of them as two different lenses *that they put on*: "the only satisfactory way to approach the problem of 2 Corinthians is to fasten upon particular questions and view them from both sides, the literary and the historical, in as great detail as possible."[57] What this has meant is that the letters are normally treated as *witnesses to* the historical situation, which is the interpreter's ultimate goal, with literary analysis employed as a means to that end.[58] But this amounts to a dichotomizing of text and event that obscures precisely what was so markedly and remarkably going on in Paul's relationship with the Corinthians: a debate over the meaning, appropriateness, and intentions of Paul's letters themselves. A more deliberate coalescence of the tasks of

---

[57]Barrett, *The Second Epistle to the Corinthians*, 18.

[58]A very good example of this is the recent article by Taylor ("Composition and Chronology of Second Corinthians"). After presenting his hypothetical list of letters and defending them on largely exegetical grounds, Taylor seeks "to locate these in the context of the development of Paul's relationship with the Corinthian church" (p. 83). Tellingly, as he does so (pp. 83–86), Taylor's account proceeds without consideration of the impact any of these letters themselves had in the unfolding course of events.

literary and historical analysis, I suggest, allows us to recognize that Paul's letters were themselves primary *agents* in the unfolding of the historical scenario (not just witnesses to it).

Furthermore, I would like to challenge the pervading assumption in Corinthian studies that there is a tremendous breach in historical situation between 1 Corinthians and 2 Corinthians which can only be accounted for by speculating that some external event (unrecorded, except for the shock waves emanating from it) drastically upset the equilibrium between Paul and his churches.[59] The wholesale adoption of the view that there must have been a profound sea change between 1 and 2 Corinthians is acutely illustrated in the fact that Furnish can state it as a methodological *mandate* of research on 2 Corinthians that "the evidence from Letter D (2 Cor 1–9) and Letter E (2 Cor 10–13) must be examined independently, and without presuming anything on the basis of the situation being addressed in Letter B (1 Cor)."[60] But doesn't this in fact abrogate sound methodology in historical and epistolographic research—the goal of which is to reconstruct the epistolary situation from all available clues? Surely to exclude 1 Corinthians entirely from the picture *on principle* is historically unwarranted, and, furthermore, would be an untenable step in the investigation of any other archive, from the Zenon papyri to the letters of Cicero or Ignatius of Antioch. Furthermore, have we fully reckoned with the important historical effects of what we know did take place between 1 and 2 Corinthians: the reception of 1 Corinthians?![61]

---

[59]A very strong influence upon scholarship in this regard has been Georgi's *Opponents of Paul*, which postulated the arrival of Hellenistic Jewish-Christian missionaries between 1 Corinthians and the next piece of the correspondence, 2:14–7:4 and 10–13. See, for example, pp. 17–18: "During the visits of Timothy and Titus the situation in the Corinthian church seems to have been calm, whereas tensions existed before and after. This break must be placed between the time period described in 1 and 2 Cor" (for one example of this assumption at work, see Furnish, *II Corinthians*, 52–54 on the "false apostles"). See further discussion on the opponents of Paul in n. 90, below.

[60]Furnish, *II Corinthians*, 50.

[61]I have hinted at this in the conclusion to *Paul and the Rhetoric of Reconciliation*, where I suggested that Paul, like others in the ancient (and modern) world who sought to reunite factions "seems, by his argument in this letter, to have 'incurred the enmity of both'" (303). Later in this essay I shall buttress this suggestion by pointing to the important role 1 Cor 16:1–4 may have played in the growing conflict. Earlier exegetes, such as Chrysostom, also assumed that 1 Corinthians set the stage for the events in 2 Corinthians, and (as is well known) postulated that the man punished in 2 Cor 2:6 was the sexual malefactor of 1 Corinthians 5 (*hom. in 2 Cor.* 4.3 [PG 61.421–22]). My solution is more complex, combining Chrysostom's assumption that there was *some* historical continuity with a reconstruction of the letters that would have been unthinkable to him.

In my judgment one should not *presume* such radical discontinuity between the epistolary situations, but should see if it is possible to account for the evolution of the tumultuous relationship on the basis of the evidence we do possess. This means taking very seriously the impact of each missive and its range of perceived meanings on the unfolding relationship between Paul and the Corinthians. On the basis of this fundamental insight—that the Corinthian situation can be largely understood as a history of successive epistolary reception, response, and counter-response—I propose the following literary reconstruction of the number and order of letters in the Corinthian archive (which have been only later redacted[62] to form the canonical 1 and 2 Corinthians):

[62] Alistair Stewart-Sykes has urged that consideration of the physical realities of archiving and editing ancient papyrus leaves and text rolls be considered as one element of the evaluation of partition hypotheses of the Pauline letters ("Ancient Editors and Copyists and Modern Partition Theories: The Case of the Corinthian Correspondence," *JSNT* 61 [1996] 53–64). On that basis Stewart-Sykes argues for the preferability of "simple" partition theories (which he defines as the combination of two documents) to "complex" ones (three or more documents), but his argument is unsatisfactory on several accounts. Because this issue of redactional activity always (justifiably) comes up when discussing partition theories, it is important to respond with some detail to this objection at the outset. First, the basis of Stewart Sykes's study is this named distinction, but no justification is given for why the number two should be the border line between "simple" and "complex," nor for the even more fundamental assumption that the *number* of original documents should be the sole factor in determining "complexity" (rather than, for instance, the arrangement or extent of adaptation of those sources required to create the resulting document). Hence Stewart-Sykes's argument becomes a tautology ("complex" = complex). Second, the author assumes a simplistic and quite debatable relationship between physical possibility and human motivation, such that for "complex theories" a scholar must be able to provide a strong redactional intention (presumably to have overridden the difficulty of the physical process [see p. 61, and esp. n. 31; and p. 64]). Third, the study unfortunately is based on old research (especially Otto Roller's 1933 study, *Das Formular der paulinischen Briefe: Ein Beitrag zur Lehre vom antiken Briefe* [BWANT 58; Stuttgart: Kohlhammer, 1933]), and actually offers not a single new piece of evidence on the question of ancient scribal practices, even overlooking such standard recent works as Harry Y. Gamble, *Books and Readers in the Early Church: A History of Early Christian Texts* (New Haven, Conn.: Yale University Press, 1995). Gamble, one should note, downplays modern readers' instinctive assumptions about the unwieldiness of scrolls (see p. 55). Fourth, the picture derived from these few sources is used to create almost a caricature of ancient scribal practice, providing the misleading picture that the Pauline redactor would have had to have an assistant (perhaps a slave) on either side of him to hold open the unwieldy rolls so he could copy them (see p. 60; what about scroll weights, placeholders, and book stands?). But contemporary with the period of the compilation of the Pauline corpus, we have Luke performing just such a "complex" literary operation of combining three sources into one. (Indeed, although Stewart-Sykes opens his essay with an approving reference to F. G. Downing, "Compositional Conventions and the Synoptic Problem," *JBL* 107 [1988] 69–85, Downing's essay results in a picture of Luke which is quite like this one. What Downing

1) Letter mentioned in 1 Cor 5:9 (not extant)	*Previous Letter from Paul* *to the Corinthians*
2) 1 Corinthians (entire)	*Deliberative Letter* *Urging Concord*
3) 2 Corinthians 8	*Fundraising Follow-up Letter*
4) 2 Cor 2:14–7:4 (minus 6:14–7:1)	*Self-Defense of the* *Maligned Messenger*
5) 2 Cor 10:1–13:10	*"The Letter of Tears"—Ironic Self-* *Defense of Apostolic Legitimacy*
6) 2 Cor 1:1–2:13; 7:5–16; 13:11–13	*Letter toward Reconciliation*
7) 2 Corinthians 9	*Final Fundraising Letter to Achaia*

This proposed theory[63] depends upon the arguments made by J. H. Kennedy, Johannes Weiss, Günther Bornkamm, and Hans Dieter Betz,[64] but my contribution (in addition to the descriptive titles, which signal my general interpretation of the genre and function of each letter) is the virtually unprecedented argument for the placement of 2 Corinthians 8 in this succession of letters. Since we have already rehearsed the major observations of literary and historical disruptions and interconnections in 2 Corinthians that point to the originally separate

---

objects to is not the *number* of sources used as a measure of complexity, but rather the *types of operations* performed on those sources.) Further, as Hans-Josef Klauck has demonstrated ("Compilations of Letters in Cicero's Correspondence," in idem, *Religion und Gesellschaft im frühen Christentum: Neutestamentliche Studien* [WUNT 152; Tübingen: Mohr Siebeck, 2003] 317–37), the Ciceronian correspondence in its edited form exemplifies many of the same editorial "complexities" as the Pauline corpus. In sum, therefore, while the reminder to consider the physical facts of editing and publication is very well taken, Stewart-Sykes's argument cannot be regarded as providing a definitive methodological standard for future research. As for its impact on the present study, the partition theory I am proposing is in large measure akin to that of Günther Bornkamm, which Stewart-Sykes actually deems "scribally feasible," if "editorially unusual"; hence even his own assessment does not discount our theory: "On practical grounds, however, this cannot be ruled summarily out of court" (p. 62). But it should perhaps be cautioned that Stewart-Sykes has not accurately understood the Bornkamm hypothesis, as he consistently misidentifies Bornkamm's "First Apology" as "the Freudenbrief" (pp. 61–62), which may lead to subsequent confusion.

[63]I have proposed this new version of the composition history of the Corinthian archive in my article "Korintherbriefe," in *Religion in Geschichte und Gegenwart* (4th ed.; ed. Hans Dieter Betz et al.; Tübingen: Mohr Siebeck, 1998–) 4:1688–94.

[64]See nn. 47–49, above. For a defense of the proposition that 1 Corinthians is a single letter, not a collection of fragments, see Mitchell, *Paul.*

composition of these seven missives, I shall focus my attention here upon my case for the novel placement and role of 2 Corinthians 8.[65] It has long been observed[66] that 2 Corinthians 8 and 9 constitute doublets—both address the issue of the collection for the saints in Jerusalem, but each appears to reflect a different stage in the process[67] (compare 8:10 and 9:2, where ἀπὸ πέρυσι in the first instance refers to the beginning of the effort and in the second to its ready completion), and an inexplicable obliviousness of one another (see especially 9:1: Περὶ μὲν γὰρ τῆς διακονίας τῆς εἰς τοὺς ἁγίους περισσόν μοί ἐστιν τὸ γράφειν ὑμῖν, "Now concerning the collection which is for the saints, it is superfluous for me to write to you"). The two texts also perhaps have in mind a different range of addressees—Corinth versus Achaia as a whole (9:2; compare 1:1). The Bornkamm hypothesis considers chapter 8 a part of the *Versöhnungsbrief* ("letter of reconciliation")—the penultimate piece of the Corinthian correspondence, followed by only chapter 9.[68] Betz argues persuasively against that hypothesis, insisting that chapter 8 is an independent composition standing apart from the letter of reconciliation, but he nonetheless follows Bornkamm in postulating that chapters 8 and 9 were the last two extant pieces of the Corinthian correspondence, written in that order.

However, the compression of the two fundraising letters into the window of time at the very end of the epistolary succession seems to me untenable for several reasons, not the least of which is that it doesn't really sufficiently reckon with the literary and historical problems which the partition hypothesis was designed to address in the first place: the difficulty of repetitive and

---

[65]Weiss (*Earliest Christianity*, 1:353, 357) did argue that 2 Corinthians 8 must precede the conflicts attested in the other letters in 2 Corinthians, but his partition theory of 1 Corinthians combined with 2 Corinthians differs in significant ways from the proposal made here. Taylor ("Composition and Chronology in 2 Corinthians") sought to revise Bornkamm's hypothesis by placing the letter in 2 Corinthians 10–13 earlier, as the first of the letters in 2 Corinthians to have been sent. Although I share his wish to find a way to combine the salient arguments of the different partition theories, I do not find his proposal convincing, particularly because Taylor places 2:14–7:4 as an unnecessary and unaccountable obstacle between "the letter of tears" of chs. 10–13 and the retrospective discussion of its meaning and reception in 2:4–9 and 7:8–13 (within Bornkamm's "letter of reconciliation"). Indeed, Taylor's reconstruction of how each letter fits into "the development of Paul's relationship with the Corinthian church" (pp. 83–86) never once refers to the effect that any letter had. This is where we can see the inescapable need to integrate the historical and literary parts of the analysis (see further below).

[66]As far back as Semler, in 1776 (see Betz, *2 Corinthians 8 and 9*, 3).

[67]See Bornkamm, "Vorgeschichte," 31: "Die Briefsituation hier und da nicht einfach die gleiche ist."

[68]Bornkamm was actually ambivalent about the placement of 2 Corinthians 8, as to whether it was part of the *Versöhnungsbrief* of 1:1–2:13; 7:5–16, or was sent soon thereafter ("Vorge-schichte," 31–32), but in either case he placed ch. 8 late in the succession of letters.

redundant fundraising appeals sent one on top of the other.[69] Moreover, placing chapters 8 and 9 in immediate succession at the end of the correspondence leaves both of these letters outside of and peripheral to the conflict between Paul and the Corinthians evidenced in the previous three reconstructed letters.[70] This is strange and problematic, given the quite conspicuous role of accusations of financial malfeasance against Paul in the disputes, which could quite logically have been connected with his most major and thoroughly documented (already in 1 Cor 16:1–4) financial undertaking: the collection for the saints in Jerusalem.

The closest and, to my mind, most remarkable indication of the temporal location of 2 Corinthians 8 is in 12:17–18, which appears to repeat *exactly* both the contents and even the language of 2 Cor 8:6, 17–18:

2 Corinthians 12:18	*2 Corinthians 8:6, 18*
παρεκάλεσα Τίτον	παρακαλέσαι ἡμᾶς Τίτον[71]
καὶ συναπέστειλα τὸν ἀδελφόν	συνεπέμψαμεν δὲ μετ' αὐτοῦ τὸν ἀδελφόν
I *urged Titus*	we *urged Titus*
and *sent with* [him] the brother.	and we *sent with* him the brother

If 12:18 does in fact refer to the same combination of envoys and authenticating letter involving Titus and the brother,[72] then quite clearly 2 Corinthians 8 must have *preceded* 2 Corinthians 10–13, and not followed it. Once one entertains that possibility, and takes seriously the extent to which each piece of the Corinthian correspondence is a response to varied interpretations (by Paul and by perhaps several different Corinthians) of some prior missive, many more, very suggestive exegetical interconnections come to the fore. Indeed, there are frequent and remarkable echoes of *1 Corinthians* in 2 Corinthians 8, which, though noted in commentaries individually, have never been

[69]Margaret Thrall recognizes but does not resolve the difficulty, nonetheless placing ch. 9 soon after ch. 8 (which she includes with chs. 1–7): "But since it [ch. 9] appears to relate to the same mission of the apostle's envoys as does ch. 8, the intervening lapse of time would not be extensive. Why, then, should a second letter have been sent at all?" (*Second Epistle to the Corinthians*, 1:43).

[70]As noted above, this objection has been maintained by interpreters such as Windisch, Barrett, Furnish, and Thrall, who insist that chs. 1–8 (9) must have preceded chs. 10–13, and also Weiss, *Earliest Christianity*, 1:353.

[71]Compare 8:17: τὴν μὲν παράκλησιν ἐδέξατο ("he accepted [my] urging").

[72]With Barrett, *Second Epistle to the Corinthians*, 325: "The coincidence in wording as well as substance makes it virtually certain that Paul is here looking back . . . upon the mission planned in chapter viii."

appreciated in the aggregate for what they might indicate about the original temporal proximity—indeed, immediate succession—of the two writings.

For instance, it is striking that the collection is termed ἡ χάρις τοῦ θεοῦ ("the gift of God"), ἡμῶν ἡ χάρις ("our gift"),[73] and ἡ χάρις αὕτη ("this gift") in 2 Corinthians 8 (8:1, 4, 6, 7, 19), just as Paul called it ἡ χάρις ὑμῶν ("your gift") in his initial instruction about the collection in 1 Cor 16:3, which quite logically preceded the effort to move the collection toward completion in 2 Corinthians 8.[74]

Most significantly, in addition to calling for the Corinthians to set up internal procedures for weekly fundraising, in 1 Cor 16:1–4 Paul also set in motion the administrative steps the Corinthians were to take to move the collection toward completion. Their responsibilities vis-à-vis the dispatch of the money they were to collect were encapsulated in the term δοκιμάζειν ("attest"): οὓς ἐὰν δοκιμάσητε δι᾽ ἐπιστολῶν τούτους πέμψω ἀπενεγκεῖν τὴν χάριν ὑμῶν εἰς Ἰερουσαλήμ ("those whomever you attest I shall send [them] via letters to bring your gift to Jerusalem," 1 Cor 16:3). The Corinthians are to make attestation of *their* chosen couriers for the collection.[75]

[73]Paul also gives it a new term in 2 Corinthians 8:4, ἡ κοινωνία τῆς διακονίας ("the partnership of the ministry"), which may be one reason why the next piece of correspondence, "The Self-Defense of the Maligned Messenger," contains a sustained defense of Paul's right to be a διάκονος ("minister"; see esp. 3:4–11, and further discussion below).

[74]An interesting progression in the language Paul uses for the collection may be perceived when we read the letters in this succession: λογεία to χάρις ("collection" to "gift," 1 Cor 16:1, 3); χάρις to διακονία ("gift" to "ministry," 2 Cor 8:1, 4, 7, 19, 20); διακονία to λειτουργία ("ministry" to "service," 2 Cor 9:1, 12–13; Rom 15:16). At the first mention of the collection, in 1 Cor 16:1–4, it is twice termed a λογεία ("collection"), but never again. χάρις ("gift"), as noted above, becomes the central term carried over from 1 Cor 16:3 to 2 Corinthians 8, where it appears five times; yet in 2 Corinthians 9, χάρις ("gift") is not used of the collection specifically, but has reverted to Paul's more customary sense of God's grace given to humanity (9:8, 14, 15; this is a deliberate word play, of course). In 2 Corinthians 9 the cultic terminology λειτουργία (literally "liturgy," meaning "official service") appears for the first time, which is subsequently invoked (with the cognate substantive λειτουργός, "officiant") once again in the last extant piece of correspondence on the collection, written to Rome from Corinth (Rom 15:16).

[75]The act of authenticating is either undertaken by the Corinthians δι᾽ ἐπιστολῶν, or it is separate, understood as the basis for the apostle's subsequent act of epistolary dispatching. Although the phrase δι᾽ ἐπιστολῶν ("through/via letters") is usually taken with the verb πέμψω ("I shall send," 1 Cor 16:3), it could possibly refer to δοκιμάσητε ("you might attest"), and hence be an action of the Corinthians—to authenticate their envoys with letters of reference (I have left any comma out of the sentence in order to leave both options open; NA²⁷ includes a comma after δοκιμάσητε). Perhaps it was their expectation, generated by 1 Cor 16:3, that *they* should have the power to write letters of recommendation (ἐπιστολαὶ συστατικαί; compare 2 Cor 3:1: συστατικαὶ ἐπιστολαὶ πρὸς ὑμᾶς ἢ ἐξ ὑμῶν, "letters of recommendation to you or *from you*").

What is especially noteworthy is that these are precisely the actions that *Paul himself* performs in the letter of 2 Corinthians 8: he sends, via mandating letters, brothers whom *he* has tested and found worthy (see especially 8:22: συνεπέμψαμεν δὲ αὐτοῖς τὸν ἀδελφὸν ἡμῶν ὃν ἐδοκιμάσαμεν, "and we sent along with them our brother whom we have attested").

I suggest (as I shall develop further below) that it was Paul's taking upon himself the authority to perform these actions—which he had promised would be the prerogative of the Corinthians (1 Cor 16:3)—that led to their anger at him, suspicion about his motives, and doubt about his own credentials (hence 2 Cor 3:1–4).

Postulating that 2 Corinthians 8 immediately followed 1 Corinthians also allows us to see some striking *rhetorical parallels* between these two letters. The opening appeal of 1 Corinthians was a kind of *captatio benevolentiae* praising the Corinthian Christians' considerable "richness" in "all things,"[76] including a list of the endowments upon which they especially pride themselves: ὅτι ἐν παντὶ ἐπλουτίσθητε . . . ἐν παντὶ λόγῳ καὶ πάσῃ γνώσει ("because *in everything you were made rich . . . in all eloquence* and *in all knowledge*," 1 Cor 1:5). In 2 Corinthians 8, Paul likewise seeks to persuade the Corinthians to cultivate the new virtue embodied in contributing to αὕτη ἡ χάρις ("this gift") by enumerating at the outset their current abundance: ὥσπερ ἐν παντὶ περισσεύετε,[77] πίστει καὶ λόγῳ καὶ γνώσει καὶ πάσῃ σπουδῇ καὶ τῇ ἐξ ἡμῶν ἐν ὑμῖν ἀγάπῃ ("just as *in everything you abound, in faith* and *eloquence* and *knowledge* and in all zeal and in the love from us among you," 2 Cor 8:7).

As in the previous letter (1 Corinthians), in 2 Corinthians 8 Paul continues to praise them for their possession of λόγος and γνῶσις ("eloquence and knowledge"), but adds the σπουδή ("zeal") he hopes will be directed toward the collection; he also adds now what was formerly missing—ἀγάπη ("love")[78]—though he omits the full complement of *their own* ἀγάπη ("love"), rhetorically holding it in abeyance until the completion of the collection, as

---

[76]On the role of praise in 1 Cor 1:4–9, see Mitchell, *Paul*, 196–97.

[77]Is the shift to περισσεύειν ("abound") in this letter about forms of "wealth" intentional? (Compare 8:9: ἵνα ὑμεῖς τῇ ἐκείνου πτωχείᾳ πλουτήσητε, "so that you might become rich through his poverty.") Perhaps this is meant to forge a deliberate connection with the Macedonians' virtuous act of περισσεύειν ("abounding," 8:2); notice also the emphatic repetition of the term in the appeal of 8:7 that frames the verse (περισσεύετε . . . ἵνα καὶ ἐν ταύτῃ τῇ χάριτι περισσεύητε, "you abound . . . so that also in this gift you might abound"), and the antitheses of 8:14 (περίσσευμα / ὑστέρημα, "abundance" / "lacking").

[78]I.e., a reference to *his* love for them (ἡ ἐξ ἡμῶν ἐν ὑμῖν ἀγάπη, "the love from us among you"; compare the anomalous final blessing of 1 Corinthians: ἡ ἀγάπη μου μετὰ πάντων ὑμῶν ἐν Χριστῷ Ἰησοῦ, "my love be with you all in Christ Jesus" [16:24]).

he explicitly states in 8:8 (τὸ τῆς ὑμετέρας ἀγάπης γνήσιον δοκιμάζων, "testing the genuineness of your love"), and reiterates in the conclusion to the letter in 8:24 (ἔνδειξιν τῆς ἀγάπης ὑμῶν... ἐνδεικνύμενοι, "making a manifestation of your love manifest").

In the same fashion the argument for ἰσότης ("equality") between περίσσευμα and ὑστέρημα ("abundance and lacking") in 8:13–15 surely derives more pungency when read as a direct follow-up to the extravagant praise of 1 Cor 1:7 (ὥστε ὑμᾶς μὴ ὑστερεῖσθαι ἐν μηδενὶ χαρίσματι, "so that you might be lacking in no spiritual gift"), and supplies the missing premise of the identity of the Corinthians' sure περίσσευμα, "abundance" (in wealth)[79] and threatened ὑστέρημα, "deficit" (in spiritual attainments).

Three other appeals in 2 Corinthians 8 were also found in 1 Corinthians 7, both of which are reflective of a rhetorical position of conciliation that will be noticeably absent in the succeeding missives in 2 Corinthians:

2 Cor 8:8	Οὐ κατ' ἐπιταγὴν λέγω
	I do not say [this] *by way of command*
1 Cor 7:6	Τοῦτο δὲ λέγω κατὰ συγγνώμην οὐ κατ' ἐπιταγήν
	I say this as a concession, *not by way of command*[80]

2 Cor 8:10	καὶ γνώμην ἐν τούτῳ δίδωμι
	I give an opinion in this
1 Cor 7:25	γνώμην δὲ δίδωμι
	I give an opinion

2 Cor 8:10	τοῦτο γὰρ ὑμῖν συμφέρει
	for *this* is *advantageous to you*
1 Cor 7:35	τοῦτο δὲ πρὸς τὸ ὑμῶν αὐτῶν σύμφορον λέγω
	and *this* I say *for your very own advantage*

This correspondence is all the more striking when one realizes that all three of these emphatic appeals are used in the genuine Pauline letters *only in these two letters*. How can these extensive common locutions and parallels between 1 Corinthians and 2 Corinthians 8 be explained? Quite simply by rhetorical practice. It is customary to build upon shared premises and existing commitments in persuasive arguments. Because both 1 Corinthians and

---

[79]Paul's argument by appeal to regional identities may be intended to resonate with the commonplace of the legendary wealth of Corinth (see, e.g., Strabo 8.6.19–20 on ἀφνειός Κόρινθος ["rich Corinth"], quoting the venerable testimony of the *Iliad* 2.570, and updating it for his own day, after the Roman rebuilding commenced in 44 B.C.E.).

[80]See also 1 Cor 7:25: ἐπιταγὴν κυρίου οὐχ ἔχω, γνώμην δὲ δίδωμι ("I do not have a command of the Lord, but I give an opinion").

2 Corinthians 8 are deliberative arguments,[81] we should expect that Paul would employ some of the same strategies in the two, as he seeks on successive occasions to move the Corinthians from where they are to a new position on the policy decision to which he is most concerned to persuade them. In the former case he appeals for unity in the face of division; in the latter case for generosity, urging them to extend their largess of wealth in some categories to others, i.e., to give freely to the collection for the saints in Jerusalem. In both instances he relies on similar deliberative forms of persuasion.

One could argue that the parallels I have noted are not an indication of temporal juxtaposition or sequencing; since all these letters are written by the same author to the same recipients, we would naturally expect some consistency of expression and diction. But the Corinthian correspondence in particular evinces such sharp changes in tone, style, and rhetorical approach that it becomes more pressing and more historically probable to regard similar approaches as representing (at least in Paul's mind) a proximate stage of the relationship which reflects the same tenor of events and communications between them—that is, a time when Paul can urge specific behaviors and policies on the Corinthians. In the letters to come, the main topic will become the advisor Paul himself, his legitimacy, and his defense against specific charges. With that in mind, I shall now posit the historical scenario which can plausibly account for this placement of 2 Corinthians 8 between 1 Corinthians and the "First Apology" of 2 Cor 2:14–7:4.

If 2 Corinthians 8 is the next piece of the Corinthian correspondence after 1 Corinthians, as I have proposed, Paul has evidently deviated in two very serious ways from the plan he set in motion in 1 Cor 16:1–4:

1) He has sent Titus and "the brother" rather than come himself, apparently having stayed in Macedonia rather than passing through it on his way to Corinth (1 Cor 16:5–7; cf. 2 Cor 8:1, likely written from Macedonia).

2) *He* has chosen the delegates himself (τὸν ἀδελφὸν ἡμῶν ὃν ἐδοκιμάσαμεν, "the brother whom we have attested," 2 Cor 8:22), rather than allowing the Corinthians to do so (οὓς ἐὰν δοκιμάσητε, "those whomever you have attested," 1 Cor 16:3).

Added to this, he chose in 2 Corinthians 8 what was likely a risky rhetorical strategy—praising the Macedonians (whom he appeared to favor over the Corinthians, since he stayed with them instead of journeying on to Corinth) and calling on their Achaian regional rivals to try to match their generosity.

---

[81]See Mitchell, *Paul*, 20–64 on 1 Corinthians; and Betz, *2 Corinthians 8 and 9*, 41–70 on 2 Corinthians 8:1–15 as "the advisory section" (he regards 8:16–23 as "the legal section: commendation and authorization of the envoys").

There is evidence that Paul is aware of, or worried about, causing offense by these tactics and by the change in approach from that laid out in his prior letter (1 Corinthians 16): (1) He softens the διέταξα ("I commanded") and imperative ποιήσατε ("do") of 1 Cor 16:1 to οὐ κατ᾽ ἐπιταγὴν λέγω ("I do not say this by way of command"), as we have seen,[82] and repeatedly emphasizes the *voluntary* nature of participation in the fund drive (αὐθαίρετοι/τος, "voluntary," in 2 Cor 8:3, 17).

(2) He avers that the collection is for *their* benefit, hence, by implication, not *his* (2 Cor 8:10, 14), just as his eagerness for its success (προθυμία in 8:19) is directed toward *the Lord's* glory, not his own (8:19, 23).[83]

(3) He corrects against an interpretation of 1 Cor 16:1–4 that might take it as a mandate to give to the point of economic hardship (2 Cor 8:12–13).[84]

(4) He issues a preemptive assertion of his uprightness in these financial arrangements and dealings, both in deed and in intention (στελλόμενοι τοῦτο, μή τις ἡμᾶς μωμήσηται ἐν τῇ ἁδρότητι ταύτῃ τῇ διακονουμένῃ ὑφ᾽ ἡμῶν, "avoiding this, lest anyone might find fault with us in the matter of this abundance which is being served up by us," 2 Cor 8:20–21).

It appears, therefore, that Paul has real or, at the very least, hypothetical knowledge about how the Corinthians have responded to 1 Corinthians, and in particular to its final instructions on the collection. He writes the letter in 2 Corinthians 8 to activate and justify a new plan for the completion of the collection, hoping that his persuasive tone of "opinion-giving," rather than commanding (compare Philemon 8–9), joined with his deliberative appeal to advantage by reference to the Macedonians as the παράδειγμα ("example"), will lead the Corinthians to do likewise (and perhaps justify his change of plans at not coming personally). The historical and rhetorical progression from 1 Corinthians to 2 Corinthians 8 is smooth and logical.

The same can be said for the transition from 2 Corinthians 8 to the next missive (according to my proposal), 2 Cor 2:14–7:4, which makes tremendous sense as Paul's reply to the escalation of Corinthian offense that Paul's letter of 2 Corinthians 8 had caused. They have apparently read that letter as an

---

[82]See also 8:10: καὶ γνώμην ἐν τούτῳ δίδωμι ("and I give an opinion in this").

[83]This is an appeal which Paul will tellingly repeat in the next letter: τὰ γὰρ πάντα δι᾽ ὑμᾶς, ἵνα ἡ χάρις πλεονάσασα διὰ τῶν πλειόνων τὴν εὐχαριστίαν περισσεύσῃ εἰς τὴν δόξαν τοῦ θεοῦ ("For everything is for your sakes, so that the gift/grace, having increased through the many, might cause thanksgiving to abound for the glory of God," 2 Cor 4:15).

[84]In particular this may be because Paul appeared to set in motion a perpetual fundraising campaign, rather than a situation-specific or interim measure (see 1 Cor 16:2: κατὰ μίαν σαββάτου, "one week to the next").

arrogant overreaching of authority by Paul. In particular, his having written a letter of recommendation and authorization for Titus and the brother[85] has led the Corinthians to ask what right or legitimacy Paul had to do so, when he had provided no such letters *for himself* (hence his reply in the next letter: "do we have need of συστατικιαὶ ἐπιστολαί ["letters of recommendation"] to you or from you?" [3:1–3]).[86] Who put *him* in charge of the collection which he was now describing as διακονουμένη ὑφ᾽ ἡμῶν ("being served up by us," 2 Cor 8:19, 20)? What justifies his claim to have such a διακονία ("service-ministry" or "courier-ministry"),[87] to be worthy to δοκιμάζειν ("attest") others, to write with such παρρησία ("boldness," 3:12; 7:4)? From where does his ἱκανότης ("competency") to write such a letter of reference and to organize such a collection come (3:5–6)? Most importantly, the key charge against which Paul defends himself in 2:14–7:4 is financial impropriety and deception, due precisely to the incongruity the Corinthians perceived between 1 Corinthians and 2 Corinthians 8: that the man who boasted that he took no pay from the Corinthians for his ministry among them (1 Corinthians 9) nevertheless, when absent, sent letters asking for their money to be given into the hands of his own henchmen. To be sure, Paul would say (in a heartbeat) that the money was not for him, but for the saints in Jerusalem, but might the Corinthians not have perceived an inconsistency in policy that led some to wonder if Paul were καπηλεύειν τὸν λόγον τοῦ θεοῦ ("peddling the word of God," 2 Cor 2:17) or περιπατεῖν ἐν πανουργίᾳ ("behaving in a guileful manner," 2 Cor 4:2)? Put thus on the defensive, Paul must claim *his own* letter of recommendation (the Corinthians themselves), devalue the currency of

---

[85]See Betz, *2 Corinthians 8 and 9*, 70–86 on the conventional form of 8:16–17.

[86]This interpretive move by the Corinthians rests upon the very logic of ancient diplomatic and mediatorial practices within which letters of recommendation are embedded: that each person is accorded the authority of the one by whom he was sent (see Margaret M. Mitchell, "New Testament Envoys in the Context of Greco-Roman Diplomatic and Epistolary Conventions: The Example of Timothy and Titus," *JBL* 111 [1992] 661–82, esp. 647–51). Hence any authority Paul would delegate to Titus or the brother must come from somewhere—in this case, Paul will argue, from God, by whom he was selected as a διάκονος, "minister" or "envoy" (per the lexical argument of John N. Collins, *Diakonia: Re-Interpreting the Ancient Sources* [New York: Oxford University Press, 1990] 195–212). That the Corinthians should have made this inference was due also to Paul's own use of the term to describe his role (see next note).

[87]The ubiquity of the term and its cognates in 2:14–7:4 (3:3, 6, 7, 8, 9 bis; 4:1; 5:18; 6:3, 4) and its importance for understanding this letter have been demonstrated in the significant works of Georgi (*Opponents*, 27–32), and especially Collins (*Diakonia*, 73–212). I am the first to argue that it has arisen precisely because of Paul's explicit reference to the collection as a διακονία ("service-ministry" or "courier-ministry"), which he makes for the first time in 2 Cor 8:4.

written texts in the first place, and claim divine, spiritual authorization of his διακονία (3:3–6, and full context). The decisive piece of evidence showing the complete correspondence between 2 Corinthians 8 and the next letter, 2 Cor 2:14–7:4, is 6:3–4, from which we can see clearly how the Corinthians interpreted the former: Μηδεμίαν ἐν μηδενὶ διδόντες προσκοπήν, ἵνα μὴ μωμηθῇ ἡ διακονία, ἀλλ᾽ ἐν παντὶ συνιστάντες ἑαυτοὺς ὡς θεοῦ διάκονοι ("Giving no offence to anyone, lest fault be found with the service-ministry, but in everything recommending ourselves as ministers of God").[88]

Naturally, to demonstrate fully my thesis about the progression of letters from Paul to the Christians at Corinth, I would need to go through each letter in turn and show how it responds to a Corinthian reading of the prior letter, as well as to personal visits made or missed. That is the task for a much wider canvas than this essay,[89] but I shall give a brief overview of the intertwining of texts and events in the unfolding of this epistolary narrative.

Proposed Reconstruction of the Letters and Historical Scenario

(1) *Letter mentioned in 1 Cor 5:9 (not extant)*: calling for separation from unethical persons.

> *Corinthian reaction*: misunderstanding and call for clarification; divisions on many levels due to a range of factors (socioeconomic, geographic, religious, gender-based); resistance by some to Paul's advice, at least in one case (1 Corinthians 5), which appears to have some measure of community support (1 Cor 5:2, 6).

(2) *1 Corinthians (entire)*: including clarification of earlier letter (1 Cor 5:9–11), overarching call for unity, inauguration of the collection, and a promise to visit in the near future (1 Cor 4:19; 16:5–9).

> *Corinthian reaction*: hard to tell, because Paul may not have read it correctly. Likely they viewed his appeals to imitate him as "self-recommendation" (if 2 Cor 3:1; 5:12 may be taken as a later, accumulated reaction), and perhaps they were worried by the apparent contradiction of 1 Cor 9:15–18 and 16:1–4.

---

[88]Compare 8:20: στελλόμενοι τοῦτο, μή τις ἡμᾶς μωμήσηται ἐν τῇ ἁδρότητι ταύτῃ τῇ διακονουμένῃ ὑφ᾽ ἡμῶν ("avoiding this, lest someone might find fault with us in the matter of this abundance which is being served up by us").

[89]I have made a start on that formidable project in my essay, "The Corinthian Correspondence and the Birth of Pauline Hermeneutics," in *Paul and the Corinthians: Studies on a Community in Conflict: Essays in Honour of Margaret Thrall* (ed. T. J. Burke and J. K. Elliott; NovTSup 109; Leiden: Brill, 2003) 17–53.

(3) *2 Corinthians 8*: Paul takes the helm and, instead of coming himself, stays in Macedonia and sends his own authenticated delegates to deliver the collection.

Corinthian reaction: anger at Paul's usurpation of their role and suspicion that one who had no letters of recommendation himself should write one for others.

(4) *2 Cor 2:14–7:4 (minus 6:14–7:1)*: Paul's first defense against charges of lack of authorization and divine authority, written as a call for proper reception of the envoy of Christ when he arrives in person (7:2).

Visit in Corinth: leads to humiliation for Paul (12:21; 13:2); Corinthians influenced by those who point to Paul's poor personal appearance and lack of skills in oral speech (10:10; 11:6; 12:7), especially when compared with "super-duper apostles" (11:6–7).[90]

---

[90]My emphasis in this essay is on the role of the letters themselves in the unfolding of events, which can, I think, go a long way toward explaining the progression of the relationship between Paul and the Corinthians. The effect of this is to minimize (though not reject entirely) the need for explanations based solely upon a hypothetical wholesale incursion from the outside, which has been the standard scholarly approach to the perceived chasm between 1 and 2 Corinthians (especially under the influence of Georgi's *Opponents of Paul*). As 2 Cor 11:5 apparently shows (also 10:12–18), at some point competing missionaries were known in Corinth, and hence obviously did play some role in the history. But we are perhaps wrong to think of this as a single, cataclysmic and (therefore) datable event. 1 Corinthians itself provides ample evidence that from the earliest period multiple Christian missionaries (Apollos, possibly Cephas) moved in and out of Corinth over an extended period of time, and the Jerusalem apostles were already stock knowledge (1 Cor 9:5). There is a noticeable shift in Paul's rhetorical strategy between 2:14–7:4, where he constructs a σύγκρισις ("rhetorical comparison") between "Paul perceived" (by the Corinthians) and "Paul actual," and 2 Corinthians 10–13, where the σύγκρισις is between himself and οἱ ὑπερλίαν ἀπόστολοι ("the super-duper apostles," 2 Cor 11:5; 12:11). But this difference need not correspond with a single particular event (i.e., a "missionary incursion" from the outside) so much as an interpretive move on the part of one influential Corinthian to invoke the "super-duper apostles" as the rhetorical standard by which Paul should be measured. That may have taken place at any time—not just when those missionaries were present in Corinth. The present essay cannot resolve all the considerable issues involved in the question of the "opponents" in 2 Corinthians 10–13, but I can say in favor of my appeal for caution about reconstructing a single "event" between the letters that the rhetoric of 2 Corinthians 10–13 is not designed to call the Corinthians to expel any outsiders from their midst, but rather to turn them toward obedience to him as a true apostle, even as measured by the criteria they are currently using. Paul makes this appeal after a visit to Corinth in which he was humiliated. What is striking is that in that passage (2 Cor 12:20–21), the worst prospect Paul can imagine is further humiliation for himself and more divisiveness among the Corinthians, but *not* a full-scale defection to a "different gospel" (à la Galatians) espoused by missionaries who are currently active at Corinth.

(5) *2 Corinthians 10:1–13:10*: Paul's second defense against more urgent charges of his lack of δοκιμή ("attestation") to be a true apostle, and consequent suspicion about his financial undertakings; letter sent with Titus as personal mediating envoy.

Corinthian reaction: they welcome Titus, hear his message, and repent (7:7, 9, 15), also censuring the one who incited them against Paul (2:5–8; 7:12). But they still wonder if Paul is truly their friend, since he wrote a letter that caused them grief (7:8–12) and did not carry out the visit he promised to make to them (1:15–2:1; see also 12:14; 13:1).

(6) *2 Cor 1:1–2:13; 7:5–16; 13:11–13*: the letter toward reconciliation that completes the unifying process by a soft-toned self-defense of his goodwill for the Corinthians throughout, and of his sincerity, even in the face of changed travel plans.

Corinthian reaction: apparently they are mollified and restored in relationship to Paul, since when he writes next he is confident enough to resume the collection effort, and is no longer defending his conduct or exegeting past letters.

(7) *2 Corinthians 9*: the storms now passed, Paul leaves debates about epistolary meaning behind, and sets in motion the final stages of the collection for the saints in Jerusalem from all the province of Achaia.

Corinthian reaction: they (Achaians) contribute to the collection effort alongside the Macedonians (Rom 15:26), and welcome Paul on his next visit. His restoration to a position of respect and authority may be seen in his enfranchisement at Corinth on his final visit there, from which he writes to the Romans. While there he is a guest in the house of the prominent Corinthian Gaius (Rom 16:23), one of his original baptisands (1 Cor 1:14), who has a house large enough to host a meeting of the whole ἐκκλησία ("assembly/church," Rom 16:23), and is closely associated with Erastus, ὁ οἰκονόμος τῆς πόλεως ("the treasurer of the city"), and Phoebe, a leader and patron (προστάτις) from Cenchreai (Rom 16:1–2).

Concluding Reflections and Topics for Conversation

The collection of extant letters from Paul to Corinth from the 50s C.E. constitutes a literary-historical artifact of immensely complex proportions that may have much to contribute to a study of religion in the early imperial period. My thesis is that many of the puzzles posed by these documents can be reasonably addressed if the letters are put in their right temporal succession and, above all, if we take seriously the extent to which the letters themselves, and their controversial and ambiguous sets of meanings, fomented the conflict and facilitated the reconciliation that ultimately ensued. The result is a rare glimpse into an intensely heated and dramatic turn of events involving a tiny fraction of the population of Roman Corinth and a provocative outsider who offered them τὸ μυστήριον τοῦ θεοῦ ("the mystery of God," 1 Cor 2:1). They accepted, and in so doing entered a hermeneutical whirlwind that would continue to the present.

In addition to providing documentary evidence of one urban religious cult at Corinth in the first century, this foray into the literary and historical complexities of the Corinthian correspondence touches on some key topics for comparative research within the broader framework of this volume on urban religion in Roman Corinth. I would like to articulate these in the form of seven questions for ongoing conversation and research.

(1) The thesis I have proposed in this paper assumes a high level of literary engagement in the religious life of the early Corinthian Christians.[91] Is this paralleled among other Corinthian religious associations, or is it rare or even unique? Is it even possible, on the basis of extant information, to answer this question? What other literary and nonliterary media were used to perform some of these same functions, or different ones, among other Corinthian cults? Did any other Corinthian cults or associations employ letters to such a degree? Did they engage in close exegesis of other texts to any similar measure?

(2) The epistolary nature of the extant literary evidence for early Corinthian Christianity was at least initially due to the translocal nature of this religious group, rooted in the itinerary of its missionary personnel. Are there any analogies among the Greco-Roman cults at Corinth in this period for such translocal communication between urban religious cults in various parts of the Empire?

---

[91]On the question in general, see the valuable study of Gamble, *Books and Readers in the Early Church.*

(3) On the basis of Rom 16:23 (which mentions Gaius, who, Paul says, is ὁ ξένος μου καὶ ὅλης τῆς ἐκκλησίας, "my host and that of the entire assembly/church"),[92] most scholars believe the Corinthian Christians assembled for their "lordly supper" and worship service in private homes. Would these Christian "house churches" have been the only Corinthian religious associations to have done so? In 1 Cor 14:23 Paul presumes that ἄπιστοι ("unbelievers") might enter into a Christian worship service in Corinth. Would the presence of such activities as sacred songs, readings, prophecies, and interpretative acts (which Paul describes in 1 Cor 14:26) in a domestic setting be inherently shocking to these persons? Would such acts fit, for instance, within the social expectations of family religious rituals, or of an after-dinner symposium?[93]

(4) 1 Cor 7:17–24 makes it clear that there were slaves (and probably slaveowners) among the Corinthian Christians. Later 1 Tim 6:1–2 (and also Paul's own letter to Philemon) will show that the confusion in norms this caused the Christian community was considerable.[94] Did worshipers of other cults at Corinth also stand side by side as slaves and slave-owners? Did this pose social tensions or stress? Would it have been a distinguishing mark of Christians, or not?

(5) Is Paul's concern for keeping women in their places in 1 Cor 11:2–16 and 14:33–36 paralleled in other Corinthian religious groups? What patterns of women's participation and activity can be documented for them? Would Corinthian women have found Paul's ἐκκλησία ("assembly/church") recognizable religious terrain, or something novel?[95]

(6) One aspect of the translocal phenomenon of Christian groups I have noted is the way Paul plays on a competitive spirit between the Christians of Achaia and those of Macedonia in his pleas for the collection.[96] Is such

---

[92]And also the references to συνέρχεσθαι ἐπὶ τὸ αὐτό (" 'come together' in the same place") in 1 Cor 11:20 and 14:23; compare 11:18: συνερχομένων ὑμῶν ἐν ἐκκλησίᾳ ("when you 'come together' in assembly").

[93]This was argued by Stephen M. Pogoloff, *Logos and Sophia: The Rhetorical Situation of 1 Corinthians* (SBLDS 134; Atlanta, Ga.: Scholars Press, 1992), on which see my review in *CBQ* 55 (1993) 819–20.

[94]See the important study by J. Albert Harrill, *The Manumission of Slaves in Early Christianity* (HUT 32; Tübingen: Mohr Siebeck, 1995).

[95]Again on this question there is much literature, but no consensus. See, for instance, Ross Kraemer, *Her Share of the Blessings: Women's Religions among Pagans, Jews and Christians in the Greco-Roman World* (New York: Oxford University Press, 1992); and Wire, *Corinthian Women Prophets*.

[96]See p. 330, above.

regional rivalry (independent of religious groups) between the two locales attested in the archaeological and literary record?[97] Can we find other instances of the employment of such territorial politics to spur competition among religious adherents in different sites? How does provincial loyalty function in ancient "identity politics," and in relation to what other terms or notions, particularly religious activities or allegiances?

(7) Religious charlatanry is of course well attested in the literary record of antiquity.[98] The Corinthian archive shows both the considerably ambitious financial projects the Pauline churches engaged in, and the intense sensitivity all shared about who was handling the money, how they were authenticated, and whether they could be trusted. Do we have other documentary evidence from Corinth in particular about financial administration and concomitant anxieties that might be comparable?[99]

[97]For instance, would their division (again) into two separate Roman senatorial provinces by Claudius in 44 c.e. have been an important part of the background even for the small Christian groups in the next decade? (For the general history of the provinces, see Betz, *2 Corinthians 8 and 9*, 49–53, with references to further literature.)

[98]Lucian's *Alexander* and *Peregrinus* are perhaps the most well-known examples.

[99]I would like to take this opportunity to thank the organizers of the conference, and all the participants, for lively and instructive conversation that aided my thinking on the set of problems I engage in this essay considerably. I would also like to express gratitude to Hans Dieter Betz, Scott Bowie, Paul Duff, Hans-Josef Klauck, Wayne Meeks, and Calvin Roetzel for valuable feedback and critiques of my argument as I revised this paper for publication.

CHAPTER TWELVE

The Silence of the Apostle

Helmut Koester

There are so many things that scholars today would like to know about Corinth and the early church in that important city in the middle of the first century C.E.[1] What was the social structure of that new community? Was it composed of mostly poor people and slaves, or did it also include some wealthy people and some members who belonged to the curia? What kind of business were they pursuing? Were they native Corinthians or Jews, or were they recent immigrants into this still-growing city? What were their political and social ambitions? Did they think that they had some responsibility for reforming the urban society to which they belonged? How was the church at Corinth, which evidently continued as a strong community throughout the following decades, organized? What kind of people were the leaders? Were they slaves, fishermen, tentmakers, bankers, or city councillors? Did the leaders include women, or men of the upper classes? Unfortunately, our best informant on the first-century church at Corinth is silent on many of these topics.

To be sure, some information can be gleaned from the letters of Paul. Erastos, the city treasurer, whose greetings Paul sends from Corinth (Rom 16:23), was certainly a member of the ruling class. He is most likely identical with the

---

[1]Translations of biblical texts are my own. Citations from the *Gospel of Thomas* follow the translation of Hans-Gebhard Bethge et al., in Stephen J. Patterson and James M. Robinson, *The Fifth Gospel: The Gospel of Thomas Comes of Age* (Harrisburg, Pa.: Trinity Press International, 1998).

Erastus of a first-century C.E. inscription found in the pavement of a square near the theater of Corinth.[2]

> ERASTUS PRO AEDILIT[AT]E
> S(ua) P(ecunia) STRAVIT
>
> Erastus, in return for his aedileship,
> laid the pavement at his own expense

But in Romans 16, Paul mentions Erastus and his title in passing, together with other people who were his relatives or his hosts—almost as if that dignifying title meant nothing to him. First Corinthians 1:26 is famous for its statement that not many in the Corinthian church were wise, powerful, or of noble birth, but that would have been true for any community or association representing a cross section of the society. Paul's comment is not in itself without value, because it certainly confirms that it was not just poor people and slaves who were attracted to this new community. Slaves must have been a part of the church, since Paul discusses the question of manumission with respect to the status of being "in Christ" in 1 Cor 7:21–24. Women were not just members of the community but also held positions as prophets and leaders of worship (1 Cor 11:5); Paul discusses the question of whether they should wear some kind of headdress when they perform such functions.[3]

The book of Acts does not help very much in supplementing that meager information. Acts 18 tells about Aquila and Priscilla, Jewish people who had been expelled from Rome, whom Paul met in Corinth. They were tentmakers like Paul (vv. 2–4), and they helped Paul to get established in the Corinthian synagogue, from which he was eventually expelled (v. 6). The leader of that synagogue, Crispus, became a member of the new community (v. 8). That Paul was eventually forced by the Roman proconsul Gallio to leave Corinth (vv. 12–17) seems to give a firm date for the Pauline chronology. Aquila and Priscilla are certainly historical persons because they are also mentioned by Paul in Romans 16:3, but otherwise the information that can be gleaned from the book of Acts is problematic. The fragmentary inscription about the "Synagogue of the Hebrews" ([Συνα]γωγὴ Ἐβρ[αίων]) does not help very much, because its date is uncertain.[4]

---

[2]John Harvey Kent, *The Inscriptions, 1926–1950* (Corinth VIII.3; Princeton, N.J.: ASCSA, 1966) 99–100; and Steven Friesen et al., "Corinth A," in *ARNTS*, vol. 1, no. 37.

[3]For a discussion of the social composition of early communities such as Corinth, see Wayne A. Meeks, *The First Urban Christians: The Social World of the Apostle Paul* (New Haven, Conn.: Yale University Press, 1983).

[4]Benjamin Dean Meritt, *Greek Inscriptions* (Corinth VIII.1; Cambridge, Mass.: Harvard University Press, 1931) 78; and John Lanci et al., "Corinth B," in *ARNTS*, vol. 2, no. 13.

In any case, the Apostle is silent about so many things that we would like to know. The reason is obvious: As far as the present society and its political and social structures are concerned, Paul shows no interest whatsoever. He is only concerned with questions related to internal relations within the new eschatological community. Individuals should serve the Lord, no matter what their social situation was when they were called (1 Cor 7:21–24). Yes, writes Paul, it is good for a slave to have the opportunity of manumission. But that goodness does not imply a criticism of the social institution of slavery. Rather, manumission is good for a Christian slave, because a free person has a better opportunity to serve the Lord fully.[5] For Paul, the institution of slavery is not a social concern.

This does not mean that the Apostle considers hierarchical organization and the social inequalities of the Roman world to be good or just. On the contrary, the Roman world and society well deserve to pass away. The community of the new age should already in the present time disregard differentiations according to social, ethnic, and gender categories (Gal 3:28). If Rome preaches "peace and security"—a typical propaganda slogan of the imperial establishment—it is in for a real surprise when the day of the Lord comes: there will be no escape![6] Paul has no doubt that the Roman empire will come to an end. It is part of a world that is dominated by sin and death, a world that is transitory and ruled by Satan, the god of this world. This world will come to an end at the appearance of Christ. Given Paul's expectation of Christ's imminent parousia, any human attempt to reform this world and its social and political structures or to start a revolution in an attempt to overthrow these unjust institutions would have appeared to Paul as utter folly.

If the Apostle believes that reform or revolution for the betterment of this world and its society does not make any sense, does he only proclaim a message of personal salvation for the individual? The answer to this question is a resounding "no." Personal religious experience or the ideals of education and the formation of a better human character have no place in Paul's thought. The purpose of Paul's correspondence is to describe a path that neither leads to a sociopolitical reform nor offers an individual religious experience. His message is best characterized as an invitation to participate in the community of the new age. While 1 Corinthians is not addressing the

---

[5]S. Scott Bartchy, Mallon chrēsai: *First-Century Slavery and the Interpretation of 1 Corinthians 7:21* (1973; SBLDS 11; Atlanta, Ga.: Scholars, 1985).

[6]1 Thess 4:3; see Helmut Koester, "From Paul's Eschatology to the Apocalyptic Schemata of 2 Thessalonians," in *The Thessalonian Correspondence* (ed. Raymond F. Collins; BETL 87; Leuven: Leuven University Press, 1990) 449–50.

ills of society in general, it does warn that the search for personal religious experience and the exercise of religious freedom can threaten the building of the community of the new age.

I am quite aware of the inherent problems associated with any attempt to reconstruct the position of the people addressed by Paul on the basis of his arguments against them. The rhetorical character of Paul's arguments implies that his depiction of the opponents cannot be taken as an unbiased description of their behavior and opinions.[7] Nevertheless, in order to understand Paul's arguments, it is necessary to attempt such a reconstruction of what took place in Corinth between Paul's departure and the time when Paul received information from the people of Chloe (1 Cor 1:11). According to 1 Cor 5:9, Paul must have written an earlier letter to Corinth, to which the Corinthians responded with a letter that raised some additional questions. Unfortunately, we do not know what the occasion of that earlier letter was; nor do we know much about the content of the letter from Corinth, except that it must have contained some inquiry about marriage (1 Cor 7:1). It is also evident that a Christian teacher named Apollos—Acts 18:24 characterizes him as a learned Jew from Alexandria—had been teaching in Corinth after Paul's departure.

Paul had received information from Corinth through two different delegations and through a letter written by the Corinthians. From the delegation of Chloe's people he had learned that there were divisions and competitions between various groups in Corinth (1 Cor 1:11–13). The character of these divisions has long been a subject of scholarly debate and speculation. I shall not discuss the various hypotheses here[8] except to say that it seems clear that there were not rival "parties" competing in Corinth, but that Paul cites the claims of several authorities, who may or may not have been active in Corinth. The keys to understanding these claims are that Paul here emphasizes that he has not come to baptize; and that the first chapters of the letter allude to several statements that also appear as wisdom sayings in the tradition of the sayings of Jesus, especially those preserved in the *Gospel of Thomas*. Moreover, in the first four chapters of 1 Corinthians, Paul uses a number of terms that he uses elsewhere not at all, or only very rarely. I repeat here some observations

---

[7]On the rhetoric of 1 Corinthians, see especially Margaret M. Mitchell, *Paul and the Rhetoric of Reconciliation: An Exegetical Investigation of the Language and Composition of 1 Corinthians* (HUT 28; Tübingen: Mohr Siebeck, 1991).

[8]See Hans Conzelmann, *1 Corinthians: A Commentary on the First Epistle to the Corinthians* (Hermeneia; Philadelphia: Fortress, 1975) 33–34.

that I have published previously,[9] but I shall go a bit further in discussing the consequences of those previous observations.

The special terms used by Paul in 1 Corinthians 1–4 are: "to keep secret" (ἀποκρύπτειν, 2:7); "to hide" (κρύπτειν, 4:5); "to uncover" (ἀποκαλύπτειν, 2:10; 3:13); "to reveal" (φανεροῦν, 4:5); and "unlearned, immature" (νήπιος, 3:1). Most striking is the frequent use of the words "wise" (σοφός) and "wisdom" (σοφία), which occur twenty-six times in the first four chapters of the letter, but only a total of nine times in all other chapters of the entire Pauline correspondence. This terminology alludes to a saying in the synoptic tradition that both Matthew (11:25–26) and Luke (10:21) evidently drew from the Synoptic Sayings Gospel (Q):

> I praise you, Father, Lord of heaven and earth, for you have hidden (ἔκρυψας) these things from the wise and clever (σοφῶν καὶ συνετῶν), and have revealed (ἀπεκάλυψας) them to the unlearned (νηπίοις).

The close relationship of this saying to 1 Corinthians 1:19 had already been observed by Adolf von Harnack and Eduard Norden.[10] The latter observed that the formulaic language of this saying belongs to a tradition of religious language that spans the entire spectrum from the Wisdom of Solomon to the *Corpus Hermeticum*. The hendiadys σοφοὶ καὶ συνετοί in this saying of Jesus appears nowhere else in the New Testament, but both terms occur in parallelism in 1 Cor 1:19 in a quotation introduced by Paul with "it is written":

> I will destroy the wisdom of the wise, and the cleverness of the clever I will thwart (ἀπολῶ τὴν σοφίαν τῶν σοφῶν καὶ τὴν σύνεσιν τῶν συνετῶν κρύψω).

Paul quotes here the Septuagint text of Isa 29:14. It appears that Paul invokes this verse to protest the use of this saying of Jesus by the Corinthians, who claimed that they were once the "unlearned," but had now acquired wisdom and had become wise. The terminology of this saying is also reflected in 1 Cor 2:7, where Paul says "we speak God's wisdom, which has been hidden in a mystery" (λαλοῦμεν θεοῦ σοφίαν ἐν μυστηρίῳ τὴν ἀποκεκρυμμένην).

---

[9]Helmut Koester, "Gnostic Writings as Witnesses for the Development of the Sayings Tradition," in *The School of Valentinus* (ed. Bentley Layton; vol. 1 of *The Rediscovery of Gnosticism*; Numen Supplement 41; Leiden: Brill, 1980) 238–61; and idem, *Ancient Christian Gospels: Their History and Development* (Philadelphia: Trinity Press International; London: SCM, 1990) 55–62.

[10]Adolf von Harnack, *The Sayings of Jesus* (New York: G. P. Putnam, 1908) 272–310; and Eduard Norden, *Agnostos Theos* (1912; Darmstadt: Wissenschaftliche Buchgesellschaft, 1956) 277–308.

Texts from the *Gospel of Thomas* provide additional evidence that the Corinthians were using sayings of Jesus to justify their claim to possess hidden wisdom. Most prominent are sayings 5 and 6:

> Come to know what is in front of you,
> and that which is hidden from you will become clear to you.
> For there is nothing hidden that will not become manifest.
> (*Gos. Thom.* 5)

> For everything is disclosed in view of <the truth>.
> For there is nothing hidden that will not become revealed.
> And there is nothing covered that will remain undisclosed.
> (*Gos. Thom.* 6)

Paul relies on the same language when he writes, "The Lord will bring to light the things now hidden in darkness and will disclose the purposes of the heart" (1 Cor 4:5). Another saying from the *Gospel of Thomas* is also paralleled in 1 Cor 2:9, where Paul quotes as "Scripture"—though to what "scripture" he is referring has remained a conundrum—the following:

> What eye has not seen
> and ear has not heard,
> nor has it risen in the human heart,
> what God has prepared for those who love him.

Gos. Thom. 17 attributes this saying to Jesus:

> I will give you what no eye has seen,
> and what no ear has heard,
> and what no hand has touched,
> and what has not occurred to the human mind.

The tradition of the sayings of Jesus preserves yet other sayings in which Jesus speaks with the voice of heavenly wisdom. But that topic cannot be further explored here. In the *Gospel of Thomas,* which contains no reference to Jesus' death on the cross, revelation through Jesus' words is the primary message of salvation. Those who discover that wisdom is hidden in themselves are being saved by that very knowledge, and the one who is perfected will stand as the solitary one (ⲙⲟⲛⲁⲭⲟⲥ) and will not taste death. Those who seek and find that hidden wisdom will become kings and rule over the All (*Gos. Thom.* 2). If some of the Corinthians understood salvation in the same way, it explains Paul's ridicule of this religious posture in 1 Cor 4:8:

You are already satisfied! Already you have become rich! Without us
you have become kings! Oh, that you had become kings, so that we
might be kings with you!

But then Paul continues (vv. 9–10):

For it seems to me that God has exhibited us apostles as last of all. . . .
We are fools for the sake of Christ, but you are wise in Christ.

The Corinthians' reliance on sayings of Jesus would explain why Paul can
say that some of them claim that they "belong to Christ" (1 Cor 1:12). That
others say that they "belong to Peter" or "belong to Apollos" implies that they
were quoting apostles, under whose authority these sayings were transmitted.
Such transmission of authoritative sayings of Jesus under apostolic names was
apparently not uncommon. The *Gospel of Thomas* itself attests the practice,
and Papias, bishop of Hierapolis, reports early in the second century that he
has inquired about what Jesus said from those who had followed the apostles
and remembered what they had heard from them.[11] Furthermore, Papias refers
to a collection of sayings that was made by Matthew.[12]

If the Corinthians used such sayings of Jesus as a basis for their claim to
salvation, it is curious that Paul never refers to such statements as sayings of
Jesus, but rather only alludes to them or quotes them instead as "Scripture."
Evidently, Paul does not allow such sayings to carry the authority of Jesus,
and thus he denies the Corinthians the right to rely on such sayings. For Paul,
the mystery that is being revealed is never a saying of Jesus but the message
of the cross (1 Cor 1:17–18). Although Paul knows such sayings of Jesus,
they are never referred to as saving authorities. His message of Christ crucified does not permit Jesus to stand as an authority for sayings that have the
power to save. What is at stake here is a fundamental religious conflict that
has far-reaching social consequences.

The religion of salvation through the communication of divine saving
wisdom is primarily concerned with the individual, not with a community.
It promises to the individual spiritual gifts in this life and immortality after
death. This corresponds to the message of the typical Hellenistic mystery
religions. In speaking about the Mysteries of Eleusis, Cicero says that they
give more joy for this life and hope for the life hereafter. The story of Lucius
reports that when he was initiated into the mysteries of Isis at Kenchreai,
the eastern port of Corinth, he was promised that the goddess would be with

---

[11]Eusebius, *Hist. eccl.* 3.39.3–4.
[12]Ibid., 3.39.15–16.

him even at the threshold of Hades.[13] For some of the Corinthians, the new religion from Palestine had become another opportunity to gain a better life now—a life of which they could boast—along with a guarantee of immortality to come. In terms of the traditional definitions, this is eschatology collapsed into the present experience of the individual.

We can also infer that the communication of sayings of Jesus as secret wisdom was connected to an act of mystery initiation. Some of the Corinthians apparently understood baptism as such an initiation rite. That would explain why Paul takes pains to say that he had not come to baptize. He first states that he had not baptized anyone in Corinth—and then remembers with some embarrassment that he did indeed baptize Crispus and Gaius and the house of Stephanas (1 Cor 1:14–16). These Corinthians must have considered the person who baptized them as their mystagogue, thus claiming that they "belonged" to such apostles as Apollos or Paul, or that in the process of initiation, namely in baptism, they had received the wisdom sayings of Jesus directly or under the authority of Peter.

Paul, however, was a champion of an eschatological message that could not be collapsed into the present religious experience of the individual. The message that he preaches does not lead into a mystery initiation. It is an eschatological message proclaiming the turning point of the ages that has come with the cross and resurrection of Christ, and it has consequences for the understanding of the present time *and* of the future. Most of all, this message does not address the religious experience of the individual, nor is it concerned with personal salvation and immortality. The entire polemic of 1 Corinthians must be seen as an argument against understanding the new message about Jesus as a mystery religion, and as a plea for understanding the "new existence" as entrance into the community of the new age. Demonstration of the individual possession of lifesaving wisdom in this world as well as for the time after death is therefore not legitimate, because focus on individual salvation destroys, rather than builds, the community of the new age. In this context, Paul develops two different but interlocking criteria for determining proper conduct: first, conduct in the present life must conform to whatever can be considered as good and proper with respect to the standards of the society in general; and second, conduct must be subservient to the demands and sensitivities of the new community, even if those sensitivities require the abandonment of cherished religious possessions.

---

[13]Apuleius, *Metam.* 11.21.6–7; see also 23.8–9.

I will briefly point out some features relating to both of these aspects: conduct according to the reasonable standards of goodness for life in this world, and the requirements arising from membership in the community of the new age. Conduct such as sexual intercourse with the wife of one's father is completely unacceptable because that is not even tolerated by society at large (1 Cor 5:1–5). Marriage, though an institution of this world, is to be taken seriously as a partnership, in which sexual intercourse is a necessary ingredient as long as it is recognized that both wife and husband are partners respecting each other's dignity and equality (1 Cor 7:2–5). Living in ascetic partnership[14] does not make anyone more holy, and if such a partnership becomes problematic, it is advisable to get married and accept sexual relations and all the other cares that come with marriage (1 Cor 7:25–38). I should add here that secular judicial authority needs to be respected, as Romans 13 argues—if those verses indeed come from the pen of the Apostle—but it is much better when members of the community settle their quarrels before their own court (1 Cor 6:1–8). Both respect for secular authority and the institution of a court of the community are inherited from diaspora Judaism. Paul does not advise slaves to rebel against their masters, but if the opportunity of manumission arises, it should be seized, because one can serve the Lord even more efficiently as a free person (1 Cor 7:21–24).

Some practices that Paul rejects straddle the line between violation of general good moral conduct and violation of the membership in the new community. The practice of going to prostitutes (did the strong ones in the Corinthian community actually do that?) is not only immoral but also incompatible with being a member of Christ, to whom our bodies—that is, "persons"—belong (1 Cor 6:12–20). With respect to participation in meals of meat that had been sacrificed to idols (1 Cor 8 and 10), Paul seems ambivalent. On the one hand, the idols are nothing, so meat sacrificed to them cannot be harmful. On the other hand, participation in such meals also implies membership in the wrong kind of community. The issue becomes critical if such behavior violates the conscience not only of the weak people in the community but also of outsiders, who may doubt the seriousness of the believer's claim to be a member of an altogether different community that is committed to the worship of the one and only living God of the Scriptures of Israel.

Paul's foremost concern is to build the new community of believers, the *ekklēsia*, which is the body of Christ. Baptism is not a mystery rite

---

[14]I do think that Paul is talking about *virgines subintroductae* in 1 Corinthians 7, although that is controversial. See Conzelmann, *1 Corinthians*, 131–38.

but the incorporation of an individual into that body (1 Cor 12:12–13). It is an act that has definite social consequences. It is not accidental that in 1 Corinthians 12 Paul uses an image that is drawn from the realm of the social and political world. All members of that "body" must serve each other for the common good and recognize the equal dignity of fellow members. The charter for this new community, quoted by Paul in Gal 3:28—"There is no longer Jew or Greek, there is no longer slave or free, there is no longer male and female; for all of you are one in Jesus Christ"—is also applicable to Corinth. The body of Christ cannot exist if there is spiritual competition among its members or if some people claim that their gifts elevate them over others. It is only in the non-Pauline Epistle to the Colossians that the body of Christ becomes a mystical-cosmic image with Christ as the head of that body. In Paul's words to the Corinthians, the body of Christ does not have a head that is superior to the other members.

This body of Christ is nourished by the Eucharist, the common meal. The cup of blessing is a participation in the blood of Christ, that is, in his death, which is the sacrifice that establishes the new covenant. The bread that is broken is a participation in the body of Christ, that is, the community (1 Cor 11:23–25). Since there is one bread, we the many are one body (1 Cor 10:16–17). The body of Christ here is not the bread of the Eucharist, into which Jesus' body has mysteriously been changed. Rather, as Günther Bornkamm showed half a century ago in a seminal article,[15] the bread that is shared is the symbol of the new community. In his criticism of the Corinthians' celebration of the Eucharist, Paul accuses them of neglecting the poor (1 Cor 11:20–22). In the crucial sentence of 1 Cor 11:29 ("For all who eat and drink without discerning the body, eat and drink judgment upon themselves"), "without discerning the body" means not recognizing that the body of Christ is the new community. Chapter 12 confirms this point by using social terminology to describe the church as the body of Christ.

The next chapter (1 Corinthians 13) then explicates the thesis of 1 Corinthians 8 that "Gnosis puffs up, but love builds up" by juxtaposing the typical religious gifts of the spirit with love. It is not a hymn but a carefully crafted didactic poem.[16] Precisely those spiritual gifts that are characteristic of the exercise of piety and religious experience—namely prophecy, speaking in

---

[15]Günther Bornkamm, "Lord's Supper and Church in Paul," in *Early Christian Experience* (trans. Paul L. Hammer; New York: Harper & Row, 1969) 123–60; the German original appeared in 1956.

[16]Idem, "The More Excellent Way (1 Corinthians 13)," in *Early Christian Experience*, 180–93; see also Conzelmann, *1 Corinthians*, 216–31.

tongues, and gnosis—have no share in eternity: they will pass away. Love will remain because it is the "superior way," through which the community of the new age can be built. This community is for Paul not a program for social and political reform. Rather, it is the only way in which the expected new world can find its real expression already in the present time. This is the core of Paul's realized eschatology. It is not a new religion and therefore does not compete with other religions. Paul is so certain that Christ will confirm this utopian program upon his future return that he does not even consider it worthwhile to enter into debate with the present unjust, hierarchical, and oppressive social order of the Roman world.

Chapter Thirteen

Prospects for a Demography of the Pauline Mission: Corinth among the Churches

Steven J. Friesen

A great deal of work has been done in the last quarter century on the social status of the Pauline congregations. In this essay, I point out two problems with the results of that work: it has produced conclusions about the Pauline assemblies based on an exceedingly narrow range of data from the New Testament; and it has not made effective use of research on society and economy in the Roman Empire, preferring instead to employ vague, undefined polarities such as high status/low status, upper-class/lower-class, rich/poor, etc. I argue that we will produce better descriptions of the Pauline assemblies if we examine the biases of the New Testament evidence and pay more attention to poverty and wealth in the Roman Empire.

Recent Work on the Social Status of Pauline Assemblies

For the greater part of the twentieth century, scholars tended to conclude that Paul's churches were composed almost entirely of people from the lowest strata of society. The leading proponent of this view was Adolf Deissmann, who concluded that the overwhelming majority of people in Paul's assemblies came from the middle and lower classes. Of Corinth in particular Deissmann said, "Even the holes and corners of the slums of this cosmopolitan city had witnessed conversions."[1]

In the late 1970s, however, Abraham Malherbe detected a sea change in the study of Paul's churches:

> It appears from the recent concern of scholars with the social level of early Christians, that a new consensus may be emerging. This consensus . . . is quite different from the one represented by Adolf Deissmann, which has held sway since the beginning of the century. The more recent scholarship has shown that the social status of early Christians may be higher than Deissmann had supposed.[2]

Other luminaries in this new consensus—along with Malherbe himself—include Gerd Theissen[3] and Wayne Meeks.[4] While they had different emphases, all three shared a common conclusion: "Representatives of the emerging consensus on the social status of early Christians view the church as comprising a cross section of most of Roman society."[5]

For the last quarter century, this "cross section consensus" about the Pauline churches has mostly held sway.[6] I do not advocate a return to the older

---

[1]Adolf Deissmann, *Paul: A Study in Social and Religious History* (2d ed.; New York: Harper & Brothers, 1927) 241–44. Deissmann also recognized, however, that there were some "well-to-do Christians," men and women whose homes were large enough to host meetings and traveling apostles like Paul. Scholars who objected to the conclusion that the churches were composed almost entirely of people from the lower strata of society include Floyd V. Filson ("The Significance of the Early House Churches," *JBL* 58 [1939] 105–12, esp. 111) and Edwin A. Judge (*The Social Pattern of Christian Groups in the First Century* [London: Tyndale, 1960]).

[2]Abraham J. Malherbe, *Social Aspects of Early Christianity* (2d ed.; Philadelphia: Fortress, 1983) 31. The first edition was published in 1977.

[3]Gerd Theissen, *The Social Setting of Pauline Christianity: Essays on Corinth* (Philadelphia: Fortress, 1982).

[4]Wayne Meeks, *The First Urban Christians: The Social World of the Apostle Paul* (New Haven, Conn.: Yale University Press, 1983).

[5]Malherbe, *Social Aspects*, 86–87. There were, of course, differences among these scholars. Malherbe (esp. 29–59) focused more on the level of education implied by Paul's rhetoric. Meeks (*First Urban Christians*, 72–73) concentrated more on the congregations, describing them as a mix of all levels of society except for "the extreme top and bottom." Theissen (*Social Setting*, 94–96) emphasized the gap between the ordinary church members from the lower classes and Paul's associates, whom he described as members of the upper class with "high social status."

[6]There have, of course, been dissenters, including Ekkhard Stegemann and Wolfgang Stegemann, *The Jesus Movement: A Social History of Its First Century* (Minneapolis: Fortress, 1999), esp. 288–303; and Justin Meggitt, *Paul, Poverty and Survival* (Edinburgh: T&T Clark, 1998).

view of the assemblies as the dregs of society. Those reconstructions were wrong, for they tended to romanticize the poor, or to assume that models for modern industrial economies also describe ancient agrarian economies. My point is this: The cross section consensus has been based largely on evidence from Corinth and from Romans 16.[7] Moreover, the consensus has tended to neglect the fact that nearly everyone in the Roman Empire was poor, and so modern reconstructions of Paul's communities have been moving members of Paul's assemblies up the social ladder.

THE BIAS OF THE NEW TESTAMENT TEXTS IN FAVOR OF CORINTH

One problem that generally goes unrecognized in the study of the Pauline churches is that we have very little reliable information from any of Paul's churches. Specialists tend to make pan-Pauline generalizations without acknowledging the gaps in our evidence about the assemblies. One basic question has not been asked: How many people do we know about from each of Paul's churches? In order to help me answer questions like this, I built a database that records all references to individuals and groups in the canonical Pauline literature (the undisputed letters of Paul, the disputed letters, the Pastoral Epistles, and Acts).[8] We have information about Paul's relationship to a total of forty-five cities.[9] These cities may be sorted into three categories: cities in which Paul founded an assembly; cities in which Paul had contact with an assembly founded by someone else; and cities through which Paul apparently passed without significant contact. The historical value of the references to these cities varies greatly, but the list gives us a starting place in our analysis of the tradition.

---

[7]The differences between Deissmann and the new consensus are actually less clear and also more complicated than this. For a more extensive comparison, see my "Poverty in Pauline Studies: Beyond the So-Called New Consensus," *JSNT* 26 (2004) 323–61.

[8]The development of the database to its current state was made possible by a Society of Biblical Literature Research and Technology Grant, and by a grant from the Research Council of the University of Missouri-Columbia. My eventual goal is to develop a "Digital Demography of the Early Churches," a database dealing with all the information known to us about individuals in the first-century churches.

[9]The undisputed letters of Paul only provide evidence for Paul's presence in eleven of those cities, but nowhere does he attempt a complete list of the places he has visited.

Cities where Paul founded assemblies	Cities where Paul contacted assemblies founded by others	Cities where Paul traveled without significant contact
Antioch (Pisidia)	Antioch (Syria)	Amphipolis
Athens?	Caesarea Maritima	Antipatris
Beroea	Damascus	Apollonia
Cenchreae	Jerusalem	Assos
Colossae	Ptolemais	Attaleia
Corinth	Puteoloi	Cos
Derbe	Rome	Fair Havens
Ephesos	Sidon?	Roum of Appius
Iconium	Tyre	Miletus
Laodicea?		Myra
Lystra		Mytilene
Paphos		Neapolis
Philippi		Patara
Salamis?		Pera
Tarsus		Rhegium
Thessalonica		Rhodes
Troas		Samos
		Syracus
		Three Taverns

Fig. 13.1 Three types of cities associated with Paul in the New Testament. It is uncertain whether Paul founded assemblies in Athens, Laodicea, Salamis, and Sidon. I have marked each of these cities with a question mark and placed each in the more probable category.

My interest is in the cities where Paul is said to have founded assemblies. How many people do we know of from each city? Do we have a representative sample from the congregations upon which to base conclusions about their social status? The database makes it easy to answer these questions after we settle two preliminary problems. One problem is whether to count references only from the seven undisputed letters of Paul, or to include all letters attributed to Paul, as well as the Acts of the Apostles, as reliable sources for prosopographic information. My opinion is that we should only use the undisputed letters, but I have also included the other information for comparison.

The other preliminary problem is whether we should include Romans 16. Specialists are divided about whether this chapter was originally part of the letter to Rome, or whether it was originally written to the Ephesian saints and then included by mistake in copies of the letter to Rome.[10] My conclusion is

---

[10]If the chapter was originally destined for Ephesos, then it would have been appended to the letter to Rome at an early stage in the transmission of the letter. For a summary of the arguments, see Joseph A. Fitzmyer, *Romans* (AB; New York: Doubleday, 1993) 55–67. For a

that Romans 16 was intended for the Roman assemblies and not for those in Ephesos. Since opinions on the issue are divided, however, I have indicated at the bottom of figures 13.2, 13.5, and 13.6 the totals for Ephesos when the names from Romans 16 are included.[11] I have also indicated in those figures the totals for Rome, even though it was technically not a part of the Pauline mission.

No matter how you decide those two small-scale problems, the overall pattern is clear: we have no prosopographic information from most of the cities (fig. 13.2, p. 356). In fact, the evidence is concentrated in Corinth and either Ephesos or Rome. Much of what we have been told about the social status of Pauline assemblies is based primarily on two extraordinary cities. We have been misled by the bias of our sources toward Corinth.

But that is not the worst of it.

THE BIAS OF THE TEXTS IN FAVOR OF TRAVELING LEADERS

Figure 13.2 (p. 356) does not give us enough detail. If our interest is in the demography of the Pauline assemblies, we need to ask how many of these references to individuals indicate long-term *residents* of local assemblies and how many indicate *traveling* leaders. The database demonstrates that there were significant differences between these two groups that require us to consider them separately in our analysis.

For example, one significant difference between travelers and residents in the Pauline assemblies is ethnicity: the missionaries tended to be Jewish, and the residents tended to be Gentile. A search of the undisputed Pauline letters yields references to thirty individuals who traveled to assemblies in other cities, and forty-five individuals who were resident members of an assembly in a particular city.[12] These individuals can be categorized according to ethnicity as follows:

---

comparison of the names in Romans 16 with the inscriptions of Rome and Ephesos, see Peter Lampe, *Die stadtrömischen Christen in den ersten beiden Jahrhunderten: Untersuchungen zur Socialgeschichte* (2d ed.; Tübingen: Mohr Siebeck, 1989) 124–35.

[11]Helmut Koester, "Ephesos in Early Christian Literature," in *Ephesos, Metropolis of Asia: An Interdisciplinary Approach to Its Archaeology, Religion, and Culture* (ed. idem; Valley Forge, Pa.: Trinity, 1995) 122–24.

[12]There are 4 individuals who are included in both categories because we know where they lived and we know of some travel they undertook: Phoebe (Rom 16:1–2); and Stephanas, Achaicus, and Fortunatus, the three travelers from 1 Cor 16:17–18. The name "Achaicus" suggests he was a Greek slave or freedman; the ethnicities of the other three are unknown.

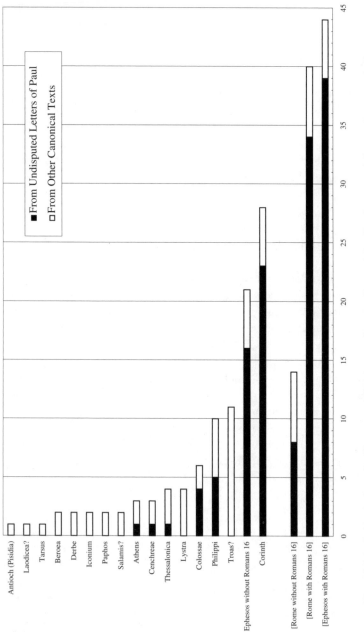

Fig. 13.2 Individuals from Pauline assemblies known from undisputed Pauline letters and from other canonical texts. Calculations do not include Paul. Question marks indicate cities whose assemblies may not have been founded by Paul.

	Jews	Gentiles	Ethnicity unknown	Total
Transients	14	4	12	30
Residents	4	24	17	45

Fig. 13.3 Ethnicity of travelers and residents in Pauline congregations, by individuals. Based on undisputed letters; includes Paul.

The same data can be rendered as percentages to facilitate comparison:

	Jews	Gentiles	Ethnicity unknown	Total
Transients	47%	13%	40%	100%
Residents	9%	53%	38%	100%

Fig. 13.4 Ethnicity of travelers and residents in Pauline congregations, by percentages. Based on undisputed letters; includes Paul.

Three provisos are in order. First, we should note that most of the references to individuals do not specify ethnicity, and sometimes it is only inferred as probable from the context.[13] Second, the inclusion of Romans 16 is an important consideration, since many of the references come from that chapter.[14] Third, I have omitted references to Antioch on the Orontes, Damascus, and Jerusalem since these assemblies preceded Paul's mission and were not, strictly speaking, a part of it.[15] In spite of the tentative nature of the evidence, however, the difference in the ratios of Jews and Gentiles is significant. Of the eighteen transients whose ethnicity is known, fourteen were Jews (78% of those known) and four were Gentiles. Of the twenty-eight residents whose ethnicity is known, four were Jews (14% of those known) and twenty-four were Gentiles.

Having established that there were significant differences in ethnicity between the missionaries and the residents in the Pauline assemblies, we can return to the question, "How many residents do we know about from

[13]The Jewish saints tend to be identified overtly in the text. Gentile saints, on the other hand, are often identified by implications in the text, such as names based on places (e.g., "Persis"). In Romans 16, Paul seems intent on noting if people are Jewish, and so I accept the conclusion of Lampe (*Die stadtrömische Christen*, 58) that if Paul did not identify the person as Jewish in Romans 16, then the man or woman was probably Gentile.

[14]The decision on whether to include or to exclude Romans 16 from the calculations is difficult. I decided to include it because the data are important no matter which theory about the chapter's original destination is correct. If the chapter was intended for Rome, the people mentioned are all known to Paul and so they probably do not deviate far from the subculture of the Pauline assemblies. If Romans 16 was written to Ephesos, then it would be wrong to exclude it.

[15]This omission is important because it removes Cephas, James, and John, who would otherwise be included in the category of resident participants in a Pauline assembly. The omission does not affect the statistics in any other way.

the assemblies founded by Paul?" When we look at this feature, the overall pattern is downright shocking (fig. 13.5). Based on the undisputed letters, we do not know any local saints from twelve of the seventeen cities. We know of one resident from Cenchreae, perhaps one more from Ephesos, and four from Philippi, but sixteen from Corinth. Even when we go beyond Paul's undisputed letters to include references from all canonical texts, the only cities where we have much information about locals are Philippi and Corinth (fig. 13.6). The case of Ephesos is particularly surprising. It was perhaps the most important center for Paul's work, yet without Romans 16 we know of only two individuals from the Ephesian churches. If we include Romans 16, nearly half of our information is still about the traveling leaders.[16]

To sum up, the consensus of the last two decades that the Pauline churches contained a cross section of social levels from mainstream society is not based on a cross section of Paul's churches. A nuanced examination of the assemblies for which we have evidence indicates that we have no reliable information about individuals from most of the churches he founded. We have one large block of evidence from the assemblies in Corinth. We have another large block of material from Romans 16, which is difficult to locate (maybe Rome, maybe Ephesos). For the Macedonian assemblies, who played a major role in Paul's mission, the undisputed letters mention no individuals from Thessalonica and only four individuals from Philippi. Moving to Asia, we find that Paul mentions only one individual from Ephesos, which was his premier location in the province. The Galatian churches are of crucial importance because they represent some kind of boundary for the Pauline mission. They provide examples of churches where the Pauline mission was in jeopardy and probably unsuccessful, yet Paul does not provide us with any references to any individuals there to help us build our theories.

But even *that* is not the worst of it.

BIASES AGAINST THE POOR

It may be that the poor are blessed with the kingdom of God, but in Pauline studies the poor have been doubly afflicted in recent decades. One affliction is that our ancient texts tend to overlook the poorest saints. We have shown that the New Testament texts overemphasize traveling leaders above residents.

---

[16]Since individuals like Barnabas, Silas/Silvanus, and Timothy show up as transients in several cities, the total number of known transients is less than the bars in figs. 13.5 and 13.6 (p. 360) imply.

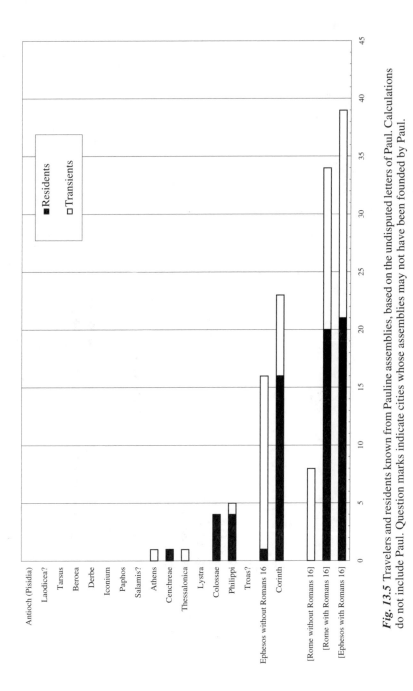

Fig. 13.5 Travelers and residents known from Pauline assemblies, based on the undisputed letters of Paul. Calculations do not include Paul. Question marks indicate cities whose assemblies may not have been founded by Paul.

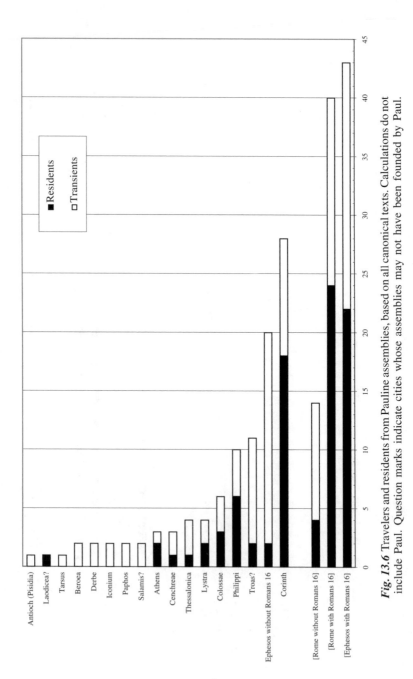

Fig. 13.6 Travelers and residents from Pauline assemblies, based on all canonical texts. Calculations do not include Paul. Question marks indicate cities whose assemblies may not have been founded by Paul.

We could also demonstrate that the texts talk more about local leaders than about other resident members of the assemblies, or that the texts talk more about men than about women. Or consider the case of children: How many children were there in the Pauline assemblies? They may well have comprised half the individuals in the congregations. How many children do we know about from the Pauline congregations? None. The same is certainly true of the poorest members of the Pauline assemblies. The poor were present in the congregations, but the texts hardly mention them.[17]

One important exception is 1 Corinthians 11:17–32, which does mention poverty. In 1 Corinthians 11, Paul discusses the proper observance of the Lord's Supper, so it is the earliest known text about the central ritual of the Pauline assemblies. The reason Paul wrote about the topic was the disregard for the poor shown by some Corinthians. Some people did not have food and some did, and those who had food would not share.[18] The refusal to share with the poor violated Paul's understanding of the Lord's Supper, it denied the intended character of the Pauline assemblies, and it disregarded his hope for the end of the age. But we now owe the poor Corinthian saints a debt of gratitude: without their humiliation in first-century Corinth, we today would have no idea how Paul instructed his assemblies to observe the Lord's Supper.[19]

The second affliction of the poor is modern. The consensus of the last two decades regarding the "Pauline church as a cross section of society" has caused the poor to disappear from our view. The precise mechanism by which we have swept the poor out of sight is, paradoxically, our focus on the description of social status.

One of the major contributions of the current consensus has been a better understanding of the concept of status. One crucial insight from Wayne Meeks's landmark study, *The First Urban Christians*, is that social status is multidimensional: that is, social status is determined by several variables such

---

[17]For a more complete treatment of poverty in these churches, see Friesen, "Poverty in Pauline Studies."

[18]One trend in the interpretation of this text is to ignore the economic factors and concentrate on the history and meaning of the ritual (Hans Conzelmann, *1 Corinthians* [Hermeneia; Philadelphia: Fortress, 1975] 192–203). Another trend is to assume that wealthy members of the church were hosting this meal in their large atrium house, and that they assigned quantities and qualities of food according to social status (Theissen, *Social Setting*, 145–68; Richard B. Hays, *First Corinthians* [Louisville, Ky.: John Knox, 1997] 195–97; and Gordon D. Fee, *The First Epistle to the Corinthians* [NICNT; Grand Rapids, Mich.: Eerdmans, 1988] 531–34, 541–45). Meggitt (*Paul, Poverty and Survival*, 118–22) rightly notes, however, that there is no reference in the text to wealthy individuals nor to large houses.

[19]Hays (*First Corinthians*, 203) notes this irony.

as "ethnic origins, *ordo*, citizenship, personal liberty, wealth, occupation, age, sex, and public offices or honors."[20] We might also add other categories to this list: patron/client relationships, marital status, family lineage (noble or common), and socialization into elite protocol; but the exact content of the list is not crucial at this point. The important point is that Meeks turned the rather crude concept of "status" into a more complex set of features, which should allow us to describe the Pauline congregations with more nuance.

There is, however, a serious drawback to this schema: social status defined in this way is unmeasurable. Three impediments prevent a multidimensional understanding of social status from being a precise tool for measurement. First, there are too many dimensions for the concept to be accurate. Second, the dimensions have no defined relationships to each other, so there is no set pattern for evaluating them and arriving at someone's social status. Furthermore, we rarely know more than one of these things about anyone in the first-century churches, so conclusions tend to be inconclusive. To make matters even more difficult, when scholars address issues of wealth and poverty within this framework, the economic question almost always dissolves into a question of status.

Given these shortcomings, there are two things that specialists could have done but have not. First, specialists could have engaged in systematic discussion of the dimension of wealth. It is, after all, the most important component of social status.[21] A weakness in any other dimension of social status could be overcome by wealth within a couple of generations, but poverty would have precluded high social standing. Wealth was the crucial factor that allowed families and individuals to control government, society, and religion for their own ends. Second, specialists could have developed nuanced scales for describing levels of poverty and wealth.[22] Instead, most specialists use only two opposing terms—rich or poor—instead of employing a graduated series of terms to describe more accurately the situations of the vast majority of people in the Roman Empire.

---

[20]Meeks, *First Urban Christians*, 53–55.

[21]There is very little systematic discussion of poverty and wealth in the "new consensus" about Pauline congregations. There are brief descriptions of social status, extended discussions of social status, pyramid diagrams showing levels of social status, and arguments about social status. New Testament scholars, however, seem reluctant to discuss money. There are a few discussions of it, but I have yet to find a typology of categories of wealth, or a pyramid diagram illustrating the ratios of rich and poor in the communities.

[22]Stegemann and Stegemann (*Jesus Movement*, 7–95) came close to constructing such a scale, and it is a very valuable resource. Their scale, however, measures social stratification, with some categories defined in economic terms and other categories defined in terms of nobility or offices.

Let me illustrate these problems by returning to the Lord's Supper passage in 1 Corinthians 11:17–32 and giving examples of how it has been handled by Theissen and Meeks. Gerd Theissen discussed the passage in economic terms, but restricted himself to the polarized categories of rich and poor:

> It can be assumed that the conflict over the Lord's Supper is a conflict between poor and rich Christians. The cause of this conflict was a particular habit of the rich. They took part in the congregational meal which they themselves had made possible, but they did so by themselves—possibly physically separated from the others and at their own table.[23]

Within a few pages, however, the economic factors disappear into a discussion of social status. Notice how the following paragraph from Theissen's study starts out as a discussion of economic factors, but then mutates into a discussion of status. Poverty vanishes before our eyes:

> The core of the problem was that the *wealthier* Christians made it plain to all just how much the rest were dependent on them, dependent on the generosity of those who were better off. Differences in menu are a relatively timeless symbol of *status and wealth*, and those not so well off came face to face with their own *social inferiority* at a most basic level. It is made plain to them that they stand on the lower rungs of the *social ladder.*[24]

For another example of these problems, I turn to Wayne Meeks, who discussed 1 Corinthians 11 and focused on the phrase "those who do not have" in v. 22. Meeks wrote that "this verse makes it clear that the basic division is between the (relatively) rich and the (relatively) poor."[25] Here we see Meeks edging toward the realization that graduated categories of relative poverty and wealth are needed in order to describe the Corinthian assemblies. Just a few pages later, however, in the conclusion of the chapter, the poor disappear from Meeks's analysis. Speaking about the assemblies, he says the following:

> The extreme top and bottom of the Greco-Roman *social* scale are missing from the picture. It is hardly surprising that we meet no landed aristocrats, no senators, *equites*, nor (unless Erastus might qualify) decurions. But there is no specific evidence of people who are *destitute.* . . . There may well have been members of the Pauline communities who lived at the subsistence level, but we hear nothing of them.[26]

---

[23]Theissen, *Social Setting*, 151.
[24]Ibid., 160; emphasis added.
[25]Meeks, *First Urban Christians*, 68.
[26]Ibid., 73; emphasis added. Meeks's argument on pp. 68–73 is that these "Christians" in Corinth measured high in wealth but lower in other categories of status. This variance across

Here we see the same conceptual problem: are we discussing wealth or status? And once again, a social description of the Pauline assemblies allows us to ignore the poor saints. Within a few pages we go from recognizing people without food to denying that there is evidence for people living at the subsistence level.

There is a way out of this problem. We need to elaborate on what Meeks implied above: we need to start measuring gradations of the most important dimension: wealth (or more precisely, the lack thereof). But first, a proviso. I am not trying to reduce status to an economic consideration. I am simply pointing out that wealth is the most important component of status, and the one least likely to be addressed systematically by New Testament scholars. This topic—poverty and wealth in the Pauline congregations—occupies the final section of this essay.

POVERTY AND PAUL'S CHURCHES

I have developed a working model for describing poverty in the Roman Empire. It is based on recent descriptions of the imperial economy as preindustrial and agrarian.[27] In such a society, almost everyone lives near the level of subsistence, but there is a very small wealthy elite that controls commerce and politics. In between the masses and the elite there is no economic middle class, because a preindustrial society has so few economic mechanisms for gaining significant wealth. Some people do, however, manage to achieve moderate surplus income for various reasons, and these people occupy the large gap between the elite and the masses. Ramsay MacMullen summarized this kind of society as follows:

> We have at the top of Roman society a quite minute but extraordinarily prominent and rich nobility, itself split into a higher (senatorial) and a lower (equestrian) stratum; at the bottom, a large mass of the totally indigent, mostly free but partly slave; and strung out between the extremes a variety too heterogeneous to be called in any sense a middle class.[28]

---

the different categories of their status meant that such Christians possessed an ambiguous status overall; and this ambiguity led to tension between those Christians and mainstream society. He concludes that the leaders in Paul's assemblies tended to be such people with a high degree of inconsistency among the various dimensions of status.

[27]Tenney Frank, *Rome and Italy of the Empire* (Paterson, N.J.: Pageant Books, 1959); Richard Duncan-Jones, *The Economy of the Roman Empire: Quantitative Studies* (2d ed.; New York: Cambridge University Press, 1982); and M. I. Finley, *The Ancient Economy* (2d ed.; Berkeley: University of California Press, 1985).

[28]Ramsay MacMullen, *Roman Social Relations, 50 B.C. to A.D. 284* (New Haven, Conn.: Yale University Press, 1974) 93–94.

This general description is widely accepted and not particularly controversial. For our purposes, however, a refinement is desireable. MacMullen and most others tend to settle for a polar view of the ancient economy: rich and poor, plus a few marginal percentage points of the population in between. Since over 90% of the population of the empire was poor, we should define some gradations of poverty to allow greater precision. Ekkhard and Wolfgang Stegemann have called attention to ancient sources that note differences between a poor person who lived at the subsistence level (πένης) and one who lived below subsistence (πτωχός).[29] I have thus divided "poor" into three subcategories—"near subsistence level," "at subsistence level," and "below subsistence level"—which together include most of the population of the empire. Those near subsistence level include people who have a reasonable hope of providing their families a little more than the average caloric needs of human bodies; those at subsistence level occasionally slide below the average needs of human bodies; and those below subsistence level cannot regularly procure the amount of food necessary to sustain the body.

Thus I have constructed a seven-level "Poverty Scale" (PS):

PS 1	*Imperial Elite*	imperial dynasty, Roman senatorial families, some retainers, local royalty, some freedpersons
PS 2	*Regional or Provincial Elites*	equestrian families, provincial officials, some retainers, some decurial families, some freedpersons, some retired military officers
PS 3	*Municipal Elites*	most decurial families, wealthy men and women who do not hold office, some freedpersons, some retainers, some veterans, some merchants
PS 4	*Moderate Surplus Resources*	some merchants, some traders, some freedpersons, some artisans (especially those who employ others), military veterans
PS 5	*Near Subsistence Level*	many merchants and traders, regular wage earners, artisans, large shop owners, freedpersons, some farm families
PS 6	*At Subsistence Level*	small farm families, laborers (skilled and unskilled), artisans (especially those employed by others), wage earners, most merchants and traders, small shop/tavern owners
PS 7	*Below Subsistence Level*	some farm families, unattached widows, orphans, beggars, disabled persons, unskilled day laborers, prisoners

[29]*Jesus Movement*, 70–71.

In order to keep these categories in perspective, remember that the top three categories comprised about 1% of the empire's total population. The generally accepted figure for the population of the Roman Empire in the first century C.E. is between 50 and 60 million. Alföldy estimated that the elite made up less than one percent of the population: i.e., the no more than 200,000 adult males who were senators, equestrians, and local decurions, plus their wives and children.[30] Since Paul's assemblies were in large urban areas that had a slightly higher proportion of wealthy inhabitants, we need to adjust the percentages a bit for cities of 10,000 or more inhabitants. Figure 13.7 illustrates the approximate proportion of the empire's population residing at each level of the Poverty Scale:

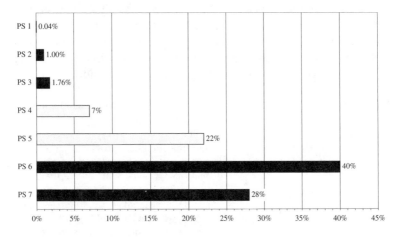

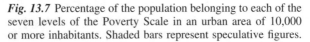

Fig. 13.7 Percentage of the population belonging to each of the seven levels of the Poverty Scale in an urban area of 10,000 or more inhabitants. Shaded bars represent speculative figures.

This sort of graduated measure of poverty (not "status") is exactly what has been missing from discussions of the social status of Pauline communities in recent years. Without such a graduated scale, the discussions are often confused, because modern interpreters are restricted to only two polarized categories: if someone in Paul's churches was not as poor as someone else, they must have been rich.

[30]Géza Alföldy, *The Social History of Rome* (2d ed.; Baltimore, Md.: Johns Hopkins University Press, 1988) 115–27, 147. MacMullen's figures (*Roman Social Relations*, 88–89) are similar. For a detailed explanation of the calculations, see Friesen, "Poverty in Pauline Studies," 340–47.

The Poverty Scale allows us to return to the embarrassing Lord's Supper of the Corinthian assembly and to construct a better scenario for the problems to which the text alludes. This essay is not the setting for a full exposition of the text. We can, however, make some progress on the focused question of the economic implications of the text. First, notice that no one is described as being rich. Paul's rhetorical question in 1 Cor 11:22 assumes that people in the congregation had places to live, but *oikia* does not imply a large home or even home ownership.[31] Paul simply assumes that homelessness was not an issue in the assembly. The only economic distinctions made are between those who have food for a meal and those who do not. In the Roman Empire, this does not indicate a schism between rich and poor. It is, rather, a schism between the poor (PS 5–6) and the very poor (PS 6–7). Or, to put it in terms of the economic model outlined earlier, it indicates that a significant number in the Corinthian assembly were living in subsistence poverty or desperate poverty, and that they were not being cared for by those not quite so impoverished (probably by those just above subsistence level or those with moderate surplus resources).

This interpretation is supported by economic information in Paul's letters. I have incorporated this graduated scale of poverty and wealth into the database, and it allows us to draw some conclusions about the Corinthian saints (fig. 13.8, p. 368).

(1) The majority of the saints in the Corinthian assemblies were poor. A broad search of Paul's undisputed letters produces references to seventy-three groups and seventy-two individuals.[32] When we remove those for which we have no indications of economic situation, we are left with references to ten individuals and eight groups.[33] These include two individuals who clearly have moderate disposable income (PS 4); five individuals who may have been at either level 4 or 5; and three individuals and eight groups who are clearly poor (PS 5–7). This is not a great deal of evidence, but the distribution suggests that we are dealing mostly with people living near the subsistence level. The fact that the references to groups tend to place them further down the economic scale implies that the general economic situation of saints was also lower on the scale. The only clear references to people above the level of poverty are to individuals (not to groups).

---

[31]Meggitt, *Paul, Poverty and Survival*, 120–21.

[32]Syria and Judea are omitted from this search.

[33]I also omit here the references to those who have food in 1 Cor 11:20–34, since this is too vague to be of use. It could refer to someone in any category except desperate poverty. Expanding the search to include the deuteropauline and Pastoral Epistles only adds two names to the list: Nympha (Col 4:15) and Onesiphorus (2 Tim 1:16–17), both of whom would probably be ranked at 4 or 5 on the Poverty Scale.

PS	Name	Location	Reference
4	(Chloe)	Corinth	1 Cor 1:11
4	Gaius	Corinth	Rom 16:23
4–5	Erastus	Corinth	Rom 16:23
4–5	Philemon	Colossae?	Phlm 4–22
4–5	Phoebe	Cenchreae, Rome	Rom 16:1–2
4–5	Aquila	Rome (or Ephesos?)	Rom 16:3–5
4–5	Prisca	Rome (or Ephesos?)	Rom 16:3–5
5	Chloe's people	Ephesos	1 Cor 1:11
5–6	Stephanas	Ephesos	1 Cor 16:17–18
5–6	The household of Stephanas	Corinth	1 Cor 16:15–16
5–6	(Many) saints	Corinth	1 Cor 16:1–2
5–6	Assemblies	Galatia	1 Cor 16:1–2
5–7	(Many) brothers (and sisters)	Thessalonica	1 Thes 4:11
6	(Many) saints	Corinth	2 Cor 8:12–15
6	Assemblies	Macedonia	2 Cor 8:1–6
6	Paul	Corinth	2 Cor 11:1–21
6	Paul	Thessalonica	1 Thes 2:1–12
6	Paul	Rome? Ephesos? Caesarea?	Phil 4:12–13
6–7	Onesimus	Ephesos? Rome?	Phlm 10–19
6–7	Those lacking food for the Lord's Supper	Corinth	1 Cor 11:22
7	Paul	Rome? Ephesos? Caesarea?	Phil 2:25–30

Fig. 13.8 Individuals and groups from the Pauline mission ranked according to the Poverty Scale (PS). Chloe is included even though it is not certain that she was a participant in the assemblies.

(2) It appears that some of the resident leaders in the Pauline churches had moderate disposable income, and hence were probably somewhat above average in status as well. Some leaders were poor, however, as was Paul himself.

(3) There is no clear evidence from Paul's letters that any of the members of Paul's assemblies were rich. The two possible exceptions are Phoebe and Erastus. From what we know of the general economy, however, the odds are greatly against this. If approximately 97% of an urban population did not belong to the wealthy elite, then we should assume that Phoebe and Erastus were not rich unless very strong evidence to the contrary can be produced. In the case of Phoebe, there is clearly not enough evidence. In Rom 16:1–2 she is

described as a leader (προστάτις) in the Cenchraea assembly and a patron of Paul and many in the church. This only places her at level 4 or 5.[34] Nor is it responsible to assume that Erastus (Rom 16:23) was a member of the municipal elite. As Meggitt and others have pointed out, οἰκονόμος τῆς πόλεως ("city steward") was probably not a municipal office.[35] Furthermore, there is at least one inscription from Thessalonica that uses this same Greek title for a poor city slave.[36] The inscription from Corinth that mentions an aedile named Erastus has probably influenced the modern discussion too greatly. The inscription itself is fragmentary and it has no clear connection to the Erastus of Romans 16 except the fragmentary name.[37]

(4) While most of the evidence comes from Corinth, it is probably representative for other Pauline assemblies as well for two reasons: it matches the scattered evidence from Thessalonica, Ephesos, and perhaps Colossae; and it fits our general knowledge of poverty in the Roman Empire.

CONCLUSIONS

What then can we say about the prospects for a demographic description of the Pauline assemblies? Several things:

(1) Arguments about the social standing of the Pauline congregations have not taken account of the fact that our evidence is almost exclusively from Corinth, with another significant body of evidence coming either from Rome or from Ephesos.

(2) The problem of the narrow range of data has been compounded by another problem: a lack of attention to poverty and wealth in the Roman world. Rather than focusing solely on the social status of the churches, we need to pay attention to levels of poverty and wealth.

(3) The best current economic model for Roman imperial society is that most people in the empire were poor, that about 3% of an urban population was rich, and that there was no economic middle class.

---

[34]Paul would not have written a letter of commendation for Chloe if she were a member of the wealthy elite, for her social standing would have been much higher than his (Meggitt, *Paul, Poverty and Survival*, 148).

[35]Ibid., 135–41. Theissen (*Social Setting*, 75–83) has a long discussion showing that the evidence is inconclusive, and then inexplicably concludes that there is no reason not to think that Erastus was indeed part of the municipal elite.

[36]*ArchDelt* 35 (1980) B369. The slave Longinus had a small inscription made for the grave of his wife Artemidora. He was not a Roman citizen.

[37]Meggitt (*Paul, Poverty and Survival*, 140–41) points out that the inscription could refer to someone named [Ep]erastus.

(4) Viewed from this perspective, Paul's congregations were probably composed mostly of individuals living near, at, or below subsistence level. Leadership within the congregations seems to have come mostly from the families of those living near subsistence level and those with moderate surplus resources.

(5) There are no convincing arguments to suggest that Paul's congregations contained any members from the wealthy 1% of the empire's population.

CHAPTER FOURTEEN

Paul's Assembly in Corinth: An Alternative Society

Richard A. Horsley

Much of what we are doing in New Testament studies these days involves rethinking not simply our fundamental assumptions and categories, but the very paradigm by which we identify issues and formulate solutions. We inherited from the Enlightenment a separation of religion from political and economic life. Then the nineteenth-century founding fathers of the field, such as Ferdinand Christian Baur, constructed the paradigmatic scheme of how a universalistic and spiritual religion, Christianity, developed and broke away from the particularistic, parochial, and overly political religion of Judaism. We now recognize the latter model as an anti-Semitic carica-ture with tragic historical consequences. Yet the paradigm of one religion, Christianity, emerging from another, Judaism, and that paradigm's attendant assumptions and concepts, persists, particularly in theologically influenced interpretations of Paul.

In attempting to re-examine and rethink how to understand Paul's mission, in particular his mission in Corinth in the early 50s C.E., I am struggling to find an alternative to the residual conceptual apparatus of this previously dominant paradigm of emergent "Christianity." This essay is merely one meditative moment in a much broader project. After some critical reflection on how the Pauline mission does not seem comprehensible in terms still current in the field, I will explore some alternative lines of historical analysis that lead to a reconstruction of Paul's mission as an attempt to catalyze the formation of an alternative society over against the Roman imperial order. The focus will be on Paul's mission in Corinth, and particularly on 1 Corinthians, the letter most frequently used in recent constructions of "Pauline Christianity" and "the first urban Christians."

A consistent rhetorical approach to Paul's letters (and other ancient literary sources) is crucial to the search for an alternative to the problematic older conceptual apparatus. The old, theologically determined approach tended to read Paul's letters as collections of theological statements and/or information available on the surface of the text. Paul's letters, however, consist of (sequences of) arguments intended to persuade groups of people, some of whom disagreed with Paul's viewpoint. Learning from the recent revival of rhetorical criticism, not only can we take into account the particular rhetorical situation (and historical situation) of each letter, but we can also be more sensitive to the subtleties and nuances, even the ironies and innuendos, of Paul's arguments.[1] In the limited compass of a single essay, it is not possible to deal explicitly with the overall argument of each of Paul's letters, so I will rely on my own and others' more focused explorations of particular arguments in particular letters.[2]

Paul Was Not a Christian

Among other critics of the received paradigm and its central concepts, Dieter Georgi has argued that what he calls "the early church" was "a Jewish migration," not a new religion.[3] He insists that the terms "Christian" and "Christianity" are historically inappropriate in reference to the first few generations of the followers of or believers in Jesus (Christ). The terms do not appear at all in the earliest documents from Jesus movements. Luke says that "in Antioch Jesus' followers were first called 'Christians'" (Acts 11:26), yet does not say when, and he later puts the term in the mouth of King

[1] See especially Elisabeth Schüssler Fiorenza, "Rhetorical Situation and Historical Reconstruction in 1 Corinthians," *NTS* 33 (1987) 386–403; Antoinette C. Wire, *The Corinthian Women Prophets* (Minneapolis: Fortress, 1990); Margaret M. Mitchell, *Paul and the Rhetoric of Reconciliation: An Exegetical Investigation of the Language and Composition of 1 Corinthians* (1991; Louisville, Ky.: Westminster/John Knox, 1993); and Richard A. Horsley, "Rhetoric and Empire—and 1 Corinthians," in *Paul and Politics: Ekklesia, Israel, Imperium, Interpretation* (Harrisburg, Pa.: Trinity Press International, 2000).

[2] On 1 Corinthians, see Richard A. Horsley, *1 Corinthians* (Abingdon New Testament Commentaries; Nashville, Tenn.: Abingdon, 1998).

[3] Dieter Georgi, "The Early Church: Internal Jewish Migration or New Religion?," *HTR* 88 (1995) 35–68.

Agrippa II (Acts 26:28). Yet neither in the latter passage nor in 1 Pet 4:16 or *Did.* 12:4 does the term "Christian" denote "membership in a certain religious community, and even less in a separate religion."[4] In the letters of Ignatius, however, the term appears more frequently, and Tacitus (*Ann.* 15:44), Pliny (*Ep.* 10.96–97), and Suetonius (*Nero* 16.2) also use the term. Thus, "Christian" appears at first only in documents associated with the areas of Rome and Asia Minor between 90–120 C.E., some sixty to ninety years after Jesus' ministry and crucifixion.

Most important for the purposes of this essay, Paul himself does not have a concept of "Christians" as separate from Israel or of "Christianity" as a separate religion. It is therefore utterly anachronistic and unhistorical for us to continue to use the terms "Christianity" or "Pauline Christianity" in discussions of Paul, his mission, and the *ekklēsiai* that he helped catalyze. Nor does Paul have a concept of "religion," much less "a religion," that he is supposedly propagating. That is a modern anachronism. Paul's mission and the communities he helped catalyze in cities of the eastern Roman Empire may have led historically toward the development of a religion that became known as "Christianity," just as English colonization of the Atlantic seaboard in North America preceded the breakaway of those colonies from the English king and the formation of the United States as a federal republic. But just as we cannot intelligibly speak of the Jamestown or Plymouth or Massachusetts Bay colonies as parts of United States history proper, so we cannot, with historical intelligibility, speak of Christianity in Paul's lifetime. While many may continue to speak of such a thing, given the inertia of the academic world, "Pauline Christianity" is a religious and theological projection. There never was such a historical entity! We have yet to construct a conceptual apparatus by which to comprehend the Pauline mission in its historical context and in historically appropriate terms.

Yet another compelling reason that we cannot continue to think in terms of Pauline Christianity as if it consisted of cohesive "churches" and a coherent "symbol system" or "theology" or "social world" is the ad hoc rhetorical character of Paul's letters. In these letters Paul is attempting to persuade particular groups of people whom he has previously taught to take particular views or actions different from those they are evidently inclined to take. Judging from the Corinthian correspondence in particular, from which scholars derive so much of their picture of "Pauline Christianity," Paul's attempts at persuasion were not particularly successful. Therefore, our primary sources,

---

[4]Ibid., 39.

Paul's letters, provide only one side of a multifaceted discussion or struggle in a movement that had yet to develop much coherence, even in particular localities. We know what Paul wanted his readers to think and do, but have only glimpses of their views and actions, which often were not to Paul's liking. What we can investigate and critically reconstruct is Paul's view of his mission and how he would like the *ekklēsiai* to think and act.

Not only is "Christianity" a misleading anachronism when it comes to understanding Paul and his mission and his community in Corinth, but so also is "Judaism." There was simply no religion called "Judaism" at the time. Paul, like the community that produced the Dead Sea Scrolls before him and like the rabbis after him, understood himself as belonging to the people of Israel. At the time of Paul, Israel was a people subjected to imperial rule. A million or so individuals still resided in the village communities of the historical homeland of Palestine, mostly under the Jerusalem temple-state that had been established and perpetuated as an instrument of Persian, Ptolemaic, Seleucid, and finally Roman imperial rule; many more were dispersed among various cities of the Roman and Parthian empires and living in various degrees of acculturation or assimilation to the dominant culture. What came to be known as "rabbinic Judaism," which is often projected back into the time of Jesus and Paul, developed only gradually, many centuries after Paul. Prior to and contemporary with Paul there were various "Jewish" movements and writings in Palestine and various communities and writings from the diaspora.

One of the principal ways in which both "Christianity" and "Judaism" are misleading concepts that block rather than facilitate historical understanding is that they are understood as religions, with all the peculiar modern Western connotations of religion as separate from political and economic life. Even though leading scholars in the field of New Testament studies are striving mightily to move past the previous anti-Semitic construction of Judaism as a decadent parochial religion obsessed with the Law, they still construct Judaism as a monolithic religion.[5] Even though leading scholars have discovered the social world, along with the social sciences that can be utilized to understand it, and recognize that Paul's letters were not theological treatises, they still construct Pauline Christianity as if it were an already existing definable religion.[6] And apparently because religion in the modern West is separate from political and economic affairs—indeed, more or less subject to

[5]E.g., E. P. Sanders, *Judaism: Practice and Belief, 63 BCE–66 CE* (Philadelphia: Trinity Press International, 1992).

[6]E.g., Wayne A. Meeks, *The First Urban Christians: The Social World of the Apostle Paul* (New Haven, Conn.: Yale University Press, 1983).

an agreement not to conflict with political and economic affairs—scholarly constructions often simply ignore (or avoid) implications in the sources of engagement with political-economic affairs, particularly any implications of conflict with the dominant political-economic order.

Projection of "Judaism" and "Christianity" onto the circumstances and processes of the Pauline mission obscures several aspects of historical reality. One such aspect is the instrumental role of religious practices such as rituals and symbols, and even architecture and public festivals, not just in legitimating political-economic power, but in constituting political-economic power relations in Greek and Roman cities. From the side of classicists, who never seemed to take religion seriously, have recently come some significant compelling arguments that not only should our concept of religion be expanded to include artistic, architectural, and numismatic representations in public space, but also that, contrary to the modern assumptions that we project onto antiquity, power can work through religious institutions and representations.[7] What held the empire together in the cities of the Pauline mission, such as Corinth and Ephesos, was not standing armies, which were absent, or an imperial bureaucracy, which was minimal, but the imperial religion expressed in temples, shrines, statues, inscriptions, and games.

Another important aspect of ancient reality that has been obscured by projecting onto the time of Paul the notion of "Judaism" and "Christianity" as religions is that diaspora Jewish communities and assemblies of Christ-believers possessed many more dimensions than merely the religious. Decrees by Roman officials concerning ethnic communities of Judeans living in Greek cities cited by Josephus provide significant illustrations. A decree concerning the *Ioudaioi* in Delos guarantees their practices of assembling together and holding common meals in accordance with their ancestral customs and ordinances (*Ant.* 14.213–16), and these practices could conceivably be encompassed within the modern concept of religion. But the treatment of these "Judeans" in Delos as different from the *thiasoi* or "voluntary associations" (as the term is misleadingly translated) which were forbidden to assemble, would not appear to be explainable merely by Roman political favoritism, partly because similar arrangements were made in other cities. In some of those other arrangements, as in the province of Asia, the *Ioudaioi* were

[7]See especially Simon R. F. Price, *Rituals and Power: The Roman Imperial Cult in Asia Minor* (Cambridge: Cambridge University Press, 1984); and Paul Zanker, *The Power of Images in the Age of Augustus* (Ann Arbor, Mich.: University of Michigan, 1988); excerpts from both are reproduced in Richard A. Horsley, ed., *Paul and Empire: Religion and Power in Roman Imperial Society* (Harrisburg, Pa.: Trinity Press International, 1997) 47–71, 72–86.

exempted from military service and permitted to carry on their lives according to their ancestral customs (*Ant.* 14.223–27). Most telling is the decree to the magistrates, council, and citizenry of Sardis:

> Our Judean citizens (Ἰουδαῖοι πολῖται ἡμέτεροι) pointed out that from the earliest times they have had an association of their own (σύνοδον . . . ἰδίαν) in accordance with their ancestral laws and a place of their own, in which they decide their affairs and disputes with on another; and [they are permitted] to do so. (*Ant.* 14.235)

The Judeans resident in Sardis, at least, and probably those in other cities as well, were clearly more than religious communities. They were, rather, semi-independent ethnic communities that ran their own affairs according to ancestral Israelite traditions rather than according to the laws of particular cities.[8] This appears to be the long-standing arrangement that the huge Jewish population in Alexandria had enjoyed for generations, the alteration of which Philo protests in his appeal to the emperor Gaius. Insofar as Saul/Paul grew up in just such a (semi-)self-governing Judean community conducting its own affairs according to ancestral customs, he may have derived from that experience some of his sense of how the communities he catalyzed might operate in the cities of the Roman empire.

Yet another and closely related aspect of ancient multiethnic and multicultural life in the cities of the Roman empire that may be blocked from view by the modern concept of a religion called "Christianity" is that those ethnic communities may well have stood at least in tension with, and perhaps even in resistance to, the dominant religious-political (and economic) order. The field of New Testament studies is heavily influenced by Lutheran theology, in which the "two kingdoms" do not interact; this separation of the kingdoms has operated primarily in modern Western societies where the separation of church and state is simply assumed. In ancient Judea, however, the activist Pharisees and other teachers who headed the "Fourth Philosophy" resistance in 6 C.E. were adamant that they could not possibly "render to Caesar" the tribute he demanded since they had God as their exclusive lord and master. And that enables us to understand Jesus' cagey statement regarding the tribute to Rome in its ancient religious-political-economic context rather than in its Christian theological sense: according to the ancestral Israelite laws presupposed by Jesus and other Galilean and Judean peasants, the category of "the things that are God's" includes everything, and Caesar had no legitimate claim at

---

[8]A. Thomas Kraabel, "Unity and Diversity among Diaspora Synagogues," in *The Synagogue in Late Antiquity* (ed. Lee I. Levine; Philadelphia: ASOR, 1987) 51–55.

all. Judeans and Galileans, of course, engaged in repeated rebellions against Roman rule in Palestine. Judean communities resident in Greek-speaking cities of the Roman Empire may have been acculturated or even assimilated in varying degrees to the dominant imperial order. Yet they may also have engaged in various modes of resistance to that order, at least insofar as they attempted to cultivate ancestral customs and laws.

THE LIMITATIONS OF "SOCIAL WORLD" STUDIES

Although they have not challenged the dominant paradigm governing questions and solutions, leading scholars in the field have nevertheless taken some significant steps to broaden the approach to Paul's letters by supplementing theological interpretation with sociological analysis. By borrowing primarily from functionalist sociology, however, they merely reinforce the dominant, and historically inappropriate, conceptualizations of the field. That is, by applying functionalist sociology, which was developed to explain the coherence of large modern social systems, to "Pauline Christianity" as if it were an already-developed social (sub-)system, influential scholarly pioneers such as Gerd Theissen and Wayne Meeks further reify an unhistorical construct and exclude almost by definition any consideration of historical political-religious conflict.[9] The "new consensus" on the social status of early/"Pauline" "Christians" as representing more or less a "cross section" of Roman imperial society (except for the very top and the utterly destitute), based largely on Theissen's analysis of (misread) social clues in 1 Corinthians, is yet another set of assumptions from modern Western society projected onto Paul's letters.[10] Attempts to describe the "social structure" of the "Christian" congregations by comparison with other "groups and organizations of the Greco-Roman city to which they bear a family resemblance" turn out in fact to beg the question all the more urgently. In a synthetic sociological study that has become a touchstone in the field, Meeks has explored four kinds of groups as "models": households, voluntary associations, synagogues, and philosophical schools. Putative correspondences between these four kinds of

---

[9]Gerd Theissen, *The Social Setting of Pauline Christianity: Essays on Corinth* (Philadelphia: Fortress, 1982); and Meeks, *First Urban Christians*.

[10]See further Steven J. Friesen's essay in this volume (pp. 351–70); Justin Meggitt, *Paul, Poverty and Survival* (Edinburgh: T&T Clark, 1998); and the exchange between Meggitt and Dale B. Martin in *JSNT* 84 (2001) 51–64, 85–94.

groups and Paul's groups are matched or outnumbered by differences between the other Greco-Roman organizations and Paul's groups.

References in 1 Corinthians and other letters indicate that "the whole assembly (*ekklēsia*)" (1 Cor 14:23; compare 11:20) was comprised not just of individuals, but also of subunits of ("assemblies" at) particular "households" (1 Cor 1:16; Rom 16:23). Households provided the meeting places for his nascent communities. But Paul is adamant that his assemblies not be reduced to or dominated by (particular) households.

Meeks finds "some important similarities" between the Pauline groups and voluntary associations, which upon closer inspection turn out to be points of difference rather than similarities.[11] That both were "small groups" is hardly a distinctive similarity.

That membership in both was "by the free decision to associate rather than by birth" he immediately qualifies for "the associations" by adding such factors such as ethnic connection and "profession"; and it appears that whole households joined the Pauline *ekklēsiai*. Do we really know, beyond Paul's association with Prisca and Aquila, how important "common trade and craft" was in the Pauline *ekklēsiai*? "Both had a more or less important place for rituals and cultic activities, and also engaged in common meals," writes Meeks. But Paul's letters and Acts give virtually no importance to rituals like those of the associations, and the Lord's Supper is hardly a common meal that in any significant way resembles those of the *thiasoi*. It is not at all clear that the Pauline communities "depended on the beneficence of wealthier persons who acted as patrons," as did many *thiasoi/collegia*. Meeks himself is quick to point out that the Pauline congregations did not reward patrons with honorific titles and inscriptions. Yet he argues that *collegia* practiced democratic internal governance in ways similar to the Pauline communities, something hard to square with Paul's portrayal of charismatic leadership, particularly in 1 Corinthians 12 and 14.

Meeks also finds "important differences" between Pauline communities and "voluntary associations."[12] The former were "exclusive and totalistic,"

---

[11]All quotations in this and the following paragraphs are from Meeks, *First Urban Christians*, 78.

[12]Ibid., 78–79. But the "extraordinarily thoroughgoing resocialization" he sees involved in being "baptized into Christ Jesus" is hardly the picture one would derive from the Corinthian correspondence! See the full discussion of socialization, etc., in Peter L. Berger and Thomas Luckmann, *The Social Construction of Reality* (Garden City, N.Y.: Doubleday, 1966) 129–63. Resocialization could hardly have been accomplished by a few outsiders resident among a few dozen Corinthians for eighteen months. Given the diversity of views and disagreements evident in 1 Corinthians, the Corinthians would appear to have undergone no more than a "secondary socialization" in the missions of Paul and others among them.

in dramatic contrast with clubs and cultic associations. He also claims that Pauline communities were "more inclusive in terms of social stratification" than the socially homogeneous "voluntary associations," which seems overstated, because of his estimate of the range of social status involved in the former. A more recent analysis of the associations concludes that the majority "were composed of the urban poor, slaves, and freedmen."[13] In a more significant difference, whereas most clubs were exclusively male, and a few were exclusively female,[14] the Pauline communities included both men and women, as well as slave and free. Often the associations and their practices (primarily social, such as drinking), were sponsored by highly placed and wealthy patrons whom the association, in return, would honor with inscriptions, statues, and honorific titles. Moreover, members could achieve within the tiny circle of their associations some of the same honorific titles that were confined to the city elite under the Roman imperial order. By contrast, the assemblies Paul was catalyzing had no such wealthy patrons; the economic and social status of figures such as Gaius and Stephanas in Pauline communities has been exaggerated in recent studies. And judging from 1 Corinthians, Paul was adamantly opposed to relations among members of his *ekklēsiai* that resembled patronage and special honors.[15] Particularly striking is the "almost complete absence of common terminology" from the surviving descriptions of the Pauline communities and the "voluntary associations" noted by Meeks. And surely of great significance were the "extra-local linkages" of the Pauline movement, which could be more appropriately described as interethnic or international.[16]

Certainly the most telling contrast, one particularly significant for my attempt at a more comprehensive analysis of the relation of Paul's mission

---

[13]John S. Kloppenborg, "Collegia and Thiasoi: Issues in Function, Taxonomy, and Membership," in *Voluntary Associations in the Graeco-Roman World* (ed. idem and Stephen G. Wilson; London: Routledge, 1996) 23.

[14]Ibid., 25.

[15]Horsley, *1 Corinthians*; and Richard A. Horsley, "1 Corinthians: A Case Study of Paul's Assembly as an Alternative Society," in Horsley, ed., *Paul and Empire*, 249–51. Patronage relations in the Corinthian assembly are somewhat exaggerated in Jon K. Chow, *Patronage and Power* (Sheffield: Sheffield Academic Press, 1992), excerpted in *Paul and Empire*, 104–25.

[16]In elaborating the many significant ways in which *thiasoi* and *collegia* simply do not directly illuminate the Pauline communities, much less provide the pattern into which they fit, we might add to Meeks's list of differences one more: that Paul's *ekklēsiai* lacked the formal organization and set of rules that characterized the "voluntary associations." See Stephen G. Wilson, "Voluntary Associations: An Overview," in *Voluntary Associations in the Graeco-Roman World* (ed. John S. Kloppenborg and idem; London: Routledge, 1996) 9. Wayne O. McReady's position ("*Ekklesia* and Voluntary Associations," in ibid., 59–73) is merely a less critical derivative of Meeks's.

to the broader Roman imperial order, comes from Stanley Stowers's reflections on "Pauline Christianity." He points out that scholars who argue that Greek and Roman "voluntary associations" organized by common trade or household or a particular deity provide illuminating comparisons for "Pauline Christianity" often neglect the practices most central to these groups and their connection to the whole broader political-religious context of the particular cities in which they functioned.[17] In the most fundamental sense, the modern concept that a person exercises choice in joining a religious group such as a voluntary association is simply not applicable to the institutions of ancient Greek and Roman religion, including *thiasoi* and *collegia*. For the god(dess) of a particular "association" (e.g., Athena of the woolworkers) was one that (already) belonged to the familiar family of the gods, even if that deity was an ostensibly foreign figure such as Isis, who had been incorporated into the religious networks of many cities. In Greek and Roman practice, "the basic unit of the religion was not the cult of a particular god, but primarily the gods and rites of a particular city" or ethnic group. "Reciprocity with the gods was embedded in the practical skills for coping with life that were evoked by the situations and contexts that these ancient polytheists encountered."[18] Of course the *thiasoi* and *collegia* were local (and not interpolitical or international, as was the series of *ekklēsiai* catalyzed by Paul), since the deities concerned (and/or their patrons) were integral parts of the local religious universe. "A host of ritual practices helped to construct Greek ethnicity, including patterns of intergenerational continuity, and wove religion into areas that moderns cordon off as economic, political, and social."

Stowers has recently reflected on another of Meeks's models, comparing "Pauline Christianity" to Greek philosophical schools, finding the comparison more telling than did Meeks.[19] It is not clear, however, that their points of comparison, other than the "radical social formation," are central features of Paul's stated concerns about his *ekklēsiai*. Most of the points of similarity Stowers identifies seem to emphasize the individual self and intellectual practices far more than Paul does. Indeed, in 1 Corinthians Paul sharply criticizes "the notion of the wise man" in his transcendent enlightenment, which appears to have been central to the alternative "gospel" that Apollos taught among Corinthians in Paul's absence.[20]

---

[17]Stanley K. Stowers, "Does Pauline Christianity Resemble a Hellenistic Philosophy?," in *Paul Beyond the Judaism/Hellenism Divide* (Louisville, Ky.: Westminster/John Knox, 2001) 87.

[18]This and the following quotation are from ibid., 88.

[19]Meeks, *First Urban Christians*, 81–84; and Stowers, "Pauline Christianity," 89–95.

[20]Horsley, *1 Corinthians*, 43–65.

Meeks found that the diaspora synagogue was "the nearest . . . model" for "the urban Christian groups"—perhaps because Paul himself had been influenced by such a Judean ethnic assembly in Tarsus. Meeks wrote twenty years ago, and his picture of what went on in Judean ethnic assemblies requires some updating in light of recent research; his points of similarity and difference between Judean and Christian assemblies need to be revised.[21] Yet Paul's expectations for his *ekklēsiai* differ from the ethos of typical Greek and Roman groups in ways that seem to be dependent on the model of the diaspora synagogue. Nevertheless, Meeks finds little evidence of Pauline "imitation of the specific organization of the synagogue."[22]

Critical review of these "models" thus suggests that they offer far less by way of "significant analogies" than Meeks thought. Indeed, this review suggests far more strongly than Meeks did that we must look for the distinctive features of the *ekklēsiai* that Paul advocated within his letters themselves, which were designed to foster the commitment and solidarity of his communities.

Broadening the Approach

Those who attempt to understand Hellenistic Jewish *synagōgai* and post-Pauline *ekklēsiai* as primarily religious communities do have a point, insofar as they call attention to the direction of later historical development. In order to appreciate the religious aspects, however, we must consider the broader Roman imperial context and the effects of imperial power on subject peoples. The cultural expressions on which New Testament scholars usually (but not always) focus come from people subject to the Roman Empire. Jews (such as Paul's parents and his coworkers Priscilla and Aquila) were in the diaspora because imperial practice or its effects had displaced them. Judea was ruled by Herod and the high priests because the Romans, after conquering the area, placed and retained them in positions of power and privilege.

Historically, subject peoples became the sources of and often the producers of cultural phenomena that could be called religion—that is, those phenomena were no longer embedded in and articulated with the political-economic aspects of those peoples. Egyptian cultural material was extracted from its

[21]E.g., Stowers, "Pauline Christianity"; and Margaret Williams, *The Jews among the Greeks and Romans: A Diasporan Sourcebook* (Baltimore, Md.: Johns Hopkins University Press, 1998).

[22]Meeks, *First Urban Christians*, 81.

context and used in the development of the Isis mysteries, which no longer had much to do with the flooding of the Nile and the growth of crops along its banks or the political economy of hierarchical Egyptian society headed by the pharaoh. In the *Wisdom of Solomon* and Philo's treatises, Jewish intellectuals still cultivated the cultural heritage of the Torah, now circulated in Greek translation as the Law. They understood the exodus, which had originally been the story of Israel's origins in an escape from foreign rule in Egypt, as the story of the soul's escape from the burdensome body into immortality, while the water from the rock and the manna provided in the wilderness became symbols of the ethereal Wisdom that affords immortality to the soul. That was indeed a religion of individual salvation. Insofar as the imperial order denied political participation and expression to subject peoples, particularly people in the cities, their cultural expressions came to resemble what modern Westerners understand as religion: beliefs, rituals, and "voluntary associations" separated from political-economic life, and thus without political-economic implications that would be disruptive to the dominant imperial order.

By no means, however, were all cultural contents of subject peoples "liberated" from their social embeddedness. Indeed, some cultural contents were grounded in and helped fuel cultural and political resistance to Roman imperial control. In Second Temple Judea, scribal circles such as the *maśkîlîm* who contributed to the book of Daniel still believed that their god was in control of international affairs and the course of history, despite the successful Seleucid imperial suppression of Judean resistance in which some of their members were killed. Given the overwhelming power of the imperial armies, these authors of the apocalyptic visions in Daniel 7–12 simply had to defer God's ultimate assertion of control of history to the future. But because they were able to project God's rule into the future and to act on the conviction that it was certain and imminent, the *maśkîlîm* and others were able both to hold their society together in loyalty to their traditional way of life and to resist imperial attempts at suppression, in a sequence of events leading to the Maccabean Revolt.[23] Diaspora Jewish communities such as the

---

[23]For a solid, basic treatment of the book of Daniel and its historical circumstances and implications, see John J. Collins, *The Apocalyptic Imagination* (New York: Crossroad, 1984) ch. 3. For an attempt to further discern the "earthly circumstances" of the "apocalyptic imagination" in Judean apocalyptic literature, see Richard A. Horsley, "The Kingdom of God and the Renewal of Israel," in *The Origins of Apocalypticism in Judaism and Christianity* (ed. John J. Collins; vol. 1 of *The Encyclopedia of Apocalypticism*; New York: Continuum, 2000), esp. 304–9.

one in Alexandria also cultivated their ancestral laws, which for the literate elite had become embodied in the Septuagint; this cultivation of traditions was one of the principal factors that enabled them to sustain their identity as a people different from the dominant imperial society.

PAUL'S UNDERSTANDING OF HIS MISSION AND ASSEMBLIES

Paul comes from just this background. Not only was he from a diaspora community, but he spent apparently formative time in Jerusalem associating with scribal circles (Phil 3:5; compare Gal 1:13–14). Although we have no detailed knowledge of what Saul/Paul himself was doing in Jerusalem in his earlier years, we do have a general sense of imperial power relations and of the particular political-religious manner in which Judean scribal circles were responding. A comparison with the response of Greek cities to Roman imperial power is instructive. As Price points out, the dominant elite of the Greek cities, who were also subjected by Rome, responded to the new imperial power that, more than any other, was determining their lives by including honors to and celebrations of the emperor within their traditional civil religion: installing statues of the emperor in temples of other gods, erecting shrines to the emperor, and constructing temples to the emperor at prominent places in public space.[24] They incorporated the presence of the emperor into traditional civic life. By contrast, although Herod also erected temples and huge statues to Caesar in Caesarea and Sebaste, and dared moreover to erect a golden Roman eagle over the gate of the temple, and although the priests sacrificed in the temple on behalf of (not to) Roma and Caesar, Judean scribal and scholarly circles rejected the imperial power as a threat to their exclusive loyalty to the god of Israel.[25] When Herod lay dying in 4 B.C.E., some scholars instructed their students to cut down the Roman eagle from over the temple gate (Josephus, *B.J.* 1.648–55; *Ant.* 17.149–67). At the imposition of direct Roman rule ten years later, some of the more radical teachers and Pharisees organized a refusal to render up the tribute as tantamount to the service of a lord and master other than their true lord and master, God (*Ant.* 18.4–10, 23–24). And early in Paul's career as a newly commissioned apostle of Jesus Christ, Judea and Galilee came perilously close to general revolt when Gaius

---

[24]Price, *Rituals and Power.*

[25]I have analyzed and discussed the following movements in a variety of publications, including *Jesus and the Spiral of Violence* (San Francisco: Harper & Row, 1987) 61–89, 110–16.

attempted to place his statue in the temple (*Ant.* 18.261–84). To take just those few illustrations, it is clear that many Judeans could not easily adjust to their subjection to Roman rule. The Judean atmosphere of movements of renewal and resistance seems to have been compelling also to diaspora Jews who had come to Jerusalem, apparently on pilgrimage. A number of Jews from diaspora communities, such as Stephen and Philip, quickly joined and even became key leaders in the movement focused on Jesus that was centered in Jerusalem (Acts 6).

I suspect that well before Paul received his commission for the mission to the peoples in an *apokalypsis* of Christ, he had already acquired a perspective on history similar to that which we see in the book of Daniel and which motivated scribal circles in Jerusalem. By the time he wrote his letters, relatively late in his mission, he had clearly reflected a great deal on the gospel he had received in that *apokalypsis*: God was bringing history to fulfillment in the crucifixion-resurrection and parousia of Christ.[26] We can see best perhaps in his argument in Galatians 3–4 how Paul thought about the world situation. History ultimately was moving not through Rome, but through Israel. Despite the Romans being currently in control, God had already set in motion the fulfillment of the promise to Abraham, whereby all peoples would receive blessings through Abraham's seed. In the crucifixion and resurrection of Jesus Christ, who was thus revealed as Abraham's seed, God had brought about the fulfillment of the promise to Abraham. Now, therefore, all other peoples, in addition to Israel, could inherit the promised blessings. In his *apokalypsis*

---

[26]The broad historical sweep of Paul's gospel and its religious-political implications for the imperial order in which he was situated are often ignored and obscured in the standard Christian theological approach that focuses on the ostensible breakthrough to a new religion. This is vividly illustrated by Meeks's synthesis of standard Pauline theology and functionalist sociology. His last chapter, on "Patterns of Belief," is focused in terms of what became the key points of the Christian creed, "One God, One Lord, One Body." "Apocalyptic" is reduced to "language" that has "functions" only within "the Pauline groups" (*First Urban Christians*, 171–72). Analysis remains strictly on an abstract cultural level, with no mention of the concrete experience of the Judeans and other peoples under Roman imperial rule. The Pauline "Christians" face a vaguely described "new situation" where "their symbolic universe no longer makes sense," so that they respond to a "millennial myth" (ibid., 173). Left unmentioned in the marshaling of comparative social scientific theory and concepts is that the anthropological studies referred to deal with movements among peoples undergoing the impact of Western European imperial conquest and takeover. Typical of theologically-oriented late-twentieth-century scholars who are uncomfortable with apocalyptic, Meeks apparently cannot discern that Judean apocalyptic thinking was focused explicitly on attempting to understand and envision an end to alien imperial rule. Accordingly, toward the end of the chapter, he insists that "there is no hint anywhere that Roman imperialism is a cause of the evil state of the present age" (ibid., 189).

of Christ, Paul had been commissioned as the apostle to bring this gospel to the (other) peoples. And, for all his talk of preaching, Paul understood his mission in terms of establishing "assemblies" (*ekklēsiai*) among the peoples. In many ways, the most driving concern evident in his letters is to keep those assemblies he established intact until the coming of the Lord.

In 1 Corinthians, Paul's whole argument (or sequence of arguments) is both framed by and peppered with his focus on God's fulfillment of history in the Christ-events of crucifixion, resurrection, and parousia or "day of the Lord."[27] In these arguments he presupposes and articulates a Judean apocalyptic perspective. In the opening of the first long argument, 1 Corinthians 1–4, Paul insists that the crucifixion of Christ has become the turning point of the ages, from "this age" to the next, according to God's *mystērion*, his plan for the fulfillment of history (1:20; 2:6, 8; compare Daniel 2 [LXX]). Paul concludes this sequence of arguments with a reassertion of the reality of the resurrection of the dead and the apocalyptic *mystērion* of the Lord's coming (1 Corinthians 15). Throughout the letter as well, Paul reminds the Corinthians periodically of the historical (eschatological) crisis, with references to the impending judgment (3:12–15; 4:5; 5:5; 6:2–3); to the foreshortened time in which the present order is passing away (7:29, 31); to "the ends of the ages" having come upon them (10:11); and to the Lord's coming as it is anticipated in every celebration of the Lord's Supper (11:26).

Because New Testament interpreters usually assume that they are reading about the formation of a religion, we have tended to miss just how politically Paul conceives of the events by which this age is waning and the next being inaugurated. Culture is involved, of course. But when Paul refers to "the wise, the powerful, and those of noble birth"—who are being shamed by God!—he is referring to (the self-image of) the political as well as the cultural elite of a city such as Corinth. Even more important to re-examine is the reference to "the rulers of this age, who are doomed to perish" and who have been outwitted by God's mystery (2:6–8), and every "rule and authority and power" (*archē, exousia, dynamis*) that Christ will destroy in Paul's portrayal of the end (15:24–28). The previously dominant reading, which understands this portrayal exclusively in terms of cosmic or transcendent spiritual powers, is now yielding to serious consideration that Paul may also be referring here to the actual Roman rulers of this age, even if he did not have Pontius Pilate explicitly in mind. Apocalyptic literature does indeed speak of cosmic forces, but those forces are closely related to, and even in

---

[27]In the following paragraphs I am depending on my analysis and exegesis in *1 Corinthians*.

control of, imperial political forces, which is what the Judean apocalyptic visionaries are attempting to understand and explain.[28]

Some time ago Helmut Koester drew attention to the passage in 1 Thess 5:1–11 where Paul juxtaposes what is clearly Judean apocalyptic language ("children of light," and "helmet" and "breastplate") with terms that, on closer examination, come from the imperial cult and propaganda ("peace and security," *eirēnē kai asphaleia/pax et securitas*).[29] The eschatological struggle that Paul portrays in apocalyptic terms is waged precisely against the Roman imperial order, which claims to offer "peace and security." "Destruction will suddenly come upon" those who tout the benefits of empire. Paul insists that his community is engaged in a struggle against that order.

Indeed, in recent years we are coming to recognize that Paul borrowed a great deal of his key terminology from the Roman imperial cult and propaganda. Along with Helmut Koester, Dieter Georgi has taken the lead in helping us discern that and how Paul uses this borrowed imperial political-religious language.[30] Even if there is some influence from the Second Isaiah on the term "gospel," and from the Torah on the concept of "righteousness/justice," nevertheless, in the context of his mission in Corinth and other Greek cities, these and many other key terms would have resonated with Paul's hearers because of their role in imperial cult.[31] For example, *euangelion* was the "gospel" of Augustus, the imperial lord and savior, who had brought "salvation" (*sōtēria*) and "peace and security" (*eirēnē kai asphaleia/pax et securitas*) to the whole world. *Pistis/fides* was the "loyalty" or faithfulness of Caesar/Rome, to be reciprocated by the "loyalty" of her subjects.

Paul, however, does not simply borrow these terms and apply them to Jesus Christ and his relationship to believers. Paul rather uses these terms to present Jesus Christ as the lord and savior who has displaced Caesar as lord and savior.[32] Paul himself proclaims the gospel of Christ in such a way that it stands diametrically opposed to the rule of Caesar. And that is nowhere

[28]Explained more fully in Horsley, "The Kingdom of God and the Renewal of Israel," 304–9.

[29]Helmut Koester, "From Paul's Eschatology to the Apocalyptic Schemata of 2 Thessalonians," in *The Thessalonian Correspondence* (ed. Raymond F. Collins; Leuven: Leuven University Press, 1990), excerpted in Horsley, ed., *Paul and Empire*, 158–66.

[30]Dieter Georgi, *Theocracy* (Minneapolis: Fortress, 1990), excerpted in Horsley, ed., *Paul and Empire*, 148–58.

[31]On the imperial cult in Corinth/Achaia, see Susan E. Alcock, *Graecia Capta: The Landscapes of Roman Greece* (Cambridge: Cambridge University Press, 1993) 181–99.

[32]Besides my exegesis in *1 Corinthians*, see N. T. Wright, "Paul's Gospel and Caesar's Empire," in Horsley, ed., *Paul and Empire*, 160–83.

more vividly articulated than in the opening of Paul's first long argument in 1 Corinthians 1–4, where the despicable, shameful death of Christ on the cross, the instrument of torturous death for slaves and provincial rebels, has become the means by which God brought the imperial "rulers of this age" to imminent judgment. As we are learning from increasingly sophisticated rhetorical criticism of 1 Corinthians,[33] Paul's main concern in this long opening section of the letter is that the whole assembly be united in the same mind and the same purpose. The principal language and the rhetorical form of the argument is borrowed from standard Greek and Roman discourse on the concord necessary for the cohesion and welfare of a city. The usual function of such discourse and its rhetorical performance in public space, of course, was the maintenance of the Roman imperial order. Paul is utilizing this discourse to shore up the concord of his alternative *ekklēsia* that stands in solidarity over against the imperial order. That is, grounded in their trust/faith that God (in his "wisdom in a mystery") had indeed brought the imperial rulers of this age to imminent judgment in the foolishness of Christ's crucifixion, the lowly Corinthians themselves can persist as a community in mutually supportive solidarity. The next steps of Paul's argument spell this out in particular ways.

Before moving to those next steps of the argument in 1 Corinthians, it may be useful to revisit the parallel argument in 1 Thessalonians 5. As Koester points out, in Paul's deployment of apocalyptic language over against the imperial claims, the members of the Thessalonian assembly "are already children of the light, a community of realized eschatology."[34] "In faith, love, and hope the 'day' becomes a reality in the life of the community . . . in which the future is becoming a present reality." Here, says Koester, is "a community which realizes the presence of the eschatological future in its *oikodome* (5:11). . . . [This] is certainly utopian, especially in its political implications. But that . . . was exactly what Paul was talking about."[35] In a parallel way, Paul in 1 Corinthians is urging the assembly to live as a community that is already anticipating the realization of the eschatological future in its present lifestyle. This seems fairly clear in the next steps of Paul's argument, in 1 Corinthians 5; 6:1–11; 7; and 8–10.[36]

---

[33]See the references in n. 1, above.

[34]Koester, "Imperial Ideology," 163.

[35]Ibid., 165.

[36]Again I am leaning heavily on my previous exegesis in *1 Corinthians*; see also Horsley, "1 Corinthians: A Case Study," 242–52.

In addressing the case of a man's relationship with his stepmother (1 Corinthians 5), Paul has two main concerns. The assembly must exercise rigorous internal communal discipline in maintaining strict ethical standards. This rigor and the communal-spiritual-apostolic presence-in-absence parallel those of both the Gospel of Matthew (chapter 18) and the Qumran community (1QS). But the community members must also remain open to outsiders in day-to-day interaction because they are still *in the world*. They are not to "go out of the world." Paul is thinking very clearly of a "this-worldly" community, not an "other-worldly" spiritual life. He may also have had continuing recruitment in mind.

Paul's argument forbidding the Corinthians to take grievances to the civil court (1 Cor 6:1–11) may be the most telling indication that he is thinking in terms of the assembly as, in effect, an alternative society, already living in the new age while anticipating its full blossoming in the near future. He seems to be saying that they are to conduct their own community affairs in virtually complete independence of "the world," the established sociopolitical order. Many commentators have projected the modern Western separation of church and state (or is it the Lutheran theological "two kingdoms" concept?) onto Paul's argument here. But that does not seem to fit at all. In this argument, Paul diametrically opposes the assembly of "saints"—the community that maintains justice in its social relations—to the "unjust" of "the world." He is painting with a very broad brush, so it is impossible to tell precisely what he has in mind. Peter Garnsey has certainly laid out abundant evidence for the prejudice of the courts of the empire in favor of the elite (*honestiores*) on the one hand, and against the ordinary people (*humiliores*) on the other.[37] Interestingly enough in this connection, Paul's list of "the unjust" who will surely not inherit the kingdom of God features the economic injustices of coveting and theft (which also evokes the Mosaic covenantal tradition). This suggests that the conflict between community members involved economic issues and/or that Paul viewed the courts and those who used them as engaged in economic injustice.

Paul's principal argument for why the Corinthian assembly must deal with its own cases internally, without recourse to the civil courts, is a vivid illustration of how he understands the present life of the community as already embodying, by anticipation, the justice that will be fully realized in the future judgment and inheritance of "the kingdom of God." The rhetorical question

---

[37]Peter Garnsey, *Social Status and Legal Privilege in the Roman Empire* (Oxford: Clarendon, 1970).

"Do you not know?" indicates that he had already taught them that they, the saints, would be involved in the judgment of the world and even of angels. The closing statement of this short argument—that they had been washed, sanctified, and justified (in baptism?) and empowered by the Spirit (6:11)— then reinforces this point that the assembly members were already living a common life sharply different from their previous one in the world.

The similarities between Paul's insistence here that his assembly handle its own internal disputes and the parallel provisions articulated in Matt 18:15–22 as well as in the *Rule of the Community* from Qumran (1QS 5:25–6:1; compare CD 9:2–8) suggest that Paul is extending traditional Judean/Israelite procedure, or at least the practice of renewal movements grounded in Israelite tradition. That the language of 1 Cor 6:1–6, which includes some awkward expressions in Greek, appears to be rooted in the traditional Israelite self-governance provisions as articulated in Exod 18:13–26 and Deut 1:9–17; 16:18–20; 17:8–13 (LXX; compare the odd Greek expression in 1 Cor 6:5b to Deut 1:16), suggests that Paul may be following what was a standard practice of self-governance among diaspora Jewish communities (as mentioned above). Finally, the motif of the righteous/saints who will participate in the eschatological judgment of the sinners, particularly of "the nations/kings"—a standard feature of apocalyptic literature concerned with the solution to Israel's subjugation by foreign imperial rulers (*1 En.* 1:9; 38:5; 1QpHab 5:4–5)—suggests fairly strongly that Paul sees his assembly as a community in opposition to the Roman imperial order here, just as he does earlier in the letter (1 Cor 2:6–8). Paul adapted and extended to his assemblies among the other peoples some of the mechanisms of self-governance and motifs of resistance that had already been developed by diaspora Jewish communities and Judean scribal circles in their efforts to resist Roman imperial domination.

In this connection we should also take a sidelong glance at another key statement by Paul, made in the climax of his argument in Philippians 3, a passage loaded with political and indeed imperial language deployed in another apocalyptic scenario. In keen anticipation of the coming of the Lord Jesus Christ as the (true) "Savior" endowed with "the power that enables him to make all things subject to himself" (v. 21), Paul declares that "our *politeuma* is in heaven" (v. 20).[38] That is, he reminds the Philippians that they are already living (and are to live) according to their true "government" or "constitution," that which already exists in heaven with the counterimperial Savior. Paul may well have known the term *politeuma* from the arrangements enjoyed by

---

[38]Wright, "Paul's Gospel and Caesar's Empire," 173–81.

Hellenistic Jewish communities. But Paul's concern here is more than simply a parallel to the practice whereby Jewish diaspora communities conducted their own internal affairs independently, insofar as the Roman authorities would allow. Paul's insistence that the community handle its own disputes internally seems to be a more complete declaration of independence and autonomy from the established (Roman imperial) order, in this case in Corinth. Thus it seems comparable, rather, to the more complete independence of the Qumran community, which handled all its own affairs internally (1QS 5:25–6:1), and to the practice of the Matthean community (Matt 18:15–22).

Paul's next argument in 1 Corinthians, on sexual relations and marriage (chapter 7), embodies among other things a struggle to discern the relationship between the assembly members' previous life and their current life in the community of the new age. In a nutshell, given the main focus of the argument on sexual relations in marriage and especially the other two examples cited in 1 Cor 7:17–24, Paul is struggling to figure out how to apply the principles articulated in the baptismal formula cited in Gal 3:28 ("no longer Jew or Greek, no longer slave or free, no longer male and female" in Christ). Most significant for the question at hand, perhaps, is the status of slaves. Jews and Greeks are included in the new community of Christ through faith, with no need to change their ethnic status. But when he considers slaves, Paul sees the problem and makes an exception to his general rule of thumb here, just as he has done in every previous paragraph of this argument. Slaves may not have much choice in the matter of their potential freedom. But, says Paul, if they do have a chance to become free, they should "by all means take it" (1 Cor 7:21), for people should not be slaves of human masters.[39]

The second point of importance for this essay that Paul makes in this argument is his statement that because "the appointed time has grown short," since "the present form of this world is passing away," "those who buy [should be] as though they had no possessions, and those who deal with the world as though they had no dealings with it," etc. (1 Cor 7:29–31). The life of those who have formed the community of the new age in Corinth are no longer really part of "the world," although they are still living in it. To use the old cliché, they are in but not of the world. Their life is still located in the world, and it is very much a communal life of social relations. But the assembly is to embody within itself transformed social relations of righteousness and justice.

---

[39]Horsley, *1 Corinthians*, 100–4.

Once we begin to construct an alternative to the standard paradigm of "Pauline Christianity" as a universal religion replacing parochial Judaism, we can recognize yet another extended argument of 1 Corinthians as an example of Paul's insistence that his assembly be an alternative community separate from the dominant order. It has been important to the prevailing view of Paul as having broken with the strictures of Jewish law to see him as sharing the enlightened view of the "strong" behind the argument in 1 Corinthians 8–10. Paul himself could not possibly still be an advocate of Jewish purity codes and dietary restrictions! He is simply advocating consideration toward one's less enlightened "weak" brother or sister who still has scruples about food offered to idols.

Stanley Stowers's recent re-examination of sacrifices in Greek and Roman society, however, reminds us that "sacrifices to idols" were central to community life at every level of society, from family and association gatherings to citywide celebrations, including the imperial cult—which by Paul's time had probably become one of the most prominent forms of religious expression in cities such as Corinth, Ephesos, and Philippi.[40] These most fundamental of Greek religious expressions were hardly just a matter of personal belief, but were inseparable from, and indeed constitutive of, political, economic, and social relations in the society. "Food offered to idols," moreover, would most often refer to food eaten in a temple, not that sold in the market (after being sacrificed in a temple). Read with critical attention to the rhetorical structure of the overall argument in 1 Corinthians 8–10, the climax and main point comes not in the concession at the very end, but in 10:14–22. In the *political* (not "sacramental") realism of this climactic step in the argument, he insists that it is impossible for members of the assembly to *share in* the ("bodily") solidarity (*koinōnia*) of the body and blood of Christ and also in that of other gods, demons, or lords! As is evident again later in 1 Corinthians 12, "body" was a standing political metaphor for the "body politic" of a Greek or Roman *polis/civis*. Over against the dominant imperial society, whose network of overlapping sociopolitical bonds was established in sacrifices to its interrelated network of gods, Paul's assembly was to maintain its own distinctive and exclusive solidarity. Paul was prohibiting the members of his assembly from participating in the fundamental forms of sociopolitical

[40]Stanley K. Stowers, "Greeks Who Sacrifice and Those Who Do Not: Toward an Anthropology of Greek Religion," in *The Social World of the First Christians: Essays in Honor of Wayne A. Meeks* (ed. L. Michael White and O. Larry Yarbrough; Minneapolis: Fortress, 1995) 293–333.

relations in Corinthian and Roman imperial society. His *ekklēsia* was to constitute an alternative society.

CONCLUSION

It should be clear from this re-examination of the imperial context of Paul's mission, Israelite/Judean resistance to the Roman imperial order, and Paul's concerns about his communities, particularly that in Corinth, that the common assumption in New Testament research—typified in Meeks's comment that sociopolitical factors, especially Roman imperialism, did not determine Paul's stance toward "the present evil age" from which Christ had set them free[41]—is a projection of the modern separation of religion from political and economic affairs. Political-economic and religious dimensions were inseparable both in Paul's understanding of his mission and communities and in the Roman imperial order that constituted the context in which he worked. Once we break with the standard Western theological paradigm that has historically dominated New Testament studies, however, then a number of important observations that Meeks and others have made fall into place and yield a very different picture of Paul's mission and assemblies: Paul was promoting not just another religious cult, but an alternative society over against the dominant imperial order.

Recognizing that neither the household, nor voluntary associations, nor Jewish synagogues, nor philosophical schools provided an adequate comparative model for what he called "Pauline Christianity," Meeks finally examined Paul's own language, albeit eclectically, without proceeding letter by letter. In addition to Paul's extensive "language of separation," which he explained in terms of a sectarian mentality, Meeks isolated the distinctive terms in which Paul addressed his assemblies. Particularly prominent are the "saints" or "holy ones," along with the closely related "elect" who are "called," and the kinship language of "brothers (and sisters)."[42] Both the language of election and that of kinship employ biblical terms for the people of Israel. Paul's understanding of and address to his assemblies is thus thoroughly grounded in Israelite tradition, as is his understanding of the crisis in world history as the prelude to the fulfillment of the promises to Abraham, which drives his whole mission. He understands his mission and assemblies in terms of an extension

---

[41]Meeks, *First Urban Christians*, 189.
[42]Ibid., 84–103.

or expansion of the people of Israel, through which God's promises to all peoples was now being realized in the Christ events. It would be yet another modern Western projection and anachronism to pretend to reduce "the saints" and the "brothers (and sisters)" to merely their religious dimension. Meeks, finally, sees that Paul's communities were all participating in a wider movement.[43] Not only do the *ekklēsiai* have a distinct political aura, almost in mimicry or parody of the assembly of free adult male citizens of a Greek city; in Paul's reference to all of those communities together as the *ekklēsia*, they also comprise "a worldwide people." And that can only be an extension of the biblical Israel, the *ekklēsia tou kyriou* (ἐκκλησία τοῦ κυριοῦ, translating קהל יהוה, the "assembly of YHWH"), the whole people of Israel. But that is hardly a "cultic assembly." It has no cult. It is rather an international movement of sociopolitical communities. They are certainly not economically self-sufficient, as were the village communities in which Jesus carried out his mission. That far more was involved than the cultural dimension alone is vividly illustrated by the economic dimension evident in relations between the individual assemblies. Although Paul apparently declined to accept support from a community during the time in which he was on mission there, in contrast to other apostles (1 Cor 9:3–18), it is evident that various communities did supply financial assistance to the apostles' missions elsewhere, as they spread the movement more widely. Most significant, perhaps, was the collection for (the poor among) the saints in Jerusalem, the central assembly in the Palestinian Israelite home base of the movement. Here was a horizontal international movement of economic resources from one assembly of poor people to another, dramatically different from the vertical movement of resources—in the form of tribute to Rome and patronage pyramids—that structured the larger Roman imperial order. Paul, at least, understands the *ekklēsiai* as local communities of a broader social order in-the-making that stands as an alternative to the Roman imperial order, the world that is passing away.

As my final point, in contrast to the anachronistic notion of "Pauline Christianity" as an already formed "religion," I emphasize that this was still a movement that had not yet reached any degree of stability as a new social formation. Perhaps the operative concept here is "movement," as can be seen best perhaps in the way its leaders went about their community-building. Paul worked in teams, apparently mostly with others originally from diaspora Jewish communities. For years he had worked with Barnabas out of Antioch. In

---

[43]Ibid., 107–10.

Macedonia he worked with Timothy and Silvanus (1 Thess 1:1; 2 Cor 1:19). In Corinth and again in Ephesos he formed a special collaborative bond with Prisca and Aquila. Significantly, and contrary to previous images of their missionary activity, especially preaching, they avoided the public "market-place" of religious competition (2 Cor 2:17). They focused their energies in intensive interaction with small groups in people's households. As mentioned above, the movement in Corinth and Ephesos, at least, took the form of sub-assemblies based in particular households (e.g., of Prisca and Aquila, or of Stephanas: Rom 16:5; 1 Cor 16:15, 19). That Paul makes a distinction between these smaller groups and "the whole assembly" suggests that the household-based "assemblies" functioned separately in some respects. And that in turn suggests that the heads of households, such as Stephanas and Gaius, operated as coworkers with Paul, Prisca, and others. Moreover, that there was another "assembly" only a short distance from Corinth itself at the seaport of Cenchreae, where Phoebe was principal leader (Rom 16:1), indicates how the movement spread out into satellite towns and perhaps villages. Indeed, Paul at times refers to a whole network of communities in Achaia or Macedonia, not just Thessalonike or Corinth (2 Cor 9:2, 4). The picture that emerges from these brief references is one not of a religious cult, but of a movement comprised of cells spreading through a whole province and centered perhaps in larger assemblies such as those in Corinth, Thessalonike, and Ephesos.

In sum, Paul did not found a religion, much less convert from one religion to another. Paul rather helped spearhead what can be understood as an international anti-imperial movement of communities that he saw as constituting an alternative society of justice, co-operation, and mutuality opposed to the Roman imperial order, which was finally being terminated through God's action in Christ. Paul did not urge his assemblies to attempt to change "the world," e.g., to challenge, much less abolish, slavery in the larger world. After all, that was "passing away." But Paul did insist to the Corinthians and to other assemblies that in the Christ events, God had brought about the turn of the ages, which meant that the empire's days were numbered, that "the rulers of this age [were] doomed to perish" (1 Cor 2:6), and that a new age was being established in the imminent realization of the kingdom of God. The assemblies Paul helped to organize owed their allegiance to Christ, the true emperor enthroned in heaven, who was about to "destroy every ruler, authority, and power" (1 Cor 15:24). The assemblies, meanwhile, were to be the realizations already, now in this world, of the "government" or "constitution" or "commonwealth" already established in heaven by the true or real

Savior, over against the Roman imperial savior and his "peace and security."
It is difficult to understand how Paul's stance could be described as "social
conservatism." He did not make a frontal assault on the Roman imperial order.
But insofar as his message to his assemblies may have taken root, it would
have been subversive in the sense that he urged them insofar as possible not
to participate in the broader imperial order, not simply in religious matters,
but in social, political, and economic affairs as well.

CHAPTER FIFTEEN

Civic Identity in Roman Corinth and Its Impact on Early Christians

James Walters

In this essay, I will relate two trends in the study of Roman Corinth and Roman rule in the provinces to two characteristics of the early Christian community in Corinth as reflected in the Pauline correspondence, 1 Corinthians in particular.[1] The two trends in the study of Roman Corinth are:

(1) Refounded Corinth was a more typical Roman colony with a stronger Roman character than has been assumed.

(2) The civic identity of Roman Corinth began to change during the Augustan period and accelerated throughout the second century as the city became increasingly integrated into the surrounding Greek world, a transition already evident by the time of Claudius.

The two characteristics of the Christian community are:

(1) Compared to other Pauline churches, there was a notable lack of conflict between Christians and outsiders at Corinth.

(2) The considerable conflict within the Christian community at Corinth was related to the varying status levels of its members.

[1] I would like to extend special thanks to Professor James Rives, who provided helpful feedback on both an early and a late draft of this essay.

In the Corinthian correspondence, there is a curious lack of reference to conflict with outsiders, even though references to contact between insiders and outsiders are more common in 1 Corinthians than in any of Paul's other letters. Comparing 1 Corinthians with other Pauline letters illustrates how sharp the differences are. Take 1 Thessalonians as an example. Paul reminds believers of his previous warning that they would suffer persecution and indicates that his prediction had already been realized:

> We sent Timothy, our brother and co-worker for God in proclaiming the gospel of Christ, to strengthen and encourage you for the sake of your faith, so that no one would be shaken by these persecutions. Indeed, you yourselves know that this is what we are destined for. In fact, when we were with you, we told you beforehand that we were to suffer persecution; so it turned out, as you know. (3:2–5)[2]

Moreover, in the letter's thanksgiving, Paul explicitly associates the Thessalonians' suffering with his own suffering and with that of Jesus himself:

> And you became imitators of us and of the Lord, for in spite of persecution (θλίψει) you received the word with joy inspired by the Holy Spirit, so that you became an example to all the believers in Macedonia and in Achaia. (1:6–7)

Although θλῖψις can signify mental distress as well as physical suffering,[3] Paul's association of their experiences with his own suffering suggests serious opposition, given the description of his own suffering in the same lettter:

> You yourselves know, brothers and sisters, that our coming to you was not in vain, but though we had already suffered and been shamefully mistreated at Philippi, as you know, we had courage in our God to declare to you the gospel of God in spite of great opposition (ἀγῶνι). (2:1–2)

---

[2]Biblical quotations follow NRSV unless otherwise indicated.

[3]Abraham J. Malherbe prefers to translate θλῖψις as "distress" and relates it to psychological factors associated with conversion (*Paul and the Thessalonians* [Philadelphia: Fortress, 1987] 46–52). Although I think Malherbe is correct to identify such factors as belonging to Paul's use of θλῖψις in 1 Thessalonians, they surely do not exhaust its meaning. The term should also be associated with broader experiences of external opposition. For a recent treatment of this issue with bibliography, see Craig Steven De Vos, *Church and Community Conflicts: The Relationships of the Thessalonian, Corinthian, and Philippian Churches with Their Wider Civic Communities* (SBLDS 168; Atlanta, Ga.: Scholars, 1999) 155–75. Robert Jewett's study of the Thessalonian situation as one marked by "millenarian radicalism" understands θλῖψις to include external persecution; however, this datum does not play a large role in his treatment of the letter (*The Thessalonian Correspondence: Pauline Rhetoric and Millenarian Piety* [Philadelphia: Fortress, 1986] 93–94, 176–78).

Moreover, Paul offers the Thessalonian Christians explicit instructions regarding how they should behave toward outsiders:

> We urge you . . . to aspire to live quietly, to mind your own affairs, and to work with your own hands, as we directed you, so that you may behave properly toward outsiders and be dependent on no one. (4:10b–12)

These instructions are reminiscent of exhortations in 1 Peter that discourage Christians from behaviors that attract unfavorable attention or exacerbate conflict with outsiders (2:11–3:22). The concluding exhortation directing the Thessalonian Christians not to "repay evil for evil, but always seek to do good to one another *and to all*," should be interpreted in the same light (1 Thess 5:15; emphasis added).[4]

The starkly apocalyptic outlook of 1 Thessalonians encouraged believers to view their social alienation as normal by interpreting their experiences of suffering as a kind of social dualism that only reflected the larger cosmic dualism which was its source (see 5:1–11). Hence, social harassment validated the apocalyptic outlook of the Thessalonians while this same apocalyptic outlook provided them with the key for interpreting the actions of their harassers.[5]

In 1 Corinthians, on the other hand, there is no reference to Corinthian Christians suffering at the hands of outsiders.[6] On the contrary, Paul indicates that Corinthian Christians receive invitations to dine with outsiders in their homes or in other communal meal settings (10:27–11:1). Some apparently attend—or believe that it is appropriate for Christians to attend—cultic meals in temple settings (8:7–13). And not only do believers move freely among outsiders, outsiders also move freely among the believers. In 1 Corinthians 14, Paul counsels against speaking in tongues when there is no one to interpret because unbelievers may spontaneously enter the house where the Christians are gathered and "think you are mad" (v. 23). In 1 Cor 6:1–11, Paul counsels the Corinthian believers against taking their legal disputes before outsiders. In the Gospel of Matthew, similar counsel is aimed at preventing discrimination:

---

[4]John Barclay ("Conflict in Thessalonica," *CBQ* 55 [1993] 514)—like most students of early Christian persecution—identifies the likely causes of the social harassment Christians experienced to have included sudden abandonment of Greco-Roman religion, familial betrayal/disruption, the exclusivity of the Christians' religion, and the belief of their peers that Christians' failure to honor the gods was the cause of misfortune.

[5]On this point, see ibid., 518. Barclay uses this interpretive circle to argue for the authenticity of 2 Thessalonians as a document that illustrates what could happen if Paul's converts took his apocalyptic symbols further than he did (525–29).

[6]De Vos, *Church and Community Conflicts*, 205–14.

"Come to terms quickly with your accuser while you are on the way to court with him, or your accuser may hand you over to the judge, and the judge to the guard, and you will be thrown into prison" (Matt 5:25). But in Corinth, the issue is not discrimination; rather, the Corinthian Christians (in Paul's view) have undue confidence in the Corinthian legal system, and Paul reads that confidence as a shameful commentary on their lack of faith in the Christian community's ability to adjudicate disputes among its own members.

Whereas in 1 Thessalonians Paul explicitly associates his own experiences of suffering with those of his readers, in 1 Corinthians he explicitly *disassociates* his experiences of suffering from the experiences of his readers:[7]

> Already you have all you want! Already you have become rich! Quite apart from us you have become rich! Indeed, I wish that you had become kings, so that we might be kings with you! For I think that God has exhibited us apostles as last of all, as though sentenced to death, because we have become a spectacle to the world, to angels and to mortals. We are fools for the sake of Christ, but you are wise in Christ. We are weak, but you are strong. You are held in honor, but we in disrepute. To the present hour we are hungry and thirsty, we are poorly clothed and beaten and homeless, and we grow weary from the work of our own hands. When reviled, we bless; when persecuted, we endure; when slandered, we speak kindly. We have become like the rubbish of the world, the dregs of all things, to this very day. (4:8–13)

Although Paul presents the relationship between the Thessalonian Christians and outsiders as one characterized by conflict, he portrays the Corinthian Christians' relations with outsiders as conflict-free, even convivial. How does one account for this difference, especially in light of the temporal proximity of Paul's missions to these cities, according to most Pauline chronologies? This essay looks for an explanation in the evolving civic identity of Roman Corinth.

THE REFOUNDING OF CORINTH

Old Corinth was destroyed in 146 B.C.E. by the Roman general Mummius. Julius Caesar refounded the city as a Roman colony in 44 B.C.E.. Scholars have sometimes assumed that Roman Corinth was not a typical Roman colony,

---

[7]John Barclay, "Thessalonica and Corinth: Social Contrasts in Pauline Christianity," *JSNT* 47 (1992) 57.

but rather more of a refounding and continuation of the Greek city that the Romans destroyed a century earlier. However, more recent analyses of the city's refoundation and development have stressed that Corinth was more or less a conventional Roman colony.[8] It is important to recognize that Roman colonies were centers of Roman presence and influence, "mini-Romes" that mirrored the religious institutions of the city of Rome more closely than any other setting outside Rome, with the exception of the Roman army.[9] Both the design and the extent of this mirroring is illustrated in the colonial charter of the colony Caesar founded, also in 44 B.C.E., at Urso in southern Spain:[10]

> Whosoever shall be appointed *pontifices* and *augures* from the colony Genetiva by Caius Caesar (or by whoever establishes the colony on Caesar's instruction) let them be *pontifices* and *augures* of the colony Genetiva Julia; let them be *pontifices* and *augures* in the colleges of the said colony, possessing all the best rights that pertain or shall pertain to the *pontifices* and *augures in every colony*. Let those *pontifices* and *augures*, who shall be members of each college, and their children be sacredly guaranteed freedom from military service and public obligations, *in the same way as a pontifex is and shall be in Rome* [emphasis added].

Not only was the colony to have the same two priestly groups as did Rome (*pontifices* and *augures*), they were to be regulated by the same criteria as in Rome right down to their exemption from military service, their attire, and their seating at games.[11] Roman officials had even devised foundation rituals for colonies that echoed the mythical foundation of Rome: auspices were taken, and the founder ploughed a furrow around the site to mark the *pomerium*.[12]

No doubt Corinth was refounded on the basis of a colonial charter similar to that of Urso. Woolf refers to such charters as a colony's "blueprint for civilized life" and the "main means by which Romans could impose new *mores*"—culture, manners, behavior, morality.[13] Colonies, however, did not develop as "mini-Romes" simply because they had a Roman charter; rather,

---

[8]Mary E. Hoskins Walbank, "The Foundation and Planning of Early Roman Corinth," *JRA* 10 (1997) 95–130.

[9]Mary Beard, John North, and Simon Price, *Religions of Rome* (2 vols.; Cambridge: Cambridge University Press, 1998) 1:328.

[10]*ILS* 6087, 64–67; *CIL* II.5, 439, 64–67, in Beard et al., *Religions of Rome*, 2:243.

[11]Ibid., 1:328.

[12]Ibid., 1:329.

[13]Greg Woolf, *Becoming Roman: The Origins of Provincial Civilization in Gaul* (Cambridge: Cambridge University Press, 1998) 72.

the Roman character of these cities was guaranteed by a Roman population. Colonists would have felt at home in Corinth because their fellow citizens shared values and tastes reflected in everything from architecture to crockery to ideas regarding education and civic responsibility.[14]

Although there is archaeological and literary evidence to suggest that Corinth was minimally inhabited during the century between its destruction and refoundation, these locals would have been forced to relocate before the settlers arrived. Based on comparisons with Carthage and assumptions regarding available land and average allotments (20–30 acres), it is likely that Corinth was settled by 12,000–16,000 colonists.[15]

Ancient sources indicate that Corinth's Roman settlers were mostly freedmen and veterans.[16] The reference to the settlers as "good-for-nothing slaves" by Crinagoras of Mytilene (during the Augustan period) reflects both their identity as Roman freedmen as well as Greek attitudes toward their new "superiors."[17] Pausanias underscored the discontinuity between the population of the Greek city and that of the Roman city when he wrote that the city is "no longer inhabited by any of the old Corinthians."[18]

In her study of Roman Corinth, Mary Walbank emphasized the "newness" of the Roman city by making six assertions:[19]

(1) The political functions and civic buildings of the old city were destroyed.

(2) There is no evidence that previous inhabitants had any connection to the new colony.

(3) There is no evidence that the new colonists were connected to the city's Greek past.

(4) There was little incentive for colonists to seek connections with the native population of Achaia.

---

[14]Ibid., 2.

[15]Although land division (centuriation) has been a debated issue in studies of Roman Corinth, there is no compelling reason to doubt that Corinth was laid out according to standard procedures for a Roman colony. See David Romano, "Post 146 B.C. Land Use in Corinth, and Planning of the Roman Colony of 44 B.C.," in *The Corinthia in the Roman Period* (ed. Timothy E. Gregory; JRASup 8; Ann Arbor, Mich.: Journal of Roman Archaeology, 1993) 9–30; as well as Romano's essay in this volume (pp. 25–59).

[16]For a presentation of the ancient sources and their interpretation, see Walbank, "Foundation and Planning," 97–99.

[17]A. S. F. Gow and D. L. Page, eds., *The Greek Anthology* (London: Cambridge University Press, 1968) 1:220–21. See also Cicero, *Att.* 16.16.11; and Strabo 8.6.23.

[18]Pausanias 2.1.2.

[19]Walbank, "Foundation and Planning," 95–96, 107.

(5) Leading families in Greece who had acquired Roman citizenship (e.g., the Euryclids of Sparta) could gravitate to Corinth.

(6) Connections with Rome were more important to these colonists than connections to Achaia.

Colonia Laus Iulia Corinthiensis was not refounded as some sort of Greek version of a Roman colony, but as a conventional Roman colony. Indeed, Antony Spawforth calls Roman Corinth's aggressive *romanitas* one of the colony's most striking features during the early Principate.[20] However, because Roman colonies functioned as important sites for interaction between Romans and locals,[21] the foundation of Roman Corinth was only the beginning of the dialogue that would determine Corinth's civic identity.

THE DEVELOPMENT OF ROMAN CORINTH

Although it is appropriate to call refounded Corinth a "mini-Rome" and to emphasize its discontinuity with old Corinth, Roman Corinth was not founded on the Tiber, but on the site of one of Greece's illustrious old cities. Even early on there must have been a sizeable Greek population. Some of these Greeks would have come from other cities in the Greek East while others made their way to Corinth from surrounding towns and the countryside. Some of these Greeks would have already possessed Roman citizenship while others did not.[22] Bowersock pointed out long ago that Romans with interests in the Greek East often depended on Greek clients to look after their interests: "A Greek, by virtue of his very intimacy with his patron, had an unrivalled opportunity to look after the best interests of such eastern cities as he chose to support, while at the same time he earned gratitude and honour among those Greeks who experienced his patron's benefactions."[23]

Moreover, some of the city's Greek past did survive into the Roman period. The Romans obviously used the same site and reused some of the structures from the old city that were not destroyed. It is clear, for example,

[20]A. J. S. Spawforth, "Roman Corinth: The Formation of a Colonial Elite," in *Roman Onomastics in the Greek East: Social and Political Aspects* (ed. A. D. Rizaki; Μελετήματα 21; Athens: Research Center for Greek and Roman Antiquity; Paris: de Boccard, 1996) 175.

[21]Woolf, *Becoming Roman*, 103.

[22]See Spawforth's catalogue of duovirs in "Roman Corinth," 175–82.

[23]G. W. Bowersock, *Augustus and the Greek World* (Oxford: Clarendon, 1965) 30.

that the archaic temple, the South Stoa, and the theater were reused. Besides the Temple of Apollo, at least four other sanctuaries from the old city were revived: the Sanctuary of Demeter and Kore; the Asklepieion; the Sanctuary of Aphrodite on Acrocorinth; and the Sanctuary of Poseidon on the Isthmus.[24] In addition, Betsey Robinson has shown that two fountains, the Fountain of Peirene and the Fountain of Glauke, continued to evoke the city's Greek traditions in the Roman period.[25] Perhaps no other feature of Corinth's civic life connected the Roman city's identity to its Greek past as did the Isthmian games, the second greatest of the Panhellenic festivals.[26]

Yet the fact that there was some continuity between Roman Corinth and its Greek past does not mean that the city's identity and the functions of its surviving structures remained unchanged. Excavations of the Demeter and Kore sanctuary have vividly illustrated the extent to which even surviving structures could change.[27]

How is one to imagine the cultural identity of Roman Corinth in the first century C.E. in light of its refoundation as a Roman colony on the site of one of Old Greece's most illustrious cities?[28] The question of how different subject peoples responded to Roman rule and influence has been a hot topic in Roman studies in recent years. The use of the term "Romanization" to describe this process has substantially declined because Romanization is too one-sided in its characterization of what was no doubt a more complex

---

[24]See the essay by Nancy Bookidis in this volume (pp. 141–64).

[25]See the essay by Betsey Robinson in this volume (pp. 111–40).

[26]On the basis of numismatic evidence Elizabeth Gebhard has argued that the Corinthians were already back in control of the Isthmian games by the time of their celebration in 40 B.C.E.; see "The Isthmian Games and the Sanctuary of Poseidon in the Early Empire" in *The Corinthia in the Roman Period* (ed. Timothy E. Gregory; JRASup 8; Ann Arbor, Mich.: Journal of Roman Archaeology, 1993) 82. Regarding the prestige of the province of Achaia in the Greek world because of the status of its agonistic festivals, see Antony Spawforth, "Agonistic Festivals in Roman Greece," in *The Greek Renaissance in the Roman Empire: Papers from the Tenth British Museum Classical Colloquium* (ed. Susan Walker and Averil Cameron; ICSBSup 55; London: University of London, 1989) 193–97.

[27]Ronald S. Stroud, "The Sanctuary of Demeter on Acrocorinth in the Roman Period," in *The Corinthia in the Roman Period* (ed. Timothy E. Gregory; JRASup 8; Ann Arbor, Mich.: Journal of Roman Archaeology, 1993) 72–73. See also the essay by Nancy Bookidis in this volume (pp. 141–64).

[28]"Cultural identity" is increasingly viewed as a dynamic, a "complex process of construction, negotiation and contestation," rather than a set of static attitudes (Rebecca Preston, "Roman Questions, Greek Answers: Plutarch and the Construction of Identity," in *Being Greek under Rome* [ed. Simon Goldhill; Cambridge: Cambridge University Press, 2001] 88). For developments in the meaning of "cultural identity" in contemporary studies and problems of definition, see Simon Goldhill, "Introduction: Setting an Agenda," in ibid., 15–20.

interaction. Contemporary studies regularly index this complexity by referring to the process as a dialogue, not a monologue.[29]

Susan Alcock's study of Roman Greece under the title *Graecia Capta* lumped Greece together with other parts of the empire that had been subjugated by the Romans. This was intended to correct the tendency of classical historians to treat the Greeks under Roman rule as a special case.[30] However, in a 1997 essay she cautions against taking her earlier approach too far:

> Significant differences *do* separate the Greeks from other peoples defeated by Rome, even if these lie more in the realm of perception and of attitude than in tangible matters. Maintenance of a separate cultural identity, one insistent upon "specialness" and privilege, colored the Greek relationship to Rome, and their responses to Roman rule. In return, Romans maintained the Greeks in a "cognitive position," vis-à-vis themselves, unlike that of any other conquered people. Throughout the early imperial period, Greeks and Romans were engaged in a tense dialogue of "cultural mapping," of mutual self-definition and aggressive maintenance of boundaries.[31]

A number of classical scholars have recently reasserted the Greek side of this dialogue. In his essay "Becoming Roman, Staying Greek," Greg Woolf writes, "Greeks felt themselves to be Greeks, in a sense that was not wholly compatible with being Roman, while at the same time adopting much Roman material culture."[32] Alcock sees evidence of reluctance on the part of Achaian elites to seize opportunities that Roman rule offered them because of their control of local power networks as compared to their North African counterparts.[33] Therefore, she asserts that because there was a "dialogue between imperial power and subject people," historians must "look for material traces of a dialogue between Roman and Greek."[34]

Antony Spawforth has been especially productive in locating such material traces. His contextualization of the Argive letter protesting payments that

---

[29]Even the use of the word "resistance" has been challenged as a descriptive category for local responses to Roman presence because resistance presumes a clash, and therefore assumes Romanization (Woolf, *Becoming Roman*, 22).

[30]Susan E. Alcock, *Graecia Capta: The Landscapes of Roman Greece* (Cambridge: Cambridge University Press, 1993).

[31]Eadem, "Greece: A Landscape of Resistance?," in *Dialogues in Roman Imperialism: Power, Discourse, and Discrepant Experience in the Roman Empire* (ed. D. J. Mattingly; JRASup 23; Ann Arbor, Mich.: Journal of Roman Archaeology, 1997) 109.

[32]Greg Woolf, "Becoming Roman, Staying Greek: Culture, Identity and the Civilizing Process in the Roman East," *PCPS* 40 (1995) 128.

[33]Alcock, "Greece: A Landscape of Resistance?," 110.

[34]Ibid., 109.

Argos was compelled to make in support of wild beast shows in Corinth;[35] his essays on agonistic festivals,[36] particularly the Panhellenia;[37] and especially his prosopographical analysis of the duoviral coinage from Corinth[38] contain important traces of this dialogue between Greeks and Romans.

The Argive letter, dated by Spawforth to the late first century C.E., illustrates the local tensions that resulted from Rome's civic and administrative presence in Achaia. A Greek notable wrote the letter to the Roman governor on behalf of Argos, requesting a special hearing.[39] The issue involved payments that Corinth had collected from Argos for the past seven years towards the cost of spectacles, including wild-beast shows that were staged in Corinth. Such shows in the Greek East were characteristic of celebrations for the Roman imperial cult. The Argives were asking for the right to present their case to the governor. They had been turned down four years earlier and were probably attempting to get a new hearing before a new governor. They wanted to claim an exemption from the payments because of their obligation to fund their own Panhellenic games. In support of this claim they offered four arguments:

(1) Elis and Delphi have a similar exemption.

(2) The payments are used to support spectacles that are neither Greek nor ancient—namely, wild-beast shows.

(3) Corinth is richer than Argos.

(4) Because they are neighbors, Corinth should show special love for Argos.

For Argos to describe wild beast shows at Corinth as spectacles "neither Greek nor ancient" underscores a certain alien status of Roman Corinth vis-à-vis its Greek neighbors that could be exploited in a pinch.

---

[35]A. J. S. Spawforth, "Corinth, Argos, and the Imperial Cult," *Hesperia* 63 (1994) 211–32.

[36]Spawforth, "Agonistic Festivals," 193–97.

[37]A. J. S. Spawforth, "The World of the Panhellenion: I. Athens and Eleusis," *JRS* 75 (1985) 78–104; and idem, "The World of the Panhellenion: II. Three Dorian Cities," *JRS* 76 (1986) 88–105.

[38]Idem, "Roman Corinth," 167–82.

[39]This letter is preserved in the correspondence of the emperor Julian, but Bruno Keil ("Ein Λόγος συστατικός," *Nederlands archief voor kerkgeschiedenis* [1913] 1–41) argued that it was written between 80 and 130 C.E. In the letter, the Argives contrast the rights of Old Greece with those that the Corinthians "seem to have received recently from the sovereign city . . . [namely,] secure advantages . . . since it received the Roman colony." In other words, the refoundation seems to be a recent event. More recently Spawforth ("Corinth, Argos," 211–32) has taken up Keil's argument and has attempted to locate the tension between Argos and Corinth in a more specific situation.

The tension reflected by the letter is not surprising. Roman Corinth's superior status depended on its special relation to Rome as a colony and as the seat of the Roman provincial government. Neighboring cities, on the other hand, continued to compete with one another for status according to more traditional horizontal patterns—appealing to their illustrious past, for example—as well as a developing vertical pattern expressed by interest in Roman religion—especially by the elite—and particularly by their interest in the imperial cult.[40]

Another aspect of life in Roman Corinth that reflects the dialogue between Greek and Roman identities is the city's rich agonistic history. Cartledge and Spawforth demonstrated that the agonistic life of Roman Sparta was largely the creation of the imperial period.[41] This datum—together with Hadrian's support of the Panathenaic games and his creation of the Panhellenia, the Hadriania, the Olympia, and the Antinoeia in Eleusis—indicates clearly that Greek agonistic festivals played a key role in negotiating between local traditions and the realities of Roman power. Spawforth writes, "At this social level, the appeal of *agones*, which celebrated traditional categories of Greek cultural activity, often in association with old local cults, can be seen in part as an aspect of the attachment to civic tradition so marked among the Greek urban elites in the second and third centuries."[42] Onno van Nijf has recently explained how Greek festive culture served both the interests of local elites and the interests of Rome during the Roman period:

> [Greek festive culture] mobilized the resources of a glorious Greek past enabling urban elites to display their social superiority in several ways. But at the same time it was clearly focused on Rome and the emperor, who ultimately underwrote the hierarchical world view of which it was an expression. Festivals (in the Roman period) were in many important respects an invented tradition that effectively blurred the boundaries between Greek and Roman.[43]

Nijf also suspects that local elites, as well as upwardly mobile individuals, resorted to athletic competition as an alternate means of acquiring Greek

[40]It is an interesting paradox that although Roman rule undermined the authority of Greek elites by its interventions into local affairs, it also legitimated the authority of the same Greek elites and provided them with opportunities for empire-wide careers that increased their status (Preston, "Roman Questions, Greek Answers," 91).

[41]Paul Cartledge and Antony Spawforth, *Hellenistic and Roman Sparta* (London: Routledge, 1989) ch. 13.

[42]Spawforth, "Agonistic Festivals," 196–97.

[43]Onno M. van Nijf, "Local Heroes: Athletics, Festivals and Elite Self-Fashioning in the Roman East," in *Being Greek Under Rome* (ed. Simon Goldhill; Cambridge: Cambridge University Press, 2001) 334.

identity and status because the literary/rhetorical route to *paideia* was a steeper climb.[44]

By establishing the Caesarean games at Corinth and by celebrating them in conjunction with the Isthmian games, the Romans guaranteed the status of the imperial games.[45] Moreover, the Caesarean games associated the more horizontal patterns of status (the competition for status between Greek cities) with the more vertical pattern (status resulting from a city's connections with Rome), further blurring the boundaries between Greek and Roman.[46]

Spawforth's prosopographical analysis of the duoviral coinage from Corinth adds a critical element for our understanding of this Greek and Roman dialogue during the first century C.E. Of the forty-two extant names, Spawforth has identified nine as probably from freedman stock (19%), three probably from veteran families (6%), fourteen from the milieu of *negotiatores* (29%), four provincial Greek notables (8%), one elite Roman (2%), and nine that cannot be determined (19%).[47] Although there is much in this list that clamors for our attention—for example, the high percentage of *negotiatores* and freedmen—it is the Greek notables that primarily concern us here.

What Spawforth finds significant about the Greek notables who are attested in the coinage is their late arrival. Five Greek notables—one other is known from an inscription—show up as magistrates, but not until the reigns of Claudius and Nero.[48] By placing the appearance of these Greek notables as magistrates within the context of the hostilities toward Roman Corinth expressed in the Augustan Crinagoras text and in the Argive letter, Spawforth argues that the icy relations between Greek cities and Roman Corinth began to thaw—at the latest—around the time of Claudius, as the city itself was becoming more integrated into its Greek context:[49] "The appearance of

---

[44]Ibid.

[45]Spawforth ("Agonistic Festivals," 195) points out that unlike the other Caesarean games established under Augustus in cities of Achaia, the Caesarea at colonial Corinth attracted a worldwide competition because—at least in part—they were celebrated in conjunction with the "renowned Isthmian festival."

[46]Of course, the fact that the highest honor for a Corinthian citizen was the post of *agōnothetēs* of the Isthmian games—not the *duovir quinquennalis* as one would expect—suggests that in Corinth, receiving honor from the entire Greek world mattered (Donald Engels, *Roman Corinth: An Alternative Model for the Classical City* [Chicago: University of Chicago Press, 1990] 97).

[47]Spawforth, "Roman Corinth," 169.

[48]Ibid., 174.

[49]Ibid., 173–75. Although Spawforth is cautious in suggesting reasons for the thaw, he suspects that the ambitions of some for Roman offices played a role, as did Roman administrative initiatives during the period that promoted the importance of the colony within the province. These would include the re-creation of the province of Achaia in 44 C.E.—increasing

outside notables as office-holders from Claudius on marks a significant step in the integration of this enclave of Romanitas into the surrounding Greek world."[50]

In his recent book *After Paul Left Corinth*, Bruce Winter takes issue with Spawforth's claim, suggesting that the appearance of these Greek notables as magistrates only demonstrates that these Greeks were becoming "Roman"; it does not indicate, according to Winter, that Corinth was becoming more "Greek." However, this is the very sort of one-sided understanding of "Romanization" that modern studies are attempting to correct. No doubt these Greek elites were becoming more Roman, while, at the same time, Corinth was becoming more Greek. Woolf nuances the issue carefully when he writes, "Becoming Roman was not a matter of acquiring a ready-made cultural package, then, so much as joining the insiders' debate about what that package did or ought to consist of at that particular time."[51] Hence, mastering Roman culture not only gave locals the means for achieving their ambitions, "but also played a part in determining what those ambitions were."[52]

What does the presence of local Greek elites in the membership of the *ordo decurionum*, the "town council" of Corinth—even as duovirs—say about the dialogue between Romans and Greeks noted above, particularly with regard to its impact on the exercise of religion? The foundation charter of the Roman colony at Urso—and no doubt Corinth's charter as well—designated the decurions as those who would exercise authority over religion in the colony. Therefore, it was the local decurions themselves, the city's *ordo*, who actually managed public cults and collegia. It was their responsibility to select, organize, and arrange the finances of civic cults.[53]

How a city's local elite controlled public religion and how their control changed under the empire is the subject of a book by James Rives that focuses on Roman Carthage, a Roman colony founded by Caesar during the same period as Corinth.[54] Rives claims that when the Roman republic gave way to the empire, the situation of the individual vis-à-vis the government changed: individuals no longer participated in government in quite the same way, because government became what the emperor and a few other people did. Because a

---

the Roman governor's presence in Corinth—and Corinth's role as a major center of the Achaian League and host of the imperial cult (instituted around 54 C.E.).

[50]Spawforth, "Roman Corinth," 175.

[51]Woolf, *Becoming Roman*, 11.

[52]Ibid., 13.

[53]Ibid., 224–25.

[54]James Rives, *Religion and Authority in Roman Carthage: From Augustus to Constantine* (New York: Oxford University Press, 1995).

city's political and religious lives were not separate, this change affected the city's religious identity. Individuals now had a civic religious identity that was shaped by the *sacra publica* of their respective city, but also a supra-civic religious identity shaped by their connections with Rome. Rives argues that this supra-civic religious identity gradually undermined local religious identity in Carthage because there was no longer the same impetus for city leaders to make a sharp distinction between their city's cults and those of other cities. Because the civic model of religion was virtually the only model around, its erosion "led to an increasing divergence between civic and religious identity and a decline in social and political control of religion."[55] In other words, with regard to the management of civic religion, this evolution led to a less exacting *ordo* with a resulting proliferation of private cults. Rives writes, "Because the elite had less reason to interfere with the private religious activities of those who lived in their city individuals were to a large extent able to define their own religious identities as they pleased."[56]

This helps to account for a development in religious identity during this period that John North drew attention to when he wrote, "We can illuminate the religious history of this period best by recognizing a new religious situation, in which the individual had to make his or her own choices and in which, as a result, the location of religious power became far more contentious, far more open to negotiation than it had been in the traditional Graeco-Roman world."[57]

When Corinth was refounded as a Roman colony, the Greek civic identity of old Corinth was destroyed. The civic identity of the new city was initially strongly Roman, reflecting the blueprint of its colonial charter and its predominate Roman population. But the civic identity of Roman Corinth was changing rapidly during the first century C.E., and these changes resulted in a growing ambiguity in the population's civic religious identity, producing decurions and magistrates who were less likely to police private religious associations in the city.[58] This resulted in a socioreligious context in which private religious associations and their members were not viewed with the same level of suspicion with which they would have been viewed in other cities—like Thessalonike, for example.

---

[55]Ibid., 14.

[56]Ibid., 173.

[57]John North, "The Development of Religious Pluralism," in *The Jews among Pagans and Christians in the Roman Empire* (ed. Judith Lieu, John North, and Tessa Rajak; New York: Routledge, 1994) 187.

[58]For other evidence of an evolution of civic identity in Roman Corinth, see Engels, *Roman Corinth*, 95–113.

The Impact on the Early Christians

In order to establish what impact the evolution of Corinth's civic identity may have had on the early Christian community at Corinth, it will be necessary to show that the lack of conflict between Christians and outsiders noted at the outset of this study was responsible—at least in part—for internal conflicts within the Christian community. It is the interrelation between these two characteristics of the Christian community—lack of external conflict, presence of internal conflict—that is the key.

Scholars have long recognized that intracommunal conflict was a major problem confronted by Paul in 1 Corinthians.[59] The extent of the problem—as Paul perceived it—is indicated by Margaret Mitchell's reading of the letter. She argues that 1 Corinthians is a compositional unit in which factionalism is the central topic throughout.[60] The thesis of the entire letter appears in 1:10: "Now I appeal to you, brothers and sisters, by the name of our Lord Jesus Christ, that all of you be in agreement and that there be no divisions among you, but that you be united in the same mind and the same purpose." Her analysis has Paul moving from the censure of factionalism in 1:18–4:21 to a case-by-case treatment of divisive issues about which Paul has specific advice in 5:1–15:57. According to Mitchell, Paul constructed the argument by first focusing on divisive issues that were raised by relations between the Corinthian Christians and outsiders (i.e., πορνεία, 5:1–7:40; and εἰδωλόθυτα, 8:1–11:1), followed by a treatment of the divisive issues raised by relations within the community itself (i.e., gathering for worship, 11:2–14:40; and the resurrection of the dead, 15:1–58).

Although Mitchell limits her analysis to examining Paul's rhetorical strategy in 1 Corinthians, her recognition that "the first set of contested issues [5:1–11:1] is entirely concerned with the integrity of the social/political boundaries of the church" hints at the sort of connection I am suggesting.[61] Mitchell sees Paul's rhetoric as an attempt to heighten group consciousness and to encourage an approach to decision-making that considers the Christian community as the fundamental context for such judgments. The reason Paul's

---

[59]For the range of scholarly views regarding the nature of the conflict, see John Hurd, *The Origin of 1 Corinthians* (Macon, Ga.: Mercer University Press, 1983) 95–107.

[60]Margaret M. Mitchell, *Paul and the Rhetoric of Reconciliation: An Exegetical Investigation of the Language and Composition of 1 Corinthians* (1991; repr., Louisville, Ky.: Westminster/John Knox, 1993) 182. Mitchell reads 1 Corinthians as deliberative rhetoric encouraging concord and reflecting the traditional rhetorical strategies and *topoi* of *homonoia* speeches.

[61]Ibid., 228.

argument pursues unambiguous definitions of "who is in" and "who is out" of the group is precisely because the boundaries of the community are blurry. It is noteworthy that in 1 Cor 5:9–13, Paul presses the Corinthian Christians to take action against the man sleeping with his stepmother by contrasting action that is appropriate relative to "insiders" with action appropriate relative to "outsiders": God judges outsiders (τοὺς ἔξω); the community judges insiders (τοὺς ἔσω).

Although there is a long and distinguished tradition in New Testament scholarship of explaining factionalism within the Corinthian church by attempting to discern the differing theological beliefs of rival teachers and factions, a more promising approach focuses on the particular question of the relationship between weak group boundaries and factionalism in the Christian community. Because this approach pays attention to the rhetorical strategy of the entire letter, it involves far less speculation than reconstructions of the parties of Paul, Peter, Apollo, and Christ.[62]

Social-scientific approaches to 1 Corinthians have found considerable evidence for weak group identity in the letter. Bruce Malina, applying Mary Douglas's group / grid model to the Christian community in Corinth, concluded that the community was "weak group" and "high grid."[63] By categorizing them as "weak group," Malina is suggesting that they were characterized by individualism and shallow group identity. Consequently, the boundaries distinguishing "who was in" and "who was out" lacked clarity. By categorizing them as "high grid," Malina is suggesting that individuals in the church tended to assent to the norms and values of the surrounding society.

Recently, Edward Adams, in a study of Paul's cosmological language, has argued—largely on the basis of Malina's analysis—that Paul's primary concern in 1 Corinthians is precisely the weak group boundaries of the Christian community itself, not factions within the community, as Mitchell claimed. Adams comes to this conclusion because he thinks that the problem of weak boundaries "underlies the internal divisions of the congregation."[64] On the latter point I believe Adams is correct. But just because weak group boundaries represent an underlying cause—or even *the* underlying cause—of at least some of the factions, it must not automatically be concluded that weak group boundaries were the focus of Paul's argument. To assume such

[62] 1 Cor 1:12; see Hurd, *Origin of 1 Corinthians*, 95–107, with bibliography.

[63] Bruce J. Malina, *Christian Origins and Cultural Anthropology: Practical Models for Biblical Interpretation* (Atlanta, Ga.: John Knox, 1986) 17–19, 45–54.

[64] Edward Adams, *Constructing the World: A Study in Paul's Cosmological Language* (Edinburgh: T&T Clark, 2000) 99.

a direct relation fails to distinguish literary questions from historical questions. Mitchell is still correct, in my view, that factionalism is the central topic throughout the letter.[65]

It has long been recognized that Pauline communities attracted members from differing social locations to an extent that was exceptional in the Greco-Roman world.[66] At Corinth, however, this characteristic of early Christianity was even more pronounced and appears to have been directly connected to the problem of factionalism.[67] How they were related is suggested in a recent book by Craig Steven De Vos. De Vos draws a contrast between the social contexts of early Christianity in Thessalonike and Corinth that parallels the contrast drawn at the outset of this essay. Moreover, he also sees a correlation between the high level of internal conflict and the lack of conflict with outsiders. Using a "culture of conflict" theory, he attempts to account for the different relations between Christians and outsiders in Thessalonike, Philippi, and Corinth as reflected in Paul's letters to churches in these cities.[68] He argues that Corinth "by its very nature" would have been more tolerant than Thessalonike because of its recent origin and more mixed population of Greeks and Romans.[69] Of particular interest is his observation that a "strong pattern of cross-cutting ties" resulting from interactions between persons of various social strata in Corinth would have resulted in less conflict between Christians and outsiders, but more conflict between insiders.[70] In other words, the cross-cutting ties that decreased conflict between Christians and outsiders resulted in increased conflict among insiders, because the more diverse Christian community had

---

[65]Mitchell, *Paul and the Rhetoric of Reconciliation*, 301.

[66]Wayne Meeks, *The First Urban Christians: The Social World of the Apostle Paul* (New Haven, Conn.: Yale University Press, 1983) 79. Of course, this does not mean that "many" in the Corinthian church were "wise by human standards," "powerful," or "of noble birth" (1 Cor 1:26).

[67]Gerd Theissen, *The Social Setting of Pauline Christianity: Essays on Corinth* (ed. and trans. J. H. Schütz; Philadelphia: Fortress, 1982) 102–10. See also Peter Lampe, "Das korinthische Herrenmahl im Schnittpunkt hellenistisch-romischer Mahlpraxis und paulinischer Theologie Crucis (1 Kor 11, 17–34)," *ZNW* 82 (1991) 183–213.

[68]De Vos's analysis is an adaptation of the conflict theory of M. H. Ross (*The Culture of Conflict: Interpretations and Interests in Comparative Perspective* [New Haven, Conn.: Yale University Press, 1993]).

[69]De Vos, *Church and Community Conflicts*, 295.

[70]"Cross-cutting ties" are contrasted with "reinforcing ties." The latter occur when there is overlap between one's kin, one's neighbors, and one's social groups and political affiliations. The former occur when the overlap is limited because there is more variety in these relations (ibid., 22).

relatively fewer reinforcing ties—and, consequently, weaker internal bonds.[71] Moreover, it was these same cross-cutting ties that allowed the Christian community to continue to attract converts from various social strata.

Dale Martin's book, *The Corinthian Body*, goes further in explaining how early Christianity's attraction of converts from various social strata affected the Christian community reflected in 1 Corinthians. Building on the work of Gerd Theissen, Martin argues that Paul's conflict with the "strong" in 1 Corinthians—and the larger tensions between the "weak" and "strong" at Corinth—resulted from their conflicting ideologies of the body, conflicts that were related to their differing social positions in the Greco-Roman world.[72] By relating disease etiologies to Greco-Roman education, particularly the role of such education in freeing students from unreasonable fears, Martin claims that Paul's concern with pollution reflects the outlook of the lower classes in the Greco-Roman world:[73] the demonizing of flesh (σάρξ) that resulted from Paul's apocalyptic dualism caused him to pursue measures that would protect bodies from pollution—human bodies as well as that of the church, the body of Christ. Concerning Paul's discussion in 1 Corinthians 5 of the man who was sleeping with his stepmother, Martin writes:

> The differences between Paul and the Strong, I would argue, lie not in moral strictness on the one hand and laxity on the other but in degree of concern about pollution and boundaries. Because Paul fears pollution, he is anxious to maintain firm boundaries; because the Strong do not share his fears, they are less concerned with boundaries.[74]

As new studies of the Corinthian correspondence continue to trace the divisions at Corinth to the differing social locations of community members, an important question arises: How did persons from such diverse social locations end up in the same religious association in Corinth—even to an extent that may have exceeded the range of diversity in other early Christian communities?[75]

[71]Rodney Stark's analysis ("Christianizing the Urban Environment: An Analysis Based on 22 Greco-Roman Cities," *Sociological Analysis* 52 [1991] 80) also suggests that Christians would have endured less conflict in ancient Corinth because the larger a city's population, the easier it is to assemble a deviant subculture—because there are more deviants to draw from—and the harder it is to resist such groups. The latter is true because the larger the city, the less likely it is that the "plausibility structure" of the society will be coextensive with that of the city as a whole.

[72]Dale B. Martin, *The Corinthian Body* (New Haven, Conn.: Yale University Press, 1995) 197.

[73]Ibid., 139–97.

[74]Ibid., 173–74.

[75]Of course, those of relatively high status in the Corinthian church were not those at the top of the Roman social scale: senators, equestrians, and decurions. It is interesting that

I am convinced that the social diversity of the Corinthian church was related to the lack of external pressure that Christians experienced from outsiders. A lack of external pressure would have resulted in a more diverse community of Christians because the commitment threshold that potential converts faced was lower. Some Corinthian Christians would no doubt have been more reluctant to convert if the decision to embrace Christianity were made in the context of greater social hostility—as was apparently the case in Thessalonike. Gerd Theissen was correct when he pointed out that the wealthier members of the Christian community in Corinth would have found the avoidance of "consecrated meat" and ritual dining especially problematic, because their status and network of relations would have necessarily involved them in such dining situations.[76] If, at the time of their conversions, these Christians had understood that their decision would have brought an end to such invitations—because their peers would be so disturbed by their membership in the Christians' private religious association—or that they could no longer accept such invitations because they were Christians, no doubt fewer would have converted.[77] This, of course, would have resulted in a less diverse Christian community, one lacking the network of social relations that would have facilitated the attraction of converts from various social strata.

The case of Erastus, the "city treasurer" (ὁ οἰκονόμος τῆς πόλεως, Rom 16:23) and a Christ-believer in Corinth, illustrates the situation I have sketched above. He is the only Christian ever mentioned by Paul who bears an official title that indexes his status by a marker not drawn from his role within the Christian community.[78] Although the precise implications of the title have been long disputed, the discovery of a Latin inscription recognizing a certain "Erastus" who paved a courtyard associated with the theater in Corinth "in return for his aedileship" has sharpened the debate.[79] J. H. Kent concluded that the phrase Paul used to describe Erastus was one that would

---

Wayne Meeks's attempt to estimate the social level of the Pauline Christians by means of prosopographical analysis (*First Urban Christians*, 55–74) depends heavily on persons of relatively high status who happened to be connected to Corinth.

[76]Theissen, *Social Setting*, 130–31.

[77]Bruce Winter (*Seek the Welfare of the City: Christians as Benefactors and Citizens* [Grand Rapids, Mich.: Eerdmans, 1994] 166–77) correctly recognizes the status implications of ritual dining, but he connects the issues in 1 Corinthians 8 too directly to the "right" claimed by some Corinthian Christians to attend banquets associated with the Isthmian games.

[78]Meeks, *First Urban Christians*, 58–59.

[79]Restored by John Harvey Kent (*The Inscriptions, 1926–1950* [Corinth VIII.3; Princeton, N.J.: ASCSA, 1966] no. 232) as [*praenomen nomen*] *Erastus pro aedelit[at]e s(ua) p(ecunia) stravit*, "Erastus laid [the pavement] at his own expense in return for his aedileship."

have been appropriate to someone performing the tasks of an aedile in Corinth.[80] Gerd Theissen, however, proposed that although both descriptive titles refer to the same Erastus, they document two different offices he held successively in Corinth: first, οἰκονόμος τῆς πόλεως, and later, aedile.[81] If Theissen's interpretation of the data is correct, Erastus's election as an aedile not only indicates his status, but also the Corinthian *ordo*'s relative comfort with electing an aedile who was also a Christian. Of course, Erastus also represents rather clearly a Christ-believer in Corinth whose status and advancement necessarily required him to participate in activities that threatened "the weak" and the unity of the church.[82]

CONCLUSION

The relationship between the two trends in the study of Roman Corinth and the two characteristics of the Christian community at Corinth noted at the outset of this essay should now be apparent. The lack of conflict between the Corinthian Christian community and outsiders was—at least in part—the result of the changing civic identity of Roman Corinth noted above. This evolution of civic identity created ambiguity in the city's religious identity, leaving individuals and groups more freedom to define their own religious identities. The resulting climate was one in which early Christians—and other private religious associations—could assemble in their household gatherings without the same level of suspicion or hostility that existed in other cities, such as Thessalonike, for example.

Paradoxically, the lack of conflict with outsiders resulted in more internal conflicts, because potential converts faced fewer of the social pressures that would have deterred persons of status from converting. Corinth—and the Corinthian Christian community—permitted persons of varying social strata, varying levels of commitment, and varying sorts of allegiances to identify in some measure with the church. Conflict was inevitable!

---

[80]See the review of Kent's analysis in Theissen, *Social Setting*, 80–83.

[81]Ibid.

[82]Meeks (*First Urban Christians*, 69) is correct to point out that "for an Erastus [i.e., a person seeking upward mobility], if indeed he was the rising public servant who in a few years would be an aedile in charge of all the Corinthian meat-markets, a restriction of his social intercourse to fellow Christians would mean a drastic reduction of his horizons and a disruption of his career."

When the Corinthian Christians gathered to eat the Lord's Supper, their experience of communal dining was such a disaster that Paul refused even to grant that it really was the "Lord's Supper" that they were eating (1 Cor 11:20). As Gerd Theissen demonstrated, Paul's description of the meal shows that the Corinthian Christians were, while dining, making social distinctions that elevated those of higher status by serving them more and better foods while those of inferior status were deprived.[83] Paul's charge that the way the meal was conducted "humiliate[d] those who have nothing" (1 Cor 11:22) indicates without question that divisions at Corinth were related to the differing socioeconomic levels of the church's members. How did persons of such differing status end up in the same private religious association? The Pauline mission and the appeal of early Christianity were no doubt important factors. However, this essay suggests that the evolution of Roman Corinth's civic identity had something to do with it as well.

The extent to which such changes affected Paul's mission to Corinth may have been a surprise even to Paul. It may be appropriate to read Paul's Corinthian correspondence as a commentary on the failure of Paul's mission to produce house churches with stable boundaries when there was not sufficient external pressure to reinforce them.[84] Without circumcision, dietary laws, and Sabbath observance, Paul's church plantings may have been more dependent on conflict with outsiders than he realized—at least before he came to Corinth!

---

[83]Ibid., 145–74.

[84]Barclay ("Thessalonica and Corinth," 69–73) argues that Paul's apocalyptic message did not take hold in Corinth precisely because the community lacked the external pressure necessary to reinforce the apocalyptic outlook he sought to communicate.

Chapter Sixteen

Archaeological Evidence for Early Christianity and the End of Hellenic Religion in Corinth

G. D. R. Sanders

Athens, as a university town in late antiquity, is now acknowledged to have relinquished its ties to Hellenic deities slowly and quite reluctantly. One may well assume that Corinth, as the capital of the province of Achaia, conformed to governmental monotheistic policy far more quickly. The intent of this essay is to present some archaeological evidence, in the light of more recent research, for religious practices in Corinth during the period circa 300–600 C.E.[1] The data suggest that Hellenic deities were still worshiped,

---

[1] Richard M. Rothaus (*Corinth, the First City of Greece: An Urban History of Late Antique Cult and Religion* [Leiden: Brill, 2000] 32–38) stresses the tenacity of Hellenic religion in Greece and summarizes the more recent literature. The excavated evidence from Corinthian sanctuaries is, with one important exception, poor and inconclusive. The sanctuary of Demeter and Kore, however, was meticulously excavated and has been published in considerable detail in Elizabeth G. Pemberton, *The Sanctuary of Demeter and Kore: The Greek Pottery* (Corinth XVIII.2; Princeton, N.J.: ASCSA, 1989); Kathleen W. Slane, *The Sanctuary of Demeter and Kore: The Roman Pottery and Lamps* (Corinth XVIII.2; Princeton, N.J.: ASCSA, 1990); Nancy Bookidis and Ronald S. Stroud, *The Sanctuary of Demeter and Kore: Topography and Architecture* (Corinth XVIII.3; Princeton, N.J.: ASCSA, 1997); and Gloria S. Merker, *The Sanctuary of Demeter and Kore: Terracotta Figurines of the Classical, Hellenistic and Roman Periods* (Corinth XVIII.4; Princeton, N.J.: ASCSA, 2000). The sanctuary was violently destroyed at the end of the fourth century (Bookidis and Stroud, *Sanctuary of Demeter,* 438–40). Like the

at least privately and in domestic situations, late into the fourth century.[2] They also suggest that public expressions of Christian identity, in the form of burial customs, architecture, and iconography, became manifest no earlier than the late fifth century.

RECENT FINDS IN THE PANAYIA FIELD

Excavation in the Panayia Field, southeast of the forum, began in 1995 (fig. 16.1).[3] The largest monument exposed is a late urban *domus* (fig. 16.2, p. 422). The construction of this building can be closely dated to after 262 C.E. by coins in a well that was sealed off by the construction of the walls. Four coins in the debris of ash and collapsed roofing date the destruction of the building to some time after the reign of Julian, perhaps around 370 C.E. The house incorporates two geometric mosaic floors, two peristyles (one with a Euripus stream), a long narrow pool, and two fountains within its fourteen identified spaces. Of the painted decorations, two lively figures of Nike were found in close proximity on the north side of the same room and are clearly part of the same decorative program (fig. 16.3, p. 423). They are a little less than half life-size, and are depicted naturalistically with emphasis given to their corporeality and movement. They are not wallpaper representations but rather were designed to be seen as figures which interact with the true architectural space in which they are set. Each figure carries a palm in her left hand and a wreath in her right. Facing the wall, the viewer saw the Nike on the right standing contraposto offering her wreath to her right, and the Nike on the left descending with drapery billowing in the wind to offer her wreath across her body to her left. If these flanked a door, the owner of the house could, when joining visitors waiting in this room, pause and be understood

---

Asklepieion, the site became the focus for Late Antique tile graves (ibid., 381–91) that appear to contain Christians, based on the placement of hands and the orientation of the body. Of the twenty-nine graves, only two belonged to adult males. This fact prompted Bookidis and Stroud (ibid., 390–91) to suggest that the memory of the place as one hospitable to women and children persisted. The Asklepieion may have had a similar attraction by association. I discuss recent changes in our perception of Corinth's Late Antique history and archaeology in "Problems in Interpreting Rural and Urban Settlement in Southern Greece, AD 365–700," in *Landscapes of Change: The Evolution of the Countryside from Late Antiquity to the Early Middle Ages* (ed. Neil Christie; Aldershot: Ashgate, 2004) ch. 5.

[2] A number of prominent late-fourth-century Corinthians worshiping Hellenic deities are known from the sources. See Rothaus, *Corinth, the First City*, 13–17 for a discussion.

[3] G. D. R. Sanders, "A Late Roman Bath at Corinth: Excavations in the Panayia Field 1995–96," *Hesperia* 68 (1999) 441–80.

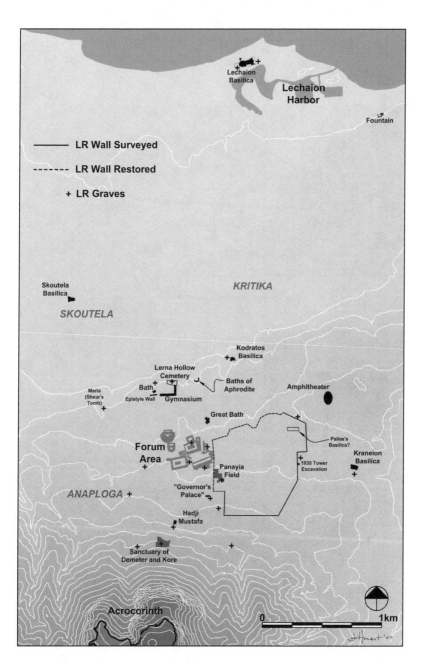

Fig. 16.1 Late Antique Corinth, from Acrocorinth to the Gulf of Corinth.

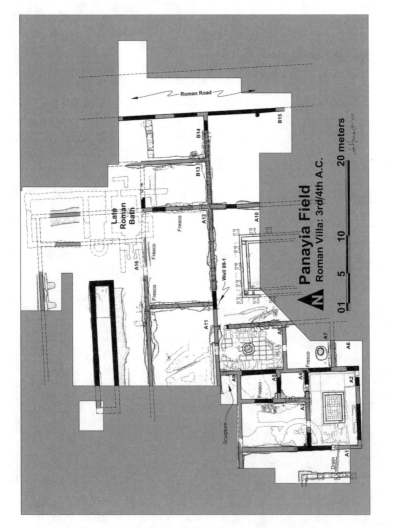

Fig. 16.2 Panayia Field. Plan of Late Antique *domus.*

Fig. 16.3 Panayia field. Fresco depicting a Nike.

to be the recipient of the wreaths. He was, perhaps, a victorious general or some musical or athletic victor in the games.[4]

In another room is a collection of important small-scale white marble sculptures that fell to the floor in the event that destroyed the building. They include Herakles Farnese, Pan, Europa, Dionysos, two Artemises, two Asklepios figures, and a seated Roma. Roma is seated with her right breast exposed (fig. 16.4). Her left hand is raised and clearly once held a staff or spear. A dowel in her right hand suggests she was holding something—perhaps an orb or a *phiale*. She and several other pieces preserve red adhesive for gold leaf and even traces of the gold leaf, which gave the figures a chryselephantine appearance. They may be considered to be copies of cult images. The smaller of the two Asklepios figures is rendered in a fashion resembling Late Antique ivory relief. The theory that these may be some kind of antique or art collection is perhaps resonant of a twentieth-century Christian rationalization of images of Hellenic deities in the first Christian century. A better explanation is that they served a more mundane function and that they represent the personal and civic divinities revered by the household.[5]

Some of the sculptural figures, including the Roma, certainly belong to the fourth century while others are probably earlier. If this was the house of a late-fourth-century non-Christian household, it is not extraordinary. Three small-scale statues found by Robert Scranton in 1947 in the tile debris of a structure destroyed by fire about 70 m to the north include a Zeus, Hades, or bearded philosopher; a Dionysos; and a Capua Aphrodite.[6] Although the figures are earlier, the destruction appears to have been contemporary with that of the Panayia *domus*. The glass opus sectile panels from Kenchreai representing Nilotic scenes and philosophers in what was identified as an Isis temple are also contemporary.[7]

---

[4]The wall paintings form part of Sarah Lepinski's forthcoming doctoral thesis and she may well have different ideas about the significance and intent of the imagery and their presentation. The walls of the house were completely removed or in places reduced to the foundations by builders recovering building stone in the sixth century. Very few thresholds or indications of thresholds of the house have been preserved and the reconstruction of a door between the Nike panels is conjectural.

[5]This material is to be published by Lea Stirling. She may or may not agree with my assessment of the significance of their presence.

[6]Oscar Broneer, "Investigations at Corinth, 1946–1947," *Hesperia* 16 (1947) 243–46, plate 65.30, MF-9034, standing figure; plate 65.29, MF-9035, Dionysos; and plate 64.28, S-2548, Aphrodite Hoplismeni.

[7]Leila Ibrahim, Robert Scranton, and Robert Brill, *The Panels of Opus Sectile in Glass* (vol. 2 of *Kenchreai, Eastern Port of Corinth*; Leiden: Brill, 1976).

Fig. 16.4 Panayia Field. Small-scale statue of Roma.

Over the remains of the Panayia *domus*, severely damaging the mosaic floors and with no reference to the existing walls, were found the remains of a building of the type often designated as "philosopher's house" and usually considered to be a fourth-century style (fig. 16.5, southwest corner).[8] The apse of the building is a space designed to accommodate a D-shaped sigma table, sometimes called an "agape table," and radiating dining couches; it is thus part of a Late Antique dining room. At first, this building appeared from the coins and pottery on the floors to date ca. 400 C.E., but a coin of ca. 450 C.E. on the earliest floor suggested differently. In conjunction with Kathleen Slane's evidence from east of the theater, this evidence has caused us to reconsider Corinth's Late Roman pottery chronology, and together we have started a reappraisal, down-dating assemblages. Now our sequences extend deep into the seventh century, whereas five years ago we could barely reach 600.[9] Such changes radically affect how we understand Late Antique monuments and later history at Corinth.

A small bathhouse on the site consists of an entrance hall, an apodyterium with two apsidal frigidarium tubs, a tepidarium, and a caldarium with three hot baptisteria or tubs (fig. 16.5, north). The building had opus sectile floors and marble revetment walls, and it was painted red on the outside. The impression of a *testudo alveolorum* for maintaining the heat of the water was found adjacent to the furnace in the third hot tub, and the impressions of lead pipes supplying water to the other two hot tubs are preserved. The provision of steam facilities and the choice of water temperatures leads one to conclude that the small tubs were not so much for modesty's sake but for individual control of one's bathing environment. On the evidence of pottery in the strata below the concrete floor and of a coin and pottery in the levels into which the foundations were cut, the bath dates to the mid-sixth century.[10] Thus there are several small baths in Corinth previously dated to the third, fourth, and fifth centuries that we should now, on the evidence of construction techniques and form, date to the sixth century.[11] The bath's construction

---

[8]Sanders, "Late Roman Bath," fig. 2.

[9]Sanders, "Problems in Interpreting Rural and Urban Settlement"; and Kathleen W. Slane and G. D. R. Sanders, "Late Roman Horizons Established at Corinth," *Hesperia*, forthcoming.

[10]Sanders, "Late Roman Bath."

[11]D. Ch. Athanasoulis, "Λουτρική ενκατάσταση στην Κοκκινόρραχι Σπάρτης," *Πρακτικά του Ε΄ Διεθνούς Συνεδρίου Πελοποννησιακῶν Σπουδῶν* 2 (1998) 209–44; Sanders, "Late Roman Bath"; and Jane Biers, "Lavari Est Vivere: Baths in Roman Corinth," in *Corinth: The Centenary, 1896–1996* (ed. Charles K. Williams II and Nancy Bookidis; Corinth XX; Princeton, N.J.: ASCSA, 2003) 303–19.

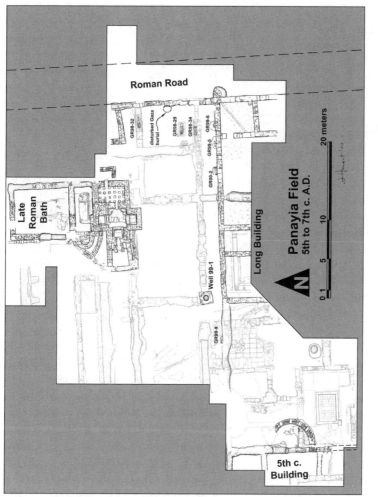

Fig. 16.5 Panayia Field, showing development from the fifth to seventh centuries.

is reminiscent too of that of the great basilicas of Corinth, and its form and its plan is close enough to the baptistery of the Lechaion Basilica for it to be taken as a kind of copy of its architecture (see fig. 16.10, p. 438). Certainly baptism and bathing are closely enough linked for the former to take place in structures usually reserved for the latter.[12]

Another structure to the south of the bath bears no relation to it, except that they border a common parcel of land (fig. 16.5, south). Little is known about the function of this long building because the limits of the property have precluded fuller exploration, although it may have had some ecclesiastical function. It extends almost 50 m east-west on the same orientation as the bath, and it had basement rooms to the east but not to the west. Its construction is similar to that of the bath, and to judge from the fill of robber trenches from which its fabric largely derived and which its wall foundations physically cut, this too dates to the sixth century. Inside one of the basement rooms, the plasterer has incised fish with his trowel (fig. 16.6). Similarly incised fish adorn the trans-isthmian wall, walls in the South Stoa, the hemicycle on the Lechaion Road, a small bath near Sparta, and a basilica at Chersonisos on Crete; at least fifteen are incised in the walls of the Lechaion Basilica.[13] Outside along the face of the wall are several burials that must postdate its construction in the mid-sixth century. These include graves of neonates, each placed within a Gaza amphora coffin. Our new chronology for ceramics indicates that Gazas were imported to Corinth from the mid-fifth century but became one of the dominant forms towards the end of the sixth century.[14] The latest graves in the area date to the seventh century and contain small containers for liquids associated with the graveside burial liturgy.[15]

The undramatic appearance of recent discoveries in the Panayia Field in fact belies the questions that the stratigraphy raises. It has yielded a late-fourth-century crèche of domestic, non-Christian religious sculpture; it has helped modify pottery chronologies; it has provided sixth-century architectural parallels for baths and basilicas; and it has furnished well-dated graves that help put less certainly dated graves in perspective.

---

[12]For example, the bath under the basilica of Ayios Demetrios in Thessalonike that was used to imprison the saint and later, because of its association with him, used as a baptistery.

[13]For a full list of comparanda, see Athanasoulis, "Λουτρική."

[14]Slane and Sanders, "Late Roman Horizons."

[15]James Wiseman, "Excavations at Corinth: The Gymnasium Area, 1966," *Hesperia* 36 (1967) 417–20; idem, "Excavations in Corinth, the Gymnasium Area, 1967–1968," *Hesperia* 38 (1969) 79–87; and idem, "The Gymnasium Area at Corinth, 1969–1970," *Hesperia* 41 (1972) 8–9.

Fig. 16.6 Panayia Field. Two fish incised in the plasterwork of the sixth-century long building.

BURIAL PRACTICES

Many sixth- and seventh-century graves[16] are known from excavations in and around the Asklepieion conducted in the 1930s and 1960s (fig. 16.7).[17] In the Lerna Court immediately to the west of the sanctuary is a dense concentration of some 250 tile graves, interspersed with about 15 infant burials in Gaza amphoras (fig. 16.8a, p. 432), dug into a deposit of earth about 1 m deep that had accumulated over the court. The graves appear to be set out in discrete—but sometimes overlapping—plots, leaving large spaces free, perhaps for a burial liturgy and attendant mourners. In the center of the court was found a sigma or agape table (fig. 16.9, p. 433; see fig. 16.7 for its location in the Asklepieion). Tables of a similar type were also found in the hemicycle on the Lechaion Road, in the Peribolos of Apollo, and in the Kenchrean Gate Basilica. It is generally thought that these tables were not restricted to domestic dining but were also used for a funerary meal. Depending on the size of the deceased, the tile graves consisted of up to four complete Lakonian roof tiles which, where complete, measure about 85 by 35 cm (fig. 16.8b, p. 432). The tiles were set on edge and rested against each other to form a tent. Sometimes covering tiles were placed over the ridge, and occasionally the ends were closed with fragmentary tiles. A handful of these tile graves were furnished with a vaulted mound measuring approximately 2.0 by 1.0 m, some 20 cm high and covered with a 3-cm-thick layer of stucco. The tiles used have the same general dimensions as the tiles used for the sixth-century tile graves found in the Panayia Field. The dead were laid out extended on their back and oriented east-west with their heads to the west. The hands, as appears to be customary in later Christian burials, were placed on the abdomen. No grave furnishings, such as libation vessels, were found with the deceased. On the evidence of the Gaza amphora coffins, we should date the burials no earlier than the late fifth century and, more probably, in the sixth century.

[16]On burial practices of the first through fifth centuries C.E. at Corinth, see the essay by Mary E. Hoskins Walbank in this volume (pp. 249–80).

[17]Carl Roebuck, *The Asklepieion and Lerna* (Corinth XIV; Princeton, N.J.: ASCSA, 1951); Corinth Notebooks 122 (1931), 126 (1932), 136 (1933), and 138 (1934); Wiseman, "Excavations, 1966," 417–20; idem, "Excavations, 1967–1968," 79–87; and idem, "Excavations, 1969–1970," 8–9. Rothaus (*Corinth, the First City*, 47–52) provides an interesting discussion of this cemetery and its relationship to the temple. I would date the lamps and tombs a little later than he does, and I do not read the use of the Asklepieion as a Christian colonization and deterrent to the worship of Hellenic deities. Church dogma seems to have left popular belief in both evil and benevolent *daimones* unscathed in many parts of Greece; see Charles Stewart, *Demons and the Devil: Moral Imagination in Modern Greek Culture* (Princeton, N.J.: Princeton University Press, 1991).

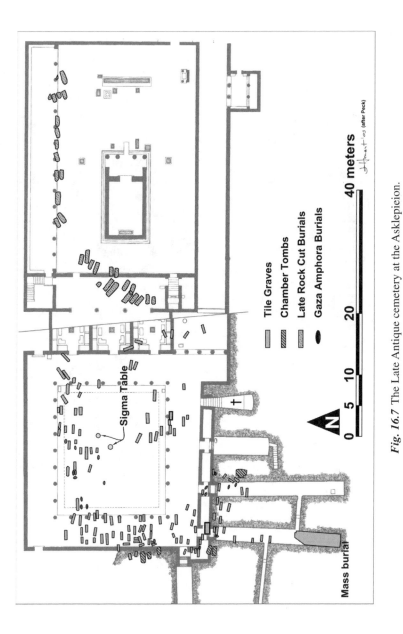

Fig. 16.7 The Late Antique cemetery at the Asklepieion.

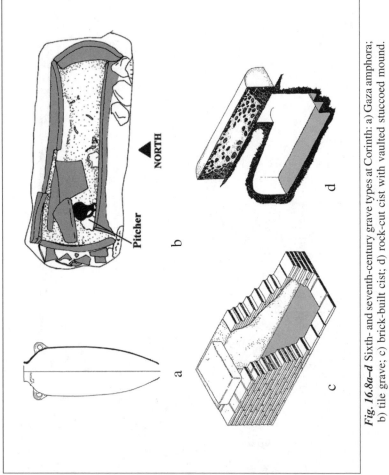

Fig. 16.8a–d Sixth- and seventh-century grave types at Corinth: a) Gaza amphora; b) tile grave; c) brick-built cist; d) rock-cut cist with vaulted stuccoed mound.

Fig. 16.9 Agape table from Corinth.

Inside one of the chambers of the Lerna Fountain on the south side of the court was found what has been interpreted as a memorial chapel (fig. 16.7, bottom center). Coins of Constans II under a built bench show that it remained in use at least into the second half of the seventh century.[18] Another of the chambers contained scores of primary burials (fig. 16.7, bottom left). Notwithstanding the orderly layout of inhumations, including some infants in Gaza amphoras, it was originally suggested that this may have been a plague pit dating to the Justinianic plague of 542.[19] Re-examination of the coins therein, however, demonstrates that some of the burials belong at least to the reign of Justinian's successor, Justin II (565–578). Associated lekythoi also appear to date to the latter part of the sixth century.

On the higher ground to the east of the court of the Lerna Fountain, rock-cut tombs skirt the edges of the Asklepieion court on the edge of the scarp (fig. 16.7, top right). The tombs are oriented east-west with an entrance from above at the east end. The burials were laid out with the head to the west. Some of the sixty-five fragmentary and complete epitaphs from the excavation were found on the Asklepieion plateau. These record details such as the owner and the owner's trade, the seller and the seller's trade, the price of one and one half solidi, and the occupants and the date of their death by month and year of indiction. The owners and occupants were not the great and the good but ordinary people such as gardeners, goatherds, and bath attendants. In one case, a burial inscription was found in one of the rock-cut tombs. It reads "<Inscribed seriphed cross> A sepulcher belonging to Eusebios the Anatolian, a shoe and clothing merchant, purchased from Leonidios the fuller. Here lies Noumenis of blessed memory who died the fifth day of the month of June, in the sixth year of the indiction <Inscribed seriphed cross>." [20] The grave contained four skeletons and was dated in the Corinth publications to the fourth century on the strength of two nearby lamps.[21] These lamps we would now place no earlier than the mid-sixth century. In this context, the inscription is also very informative. It reads as a legal document and, like papyri in which indictions started to appear alone or with regnal year after

---

[18]Roebuck, *Asklepieion*, 169.

[19]Ibid., 164.

[20]John Harvey Kent, *The Inscriptions, 1926–1950* (Corinth VIII.3; Princeton, N.J.: ASCSA, 1966) no. 522.

[21]Roebuck, *Asklepieion*, plate 67.1, L-2908, Broneer type XXIX.4, and a Broneer type XXXI. Similar inscriptions (Kent, *Inscriptions*, nos. 531 and 552) dated by indiction were apparently associated with a nearby grave with three Broneer type XXXI lamps. See Corinth Notebook 122 (131) 79, 81, 92, and 94.

the discontinuation of the *fasti consulares* and the publication of Justinian's *Nov*. 47, these gravestones dated by indiction alone should date no earlier than the mid-sixth century.[22] The Roman church, under whose jurisdiction Corinth fell, adopted the indiction for establishing the dates of documents during the reign of Pope Pelagius II (579–590). Unlike the tile graves of the Hollow, the rock-cut graves were regularly used for multiple burials and frequently contained small pitchers and lekythoi.

To the west of the Lerna Hollow, the graves resemble those on the Asklepieion terrace to the east.[23] These too are multiple-burial, rock-cut cists. Although they were close to the surface and thus exposed to modern plowing, several graves preserved vaulted stuccoed mounds heaped over them, one or two of which were incised with a cross in the stucco (fig. 16.8d). Large quantities of fragmentary lamps were found in the mounds and many complete lamps were found around the tombs. Small pitchers and lekythoi are common; one grave contained eight bodies, with which were seven such libation vessels, an imported red-slipped pitcher, and an imported red-slipped bowl stamped with a cross. The pottery dates the use of the grave to ca. 600.[24]

The rock-cut graves of the Asklepieion district anticipate tomb types of the mid seventh to late eighth centuries. These later tombs were for multiple burials and were built of spolia; such tombs were either equipped with a built vault with an entrance hole at the east end or simply covered with squared slabs. They also frequently contain small pitchers. Late-seventh-century graves sometimes have Syracuse-type belt buckles associated with the deceased. One such grave in the Kenchreian Gate Basilica had a Syracuse belt buckle and two coins of Constans II.[25] Eighth-century burials occasionally

[22]K. A. Wolp ("Indictions and Dating Formulas in the Papyri from Byzantine Egypt A. D. 337–540," *Archiv für Papyrusforschung und verwandte Gebiete* 33 [1987] 96) suggested that the indiction dating of papyri with consular year or reintroduced regnal year followed Justinian I's *Nov*. 47 in 537. The *fasti consulares* was abandoned in 535 in the East and 541 in the West. Only two gravestones from Corinth are dated by consular or regnal year in addition to indiction. SEG XXIX, 310 is dated to the third year of the reign of Justinian in 529 C.E., while SEG XXXI, 288 dates to 524 C.E. based on consular year. I thank Ben Millis for drawing my attention to these latter references.

[23]Wiseman, "Excavations, 1966," 417–20; idem, "Excavations, 1967–1968," 79–87; and idem, "Excavations, 1969–1970," 8–9.

[24]Corinth Notebook 136 (1933). The bowl is an Askra Ware bowl as Sanders, "Late Roman Bath," no. 5; and Slane and Sanders, "Late Roman Horizons," no. 3.16. The pitcher is as ibid., no. 3.17.

[25]D. I. Pallas, "Données nouvelles sur quelques boucles et fibules considérées comme avares et slaves et sur la Corinthe entre le VIᵉ et le IXᵉ s.," *Byzantino-bulgarica* 7 (1981) 298 and n. 18.

have Corinth-type buckles and a selection of weapons, jewelry, and libation vessels.[26] They tend to cluster in the region of the former forum. What was the function of the pottery found in the tombs? The lekythoi and pitchers are clearly not offerings, but they may well have been used in the burial liturgy. In modern Orthodox practice, the priest anoints the body of the deceased with oil, water, and wine at the graveside. The containers are now plastic bottles which are discarded after use, but until the recent past, ceramic pitchers were used. These were broken at the gravesite or placed within the grave to prevent reuse. The dish in one of the graves may have been for kalyva—boiled whole grains mixed with pomegranate seeds—or some such dish. These practices seem to relate to pre-Christian Greek burial liturgy. The absence of liturgical vessels in the sixth-century tile graves in the Lerna Court and in many later cist graves on the low hills to the east and west may reflect subtle differences in burial practice. The appearance of vessels in the later sixth century perhaps indicates a degree of syncretism, as the last convinced worshipers of Hellenic deities were reconciled to placing a Christian front on their beliefs and practices. Alternatively, the vessels could reflect the appearance of a more rustic or foreign population in the urban community. Then again, the absence of vessels does not preclude their use and their disposal elsewhere.

Vast quantities of lamps have been found in the Asklepieion cemetery. The large majority are Broneer types 28 and 31 with rather fewer examples of types 29 and 32.[27] Many—but by no means all—have Christian symbols (usually a cross) decorating the discus. On Attic lamps of Broneer type 28, Christian symbols only start appearing after the second quarter of the fifth century. Other subjects on these Attic lamps, such as gladiator and bear and simple rosettes, remained popular to the end of the fifth century, while the common shell pattern, symbolic of Aphrodite and later of the resurrection, continued well into the sixth century.[28] Most of the lamps in the area of the

---

[26]Anna Avraméa, *Le Péloponnèse du VIe au VIIIe siècle: Changements et persistances* (Byzantina Sorbonensia 15; Paris: Publications de la Sorbonne, 1997) 86–96; H. S. Robinson, "Excavations at Corinth: Temple Hill, 1968–1972," *Hesperia* 45 (1976) 222; Charles K. Williams II, Jean MacIntosh, and Joan E. Fisher, "Excavations at Corinth, 1973," *Hesperia* 43 (1974) no. 8; and Charles K. Williams II and Joan E. Fisher, "Corinth, 1974: Forum Southwest," *Hesperia* 44 (1975) no. 2, plate 57a.

[27]Oscar Broneer, *Terracotta Lamps* (Corinth IV.2; Cambridge, Mass.: ASCSA, 1930) 102–21.

[28]Arja Karivieri, *The Athenian Lamp Industry in Late Antiquity* (Papers and Monographs of the Finnish Institute at Athens 5; Helsinki: Foundation of the Finnish Institute at Athens, 1996).

Asklepieion are Corinthian imitations of Attic post-glazing and North African lamps. Since the Corinthian lamp industry seems to have been in total abeyance in the first half of the fifth century, we should date the Corinthian imitations of Attic lamps no earlier than about 450 and probably after 475. They continue well into the sixth century. The North African imitations start in the sixth century and continue at least to the middle of the seventh century.[29] The Asklepieion cemetery provides evidence for Christian burial practices which can be identified as such only from the late fifth century, if not later. The tomb types are the beginning of a tradition which continues at least into the eighth century. The graveside liturgy included the lighting of vigil lamps that were presumably renewed periodically. It appears to have included anointing at the time of burial and a communal sharing of a token meal, perhaps only at the funeral or possibly also at intervals thereafter.

THE CHRISTIAN BASILICAS

I turn now to the evidence of the Christian basilicas—primarily the Lechaion Basilica excavated by the late Demetrios Pallas in the 1950s (fig. 16.10, p. 438).[30] The basilica is built on a sand spit separating the inner basins of Lechaion Harbor from the sea. It consists of a three-aisled structure with two atria at the west end and a transept and single apse at the east end. The total length from outer atrium to apse is 180 m and is comparable to the size of the original basilica of Saint Peter in Rome. It counts among the largest such structures anywhere. Indeed, the length and height of the building made it a prominent landmark for those looking towards the sea from the city and for travellers arriving by land and sea. As in all of the basilicas at Corinth and a great many found in Greece, the nave is divided from the aisles by the high stylobate of the colonnade and by screens between the columns. Clearly, there was an intent to separate the congregation in the aisles from activity in the nave. Galleries above the aisles were accessed by stairwells outside the basilica immediately to the north and south of the inner atrium. The basilica is constructed of rubble and cement in a manner like the bath and the long building at Panayia, and fish have been incised in the grouting inside and out, even on places which were intended to be covered. The floors

---

[29]Slane and Sanders, "Late Roman Horizons."

[30]For a summary of the bibliography, see D. I. Pallas, "Korinth," *Reallexikon zur Byzantinischen Kunst* (Stuttgart: Hiersemann, 1966–) 4:745–811.

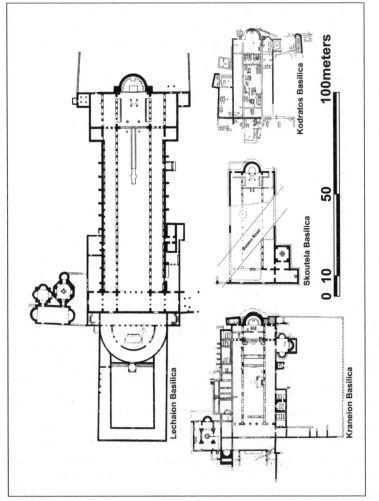

Fig. 16.10 Basilicas at Corinth.

were paved with opus sectile panels and the lower walls were clad with marble revetment. The uniform order of columns, capitals, and screens is of Proconnesian marble and therefore appears, as indeed the whole church may have been, an imperial donation.

It has plausibly been suggested that the basilica is dedicated to Saint Leonidas, who was hung at Corinth, and the seven virgins who mourned his death and were themselves executed by drowning when the corpse of Leonidas was dumped off the coast of Lechaion. Pallas has suggested that the baptistery, which resembles the Panayia Bath in many respects, was originally a martyrium erected near the spot where the eight bodies miraculously washed ashore. Despite this connection, the basilica was not a cemetery church, for there are only four graves associated with it. One of them, a brick-built cist against the exterior of the apse, is that of the presbyter Thomas. The form of the grave and its contents indicate that he died towards the end of the sixth century.[31]

The date of the basilica is a significant issue. From a coin of Marcian (450–457) discovered in the foundations of the basilica, Pallas established that the building was started no earlier than the sixth decade of the fifth century. A coin of Anastasius I (491–518) was found under a section of the interior pavement, showing that it was substantially complete at or after the turn of the century. A coin of Justin I (518–527) discovered in the foundations of the outer atrium, which does not bond with the basilica, shows that additions were still being made in or after the first quarter of the sixth century.[32] In other words, Pallas concluded that the basilica may have been complete by ca. 525 and that it was destroyed by the 552 earthquake centered on Chaironeia, which we now know did not affect Corinth.[33] However, if this basilica that was founded on sand and not on rock was built that early, then it should have been destroyed by the 525 earthquake, which Procopius explicitly says

[31]D. I. Pallas, "Ἀνασκαφή Βασιλικῆς ἐν Λεχαίω," *Prak* (1956) 177–78 and plate 72b.
[32]Pallas, "Korinth."
[33]The earthquake of 551/52 and the attendant tsunami are described by Procopius (*Bell. Goth.* 8.16–25), who reports damage in Achaia, Boeotia, and the region of the Alkionides and Malaic Gulfs. Procopius specifies that Chaeroneia and Coroneia, both in western Boeotia; Patras and Naupaktos, both at the west end of the Corinthian Gulf; and Echinus and Scarphea on the Malaic Gulf were destroyed. Indeed, at Corinth it is now clear that only earthquakes with their epicenter in the immediate region of the city, such as that of 1858, and not those with their epicenter in the Corinthian Gulf—let alone in central Greece—have caused damage to the city's fabric; see N. N. Ambraseys and A. Jackson, "Seismicity and Associated Strain of Central Greece between 1890 and 1988," *Geophysical Journal International* 101 (1990) 663–708.

did severe damage to Corinth.[34] There is, however, no observable destruction debris in or around the building except in the apse at the east end. Indeed, mid-sixth-century structures were built up against the unobstructed south side of the south aisle, but not within the aisle itself. These observations suggest that either the Lechaion basilica was only completed after the 525 earthquake, or that it was inexplicably unaffected by the earthquake. The tomb of the presbyter Thomas shows that the basilica remained in use until ca. 600 and later.

There are three other basilicas at Corinth known from excavation. These share the division of nave from aisles and of lower story from upper story. The Kraneion Basilica (fig. 16.10) resembles the Lechaion Basilica but on a much smaller scale.[35] It lacks an atrium but does have a baptistery on its north side. It is a cemetery church with ample evidence of vaulted brick-built cist graves over a large area: to the south, to the west, and within burial monuments added to and accessing the aisles. A complete sigma table was found in the cemetery to the south. This basilica is dated to the sixth century, and the lamps, pitchers, and coins in the graves indicate that burials continued well into the seventh century. The sixth century basilica of Saint Kodratos is a three-aisle building without atrium or baptistery (fig. 16.10).[36] It, too, is a cemetery church with mausolia attached to the aisles and graves within the aisles and nave, including that of Bishop Eustathios. The Skoutela Basilica has three aisles and a baptistery but was not used as a cemetery church (fig. 16.10).[37] It is also a sixth-century foundation. Finally, the remains of a cement and rubble structure thought by Pallas to be an important basilica close to the amphitheater were further investigated by the American School in December 2000. Remote-sensing survey and examination of the standing remains show this to be a circular or octagonal building 12 m in diameter attached to a rectangular structure 20 m square.[38] To judge from the density of built cist graves to the north of the city walls close by, this building may well be a martyrium.

The division of the aisles from the nave and the galleries from the ground floor has caused some confusion over who in the congregation went where. The solution may be relatively simple. Generally in the East, the rule of entry

[34]Procopius, *Anec.* 18.41–44.

[35]J. M. Shelley, "The Christian Basilica near the Cenchrean Gate at Corinth," *Hesperia* 12 (1943) 166–89; Pallas, "Korinth."

[36]E. G. Stikas, "Ἀναγραφή κοιμητηριακής βασιλικής Παλαίς Κορίνθου," *Prak* (1966) 51–56; Pallas, "Korinth."

[37]Ibid.

[38]Ibid., 764.

into the church was *seniores priores*: the bishop entered first, followed by the clergy and finally the congregation. The reason that the nave of Corinthian churches was segregated from the aisles can be explained by the fact that Corinth was under Rome until the eighth century and the rule *juniores priores* prevailed. The congregation entered first and filed into the aisles, perhaps women on one side and the men on the other. From here they were afforded a ringside view of the approach of the Gospels, the bishop, and the attendant clergy down the nave and into the sanctuary. During the Liturgy of the Faithful, the empty nave enabled efficient distribution of the Eucharist over the nave barrier. If we believe that the galleries, or *catechumena*, as they were termed at the Council of Trullo in the eighth century, were indeed reserved for catechumens, then members of this group were able to make an orderly exit down the stairwells into the atrium at the end of the Liturgy of the Word.

Three of the Corinth basilicas have cruciform baptismal fonts, the design of which—if functionality was a factor in that design—suggests a more total immersion baptism of adult catechumens than is indicated by other forms of font design. It is of interest that the cruciform font at Lechaion was subsequently replaced by a new font placed in one corner, access to which was considerably more restricted. The galleries at Lechaion afford as much space to catechumens as to the baptized in the aisles below. We know that adults often put off baptism until late in life, but one can also speculate that a large number of Corinthians were late in adopting Christianity. This neglect may have required urgent remedial action in the early sixth century.

We have no evidence whatsoever at Corinth for buildings dedicated to Christian worship before about 475. In the sixth century, the buildings that were erected provided an inordinate amount of space for adult catechumens, suggesting a large population of unbaptized Corinthians. Of the four excavated basilicas, three have baptismal facilities.

Conclusions

In this essay, I have presented the latest hard evidence for the worship of Hellenic deities at Corinth. Although we can surmise that low-key worship continued at the Demeter precincts and at the Asklepieion until the end of the fourth century, thereafter their use is difficult to demonstrate archaeologically. The destruction of the Panayia *domus* sculptures ca. 370 is as far as we can push at present. Hard archaeological evidence for Christian worship, such as Christian decorations on lamps, basilicas, and recognizable Christian burial practices, all appear no earlier and plausibly much later than ca. 475. Only in the sixth century is there a sense that Christianity has prevailed. The question of what happened during the intervening generations invites solution. With a new chronological tool at our disposal—a better understanding of Late Roman pottery—I hope that dating will not be a source of doubt for long.

Answering the question of what caused these changes as late as the sixth century is difficult to answer. David Turner has written of the extreme reactions of Christians to natural disasters in the eighth century. He argues that the violent eruption of Thera in 726 caused Leo III to issue an edict promoting the removal of icons.[39] The plague of 746/7 caused Leo's successor, Constantine V, to suspend temporarily his iconoclastic campaign. When he realized that it was iconophiles and not the icons who were to blame for God's vengeance, Constantine attacked the philosophy, the objects, and their worshipers with a vengeance after 750.[40] In the second quarter of the sixth century, Corinthians experienced an extended period of demoralizing natural phenomena that reduced their city and its population to a fraction of what they had once been. The 525 earthquake was followed by a severe global climatic event that endured from ca. 536 to ca. 545. This event is thought to have triggered famine and perhaps to have precipitated the plague of 542 that Procopius credits with killing half of those who survived the earthquake in 525.[41] Finally, a much later and therefore perhaps questionable source, the tenth-century *Chronography* of Bishop Elias of Nisibis, records that an earthquake in 543 destroyed the walls of Corinth.[42] With Poseidon, Demeter, and Asklepios unable to avert these disasters, Corinthians may have had cause to reflect on the relative potency of the Christian God. Combined with mounting pressure from Justinian for Jews, worshipers of Hellenic deities, and others to convert, and for heretics to conform to Orthodoxy (which was often more than a threat of force), these natural disasters may have persuaded many Corinthians to accept Orthodox Christianity in the mid-sixth century.

---

[39]David Turner, "The Politics of Despair: The Plague of 746–747 and Iconoclasm in the Byzantine Empire," *BSA* 85 (1990) 421.

[40]Ibid., 428–29.

[41]Procopius, *Bell. Goth.* 4.14.5–6; M. G. L. Baillie, "Dendrochronology Raises Questions about the Nature of the AD 536 Dust-Veil Event," *The Holocene* 4 (1994); idem, *A Slice through Time: Dendrochronology and Precision Dating* (London: Batsford, 1995) 91–107; M. G. L. Baillie and M. A. R. Munro, "Irish Tree Rings, Santorini, and Volcanic Dust Veils," *Nature* 332 (1988) 344–46; R. B. Stothers, "Mystery Cloud of AD 543," *Nature* 307 (1984) 344–45; and R. B. Stothers and M. R. Rampino, "Volcanic Eruptions in the Mediterranean before AD 630 from Written and Archaeological Sources," *Journal of Geophysical Research* 88 (1983) 6357–71.

[42]Avraméa, *Le Péloponnèse*, 46.

CHAPTER SEVENTEEN

Ecclesiastical Ambiguities: Corinth in the Fourth and Fifth Centuries

Vasiliki Limberis

Gilbert Dagron has argued that Christianizing the ancient city required four things: the building of churches, the burial of bodies inside the city, the rise of the social prestige and civic responsibilities of the bishop and clergy, and finally the local foundation of cults of saints and relics.[1] The city of Corinth is no exception to this rule. In this essay, I assume that there was a secure infrastructure of buildings, Christian cemeteries and martyria, and city planning in place by the late fifth and early sixth centuries.[2] I will address the third and fourth of Dagron's categories, sketching in some detail the status of the Corinthian church in the fourth and fifth centuries from the institutional vantage point. I focus first on episcopal records, and then on hagiography,

---

[1]Gilbert Dagron, "Christianisme dans la ville byzantine," *DOP* 31 (1977) 4.

[2]See Eric A. Ivison, "Burial and Urbanism at Late Antique and Early Byzantine Corinth," in *Town in Transition: Urban Evolution in Late Antiquity and the Early Middle Ages* (ed. Neil Christie and S. T. Loseby; Hants, England: Aldershot, 1996) 99–126, esp. 103. In Corinth, shrines and cemeteries are first associated in the fifth century. Martyria and cemetery basilicas began to be constructed; they were all built over tombs of saints and cemeteries outside the walls. Excavations near Kenchreai Gate at Kraneion show a basilica dating to the late fifth or early sixth century, outside the fifth-century city boundaries. The earliest seems to be the St. Kodratos martyrium basilica (mid-fifth century) on the site of the North Cemetery (55 burials). The basilica was destroyed in 550/51. The Sanctuary of Asklepeios, the Shrine of the Sacred Spring at Lerna, and the gymnasium all became Christian cemeteries between the fourth and sixth centuries. That the Sacred Springs and Fountain of Lamps were gradually Christianized as ἁγιασμά is very likely.

which invites us to look at the Corinthian community's Christian identity from a more self-conscious description. Hagiography plays a very important role, because although the lives of the saints are legendary, they help to bind a "spatial unity and coherence" into the city and its stones, vivifying them with the lives of people and the importance of events.[3] These lives bring a sense of the sacred to the ancient city.

CORINTH UNDER ROME

The church inherited its divisions and "spheres of influence" from the restructuring of the government by Diocletian. This emperor had broken up the large provinces into dioceses, each of which was under one civil ruler, the vicar. The dioceses were grouped into four vast prefectures, each under a praetorian prefect: Gaul, Italy, Illyricum, and the Oriens. In the east, the highest-ranking official was the praetorian prefect in Constantinople, while the second-highest was the prefect of Illyricum; in the west, the praetorian prefect in Italy ranked above the prefect of Gaul. The prefects appointed governors for the provinces, which were smaller than the dioceses, and these governors were responsible for making laws.[4]

The prefecture of Illyricum, the smallest of the four, must be distinguished from the broader geographical region of Illyricum, which originally contained three dioceses.[5] One of these dioceses, the Pannonias, comprising roughly the area of modern Serbia, Croatia, and Montenegro, belonged to the prefecture of Italy.[6] The other two dioceses of this region, the Moesias and the Thraces, belonged to the prefecture of Illyricum. Originally, Corinth was in the diocese of the Moesias, which contained the provinces of Moesia, Dacia, Macedonia, Epirus, Achaea, and Crete.[7] However, Constantine I divided the Moesias into the dioceses of Dacia and Macedonia, and thus Corinth was subsequently part of the diocese of Macedonia.

The organization of ecclesiastical government imitated that of civil government. Every city had a bishop, and every province had a metropolitan,

---

[3]Dagron, "Christianisme," 8.

[4]J. B. Bury, *The History of the Later Roman Empire* (1889; repr., 2 vols., New York: Dover Publications, 1958) 1:25–28.

[5]A. H. M. Jones, *The Later Roman Empire* (2 vols.; Oxford: Basil Blackwell, 1964) 1:47.

[6]Antoine Bon, *Le Péloponnèse byzantin jusqu'en 1204* (Paris: Presses Universitaires de France, 1951) 3.

[7]Jones, *Later Roman Empire*, 1:47.

who resided in the capital.[8] An exarch was higher than a metropolitan and corresponded to the vicar of the civil diocese. Corinth was in the province of Achaia, the ecclesiastical diocese of Moesia or Macedonia (depending on the year), and the prefecture of Illyricum. Following civil government from the first century onward, ecclesiastical geography placed the prefecture of Illyricum under the authority of Italy, so that all the churches of mainland Greece were under the bishop of Rome. Clement of Rome, circa 90 C.E., writes of the troubles he had with his parishioners in Corinth.[9] Even at the end of the fourth century (379–395), when the civil governments of Corinth joined the eastern empire, ecclesiastically the city remained under Rome. And even when Justinian separated Achaia from the prefecture of Illyricum (between 535 and 545), the archbishop of Corinth remained under Roman ecclesiastical jurisdiction.[10] It is generally thought that the complete separation of Illyricum from Rome did not take place until 733.[11] Moreover, from the period of Diocletian until the tenure of Pope Leo I (440–460), the bishop of Thessaloniki continued to act as vicar of the bishop of Rome, since the ecclesiastical vicar was roughly parallel to a praetorian prefect.[12]

From the time of Pope Damascus (366–384), it had been customary for the papacy to maintain relations with the bishop of Thessaloniki in a most controlling manner. Acholius was installed as bishop of Thessaloniki by Pope Damascus in 380.[13] Moreover, by making Acholius a papal vicar, "his personal deputy for the Illyriam provinces," Damascus made significant inroads into preserving Rome's jurisdiction on the Greek mainland against the growing claims of authority by the see of Constantinople.[14]

After the accession of Pope Siricius (384–399), Rome's interest in preserving this relationship in the east became more important, given the imperial government's indecisiveness on the status of the prefecture of Illyricum.[15]

---

[8]Bury, *History of the Later Roman Empire*, 1:64.

[9]*ANF* 1:1–21.

[10]Bon, *Le Péloponnèse byzantin*, 8.

[11]Georges Ostrogorsky, "Byzantine Cities in the Early Middle Ages," *DOP* 13 (1959) 53 n. 22.

[12]Bon, *Le Péloponnèse byzantin*, 8; Charles Pietri, "La géographie de l'Illyricum ecclesiastique et ses relations avec l'Eglise de Rome (Vᵉ–Vⁱᵉ siecles)," in *Villes et Peuplement dans l'Illyricum Protobyzantin* (Rome: Palais Farnese, L'École française de Rome, 1984) 24–25; and Leo the Great, *Ep.* 5.4, 6.5, 13 (PG 54:614–16, 663–66; trans. Edmund Hunt, *Saint Leo: Letters* [FoC 34; New York: Fathers of the Church, 1957]).

[13]W. H. C. Frend, *The Rise of Christianity* (Philadelphia: Fortress, 1984) 628.

[14]Ibid.

[15]Charles Pietri, *Roma Christiana* (2 vols.; Rome: L'École française de Rome, 1976) 2:1071–75.

Since 388, Macedonia and Dacia had sometimes belonged to Milan, and sometimes to Constantinople, with regard to civil administration. By the accession of Theodosius I in 401, Macedonia, which contained Thessaloniki, was effectively part of the prefecture of Oriens.

Pope Siricius was not the only western bishop to continue to correspond with and to influence Bishop Anysius of Thessaloniki. During the late 380s, the doctrine of a certain Bishop Bonosus of Sirmium came to the attention of western bishops. After much scrutiny, Bonosus was condemned at the council of Capua in 391 for his denial of the perpetual virginity of Mary. Not only did Pope Siricius prevail upon Bishop Anysius of Thessaloniki to condemn the heretic Bonosus; Ambrose, bishop of Milan, also succeeded in persuading all the Macedonian bishops to depose Bonosus.[16]

By the time of Pope Innocent I (402–404), increasingly numerous barbarian invasions preoccupied both secular and ecclesiastical leaders. Due to these pressures and his strong claims for the papacy, Innocent lost no time in corresponding with Bishop Anysius of Thessaloniki, in part to ensure that Rome's interests would still be carried out as had been the case under his predecessors, Damascus and Siricius.[17] A good example of such cooperation is the allegiance between Illyricum and Rome in the controversy over John Chrysostom. All of the bishops of Illyricum had sided with Rome in the see's opposition to the deposition of John Chrysostom (403–404).[18] In keeping with their loyalties to Rome, they were accustomed to ignoring Constantinople.[19]

When Rufus was installed as bishop of Thessaloniki at Anysius's death in 407, Pope Innocent acted quickly by sending him a letter spelling out the nature of the vicariate.[20] According to Innocent, the bishop of Thessaloniki was *primus inter primates* and thus had the authority to decide which cases must proceed to the pope. The vicar could convoke councils and had the power to control the relations of metropolitans with other churches.[21] It could be argued that this concept of the papal right to delegate a metropolitan's jurisdiction was directly modeled on the imperial system.[22] What was unique in this arrangement was that the bishop of Thessaloniki acted as a vicar of the pope, commissioned by him. The power was not intrinsic to the see of Thessaloniki

---

[16]Ambrose, *Ep.* 56 (PL 16:1171), cited in Pietri, *Roma Christiana*, 2:1079.
[17]Pietri, *Roma Christiana*, 2:1086–87.
[18]Frend, *Rise of Christianity*, 752.
[19]Pietri, *Roma Christiana*, 2:1088–91.
[20]Innocent, *Ep.* 1 (PL 20:463–66).
[21]Pietri, *Roma Christiana*, 2:1086–88.
[22]Ibid., 2:1095.

itself. In this way, Innocent succeeded in preserving Rome's ecclesiastical influence on the Greek mainland over and above Constantinople's claims. The ramifications of these policies were tested in Corinth, when in 419 there was a contested ecclesiastical election in the province of Achaia. Several years earlier, a former priest of Corinth, Perigenes, had been duly elected and consecrated as bishop of Patras. But the people of Patras did not want Perigenes as their bishop, and they ran the prelate out of town. Known and respected in Corinth, he returned there, although he was, canonically speaking, a bishop "estranged from his see." Nevertheless, the Corinthian Christians, pleased to have him back, took canonical matters into their own hands.[23]

When the metropolitan of Corinth—the very bishop who had consecrated Perigenes to the episcopal seat of Patras—died, the laity and clergy of Corinth elevated Perigenes to the head of the Corinthian church. Needless to say, Perigenes' irregular canonical state was analogous to bigamy. Canon 16 of the Council of Nicaea plainly forbade the translation of any clergy from one parish or see to another "on pain of excommunication."[24] Although this was highly irregular, the bishops of Achaia and those of neighboring provinces convoked a synod at Corinth. Even though some of the Thessalian bishops demanded strict adherence to the canon, the majority decided to keep Perigenes as metropolitan. Whether they were in too much of a hurry or worried about his disapproval, they neglected to consult the pope's vicar, Rufus, the bishop of Thessaloniki. They appealed directly to Rome, begging Pope Boniface to approve their beloved Perigenes.

Surprisingly, Pope Boniface decided in favor of the Achaian majority, against the canons of Nicaea. His decision rested on the proviso that Rufus, as his vicar, approve the elevation of Perigenes to Corinth. In this way he was taking the opportunity to reinforce the papal vicariate in Thessaloniki. He sent a letter to the synod in Corinth to inform them of his decision, and another to Rufus to appoint him as his representative. In the meantime, Boniface was researching the archives for precedents that would justify his decision to authorize Rufus of Thessaloniki to partake of the *sollicitudo* and the *cura pontificales*. In truth, Boniface did not linger long over the archival records; rather, he confirmed that, in the past, this very bishop of Thessaloniki had been quite cooperative with the aims of Rome.[25] As vicar of the pope, the bishop of Thessaloniki was to insure that all the territory of Macedonia and Achaia honored the wishes of Christian Rome.

---

[23]My account of Perigenes follows ibid., 2:1106–8.
[24]*NPNF*[2] 14:21.
[25]Pietri, *Roma Christiana*, 2:1108.

Through several more letters, Boniface prevailed in his declaration that Perigenes was indeed bishop of Corinth, and he confirmed as well the vicariate status of the bishop of Thessaloniki. A minority of bishops was still hostile to him and to the vicariate status of Rufus, but for the meantime Boniface believed that the re-establishment of the vicariate would restore peace. How wrong he was!

In 421, the Thessalian bishops, although a minority, did not let the matter rest. As the most incensed members of the opposition to Rome, the Thessalian bishops called upon Emperor Theodosius II on behalf of the bishops of Illyricum. From their point of view, the synod of Corinth was fraudulent, and they questioned Rufus's authority. They also called upon Bishop Atticus of Constantinople, under whose jurisdiction they had been for the past forty years. An exchange between Atticus and Boniface ensued, with the latter accusing the former of "presumptuousness."[26]

Theodosius wanted to resolve this situation as soon as possible. The fact that he was still angry at the memory of the papacy's intervention on behalf of John Chrysostom (when his father had exiled the bishop and Atticus was elected in his stead) did not help matters. Theodosius's own uncle, Honorius, emperor of the west, had taken the pope's side in the matter. Theodosius did not hesitate, and on 14 July 421 he issued this imperial legislation:

> The Same Augustuses to Phillipus, Praetorian Prefect of Illyricum: We command that the ancient practice and the pristine ecclesiastical canons which have been in force up to the present shall be observed throughout all the provinces of Illyricum and that all innovations shall cease. Then, if any doubt should arise, such cases must be reserved for the synod of priests and their holy court, not without the knowledge of the most reverend man of the sacrosanct law, the Bishop of the City of Constantinople, which enjoys the prerogative of ancient Rome.[27]

Not one to miss an opportunity, Boniface responded to the emperor's challenge by calling on precedent again, this time in the person of Theodosius's uncle in Ravenna, Emperor Honorius. The latter willingly took up the pope's cause, and included Boniface's accusations in his own letter to his nephew. Not only had Boniface censured the Illyrian bishops for intrigue and innovation, he accused Bishop Atticus of pretentiousness, since he was opposing canonical tradition and only defending the privileges and interests of his own see of Constantinople. While admonishing him, Honorius stated his own position in

---

[26]Boniface, *Ep.* 13 (PL 20:770, cited in Pietre, *Roma Christiana*, 1113).

[27]*Codex Theodosianus* 16.2.45. Translated by Clyde Pharr, *The Theodosian Code and Novels and the Sirmondian Constitutions: A Translation with Commentary* (Princeton, N.J.: Princeton University Press, 1952) 449.

a letter to his younger nephew, saying that he was trying to "keep the peace of divine protection, especially for Rome, the city of the Principate."[28] Honorius's intervention succeeded in halting Theodosius's impetuousness. The younger emperor wrote his uncle a conciliatory letter. In it he did not exactly capitulate, but he seconded his uncle's deference to Rome, declaring that he must bow to the ecclesiastical canon and tradition. He said that he rejected the claims of the bishops of Illyricum, preferring to preserve the "ancient state of things." Although in the short run it looked as if Theodosius had lost, he had only yielded. In the long run, the law remained in the codices, and it would prove quite troublesome to such papal claims in the future.

By 422, at the end of his reign, Pope Boniface had succeeded in institutionalizing the vicariate of Thessaloniki. Although it had been hastily established by Pope Innocent at the beginning of the fifth century to take care of immediate problems, Boniface called on the tradition of the vicariate as if it were a venerable institution. Through his quick intervention, Boniface had managed the emperor and condemned Atticus for ambition. Theodosius had retreated diplomatically, permitting the pope to make a strong re-entry.

CORINTH'S SAINTS

Christians of late antiquity localized the holy in their cities as physical examples of their faith and as an insurance of local divine protection. This practice is clear in the descriptions of holy lives honored by the Corinthians as examples of Christian virtue. Four were martyred during the third century, while another provides an example of how criteria for sainthood changed after the Constantinian settlement. The current study draws from several hagiographical collections: the *Syriac Martyrology* of Palladius (circa 411),[29] the *Hieronymian Martyrology* (ca. 450–600),[30] the *Parvum Romanum* (ninth century),[31] the *Synaxarion Constantinopolitanae* (800–900), and the *Menologion* (800–900). The saints treated here were either from Corinth or were honored in Corinth for some heroic witness. Interestingly enough, the

[28]Correspondence between Boniface and Honorius, *Ep.* 10–11 (PL 20:769–71, cited in Pietri, *Roma Christiana*, 2:1118–19).

[29]Hans Lietzmann, *Die drei altesten martyrologien* (Bonn: Marcus and Weber, 1911).

[30]For the *Hieronymian Martyrology*, see Hugh Jackson Lawlor, ed., *The Psalter and Martyrology of Ricemarch* (2 vols.; London: Harrison and Sons, 1914).

[31]For the *Parvum Romanum*, see Henri Quentin, ed., *Les Martyrologes historiques du Moyen Age* (Paris: Librairie Victor Le Coffre, 1908) ch. 6.

Corinthians appear not to have honored Paul with either a church or a place of pilgrimage. This may be because it was Apollos who was remembered as the first bishop of the city. Honors to Paul are found in Seleucia as well as in the famous cult of St. Thecla in Asia Minor. Omitted in this study are three male martyrs, all from Corinth, who are mentioned in the *Parvum Romanum* but were never included in the *Synaxarion* or the *Menologion*. They are Crispus and Gaius, honored together on 4 October,[32] along with the deacon Tymonis, honored on 19 April.[33]

A word of caution must be inserted, however, about using hagiography as a "historical" source in the post-Enlightenment sense of the word. Gregoire warns that "there is nothing more commonplace in hagiography than attaching passions of saints of unknown provenance and date to the Decian persecutions."[34] This is the case with at least one example from Corinth. We are also warned that "many striking episodes which an inexperienced reader would be tempted to take for original inventions are mere reminiscences or floating traditions which cling sometimes to one saint, and then sometimes to another."[35] The lives of the saints are useful for understanding how Corinth fared in the attribution of saints for the church, and, especially where there is outside evidence, whom the Corinthians honored as holy in their own city.

The first is Saint Leonidas and his seven companions—all women—who were martyred in Corinth under the consul Venustus around 240. The earliest martyrologies, the Syriac (ca. 411) and the Hieronymian, as well as the oldest synaxaries of the Orthodox church, place the feast of Leonidas and his companions on 16 April.[36] This saint has a very interesting history, *post sanctum*. To this day, however, Saint Leonidas is honored in the Orthodox church as an archbishop of Athens on 15 April, instead of 16 April.[37] François Halkin, in that wonderfully ineluctable way of the Bollandists, unraveled the lives of the Saints Leonidas, demonstrating that the two men had been conflated in the thirteenth century.[38] Leonidas's transformation into an Athenian bishop speaks to the ease with which Athens eclipsed Corinth at a much later date.

---

[32]Ibid., 442, "Corinthi, crispi et gaii."

[33]Ibid., 424, "Corinthi tymonis diaconi de VII."

[34]Henri Gregoire, *Les persécutions dans l'Empire romain* (Brussels: Palais des Academies, 1950) 158.

[35]Hippolyte Delehaye, *Legends of the Saints* (trans. V. M. Crawford; London: Longmans, Green, and Co., 1907) 28.

[36]Idem, *Les origines du culte des martyrs* (Brussels: Société des Bollandistes, 1933) 262.

[37]In some calendars it is celebrated on April 15, in others on April 16.

[38]François Halkin, "Saint Léonide et ses sept compagnes martyrs à Corinthe," in *Recherches et documents d'hagiographie byzantine* (Subsidia Hagiographica Graeca 51; Brussels: Société des Bollandistes, 1971) 60–66; Halkin provides an edition of the account of Leonidas and

Leonidas of Corinth had seven women companions: Nike, Chariessa, Nounexia, Vasilissa, Galina, Kalle, and Theodora. Leonidas and the seven virgin women were known in Corinth for their fasting, continual prayer, and rather bold preaching in town. Eventually, they were all arrested for their activities, and the virgins were separated from Leonidas. When they were brought before the consul, the magistrate demanded that Leonidas sacrifice to the gods. Twice he was warned that unless he performed the proper sacrifice, he would be tortured. Leonidas gave a rather philosophical response, maintaining that while the body is perishable and liable to be destroyed by things of a similar nature, a soul, being invulnerable, will perceive rational things all the better once it is set free from material things.[39] Of course the Roman leaders of Corinth just stared in amazement at the young man, who appeared utterly mad to them.

The leader then ordered that Leonidas be taken elsewhere, and he had the seven virgins brought before him. He told the women, "Leonidas, who at first was in error, now promises to sacrifice."[40] Recognizing the deception, the women replied that they would indeed sacrifice—but to God and his son, Jesus Christ, for it was to these that Leonidas had promised to sacrifice, and not to the idols.[41] The leader pressed them further, urging them to sacrifice to the twelve gods who protect the whole world. But the virgins replied that these so-called gods were but matter shaped in human form, unable to see or move.[42]

The Corinthian leader became very angry and sent the virgins off to prison. He ordered Leonidas brought back, failed again to convince him to sacrifice, and then sent him off to be tortured by fire and flogging. The leader then ordered that the virgins be returned for further questioning, which included *double entendres* of an obviously sexual nature. He asked them, "Of what rank and family are you? And what kind of interaction (κοινωνία) do you have with Leonidas?" They answered that they were "Christians (χριστιαναί), just as our companion

---

his companions found in MS Patmos 254. The *Acta Sanctorum* mentions Leonidas, bishop of Athens, on 15 April (*de Sancto Leonide, Episcopo Athenarum in Graecia, AASS* 15 April, 374–75) and Leonidas of Corinth on 16 April (*de SS. Callisto, Charisio, Leonide, Christiana, Galla, Theodora, Lota, Tertia, Caristo, item Chariessa, Nice, Gallena, Nunechia, Basilissa, Cali. Martyribus Corinthi in Achaia, AASS* 16 April, 399–401). The *Menologion* (PG 117:405) remembers Leonidas and the seven companions, martyred on 16 April. Curiously, the Florus of Lyons recension does not mention Leonidas on 16 April but rather notes, "Apud Corinthum, Calisti et Carisi, cum alius septum, omnum in mare mensorum" (Quentin, *Les Martyrologes*, 330).

[39]Ibid., 63–64.
[40]Ibid., 64.
[41]Ibid., 65.
[42]Ibid.

(συνέταιρος) Leonidas is." They further maintained that although they were separate in physical family and in nature, they were one in manner and joined together in faith. Hearing this, the consul promised them the same punishment as Leonidas. After they were flogged, each of them was chained, weighted down with rocks, and thrown into the sea. After a day or so their bodies washed up onto the beach. Pious men gathered up their remains, buried them, and built a holy shrine above their bodies where, the account concludes, the saints were honored by the faithful and worked an endless series of cures.[43]

The baptistery of the great Lechaion Basilica was perhaps the original martyrion of Leonidas.[44] It was constructed in the early fifth century, near the beach of Lechaion. The basilica itself was built later, in the mid-sixth century, and rebuilt a century afterward. It is believed to have been dedicated to St. Leonidas and his companions. It is the largest basilica yet found in Greece, measuring 180 m in length. The expensive mosaics and costly marble of every hue with which it was decorated are evidence of Christianity's emerging social and financial influence in the city. Prominent Christians were acting as *curiales* in beneficence for Corinth, while sacralizing it.

St. Kodratos is probably the most famous of the saints of Corinth, remembered in the calendar on 10 March.[45] But there are considerable problems with his vita. To begin with, there are at least four different individuals named Kodratos who have been confused with each other. One was the author of an apology in the second century, one was bishop of Athens, another was a prophet of Asia, and the fourth was a martyr of Corinth.[46] According to Eusebius's *Ecclesiastical History*, Kodratos was an apologist in Athens. Jerome identified this apologist with the bishop of Athens.[47] It is also likely that a certain "Isocrates" named by Pseudo-Pionius in a series of transmitters of the *Life of Polycarp* is in fact a textually corrupt reference to Kodratos of Corinth, whom Pseudo-Pionius knew as a Decian martyr.[48]

In the *Parvum Romanum*, the Corinthian saint is remembered as "Quadratus martyr" on 26 May.[49] In the *Carthaginian Martyrology*, which includes

[43]Ibid.

[44]Donald Engels, *Roman Corinth: An Alternative Model for the Classical City* (Chicago: University of Chicago Press, 1990) 119.

[45]*AASS, de Sanctis Martyribus Codrato, Dionysio, Cypriano, Anecto, Paulo, Crescente, Corinthi in Peloponneso,* 10 March, 4–11; *Menologion,* 10 March, Ἄθλησις τῶν ἁγίων μαρτύρων Καδράτου, Κυπριανοῦ, καὶ τῶν σὺν αὐτοῖς (PG 117:345–48).

[46]Gregoire, *Les Persecutions,* 159.

[47]Eusebius, *Hist. Eccl.* 4.3; Jerome, *De vir. illust.* 19–20.

[48]Gregoire, *Les Persecutions,* 158–60.

[49]Quentin, *Les Martyrologes,* 428.

saints from outside that region, a St. Quadratus is honored on 20 August.[50] The Florus of Lyons recension of the *Roman Martyrology* also names on 26 May, "Athenis quadrati discipuli apostolorum."[51] The following account of Kodratos's career is drawn from the *Menologion*.[52]

Under the persecutions of Decius and Valerian (249–259), the Christians of Corinth were particularly hard-pressed. To escape capture, many Christians fled to the mountains, as did a young woman who was pregnant. She hid there for some time, ultimately giving birth to a baby boy in her hideaway. Soon she died, but her baby boy was "nourished by the clouds above him with both water and food." As time went by, he grew up and came to be known as "Holy Kodratos." Many started coming to him for Christian instruction in the truth, including Kyprianos, Dionysios, Anektos, Paul, and Kriskes. Their fame spread from the mountains into town, and soon they were denounced and arrested, then tortured and decapitated. The relics of Kodratos were placed in a church later identified with the Cemetery Basilica, north of the city, built in the late fourth century. There the relics could act as a vanguard for Corinth. The name "Saint Kodratos" was found inscribed on a lintel of the basilica.[53]

Kodratos's follower Dionysios, however, seems to have escaped the first roundup. He continued his Christian life, and soon was denounced to the archon of Corinth as "one of those who were familiar with holy Kodratos, for not having obeyed the mandate of the emperor, and looking down on the great gods."[54] There follows in the short vita a résumé of Dionysios's teaching: "He proclaims some other god who was crucified, saying that he was the maker of heaven and earth and sea, and all creatures in them, the very one who would, in the future, come out of heaven and judge the living and the dead, and give back to each according to his works."[55] After being given one more chance to renounce Christ, Dionysios was killed with a sword.

The *Menologion* honors Victorinus and his six companions, martyred in Corinth, on 31 January.[56] Again, the violence took place during the Decian persecutions. Victorinus, Victor, Nikesopos, Claudianus, Diodorus, Serapion, and Papias were handed over to Tertius the proconsul. The vita makes a point

[50]Lietzmann, *Altesten martyrologien,* 5.
[51]Quentin, *Les Martyrologes,* 428.
[52]*Menologion,* PG 117:345–48.
[53]Engels, *Roman Corinth,* 119.
[54]Ibid.
[55]καὶ ἀποδοῦναι ἑκάστῳ κατὰ τὰ ἔργα αὐτοῦ.
[56]Ἄθλησις τοῦ ἁγίου μάρτυρος Οὐικτωρίνου καὶ τῶν σὺν αὐτῷ ἓξ ἁγίων (*Menologion,* PG 117:288).

of stating that Tertius tortured them very fiercely. Victorinus had his right eye gouged out, his hands and feet cut off, and he was put into a large mortar stone and pounded to death. Victor, having had his tongue excised, was also crushed in the mortar stone. Nikesopos was squeezed so hard that blood ran from his nose. After being hung by his hair, he too was killed in the mortar stone. Claudianus died by hanging after his feet and hands were cut off. Diodorus was burned. Serapion was hung upside down and decapitated. And Papias had his limbs removed, was stoned, and finally was thrown into an abyss.

In the *Lausiac History*, Palladius repeats from the "book of Hippolytus" the story of a martyr who died to rescue a woman from a brothel.[57] Although the author does not name the persecutors, it is likely that the martyrdom occurred under Diocletian. The woman was a beautiful virgin, of a prominent family in Corinth, who practiced an ascetic life. She was denounced to the pagan magistrate "as one who blasphemed both the times and the emperors and spoke ill of the idols." But everyone who set eyes on her praised her beauty. The magistrate was no exception. He was inflamed with erotic passion for her, and devised a suitable torture because of it. He ordered her to be taken to a brothel, and required a daily payment of three pieces of money in exchange for her services. And so she was dragged off. But when men begged her for her favors, she put them off by saying that she had an offensive sore, and that she feared they would hate her because of it. She pleaded for a few days' respite, promising that she would then render them her services for free. Then she began her fervent prayer to God.

God answered her prayers by inspiring a young man, the *magister officiorum* (νεανίσκος μαγιστριανός), with a zeal for martyrdom so that he would help her in her plight. The man worked out a deal with her keeper so that he could spend the night with her. To her surprise, the young man told her to get up, disrobe, put on his clothes, and sneak out of the brothel veiled in his cloak. The next day, the keeper discovered the plot and immediately had the young man thrown to the beasts. Thus, writes Palladius, "He became a martyr in two senses, both for his own sake and for the sake of that blessed one."

The lurid tale of St. Helikonis of Thessaloniki, whose passion is attested in none of our martyrologies, reached its painful conclusion at Corinth. Her struggle took place under the emperors Gordian III (238–244) and Philipus Iulius (244–249), and her martyrdom is remembered on 28 May.[58] Her vita

---

[57]Palladius, *Lausiac History*, ch. 65 (trans. W. Lowther Clarke; London: SPCK, 1918) 171–73.

[58]*AASS, de S. Heliconide Martyre*, 28 May, 728–31; and *AASS, Propylaeum Novembris, Synaxarium Ecclesiae Constantinopolitanae* (1902) 713–14.

relates that a terrible persecution broke out against Christians, and that orders were sent throughout all the prefectures, which included Achaia and Macedonia. Helikonis was arrested and sent to Corinth to appear before the duke, Perinius. She would not bow down or make sacrifices to the idols, but courageously proclaimed Christ as the true God.

Thus a series of truly hideous tortures followed. Her persecutors tied her to the harness of a yoke of oxen and dragged her on the ground. Next, they threw her in the middle of burning coal, tar, and oil, but she did not suffer. They lit a fire around her and shaved her head. Undeterred, she went into the temple of idols and through her prayers hurled down the statues of Athena, Zeus, and Asklepios. Because of that they cut off her breasts. Finally she was led to the proconsul, Justinus. She still refused to sacrifice, and so they threw her in a furnace. As pieces of her flesh fell away, the archangels Michael and Gabriel gathered them. The persecutors threw what was left of Helikonis to the wild beasts, but the beasts did not approach her. Instead, one hundred and twenty of the guards died. Finally, because she had defied death, her tormentors decapitated her.

I would like to end this treatment of the saints of Corinth with the life of St. Kyriakos the Anchorite, who is remembered in the calendar on 30 September.[59] His vita is a long and rather tedious account of a holy man who grew up in Corinth and went to Palestine in search of the monastic life. Besides the account of his life, which includes accounts of visitors from Corinth to his monastery in Palestine, this vita is a wonderful contrast to the four martyrdoms of the third century. Though the details of the vita are quotidian at worst and overly concerned with Origenist theology at best, it does tell us that the church in Corinth was well respected, well known, and had some connections. Kyriakos was born to a priest named John and his wife, Eudoxia, at the end of the reign of Theodosius II, who died in 450. His mother Eudoxia's brother Peter was the metropolitan of Corinth, whose correspondence with Pope Leo VII has been preserved.[60]

Above all, these bits of information tell us that there was a growing ecclesiastical upper class of which Kyriakos's family was intrinsically a part. Perhaps his father "married up," since his wife's family included the metropolitan. In any case, the life of Kyriakos sheds light on a thriving Christian community in the fifth-century capital of Achaia that was, however, not without its ecclesiastical irregularities. Corinthian clergy are not known for any significant

---

[59]Βίος καὶ πολιτεία τοῦ ὁσίου πατρὸς ὑμῶν Κυριάκου τοῦ ἀναχωρήτου, PG 115:919–44.

[60]Hunt, *St. Leo the Great: Letters,* esp. 149–50.

contribution to doctrinal controversies. Nevertheless, the vita of Kyriakos does contain a good deal of theological sparring on the merits of Origenist theology. Of course Kyriakos's positions are fully Orthodox.

Conclusion

From this evidence we can say quite a bit about Christian Corinth in the fourth and fifth centuries. First of all, although Corinth was a vibrant, well-established community, the city was definitely circumscribed by its provincial status. Bishops in this period gradually took on the roles of the now disappearing *curiales*. The elites now included the clergy. Ranking of ecclesiastical officials mirrored the offices of the state, which was growing ever weaker on the local level. Justinian's legislation from 535 to 556 implicitly acknowledges the centralizing policies of the imperial government, which had been growing for over a century. These laws virtually eliminated provincial power: bishops filled the gap as a real substitute for municipal magistrates.[61] This is evident in Corinth in the building of new houses and in new plans for churches and cemeteries in the city. These activities reveal the bishops' active sponsorship of and participation in the renovation of the city.[62]

It appears, however, that Corinth was a victim of the tension between growing imperial centralization and Rome's own growth of ecclesiastical power, which sought to check Constantinople's centralization policies. Corinth was caught both geographically and politically in the vise between papal power in the west and imperial power in the east. Illyricum's difficult position was reflected in its inability to act as an independent ecclesiastical entity. The Perigenes affair also shows that the local clergy and people were likely to take matters into their own hands, despite the traditions of Rome or the councils of Nicaea.

The hagiography of Corinth gives a more intimate—if more ideological—view of Corinth's Christian identity. St. Kodratos, St. Leonidas, and their companions sacralized the city early on with shrines and martyria that acted as cemeteries for socially prominent believers, as well as centers of pilgrimage and healings. From the evidence in the *Synaxarion* and *Menologion*, Corinthian Christians suffered in remarkable ways during the

---

[61]Dagron, "Christianisme," 20; Justinian, *Nov.* 15, 86, 128, 134.3.

[62]Mark Whittow, "Ruling the Late Roman and Early Byzantine City: A Continuous History," *Past and Present* 129 (1990) 28–29.

Decian persecutions; perhaps this is because it was a provincial capital. The theology in the martyrdoms is an interesting blend of first-century Christian kerygma, third-century "us against the world" apocalyptic martyrdom, and post-Constantinian growth of the cult of the saints. The lives of the saints tell us that Corinth saw itself as a thoroughly Christian city, bearing witness *locally* to the Christian life.

Finally, as we have seen in the life of St. Kyriakos, Corinth had a growing stratum of high-status clergy. His vita shows the Corinthian church in communication with famous monasteries in Palestine as well. Because of its status as a provincial capital, Corinth was overshadowed by larger cities and their charismatic bishops during the fourth and fifth centuries. The evidence shows that Corinth, albeit quiet and provincial, was a vibrant city with a strong Christian identity that was already well established and continued to grow in this period.

Bibliography

Adams, Edward. *Constructing the World: A Study in Paul's Cosmological Language*. Edinburgh: T&T Clark, 2000.

Agusta-Boularot, Sandrine. "Fontaines et fontaines monumentales en Grèce de la conquête romaine à l'époque flavienne: permanence ou renouveau architectural?" Pages 167–236 in *Constructions publiques et programmes édilitaires en Grèce entre le IIᵉ siècle av. J.-C. et le Iᵉʳ siècle ap. J.-C.* Edited by Jean-Yves Marc and Jean-Charles Moretti. BCHSup 39. Paris: de Boccard, 2001.

Aitken, Ellen Bradshaw, and Jennifer K. Berenson MacLean, eds. *Flavius Philostratus: Heroikos*. Atlanta, Ga.: Society of Biblical Literature, 2001.

Alcock, Susan E. *Graecia Capta: The Landscapes of Roman Greece*. Cambridge: Cambridge University Press, 1993.

———. "Greece: A Landscape of Resistance?" Pages 103–16 in *Dialogues in Roman Imperialism: Power, Discourse, and Discrepant Experience in the Roman Empire*. Edited by D. J. Mattingly. JRASup 23. Ann Arbor, Mich.: Journal of Roman Archaeology, 1997.

———. "The Heroic Past in a Hellenistic Present." Pages 20–34 in *Hellenistic Constructs*. Edited by Paul Cartledge, Peter Garnsey, and Erich Gruen. Berkeley: University of California Press, 1997.

———. "The Pseudo-History of Messenia Unplugged." *TAPA* 129 (1999) 333–41.

Alexiou, Margaret. *The Ritual Lament in Greek Tradition*. Cambridge: Cambridge University Press, 1974.

Amandry, Michel. *Le monnayage des duovirs corinthiens*. BCHSup 15. Paris: de Boccard, 1988.

Amato, Eugenio. *Studi su Favorino: Le orazioni pseudo-crisostomiche*. Salerno: Edisud, 1995.

Ambraseys, N. N., and A. Jackson. "Seismicity and Associated Strain of Central Greece between 1890 and 1988." *Geophysics Journal International* 101 (1990) 663–708.

d'Ambrosio, A. "Termopolio e Casa di Le Betuzio Placido." Pages 109–13 in *Pompei: Abitare sotto il Vesuvio*. Edited by Mariarosaria Borriello et al. Ferrara: Ferrara arte, 1996.

Ameling, Walter. *Herodes Atticus*. 2 vols. Hildesheim: Georg Olms, 1983.

Anderson, J. K. "Corinth: Temple E Northwest, Preliminary Report, 1965." *Hesperia* 36 (1967) 1–12.

Anderson, M. L. "The Villa of P. Fannius Synistor at Boscoreale." *Metropolitan Museum of Art Bulletin: Pompeian Frescoes in the Metropolitan Museum of Art* (1987/1988) 16–35.

Arce, Javier. *Funus Imperatorum: los funerales de los emperadores imperiales*. Madrid: Alianza, 1988.

Arcellaschi, André. *Médée dans le théâtre latin d'Ennius à Sénèque*. Collection de l'École française de Rome 132. Rome: L'École française de Rome, 1990.

Arnim, Hans von (Johannes de Arnim). *Dionis Prusaensis quem vocant Chrysostomum quae exstant omnia*. 2 vols. Berlin: Weidmanns, 1893–1896.

Asgari, N. "Die Halbfabrikate kleinasiatischer Girlandensarkophage und ihre Herkunft." *AA* (1977) 329–80.

———. "Helenistik ve Roma Çağlarında Anadolu Ostotekleri." Ph.D. diss., Istanbul University, 1965.

Astour, Michael G. *Hellenosemitica*. 2d ed. Leiden: Brill, 1967.

Athanasoulis, D. Ch. "Λουτρική εγκατάσταση στην Κοκκινόρραχι Σπάρτης." *Πρακτικά του Ε' Διεθνούς Συνεδρίου Πελοποννησιακών Σπουδών* 2 (1998) 209–44.

Audin, A. "Inhumation et incinération." *Latomus* 19 (1960) 312–22, 518–32.

Avraméa, Anna. *Le Péloponnèse du VIᵉ au VIIIᵉ siècle: Changements et persistances*. Byzantina Sorbonensia 15. Paris: Publications de la Sorbonne, 1997.

Babelon, Ernest. *Description historique et chronologique des monnaies de la République romaine vulgairement appelées monnaies consulaires*. 2 vols. Paris: Rollin et Feuardent, 1885–1886.

———. *Le trésor d'argenterie de Berthouville près de Bernay*. Paris: Lévy, 1916.

Baillie, M. G. L. "Dendrochronology Raises Questions about the Nature of the AD 536 Dust-Veil Event." *The Holocene* 4 (1994) 212–17.

———. *A Slice through Time: Dendrochronology and Precision Dating*. London: Batsford, 1995.

Baillie, M. G. L., and M. A. R. Munro. "Irish Tree Rings, Santorini, and Volcanic Dust Veils." *Nature* 332 (1988) 344–46.

Bakirtzis, Charalambos. "Περί του συγκροτήματος της Αγορας της Θεσσαλονίκης." Pages 257–69 in *Archaia Makedonia II*. Thessaloniki: Institute for Balkan Studies, 1977.

Bakker, Jan T. *Living and Working with the Gods: Studies of Evidence for Private Religion and Its Material Environment in the City of Ostia (100–500 AD)*. Dutch Monographs on Ancient History and Archaeology 12. Amsterdam: J. C. Gieben, 1994.

Barclay, John. "Conflict in Thessalonica." *CBQ* 55 (1993) 512–30.

———. "Thessalonica and Corinth: Social Contrasts in Pauline Christianity." *JSNT* 47 (1992) 512–30.

Barigazzi, Adelmo. "Favorino di Arelate." *ANRW* II.34.1 (1993) 556–81.

———. *Favorino di Arelate: Opere: Introduzione, Testo Critico e Commento*. Testi greci et latini con commento filologico 4. Florence: Lelice Le Monnier, 1966.

Barnes, Ethne. "The Dead Do Tell Tales." Pages 435–43 in *Corinth: The Centenary, 1896–1996*. Edited by Charles K. Williams II and Nancy Bookidis. Corinth XX. Princeton, N.J.: ASCSA, 2003.

Barrett, C. K. "Paul's Opponents in 2 Corinthians." Pages 60–86 in *Essays on Paul*. Philadelphia: Westminster, 1982.

———. *The Second Epistle to the Corinthians*. HNTC. New York: Harper & Row, 1973.

Bartchy, S. Scott. Mallon chrēsai: *First-Century Slavery and the Interpretation of 1 Corinthians 7:21*. SBLDS 11. 1973. Repr., Atlanta, Ga.: Scholars, 1985.

Bartoli, A. "Il culto della Mater Deum Magna Idaea e di Venere Genitrice." *Mem. Pont.* 6 (1947) 229–39.

Barton, Carlin. "Savage Miracles: Redemption of Lost Honor in Roman Society and the Sacrament of the Gladiator and the Martyr." *Representations* 45 (1994) 41–71.

———. "The Scandal of the Arena." *Representations* 27 (1989) 1–36.

———. *The Sorrows of the Ancient Romans: The Gladiator and the Monster*. Princeton, N.J.: Princeton University Press, 1993.

Barton, I. M. "Capitoline Temples in Italy and the Provinces (Especially Africa)." *ANRW* II.12.1 (1982) 259–342.

Beard, Mary, and John Henderson. "With This Body I Thee Worship: Sacred Prostitution in Antiquity." Pages 56–79 in *Gender and Body in the Ancient Mediterranean*. Edited by Maria Wyke. Malden, Mass.: Blackwell, 1998.

Beard, Mary, John North, and Simon Price. *Religions of Rome*. 2 vols. Cambridge: Cambridge University Press, 1998.

Beaumont, Lesley. "Born Old or Never Young? Femininity, Childhood, and the Goddesses of Ancient Greece." Pages 71–95 in *The Sacred and the Feminine in Ancient Greece*. Edited by Sue Blundell and Margaret Williamson. New York: Routledge, 1998.

Bees, Nikos A. *Corpus der griechisch christlichen Inschriften von Hellas: Inschriften von Peloponnes: Bd. 1, Isthmos-Korinthos*. Vol. 1 of *Inscriptiones graecae christianae veteres et byzantinae*. Chicago: Ares, 1978.

Benson, J. L. "Human Figures in Later Protocorinthian Vase Painting." *Hesperia* 64 (1995) 163–77.

Berger, Peter L., and Thomas Luckmann. *The Social Construction of Reality*. Garden City, N.Y.: Doubleday, 1966.

Bergmann, B. "Rhythms of Recognition: Mythological Encounters in Roman Landscape Painting." Pages 81–107 in *Im Spiegel des Mythos: Bilderwelt und Lebenswelt*. Edited by Franceso de Angelis and Susanne Muth. Wiesbaden: L. Reichert, 1999.

Bergquist, Birgitta. *Heracles on Thasos*. Boreas 5. Uppsala: University of Uppsala, 1973.

Berthiaume, Guy. *Les rôles du mágeiros: Étude sur la boucherie, la cuisine et le sacrifice dans la Grèce ancienne*. Mnemosyne 70. Leiden: Brill, 1982.

Betz, Hans Dieter. *Der Apostel Paulus und die sokratische Tradition: Eine exegetische Untersuchung zu seiner 'Apologie' 2 Kor 10–13*. BHT 45. Tübingen: Mohr Siebeck, 1972.

———. *2 Corinthians 8 and 9: A Commentary on Two Administrative Letters of the Apostle Paul*. Hermeneia. Philadelphia: Fortress, 1985.

———. *Galatians*. Hermeneia. Philadelphia: Fortress, 1979.

Bieringer, Reimund, and Jan Lambrecht. *Studies on 2 Corinthians*. BETL 112. Leuven: Leuven University Press, 1994.

Biers, Jane. "Lavari Est Vivere: Baths in Roman Corinth." Pages 303–19 in *Corinth: The Centenary, 1896–1996*. Edited by Charles K. Williams II and Nancy Bookidis. Corinth XX. Princeton, N.J.: ASCSA, 2003.

Bird, Phyllis. "'To Play the Harlot': An Inquiry into an Old Testament Metaphor." Pages 75–84 in *Gender and Difference in Ancient Israel*. Edited by Peggy L. Day. Minneapolis: Fortress, 1989.

Blegen, Carl William, Oscar Broneer, Richard Stillwell, and Alfred Raymond Bellinger. *Acrocorinth: Excavations in 1926*. Corinth III.1. Cambridge, Mass.: ASCSA, 1930.

Blegen, Carl William, Hazel Palmer, and Rodney S. Young. *The North Cemetery*. Corinth XIII. Princeton: ASCSA, 1964.

Blok, Josine H. *The Early Amazons*. Leiden: Brill, 1995.

Boardman, John. *Athenian Red Figure Vases: The Archaic Period*. London: Thames and Hudson, 1975.

———. *Greek Art*. New York: Praeger, 1964.

Bon, Antoine. *Le Péloponnèse byzantin jusqu'en 1204*. Paris: Presses universitaires de France, 1951.

Bonnet, C. "Le culte de Leucothéa et de Mélicertes en Grèce, au Proche-Orient et en Italie." *Studi e Materiali* 10 (1986) 33–71.

Bookidis, Nancy. "The Sanctuaries of Corinth." Pages 247–60 in *Corinth: The Centenary, 1896–1996*. Edited by Charles K. Williams II and Nancy Bookidis. Corinth XX. Princeton, N.J.: ASCSA, 2003.

Bookidis, Nancy, and J. E. Fisher. "Sanctuary of Demeter and Kore on Acrocorinth. Preliminary Report V: 1971–1973." *Hesperia* 43 (1974) 267–307.

Bookidis, Nancy, and Ronald S. Stroud. "Apollo and the Archaic Temple at Corinth." *Hesperia*, forthcoming.

————. *Demeter and Persephone in Ancient Corinth.* American Excavations in Old Corinth, Corinth Notes 2. Princeton, N.J.: ASCSA, 1987.

————. *The Sanctuary of Demeter and Kore: Topography and Architecture.* Corinth XVIII.3. Princeton N.J.: ASCSA, 1997.

Bornkamm, Günther. "Lord's Supper and Church in Paul." Pages 123–60 in *The Early Christian Experience.* Translated by Paul L. Hammer. New York: Harper & Row, 1969.

————. "The More Excellent Way (1 Corinthians 3)." Pages 180–93 in *The Early Christian Experience.* Translated by Paul L. Hammer. New York: Harper & Row, 1969.

————. "Die Vorgeschichte des sogennanten zweiten Korinterbriefes." Pages 7–36 in *Sitzungsberichte der Heidelberger Akademie der Wissenschaften, Philologisch-historische Klasse.* Heidelberg: Winter, 1961.

Bourgeois, Claude. *Divona.* 2 vols. Paris: de Boccard, 1991–1992.

Bowersock, Glen W. *Augustus and the Greek World.* Oxford: Clarendon, 1965.

————. *Greek Sophists in the Roman Empire.* Oxford: Clarendon, 1969.

Boyce, George K. *Corpus of the Lararia of Pompeii.* MAAR 4. Rome: American Academy in Rome, 1937.

Brelich, Angelo. *Paides e Parthenoi.* Rome: Edizioni dell'Ateneo, 1969.

Broneer, Oscar. "Excavations at Isthmia: Fourth Campaign, 1957–1958." *Hesperia* 28 (1959) 299–343.

————. "Hero Cults in the Corinthian Agora." *Hesperia* 11 (1942) 128–61.

————. "Investigations at Corinth, 1946–1947." *Hesperia* 16 (1947) 233–47.

————. *Isthmia: Topography and Architecture.* Isthmia 2. Princeton, N.J.: ASCSA, 1973.

————. "The Isthmian Victory Crown." *AJA* 66 (1962) 259–63.

————. *The Odeum.* Corinth X. Cambridge, Mass.: ASCSA, 1932.

————. *The South Stoa and Its Roman Successors.* Corinth I.4. Princeton, N.J.: ASCSA, 1954.

————. *Terracotta Lamps.* Corinth IV.2. Cambridge, Mass.: ASCSA, 1930.

————. *Terracotta Lamps.* Isthmia 3. Princeton, N.J.: ASCSA, 1977.

Brown, Christopher. "The Prayers of the Corinthian Women." *GRBS* 32 (1991) 5–14.

de Budé, Guy. *Dionnis Chrysostomi Orationes.* 2 vols. Leipzig: B. G. Tuebner, 1916–1919.

Burkert, Walter. *Greek Religion.* Translated by John Raffan. Cambridge, Mass.: Harvard University Press, 1985.

Burkert, Walter. *Homo Necans: The Anthropology of Ancient Greek Sacrificial Ritual and Myth*. Translated by Peter Bing. Berkeley: University of California Press, 1983.

Bury, J. B. *The History of the Later Roman Empire*. 1889. 2 vols. Repr., New York: Dover Publications, 1958.

Cadbury, H. J. "The Macellum at Corinth." *JBL* 53 (1934) 134–41.

Callahan, C. K., and A. Bertini Malgarni. "Übersehene Favorin-Fragmente aus einer Oxforder Handschrift." *Rheinisches Museum für Philologie* 129 (1986) 170–84.

Calza, Guido. *La Necropoli del porta di Roma nell'Isola Sacra*. Rome: Instituto di Archeologiae Storia dell'Arte, 1940.

Camp, John M. *The Athenian Agora: Excavations in the Heart of Classical Athens*. 2d ed. London: Thames & Hudson, 1992.

Campbell, Brian. *The Writings of the Roman Land Surveyors*. London: Society for the Promotion of Roman Studies, 2000.

Capps, Edward, Jr. "Pergamene Influence at Corinth." *Hesperia* 7 (1938) 539–56.

Carpenter, Rhys, and Antoine Bon. *The Defenses of Acrocorinth and the Lower Town*. Corinth III.2. Cambridge, Mass.: ASCSA, 1936.

Carpenter, T. H. "Images and Beliefs: Thoughts on the Derveni Krater." Pages 50–59 in *Periplous: Papers on Classical Art and Archaeology Presented to Sir John Boardman*. Edited by G. R. Tsetskhladze, A. J. N. W. Prag, and A. M. Snodgrass. London: Thames and Hudson, 2000.

Cartledge, Paul. "Herodotus and 'the Other': A Meditation on Empire." *Echos du Monde Classique/Classical Views* 34 = n.s. 9 (1990) 27–40.

Cartledge, Paul, and Antony Spawforth. *Hellenistic and Roman Sparta*. London: Routledge, 1989.

Castiglione, L. "Isis Pharia: Remarque sur la statue de Budapest." *Bulletin Musée hongrois des Beaux-Arts* 34–35 (1970) 37–55.

Childe, Vere Gordon. "Directional Changes in Funerary Practices during 50,000 Years." *Man* 45 (1945) 13–19.

Chow, John K. *Patronage and Power: A Study of Social Networks in Corinth*. Sheffield: Sheffield Academic Press, 1992.

Christol, Michel, and Thomas Drew-Bear. "Documents latins de Phrygie." *Tyche* 1 (1986) 41–87.

Clavel-Lévêque, Monique, et al. *Atlas historique des cadastres d'Europe*, vols. 1–2. Publications of the Action COST G2 "Paysages anciens et structures rurales." Luxembourg: Offices des publications officielles des Communautés européennes, 1998– .

Clinton, Kevin. "Stages of Initiation in the Eleusinian and Samothracian Mysteries." Pages 50–78 in *Greek Mysteries: The Archaeology and Ritual of Ancient Greek Secret Cults*. Edited by M. B. Cosmopoulos. London: Routledge, 2003.

Coarelli, Filippo. *I santuari del Lazio in età repubblicana*. Rome: La Nuova Italia Scientifica, 1987.

Cole, Susan Guettel. "Domesticating Artemis." Pages 27–43 in *The Sacred and the Feminine in Ancient Greece*. Edited by Sue Blundell and Margaret Williamson. New York: Routledge, 1998.

Collins, John J. *The Apocalyptic Imagination*. New York: Crossroad, 1984.

Collins, John N. *Diakonia: Re-Interpreting the Ancient Sources*. New York: Oxford University Press, 1990.

Das Cömeterium der sieben Schläfer. FiE 4.2. Vienna: Österreichisches Archäologisches Institut, 1937.

Congès, A. R. "Culte de l'eau et dieux guérisseurs en Gaule romaine." *JRA* 7 (1994) 396–407.

Conzelmann, Hans. *1 Corinthians: A Commentary on the First Epistle to the Corinthians*. Hermeneia. Philadelphia: Fortress, 1975.

————. "Korinth und die Mädchen der Aphrodite." *Nachrichten der Akademie der Wissenschaften in Göttingen* 8 (1967) 247–61.

Cook, A. B. *Zeus: A Study in Ancient Religion*. 3 vols. in 5. Cambridge: Cambridge University Press, 1914–1940.

Cormack, Sara. "Funerary Monuments and Mortuary Practice in Roman Asia Minor." Pages 137–56 in *The Early Roman Empire in the East*. Edited by Susan Alcock. Oxford: Oxbow, 1997.

Couchoud, P. L., and J. Svoronos. "Le monument dit 'des taureaux' à Délos et le cult du navire sacré." *BCH* 45 (1921) 270–94.

Couilloud, Marie-Thérèse. *Les monuments funéraires de Rhénée*. Délos 30. Paris: de Boccard, 1974.

Craig, J. D. "Plautus, *Rudens* 160–162." *CR* 40 (1926) 152–53.

Crawford, Michael H., ed. *Roman Statutes*. 2 vols. BICSSup 64. London: University of London, 1996.

Croisille, J.-M. *Poésie et art figuré de Néron aux Flaviens*. Collection Latomus 179. Brussels: Latomus, 1982.

Crook, John A. *Law and Life in Ancient Rome*. Ithaca, N.Y.: Cornell University Press, 1967.

Cummer, W. Willson. "A Roman Tomb at Corinthian Kenchreai." *Hesperia* 40 (1971) 205–31.

Cumont, Franz. *Lux Perpetua*. Paris: Geuthner, 1949.

————. *Recherches sur le symbolisme funéraire des Romains*. Paris: Geuthner, 1942.

Dagron, Gilbert. "Christianisme dans la ville byzantine." *DOP* 31 (1972) 1–25.

D'Arms, J. H. "P. Lucilius Gamala's Feasts for the Ostians and Their Roman Models." *JRA* 13 (2000) 192–200.

Dautzenberg, Gerhard. *Urchristliche Prophetie: Ihre Erforschung, ihre Voraussetzung im Judentum und ihre Struktur im ersten Korintherbrief.* BWANT 104. Stuttgart: Kohlhammer, 1975.

Daux, Georges. "Chronique des fouilles." *BCH* 89 (1965) 694–97.

————. "Chronique des fouilles et découvertes archéologiques en Grèce en 1962." *BCH* 87 (1963) 689–878.

Davidson, G. R. "A Hellenistic Deposit at Corinth." *Hesperia* 11 (1942) 105–27.

————. *The Minor Objects.* Corinth XII. Princeton, N.J.: ASCSA, 1952.

Davies, Glenys. "Burial in Italy up to Augustus." Pages 13–19 in *Burial in the Roman World.* Edited by Richard Reece. London: Council for British Archaeology, 1977.

Dawson, Christopher M. *Romano-Campanian Mythological Landscape Painting.* YaleClSt 9. New Haven, Conn.: Yale University Press, 1944.

Deissmann, Adolf. *Paul: A Study in Social and Religious History.* 2d ed. New York: Harper & Brothers, 1927.

Delehaye, Hippolyte. *Legends of the Saints.* Translated by V. M. Crawford. London: Longmans, Green, and Co., 1907.

————. *Les origines du culte des martyrs.* Brussels: Société des Bollandistes, 1933.

De Martino, Ernesto. *Morte e pianto rituale nel mondo antico.* Torino: Edizioni scientifiche Einaudi, 1958.

Derderian, Katharine. *Leaving Words to Remember: Greek Mourning and the Advent of Literacy.* Leiden: Brill, 2001.

Des Courtiles, J., A. Gardeisen, and A. Pariente. "Sacrifices d'animaux à Hérakleion de Thasos." *BCH* 129 (1996) 799–820.

Despines, Georgios. "Το αντίγραφο της Αθηνάς Medici του μουσείου Θεσσαλονίκης." Pages 257–69 in *Archaia Makedonia II.* Thessaloniki: Institute for Balkan Studies, 1977.

De Vos, Craig Steven. *Church and Community Conflicts: The Relationships of the Thessalonian, Corinthian, and Philippian Churches with Their Wider Civic Communities.* SBLDS 168. Atlanta, Ga.: Scholars, 1999.

DeWaele, J. "The Sanctuary of Asklepios and Hygieia at Corinth." *AJA* 37 (1933) 417–51.

Dewar, Michael, ed. *Statius, Thebaid IX.* Oxford: Clarendon, 1991.

Dindorf, Ludwig. *Dionis Chrysostomi Orationes.* Leipzig: B. G. Teubner, 1857.

Dinsmoor, W. B. "The Largest Temple in the Peloponnesos." Pages 104–15 in *Commemorative Studies in Honor of Theodore Leslie Shear. Hesperia* Supplement 8. N.p.: ASCSA, 1949.

Dixon, Michael D. "Disputed Territories: Interstate Arbitration in the Northeast Peloponnese, ca. 250–150 B.C." Ph.D. diss., Ohio State University, 2000.

————. "A New Latin and Greek Inscription from Corinth." *Hesperia* 69 (2000) 335–42.

Dobrov, Gregory W., ed. *The City as Comedy: Society and Representation in Athenian Drama*. Chapel Hill: University of North Carolina Press, 1997.

Dörpfeld, W. "Der Tempel in Korinth." *AM* 11 (1886) 297–308.

Doukellis, Panagiotis N. "Le territoire de la colonie romaine de Corinthe." Pages 359–90 in *Structures rurales et sociétés antiques: actes du colloque de Corfou, 14–16 mai 1992*. Edited by Panagiotis N. Doukellis and Lina G. Mendoni. Paris: Belles Lettres, 1994.

Dow, Sterling. "Corinthiaka." *AJA* 46 (1942) 69–72.

Downing, F. G. "Compositional Conventions and the Synoptic Problem." *JBL* 107 (1988) 69–85.

Duff, A. M. *Freedmen in the Early Roman Empire*. Oxford: Oxford University Press, 1928.

Duff, Paul B. "Apostolic Suffering and the Language of Processions in 2 Corinthians 4.7–10." *BTB* 21 (1991) 158–65.

———. "Metaphor, Motif, and Meaning: The Rhetorical Strategy behind the Image 'Led in Triumph' in 2 Cor 2:14." *CBQ 53* (1991) 79–92.

———. "The Mind of the Redactor: 2 Cor 6:14–7:1 in Its Secondary Context." *NovT* 35 (1993) 160–80.

———. "The Transformation of the Spectator: Power, Perception, and the Day of Salvation." *SBLSP* 26 (1987) 233–43.

Dunand, Françoise. *Le culte d'Isis dans le bassin oriental de la Méditerranée*. 3 vols. EPRO 26. Leiden: Brill, 1973.

Dunbabin, T. J. "Bellerophon, Herakles and Chimaera." Pages 1164–84 in *Studies Presented to David Moore Robinson*, vol. 2. Edited by G. E. Mylonas and D. Raymond. 2 vols. Saint Louis: Washington University, 1953.

Duncan-Jones, Richard. *The Economy of the Roman Empire: Quantitative Studies*. 2d ed. New York: Cambridge University Press, 1982.

Dunn, F. M. "Euripides and the Rites of Hera Akraia." *GRBS* 35 (1995) 103–15.

Edwards, C. M. "The Arch over the Lechaion Road at Corinth and Its Sculpture." *Hesperia* 63 (1994) 263–308.

———. "Greek Votive Reliefs to Pan and the Nymphs." Ph.D. diss., New York University, 1985.

———. "Tyche at Corinth." *Hesperia* 59 (1990) 529–42.

Edwards, G. Roger. *Corinthian Hellenistic Pottery*. Corinth VII.3. Princeton, N.J.: ASCSA, 1975.

Edwards, K. M. *Coins, 1896–1929*. Corinth VI. Cambridge, Mass.: ASCSA, 1933.

Eitrem, S. "Leukothea 6." *RE* 12 (1925) cols. 2294–95.

———. "A Purification Rite and Some Allied 'rites de passages.'" *Symbolae Osloenses* 25 (1947) 36–53.

Ekroth, G. "Altars in Greek Hero-Cults: A Review of the Archaeological Evidence."
Pages 117–30 in *Ancient Greek Cult Practice from the Archaeological Evidence*.
Edited by R. Hägg. Stockholm: Svenska Institutet i Athen, 1998.

———. *The Sacrificial Rituals of Greek Hero-Cults in the Archaic to the Early Hellenistic Periods*. Stockholm: University of Stockholm, 1999.

Elderkin, G. W. "The Fountain of Glauce at Corinth." *AJA* 14 (1910) 19–50.

Emperius, Adolph Karl Wilhelm. *De Oratione Corinthiaca falso Dioni Chrysostomo adscripta*. Braunschweig: G. Westermann, 1832. Repr. in *Opuscula philologica et historica*. Edited by F. G. Schneidewin. Göttingen: Librariae Dieterichiana, 1847.

———. *Dionis Chrysostomi: Opera graece*. Braunschweig: G. Westermann, 1844.

Engels, Donald. *Roman Corinth: An Alternative Model for the Classical City*.
Chicago: University of Chicago Press, 1990.

Erdemgil, S., et al. *Ephesus Museum*. Istanbul: Dogü Publications, 1999.

——— *Ephesus Museum Catalogue*. Istanbul: n.p., 1989.

Eustratiou, Kleopatra. "Chronika." *ArchDelt* 44 (1989) 76 and plate 56.

Fabrizii-Reuer, Susanne. "Gräber im Bereich der Via Sacra Ephesiaka." Pages
461–64 in *100 Jahre österreichische Forschungen in Ephesos: Akten des Symposions Wien 1995*. Edited by Barbara Brandt and Karl R. Krierer. Vienna: Österreichische Akademie der Wissenschaften, 1999.

Fabrizii-Reuer, Susanne, and Egon Reuer. "Die Ergebnisse der anthropologischen Untersuchung von 18 kg Leichenbrand aus der Ringnekropole von Ephesos."
Pages 62–66 in *Via Sacra Ephesiaca II*. Edited by Dieter Knibbe and Gerhard Langmann. Vienna: Schindler, 1993– .

Fantham, Elaine. "The Role of Evander in Ovid's *Fasti*." *Arethusa* 25 (1992) 155–71.

Farnell, Lewis R. *The Cults of the Greek States*. 5 vols. Oxford: Clarendon, 1896–1909.

———. *Greek Hero Cults and Ideas of Immortality*. Oxford: Clarendon, 1921.

———. "Ino-Leucothea." *JHS* 36 (1916) 36–44.

Fears, J. Rufus. "The Cult of Jupiter and Roman Imperial Ideology." *ANRW* II.17.1 (1981) 3–141.

Fee, Gordon D. *The First Epistle to the Corinthians*. NICNT. Grand Rapids, Mich.: Eerdmans, 1988.

Fehr, Burkhard. "Archäologen, Techniker, Industrielle: Betrachtungen zur Wiederaufstellung der Bibliothek des Celsus in Ephesos." *Hephaistos* 3 (1981) 107–25.

Ferguson, W. S. "Attic Orgeones." *HTR* 37 (1944) 61–140.

Filson, Floyd V. "The Significance of the Early House Churches." *JBL* 58 (1939) 105–12.

Finley, M. I. *The Ancient Economy*. 2d ed. Berkeley: University of California Press, 1985.

Fischer-Bossert, Wolfgang. *Chronologie der Didrachmenprägung von Tarent. 510–280 v. Chr.* Berlin: de Gruyter, 1999.

Fisher, Eugene J. "Cultic Prostitution in the Ancient Near East? A Reassessment." *BTB* 6 (1976) 225–36.

Fitzmyer, Joseph A. *Romans.* AB. New York: Doubleday, 1993.

Flint, Valerie. "The Demonisation of Magic and Sorcery in Late Antiquity: Christian Redefinitions of Pagan Religions." Pages 277–348 in *Witchcraft and Magic in Europe, Ancient Greece and Rome.* Edited by Bengt Ankarloo and Stuart Clark. Philadelphia: University of Pennsylvania Press, 1999.

Flower, Harriet I. *Ancestor Masks and Aristocratic Power in Roman Culture.* Oxford: Clarendon, 1996.

Follet, Simone. *Athènes au IIᵉ et au IIIᵉ siècle: Études chronologiques et prosopographiques.* Paris: Belles Lettres, 1976.

Fontenrose, J. "The Sorrows of Ino and Procne." *TAPA* 79 (1948) 125–67.

Forbes Irving, P. M. C. *Metamorphosis in Greek Myths.* Oxford: Clarendon, 1990.

Fowler, H. N., and R. Stillwell. *Introduction, Topography, Architecture.* Corinth I. Cambridge, Mass.: ASCSA, 1932.

Frank, Tenney. *Rome and Italy of the Empire.* Paterson, N.J.: Pageant Books, 1959.

Frazer, J. G., ed. *Pausanias's Description of Greece.* 1897. Repr., New York: Biblo and Tannen, 1965.

Frazer, P. M. *Ptolemaic Alexandria.* 2 vols. Oxford: Clarendon, 1972.

Frend, W. H. C. *The Rise of Christianity.* Philadelphia: Fortress, 1984.

Friedrich, Paul. *The Meaning of Aphrodite.* Chicago: University of Chicago Press, 1978.

Friesen, Steven J. "The Cult of the Roman Emperors in Ephesos: Temple Wardens, City Titles, and the Interpretation of the Book of Revelation." Pages 229–50 in *Ephesos, Metropolis of Asia: An Interdisciplinary Approach to Its Archaeology, Religion, and Culture.* Edited by Helmut Koester. HTS 41. Valley Forge, Pa.: Trinity Press International, 1995.

———. "Poverty in Pauline Studies: Beyond the So-Called New Consensus." *JSNT* 26 (2004) 323–61.

Friesen, Steven, et al. "Corinth A." No. 37 in *Archaeological Resources for New Testament Studies*, vol. 1. Edited by Helmut Koester et al. 2 vols. Harrisburg, Pa.: Trinity Press International, 1994.

Friesinger, Herwig, and Friedrich Krinzinger, eds. *100 Jahre österreichischen Forschungen in Ephesos: Akten des Symposions Wien 1995.* Vienna: Österreichische Akademie der Wissenschaften, 1999.

Froning, H. "Ikonographische Tradition mythologischer Sarkophagreliefs." *JdI* 95 (1980) 322–41.

Furnish, Victor Paul. *II Corinthians.* AB 32A. Garden City, N.Y.: Doubleday, 1984.

Gadbery, Laura M. "Roman Wall Painting at Corinth: New Evidence from East of the Theater in the Roman Period." Pages 47–64 in *The Corinthia in the Roman Period*. Edited by Timothy E. Gregory. JRASup 8. Ann Arbor, Mich.: Journal of Roman Archaeology, 1993.

Gaggadis-Robin, Vassiliki. *Jason et Médée sur les sarcophages d'époque impériale*. Rome: L'École française de Rome, 1994.

Gamble, Harry Y. *Books and Readers in the Early Church: A History of Early Christian Texts*. New Haven, Conn.: Yale University Press, 1995.

Gantz, Timothy. *Early Greek Myth: A Guide to Literary and Artistic Sources*. Baltimore: Johns Hopkins University Press, 1993.

Garland, Robert. *The Greek Way of Death*. 2d ed. London: Duckworth, 2001.

Garnsey, Peter. *Social Status and Legal Privilege in the Roman Empire*. Oxford: Clarendon, 1970.

Geagan, Daniel J. "The Isthmian Dossier of P. Licinius Priscus Juventianus." *Hesperia* 58 (1989) 349–60.

———. "Notes on the Agonistic Festivals of Roman Corinth." *GRBS* 9 (1968) 69–80.

———. "Roman Athens: Some Aspects of Life and Culture, I. 86 BC–AD 267." *ANRW* II.7.1 (1979) 271–437.

Gebhard, Elizabeth R. "The Beginnings of Panhellenic Games at the Isthmus." Pages 221–37 in *Olympia 1875–2000: 125 Jahre Deutsche Ausgrabungen*. Edited by Helmut Kyrieleis. Mainz am Rhein: Philipp von Zabern, 2002.

———. "The Isthmian Games and the Sanctuary of Poseidon in the Early Empire." Pages 78–94 in *The Corinthia in the Roman Period*. Edited by Timothy E. Gregory. JRASup 8. Ann Arbor, Mich.: Journal of Roman Archaeology, 1993.

———. *The Theater at Isthmia*. Chicago: University of Chicago Press, 1973.

Gebhard, Elizabeth R., and M. W. Dickie. "Melikertes-Palaimon: Hero of the Isthmian Games." Pages 159–65 in *Ancient Greek Hero Cult: Proceedings of the Fifth International Seminar on Ancient Greek Cult, Goteborg University, 21–23 April 1995*. ActaAth 8, 16. Edited by R. Hägg. Stockholm: Svenska Institutet i Athen, 1998.

———. "The View from the Isthmus, ca. 200 to 44 B.C." Pages 261–78 in *Corinth: The Centenary, 1896–1996*. Edited by Charles K. Williams II and Nancy Bookidis. Corinth XX. Princeton, N.J.: ASCSA, 2003.

Gebhard, Elizabeth R., and F. P. Hemans. "University of Chicago Excavations at Isthmia, 1989: II." *Hesperia* 67 (1998) 1–63.

Gebhard, Elizabeth R., F. P. Hemans, and J. W. Hayes. "University of Chicago Excavations at Isthmia, 1989: III." *Hesperia* 67 (1998) 405–56.

Gebhard, Elizabeth R., and D. Reese. "Sacrifices to Poseidon and Melikertes-Palaimon at Isthmia." In *Greek Sacrificial Ritual, Olympian and Chthonian: Proceedings of the Sixth International Seminar on Ancient Greek Cult, Göteborg University, April 1997*. ActaAth 8, 17. Edited by R. Hägg. Stockholm, forthcoming.

von Geisau, H. "Palaimon." *RE* Suppl. 9 (1962) 514–15.

Georgi, Dieter. "The Early Church: Internal Jewish Migration or New Religion?" *HTR* 88 (1995) 35–68.

———. *The Opponents of Paul in 2 Corinthians*. Philadelphia: Fortress, 1986.

———. *Theocracy in Paul's Praxis and Theology*. Minneapolis: Fortress, 1991.

Gericke, T. "Die Bändigung des Pegasos." *AM* 71 (1956) 192–201.

Ginouvès, René. *Balaneutiké: Recherches sur le bain dans l'antiquité grecque*. Paris: de Boccard, 1962.

Giuliano, Antonio, ed. *Museo Nazionale Romano: Le Sculture I, 8, Parte I*. Rome: De Luca, 1985.

Glad, Clarence E. *Paul and Philodemus: Adaptability in Epicurean and Early Christian Psychagogy*. NovTSup 81. Leiden: Brill, 1995.

Glaser, Franz. *Antike Brunnenbauten (KRHNAI) in Griechenland*. Vienna: Österreichische Akademie der Wissenschaften, 1983.

Gleason, Maude W. *Making Men: Sophists and Self-Presentation in Ancient Rome*. Princeton, N.J.: Princeton University Press, 1995.

Goldberg, Marilyn. "The Amazon Myth and Gender Studies." Pages 89–100 in *Stephanos: Studies in Honor of Brunilde Sismondo Ridgway*. Edited by Kim J. Hartswicke and Mary C. Sturgeon. Philadelphia: University of Pennsylvania Press, 1998.

Goldhill, Simon. "Introduction: Setting an Agenda." Pages 1–25 in *Being Greek Under Rome*. Edited by Simon Goldhill. Cambridge: Cambridge University Press, 2001.

Gould, John. "On Making Sense of Greek Religion." Pages 1–33 in *Greek Religion and Society*. Edited by P. E. Easterling and J. V. Muir. Cambridge: Cambridge University Press, 1985.

Gow, A. S. F., and D. L. Page, eds. *The Greek Anthology*. 2 vols. London: Cambridge University Press, 1968.

Grace, V. R. "The Middle Stoa Dated by Amphora Stamps." *Hesperia* 54 (1985) 1–54.

———. "Stamped Amphora Handles Found in 1931–1932." *Hesperia* 3 (1934) 197–310.

Graf, Fritz. "Medea, the Enchantress from Afar: Remarks on a Well-Known Myth." Pages 21–43 in *Medea: Essays on Medea in Myth, Literature, Philosophy, and Art*. Edited by James J. Clauss and Sarah Iles Johnston. Princeton, N.J.: Princeton University Press, 1997.

Graindor, Paul. *Un milliardaire antique: Hérode Atticus et sa famille*. Cairo: L'Université Egyptienne, 1930.

Grandjouan, C. *Terracottas and Plastic Lamps of the Roman Period*. Agora 6. Princeton, N.J.: ASCSA, 1961.

Grant, Robert M. *Paul in the Roman World: The Conflict at Corinth*. Louisville, Ky.: Westminster/John Knox, 2001.

Gray, Vivienne. "Herodotus and the Rhetoric of Otherness." *AJP* 116 (1995) 185–211.

Grégoire, Henri. *Les persécutions dans l'empire Romain*. Brussels: Palais des Academies, 1950.

Gregory, Timothy E., ed. *The Corinthia in the Roman Period*. JRASup 8. Ann Arbor, Mich.: Journal of Roman Archaeology, 1993.

————. *The Hexamilion and the Fortress*. Isthmia V. Princeton, N.J.: Princeton University Press, 1993.

Grimal, Pierre. *Roman Cities*. Translated and edited by G. M. Woloch. Madison: University of Wisconsin Press, 1983.

Grodzynski, D. "*Superstitio.*" *REA* 76 (1974) 36–60.

Gros, Pierre, and Mario Torelli. *Storia dell' Urbanistica, il mondo Romano*. Rome: Laterza, 1994.

Gruen, Erich S. *The Hellenistic World and the Coming of Rome*. 2 vols. Berkeley: University of California Press, 1984.

Guzzo, Pietro Giovanni, ed. *Pompeii: Picta fragmenta: Decorazioni parietali dalla città sepolte*. Torino: Umberto Allemandi, 1997.

Habicht, Christian. *Pausanias' Guide to Ancient Greece*. Berkeley: University of California Press, 1985.

Hackett, Jo Ann. "Can a Sexist Model Liberate Us? Ancient Near Eastern 'Fertility' Goddesses." *Journal of Feminist Studies in Religion* 5 (1989) 65–76.

Hägg, R., ed. *Greek Sacrificial Ritual, Olympian and Chthonian: Proceedings of the Sixth International Seminar on Ancient Greek Cult, Göteborg University, April 1997*. ActaAth 8, 17. Stockholm, forthcoming.

Halkin, François. "Saint Léonide et ses sept compagnes martyrs à Corinthe." Pages 60–66 in *Recherches et documents d'hagiographie byzantine*. Subsidia Hagiographica Graeca 51. Brussels: Société des Bollandistes, 1971.

Hallett, Judith P. "Women as *Same* and *Other* in Classical Roman Elite." *Helios* 16 (1989) 59–78.

Hardie, Alex. *Statius and the Silvae*. Liverpool: F. Cairns, 1983.

von Harnack, Adolf. *The Sayings of Jesus*. New York: G. P. Putnam, 1908.

Harrill, J. Albert. *The Manumission of Slaves in Early Christianity*. HUT 32. Tübingen: Mohr Siebeck, 1995.

Hartog, François. *The Mirror of Herodotus: The Representation of the Other in the Writing of History*. Berkeley: University of California Press, 1988.

Hatzopoulos, M. B. *Cultes et rites de passage en Macédoine*. Μελετήματα 19. Athens: Κεντρον Ηελληνικης και Ρωμαικης Αρχηαιοτητος Ετηνικον Ηυδρυμα Ερευνων, 1994.

Hawthorne, J. "The Myth of Palaemon." *TAPA* 89 (1958) 92–98.

Hayes, J. W. *Late Roman Pottery*. London: British School at Rome, 1972.

Hays, Richard B. *First Corinthians*. Louisville, Ky.: John Knox, 1997.

Hayward, Chris L. "Geology of Corinth: The Study of a Basic Resource." Pages 15–42 in *Corinth: The Centenary, 1896–1996*. Edited by Charles K. Williams II and Nancy Bookidis. Corinth XX. Princeton, N.J.: ASCSA, 2003.

———. "High-Resolution Provenance Determination of Construction-Stone: A Preliminary Study of Corinthian Oolitic Limestone Quarries at Examilia." *Geoarchaeology* 11 (1996) 215–34.

Head, Barclay V. *Catalogue of the Greek Coins of Caria, Cos, Rhodes, Etc.* Catalogue of the Greek Coins in the British Museum 18. London: The Trustees, 1897.

Hedreen, G. "The Cult of Achilles in the Euxine." *Hesperia* 60 (1991) 313–30.

Henderson, John. "*Timeo Danaos*: Amazons in Early Greek Art and Pottery." Pages 85–137 in *Art and Text in Ancient Greek Culture*. Edited by Simon Goldhill and Robin Osborne. Cambridge: Cambridge University Press, 1994.

Herbert, S. "The Torch-Race at Corinth." Pages 29–35 in *Corinthiaca: Studies in Honor of Darrell A. Amyx*. Edited by Mario A. Del Chiaro. Columbia: University of Missouri Press, 1986.

Herrmann, Peter, and Kemal Ziya Polatkan. "Das Testament des Epikrates und andere neue Inschriften aus dem Museum von Manisa." *SÖAW* 265.1 (1969) 1–64.

Hill, Bert Hodge. *The Springs: Peirene, Sacred Spring, Glauke*. Corinth I.6. Princeton, N.J.: ASCSA, 1964.

Hill, Ida T. *The Ancient City of Athens: Topography and Monuments*. 2d ed. Chicago: Argonaut, 1969.

Hiller, Stefan. *Bellerophon: Ein griechischer Mythos in römischer Kunst*. Munich: W. Fink, 1969.

Hobsbawm, E. J. "Introduction: Inventing Traditions." Pages 1–14 in *The Invention of Tradition*. Edited by E. J. Hobsbawm and T. Ranger. Cambridge: Cambridge University Press, 1983.

Hock, Ronald F. *The Social Context of Paul's Ministry: Tentmaking and Apostleship*. Philadelphia: Fortress, 1980.

Hodder, Ian. *The Archaeological Process*. London: Blackwell, 1999.

———. "Economic and Social Stress and Material Culture Patterning." *American Antiquity* 44 (1979) 446–54.

———. *Reading the Past*. 2d ed. Cambridge: Cambridge University Press, 1991.

Holland, Louise Adams. *Janus and the Bridge*. PMAAR 21. Rome: American Academy, 1962.

Hollis, A. S. "Ovid, Metamorphoses 1,445ff: Apollo, Daphne and the Pythian Crown." *ZPE* 112 (1996) 69–73.

Hopkins, Keith. *Death and Renewal*. Cambridge: Cambridge University Press, 1983.

Hopkinson, Neil, ed. *A Hellenistic Anthology*. Cambridge: Cambridge University Press, 1998.

Horsley, Richard A. *1 Corinthians*. Abingdon New Testament Commentaries. Nashville, Tenn.: Abingdon, 1998.

Horsley, Richard A. "1 Corinthians: A Case Study of Paul's Assembly as an Alternative Society." Pages 242–52 in *Paul and Empire: Religion and Power in Roman Imperial Society*. Edited by Richard A. Horsley. Harrisburg, Pa.: Trinity Press International, 1997.

———. *Jesus and the Spiral of Violence*. San Francisco: Harper & Row, 1987.

———. "The Kingdom of God and the Renewal of Israel." Pages 303–44 in *The Origins of Apocalypticism in Judaism and Christianity*. Vol. 1 of *The Encyclopedia of Apocalypticism*. Edited by John J. Collins. 3 vols. New York: Continuum, 2000.

———. "Rhetoric and Empire—and 1 Corinthians." Pages 72–102 in *Paul and Politics: Ekklesia, Israel, Imperium, Interpretation*. Edited by Richard A. Horsley. Harrisburg, Pa.: Trinity Press International, 2000.

Horsley, Richard A., ed. *Paul and Empire: Religion and Power in Roman Imperial Society*. Harrisburg, Pa.: Trinity Press International, 1997.

Hueber, Friedmund J. "Beobachtungen zu Kurvatur und Scheinperspektive an der Celsusbibliothek und anderen Kaiserzeitlichen Bauten." Pages 175–200 in *Bauplanung und Bautheorie der Antike*. Diskussionen zur archäologischen Bauforschung 4. Berlin: Deutsches Archäologisches Institut, 1983.

Hunt, Edmund, trans. *The Fathers of the Church: St. Leo the Great: Letters*. New York: Fathers of the Church, 1957.

Hurd, John C. *The Origin of 1 Corinthians*. Macon, Ga.: Mercer University Press, 1983.

Ibrahim, Leila, Robert Scranton, and Robert Brill. *The Panels of Opus Sectile in Glass*. Vol. 2 of *Kenchreai, Eastern Port of Corinth*. Leiden: Brill, 1976.

Isenberg, M. "The Sale of Sacrificial Meat." *CP* 70 (1975) 271–73.

Isler-Kerényi, C. "Immagini di Medea." Pages 117–38 in *Medea nella letterature e nell'arte*. Edited by Bruno Gentili and Franca Perusino. Venice: Marsilio, 2000.

Ivison, Eric. A. "Burial and Urbanism at Late Antique and Early Byzantine Corinth." Pages 99–126 in *Towns in Transition: Urban Evolution in Late Antiquity and the Early Middle Ages*. Edited by Neil Christie and S. T. Loseby. Hants, England: Aldershot, 1996.

Jameson, M. H. "Sacrifice and Animal Husbandry in Classical Greece." Pages 87–119 in *Pastoral Economies in Classical Antiquity*. Edited by C. R. Whittaker. PCPS Sup 14. Cambridge: Cambridge Philological Society, 1988.

Jewett, Robert. "The Redaction of 1 Corinthians and the Trajectory of the Pauline School." *JAARSup* 46 (1978) 389–444.

———. *The Thessalonian Correspondence: Pauline Rhetoric and Millenarian Piety*. Philadelphia: Fortress, 1986.

Jocelyn, H. D., ed. *The Tragedies of Ennius: The Fragments*. Cambridge: Cambridge University Press, 1967.

Johnson, Franklin P. *Sculpture, 1896–1923*. Corinth IX. Cambridge, Mass.: ASCSA, 1931.

Johnson, Lora L. "The Hellenistic and Roman Library: Studies Pertaining to Their Architectural Form." Ph.D. diss., Brown University, 1984.

Johnston, Sarah Iles. "Corinthian Medea and the Cult of Hera Akraia." Pages 44–70 in *Medea: Essays on Medea in Myth, Literature, Philosophy, and Art.* Edited by James J. Clauss and Sarah Iles Johnston. Princeton, N.J.: Princeton University Press, 1997.

Jones, A. H. M. *The Later Roman Empire.* 2 vols. Oxford: Basil Blackwell, 1964.

Jones, Christopher P. "Pausanias and His Guides." Pages 33–39 in *Pausanias: Travel and Memory in Roman Greece.* Edited by Susan E. Alcock, John F. Cherry, and J. Elsner. Oxford: Oxford University Press, 2001.

———. "Philostratus' *Heroikos* and Its Setting in Reality." *JHS* 121 (2001) 141–49.

———. *Plutarch and Rome.* Oxford: Clarendon, 1971.

Jones, Rick. "A Quantitative Approach to Roman Burial." Pages 20–25 in *Burial in the Roman World.* Edited by Richard Reece. London: Council for British Archaeology, 1977.

Jordan, D. R. "Inscribed Lamps from a Cult at Corinth in Late Antiquity." *HTR* 87 (1994) 223–29.

Judge, Edwin A. *The Social Pattern of Christian Groups in the First Century.* London: Tyndale, 1960.

Kähler, Heinz. "Biblioteca." Pages 93–99 in *Enciclopedia dell'arte antica, classica e orientale,* vol. 2. 7 vols. Rome: Enciclopedia Italiana/Instituto dello Stato, 1959.

Kajava, M. "When Did the Isthmian Games Return to the Isthmus? (Re-Reading *Corinth* VIII.3, no. 153)." *CP* 97 (2002) 168–78.

Kampouri, Evangelia. "Δημόσιο κτίσμα των ρωμαϊκών αυτοκρατορικών κρόνων στο χώρο του συγκροτήματος της αρχαίας Αγοράς Θεσσαλονίκης." *Η ΘΕΣΣΑΛΟΝΙΚΗ* 1 (1985) 85–109.

Karivieri, Arja. *The Athenian Lamp Industry in Late Antiquity.* Papers and Monographs of the Finnish Institute at Athens 5. Helsinki: Foundation of the Finnish Institute at Athens, 1996.

Katzef, M. L. "The Kyrenia Ship." Pages 50–52 in *A History of Seafaring Based on Underwater Archaeology.* Edited by George Fletcher Bass. London: Thames & Hudson, 1972.

Katzef, M. L., and S. W. Katzef. "Building a Replica of an Ancient Greek Merchantman." Pages 163–75 in *Proceedings of the 1st International Symposium on Ship Construction in Antiquity.* Edited by H. E. Tzalas. Athens: n.p., 1989.

Keil, Bruno. "Ein Λόγος συστατικός." *Nederlands archief voor kerkgeschiedenis* (1913) 1–41.

Keil, Joseph. *Die Bibliothek. FiE* 5.1. Vienna: Österreichische Archäologische Institut, 1944.

Kennedy, George. *The Art of Persuasion in Greece.* Princeton, N.J.: Princeton University Press, 1963.

Kennedy, James Houghton. *The Second and Third Epistles of St. Paul to the Corinthians, with Some Proofs of Their Independence and Mutual Relation.* London: Methuen, 1900.

Kent, John Harvey. *The Inscriptions, 1926–1950.* Corinth VIII.3. Princeton, N.J.: ASCSA, 1966.

Keppie, L. *Colonization and Veteran Settlement in Italy, 47–14 B.C.* London: British School at Rome, 1983.

King, Margaret. "Commemoration of Infants on Roman Funerary Inscriptions." Pages 117–54 in *The Epigraphy of Death.* Edited by Graham Oliver. Liverpool: Liverpool University Press, 2000.

Klauck, Hans-Josef. "Compilations of Letters in Cicero's Correspondence." Pages 317–37 in *Religion und Gesellschaft im frühen Christentum: Neutestamentliche Studien.* Edited by Hans-Josef Klauck. WUNT 152. Tübingen: Mohr Siebeck, 2003.

———. *Herrenmahl und Hellenistischer Kult: Eine religionsgeschichtliche Untersuchung zum ersten Korintherbrief.* NTAbh n.s. 15. Münster: Aschendorff, 1982.

Klein, W. "Pompejanische Bilderstudien II." *ÖJh* 19–20 (1919) 268–95.

Kleiner, Diana E. E. *The Monument of Philopappos in Athens.* Rome: G. Bretschneider, 1983.

Kloppenborg, John S. "Collegia and Thiasoi: Issues in Function, Taxonomy, and Membership." Pages 16–30 in *Voluntary Associations in the Graeco-Roman World.* Edited by John S. Kloppenborg and Stephen G. Wilson. London: Routledge, 1996.

Knibbe, Dieter. "Via Sacra Ephesiaka." Pages 449–54 in *100 Jahre österreichische Forschungen in Ephesos: Akten des Symposions Wien 1995.* Edited by Herwig Friesinger and Friedrich Krinzinger. Vienna: Österreichische Akademie der Wissenschaften, 1999.

Knibbe, Dieter, and Gerhard Langmann. *Via Sacra Ephesiaca I.* BerMatÖAI 3. Vienna: Schindler, 1993.

Knibbe, Dieter, and Hilke Thür. *Via Sacra Ephesiaca II.* BerMatÖAI 6. Vienna: Schindler, 1995.

Koch, Guntram, and Hellmut Sichtermann. *Römische Sarkophage.* Munich: C. H. Beck, 1982.

Koester, Helmut. *Ancient Christian Gospels: Their History and Development.* Philadelphia: Trinity Press International; London: SCM, 1990.

———. "Ephesos in Early Christian Literature." Pages 119–40 in *Ephesos, Metropolis of Asia: An Interdisciplinary Approach to Its Archaeology, Religion, and Culture.* Edited by Helmut Koester. HTS 41. Valley Forge, Pa.: Trinity Press International, 1995.

———. "From Paul's Eschatology to the Apocalyptic Schemata of 2 Thessalonians." Pages 441–45 in *The Thessalonian Correspondence.* Edited by Raymond F. Collins. BETL 87. Leuven: Leuven University Press, 1990.

Koester, Helmut. "Gnostic Writings as Witnesses for the Development of the Sayings Tradition." Pages 238–61 in *The School of Valentinus*. Vol. 1 of *The Rediscovery of Gnosticism*. Edited by Bentley Layton. Numen Sup 41. Leiden: Brill, 1980.

————. "Imperial Ideology and Paul's Eschatology in 1 Thessalonians." Pages 158–66 in *Paul and Empire: Religion and Power in Roman Imperial Society*. Edited by Richard A. Horsley. Harrisburg, Pa.: Trinity Press International, 1997.

————. "Melikertes at Isthmia: A Roman Mystery Cult." Pages 355–66 in *Greeks, Romans, and Christians: Essays in Honor of Abraham J. Malherbe*. Edited by David L. Balch, Everett Ferguson, and Wayne A. Meeks. Minneapolis: Fortress, 1990.

Koester, Helmut, ed. *Ephesos, Metropolis of Asia: An Interdisciplinary Approach to Its Archaeology, Religion, and Culture*. HTS 41. Valley Forge, Pa.: Trinity Press International, 1995. Repr., Cambridge, Mass.: Harvard Divinity School, 2004.

————. *Pergamon, Citadel of the Gods: Archaeological Record, Literary Description, and Religious Development*. HTS 46. Valley Forge, Pa.: Trinity Press International, 1998.

Koester, Helmut, et al., eds. *Archaeological Resources for New Testament Studies*. 2 vols. Harrisburg: Trinity Press International, 1994.

Koloski-Ostrow, Ann Olga, and Claire D. Lyon. "Naked Truths about Classical Art: An Introduction." Pages 1–11 in *Naked Truths: Women, Sexuality and Gender in Classical Art and Archaeology*. Edited by Ann Olga Koloski-Ostrow and Claire D. Lyon. New York: Routledge, 1997.

König, Jason. "Favorinus' *Corinthian Oration* in its Corinthian Context." *Proceedings of the Cambridge Philological Society* 47 (2001) 140–71.

Kos, M. Šašel. "A Latin Epitaph of a Roman Legionary from Corinth." *JRS* 68 (1978) 22–25.

Kraabel, A. Thomas. "Unity and Diversity among Diaspora Synagogues." Pages 51–55 in *The Synagogue in Late Antiquity*. Edited by Lee I. Levine. Philadelphia: ASOR, 1987.

Kraemer, Ross. *Her Share of the Blessings: Women's Religions among Pagans, Jews and Christians in the Greco-Roman World*. New York: Oxford University Press, 1992.

Krauskopf, Iadwiga. "Leukothea nach den antiken Quellen." Pages 137–48 in *Akten des Kolloquiums zum Thema die Göttin von Pyrgi: archäologische, linguistische und religionsgeschichtliche Aspekte (Tübingen, 16–17 Januar 1979)*. Edited by Aldo Neppi Modona and Friedhelm Prayon. Florence: Olschki, 1981.

Kroll, W. "Melqart." *RE* Suppl. 6 (1935) cols. 293–97.

Kubinska, J. *Les monuments funéraires dans les inscriptions grecques de l'Asie Mineure*. Warsaw: Éditions scientifiques de Pologne, 1968.

————. "Les ostothèques dans les inscriptions grecques de l'Asie Mineure." *Études d'archéologie classique* 9 (1997) 7–58.

Künzl, E. "Der augusteische Silberkalathus im Rheinische Landesmuseum Bonn." *Bonner Jahrbücher* (1969) 321–92.

Kurke, Leslie. "Inventing the *Hetaira*: Sex, Politics, and Discursive Conflict in Archaic Greece." *Classical Antiquity* 16 (1997) 106–50.

Kurtz, Donna, and John Boardman. *Greek Burial Customs*. London: Thames and Hudson, 1971.

Kuttner, A. "Looking Outside Inside: Ancient Roman Garden Rooms." *Studies in the History of Gardens and Designed Landscapes* 19 (1999) 3–35.

Kyle, Donald G. *Spectacles of Death in Ancient Rome*. London: Routledge, 2001.

Kyrieleis, Helmut. "Zu den Anfängen des Heiligtums von Olympia." Pages 213–20 in *Olympia 1875–2000: 125 Jahre Deutsche Ausgrabungen*. Edited by Helmut Kyrieleis. Mainz am Rhein: Philipp von Zabern, 2002.

Lake, Kirsopp. *The Earlier Epistles of St. Paul: Their Motive and Origin*. London: Rivingtons, 1911.

Lampe, Peter. "Das korinthische Herrenmahl im Schnittpunkt hellenistisch-romischer Mahlpraxis und paulinischer Theologie Crucis (1 Kor 11, 17–34)." *ZNW* 82 (1991) 183–213.

———. *Die stadtrömischen Christen in den ersten beiden Jahrhunderten: Untersuchungen zur Socialgeschichte*. 2d ed. Tübingen: J. C. B. Mohr, 1989.

Lanci, John, et al. "Corinth B." No. 13 in *Archaeological Resources for New Testament Studies*, vol. 2. Edited by Helmut Koester et al. Valley Forge, Pa.: Trinity Press International, 1994.

Landon, Mark E. "Beyond Peirene: Toward a Broader View of Corinthian Water Supply." Pages 43–62 in *Corinth: The Centenary, 1896–1996*. Edited by Charles K. Williams II and Nancy Bookidis. Corinth XX. Princeton: ASCSA, 2003.

———. "Contributions to the Study of the Water Supply of Ancient Corinth." Ph.D. diss., University of California, Berkeley, 1994.

Lapatin, Kenneth D. S. *Chryselephantine Statuary in the Ancient Mediterranean World*. New York: Oxford University Press, 2001.

———. "Pheidias ἐλεφαντουργός." *AJA* 101 (1997) 663–82.

La Rocca, E., M. de Vos, and A. de Vos. *Guida archeologica di Pompei*. Verona: A. Mondadori, 1976.

Larsen, J. A. O. "Roman Greece." Pages 259–498 in *An Economic Survey of Ancient Rome*, vol. 4. Edited by Tenney Frank. Baltimore, Md.: Johns Hopkins University Press, 1938.

Lateiner, Donald. *The Historical Method of Herodotus*. Toronto: University of Toronto Press, 1989.

Lattimore, Richmond. *Themes in Greek and Latin Epitaphs*. Urbana: University of Illinois, 1962.

Lavagne, Henri. *Operosa antra: Recherches sur la grotte à Rome de Sylla à Hadrian*. BÉFAR 272. Paris: L'École française de Rome, 1988.

Lavecchia, Salvator. *Pindari Dithyramborum Fragmenta.* Rome: Edizioni dell'Ateneo, 2000.

Lawlor, Hugh Jackson, ed. *The Psalter and Martyrology of Ricemarch.* 2 vols. London: Harrison and Sons, 1914.

Le Bonniac, Henri. *Le culte de Cérès à Rome, des origines à la fin de la République.* Paris: C. Klincksieck, 1958.

Lehmann, Phyllis Williams. *Roman Wall Paintings from Boscoreale in the Metropolitan Museum of Art.* Monographs on Archaeology and Fine Arts 5. Cambridge, Mass.: Archaeological Institute of America, 1953.

Lesky, Albin. *A History of Greek Literature.* 2d ed. New York: Thomas Y. Crowell, 1966.

————. "Melikertes." *RE* 29 (1931) cols. 514–21.

Levi, Doro. *Antioch Mosaic Pavements.* Princeton, N.J.: Princeton University Press, 1947.

Lietzmann, Hans. *Die drei altesten martyrologien.* Bonn: Marcus and Weber, 1911.

Lightfoot, J. L. *Parthenius of Nicaea.* Oxford: Clarendon, 1999.

Lindemann, Andreas. *Der Erste Korintherbrief.* HNT 9.1. Tübingen: Mohr Siebeck, 2000.

Lindsay, Hugh. "Eating with the Dead: The Roman Funerary Banquet." Pages 67–80 in *Meals in a Social Context: Aspects of the Communal Meal in the Hellenistic and Roman World.* Edited by Inge Nielsen and Hanne Nielsen. Aarhus: Aarhus University Press, 1998.

Lintott, A. W. *Judicial Reform and Land Reform in the Roman Republic.* Cambridge: Cambridge University Press, 1992.

Lippolis, I. Baldini. "La monumentalizzazione tardoantica di Athene." *Ostraka* 4 (1995) 169–90.

Lisle, R. "The Cults of Corinth." Ph.D. diss., Johns Hopkins University, 1955.

Littlewood, R. J. "Ovid among the Family Dead." *Latomus* 60 (2001) 916–35.

Lolos, A. C. "Antike Scholien zur Antologie Graeca-Palatina." *Hellenika* 33 (1981) 374–81.

Lolos, Y. A. "The Hadrianic Aqueduct of Corinth." *Hesperia* 66 (1997) 271–314.

Loraux, Nicole. "What Is a Goddess?" Pages 11–44 in *A History of Women in the West.* Edited by Pauline S. Pantel. Cambridge, Mass.: Harvard University Press, 1992.

Maass, Ernst. "De Favorini oratione Corinthiaca." Pages 133–38 in *De biographis Graecis quaestiones selectae.* Philologische Untersuchungen 3. Berlin: Weidmannsche Buchhandlung, 1880.

————. *Griechen und Semiten auf dem Isthmos von Korinth.* Berlin: G. Reimer, 1903.

MacDonald, W. L. "Empire Imagery in Augustan Architecture." Pages 137–48 in *The Age of Augustus: Interdisciplinary Conference Held at Brown University, April 30–May 2, 1982.* Edited by Rolf Winkes. Providence, R.I.: Center for Old World Archaeology and Art, Brown University, 1985.

MacKay, P. A. "The Fountain at Hadji Mustafa." *Hesperia* 36 (1967) 193–95.

MacLachlan, Bonnie. "Sacred Prostitution and Aphrodite." *SR* 2 (1992) 145–62.

MacMullen, Ramsay. *Roman Social Relations, 50 B.C. to A.D. 284.* New Haven, Conn.: Yale University Press, 1974.

Magnelli, Enrico. "Miscellanea critica." *Eikasmos* 10 (1999) 101–17.

Makowiecka, E. *The Origin and Evolution of Architectural Form of Roman Library* [sic]. Warsaw: Wydawnictwa Uniwersytetu Warszawskiego, 1978.

Malherbe, Abraham J. "Determinism and Free Will in Paul: The Argument of 1 Corinthians 8 and 9." Pages 231–55 in *Paul in His Hellenistic Context.* Edited by Troels Engberg-Pedersen. Minneapolis: Fortress, 1995.

———. *Paul and the Thessalonians: The Philosophic Tradition of Pastoral Care.* Philadelphia: Fortress, 1987.

———. *Social Aspects of Early Christianity.* 2d ed. Philadelphia: Fortress, 1983.

Malina, Bruce J. *Christian Origins and Cultural Anthropology: Practical Models for Biblical Interpretation.* Atlanta, Ga.: John Knox Press, 1986.

Mallwitz, Alfred. *Olympia und seine Bauten.* Munich: Prestel-Verlag, 1972.

Marres, Johannes Leonardus. *Dissertatio de Favorini Arelatensis: vita, studiis, scriptis. Accedunt fragmenta.* Trajecti ad Rhenum: Kemink et filium, 1853.

Marshall, Peter. *Enmity at Corinth: Social Conventions in Paul's Relations with the Corinthians.* WUNT 2.23. Tübingen: Mohr-Siebeck, 1987.

Martin, Dale B. *The Corinthian Body.* New Haven, Conn.: Yale University Press, 1995.

———. *Slavery as Salvation: The Metaphor of Slavery in Pauline Christianity.* New Haven, Conn.: Yale University Press, 1990.

Martin, T. R. "Inscriptions at Corinth." *Hesperia* 46 (1977) 178–98.

Martini, Wolfram. "Zur Benennung der sogennanten Hadriansbibliothek in Athen." Pages 188–91 in *Lebendige Altertumswissenschaft. Festgabe H. Vetters.* Edited by Manfred Kandler et al. Vienna: Adolf Holzhausen, 1985.

Mason, H. "Favorinus' Disorder: Reifenstein's Syndrome in Antiquity?" *Janus* 66 (1979) 1–13.

Mattusch, C. C. "Corinthian Metalworking: An Inlaid Fulcrum Panel." *Hesperia* 60 (1991) 525–28.

———. "Corinthian Metalworking: The Gymnasium Bronze Foundry." *Hesperia* 60 (1991) 383–95.

Mau, August. *Pompeii: Its Life and Art.* Translated by Francis W. Kelsey. Rev. ed., 1902. Repr., New Rochelle, N.Y.: Caratzas Bros., 1982.

McCready, Wayne O. "*Ekklesia* and Voluntary Associations." Pages 59–73 in *Voluntary Associations in the Graeco-Roman World.* Edited by John S. Kloppenborg and Stephen G. Wilson. London: Routledge, 1996.

McNelis, Charles. "Greek Grammarians and Roman Society during the Early Empire: Statius' Father and His Contemporaries." *Classical Antiquity* 21 (2002) 67–94.

Meeks, Wayne A. *The First Urban Christians: The Social World of the Apostle Paul.* New Haven, Conn.: Yale University Press, 1983.

Meggitt, Justin. *Paul, Poverty and Survival.* Edinburgh: T&T Clark, 1998.

Meiggs, Russell. *Roman Ostia.* 2d ed. Oxford: Clarendon, 1973.

Menadier, Blanche. "The Sixth Century BC Temple and the Sanctuary and Cult of Hera Akraia, Perachora." Ph.D. diss., University of Cincinnati, 1995.

Meritt, Benjamin D. "Greek Inscriptions." *Hesperia* 15 (1946) 169–253.

————. *Greek Inscriptions, 1896–1927.* Corinth VIII.1. Cambridge, Mass.: ASCSA, 1931.

Merker, Gloria S. "Corinthian Terracotta Figurines:The Development of an Industry." Pages 233–46 in *Corinth: The Centenary, 1896–1996.* Edited by Charles K. Williams II and Nancy Bookidis. Corinth XX. Princeton, N. J.: ASCSA, 2003.

————. *The Sanctuary of Demeter and Kore: Terracotta Figurines of the Classical, Hellenistic and Roman Periods.* Corinth XVIII.4. Princeton, N.J.: ASCSA, 2000.

Mertens-Horn, M. "Herakles, Leukothea e Palaimon sul tempio arcaico del Foro Boario." Pages 143–49 in *Deliciae Fictiles II: Proceedings of the Second International Conference on Archaic Architectural Terracottas from Italy Held at the Netherlands Institute in Rome, 12–13 June 1996.* Edited by Patricia S. Lulof and Eric M. Moormann. Amsterdam: Nederlands Instituut te Rome, 1997.

Miller, Daniel. *Artefacts as Categories: A Study of Ceramic Variability in Central India.* Cambridge: Cambridge University Press, 1985.

Miller, Naomi. *Heavenly Caves: Reflections on the Garden Grotto.* New York: G. Braziller, 1982.

Miller, Stephen G. "A Mosaic Floor from a Roman Villa at Anaploga." *Hesperia* 41 (1972) 332–54.

Miller, Stephen G., ed. "The Shrine of Opheltes and the Earliest Stadium of Nemea." Pages 239–50 in *Olympia 1875–2000: 125 Jahre Deutsche Ausgrabungen.* Edited by Helmut Kyrieleis. Mainz am Rhein: Philipp von Zabern, 2002.

————. *Nemea: A Guide to the Site and Museum.* Berkeley: University of California Press, 1990.

Mitchell, Margaret M. "The Corinthian Correspondence and the Birth of Pauline Hermeneutics." Pages 17–53 in *Paul and the Corinthians: Studies on a Community in Conflict: Essays in Honour of Margaret Thrall.* Edited by T. J. Burke and J. K. Elliott. NovTSup 109. Leiden: Brill, 2003.

————. "Korintherbriefe." Pages 1688–94 in *Religion in Geschichte und Gegenwart,* vol. 4. Edited by Hans Dieter Betz et al. 4th ed. Tübingen: Mohr Siebeck, 1998– .

————. "New Testament Envoys in the Context of Greco-Roman Diplomatic and Epistolary Conventions: The Example of Timothy and Titus." *JBL* 111 (1992) 661–82.

Mitchell, Margaret M. *Paul and the Rhetoric of Reconciliation: An Exegetical Investigation of the Language and Composition of 1 Corinthians.* HUT 28. Tübingen: Mohr/Siebeck, 1991. Repr., Louisville, Ky.: Westminster/John Knox, 1993.

―――. "Rhetorical Shorthand in Pauline Argumentation: The Functions of 'The Gospel' in the Corinthian Correspondence." Pages 63–88 in *Gospel in Paul: Studies on Corinthians, Galatians, and Romans for Richard N. Longenecker.* Edited by L. A. Jervis and P. Richardson. Sheffield: Sheffield Academic Press, 1994.

Momigliano, Arnaldo. "The Place of Herodotus in the History of Historiography." *History* 43 (1958) 1–13.

Monceaux, P. "Fouilles et recherches archéologiques au sanctuaire des jeux isthmiques IV: Ruines d'Ephyra, le diolcos, la nécropole de Corinthe." *Gazette Archéologique* (1885) 402–12.

Morgan, C. H. "Excavations at Corinth, 1936–37." *AJA* 41 (1937) 539–52.

―――. "Investigations at Corinth, 1953—A Tavern of Aphrodite." *Hesperia* 22 (1953) 131–40.

Morgan, Catherine. *The Late Bronze Age Settlement and Early Iron Age Sanctuary.* Isthmia 8. Princeton, N.J.: ASCSA, 1999.

Morris, Ian. *Death-Ritual and Social Structure in Classical Antiquity.* Cambridge: Cambridge University Press, 1992.

Morris, S. P., and J. K. Papadopoulos. "Phoenicians and the Corinthian Pottery Industry." Pages 251–63 in *Archäologische Studien in Kontaktzonen der antiken Welt.* Edited by Renate Rolle and Karin Schmidt. Göttingen: Vandenhoeck & Ruprecht, 1998.

Murphy-O'Connor, Jerome. *St. Paul's Corinth: Texts and Archaeology.* 3d ed. Minneapolis: Liturgical Press, 2002.

―――. *The Theology of the Second Letter to the Corinthians.* New Testament Theology. Cambridge: Cambridge University Press, 1991.

Musti, Domenico, and Mario Torelli, eds. *Pausania: Guida della Grecia II.* Milan: Fondazione Lorenzo Valla/Mondadori, 1986.

Neils, Jenifer. "Others Within the Other: An Intimate Look at Hetairai and Maenads." Pages 203–26 in *Not the Classical Ideal: Athens and the Construction of the Other in Greek Art.* Edited by Beth Cohen. Leiden: Brill, 2000.

Néraudau, Jean-Pierre. "La loi, la coutume et le chagrin: réflexions sur la mort des enfants." Pages 195–208 in *La mort, les morts et l'au-delà dans le monde romain.* Edited by François Hinard. Caen: Université de Caen, 1987.

Neuerburg, Norman. *L'architettura delle fontane e dei ninfei nell'Italia antica.* Naples: G. Macchiaroli, 1965.

Newlands, C. E. *Playing with Time: Ovid and the Fasti.* Ithaca, N.Y.: Cornell University Press, 1995.

van Nijf, Onno M. *The Civic World of Professional Associations in the Roman East.* Amsterdam: J. C. Gieben, 1997.

van Nijf, Onno M. "Local Heroes: Athletics, Festivals and Elite Self-Fashioning in the Roman East." Pages 306–34 in *Being Greek Under Rome*. Edited by Simon Goldhill. Cambridge: Cambridge University Press, 2001.

Nilsson, Martin P. *Griechische Feste von religiöser Bedeutung*. Leipzig: Teubner, 1906.

Nock, Arthur Darby. "Cremation and Burial in the Roman Empire." *HTR* 25 (1932) 321–59.

————. "The Cult of Heroes." *HTR* 37 (1944) 141–74. Repr., pages 575–602 in *Essays on Religion and the Ancient World*. Edited by Zeph Stewart. 2 vols. Oxford: Clarendon, 1972.

Norden, Eduard, *Agnostos Theos*. Stuttgart: Teubner, 1912. Repr., Darmstadt: Wissenschaftliche Buchgesellschaft, 1956.

————. *Die Antike Kunstprosa*. 2 vols. 1915–1918. Repr., Darmstadt: Wissenschaftliche Buchgesellschaft, 1958.

North, John. "The Development of Religious Pluralism." Pages 174–93 in *The Jews among Pagans and Christians in the Roman Empire*. Edited by Judith Lieu, John North, and Tessa Rajak. New York: Routledge, 1994.

Ober, Josiah, and Barry Strauss. "Drama, Political Rhetoric, and the Discourse of Athenian Democracy." Pages 237–70 in *Nothing to Do with Dionysos?: Athenian Drama in Its Social Context*. Edited by John J. Winkler and Froma I. Zeitlin. Princeton, N.J.: Princeton University Press, 1990.

Oden, Robert A. *The Bible without Theology*. Urbana: University of Illinois Press, 1987.

Oliver, James H. "Flavius Pantaenus, Priest of the Philosophical Muses." *HTR* 72 (1979) 157–60. Repr. pages 62–65 in *The Civic Tradition in Roman Athens*. Baltimore, Md.: Johns Hopkins University Press, 1983.

————. "Panachaeans and Panhellenes." *Hesperia* 47 (1978) 185–91.

Orr, D. G. "Roman Domestic Religion: A Study of the Roman Household Deities and Their Shrines at Pompeii and Herculaneum." Ph.D. diss., University of Maryland, 1972.

Ostrogorsky, Georges. "Byzantine Cities in the Early Middle Ages." *DOP* 13 (1959) 47–66.

Otto, Walter Friedrich. *Die Manen, oder Von den Urformen des Totenglaubens: Eine Untersuchung zur Religion der Griechen, Römer und Semiten and zum Volksglauben überhaupt*. Berlin: J. Springer, 1923.

Page, Denys L., trans. *Euripides: Medea*. Oxford: Oxford University Press, 1967.

————. *Further Greek Epigrams*. Cambridge: Cambridge University Press, 1981.

Palagia, Olga. "Meaning and Narrative Techniques in Statue-Bases of the Pheidian Circle." Pages 53–78 in *Work and Image in Ancient Greece*. Edited by N. Keith Rutter and Brian A. Sparkes. Edinburgh: Edinburgh University Press, 2000.

Pallas, D. I. " Ἀνασκαφή Βασιλικης ἐν Λεχαίω." *Prak* (1956) 177–78 and plate 72b.

Pallas, D. I. "Données nouvelles sur quelques boucles et fibules considéreés comme avares et slaves et sur la Corinthe entre le VIe et le IXe s." *Byzantino-bulgarica* 7 (1981) 295–318.

———. "Korinth." Pages 745–811 in *Reallexikon zur Byzantinischen Kunst*, vol. 4. Edited by Klaus Wessel. Stuttgart: Hiersemann, 1990.

Palmer, Hazel. "The Classical and Roman Periods." Pages 65–327 in *The North Cemetery*. Edited by Carl William Blegen, Hazel Palmer, and Rodney Stewart Young. Corinth XIII. Princeton, N.J.: ASCSA, 1964.

Papahatzis, Nicos. *Ancient Corinth*. Athens: Ekdotike Athenon, 1983.

Parke, H. W. *Festivals of the Athenians*. Ithaca, N.Y.: Cornell University Press, 1977.

Parker, H. C. "The Romanization of Ino (*Fasti* 6, 475–550)." *Latomus* 58 (1999) 336–47.

Parker, Robert. *Athenian Religion: A History*. Oxford: Clarendon, 1996.

Pearson, Birger A. "Friedländer Revisited: Alexandrian Judaism and Gnostic Origins." Pages 10–28 in *Gnosticism, Judaism, and Egyptian Christianity*. Studies in Antiquity and Christianity. Philadelphia: Fortress, 1990.

———. "Philo, Gnosis, and the New Testament." Pages 73–89 in *The New Testament and Gnosis: Essays in Honour of Robert McL. Wilson*. Edited by A. H. B. Logan and A. J. M. Wedderburn. Edinburgh: T&T Clark, 1983.

Pearson, M. Parker. "Economic and Ideological Change: Cyclical Growth in the Pre-State Societies of Jutland." Pages 69–92 in *Ideology, Power, and Prehistory*. Edited by Daniel Miller and Christopher Tilley. Cambridge: Cambridge University Press, 1984.

Pedley, J. G. "Reflections of Architecture in Sixth-Century Attic Vase-Painting" Pages 63–80 in *Papers on the Amasis Painter and His World*. Malibu, Calif.: J. Paul Getty Museum, 1987.

Peek, Werner. *Attische Grabschriften II: unedierte Grabinschriften aus Athen und Attika*. Berlin: Akademie-Verlag, 1957.

Pemberton, Elizabeth G. *The Sanctuary of Demeter and Kore: The Greek Pottery*. Corinth XVIII.1. Princeton, N.J.: ASCSA, 1989.

———. "Ten Hellenistic Graves in Ancient Corinth." *Hesperia* 54 (1985) 271–307.

Perdrizet, Paul. *Les terres cuites grecques d'Égypte de la collection Fouquet*. Nancy: Berger-Levrault, 1921.

Perkins, Pheme. *Gnosticism and the New Testament*. Minneapolis: Fortress, 1993.

Pervo, Richard. *Profit with Delight: The Literary Genre of the Acts of the Apostles*. Minneapolis: Fortress, 1987.

Pfaff, C. A. "Archaic Corinthian Architecture." Pages 95–140 in *Corinth: The Centenary, 1896–1996*. Edited by Charles K. Williams II and Nancy Bookidis. Corinth XX. Princeton, N.J.: ASCSA, 2003.

Pharr, Clyde. *The Theodosian Code and Novels and the Sirmondian Constitutions: A Translation with Commentary*. Princeton, N.J.: Princeton University Press, 1952.

Picard, C. "L'Héraeon de Perachora et les enfants de Médée." *RA* (1932) 218–29.

Piérart, M. "Panthéon et hellénisation dans la colonie romaine de Corinthe: la 'redécouverte' du culte de Palaimon à l'Isthme." *Kernos* 11 (1998) 85–109.

Pietri, Charles. "La géographie de l'Illyricum ecclésiastique et ses relations avec l'Église de Rome (V^e–V^{ie} siècles)." Pages 21–59 in *Villes et peuplement dans l'Illyricum protobyzantin*. Rome: L'École française de Rome, 1984.

———. *Roma Christiana.* 2 vols. Rome: L'École française de Rome, 1976.

Pietsch, Wolfgang. "Außerstädtische Grabanlagen von Ephesos." Pages 455–60 in *100 Jahre österreichische Forschungen in Ephesos: Akten des Symposions Wien 1995*. Edited by Herwig Friesinger and Friedrich Krinzinger. Vienna: Österreichische Akademie der Wissenschaften, 1999.

Pietsch, Wolfgang, and Elisabeth Trinkl. "Der Grabungsbericht der Kampagnen 1992–93." Pages 33–42 in *Via Sacra Ephesiaca II*. Edited by Dieter Knibbe and Hilke Thür. BerMatÖAI 6. Vienna: Schindler, 1995.

Piganiol, A. *Les documents cadastraux de la colonie romaine d'Orange.* Gallia Sup 16. Paris: Centre national de la recherche scientifique, 1962.

Platner, Samuel B., and Thomas Ashby. *A Topographical Dictionary of Ancient Rome.* London: Oxford University Press, 1929.

Pogoloff, Stephen M. *Logos and Sophia: The Rhetorical Situation of 1 Corinthians.* SBLDS 134. Atlanta, Ga.: Scholars Press, 1992.

Pollini, John. *The Portraiture of Gaius and Lucius Caesar.* New York: Fordham University Press, 1987.

Preston, Rebecca. "Roman Questions, Greek Answers: Plutarch and the Construction of Identity." Pages 86–119 in *Being Greek under Rome*. Edited by Simon Goldhill. Cambridge: Cambridge University Press, 2001.

Price, Simon R. F. *Religions of the Ancient Greeks.* Cambridge: Cambridge University Press, 1999.

———. *Rituals and Power: The Roman Imperial Cult in Asia Minor.* Cambridge: Cambridge University Press, 1984.

Protonotariou-Deilaki, Evangelia. "Chronika." *ArchDelt* 24 (1969) 102–3.

Purcell, N. "Atrium Libertatis," *PBSR* 61 (1993) 125–55.

———. "The Ports of Rome: Evolution of a *Façade Maritime*." Pages 267–80 in *'Roman Ostia' Revisited: Archaeological and Historical Papers in Memory of Russell Meiggs*. Edited by Anna Gallina Zevi and Amanda Claridge. Rome: British School at Rome, 1996.

Quentin, Henri, ed. *Les Martyrologes historiques du Moyen Age.* Paris: Librairie Victor Le Coffre, 1908.

Quesnel, Michel. "Circonstances de composition de la seconde épître aux Corinthiens." *NTS* 43 (1997) 256–67.

Raepsaet, G. "Le Diolkos de l'isthme à Corinthe: sa trace, son fonctionnement." *BCH* 117 (1993) 233–56.

Reeder, William W. *The Severed Hand and the Upright Corpse: The Declamations of Marcus Antonius Polemo.* SBLTT 42. Atlanta, Ga.: Scholars Press, 1996.

Reese, D. S. "A Bone Assemblage at Corinth of the Second Century after Christ." *Hesperia* 56 (1987) 255–74.

Reiner, Eugen. *Die rituelle Totenklage der Griechen.* Berlin: W. Kohlhammer, 1938.

Rhodes, Robin F. "The Earliest Greek Architecture in Corinth and the 7th-Century Temple on Temple Hill." Pages 85–94 in *Corinth: The Centenary, 1896–1996.* Edited by Charles K. Williams II and Nancy Bookidis. Corinth XX. Princeton, N.J.: ASCSA, 2003.

Richardson, Lawrence Jr. *Pompeii: An Architectural History.* Baltimore, Md.: Johns Hopkins University Press, 1988.

Richardson, R. B. "The Fountain of Glauce at Corinth." *AJA* 4 (1900) 458–75.

Riethmueller, J. "*Bothros* and Tetrastyle: The *Heroön* of Asclepius in Athens." Pages 123–43 in *Ancient Greek Hero Cult.* Ed. R. Hägg. ActaAth 8, 16. Stockholm: Svenska Institutet i Athen, 1999.

Rife, Joseph. "Death, Ritual, and Memory in Greek Society during the Early and Middle Roman Empire." Ph.D. diss., University of Michigan, 1999.

Rives, James. *Religion and Authority in Roman Carthage: From Augustus to Constantine.* New York: Oxford University Press, 1995.

Rizakis, A. D. "Roman Colonies in the Province of Achaia: Territories, Land and Population." Pages 15–36 in *The Early Roman Empire in the East.* Edited by Susan E. Alcock. Oxford: Oxbow Books, 1997.

Robertson, N. "A Corinthian Inscription Recording Honors at Elis for Corinthian Judges." *Hesperia* 45 (1976) 253–66.

Robinson, Betsey A. "Fountains and the Culture of Water at Roman Corinth." Ph.D. diss., University of Pennsylvania, 2001.

Robinson, Henry S. "American Excavations at Corinth" (Chronika B1). *ArchDelt* 19 (1964) 100–2.

———. "Excavations at Corinth" (Chronika B1). *ArchDelt* 18 (1963) 76–80. French translation published in *BCH* 87 (1963) 722–28.

———. "Excavations at Corinth" (Chronika B1). *ArchDelt* 21 (1966) 133–41.

———. "Excavations at Corinth: Temple Hill, 1968–1972." *Hesperia* 45 (1976) 203–39.

———. "A Sanctuary and Cemetery in Western Corinth." *Hesperia* 38 (1969) 1–35.

Roddaz, Jean-Michel. *Marcus Agrippa.* BÉFAR 253. Rome: L'École française de Rome, 1984.

Roebuck, Carl. *The Asklepieion and Lerna.* Corinth XIV. Princeton, N.J.: ASCSA, 1951.

Rogers, Guy. *The Sacred Identity of Ephesos: Foundation Myths of a Roman City.* London: Routledge, 1991.

Roller, Otto. *Das Formular der paulinischen Briefe: Ein Beitrag zur Lehre vom antiken Briefe.* BWANT 58. Stuttgart: Kohlhammer, 1933.

Romano, David G. *Athletics and Mathematics in Archaic Corinth: The Origins of the Greek Stadion.* MAPS 206. Philadelphia: American Philosophical Society, 1993.

———. "A Circus in Roman Corinth." *Hesperia,* forthcoming.

———. "City Planning, Centuriation, and Land Division in Roman Corinth: *Colonia Laus Iulia Corinthiensis* and *Colonia Iulia Flavia Augusta Corinthiensis.*" Pages 279–301 in *Corinth: The Centenary, 1896–1996.* Edited by Charles K. Williams II and Nancy Bookidis. Corinth XX. Princeton, N.J.: ASCSA, 2003.

———. "Post 146 B.C. Land Use in Corinth, and Planning of the Roman Colony of 44 B.C." Pages 9–30 in *The Corinthia in the Roman Period.* Edited by Timothy E. Gregory. JRASup 8. Ann Arbor, Mich.: Journal of Roman Archaeology, 1993.

———. "A Tale of Two Cities: Roman Colonies at Corinth." Pages 83–104 in *Romanization and the City.* Edited by Elizabeth Fentress. JRASup 38. Portsmouth, N.H.: Journal of Roman Archaeology, 2000.

Romano, David G., and B. C. Schoenbrun. "A Computerized Architectural and Topographical Survey of Ancient Corinth." *Journal of Field Archaeology* 20 (1993) 177–90.

Romano, David G., and N. L. Stapp. "Piecing Together the City and Territory of Roman Corinth." *Archaeological Computing Newsletter (Institute of Archaeology, Oxford)* 52 (1998) 1–7.

Romano, David G., and Osama Tolba. "Remote Sensing and GIS in the Study of Roman Centuriation in the Corinthia, Greece." Pages 457–63 in *Interfacing the Past, Computer Applications and Quantitative Methods in Archaeology CAA95.* Edited by Hans Kamermans and Kelly Fennema. Analecta Praehistorica Leidensia 28. Leiden: Brill, 1996.

———. "Remote Sensing, GIS and Electronic Surveying: Reconstructing the City Plan and Landscape of Roman Corinth." Pages 163–74 in *Computer Applications and Quantitative Methods in Archaeology 1994.* Edited by Jeremy Huggett and Nick Ryan. BAR International Series 600. Oxford: Tempus Reparatum, 1995.

Romano, I. B. "A Hellenistic Deposit from Corinth: Evidence for Interim Period Activity." *Hesperia* 63 (1994) 57–104.

Ross, M. H. *The Culture of Conflict: Interpretations and Interests in Comparative Perspective.* New Haven, Conn.: Yale University Press, 1993.

Rothaus, Richard M. *Corinth, the First City of Greece: An Urban History of Late Antique Cult and Religion.* Leiden: Brill, 2000.

Rotroff, Susan I. *Hellenistic Pottery: Athenian and Imported Wheelmade Table Ware and Related Material.* Agora XXIX. Princeton, N.J.: ASCSA, 1997.

Roux, Georges. *Pausanias en Corinthie (Livre II, 1 à 15): texte, traduction, commentaire archéologique et topographique.* Paris: Belles Lettres, 1958.

Rudolph, Kurt. *Gnosis: The Nature and History of Gnosticism.* San Francisco: Harper & Row, 1983.

Saffrey, H. D. "Aphrodite à Corinthe: réflexions sur une idée reçue." *RB* 92 (1985) 359–74.

Salmon, E. T. *Roman Colonization under the Republic.* London: Thames and Hudson, 1969.

Salomon, Nanette. "Making a World of Difference." Pages 197–219 in *Naked Truths: Women, Sexuality and Gender in Classical Art and Archaeology.* Edited by Ann Olga Koloski-Ostrow and Claire D. Lyon. New York: Routledge, 1997.

Salvadori, E. "La struttura narrativa dei Matralia: Ovidio, *Fasti* vi 473–550." *Sandalion* 5 (1982) 205–21.

Salviat, F. "Orientation, extension et chronologie des plans cadastraux d'Orange." *Revue Archéologique de Narbonnaise* 10 (1977) 107–18.

Sanders, E. P. *Judaism: Practice and Belief, 63 BCE–66 CE.* Philadelphia: Trinity Press International, 1992.

Sanders, G. D. R. "A Late Roman Bath at Corinth: Excavations in the Panayia Field 1995–96." *Hesperia* 68 (1999) 441–80.

———. "Problems in Interpreting Rural and Urban Settlement in Southern Greece, AD 365–700." Chapter 5 in *Landscapes of Change: The Evolution of the Countryside from Late Antiquity to the Early Middle Ages.* Edited by Neil Christie. Aldershot: Ashgate, 2004.

Sanders, G. D. R., and I. K. Whitbread. "Central Places and Major Roads in the Peloponnese." *BSA* 85 (1990) 333–61.

Sapelli, Marina. *The National Roman Museum, Palazzo Massimo alle Terme.* Rome: Ministero per i beni culturali e ambientali/Soprintendenza archeologica di Roma, 1999.

Saumagne, Charles. " 'Iter populo debetur' . . . ." *Revue de Philologie,* 3d series, 2 (1928) 320–52.

Schachter, Albert. *Cults of Boiotia.* 4 vols. BICSSup 38.1–4. London: University of London, Institute of Classical Studies, 1986.

———. "Kadmos and the implications of the tradition for Boiotian history." Pages 143–53 in *La Béotie antique.* Edited by Gilbert Argoud and Paul Roesch. Paris: Éditions du Centre National de la Recherche Scientifique, 1985.

———. "Ovid and Boeotia." Pages 103–9 in *Essays in the History, Topography, and Culture of Boiotia.* Edited by Albert Schachter. Teiresias Supplement 3. Montreal: McGill University, Department of Classics, 1990.

Schefold, Karl. "Origins of Roman Landscape Painting." *Art Bulletin* 42 (1960) 87–96.

———. *Die Wände Pompejis: Topografisches Verzeichnis der Bildmotive.* Berlin: de Gruyter, 1957.

Schefold, Karl, and Franz Jung. *Die Urköniger: Perseus, Bellerophon, Herakles und Theseus in der klassischen und hellenistischen Kunst.* Munich: Hirmer, 1988.

Scheid, J. "Sacrifice et banquet à Rome, quelques problèmes." *MEFRA* 97 (1985) 193–206.

Schilling, Robert, trans. *Pline l'Ancien: Histoire naturelle.* Paris: Belles Lettres, 1977.

———. *La religion romaine de Vénus, depuis les origins jusqu'au temps d'Auguste.* 2d ed. Paris: de Boccard, 1982.

———. "Le sanctuaire de Venus près de Casinum." Pages 445–51 in *Perennitas: Studi in onore di Angelo Brelich.* Rome: Edizioni dell'Ateneo, 1980.

Schmithals, Walter. *Die Briefe des Paulus in ihrer ursprünglichen Form.* Zurich: Theologischer Verlag, 1984.

———. *Gnosticism at Corinth.* Translated by J. E. Steely. Nashville, Tenn.: Abingdon, 1971.

———. "Die Korintherbriefe als Briefsammlung." *ZNW* 64 (1973) 263–88.

Schmitt, M. L. "Bellerophon and the Chimaera in Archaic Greek Art." *AJA* 70 (1966) 341–47.

Schneider, K. "Isthmia." *RE* (1916) 9:2248–55.

Schrage, Wolfgang. *Der erste Brief an die Korinther.* EKK 7.1–3. Zürich: Benziger; Neukirchen-Vluyn: Neukirchener Verlag, 1991–1999.

Schüssler Fiorenza, Elisabeth. "Rhetorical Situation and Historical Reconstruction in 1 Corinthians." *NTS* 33 (1987) 386–403.

Scotton, Paul. "An Augustan Tribunal: A Seat for Gallio." *AJA* 106 (2002) 278.

———. "The Julian Basilica at Corinth: An Architectural Investigation." Ph.D. diss., University of Pennsylvania, 1997.

Scranton, Robert L. *Monuments in the Lower Agora and North of the Archaic Temple.* Corinth I.3. Princeton, N.J.: ASCSA, 1951.

Scranton, Robert L., Joseph W. Shaw, and Leila Ibrahim. *Topography and Architecture.* Vol. 1 of *Kenchreai, Eastern Port of Corinth.* Leiden: Brill, 1978.

Scully, Vincent. *The Earth, the Temple, and the Gods.* New Haven, Conn.: Yale University Press, 1979.

Seelinger, R. A. "The Dionysiac Context of the Cult of Melikertes/Palaimon at the Isthmian Sanctuary of Poseidon." *Maia* 50 (1998) 271–80.

Sellin, Gerhard. "Hauptprobleme des Ersten Korintherbriefes." *ANRW* II.25.4 (1987) 2940–3044.

———. *Der Streit um die Auferstehung der Toten: eine religionsgeschichtliche und exegetische Untersuchung von 1 Korinther.* FRLANT 138. Göttingen: Vandenhoeck & Ruprecht, 1986.

Shapiro, H. A. *Art and Cult under the Tyrants.* Mainz: Philipp von Zabern, 1989.

Shear, T. Leslie. "Excavations at Corinth." *AJA* 29 (1925) 381–97.

———. "Excavations in the North Cemetery at Corinth in 1930." *AJA* 34 (1930).

———. "Excavations in the North Cemetery in Corinth in 1931." *AJA* 35 (1931) 424–41.

Shear, T. Leslie. "Excavations in the Theatre District and Tombs of Corinth in 1929." *AJA* 33 (1929) 515–46.

———. "Excavations in the Theatre District of Corinth in 1926." *AJA* 30 (1926) 1–20.

———. *The Roman Villa*. Corinth V. Cambridge, Mass.: ASCSA, 1930.

Shelley, J. M. "The Christian Basilica near the Cenchrean Gate at Corinth." *Hesperia* 12 (1943) 166–89.

Sherwin-White, A. N. "Early Persecutions and Roman Law Again." *JTS* n.s. 3 (1952) 199–213.

———. *The Letters of Pliny: A Historical and Social Commentary*. Oxford: Clarendon, 1966.

———. *The Roman Citizenship*. Oxford: Clarendon Press, 1980.

Shoe, L. T. "The Roman Ionic Base in Corinth." Pages 300–3 in *Essays in Memory of Karl Lehmann*. Edited by Lucy F. Sandler. [New York]: Institute of Fine Arts, New York University, 1964; distributed by J. J. Augustin, Locust Valley, N.Y.

Shorrock, Robert. *The Challenge of Epic: Allusive Engagement in the Dionysiaca of Nonnus*. Mnemosyne Supplement 210. Leiden: Brill, 2001.

Siddall, R. "Lime Cements, Mortars and Concretes; The Site of Ancient Corinth, Northern Peloponnese, Greece; I: Preliminary Results from Morphologic and Petrographic Analyses. (Weiner Laboratory Internal Report; Athens, 1997)." Unpublished manuscript.

Simon, Erika. *Augustus: Kunst und Leben in Rom um die Zeitenwende*. Munich: Hirmer, 1986.

Sinn, Friederike. *Stadtrömische Marmorurnen*. Mainz: von Zabern, 1987.

Slane, Kathleen W. "Corinth's Roman Pottery: Quantification and Meaning." Pages 321–36 in *Corinth: The Centenary, 1896–1996*. Edited by Charles K. Williams II and Nancy Bookidis. Corinth XX. Princeton, N.J.: ASCSA, 2003.

———. *The Sanctuary of Demeter and Kore: The Roman Pottery and Lamps*. Corinth XVIII.2. Princeton, N.J.: ASCSA, 1990.

Slane, Kathleen W., and G. D. R. Sanders. "Late Roman Horizons Established at Corinth." *Hesperia*, forthcoming.

Slater, W. J. "Pelops at Olympia." *GRBS* 30 (1989) 485–501.

Smith, Bonnie E. *The Gender of History*. Cambridge, Mass.: Harvard University Press, 1998.

Smith, Christopher. "Worshipping Mater Matuta: Ritual and Context." Pages 136–55 in *Religion in Archaic and Republican Rome and Italy*. Edited by Edward Bispham and Christopher Smith. Edinburgh: Edinburgh University Press, 2001.

Sorensen, Marie L. S. *Gender Archaeology*. Cambridge: Polity Press, 2000.

Sourvinou-Inwood, Christiane. "Persephone and Aphrodite at Locri: A Model for Personality Definitions in Greek Religion." *JHS* 98 (1978) 101–21.

Spanu, Marcello. "Burial in Asia Minor during the Imperial Period, with Particular Reference to Cilicia and Cappadocia." Pages 169–77 in *Burial, Society and Context in the Roman World*. Edited by John Pearce, Martin Millett, and Manuela Struck. Oxford: Oxbow Books, 2000.

Spawforth, A. J. S. "Agonistic Festivals in Roman Greece." Pages 193–97 in *The Greek Renaissance in the Roman Empire: Papers from the Tenth British Museum Classical Colloquium*. Edited by Susan Walker and Averil Cameron. ICSBSup 55. London: University of London, 1989.

———. "Corinth, Argos, and the Imperial Cult. Pseudo-Julian, *Letters* 198." *Hesperia* 63 (1994) 211–32.

———. "Roman Corinth: The Formation of a Colonial Elite." Pages 167–82 in *Roman Onomastics in the Greek East: Social and Political Aspects*. Edited by A. D. Rizakis. Μελετήματα 21. Athens: Research Center for Greek and Roman Antiquity; Paris: de Boccard, 1996.

———. "The World of the Panhellenion: I. Athens and Eleusis." *JRS* 75 (1985) 78–104.

———. "The World of the Panhellenion: II. Three Dorian cities." *JRS* 76 (1986) 88–105.

Spetsieri-Choremi, A. "Library of Hadrian at Athens: Recent Finds." *Ostraka* 4 (1995) 137–47.

Stark, Rodney. "Christianizing the Urban Environment: An Analysis Based on 22 Greco-Roman Cities." *Sociological Analysis* 52 (1991) 77–88.

Stegemann, Ekkhard, and Wolfgang Stegemann. *The Jesus Movement: A Social History of Its First Century*. Minneapolis: Fortress, 1999.

Steiner, A. "Pottery and Cult in Corinth: Oil and Water at the Sacred Spring." *Hesperia* 61 (1992) 358–408.

Stephanidou-Tiveriou, Theodosia. "Une tête colossale de Titus au Forum de Thessalonique." *BCH* 125 (2001) 389–411.

Stevens, G. P. "The Fountain of Peirene in the Time of Herodes Atticus." *AJA* 38 (1934) 55–58.

Stewart, Andrew. "Imag(in)ing the Other: Amazons and Ethnicity in Fifth-Century Athens." *Poetics Today* 16 (1995) 571–97.

Stewart, Charles. *Demons and the Devil: Moral Imagination in Modern Greek Culture*. Princeton, N.J.: Princeton University Press, 1991.

Stewart-Sykes, Alistair. "Ancient Editors and Copyists and Modern Partition Theories: The Case of the Corinthian Correspondence." *JSNT* 61 (1996) 53–64.

Stikas, E. G. "Ἀναγραφή κοιμητηριακῆς βασιλικῆς Παλαιᾶς Κορίνθου." *Prak* (1966) 51–56.

Stillwell, A. N. *The Potters' Quarter*. Corinth XV.1. Princeton, N.J.: ASCSA, 1948.

Stillwell, Richard. "Excavations at Corinth, 1934–1935." *AJA* 40 (1936) 21–45.

———. *The Theatre*. Corinth II. Princeton, N.J.: ASCSA, 1952.

Stillwell, Richard, Robert L. Scranton, and Sarah Elizabeth Freeman. *Architecture*. Corinth I.2. Cambridge, Mass.: ASCSA, 1941.

Stothers, R. B. "Mystery Cloud of AD 543." *Nature* 307 (1984) 344–45.

Stothers, R. B., and M. R. Rampino. "Volcanic Eruptions in the Mediterranean before AD 630 from Written and Archaeological Sources." *Journal of Geophysical Research* 88 (1983) 6357–71.

Stowers, Stanley K. "Does Pauline Christianity Resemble a Hellenistic Philosophy?" Pages 81–102 in *Paul Beyond the Judaism/Hellenism Divide*. Edited by Troels Engberg-Pedersen. Louisville, Ky.: Westminster/John Knox, 2001.

———. "Greeks Who Sacrifice and Those Who Do Not: Toward an Anthropology of Greek Religion." Pages 293–333 in *The Social World of the First Christians: Essays in Honor of Wayne A. Meeks*. Edited by L. Michael White and O. Larry Yarbrough. Minneapolis: Fortress, 1995.

Streete, Gail Corrington. *The Strange Woman: Power and Sex in the Bible*. Louisville, Ky.: Westminster/John Knox, 1997.

Strocka, V. M. "Römische Bibliotheken." *Gymnasium* 88 (1981) 298–329.

———. "Zur Datierung der Celsusbibliothek." Pages 893–99 in *The Proceedings of the Xth International Congress of Classical Archaeology, Ankara-Izmir 23–30 September 1973*. Edited by Ekrem Akurgal. Ankara: Türk Tarih Kurumu, 1978.

Stroszeck, Jutta (with contributions from Klaus Hallof and Anna Lagia). "Kerameikosgrabung 1999." *AA* (2000) 455–93.

Stroud, R. S. "The Sanctuary of Demeter on Acrocorinth in the Roman Period." Pages 65–73 in *The Corinthia in the Roman Period*. Edited by Timothy E. Gregory. JRASup 8. Ann Arbor, Mich.: Journal of Roman Archaeology, 1993.

Taylor, N. H. "The Composition and Chronology of Second Corinthians." *JSNT* 44 (1991) 67–87.

Tenney, Frank. *Rome and Italy of the Empire*. Paterson, N.J.: Pageant Books, 1959.

Teodorsson, Sven-Tage. *Commentary on Plutarch's Table Talks*. 3 vols. Gotheborg: Acta Universitatis Gothoburgensis, 1990.

Theissen, Gerd. *The Social Setting of Pauline Christianity: Essays on Corinth*. Edited and translated by J. H. Schütz. Philadelphia: Fortress, 1982.

Thomas, Christine, and C. İçten. "The Ephesian Ossuaries and Roman Influence on the Production of Burial Containers." Pages 549–54 in *100 Jahre österreichische Forschungen in Ephesos: Akten des Symposions Wien 1995*, vol. 1. Edited by Herwig Friesinger and Friedrich Krinzinger. 3 vols. Vienna: Österreichische Akademie der Wissenschaften, 1999.

———. "The *Ostothekai* of Ephesos and the Rise of Sarcophagus Inhumation: Death, Conspicuous Consumption, and the Roman Freedmen." In *Symposium des Sarkophag-Korpus 2001*. Edited by Guntram Koch. Sarkophag-Studien. Mainz: Zabern, 2005.

Thompson, D. B. "Three Centuries of Hellenistic Terracottas, I, B and C." *Hesperia* 23 (1954) 72–107.

Thompson, Homer A., and Richard E. Wycherley. *The Agora of Athens: The History, Shape, and Uses of an Ancient City Center.* The Athenian Agora XIV. Princeton, N.J.: ASCSA, 1972.

Thornton, Bruce. *Eros: The Myth of Ancient Greek Sexuality.* Boulder, Colo.: Westview Press, 1997.

Thrall, Margaret E. *A Critical and Exegetical Commentary on the Second Epistle to the Corinthians.* 2 vols. ICC. Edinburgh: T&T Clark, 1994–2000.

Thür, Hilke. "The Processional Way in Ephesos as a Place of Cult and Burial." Pages 157–200 in *Ephesos, Metropolis of Asia: An Interdisciplinary Approach to Its Archaeology, Religion, and Culture.* Edited by Helmut Koester. HTS 41. Philadelphia: Trinity Press International, 1995.

————. " 'Via Sacra Ephesiaka': Vor der Stadt und in der Stadt." Pages 163–72 in *Steine und Wege: Festschrift für Dieter Knibbe.* Edited Peter Scherrer, Hans Taeuber, and Hilke Thür. Sonderschriften 32. Vienna: Österreichisches Archäologisches Institut, 1999.

Tobin, Jennifer L. "The Monuments of Herodes Atticus." Ph.D. diss., University of Pennsylvania, 1991.

Tomlinson, R. A. "Perachora: The Remains Outside the Two Sanctuaries: The Storage Chambers and the Fountain House." *BSA* 64 (1969) 155–258.

————. "Perachora." Pages 321–51 in *Le Sanctuaire Grec.* Edited by Albert Schachter and Jean Bingen. Entretiens sur l'Antiquité classique 37. Geneva: Fondation Hardt, 1992.

Török, Laszlo. *Hellenistic and Roman Terracottas from Egypt.* Bibliotheca Archaeologica 15/Monumenta Antiquitatis extra fines Hungariae reperta 4. Rome: "L'Erma" di Bretschneider, 1995.

Toynbee, Jocelyn M. *Death and Burial in the Roman World.* London: Thames and Hudson; Ithaca, N.Y.: Cornell University Press, 1971.

Toynbee, Jocelyn M., and John Ward-Perkins. *The Shrine of St. Peter.* London: Longmans, Green, 1956.

Travlos, Ioannes. "Τὸ τετράκογχο οἰκοδόμημα τῆς βιβλιοθήκης τοῦ Ἀδριανοῦ." Pages 343–47 in *ΦΙΛΙΑ ΕΠΗ ΕΙΣ ΓΕΩΡΓΙΟΝ Ε. ΜΥΛΩΝΑΝ,* vol. 1. 4 vols. Athens: Ἡ ἐν Ἀθήναις Ἀρχαιολογικὴ Ἑταιρεία, 1986–1989.

Treggiari, Susan. *Roman Freedmen during the Late Republic.* Oxford: Clarendon, 1969.

Turcan, Robert. "Origines et sens de l'inhumation à l'époque impériale." *REA* 60 (1958) 323–47.

————. "Les sarcophages romains et le problème du symbolisme funéraire." *ANRW* II.16.2 (1978) 1700–35.

Turner, David. "The Politics of Despair: The Plague of 746–747 and Iconoclasm in the Byzantine Empire." *BSA* 85 (1990) 419–34.

Tybout, R. A. "Domestic Shrines and 'Popular Painting': Style and Social Content." *JRA* 9 (1996).

Van Groningen, B. A. *Euphorion.* Amsterdam: Hakkert, 1977.

Verdelis, N. M. "Der Diolkos am Isthmus von Korinth." *AM* 71 (1956) 51–59.

Vikela, Eugenia. *Die Weihreliefs aus dem Athener Pankrates-Heiligtum am Ilissos: Religiongeschichtliche Bedeutung und Typologie.* Mitteilungen des deutschen archäologischen Instituts, Athenische Abteilung, Beiheft 16. Berlin: Gebr. Mann, 1994.

Vikela, Eugenia, and R. Vollkommer. "Melikertes." *LIMC* VI.1 (1982) 443–44.

Visscher, Ferdinand de. *Le droit des tombeaux romains.* Milan: Giuffré, 1963.

Vollenweider, Samuel. *Freiheit als neue Schöpfung. Eine Untersuchung zur Eleutheria bei Paulus und in seiner Umwelt.* FRLANT 147. Göttingen: Vandenhoeck & Ruprecht, 1989.

Walbank, Mary E. Hoskins. "Aspects of Corinthian Coinage in the Late 1st and Early 2nd Centuries A.C." Pages 337–49 in *Corinth: The Centenary, 1896–1996.* Edited by Charles K. Williams II and Nancy Bookidis. Corinth XX. Princeton, N.J.: ASCSA, 2003.

———. "Evidence for the Imperial Cult in Julio-Claudian Corinth." Pages 201–14 in *Subject and Ruler: The Cult of the Ruling Power in Classical Antiquity.* Edited by Alastair Small. JRASup 17. Ann Arbor, Mich.: Journal of Roman Archaeology, 1996.

———. "The Foundation and Planning of Early Roman Corinth." *JRA* 10 (1997) 95–130.

———. "The Nature and Development of Roman Corinth to the End of the Antonine Period." Ph.D. diss., Open University, London, 1986.

———. "Pausanias, Octavia and Temple E at Corinth." *BSA* 84 (1989) 361–94.

———. "What's in a Name? Corinth Under the Flavians." *ZPE* 139 (2002) 251–64.

Walker, S. E. C. "The Architectural Development of Roman Nymphaea in Greece." Ph.D. diss., University of London, 1979.

Ward-Perkins, J. B. *Roman Imperial Architecture.* New Haven, Conn.: Yale University Press, 1981.

Warland, D. "Tentative d'exégèse des fresques de la tombe 'du Plongeur' de Poseidonia." *Latomus* 57 (1957) 261–91.

Watson, Francis. "2 Cor. x–xiii and Paul's Painful Letter to the Corinthians." *JTS* 35 (1984) 324–46.

Weinberg, Saul. *The Southeast Building, the Twin Basilicas, and the Mosaic House.* Corinth I.5. Princeton, N.J.: ASCSA, 1960.

Weiss, Johannes. *Earliest Christianity.* Translated by F. C. Grant. 2 vols. New York: Harper, 1959. Translation of *Das Urchristentum.* Göttingen: Vandenhoeck & Ruprecht, 1914–1917.

Welch, Katherine. "Negotiating Roman Spectacle Architecture in the Greek World: Athens and Corinth." Pages 133–40 in *The Art of Ancient Spectacle.* Edited by Bettina Bergmann and Christine Kondoleon. Studies in the History of Art 56. Washington, D.C.: National Gallery of Art, 1999.

West, A. B. *Latin Inscriptions, 1896–1926.* Corinth VIII.2. Cambridge, Mass.: ASCSA, 1931.

West, M. L. *The East Face of Helicon.* Oxford: Clarendon, 1997.

———. "'Eumelos': A Corinthian Epic Cycle?" *JHS* 122 (2002) 109–54.

Westenholz, Joan Goodnick. "Tamar, *Qĕdēšā, Qadištu,* and Sacred Prostitution in Mesopotamia." *HTR* 82 (1989) 245–65.

White, L. Michael. "Rhetoric and Reality in Galatians: Framing the Social Demands of Friendship." Pages 307–49 in *Early Christianity and Classical Culture: Comparative Studies in Honor of Abraham J. Malherbe.* Edited by John T. Fitzgerald, Thomas H. Olbricht, and L. Michael White. NovTSup 110. Leiden: Brill, 2003.

———. "Urban Development and Social Change in Imperial Ephesos." Pages 27–79 in *Ephesos, Metropolis of Asia: An Interdisciplinary Approach to Its Archaeology, Religion, and Culture.* Edited by Helmut Koester. HTS 41. Valley Forge, Pa.: Trinity Press International, 1995.

———. "Visualizing the 'Real' World of Acts 16: Toward Construction of a Social Index." Pages 234–64 in *The Social World of the First Christians: Studies in Honor of Wayne A. Meeks.* Edited by L. Michael White and O. Larry Yarbrough. Minneapolis: Fortress, 1995.

Whittow, Mark. "Ruling the Late Roman and Early Byzantine City: A Continuous History." *Past and Present* 129 (1990) 3–29.

Wilberg, Wilhelm, et al. *Celsusbibliothek.* Forschungen in Ephesos 5.1. Vienna: Österreichische Verlagsgesellschaft, 1944.

Wilckens, Ulrich. *Weisheit und Torheit.* BHT 26. Tübingen: Mohr Siebeck, 1959.

Will, Edouard. *Korinthiaka: recherches sur l'histoire et la civilisation de Corinthe des origines aux guerres médiques.* Paris: de Boccard, 1955.

Willers, Dietrich. *Hadrians panhellenisches Programm. Archäologische Beitrage zur Neugestaltung Athens durch Hadrian.* Beiheft zur Halbjahresschrift Antike Kunst 16. Basel: Vereinigung der Freunde Antiker Kunst, 1990.

Williams, Charles K. II. "Archaic and Classical Corinth." Pages 31–45 in *Corinto e l'Occidente: Atti del trentaquattresimo convegno di studi sulla Magna Grecia.* Taranto: Istituto per la storia e l'archeologia della Magna Grecia, 1995.

———. "The City of Corinth and Its Domestic Religion." *Hesperia* 50 (1981) 408–21.

———. "Corinth, 1969: Forum Area." *Hesperia* 39 (1970) 1–39.

———. "Corinth, 1976: Forum Southwest." *Hesperia* 46 (1977) 40–81.

———. "Corinth, 1977: Forum Southwest." *Hesperia* 47 (1978) 1–39.

———. "Corinth and the Cult of Aphrodite." Pages 12–24 in *Corinthiaca: Studies in Honor of Darrell A. Amyx.* Ed. Mario A. Del Chiaro. Columbia, Mo.: University of Missouri Press, 1986.

———. "Excavations at Corinth." *Prak* 23 (1969) B1, 134–36.

Williams, Charles K. II. "Excavations at Corinth, 1968." *Hesperia* 38 (1969) 36–63.

———. "Pre-Roman Cults in the Area of the Forum of Ancient Corinth." Ph.D. diss., University of Pennsylvania, 1978.

———. "A Re-Evaluation of Temple E and the West End of the Forum of Corinth." Pages 156–62 in *The Greek Renaissance in the Roman Empire: Papers from the Tenth British Museum Classical Colloquium.* Edited by Susan Walker and Averil Cameron. BICSSup 55. London: University of London Institute of Classical Studies, 1989.

———. "The Refounding of Roman Corinth: Some Roman Religious Attitudes." Pages 26–37 in *Roman Architecture in the Greek World.* Edited by Sarah Macready and F. H. Thompson. Society of Antiquaries of London, Occasional Papers, n.s. 10. London: Society of Antiquaries of London, 1987.

———. "Roman Corinth as a Commercial Center." Pages 31–46 in *The Corinthia in the Roman Period.* Edited by Timothy E. Gregory. JRASup 8. Ann Arbor, Mich.: Journal of Roman Archaeology, 1993.

Williams, Charles K. II, and Joan E. Fisher. "Corinth, 1970: Forum Area." *Hesperia* 40 (1971) 1–51.

———. "Corinth, 1971: Forum Area." *Hesperia* 41 (1972) 143–84.

———. "Corinth, 1972: The Forum Area." *Hesperia* 42 (1973) 1–44.

———. "Corinth, 1974: Forum Southwest." *Hesperia* 44 (1975) 1–50.

———. "Corinth, 1975: Forum Southwest." *Hesperia* 45 (1976) 99–162.

Williams, Charles K. II, J. MacIntosh, and Joan E. Fisher. "Excavation at Corinth, 1973." *Hesperia* 43 (1974) 1–76.

Williams, Charles K. II, and P. Russell. "Corinth: Excavations of 1980." *Hesperia* 50 (1981) 1–44.

Williams, Charles K. II, L. M. Snyder, Ethne Barnes, and Orestes H. Zervos. "Frankish Corinth, 1997." *Hesperia* 67 (1998) 223–81.

Williams, Charles K. II, and Orestes H. Zervos. "Corinth, 1983: The Route to Sikyon." *Hesperia* 53 (1984) 83–122.

———. "Corinth, 1984: East of the Theater." *Hesperia* 54 (1985) 55–96.

———. "Corinth, 1985: East of the Theater." *Hesperia* 55 (1986) 129–205.

———. "Corinth, 1986: Temple E and East of the Theater." *Hesperia* 56 (1987) 1–46.

———. "Corinth, 1987: South of Temple E and East of the Theater." *Hesperia* 57 (1988) 95–146.

———. "Corinth, 1988: East of the Theater." *Hesperia* 58 (1989) 1–50.

———. "Excavations at Corinth, 1989: The Temenos of Temple E." *Hesperia* 59 (1990) 325–69.

Williams, Charles K. II, and Nancy Bookidis, eds. *Corinth: The Centenary, 1896–1996.* Corinth XX. Princeton, N.J.: ASCS, 2003.

Williams, Margaret. *The Jews among the Greeks and Romans: A Diasporan Sourcebook.* Baltimore, Md.: Johns Hopkins University Press, 1998.

Williams, Michael Allen. *Rethinking "Gnosticism": An Argument for Dismantling a Dubious Category.* Princeton, N.J.: Princeton University Press, 1996.

Willis, Wendell L. *Idol Meat in Corinth: The Pauline Argument in 1 Corinthians 8 and 10.* SBLDS 68. Chico, Ca.: Scholars, 1985.

Wilson, S. G. "Voluntary Associations: An Overview." Pages 1–15 in *Voluntary Associations in the Graeco-Roman World.* Edited by John S. Kloppenborg and Stephen G. Wilson. London: Routledge, 1996.

Windisch, Hans. *Der zweite Korintherbrief.* KEK 6. Göttingen: Vandenhoeck & Ruprecht, 1924.

Winter, Bruce. *Paul and Philo among the Sophists: Alexandrian and Corinthian Responses to a Julio-Claudian Movement.* 2d ed. Grand Rapids, Mich.: Eerdmans, 2002.

———. *Seek the Welfare of the City: Christians as Benefactors and Citizens.* Grand Rapids, Mich.: Eerdmans, 1994.

———. "The Toppling of Favorinus and Paul by the Corinthians." Pages 291–306 in *Early Christianity and Classical Culture: Comparative Studies in Honor of Abraham J. Malherbe.* Edited by John T. Fitzgerald, Thomas H. Olbricht, and L. Michael White. NovTSup 110. Leiden: Brill, 2003.

Wire, Antoinette Clark. *The Corinthian Women Prophets: A Reconstruction through Paul's Rhetoric.* Minneapolis: Fortress, 1990.

Wiseman, James. "Corinth and Rome I: 228 B.C.–A.D. 267." *ANRW* II.17.1 (1979) 438–548.

———. "Excavations at Corinth, The Gymnasium Area, 1965." *Hesperia* 36 (1967) 13–41.

———. "Excavations at Corinth, The Gymnasium Area, 1966." *Hesperia* 36 (1967) 402–28.

———. "Excavations in Corinth, The Gymnasium Area, 1967–1968." *Hesperia* 38 (1969) 64–106.

———. "Excavations in the Gymnasium Area. 1969–1970." *Hesperia* 41 (1972) 1–42.

———. "The Fountain of the Lamps." *Archaeology* 23 (1970) 130–37.

———. *The Land of the Ancient Corinthians.* SIMA 50. Göteborg: P. Åström, 1978.

Wiseman, T. P. "The Games of Flora." Pages 195–203 in *The Art of Ancient Spectacle.* Edited by Bettina Bergmann and Christine Kondoleon. Washington, D.C.: National Gallery of Art, 1999.

Woloch, Michael. *Roman Citizenship and the Athenian Elite, A.D. 96–161: Two Prosopographical Catalogues.* Amsterdam: Hakkert, 1973.

Wolp, K. A. "Indictions and Dating Formulas in the Papyri from Byzantine Egypt A. D. 337–540." *Archiv für Papyrusforschung und verwandte Gebiete* 33 (1987) 91–96.

Woolf, Greg. "Becoming Roman, Staying Greek: Culture, Identity and the Civilizing Process in the Roman East." *PCPS* 40 (1995) 116–43.

———. *Becoming Roman: The Origins of Provincial Civilization in Gaul.* Cambridge: Cambridge University Press, 1998.

Wright, K. S. "A Tiberian Pottery Deposit from Corinth." *Hesperia* 49 (1980) 135–77.

Wright, N. T. "Paul's Gospel and Caesar's Empire." Pages 160–83 in *Paul and Empire: Religion and Power in Roman Imperial Society.* Edited by Richard A. Horsley. Harrisburg, Pa.: Trinity Press International, 1997.

Wycherley, Richard E. *Literary and Epigraphical Testimonia.* Agora 3. Princeton, N.J.: ASCSA, 1957.

Yalouris, N. "Athena als Herrin der Pferde." *Museum Helveticum* 7 (1950) 19–101.

———. *Pegasus: Ein Mythos in der Kunst.* Mainz: Philipp von Zabern, 1987.

Yegül, F. K. " 'Roman' Architecture in the Greek World." *JRA* 4 (1991) 345–55.

Young, Frances M., and David F. Ford. *Meaning and Truth in 2 Corinthians.* Grand Rapids, Mich.: Eerdmans, 1988.

Young, Rodney S. "The Geometric Period." Pages 13–49 in *The North Cemetery.* Edited by Carl William Blegen, Hazel Palmer, and Rodney S. Young. Corinth XIII. Princeton, N.J.: ASCSA, 1964.

———. "The Protocorinthian Period." Pages 50–64 in *The North Cemetery.* Edited by Carl William Blegen, Hazel Palmer, and Rodney S. Young. Corinth XIII. Princeton, N.J.: ASCSA, 1964.

Zahn, R., ed. *Sammlung Baurat Schiller, Berlin: Werke antiker Kleinkunst: Goldschmuck, Gläser, Tonfiguren, [und] Tongefässe.* Lepke's Kunst-Auctions-Haus, Catalogue no. 2008. Berlin: Rudolf Lepke, 1929.

Zanker, Paul. *The Power of Images in the Age of Augustus.* Ann Arbor, Mich.: University of Michigan, 1988.

Maps

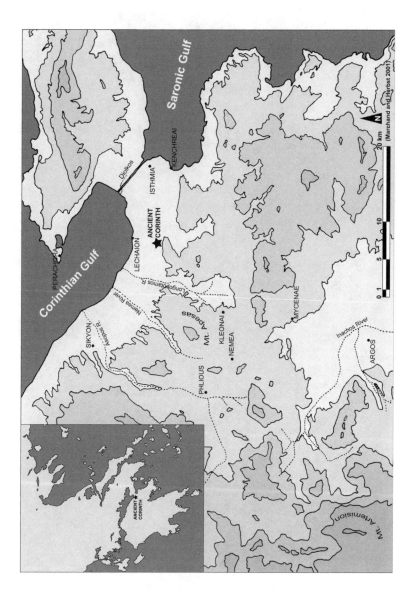

Map 1: The Corinthia

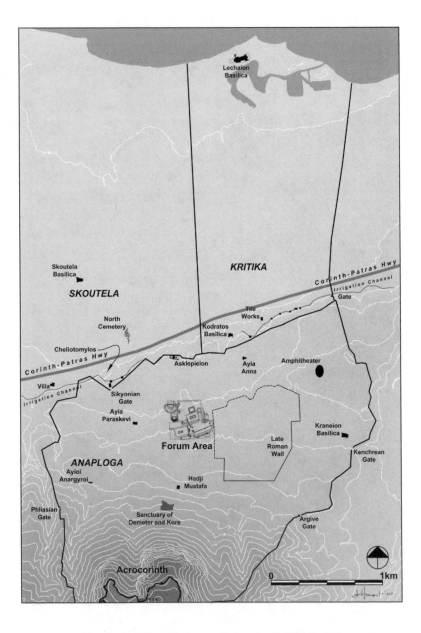

Map 2: Corinth, from Acrocorinth to the Gulf of Corinth.

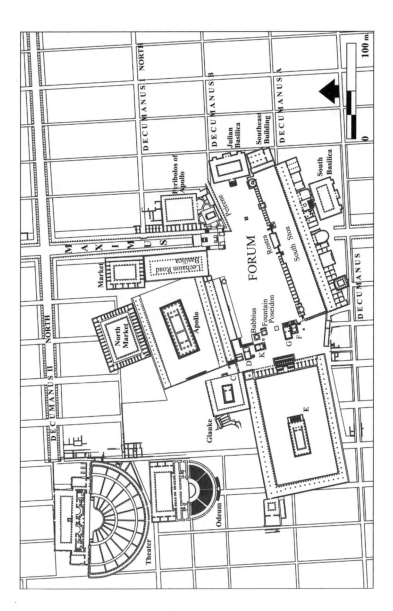

Map 3: Restored Roman city center, ca. 150 C.E.

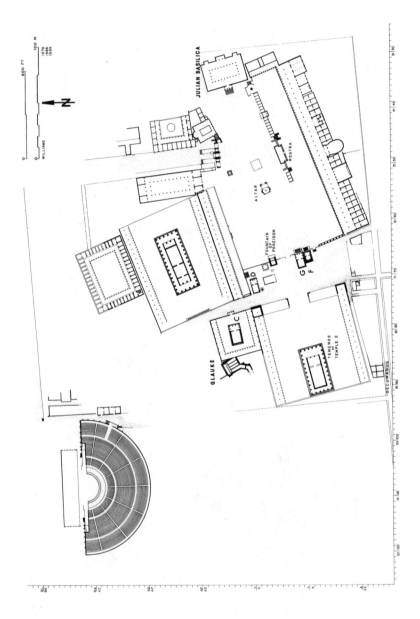

Map 4: Corinth, plan of forum, early first century C.E.

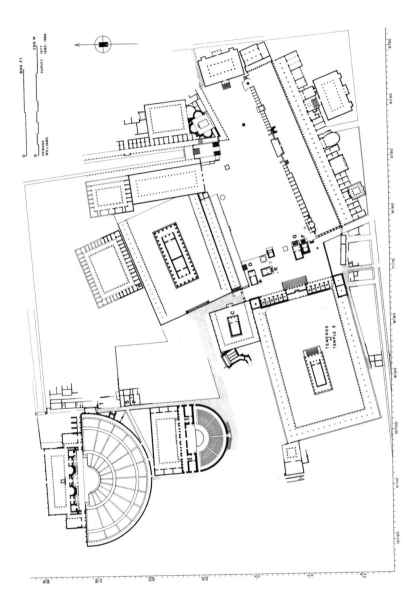

Map 5: Corinth, plan of forum, mid-second century C.E.

I Illustration Credits

Fig. 2.1   O. A. W. Dilke, *The Roman Land Surveyors: An Introduction to the Agrimensores* (New York: Barnes & Noble, 1971) 16.

Figs. 2.2–18   David Gilman Romano, Corinth Computer Project.

Fig. 2.19   David Gilman Romano, Corinth Computer Project, after D. B. Peck.

Fig. 3.1   L. Michael White.

Fig. 3.2   The University of Texas at Austin, Classics Department Photo Archives, No. SR-B-33. G. M. A. Hanfmann, *From Croesus to Constantinople* (Ann Arbor: University of Michigan Press, 1975) fig. 149. Österreichisches Archäologisches Institut, Selçuk [Efes].

Fig. 3.3   The University of Texas at Austin, Classics Department Photo Archives, No. SR-BI-21. Naples Museum.

Fig. 3.4   The University of Texas at Austin, Classics Department Photo Archives, No. SR-B19-2. Palazzo dei Conservatori, Capitoline Museum, Rome.

Fig. 3.5   Photos of fragments from John Harvey Kent, *The Inscriptions, 1926–1950* (Corinth VIII.3; Princeton, N.J.: ASCSA, 1966) plate 30; digitally reassembled by L. Michael White.

Fig. 3.6   Saul Weinberg, *The Southeast Building, the Twin Basilicas, and the Mosaic House* (Corinth I.5; Princeton, N.J.: ASCSA, 1960) plan I; digital overlay by L. Michael White.

Fig. 3.7   Ibid.; digital overlay by L. Michael White.

Fig. 3.8   Ibid., plan II.2; digital overlay by L. Michael White.

Fig. 3.9   Digital restoration by L. Michael White, based on Charles K. Williams II and O. H. Zervos, "Excavations at Corinth, 1989: The Temenos of Temple E," *Hesperia* 59 (1990) 325–69; and Nicos Papahatzis, *Ancient Corinth* (Athens: Ekdotike Athenon, 1983) 54.

Fig. 4.1–2   Betsey A. Robinson.
Fig. 4.3   Adapted from Bert Hodge Hill, *The Springs: Peirene, Sacred Spring, Glauke* (Corinth I.6) plate 9.1 (R. Stillwell).
Fig. 4.4   DAI Rome Archive, Neg. 58.2116.
Fig. 4.5   Adapted from Hill, *The Springs*, plate 9.2 (R. Stillwell).
Fig. 4.6   Bartl; DAI Rome, Neg. 57.782.
Fig. 4.7   American School of Classical Studies, Corinth Excavations.
Fig. 4.8   Adapted from Hill, *The Springs* (Corinth I.6) fig. 126.
Fig. 4.9   Adapted from Hill, *The Springs* (Corinth I.6) fig. 137.
Fig. 4.10   Koppermann; DAI, Rome, Neg. 63.545.

Fig. 6.1a   F. W. Imhoof-Blumer and P. Gardiner, *Ancient Coins Illustrating Lost Masterpieces of Greek Art: A Numismatic Commentary on Pausanias* (ed. A. N. Oikonomides; repr., Chicago: Argonaut, 1964) plate B vi.
Fig. 6.1b   Ibid., plate B v.
Figs. 6.2–6   Ino Ioannidou and Lenio Bartzioti, Corinth Excavations.
Fig. 6.7a–b   Peggy Sanders, partially based on Oscar Broneer, *Isthmia: Topography and Architecture* (Isthmia 2; Princeton, N.J.: ASCSA, 1973) plans 2 and 8.
Fig. 6.8   Peggy Sanders.
Fig. 6.9a   Elizabeth R. Gebhard, F. P. Hemans, and J. W. Hayes, "University of Chicago Excavations at Isthmia, 1989: III," *Hesperia* 67 (1998) 405–56, no. 18.
Fig. 6.9b   Ibid., no. 21.
Fig. 6.10a   Oscar Broneer, Chicago Isthmia Excavations, A 148.
Fig. 6.10b   Photos: Ino Ioannidou and Lenio Bartzioti; drawing: J. W. Hayes.
Fig. 6.11   Peggy Sanders.
Fig. 6.12   Broneer, *Isthmia: Topography and Architecture*, plate 13a.
Fig. 6.13   Ibid., plan 2.
Fig. 6.14   Ibid., plate 37a.

Figs. 8.1–3   Ino Ioannidou and Lenio Bartzioti, Corinth Excavations.
Fig. 8.4   Corinth Excavations.
Figs. 8.5–10   Ino Ioannidou and Lenio Bartzioti, Corinth Excavations.
Fig. 8.11   Charles K. Williams II.
Fig. 8.12–16   Ino Ioannidou and Lenio Bartzioti, Corinth Excavations.

Fig. 9.1   Corinth Excavations.
Figs. 9.2–4   Corinth Excavations.
Fig. 9.5   James Herbst, Corinth Excavations.
Figs. 9.6–16   Corinth Excavations.

Figs. 10.1–2	Christine M. Thomas.
Fig. 11.1	Laurie Brink, O.P.
Fig. 16.1–2	James Herbst.
Fig. 16.3	G. D. R. Sanders and James Herbst.
Fig. 16.4	Ino Ioannidou and Lenio Bartzioti.
Fig. 16.5	James Herbst.
Fig. 16.6	Ino Ioannidou and Lenio Bartzioti.
Fig. 16.7	James Herbst, additions to D. Peck.
Fig. 16.8a–d	G. Grulich, James Herbst, and G. D. R. Sanders.
Fig. 16.9	Ino Ioannidou and Lenio Bartzioti.
Fig. 16.10	James Herbst, after D. I. Pallas, "Korinth," *Reallexikon zur Byzantinischen Kunst* (Stuttgart: Hiersemann, 1966–) 4:745–811.
Map 1	Jeanette Marchand and James Herbst.
Map 2	James Herbst.
Map 3	David Gilman Romano, Corinth Computer Project
Map 4	C. K. Williams II, "Roman Corinth as a Commercial Center," in *The Corinthia in the Roman Period* (ed. Timothy E. Gregory; JRA Sup 8; Ann Arbor, Mich.: Journal of Roman Archaeology, 1993) 31–46, fig. 1 (p. 32).
Map 5	Ibid., fig. 2 (p. 34).

Index

Abraham, 384
Achaia, 15, 330, 337, 394, 398, 402–3,
    405–6, 408n45, 439n33, 445, 447
Achaian League, 22, 26, 148, 408–9n49
Achaicus, 355n12
Achilles, 176nn42–43, 179, 193n91, 194
Acrocorinth, 11, 15, 21–22, 38, 40n44, 55,
    94, 121, 146n24, 147, 150, 159n83,
    161, 164, 219, 240, 243–44n38, 245,
    404, 421
Acts of the Apostles, 61–62n2, 340,
    353–54, 372–73
Adonis, 176n42
Aelius Aristides, 71n34, 203
Aesculapius, 173
agape table, 433
agora, Athenian, 80
agora, Corinthian, 21
Agrippa II, 373
Agrippa, Marcus, 123
Akraia, Hera. See Hera
Alexandria, 376
Alkidameia, 147
altars, 34, 37, 156–57, 194, 235n27, 236
Amazons, 216n45
American School of Classical Studies at
    Athens, 14, 16, 19, 26, 221, 250n1
Amphimachos, 176
Ananke, 146
Anna Perenna, 112

Antony, Marc, 153, 163
Apheios, 112
Aphrodite/Venus, 15n14, 22, 23, 147,
    160–64, 223n2, 310
    Anadyomene, 245;
    cult of, 236, 276;
    in East Theater Street, 243–47;
    figurines of, 223, 231n17, 232;
    fresco of, 239;
    Hoplismene, 243–44n38, 245, 424n6;
    of Knidian type, 229n15, 230;
    on lamps, 436nn27–28;
    with Pan, 229;
    sacrifice to, 236;
    sanctuary of, 404, 443n1;
    statues of, 219, 243–46;
    temple of, on coins, 240;
    terracotta figurines of, 223, 245–46;
    as war goddess, 161, 212–13, 218n52,
    219–20;
    women praying to, 211–12, 213n30,
    220
    See also prostitution, cultic; cult(s),
    Roman; cult(s), Hellenistic; tem-
    ples, Hellenistic; temples, Roman
apocalyptic literature, 384–86
    See also eschatology
Apollo, 22, 142, 145, 148, 154, 157,
    163, 197n102, 310
    See also Temple of Apollo

Apollo, Clarion, 23, 153
Apollos (rival of Paul), 314, 334n90, 342, 345, 380, 450
Aquila, 340, 381, 394
Archaic Temple, 21–22, 93, 116, 128, 131, 142, 143n4, 154
Arelate (Arles), 64
Argives, 405, 406n39
Argos, 406n35
Ariadne, 167
Arion, 67, 91, 92, 99
Aristophanes, 13, 216
Artemis/Diana, 94, 144, 146, 153, 159n83, 219, 220n61, 229n15, 237n32
Artemis Korithos, 22
Artemision, 300
ash chests, 293–99, 301–4
Asklepieion
   cemetery in, 431, 419–420n1, 430n17, 435, 437;
   location of, 46, 143, 186;
   refurbishment of, 131, 404;
   worship of Hellenic deities at, 441
Asklepius/Asklepios, 22, 24, 40, 148, 159, 163, 443n2
   See also Aesculapius
Athamas, 168
Athena, 94n102, 118–20, 125, 143–44, 218, 233, 455
   Chalinitis, 146, 148, 164;
   Hippia, 146;
   terracotta bust of, 233
Athenaeus, 205, 212, 213n30
Athens, 12, 21, 64, 75, 77, 80nn52–53, 81, 94n102, 147, 257n6, 289, 302, 419, 450, 452
Atticus, bishop of Constantinople, 448
Augustus, Emperor, 23, 123, 153, 155, 157, 163, 245n40, 284, 297, 386, 408n45
Babbius Italicus, Gnaeus, 83, 84, 88, 90, 96, 104–6
Babbius Monument, 86n73, 91n91, 92n97, 93, 94n101, 97

Babbius Philinus, Gnaeus, 82n64, 84, 90, 92, 93, 95, 104–6, 187
baptism, 311, 346–47
baptismal fonts, 428n12, 439–41, 452
Barnabas, 358n16, 393
basilica(s), 437–41
   early Christian, 14, 22;
   Julian, 23, 32n24, 36, 37, 81, 82n65, 84, 86, 106–7, 156
   Kraneion, 24, 440;
   Lechaion, 24, 38, 52, 150, 437–40, 452;
   North, 154;
   St. Kodratos, 440;
   Skoutela, 24, 440;
   Twin, 81
Bellerophon, 113, 118n18, 119–20, 125, 134, 139–40, 146, 159n83
   See also Pegasos and Bellerophon
Bes, 223
Bia, 146
body of Christ, image of (soma Christou), 311n10, 347–48
Boniface, Pope, 447–48
Bonosus, bishop of Naïssus, 446
Bounos, 147
bracteates, 276
Briareus, 94–95n104
Buildings 1, 3, 5, 7. See under East Theater Street
burial practices
   afterlife and, 288, 290–91;
   burial clubs, 268;
   changes in, 261, 278, 281–82, 286–88;
   compared with Greek, 287;
   corpse position, 253, 274, 279;
   dead as malign influence and, 265, 277;
   food in, 257n6, 263, 272–73, 288, 289n36, 291
   homogenization of, 303–4;
   incense burners used in, 274–75;
   influence of Christianity on, 282–83;
   provision for the poor in, 254;
   Roman law and, 269n27;

social status in, 279–80, 281–82,
292, 298–99 (*see also* ash chests;
burials, at Ephesos vs. Corinth;
burials, Roman; cremation; grave
goods)
See also ash chests; burials, Christian; burials, Roman;
cremation; tomb(s)
burials, Archaic, 285
burials, Christian, 434–37
coffins, Gaza amphora, 428, 430, 434;
from 6th–7th c., 430, 432;
funerary meals and, 273, 430;
grave goods, lack of in, 430;
in Asklepieion, 419–20n1, 430,
431n17, 435–37;
inception of, 441–42;
of infants, 428, 434;
lamps and, 276;
tile graves, 253, 254n5, 430;
urns in, 278n49, 301n77
burials, at Ephesos vs. Corinth, 283–84,
292–302, 304
See also ash chests
burials, Roman
cemeteries, location of, 250, 254,
284–85;
dates, range of, 250;
excavation of, 249–50;
family tombs, 261, 269;
funerary monuments used in,
284n12, 290–91;
graves, 249, 252–54;
inscriptions found in, 267 (*see also*
inscriptions);
methods of, 263, 284–92, 300 (*see
also* burials, at Ephesos vs.
Corinth; cremation; tomb(s));
modesty of, in North Cemetery,
299–300
multiple, 270–77, 279;
paintings on tomb walls in, 263–65;
reuse of graves in, 266, 270–71,
286n22;

sarcophagi in, 253, 256, 270–72,
279, 286–90, 299–300, 304
secondary, 271–72
See also ash chests; cremation; skeletal remains, Roman; tomb(s)
Caesar, Julius, 135, 376, 383, 386, 400,
409
Caesarea, 185, 408n45
Camillus, 77, 79
Carthage, 402, 409–10
cemeteries, Roman. *See* burials, Roman;
tomb(s)
Cenchreae, 358
See also Kenchreai
Central Shops, 34, 55
centuriation, Flavian, 29, 50n56
See also Corinth, colonial; Corinth,
surveying under Vespasian; surveying, Roman
Cephas, 334n90
Chamaeleon of Heracleia, 212
Cheliotomylos cemetery, 299
Cheliotomylos hill, 40, 59, 249, 258,
280, 285n19
Cheliotomylos tomb, 272, 273n37,
276n41
Chloe, 342, 368, 369n34
Christian community at Corinth,
307–12, 397–98, 411–17
as alternative society, 347–48,
392–95;
autonomy of, 389–90;
conflicts in, 342, 388–89, 398–400;
earliest evidence of, 307–12;
in 4th and 5th c., 443–57;
and Paul, 310–12, 331–33, 334n90,
371–72 (*see also* Paul);
and relationship to Roman imperial
order, 379–81;
social structure of, 339–41 (*see also*
demography);
as urban religious cult, 336;
worship in, 308, 441
Christian community, early
anachronism of term, 372–77;

civic identity in, 397–403;
as extension of Israel, 392–93;
households as basis of, 378, 394;
"Pauline Christianity" as projection
    on, 373, 393;
as religious community, 381–82;
rethinking paradigm for, 371–72;
Roman imperial context of, 381;
social models for, 377–81, 392–93;
social science approaches to, 374–75
See also Eucharist
Christianity
as emerging from Judaism, 371;
inappropriateness of term, 372–77;
Orthodox, 436, 442, 450
Chrysostom, John, 277n47, 446, 448
church, at Corinth. *See* Christian com-
    munity at Corinth
Cicero, 116, 150n40, 172–73, 214, 345
Circular Monument, 36, 93, 104
cists A–F, 263, 266n20, 267n23, 268
city planning. *See* urban planning
Claudius, 84, 86, 409
Clement of Rome, 445
Code of Hammurabi, 207
coins, 14, 22, 217
altar representations on, 178;
Aphrodite temple image on, 240;
of Arcadins, 266;
of bronze, 125, 245n40;
Constantius II (mid-4th c.), 272;
Corinthian (2/1 B.C.E.), 261;
Corinthian, 240n34;
dolphin on, 184, 188;
dove on Sikyonian, 276–77;
found in grave, 261n11;
Hadrian, 197n104;
of Melikertes, 168, 180–81, 188;
from North Cemetery, 274n39;
for passage to underworld, 274, 276;
Peirenian colt on, 118;
Poseidon seated on, 183nn71–72,
    197n104;
Roman with Aphrodite, 161;
Roman denarius, 149;

Roman republican, of C. Cen-
    sorinus,149n36;
silver, 274;
as talismans, 275, 276n43, 277;
wreath on, 184;
Zeus and Athena on, 182n69
*Colonia Iulia Flavia Augusta
    Corinthiensis*, 29, 46–53
Colonia Laus Iulia Corinthiensis, 26n2,
    27–31, 151, 250, 283, 403
colony. *See* Corinth, colonial
Colossae, 369
Colossians, Letter to the, 348
communal meals, 158–59, 399,
    415n77, 158–59
communion. *See* Eucharist
community. *See* Christian commu-
    nity, early; Christian community at
    Corinth
Constantine II, 442
Corinth Computer Project, 25n1, 26n2,
    29, 50n56, 250, 403
Corinth, ancient literary sources, 61–62
See also Corinthians, Letters to the;
    Paul; Pausanias
Corinth, Christian, archaeology of
agape table, 430, 433;
bathhouse, 426, 428, 439;
coins, 420, 426, 434–35, 439–40
    (*see also* coins);
domus, 420–21;
incised fish found in, 428–29;
Lechaion Basilica, 428;
long building, 428;
material expressions of Christian
    identity, 420;
Panaiya Field excavations, 420–29;
"philosopher's house," 426;
pottery, 426, 428;
worship and, 441
See also basilica(s)
Corinth, colonial
abandonment of Hellenistic cult
    sites and, 148–49;
ancient sources on, 27n9;

centuriation, 43, 46, 50–51n56, 53, 402n15 (*see also* surveying, Roman; Corinth, surveying under Vespasian)
civic identity in, 397–400;
as compared to other Roman colonies, 401–3;
founding of, 400–3;
freedmen as settlers of, 402–3;
land allotment in, 28n13;
planning of, 30–31 (*see also* surveying, Roman);
population of, 402;
priestly groups in, 401–2;
Roman character of, 397, 401–3;
"Romanization" and, 404–5;
social models for, 377–81, 392–93
Corinth, colonial, forum of, 32–38, 43, 53–55, 59
See also library, at Corinth
Corinth, colonial, refounded
area of, 48;
city plan of, 56–57;
colonists in, 27n10, 53;
forum, changes to, 53–55;
Jewish slaves and, 51n61, 53;
roads, paving of, 55;
size in relation to original plan, 54–55;
temples, new, 55;
theater, refurbishing of, 55n71;
tombs in, 59;
villas in, 58
See also Corinth, surveying under Vespasian
Corinth, Hellenistic
agora, location of, 142–43;
art work depicting Greek deities and, 420–21, 423–24;
destruction of and aftermath, 12, 26, 148–51, 400–1;
public inscriptions from, 142–43;
worship of Greek deities and, 419–20n1, 441

Corinth, interim period, 27, 43, 46, 148–49, 150n40
Corinth, Roman
athletic facilities in, 186;
changes in city landscape, 113, 116;
circus of, 40n45;
cults in, 221–47;
cultural identity of, 404;
development of, 403–10;
Greek elites in, 407n40, 408–9;
Greek influences on, 19nn25–26, 113, 116, 397, 400–10;
relationship with Greek cities, 408–9n49;
as seat of provincial government, 407;
sketch plan of, 251
Corinth, surveying under Vespasian
centuriation of, 46n52, 48–49, 50–51n56, 55, 402n15;
grid of, 48n53, 49
See also surveying, Roman
Corinthian Gulf, 11, 48, 421
Corinthians, Letters to the
and ancient scribal practice, 323–24n62;
chronology of, 342;
literary analysis of, 312–35
occasions for, 342;
questions about urban religion raised by, 336–38;
and reconstruction of history of Corinthian church, 308–12;
rhetorical approach to, 372;
social setting of, 342;
sociological analysis of, 316–17;
temporal sequence of, 336
See also Paul, the Apostle; Christian community at Corinth: 1 Corinthians 1–4; 2 Corinthians 8
1 Corinthians 1–4, 342–45
2 Corinthians 8
historical situation of, 330–35;
as key to reconstruction of Paul's letters, 321, 323–25;

rhetorical parallels to 1 Cor,
   328n77, 329–30;
rhetorical strategy of, 330–31;
similarities to 2 Cor 9, 320, 325–26;
temporal location of, 325n65, 326,
   327n74, 328;
as transition to next letter (2 Cor
   2:14–7:4), 331–33
Cornelius Babbius, Gnaius 23, 88
Corpus Hermeticum, 343
Council of Nicaea, 447, 456
Council of Trullo, 441
Craneum, 285n17
cremation, 300–4
   afterlife and, 288, 291;
   inhumation and, 270, 300;
   meaning of, 270;
   as Roman practice, 270n32, 286,
      287n27, 292;
   in Rome, 302–3;
   social status and, 270, 286–87;
   urns, 254–56, 260, 261n11, 301n77
   See also ash chests; burials, at
      Ephesos vs. Corinth
Crete, 428
Crispus, 340, 346, 450
crucifixion of Jesus, as turning point of
   history, 384–85, 387, 393–94
cult of Isis and Sarapis, 146, 223, 225
   See also cults, Hellenistic
cults, fertility. *See* prostitution, cultic
cults, Hellenistic, 141–51
cults, pagan, 221–47
cult(s), Roman, 141
   civic, 152, 157–59, 163, 409–10;
   communal meals, 158–59n81;
   continuity with Hellenistic, 141, 159,
      162, 163n108, 164;
   Cybele and Matrona, 225, 231;
   deposition of curse tablets, 162n103;
   discussed by Pausanius, 160n87,
      161–64 (*see also* Pausanius);
   imperial, 152–57, 375–76, 383;
   inscriptions related to, 159–60, 223;
   lararia in, 245–46;

sacrifice in, 157–59, 391–92
   See also Melikertes-Palaimon;
      prostitution, cultic
Cybele, 225n5, 231
Cyclopean fountain, 21

Daedalus, 92, 94
Damascus, Pope, 445–46
Dead Sea Scrolls, 374
Decian persecutions, 453, 457
Demeter, 22, 24, 38, 50–51n56, 55n72,
   58, 149, 151, 404
Demeter and Kore, 146–49, 159n83,
   160–62, 310, 404, 419–20n1
Demetrius of Phaleron, 303
demography of Pauline communities,
   352–58, 361, 367–69
   See also poor in Christian commu-
      nities; social status
Diana. *See* Artemis
Dio Chrysostom, 62, 64, 71n34, 98n114
Diocletian, 444–45
Diodorus Siculus, 146
Diogenes the Dog, 64
Diolkos, 13, 53n62
Dionysios, bishop of Corinth, 308n4, 453
Dionysos, 153, 159n83, 164, 167–68,
   180nn59–60, 181, 424n6
   See also Melikertes
Dioscuri, 23, 173, 194n97
Donakinos, 176
Doric temple, 143

earthquakes, 12–13, 23–24, 88, 90, 161,
   227, 242–43, 246, 260, 439n33, 440
East Central Shops, 157
East Gymnasium, 76
East Theater Street, 221–22, 224, 236, 240
   Building 1, 222–28;
   Building 3, 222–28;
   Building 5, 222–37, 240, 243–44;
   Building 7, 221–23, 225, 236–44
   See also Aphrodite; cult(s), Roman
Egypt, 226n10, 381, 435n22
Eilithyia, 146

ekklēsia, 373–74, 378, 393
  See also Christian community at
  Corinth; Christian community, early
Elias, bishop of Nisibis, 442
Ephesos, 61–62n2, 64–66, 76, 77, 281,
  283, 291–99, 311, 354–55n10, 358,
  369, 394
Erastus
  inscription of, 13, 23, 339–40,
    354–55n10, 363, 369;
  social status of, 368, 415–16
Eros, 160, 218, 258n8, 260n9
eschatology, 384–85
  See also Paul, eschatology of
Eucharist
  anticipation of Christ's coming, 385;
  architecture of basilicas and, 441;
  as communal meal, 311, 378, 417;
  libretto for, in 1 Corinthians, 308;
  social status and, 361–62, 367, 417
Euphorion, 175–77
Euripedes, 116, 118nn16,18, 133, 136,
  139, 146, 168n10, 171
Europa, 424
Eurotas, 112
Evil Eye, 265

Fates, 112, 139–40, 146–47
Favorinus, 62–68, 86, 93–94n101,
  95–99, 182, 198
  "Corinthian Oration" of, 62–74,
    91–96, 98–103;
  rhetorical strategy of, 67–73;
  statue of, 66–69, 73–79
  See also library, at Corinth
figurines, terracotta, Roman cultic
  of Aphrodite, 223, 229–32;
  of Athena, 233;
  decline of quality of, 235;
  dog-shaped rattles among, 231n17,
    232, 240–41, 246–47;
  female grotesques among, 225–27;
  in Tomb X, 259
  See also East Theater Street, Build-
    ings 5 and 7

Flavius Damianus, T. , 65, 76–77
Fortuna Santa, 234
Fortunatus, 355
Forum, 53–55, 73–90
  See also Roman forum
Fountain House, 89–90, 112
Fountain of the Lamps, 112, 139
Fountain of Poseidon. *See under*
  Poseidon
fountains, 112–13, 133, 136, 139–40
  See also Peirene Fountain; Glauke
    Fountain; springs; Poseidon,
    fountain of
freedmen, 26, 29, 94–95n104, 258,
  296–302, 304, 355n12, 402–3
frescoes, 227, 229n14, 231, 233–37,
  239, 242, 261, 264–65

Gaius, in letters of Paul, 311, 335, 346,
  379, 394
Gaius, Emperor, 376
Galatia, 358
Galilee, 376, 383
Gallio, 340
Gaza amphora coffins, 428, 430, 432
Gentile, 355, 357n13
geology, 11–13
"ghost money," 276
Glauke Fountain, 93–94n101, 112–13,
  115–16, 128–40, 154, 221, 404
Glauke/Kreousa, 133–36
Gnosticism, 312–13, 343n9
  See also Gospel of Thomas; wisdom
    at Corinth
Gordian III, Emperor, 454
Gospel of Thomas, 339n1, 342–45
grave goods
  afterlife and, 289–90;
  altars, 256, 272;
  charms, 277–78;
  curse tablets, 277, 278n48, 290n41;
  figurines, 258–59, 260n9, 261;
  jewelry, 274;
  offerings 272–78, 290;
  paucity of, 276, 278, 280, 299;

present in cremation and inhumation, 291;
social stability and, 299;
unguentaria, 253–54, 258, 260, 274
See also lamps
graves. *See* burials, Archaic; burials,
Christian; burials, at Ephesos vs.
Corinth; burials, Roman; burial
practices; cists A–F; cremation;
tomb(s)
Gymnasium area, 428n15

Hadji Mustapha, 146
Hadrian, 5, 64, 66n19, 79, 80, 96–97,
98n114, 104–7, 197n104, 407
Hadrianic period, 73n41, 225n8
hagiography, 449–57
See also martyrs
Harpocrates, 223
Hektor, 176n43
Helikonis, St., 454–55
Helios, 94–96, 133, 146, 159n83, 160, 164
Hellotis, 21, 144, 148
Hephaistos, 218
Hera, 19, 94, 142, 158, 177, 218, 237
Hera Akraia, 132nn53, 55, 146n22, 159
Herakleidai, 148
Herakles/Hercules, 178n49, 194n97, 237
Herakles Farnese, 424
Herculanus, Julios Eurycles, 97
Hercules. *See* Herakles
Hermes, 234
Herod, the Great, 383
Herodes Atticus, 64, 65n14, 77, 97
Herodian, 302
Herodotus, 211, 213, 214nn34–36, 215n41
Heröon of the Crossroads, 144–45
Hesiod, 94n104
Hippia, 148
Homer 68, 94–95nn103–4, 99n116, 173
Honorius, Emperor, 448–49

Ignatius, 373
Illyricum, 444–45
Innocent I, Pope, 446

Ino, 167, 168, 170, 174, 176
inscriptions, 29, 80n52, 82nn64–65,
83–88, 89n82, 91, 96, 97, 104–10,
116, 142–43, 145, 156–60, 223,
229, 267, 269n31, 295–97,
369n36, 379
from Southeast Building, 104–22;
"Synagogue of the Hebrews," 340
See also Erastus
Isis, 14, 139, 246n42, 345, 380
and Sarapis, 146, 163, 223, 225,
310;
Pelasgia, 230
See also lamps
Isthmia, 19, 141, 185
Isthmian games, 40, 166, 169, 175–76,
182–89, 203, 402n26, 408n46
See also Melikertes-Palaimon
Isthmian Palaimon. *See* Palaimon, at
Isthmia
Isthmian sanctuary, 250
Isthmus of Corinth, 11, 51, 159, 166,
169, 178, 182

Jason, 113, 132–34, 219
Jerusalem, collection of money for,
312, 325–28, 332–33, 393
Jews, 347, 372–77, 381–84
as slaves, 51n61, 63
Josephus, 51, 383
Jove. *See* Zeus
Judaism, 374–75
Julian, Emperor, 420
Julius Caesar, 22, 27n8–9, 32, 42,
53–54
Julius Philopappos, C., 74n46, 75
Jupiter Capitolinus, 159
Justin Martyr, 283n5
Justinian, 442, 445

Kenchreai, 4, 12, 14, 19, 63–64, 68n23,
139, 250, 345, 424, 443
Kodratos, St., 440, 452, 456
Kore, 55
See also Demeter and Kore

Korinthiakos. See Favorinus, "Corinthian Oration" of
Kotyto, 144, 148
Kreon, 133
Kreousa. *See* Glauke
Kritika cemetery, 279
Kyriakos, St., 455–57

lamps, 202
  associated with Isis Pelasgia, 230;
  Attic, 436–37;
  boat-shaped, 223–25n4;
  Christian symbols on, 279;
  Fountain of the, 112, 139;
  as grave goods, 194n100, 258, 263,
    275–76;
  green glazed, 260;
  iconography on, 275–76;
  Italian, 258;
  Palaimonion type, 196, 202n112;
  terracotta, 223–25, 279n50
lararia, 234–35
Lechaion Harbor, 14, 24, 30, 43, 51, 52
Lechaion Road, 20, 22, 30, 32, 34,
  36–38, 40, 92n97, 95, 113, 116, 144,
  428, 430
Leo I, Pope, 441
Leo III, Pope, 442
Leo VII, Pope, 455
Leonidas, St., 439, 450–51n38, 456
Lerna area, 149, 430, 434–436
Leukothea, 172–73, 177–78
library, at Corinth
  and Babbius family, 96–97, 104–7
  Babbius family inscriptions, 104–7;
  Babbius family monuments, 96–97;
  evidence for, 91n91, 92, 95–96;
  identification of, 81–84;
  as setting of Favorinus's "Corinthian Oration," 74, 77–79, 80,
    81, 91–92, 93–94n101, 95–96
    (*see also* Favorinus)
Long Rectangular Building, 37, 39, 54
Longopotomos River, 48–50
Long Walls, 43

Lord's Supper. *See* Eucharist
Lucius Caesar, Lucius, 23
Luke, 312, 343

Macedonia, 330, 337, 394, 398,
  444–45, 447
Magarian bowls, 22
Mammius Maximus, Lucius, 77–78
martyrs, 449–55
  See also hagiography
Mater Matuta, 167
Matrona, 225
Matthew, Gospel of, 343, 390, 399
Medea, 113, 118, 132–38, 140, 146,
  148, 161, 163, 168
Melikertes-Palaimon, 165–203
  association with Dionysios of,
    167n7, 180–81;
  association with Hercules and
    Melqart of, 171nn20,23;
  association with Poseidon of,
    170–71, 186–89, 191–92;
  as god, 166–67, 169, 171, 173–74;
  as hero, 166, 169–70, 173–74;
  Isthmian Games and, 166–67,
    174–76, 178–79, 203;
  monument of, 92n97;
  myth of, 168–74
  mysteries of, 167, 179n54, 180–81;
  See also Melikertes-Palaimon, cult of
Melikertes-Palaimon, cult of, 174–81
  communal meals in, 194;
  continuity between Roman and Hellenistic, 203;
  dirges/laments in, 175, 176–
    77nn42–43,46, 178–81;
  nocturnal performance of, 194n100,
    202–3;
  origin of rites for, 165–67;
  and other god-hero cults, 173–
    74n33, 193n91,95, 194;
  rites of, 176–81, 203;
  sacrificial pits associated with,
    192–94, 203;

shrine associated with, 165, 187,
    189–203
See also Melikertes-Palaimon
Mesopotamia, 207, 209
Minerva. See Athena
Morai, 55
Mummius, Lucius, 6, 22, 26–27, 43, 141,
    149–50, 182n69, 250, 283, 400
Mysteries of Eleusis, 345–56
mystery religions. See cult(s), Hel-
    lenistic; Isis and Sarapis, cult of;
    Melikertes-Palaimon; Melikertes-
    Palaimon, cult of; Mysteries of
    Eleusis; wisdom at Corinth
Neptune, 116
    See also Poseidon
Nero, 14, 51, 53, 54, 84, 88–90, 104
Nike, 420, 423, 424n4, 451
Nilotic scenes, 424
North Building, 36, 37
North Cemetery, 59, 258, 268n26,
    270n32, 277n46, 278n49, 284,
    285n14, 292, 299–300
Northwest Stoa, 33n27, 34, 37, 91n91,
    154
Nymphs, 148

Octavia, 23
Odeion, 93, 132n53, 138
Orange (Aurasio), 8
Oryphas, Niketas, 13
Osiris hydreios jar, 225, 246
ostothēkai. See ash chests
Ovid, 135, 167, 172n24, 180

Painted Tomb. See under tomb(s),
Palaimon
    at Isthmia, 19, 189–203;
    lamps of, 202n112;
    Melikertes becomes, 169;
    monument of, 92n97, 172, 187;
    pits A–C of, 192n90, 194, 200–2;
    rites of, 149n83, 178, 193n92;
    Temple of, 197–98, 200n108;

tomb of, 203
    See also Melikertes-Palaimon
Palaimonion. See Melikertes-Palaimon,
    cult of
Palladius, 454
Pallas, 439
Pan, 148, 187, 229–30
Panayia Field, 420–29
Panhellenic games, 406
    See also Isthmian games
Papias, 345
Pastoral Epistles, 353, 367n33
Patras, 447
Paul, the Apostle, 283, 307–40, 352,
    359–61, 450
    and baptism, 342, 346–48;
    credentials of, 327n75, 328, 332n86;
    eschatology of, 341, 346, 349,
        383–94, 414;
    message of, 308–11, 341–42,
        346–49, 373–74, 384, 390, 399;
    mission at Corinth of, 37–72;
    in Corinth opponents of, 312–21,
        334n90 (see also Apollos)
    See also Corinthians, Letters to the;
    Christian community at Corinth
Pausanias
    on Corinth, 9, 26, 30, 61n1, 124,
        143n8, 151–52, 154, 260n9, 402;
    on Fountain of Glauke, 93–94n101,
        128, 132;
    on monuments, 92n97, 141–42n1,
        146, 181, 240;
    on mythology of Corinth, 94, 113, 167;
    on Roman-period cults, 160–61,
        163–64, 173n33, 193n93,
        197n102, 199, 203;
    on temples of Corinth, 160n87, 161
Pegasos/Pegasus, 113, 118–19, 121n26,
    125–27, 134, 139–40
Pegasos and Bellerophon
    as depicted in wall painting at
        Pompeii, 119–20, 125;
    depiction on coins of, 125;

representing Corinth, 125;
revival of myth of, 125
Peirene Fountain, 21, 22, 24, 65, 112n4,
113–27, 139–40, 404
Pelagius II, Pope, 435
Pelops, 178
Perachora, 19, 131, 132n53, 146n22,
159n83, 177
Peregenes, 447–48
Periander, 13, 92
Peribolos of Apollo. *See* Apollo
persecution of Christians, 398–400,
453, 457
Pharisees, 376
Philip, 384
Philippi, 413
Philo, 376, 382
Philostratus, 64n10, 66n18, 98n114,
178–80, 193n95
Phoebe, 311n11, 368, 369
Pindar, 116, 118–19, 125, 148n32, 168n11
Pit A, 192n90, 200
See also Palaimon
Pliny, 373
Plutarch, 64n9, 74, 97, 178n50, 179,
181n63, 193n95, 202
politics and religion in Roman era,
276–77, 374–75, 392
See also cult(s), Roman
Pompeii, 119, 125, 135n67, 156n74,
234, 244n39, 245
Pontius Pilate, 385
poor in Pauline Christian communities,
351, 353n7, 358–70
See also Christian community at
Corinth; social status
Poseidon, 197
altar to, 181;
on coins, 182n69, 183–85;
cults of, 22, 159n83;
fountain of, 23, 32, 92, 93, 95, 106,
133, 186–87;
Helios and, 94–95n104, 96;
myths of, 121, 148, 171;
pottery of, 150–51;

sanctuary of, 19, 94, 167, 192,
404n26, 310;
shrine of, 170;
temple of, 92n97, 192
Potters' Quarter, 145
pottery, 17–18, 150–1, 195, 227,
254–55n9, 258, 426, 428
See also figurines; lamps
Praxiteles, 178n50, 219n59
Prisca, 378
Priscilla, 340, 381
Procopius, 439n33, 449n41
prostitution, cultic, 147, 205–20
cessation of, 161, 245;
lack of evidence for, 205–10;
and worship of Aphrodite, 243–44
(*see also* Aphrodite)
Psyche, 260n9

Q source, 343
Qumran, 389

racecourse, 21, 36nn36–37, 144n10,
149n36
religion, Christian. *See* Christian
religion
religion, Greek. *See* cults, Hellenistic
religion, pagan. *See* cults, Hellenistic;
cult(s), Roman
religion, Roman imperial. *See* cult(s),
Roman
religion, Roman. *See* cult(s), Roman
rites. *See* cults, Hellenistic; cults, pagan; cult(s), Roman
Roma, 424, 425
Roman forum, 20, 33, 35, 54, 81, 85,
87, 90, 157, 221
Rome, 22, 26–27, 79, 124, 135, 157,
354–55n10, 386, 403, 405–6, 445,
447
Rufus, 447

Sacred Spring, 20–22, 36, 112n3, 139,
144, 149n36, 153, 186n79, 443n1
sacrifice, 161, 193nn94, 95, 194nn96

sanctuary. *See* Asklepius; Demeter; Demeter and Kore; Hera; Sacred Spring

Sarapis. *See under* Isis and Sarapis

sarcophagus. *See* burials, Roman; burial, at Ephesos vs. Corinth

Sardis, 376

Saronic Gulf, 14, 48

Seneca, 135

Septuagint, 343

Severus, Emperor, 302

sex, sacred. *See* prostitution, cultic

Sikyon, 12, 18, 48, 53, 93, 128, 143, 181, 182n67, 250

Sikyonians, 148

Silvanus, 358n16, 394

Simonides, 211, 213

Siricius, Pope, 445

Sirius, 240

Sisyphos, 118, 169, 176, 180

skeletal remains, Roman, 252, 254, 257–58, 266n20, 267–68, 271
  See also burial, Roman; burial practices, Roman; tomb(s), chamber

Skoutela Basilica, 24, 440

slavery, 340, 390

social status
  and burial practices, 298–304 (*see also* burial practices)
  in Pauline Christian communities, 339–41, 351, 352nn1,5, 361–67, 378
  See also demography; poor in Christian communities

Solon, 92

Sophists, 64n11, 65, 66n16, 67n20, 235

Sospes, Antonius, 97

South Basilica, 109

South Stoa, 21–23, 32, 34n31, 36–37, 55, 81, 84, 89, 116, 141, 144, 150

Southeast Building, 32, 34n31, 37, 81–90, 91n91, 95–96, 104–5

Sparta, 64n9, 407, 428

springs, 11–12, 111–12
  See also fountains; Glauke Fountain; Peirene Fountain; Sacred Spring

Stadium, Classical, 189n88

Statius, 178, 179n53, 203

Stephen, 384

Stephanas, 346, 355n12, 379, 394

Strabo, 121, 160, 205, 213n30

subject peoples, 376, 381–82
  See also Jews

Suetonius, 373

surveying, Roman, 26–46, 48n53, 50–51n56, 53, 402n15
  at Corinth evidence for, 29, 59;
  inscriptions related to, 29;
  lex agraria and, 27, 29, 43;
  measurement system used, 38n40;
  orientation of city and, 32, 36–37;
  responsibilities of surveyors in, 28;
  role of *agrimensores* in, 27–28, 59
  See also Corinth, surveying under Vespasian

Tacitus, 373

Taenarum, 92

Temple A, 21

Temple, Archaic. *See* Archaic Temple

Temple C, 33, 37, 93, 131, 154, 155

Temple D (Tyche), 97, 153

Temple E, 23, 33, 37, 53, 54n65, 55n71, 81, 116n9, 155n60, 157n75, 158n80, 160n87, 225n7

Temple F, 23, 32, 37

Temple G, 23, 151, 153, 156

Temple Hill, 21–22, 34, 142

Temple of Apollo, 12, 34n30, 36–37, 143, 157, 197n102, 404

Temple of Palaimon. *See under* Palaimon

Temple of Poseidon. *See under* Poseidon

temples, Hellenistic
  of Aphrodite, 147;
  of Asklepios, 143, 149;

of Demeter and Kore, 146–47, 149, 151;
of Isis and Sarapis, 146;
sanctuary, Sacred Spring, 144, 149;
of Zeus Olympios, 143;
temples, Roman
of Aphrodite, 160–61;
of Asclepios, 159, 161;
civic use of, 157–59;
of Demeter and Kore, 160–63;
floor plans of, 154;
Ionic, 58;
location of, 152–62;
organized planning of, 152–53;
unidentified, 154–57;
of various major deities, 152–53;
of Zeus, 160
Teneatic gate, 146
theater, 131, 143, 160, 404
Thecla, St., 450
Theodosius, 448–49
Theophrastos, 143n8
Thessalonians, 316n42, 387, 398n3, 399n4
Thessalonika, 80, 358, 369, 394, 410, 413, 415–16, 428n12, 446–49
Tiberian period, 82, 89, 109
Tiberius, Emperor, 88
Timothy, 358n16, 394, 398
Titus, 320, 326, 330, 332n896, 335
tomb(s)
of Caetennii, 270;
chamber, 249, 255–70, 274–75n40;
K, 274–75n40;
of North Cemetery, 285–86;
QQ, 272–73, 275;
Painted, 261–70, 272–75, 289n36;

Roman type, 259;
with Sarcophagi, 270–72, 275 –79;
Trajan, 269
See also burials, Christian; cists;
burials, Roman; North Cemetery
Tyche, 310
unguentaria, 253–54, 258, 260, 274
urban planning, Roman, 26, 33–47, 42–46, 59
See also surveying, Roman
urns. *See under* cremation
Urso, 401, 409

Valerian, 453
Venus
Anadyomene, 246;
Genetrix, 32;
Hoplismene, 245
See also Aphrodite
Vibius Euelpistos, Gaius, 159
Victorinus, 453
villas, Roman, 58

West Shops, 33
wisdom at Corinth, 343–49
Wisdom of Solomon, 343, 382
women, 205–13, 220, 340, 361, 450–55
See also Aquila, Priscilla, Chloe, Phoebe
worship, 216–18
See also cults, Hellenistic; cults, pagan;
cult(s), Roman
Zeus/Jupiter/Jove, 23, 142, 148, 160, 237, 455
Zeuxippus, 22

Harvard Theological Studies

53. Schowalter, Daniel N., and Steven J. Friesen, eds. *Urban Religion in Roman Corinth: Interdisciplinary Approaches*, 2004.

52. Nasrallah, Laura. *"An Ecstasy of Folly": Prophecy and Authority in Early Christianity*, 2003.

51. Brock, Ann Graham. *Mary Magdalene, The First Apostle: The Struggle for Authority*, 2003.

50. Trost, Theodore Louis. *Douglas Horton and the Ecumenical Impulse in American Religion*, 2002.

49. Huang, Yong. *Religious Goodness and Political Rightness: Beyond the Liberal-Communitarian Debate*, 2001.

48. Rossing, Barbara R. *The Choice between Two Cities: Whore, Bride, and Empire in the Apocalypse*, 1999.

47. Skedros, James Constantine. *Saint Demetrios of Thessaloniki: Civic Patron and Divine Protector, 4th–7th Centuries C.E.*, 1999.

46. Koester, Helmut, ed. *Pergamon, Citadel of the Gods: Archaeological Record, Literary Description, and Religious Development*, 1998.

45. Kittredge, Cynthia Briggs. *Community and Authority: The Rhetoric of Obedience in the Pauline Tradition*, 1998.

44. Lesses, Rebecca Macy. *Ritual Practices to Gain Power: Angels, Incantations, and Revelation in Early Jewish Mysticism*, 1998.

43. Guenther-Gleason, Patricia E. *On Schleiermacher and Gender Politics*, 1997.

42. White, L. Michael. *The Social Origins of Christian Architecture* (2 vols.), 1997.

41. Koester, Helmut, ed. *Ephesos, Metropolis of Asia: An Interdisciplinary Approach to its Archaeology, Religion, and Culture*, 1995.

40. Guider, Margaret Eletta. *Daughters of Rahab: Prostitution and the Church of Liberation in Brazil*, 1995.

39. Schenkel, Albert F. *The Rich Man and the Kingdom: John D. Rockefeller, Jr., and the Protestant Establishment*, 1995.

38. Hutchison, William R. and Hartmut Lehmann, eds. *Many Are Chosen: Divine Election and Western Nationalism*, 1994.

37. Lubieniecki, Stanislas. *History of the Polish Reformation and Nine Related Documents*. Translated and interpreted by George Huntston Williams, 1995.

– Davidovich, Adina. *Religion as a Province of Meaning: The Kantian Foundations of Modern Theology*, 1993.

36. Thiemann, Ronald F., ed. *The Legacy of H. Richard Niebuhr*, 1991.

35. Hobbs, Edward C., ed. *Bultmann, Retrospect and Prospect: The Centenary Symposium at Wellesley*, 1985.

34. Cameron, Ron. *Sayings Traditions in the Apocryphon of James*, 1984. Reprinted, 2004,

33. Blackwell, Albert L. *Schleiermacher's Early Philosophy of Life: Determinism, Freedom, and Phantasy*, 1982.

32. Gibson, Elsa. *The "Christians for Christians" Inscriptions of Phrygia: Greek Texts, Translation and Commentary*, 1978.

31. Bynum, Caroline Walker. Docere Verbo et Exemplo: *An Aspect of Twelfth-Century Spirituality*, 1979.

30. Williams, George Huntston, ed. *The Polish Brethren: Documentation of the History and Thought of Unitarianism in the Polish-Lithuanian Commonwealth and in the Diaspora 1601–1685*, 1980.

29. Attridge, Harold W. *First-Century Cynicism in the Epistles of Heraclitus*, 1976.

28. Williams, George Huntston, Norman Pettit, Winfried Herget, and Sargent Bush, Jr., eds. *Thomas Hooker: Writings in England and Holland, 1626–1633*, 1975.

27. Preus, James Samuel. *Carlstadt's* Ordinaciones *and Luther's Liberty: A Study of the Wittenberg Movement, 1521–22*, 1974.

26. Nickelsburg, George W. E. *Resurrection, Immortality, and Eternal Life in Inter-testamental Judaism*, 1972.

25. Worthley, Harold Field. *An Inventory of the Records of the Particular (Congregational) Churches of Massachusetts Gathered 1620–1805*, 1970.

24. Yamauchi, Edwin M. *Gnostic Ethics and Mandaean Origins*, 1970.

23. Yizhar, Michael. *Bibliography of Hebrew Publications on the Dead Sea Scrolls 1948–1964*, 1967.

22. Albright, William Foxwell. *The Proto-Sinaitic Inscriptions and Their Decipherment*, 1966.

21. Dow, Sterling, and Robert F. Healey. *A Sacred Calendar of Eleusis*, 1965.

20. Sundberg, Jr., Albert C. *The Old Testament of the Early Church*, 1964.

19. Cranz, Ferdinand Edward. *An Essay on the Development of Luther's Thought on Justice, Law, and Society*, 1959.

18. Williams, George Huntston, ed. *The Norman Anonymous of 1100 A.D.: Towards the Identification and Evaluation of the So-Called Anonymous of York*, 1951.

17. Lake, Kirsopp, and Silva New, eds. *Six Collations of New Testament Manuscripts*, 1932.

16. Wilbur, Earl Morse, trans. *The Two Treatises of Servetus on the Trinity: On the Errors of the Trinity, 7 Books, A.D. 1531. Dialogues on the Trinity, 2 Books. On the Righteousness of Christ's Kingdom, 4 Chapters, A.D. 1532*, 1932.

15. Casey, Robert Pierce, ed. Serapion of Thmuis's *Against the Manichees*, 1931.

14. Ropes, James Hardy. *The Singular Problem of the Epistles to the Galatians*, 1929.

13. Smith, Preserved. *A Key to the Colloquies of Erasmus,* 1927.

12. Spyridon of the Laura and Sophronios Eustratiades. *Catalogue of the Greek Manuscripts in the Library of the Laura on Mount Athos,* 1925.

11. Sophronios Eustratiades and Arcadios of Vatspedi. *Catalogue of the Greek Manuscripts in the Library of the Monastery of Vatopedi on Mt. Athos,* 1924.

10. Conybeare, Frederick C. *Russian Dissenters,* 1921.

9. Burrage, Champlin, ed. *An Answer to John Robinson of Leyden by a Puritan Friend: Now First Published from a Manuscript of A.D. 1609,* 1920.

8. Emerton, Ephraim. *The* Defensor pacis *of Marsiglio of Padua: A Critical Study,* 1920,

7. Bacon, Benjamin W. *Is Mark a Roman Gospel?* 1919.

6. Cadbury, Henry Joel. 2 vols. *The Style and Literary Method of Luke,* 1920.

5. Marriott, G. L., ed. Macarii Anecdota*: Seven Unpublished Homilies of Macarius,* 1918.

4. Edmunds, Charles Carroll and William Henry Paine Hatch. *The Gospel Manuscripts of the General Theological Seminary,* 1918.

3. Arnold, William Rosenzweig. *Ephod and Ark: A Study in the Records and Religion of the Ancient Hebrews,* 1917.

2. Hatch, William Henry Paine. *The Pauline Idea of Faith in its Relation to Jewish and Hellenistic Religion,* 1917.

1. Torrey, Charles Cutler. *The Composition and Date of Acts,* 1916.

Harvard Dissertations in Religion

In 1993, Harvard Theological Studies absorbed
the Harvard Dissertations in Religion series.

31. Baker-Fletcher, Garth. *Somebodyness: Martin Luther King, Jr. and the Theory of Dignity,* 1993.

30. Soneson, Jerome Paul. *Pragmatism and Pluralism: John Dewey's Significance for Theology,* 1993.

29. Crabtree, Harriet. *The Christian Life: The Traditional Metaphors and Contemporary Theologies,* 1991.

28. Schowalter, Daniel N. *The Emperor and the Gods: Images from the Time of Trajan,* 1993.

27. Valantasis, Richard. *Spiritual Guides of the Third Century: A Semiotic Study of the Guide-Disciple Relationship in Christianity, Neoplatonism, Hermetism, and Gnosticism,* 1991.

26. Wills, Lawrence Mitchell. *The Jews in the Court of the Foreign King: Ancient Jewish Court Legends,* 1990.

25. Massa, Mark Stephen. *Charles Augustus Briggs and the Crisis of Historical Criticism,* 1990.

24. Hills, Julian Victor. *Tradition and Composition in the* Epistula apostolorum, 1990.

23. Bowe, Barbara Ellen. *A Church in Crisis: Ecclesiology and Paraenesis in Clement of Rome*, 1988.

22. Bisbee, Gary A. *Pre-Decian Acts of Martyrs and* Commentarii, 1988.

21. Ray, Stephen Alan. *The Modern Soul: Michel Foucault and the Theological Discourse of Gordon Kaufman and David Tracy*, 1987.

20. MacDonald, Dennis Ronald. *There Is No Male and Female: The Fate of a Dominical Saying in Paul and Gnosticism*, 1987.

19. Davaney, Sheila Greeve. *Divine Power: A Study of Karl Barth and Charles Hartshorne*, 1986.

18. LaFargue, J. Michael. *Language and Gnosis: The Opening Scenes of the Acts of Thomas*, 1985.

12. Layton, Bentley, ed. *The Gnostic Treatise on Resurrection from Nag Hammadi*, 1979.

11. Ryan, Patrick J. *Imale: Yoruba Participation in the Muslim Tradition: A Study of Clerical Piety*, 1977.

10. Neevel, Jr., Walter G. *Yāmuna's* Vedānta *and* Pāñcarātra: *Integrating the Classical and the Popular*, 1977.

9. Yarbro Collins, Adela. *The Combat Myth in the Book of Revelation*, 1976.

8. Veatch, Robert M. *Value-Freedom in Science and Technology: A Study of the Importance of the Religious, Ethical, and Other Socio-Cultural Factors in Selected Medical Decisions Regarding Birth Control*, 1976.

7. Attridge, Harold W. *The Interpretation of Biblical History in the* Antiquitates judaicae *of Flavius Josephus*, 1976.

6. Trakatellis, Demetrios C. *The Pre-Existence of Christ in the Writings of Justin Martyr*, 1976.

5. Green, Ronald Michael. *Population Growth and Justice: An Examination of Moral Issues Raised by Rapid Population Growth*, 1975.

4. Schrader, Robert W. *The Nature of Theological Argument: A Study of Paul Tillich*, 1976.

3. Christensen, Duane L. *Transformations of the War Oracle in Old Testament Prophecy: Studies in the Oracles Against the Nations*, 1975.

2. Williams, Sam K. *Jesus' Death as Saving Event: The Background and Origin of a Concept*, 1972.

1. Smith, Jane I. *An Historical and Semantic Study of the Term "Islām" as Seen in a Sequence of Qur'an Commentaries*, 1970.